Christian Writings

By

G K Chesterton

Cover Photograph: atomicjeep

ISBN: 978-1-78943-290-9

Contents

THE EVERLASTING MAN

ORTHODOXY

HERETICS

ST FRANCIS OF ASSISI

ST. THOMAS AQUINAS

THE MAN WHO WAS THURSDAY

THE EVERLASTING MAN

PREPARATORY NOTE

This book needs a preliminary note that its scope be not misunderstood The view suggested is historical rather than theological, and does not deal directly with a religious change which has been the chief event of my own life; and about which I am already writing a more purely controversial volume. It is impossible, I hope, for any Catholic to write any book on any subject, above all this subject, without showing that he is a Catholic; but this study is not specially concerned with the differences between a Catholic and a Protestant. Much of it is devoted to many sorts of Pagans rather than any sort of Christians; and its thesis is that those who say that Christ stands side by side with similar myths, and his religion side by side with similar religions, are only repeating a very stale formula contradicted by a very striking fact. To suggest this I have not needed to go much beyond matters known to us all; I make no claim to learning; and have to depend for some things, as has rather become the fashion, on those who are more learned. As I have more than once differed from Mr. H. G. Wells in his view of history, it is the more right that I should here congratulate him on the courage and constructive imagination which carried through his vast and varied and intensely interesting work; but still more on having asserted the reasonable right of the amateur to do what he can with the facts which the specialists provide.

INTRODUCTION - THE PLAN OF THIS BOOK

There are two ways of getting home; and one of them is to stay there. The other is to walk round the whole world till we come back to the same place; and I tried to trace such a journey in a story I once wrote. It is, however, a relief to turn from that topic to another story that I never wrote. Like every book I never wrote, it is by far the best book I have ever written. It is only too probable that I shall never write it, so I will use it symbolically here; for it was a symbol of the same truth. I conceived it as a romance of those vast valleys with sloping sides, like those along which the ancient White Horses of Wessex are scrawled along the flanks of the hills. It concerned some boy whose farm or cottage stood on such a slope, and who went on his travels to find something, such as the effigy and grave of some giant; and when he was far enough from home he looked back and saw that his own farm and kitchen-garden, shining flat on the hill-side like the colours and quarterings of a shield, were but parts of some such gigantic figure, on which he had always lived, but which was too large and too close to be seen. That, I think, is a true picture of the progress of any really independent intelligence today; and that is the point of this book.

The point of this book, in other words, is that the next best thing to being really inside Christendom is to be really outside it. And a particular point of it is that the popular critics of Christianity are not really outside it. They are on a debatable ground, in every sense of the term. They are doubtful in their very doubts. Their criticism has taken on a curious tone; as of a random and illiterate heckling. Thus they make current and anti-clerical cant as a sort of small-talk. They will complain of parsons dressing like parsons; as if we should be any more free if all the police who shadowed or collared us were plain clothes detectives. Or they will complain that a sermon cannot be interrupted, and call a pulpit a coward's castle; though they do not call an editor's office a coward's castle. It would be unjust both to journalists and priests; but it would be much truer of journalist. The clergyman appears in person and could easily be kicked as he came out of church; the journalist conceals even his name so that nobody can kick him. They write wild and pointless articles and letters in the press about why the churches are empty, without even going there to find out if they are empty, or which of them are empty. Their suggestions are more vapid and vacant than the most insipid curate in a three-act farce, and move us to comfort him after the manner of the curate in the Bab Ballads; 'Your mind is not so blank as that of Hopley Porter.' So we may truly say to the very feeblest cleric: 'Your mind is not so blank as that of Indignant

Layman or Plain Man or Man in the Street, or any of your critics in the newspapers; for they have not the most shadowy notion of what they want themselves. Let alone of what you ought to give them.' They will suddenly turn round and revile the Church for not having prevented the War, which they themselves did not want to prevent; and which nobody had ever professed to be able to prevent, except some of that very school of progressive and cosmopolitan sceptics who are the chief enemies of the Church. It was the anti-clerical and agnostic world that was always prophesying the advent of universal peace; it is that world that was, or should have been, abashed and confounded by the advent of universal war. As for the general view that the Church was discredited by the War--they might as well say that the Ark was discredited by the Flood. When the world goes wrong, it proves rather that the Church is right. The Church is justified, not because her children do not sin, but because they do. But that marks their mood about the whole religious tradition they are in a state of reaction against it. It is well with the boy when he lives on his father's land; and well with him again when he is far enough from it to look back on it and see it as a whole. But these people have got into an intermediate state, have fallen into an intervening valley from which they can see neither the heights beyond them nor the heights behind. They cannot get out of the penumbra of Christian controversy. They cannot be Christians and they can not leave off being Anti-Christians. Their whole atmosphere is the atmosphere of a reaction: sulks, perversity, petty criticism. They still live in the shadow of the faith and have lost the light of the faith.

Now the best relation to our spiritual home is to be near enough to love it. But the next best is to be far enough away not to hate it. It is the contention of these pages that while the best judge of Christianity is a Christian, the next best judge would be something more like a Confucian. The worst judge of all is the man now most ready with his judgements; the ill-educated Christian turning gradually into the ill-tempered agnostic, entangled in the end of a feud of which he never understood the beginning, blighted with a sort of hereditary boredom with he knows not what, and already weary of hearing what he has never heard. He does not judge Christianity calmly as a Confucian would; he does not judge it as he would judge Confucianism. He cannot by an effort of fancy set the Catholic Church thousands of miles away in strange skies of morning and judge it as impartially as a Chinese pagoda. It is said that the great St. Francis Xavier, who very nearly succeeded in setting up the Church there as a tower overtopping all pagodas, failed partly because his followers were accused by their fellow missionaries of representing the Twelve Apostles with the garb or attributes of Chinamen. But it would be far better to see them as Chinamen, and judge them fairly as Chinamen, than to see them as featureless idols merely made to be battered by iconoclasts; or rather as cockshies to be pelted by empty-handed cockneys. It would be better to see the whole thing as a remote Asiatic cult; the mitres of its bishops as the towering head dresses of mysterious bonzes; its pastoral staffs as the sticks twisted like serpents carried in some Asiatic procession; to see the prayer book as fantastic as the prayer-wheel and the Cross as crooked as the Swastika. Then at least we should not lose our temper as some of the sceptical critics seem to lose their temper, not to mention their wits. Their anti-clericalism has become an atmosphere, an atmosphere of negation and hostility from which they cannot escape. Compared with that, it would be better to see the whole thing as something belonging to another continent, or to another planet. It would be more philosophical to stare indifferently at bonzes than to be perpetually and pointlessly grumbling at bishops. It would be better to walk past a church as if it were a pagoda than to stand permanently in the porch, impotent either to go inside and help or to go outside and forget. For those in whom a mere reaction has thus become an obsession, I do seriously recommend the imaginative effort of conceiving the Twelve Apostles as Chinamen. In other words, I recommend these critics to try to do as much justice to Christian saints as if they were Pagan sages.

But with this we come to the final and vital point I shall try to show in these pages that when we do make this imaginative effort to see the whole thing from the outside, we find that it really looks like what is traditionally said about it inside. It is exactly when the boy gets far enough off to see the giant that he sees that he really is a giant. It is exactly when we do at last see the Christian Church afar under those clear and level eastern skies that we see that it is really the Church of Christ. To put it shortly, the moment we are really impartial about it, we know why people are partial to it. But this second proposition requires more serious discussion; and I shall here set myself to discuss it.

As soon as I had clearly in my mind this conception of something solid in the solitary and unique character of the divine story, it struck me that there was exactly the same strange and yet solid character in the human story that had led up to it; because that human story also had a root that was divine. I mean that just as the Church seems to grow more remarkable when it is fairly compared with the common religious life of mankind, so mankind itself seems to grow more remarkable when we compare it with the common life of nature. And I have noticed that most modern history is driven to something like sophistry, first to soften the sharp transition from animals to men, and then to soften the sharp transition from heathens to Christians. Now the more we really read in a realistic spirit of those two transitions the sharper we shall find them to be. It is because the critics are not detached that they do not see this detachment; it is because they are not looking at things in a dry light that they cannot see the difference between black and white. It is because they are in a particular mood of reaction and revolt that they have a motive for making out that all the white is dirty grey and the black not so black as it is painted. I do not say there are not human excuses for their revolt; I do not say it is not in some ways sympathetic; what I say is that it is not in any way scientific. An iconoclast may be indignant; an iconoclast may be justly indignant; but an iconoclast is not impartial. And it is stark hypocrisy to pretend that nine-tenths of the higher critics and scientific evolutionists and professors of comparative religion are in the least impartial. Why should they be impartial, what is being impartial, when the whole world is at war about whether one thing is a devouring superstition or a divine hope? I do not pretend to be impartial in the sense that the final act of faith fixes a man's mind because it satisfies his mind. But I do profess to be a great deal more impartial than they are; in the sense that I can tell the story fairly, with some sort of imaginative justice to all sides; and they cannot. I do profess to be impartial in the sense that I should be ashamed to talk such nonsense about the Lama of Thibet as they do about the Pope of Rome, or to have as little sympathy with Julian the Apostate as they have with the Society of Jesus. They are not impartial; they never by any chance hold the historical scales even; and above all they are never impartial upon this point of evolution and transition. They suggest everywhere the grey gradations of twilight, because they believe it is the twilight of the gods. I propose to maintain that whether or no it is the twilight of gods, it is not the daylight of men.

I maintain that when brought out into the daylight these two things look altogether strange and unique; and that it is only in the false twilight of an imaginary period of transition that they can be made to look in the least like anything else. The first of these is the creature called man and the second is the man called Christ. I have therefore divided this book into two parts: the former being a sketch of the main adventure of the human race in so far as it remained heathen; and the second a summary of the real difference that was made by it becoming Christian. Both motives necessitate a certain method, a method which is not very easy to manage, and perhaps even less easy to define or defend.

In order to strike, in the only sane or possible sense, the note of impartiality, it is necessary to touch the nerve of novelty. I mean that in one sense we see things fairly when we see them first. That, I may remark in passing, is why children generally have very little difficulty about the dogmas of the Church. But the Church, being a highly practical thing for working and fighting, is necessarily a thing for men and not merely for children. There must be in it for working purposes a great deal of tradition, of familiarity, and even of routine. So long as its fundamentals are sincerely felt, this may even be the saner condition. But when its fundamentals are doubted, as at present, we must try to recover the candour and wonder of the child; the unspoilt realism and objectivity of innocence. Or if we cannot do that, we must try at least to shake off the cloud of mere custom and see the thing as new, if only by seeing it as unnatural. Things that may well be familiar so long as familiarity breeds affection had much better become unfamiliar when familiarity breeds contempt. For in connection with things so great as are here considered, whatever our view of them, contempt must be a mistake. Indeed contempt must be an illusion. We must invoke the most wild and soaring sort of imagination; the imagination that can see what is there.

The only way to suggest the point is by an example of something, indeed of almost anything, that has been considered beautiful or wonderful. George Wyndham once told me that he had seen one of the first aeroplanes rise for the first time and it was very wonderful but not so wonderful as a horse allowing a man to ride on him. Somebody else has said that a fine man on a fine horse is the noblest bodily object in the world. Now, so long as people feel this in the right way, all is well. The first and best way of appreciating it is to come of people with a tradition of treating animals properly; of men in the right relation to horses. A boy who remembers his father who rode a horse, who rode it well and treated it well, will know that the relation can be satisfactory and will be satisfied. He will be all the more indignant at the ill-treatment of horses because he knows how they ought to be treated; but he will see nothing but what is normal in a man riding on a horse. He will not listen to the great modern philosopher who explains to him that the horse ought to be riding on the man. He will not pursue the pessimist fancy of Swift and say that men must be despised as monkeys and horses worshipped as gods. And horse and man together making an image that is to him human and civilised, it will be easy, as it were, to lift horse and man together into something heroic or symbolical; like a vision of St. George in the clouds. The fable of the winged horse will not be wholly unnatural to him: and he will know why Ariosto set many a Christian hero in such an airy saddle, and made him the rider of the sky. For the horse has really been lifted up along with the man in the wildest fashion in the very word we use when we speak 'chivalry.' The very name of the horse has been given to the highest mood and moment of the man; so that we might almost say that the handsomest compliment to a man is to call him a horse.

But if a man has got into a mood in which he is not able to feel this sort of wonder, then his cure must begin right at the other end. We must now suppose that he has drifted into a dull mood, in which somebody sitting on a horse means no more than somebody sitting on a chair. The wonder of which Wyndham spoke, the beauty that made the thing seem an equestrian statue, the meaning of the more chivalric horseman, may have become to him merely a convention and a bore. Perhaps they have been merely a fashion; perhaps they have gone out of fashion; perhaps they have been talked about too much or talked about in the wrong way; perhaps it was then difficult to care for horses without the horrible risk of being horsy. Anyhow, he has got into a condition when he cares no more for a horse than for a towel-horse. His grandfather's charge at Balaclava seems to him as dull and dusty as the album containing such family portraits. Such a person has not really become enlightened about the album; on the contrary, he has only become blind with the dust. But when he has reached that degree of blindness, he will not be able to look at a horse or a horseman at all until he has seen the whole thing as a thing entirely unfamiliar and almost unearthly.

Out of some dark forest under some ancient dawn there must come towards us, with lumbering yet dancing motions, one of the very queerest of the prehistoric creatures. We must see for the first time the strangely small head set on a neck not only longer but thicker than itself, as the face of a gargoyle is thrust out upon a gutter-spout, the one disproportionate crest of hair running along the ridge of that heavy neck like a beard in the wrong place; the feet, each like a solid club of horn, alone amid the feet of so many cattle; so that the true fear is to be found in showing, not the cloven, but the uncloven hoof. Nor is it mere verbal fancy to see him thus as a unique monster; for in a sense a monster means what is unique, and he is really unique. But the point is that when we thus see him as the first man saw him, we begin once more to have some imaginative sense of what it meant when the first man rode him. In such a dream he may seem ugly, but he does not seem unimpressive; and certainly that two-legged dwarf who could get on top of him will not seem unimpressive. By a longer and more erratic road we shall come back to the same marvel of the man and the horse; and the marvel will be, if possible, even more marvellous. We shall have again a glimpse of St. George; the more glorious because St. George is not riding on the horse, but rather riding on the dragon.

In this example, which I have taken merely because it is an example, it will be noted that I do not say that the nightmare seen by the first man of the forest is either more true or more wonderful than the normal mare of the stable seen by the civilised person who can appreciate what is normal. Of the two extremes, I think on the whole that the traditional grasp of truth is the better. But I say that the truth is found at one or other of these two extremes, and is lost in the intermediate condition of mere fatigue and forgetfulness of tradition. In other words, I say it is better to see a horse as a monster than to see it only as a slow substitute for a motor-car. If we have got into that state of mind about a horse as something stale, it is far better to be frightened of a horse because it is a good deal too fresh.

Now, as it is with the monster that is called a horse, so it is with the monster that is called a man. Of course the best condition of all, in my opinion, is always to have regarded man as he is regarded in my philosophy. He who holds the Christian and Catholic view of human nature will feel certain that it is a universal and therefore a sane view, and will be satisfied. But if he has lost the pose to strike wherever possible this note of what is new and strange, and for that reason the style even on so serious a subject may sometimes be deliberately grotesque and fanciful. I do desire to help the reader to see Christendom from the outside in the sense of seeing it as a whole, against the background of other historic things; just as I desire him to see humanity as a whole against the background of natural things. And I say that in both cases, when seen thus, they stand out from their background like supernatural things. They do not fade into the rest with the colours of impressionism; they stand out from the rest with the colours of heraldry; as vivid as a red cross on a white shield or a black lion on a ground of gold. So stands the Red Clay against the green field of nature, or the White Christ against the red clay of his race.

But in order to see them clearly we have to see them as a whole. We have to see how they developed as well as how they began; for the most incredible part of the story is that things which began thus should have developed thus. Anyone who chooses to indulge in mere imagination can imagine that other things might have happened or other entities evolved. Anyone thinking of what might have happened may conceive a sort of evolutionary equality; but anyone facing what did happen must face an exception and a prodigy. If there was ever a moment when man was only an animal, we can if we choose make a fancy picture of his career transferred to some other animal. An entertaining fantasia might be made in which elephants built in elephantine architecture, with towers and turrets like tusks and trunks, cities beyond the scale of any colossus. A pleasant fable might be conceived in which a cow had developed a costume, and put on four boots and two pairs of trousers. We could imagine a Supermonkey more marvellous than any Superman, a quadrumanous creature carving and painting with his hands and cooking and carpentering with his feet. But if we are considering what did happen, we shall certainly decide that man has distanced everything else with a distance like that of the astronomical spaces and a speed like that of the still thunderbolt of the light. And in the same fashion, while we can if we choose see the Church amid a mob of Mithraic or Manichean superstitions squabbling and killing each other at the end of the Empire, while we can if we choose imagine the Church killed in the struggle and some other chance cult taking its place, we shall be the more surprised (and possibly puzzled) if we meet it two thousand years afterwards rushing through the ages as the winged thunderbolt of thought and everlasting enthusiasm; a thing without rival or resemblance; and still as new as it is old.

PART I ON THE CREATURE CALLED MAN

I THE MAN IN THE CAVE

Far away in some strange constellation in skies infinitely remote, there is a small star, which astronomers may some day discover. At least I could never observe in the faces or demeanour of most astronomers or men of science any evidence that they have discovered it; though as a matter of fact they were walking about on it all the time. It is a star that brings forth out of itself very strange plants and very strange animals; and none stranger than the men of science. That at least is the way in which I should begin a history of the world, if I had to follow the scientific custom of beginning with an account of the astronomical universe. I should try to see even this earth from the outside, not by the hackneyed insistence of its relative position to the sun, but by some imaginative effort to conceive its remote position for the dehumanised spectator. Only I do not believe in being dehumanised in order to study humanity. I do not believe in dwelling upon the distances that are supposed to dwarf the world; I think there is even something a trifle vulgar about this idea of trying to rebuke spirit by size. And as the first idea is not feasible, that of making the earth a strange planet so as to make it significant, I will not stoop to the other trick of making it a small planet in order to make it insignificant. I would rather insist that we do not even know that it is a planet at all, in the sense in which we know that it is a place; and a very extraordinary place too. That is the note which I wish to strike from the first, if not in the astronomical, then in some more familiar fashion.

One of my first journalistic adventures, or misadventures, concerned a comment on Grant Allen, who had written a book about the Evolution of the Idea of God. I happened to remark that it would be much more interesting if God wrote a book about the evolution of the idea of Grant Allen. And I remember that the editor objected to my remark on the ground that it was blasphemous; which naturally amused me not a little. For the joke of it was, of course, that it never occurred to him to notice the title of the book itself, which really was blasphemous; for it was, when translated into English, 'I will show you how this nonsensical notion that there is God grew up among men.' My remark was strictly pious and proper confessing the divine purpose even in its most seemingly dark or meaningless manifestations. In that hour I learned many things, including the fact that there is something purely acoustic in much of that agnostic sort of reverence. The editor had not seen the point, because in the title of the book the long word came at the beginning and the short word at the end; whereas in my comments the short word came at the beginning and gave him a sort of shock. I have noticed that if you put a word like God into the same sentence with a word like dog, these abrupt and angular words affect people like pistol-shots. Whether you say that God made the dog or the dog made God does not seem to matter; that is only one of the sterile disputations of the too subtle theologians. But so long as you begin with a long word like evolution the rest will roll harmlessly past; very probably the editor had not read the whole of the title, for it is rather a long title and he was rather a busy man.

But this little incident has always lingered in my mind as a sort of parable. Most modern histories of mankind begin with the word evolution, and with a rather wordy exposition of evolution, for much the same reason that operated in this case. There is something slow and soothing and gradual about the word and even about the idea. As a matter of fact, it is not, touching these primary things, a very practical word or a very profitable idea. Nobody can imagine how nothing could turn into something. Nobody can get an inch nearer to it by explaining how something could turn into something else. It is really far more logical to start by saying 'In the beginning God created heaven and earth' even if you only mean 'In the beginning some unthinkable power began some unthinkable process.' For God is by its nature a name of mystery, and nobody ever supposed that man could imagine how a world was created any more than he could create one. But evolution really is mistaken for explanation. It has the fatal quality of leaving on many minds the impression that they do understand it and everything else; just as many of them live under a sort of illusion that they have read the Origin of Species.

But this notion of something smooth and slow, like the ascent of a slope, is a great part of the illusion. It is an illogicality as well as an illusion; for slowness has really nothing to do with the question. An event is not any more intrinsically intelligible or unintelligible because of the pace at which it moves. For a man who does not believe in a miracle, a slow miracle would be just as incredible as a swift one. The Greek witch may have turned sailors to swine with a stroke of the wand. But to see a naval gentleman of our acquaintance looking a little more like a pig every day, till he ended with four trotters and a curly tail, would not be any more soothing. It might be rather more creepy and uncanny. The medieval wizard may have flown through the air from the top of a tower; but to see an old gentleman walking through the air, in a leisurely and lounging manner, would still seem to call for some explanation. Yet there runs through all the rationalistic treatment of history this curious and confused idea that difficulty is avoided, or even mystery eliminated, by dwelling on mere delay or on something dilatory in the processes of things. There will be something to be said upon particular examples elsewhere; the question here is the false atmosphere of facility and ease given by the mere suggestion of going slow; the sort of comfort that might be given to a nervous old woman travelling for the first time in a motor-car.

Mr. H. G. Wells has confessed to being a prophet; and in this matter he was a prophet at his own expense. It is curious that his first fairy-tale was a complete answer to his last book of history. The Time Machine destroyed in advance all comfortable conclusions founded on the mere relativity of time. In that sublime nightmare the hero saw trees shoot up like green rockets, and vegetation spread visibly like a green conflagration, or the sun shoot across the sky from east to west with the swiftness of a meteor. Yet in his sense these things were quite as natural when they went swiftly; and in our sense they are quite as supernatural when they go slowly. The ultimate question is why they go at all; and anybody who really understands that question will know that it always has been and always will be a religious question; or at any rate a philosophical or metaphysical question. And most certainly he will not think the question answered by some substitution of gradual for abrupt change; or, in other words by a merely relative question of the same story being spun out or rattled rapidly through, as can be done with any story at a cinema by turning a handle.

Now what is needed for these problems of primitive existence is something more like a primitive spirit. In calling up this vision of the first things, I would ask the reader to make with me a sort of experiment in simplicity. And by simplicity I do not mean stupidity, but rather the sort of clarity that sees things like life rather than words like evolution. For this purpose it would really be better to turn the handle of the Time Machine a little more quickly and see the grass growing and the trees springing up into the sky, if that experiment could contract and concentrate and make vivid the upshot of the whole affair. What we know, in a sense in which we know nothing else, is that the trees and the grass did grow and that number of other extraordinary things do in fact happen; that queer creatures support themselves in the empty air by beating it with fans of various fantastic shapes; that other queer creatures steer themselves about alive under a load of mighty waters; that other queer creatures walk about on four legs, and that the queerest creature of all walks about on two. These are things and not theories; and compared with them evolution and the atom and even the solar system are merely theories. The matter here is one of history and not of philosophy so that it need only be noted that no philosopher denies that a mystery still attaches to the two great transitions: the origin of the universe itself and the origin of the principle of life itself. Most philosophers have the enlightenment to add that a third mystery attaches to the origin of man himself. In other words, a third bridge was built across a third abyss of the unthinkable when there came into the world what we call reason and what we call will. Man is not merely an evolution but rather a revolution. That he has a backbone or other parts upon a similar pattern to birds and fishes is an obvious fact, whatever be the meaning of the fact. But if we attempt to regard him, as it were, as a quadruped standing on his hind legs, we shall find what follows far more fantastic and subversive than if he were standing on his head.

I will take one example to serve for an introduction to the story of man. It illustrates what I mean by saying that a certain childish directness is needed to see the truth about the childhood of the world. It illustrates what I mean by saying that a mixture of popular science and journalistic jargon have confused the facts about the first things, so that we cannot see which of them really comes first. It illustrates, though only in one convenient illustration, all that I mean by the necessity of seeing the sharp differences that give its shape to history, instead of being submerged in all these generalisations about slowness and sameness. For we do indeed require, in Mr. Wells's phrase, an outline of history. But we may venture to say, in Mr. Mantalini's phrase, that this evolutionary history has no outline or is a demd outline. But, above all, it illustrates what I mean by saying that the more we really look at man as an animal, the less he will look like one.

To-day all our novels and newspapers will be found swarming with numberless allusions to a popular character called a Cave-Man. He seems to be quite familiar to us, not only as a public character but as a private character. His psychology is seriously taken into account in psychological fiction and psychological medicine. So far as I can understand, his chief occupation in life was knocking his wife about, or treating women in general with what is, I believe, known in the world of the film as 'rough stuff.' I have never happened to come upon the evidence for this idea; and I do not know on what primitive diaries or prehistoric divorce-reports it is founded. Nor, as I have explained elsewhere, have I ever been able to see the probability of it, even considered a priori. We are always told without any explanation or authority that primitive man waved a club and knocked the woman down before he carried her off. But on every animal analogy, it would seem an almost morbid modesty and reluctance, on the part of the lady, always to insist on being knocked down before consenting to be carried off. And I repeat that I can never comprehend why, when the male was so very rude, the female should have been so very refined. The cave-man may have been a brute, but there is no reason why he should have been more brutal than the brutes. And the loves of the giraffes and the river romance of the hippopotami are effected without any of this preliminary fracas or shindy. The cave-man may have been no better that the cave-bear; but the child she-bear, so famous in hymnology, is not trained with any such bias for spinsterhood. In short these details of the domestic life of the cave puzzle me upon either the revolutionary or the static hypothesis; and in any case I should like to look into the evidence for them, but unfortunately I have never been able to find it. But the curious thing is this: that while ten thousand tongues of more or less scientific or literary gossip seemed to be talking at once about this unfortunate fellow, under the title of the cave-man, the one connection in which it is really relevant and sensible to talk about him as the cave-man has been comparatively neglected. People have used this loose term in twenty loose ways, but they have never even looked at their own term for what could really be learned from it.

In fact, people have been interested in everything about the cave-man except what he did in the cave. Now there does happen to be some real evidence of what he did in the cave. It is little enough, like all the prehistoric evidence, but it is concerned with the real cave-man and his cave and not the literary cave-man and his club. And it will be valuable to our sense of reality to consider quite simply what that real evidence is, and not to go beyond it. What was found in the cave was not the club, the horrible gory club notched with the number of women it had knocked on the head. The cave was not a Bluebeard's Chamber filled with the skeletons of slaughtered wives; it was not filled with female skulls all arranged in rows and all cracked like eggs. It was something quite unconnected, one way or the other, with all the modern phrases and philosophical implications and literary rumours which confuse the whole question for us. And if we wish to see as it really is this authentic glimpse of the morning of the world, it will be far better to conceive even the story of its discovery as some such legend of the land of morning. It would be far better to tell the tale of what was really found as simply as the tale of heroes finding the Golden Fleece or the Gardens of the Hesperides, if we could so escape from a fog of controversial theories into the clear colours and clean-cut outlines of such a dawn. The old epic poets at least knew how to tell a story, possibly a tall story but never a twisted story, never a story tortured out of its own shape to fit theories and philosophies invented centuries afterwards. It would be well if modern investigators could describe their discoveries in the bald narrative style of the earliest travellers, and without any of these long allusive words that are full of irrelevant implication and suggestion. Then we might realise exactly what we do know about the cave-man, or at any rate about the cave.

A priest and a boy entered sometime ago a hollow in the hills and passed into a sort of subterranean tunnel that led into a labyrinth of such sealed and secret corridors of rock. They crawled through cracks that seemed almost impassable, they crept through tunnels that might have been made for moles, they dropped into holes as hopeless as wells, they seemed to be burying themselves alive seven times over beyond the hope of resurrection. This is but the commonplace of all such courageous exploration; but what is needed here is some one who shall put such stories in the primary light, in which they are not commonplace. There is, for instance, something strangely symbolic in the accident that the first intruders into that sunken world were a priest and a boy, the types of the antiquity and of youth of the world. But here I am even more concerned with the symbolism of the boy than with that of the priest. Nobody who remembers boyhood needs to be told what it might be to a boy to enter like Peter Pan under a roof of the roots of all the trees and go deeper and deeper, till he reach what William Morris called the very roots of the mountains. Suppose somebody, with that simple and unspoilt realism that is a part of innocence, to pursue that journey to its end, not for the sake of what he could deduce or demonstrate in some dusty magazine controversy, but simply for the sake of what he could see. What he did see at last was a cavern so far from the light of day that it might have been the legendary Domdaniel cavern, that was under the floor of the sea. This secret chamber of rock, when illuminated after its long night of unnumbered ages, revealed on its walls large and sprawling outlines diversified with coloured earths; and when they followed the lines of them they recognised, across that vast and void of ages, the movement and the gesture of a man's hand. They were drawings or paintings of animals; and they were drawn or painted not only by a man but by an artist. Under whatever archaic limitations, they showed that love of the long sweeping or the long wavering line which any man who has ever drawn or tried to draw will recognise; and about which no artist will allow himself to be contradicted by any scientist. They showed the experimental and adventurous spirit of the artist, the spirit that does not avoid but attempt difficult things; as where the draughtsman had represented the action of the stag when he swings his head clean round and noses towards his tail, an action familiar enough in the horse. But there are many modern animal-painters who would set themselves something of a task in rendering it truly. In this and twenty other details it is clear that the artist had watched animals with a certain interest and presumably a certain pleasure. In that sense it would seem that he was not only an artist but a naturalist; the sort of naturalist who is really natural.

Now it is needless to note, except in passing, that there is nothing whatever in the atmosphere of that cave to suggest the bleak and pessimistic atmosphere of that journalistic cave of the winds, that blows and bellows about us with countless echoes concerning the cave-man. So far as any human character can be hinted at by such traces of the past, that human character is quite human and even humane. It is certainly not the ideal of an inhuman character, like the abstraction invoked in popular science. When novelists and educationists and psychologists of all sorts talk about the cave-man, they never conceive him in connection with anything that is really in the cave. When the realist of the sex novel writes, 'Red sparks danced in Dagmar Doubledick's brain; he felt the spirit of the cave-man rising within him,' the novelist's readers would be very much disappointed if Dagmar only went off and drew large pictures of cows on the drawing-room wall. When the psycho-analyst writes to a patient, 'The submerged instincts of the cave-man are doubtless prompting you to gratify a violent impulse,' he does not refer to the impulse to paint in water-colours; or to make conscientious studies of how cattle swing their heads when they graze. Yet we do know for a fact that the cave man did these mild and innocent things; and we have not the most minute speck of evidence that he did any of the violent and ferocious things. In other words the cave-man as commonly presented to us is simply a myth or rather a muddle; for a myth has at least an imaginative outline of truth. The whole of the current way of talking is simply a confusion and a misunderstanding, founded on no sort of scientific evidence and valued only as an excuse for a very modern mood of anarchy. If any gentleman wants to knock a woman about, he can surely be a cad without taking away the character of the cave-man, about whom we know next to nothing except what we can gather from a few harmless and pleasing pictures on a wall.

But this is not the point about the pictures or the particular moral here to be drawn from them. That moral is something much larger and simpler, so large and simple that when it is first stated it will sound childish. And indeed it is in the highest sense childish; and that is why I have in this apologue in some sense seen it through the eyes of a child. It is the biggest of all the facts really facing the boy in the cavern; and is perhaps too big to be seen. If the boy was one of the flock of the priest, it may be presumed that he had been trained in a certain quality of common sense; that common sense that often comes to us in the form of tradition. In that case he would simply recognise the primitive man's work as the work of a man, interesting but in no way incredible in being primitive. He would see what was there to see; and he would not be tempted into seeing what was not there, by any evolutionary excitement or fashionable speculation. If he had heard of such things he would admit, of course, that the speculations might be true and were not incompatible with the facts that were true. The artist may have had another side to his character besides that which he has alone left on record in his works of art.

The primitive man may have taken a pleasure in beating women as well as in drawing animals; all we can say is that the drawings record the one but not the other. It may be true that when the cave-man's finished jumping on his mother, or his wife as the case may be, he loves to hear the little brook a-gurgling, and also to watch the deer as they come down to drink at the brook. These things are not impossible, but they are irrelevant. The common sense of the child could confine itself to learning from the facts what the facts have to teach; and the pictures in the cave are very nearly all the facts there are. So far as that evidence goes, the child would be justified in assuming that a man had represented animals with rock and red ochre for the same reason as he himself was in the habit of trying to represent animals with charcoal and red chalk. The man had drawn a stag just as the child had drawn a horse; because it was fun. The man had drawn a stag with his head turned as the child had drawn a pig with his eyes shut; because it was difficult. The child and the man, being both human, would be united by the brotherhood of men; and the brotherhood of men is even nobler when it bridges the abyss of ages than when it bridges only the chasm of class. But anyhow he would see no evidence of the cave man of crude evolutionism; because there is none to be seen. If somebody told him that the pictures had all been drawn by St. Francis of Assisi out of pure and saintly love of animals, there would be nothing in the cave to contradict it.

Indeed I once knew a lady who half-humorously suggested that the cave was a creche, in which the babies were put to be specially safe, and that coloured animals were drawn on the walls to amuse them; very much as diagrams of elephants and giraffes adorn a modern infant school. And though this was but a jest, it does draw attention to some of the other assumptions that we make only too readily. The pictures do not prove even that the cave-men lived in caves, any more than the discovery of a wine-cellar in Balham (long after that suburb had been destroyed by human or divine wrath) would prove that the Victorian middle classes lived entirely underground. The cave might have had a special purpose like the cellar; it might have been a religious shrine or a refuge in war or the meeting place of a secret society or all sorts of things. But it is quite true that its artistic decoration has much more of the atmosphere of a nursery than of any of these nightmares of anarchical fury and fear. I have conceived a child as standing in the cave; and it is easy to conceive any child, modern or immeasurably remote, as making a living gesture as if to pat the painted beasts upon the wall. In that gesture there is a foreshadowing, as we shall see later, of another cavern and another child.

But suppose the boy had not been taught by a priest but by a professor, by one of the professors who simplify the relation of men and beasts to a mere evolutionary variation. Suppose the boy saw himself, with the same simplicity and sincerity, as a mere Mowgli running with the pack of nature and roughly indistinguishable from the rest save by a relative and recent variation. What would be for him the simplest lesson of that strange stone picture-book? After all, it would come back to this; that he had dug very deep and found the place where a man had drawn the picture of a reindeer. But he would dig a good deal deeper before he found a place where a reindeer had drawn a picture of a man. That sounds like a truism, but in this connection it is really a very tremendous truth. He might descend to depths unthinkable, he might sink into sunken continents as strange as remote stars, he might find himself in the inside of the world as far from men as the other side of the moon; he might see in those cold chasms or colossal terraces of stone, traced in the faint hieroglyphic of the fossil, the ruins of lost dynasties of biological life, rather like the ruins of successive creations and separate universes than the stages in the story of one. He would find the trail of monsters blindly developing in directions outside all our common imagery of fish and bird; groping and grasping and touching life with every extravagant elongation of horn and tongue and tentacle; growing a forest of fantastic caricatures of the claw and the fin and the finger. But nowhere would he find one finger that had traced one significant line upon the sand; nowhere one claw that had even begun to scratch the faint suggestion of a form. To all appearance, the thing would be as unthinkable in all those countless cosmic variations of forgotten aeons as it would be in the beasts and birds before our eyes The child would no more expect to see it than to see the cat scratch on the wall a vindictive caricature of the dog. The childish common sense would keep the most evolutionary child from expecting to see anything like that; yet in the traces of the rude and recently evolved ancestors of humanity he would have seen exactly that. It must surely strike him as strange that men so remote from him should be so near, and that beasts so near to him should be so remote. To his simplicity it must seem at least odd that he could not find any trace of the beginning of any arts among any animals. That is the simplest lesson to learn in the cavern of the coloured pictures; only it is too simple to be learnt. It is the simple truth that man does differ from the brutes in kind and not in degree; and the proof of it is here; that it sounds like a truism to say that the most primitive man drew a picture of a monkey and that it sounds like a joke to say that the most intelligent monkey drew a picture of a man. Something of division and disproportion has appeared; and it is unique. Art is the signature of man.

That is the sort of simple truth with which a story of the beginnings ought really to begin. The evolutionist stands staring in the painted cavern at the things that are too large to be seen and too simple to be understood. He tries to deduce all sorts of other indirect and doubtful things from the details of the pictures, because he can not see the primary significance of the whole; thin and theoretical deductions about the absence of religion or the presence of superstition; about tribal government and hunting and human sacrifice and heaven knows what. In the next chapter I shall try to trace in a little more detail the much disputed question about these prehistoric origins of human ideas and especially of the religious idea. Here I am only taking this one case of the cave as a sort of symbol of the simpler sort of truth with which the story ought to start. When all is said, the main fact that the record of the reindeer men attests, along with all other records, is that the reindeer man could draw and the reindeer could not. If the reindeer man was as much an animal as the reindeer, it was all the more extraordinary that he could do what all other animals could not. If he was an ordinary product of biological growth, like any other beast or bird, then it is all the more extraordinary that he was not in the least like any other beast or bird. He seems rather more supernatural as a natural product than as a supernatural one.

But I have begun this story in the cave, like the cave of the speculations of Plato, because it is a sort of model of the mistake of merely evolutionary introductions and prefaces. It is useless to begin by saying that everything was slow and smooth and a mere matter of development and degree. For in the plain matter like the pictures there is in fact not a trace of any such development or degree. Monkeys did not begin pictures and men finish them; Pithecanthropus did not draw a reindeer badly and Homo Sapiens draw it well. The higher animals did not draw better and better portraits; the dog did not paint better in his best period than in his early bad manner as a jackal; the wild horse was not an Impressionist and the race-horse a Post-Impressionist. All we can say of this notion of reproducing things in shadow or representative shape is that it exists nowhere in nature except in man; and that we cannot even talk about it without treating man as something separate from nature. In other words, every sane sort of history must begin with man as man, a thing standing absolute and alone. How he came there, or indeed how anything else came there, is a thing for theologians and philosophers and scientists and not for historians. But an excellent test case of this isolation and mystery is the matter of the impulse of art. This creature was truly different from all other creatures; because he was a creator as well as a creature. Nothing in that sense could be made in any other image but the image of man. But the truth is so true that, even in the absence of any religious belief, it must be assumed in the form of some moral or metaphysical principle. In the next chapter we shall see how this principle applies to all the historical hypotheses and evolutionary ethics now in fashion; to the origins of tribal government or mythological belief. But the clearest and most convenient example to start with is this popular one of what the cave-man really did in his cave. It means that somehow or other a new thing had appeared in the cavernous night of nature, a mind that is like a mirror. It is like a mirror because it is truly a thing of reflection. It is like a mirror because in it alone all the other shapes can be seen like shining shadows in a vision. Above all, it is like a mirror because it is the only thing of its kind. Other things may resemble it or resemble each other in various ways; other things may excel it or excel each other in various ways; just as in the furniture of a room a table may be round like a mirror or a cupboard may be larger than a mirror. But the mirror is the only thing that can contain them all. Man is the microcosm; man is the measure of all things; man is the image of God These are the only real lessons to be learnt in the cave, and it is time to leave it for the open road.

It will be well in this place, however, to sum up once and for all what is meant by saying that man is at once the exception to everything and the mirror and the measure of all things. But to see man as he is, it is necessary once more to keep close to that simplicity that can clear itself of accumulated clouds of sophistry. The simplest truth about man is that he is a very strange being; almost in the sense of being a stranger on the earth. In all sobriety, he has much more of the external appearance of one bringing alien habits from another land than of a mere growth of this one. He has an unfair advantage and an unfair disadvantage. He cannot sleep in his own skin; he cannot trust his own instincts. He is at once a creator moving miraculous hands and fingers and a kind of cripple. He is wrapped in artificial bandages called clothes; he is propped on artificial crutches called furniture. His mind has the same doubtful liberties and the same wild limitations. Alone among the animals, he is shaken with the beautiful madness called laughter; as if he had caught sight of some secret in the very shape of the universe hidden from the universe itself. Alone among the animals he feels the need of averting his thought from the root realities of his own bodily being; of hiding them as in the presence of some higher possibility which creates the mystery of shame. Whether we praise these things as natural to man or abuse them as artificial in nature, they remain in the same sense unique. This is realised by the whole popular instinct called religion, until disturbed by pedants, especially the laborious pedants of the Simple Life. The most sophistical of all sophists are gymnosophists.

It is not natural to see man as a natural product. It is not common sense to call man a common object of the country or the seashore. It is not seeing straight to see him as an animal. It is not sane. It sins against the light; against that broad daylight of proportion which is the principle of all reality. It is reached by stretching a point, by making out a case, by artificially selecting a certain light and shade, by bringing into prominence the lesser or lower things which may happen to be similar. The solid thing standing in the sunlight, the thing we can walk round and see from all sides, is quite different. It is also quite extraordinary, and the more sides we see of it the more extraordinary it seems. It is emphatically not a thing that follows or flows naturally from anything else. If we imagine that an inhuman or impersonal intelligence could have felt from the first the general nature of the non-human world sufficiently to see that things would evolve in whatever way they did evolve, there would have been nothing whatever in all that natural world to prepare such a mind for such an unnatural novelty. To such a mind, man would most certainly not have seemed something like one herd out of a hundred herds finding richer pasture, or one swallow out of a hundred swallows making a summer under a strange sky. It would not be in the same scale and scarcely in the same dimension. We might as truly say that it would not be in the same universe. It would be more like seeing one cow out of a hundred cows suddenly jump over the moon or one pig out of a hundred pigs grow wings in a flash and fly. It would not be a question of the cattle finding their own grazing ground but of their building their own cattle-sheds, not a question of one swallow making a summer but of his making a summer house. For the very fact that birds do build nests is one of those similarities that sharpen the startling difference. The very fact that a bird can get as far as building a nest, and cannot get any farther, proves that he has not a mind as man has a mind; it proves it more completely than if he built nothing at all. If he built nothing at all, he might possibly be a philosopher of the Quietist or Buddhistic school, indifferent to all but the mind within. But when he builds as he does build and is satisfied and sings aloud with satisfaction, then we know there is really an invisible veil like a pane of glass between him and us, like the window on which a bird will beat in vain. But suppose our abstract onlooker saw one of the birds begin to build as men build. Suppose in an incredibly short space of time there were seven styles of architecture for one style of nest. Suppose the bird carefully selected forked twigs and pointed leaves to express the piercing piety of Gothic, but turned to broad foliage and black mud when he sought in a darker mood to call up the heavy columns of Bel and Ashtaroth; making his nest indeed one of the hanging gardens of Babylon. Suppose the bird made little clay statues of birds celebrated in letters or politics and stuck them up in front of the nest. Suppose that one bird out of a thousand birds began to do one of the thousand things that man had already done even in the morning of the world; and we can be quite certain that the onlooker would not regard such a bird as a mere evolutionary variety of the other birds; he would regard it as a very fearful wild-fowl indeed; possibly as a bird of ill-omen, certainly as an omen. That bird would tell the augurs, not of something that would happen, but of some thing that had happened. That something would be the appearance of a mind with a new dimension of depth; a mind like that of man. If there be no God, no other mind could conceivably have foreseen it.

Now, as a matter of fact, there is not a shadow of evidence that this thing was evolved at all. There is not a particle of roof that this transition came slowly, or even that it came naturally. In a strictly scientific sense, we simply know nothing whatever about how it grew, or whether it grew, or what it is. There may be a broken trail of stone and bone faintly suggesting the development of the human body. There is nothing even faintly suggesting such a development of this human mind. It was not and it was; we know not in what instant or in what infinity of years. Something happened; and it has all the appearance of a transaction outside of time. It has therefore nothing to do with history in the ordinary sense. The historian must take it or something like it for granted; it is not his business as a historian to explain it. But if he cannot explain it as a historian, he will not explain it as a biologist. In neither case is there any disgrace to him in accepting it without explaining it; for it is a reality, and history and biology deal with realities. He is quite justified in calmly confronting the pig with wings and the cow that jumped over the moon, merely because they have happened. He can reasonably accept man as a freak, because he accepts man as a fact. He can be perfectly comfortable in a crazy and disconnected world, or in a world that can produce such a crazy and disconnected thing. For reality is a thing in which we can all repose, even if it hardly seems related to anything else. The thing is there; and that is enough for most of us. But if we do indeed want to know how it can conceivably have come there, if we do indeed wish to see it related realistically to other things, if we do insist on seeing it evolved before our very eyes from an environment nearer to its own nature, then assuredly it is to very different things that we must go. We must stir very strange memories and return to very simple dreams, if we desire some origin that can make man other than a monster. We shall have discovered very different causes before he becomes a creature of causation; and invoked other authority to turn him into something reasonable, or even into anything probable. That way lies all that is at once awful and familiar and forgotten, with dreadful faces thronged and fiery arms. We can accept man as a fact, if we are content with an unexplained fact. We can accept him as an animal, if we can live with a fabulous animal. But if we must needs have sequence and necessity, then indeed we must provide a prelude and crescendo of mounting miracles, that ushered in with unthinkable thunders in all the seven heavens of another order, a man may be an ordinary thing.

II PROFESSORS AND PREHISTORIC MEN

Science is weak about these prehistoric things in a way that has hardly been noticed. The science whose modern marvels we all admire succeeds by incessantly adding to its data. In all practical inventions, in most natural discoveries, it can always increase evidence by experiment. But it cannot experiment in making men; or even in watching to see what the first men make. An inventor can advance step by step in the construction of an aeroplane, even if he is only experimenting with sticks and scraps of metal in his own back-yard. But he cannot watch the Missing Link evolving in his own back-yard. If he has made a mistake in his calculations, the aeroplane will correct it by crashing to the ground. But if he has made a mistake about the arboreal habitat of his ancestor, he cannot see his arboreal ancestor falling off the tree. He cannot keep a cave-man like a cat in the back-yard and watch him to see whether he does really practice cannibalism or carry off his mate on the principles of marriage by capture. He cannot keep a tribe of primitive men like a pack of hounds and notice how far they are influenced by the herd instinct. If he sees a particular bird behave in a particular way, he can get other birds and see if they behave in that way; but if he finds a skull, or the scrap of a skull, in the hollow of a hill, he cannot multiply it into a vision of the valley of dry bones. In dealing with a past that has almost entirely perished, he can only go by evidence and not by experiment. And there is hardly enough evidence to be even evidential. Thus while most science moves in a sort of curve, being constantly corrected by new evidence, this science flies off into space in a straight line uncorrected by anything. But the habit of forming conclusions, as they can really be formed in more fruitful fields, is so fixed in the scientific mind that it cannot resist talking like this. It talks about the idea suggested by one scrap of bone as if it were something like the aeroplane which is constructed at last out of whole scrapheaps of scraps of metal. The trouble with the professor of the prehistoric is that he cannot scrap his scrap. The marvellous and triumphant aeroplane is made out of a hundred mistakes. The student of origins can only make one mistake and stick to it.

We talk very truly of the patience of science; but in this department it would be truer to talk of the impatience of science. Owing to the difficulty above described, the theorist is in far too much of a hurry. We have a series of hypotheses so hasty that they may well be called fancies, and cannot in any case be further corrected by facts. The most empirical anthropologist is here as limited as an antiquary. He can only cling to a fragment of the past and has no way of increasing it for the future He can only clutch his fragment of fact, almost as the primitive man clutched his fragment of flint. And indeed he does deal with it in much the same way and for much the same reason. It is his tool and his only tool. It is his weapon and his only weapon. He often wields it with a fanaticism far in excess of anything shown by men of science when they can collect more facts from experience and even add new facts by experiment. Sometimes the professor with his bone becomes almost as dangerous as a dog with his bone. And the dog at least does not deduce a theory from it, proving that mankind is going to the dogs--or that it came from them.

For instance, I have pointed out the difficulty of keeping a monkey and watching it evolve into a man. Experimental evidence of such an evolution being impossible, the professor is not content to say (as most of us would be ready to say) that such an evolution is likely enough anyhow. He produces his little bone, or little collection of bones, and deduces the most marvellous things from it. He found in Java a piece of a skull, seeming by its contour to be smaller than the human. Somewhere near it he found an upright thigh-bone and in the same scattered fashion some teeth that were not human. If they all form part of one creature, which is doubtful, our conception of the creature would be almost equally doubtful. But the effect on popular science was to produce a complete and even complex figure, finished down to the last details of hair and habits. He was given a name as if he were an ordinary historical character. People talked of Pithecanthropus as of Pitt or Fox or Napoleon. Popular histories published portraits of him like the portraits of Charles the First and George the Fourth. A detailed drawing was reproduced, carefully shaded, to show that the very hairs of his head were all numbered No uninformed person looking at its carefully lined face and wistful eyes would imagine for a moment that this was the portrait of a thigh-bone; or of a few teeth and a fragment of a cranium. In the same way people talked about him as if he were an individual whose influence and character were familiar to us all. I have just read a story in a magazine about Java, and how modern white inhabitants of that island are prevailed on to misbehave themselves by the personal influence of poor old Pithecanthropus. That the modern inhabitants of Java misbehave themselves I can very readily believe; but I do not imagine that they need any encouragement from the discovery of a few highly doubtful bones. Anyhow, those bones are far too few and fragmentary and dubious to fill up the whole of the vast void that does in reason and in reality lie between man and his bestial ancestors, if they were his ancestors. On the assumption of that evolutionary connection (a connection which I am not in the least concerned to deny), the really arresting and remarkable fact is the comparative absence of any such remains recording that connection at that point. The sincerity of Darwin really admitted this; and that is how we came to use such a term as the Missing Link. But the dogmatism of Darwinians has been too strong for the agnosticism of Darwin; and men have insensibly fallen into turning this entirely negative term into a positive image. They talk of searching for the habits and habitat of the Missing Link; as if one were to talk of being on friendly terms with the gap in a narrative or the hole in an argument, of taking a walk with a non-sequitur or dining with an undistributed middle.

In this sketch, therefore, of man in his relation to certain religious and historical problems, I shall waste no further space on these speculations on the nature of man before he became man. His body may have been evolved from the brutes; but we know nothing of any such transition that throws the smallest light upon his soul as it has shown itself in history. Unfortunately the same school of writers pursue the same style of reasoning when they come to the first real evidence about the first real men. Strictly speaking of course we know nothing about prehistoric man, for the simple reason that he was prehistoric. The history of prehistoric man is a very obvious contradiction in terms. It is the sort of unreason in which only rationalists are allowed to indulge. If a parson had casually observed that the Flood was ante-diluvian, it is possible that he might be a little chaffed about his logic. If a bishop were to say that Adam was Preadamite, we might think it a little odd. But we are not supposed to notice such verbal trifles when sceptical historians talk of the part of history that is prehistoric. The truth is that they are using the terms historic and prehistoric without any clear test or definition in their minds. What they mean is that there are traces of human lives before the beginning of human stories; and in that sense we do at least know that humanity was before history.

Human civilisation is older than human records. That is the sane way of stating our relations to these remote things. Humanity has left examples of its other arts earlier than the art of writing; or at least of any writing that we can read. But it is certain that the primitive arts were arts; and it is in every way probable that the primitive civilisations were civilisations. The man left a picture of the reindeer, but he did not leave a narrative of how he hunted the reindeer; and therefore what we say of him is hypothesis and not history. But the art he did practice was quite artistic; his drawing was quite intelligent and there is no reason to doubt that his story of the hunt would be quite intelligent, only if it exists it is not intelligible. In short, the prehistoric period need not mean the primitive period, in the sense of the barbaric or bestial period. It does not mean the time before civilisation or the time before arts and crafts. It simply means the time before any connected narratives that we can read. This does indeed make all the practical difference between remembrance and forgetfulness; but it is perfectly possible that there were all sorts of forgotten forms of civilisation, as well as all sorts of forgotten forms of barbarism. And in any case everything indicated that many of these forgotten or half-forgotten social stages were much more civilised and much less barbaric than is vulgarly imagined today. But even about these unwritten histories of humanity, when humanity was quite certainly human, we can only conjecture with the greatest doubt and caution. And unfortunately doubt and caution are the last things commonly encouraged by the loose evolutionism of current culture. For that culture is full of curiosity; and the one thing that it cannot endure is the agony of agnosticism. It was in the Darwinian age that the word first became known and the thing first became impossible.

It is necessary to say plainly that all this ignorance is simply covered by impudence. Statements are made so plainly and positively that men have hardly the moral courage to pause upon them and find that they are without support. The other day a scientific summary of the state of a prehistoric tribe began confidently with the words 'They wore no clothes.' Not one reader in a hundred probably stopped to ask himself how we should come to know whether clothes had once been worn by people of whom everything has perished except a few chips of bone and stone. It was doubtless hoped that we should find a stone hat as well as a stone hatchet. It was evidently anticipated that we might discover an everlasting pair of trousers of the same substance as the everlasting rock. But to persons of a less sanguine temperament it will be immediately apparent that people might wear simple garments, or even highly ornamental garments, without leaving any more traces of them than these people have left. The plaiting of rushes and grasses, for instance, might have become more and more elaborate without in the least becoming more eternal. One civilisation might specialise in things that happened to be perishable, like weaving and embroidery, and not in things that happen to be more permanent, like architecture and sculpture. There have been plenty of examples of such specialist societies. A man of the future finding the ruins of our factory machinery might as fairly say that we were acquainted with iron and with no other substance; and announce the discovery that the proprietor and manager of the factory undoubtedly walked about naked--or possibly wore iron hats and trousers.

It is not contended here that these primitive men did wear clothes any more than they did weave rushes; but merely that we have not enough evidence to know whether they did or not. But it may be worthwhile to look back for a moment at some of the very few things that we do know and that they did do. If we consider them, we shall certainly not find them inconsistent with such ideas as dress and decoration. We do not know whether they decorated other things. We do not know whether they had embroideries, and if they had the embroideries could not be expected to have remained. But we do know that they did have pictures; and the pictures have remained. And there remains with them, as already suggested, the testimony to something that is absolute and unique; that belongs to man and to nothing else except man; that is a difference of kind and not a difference of degree. A monkey does not draw clumsily and a man cleverly; a monkey does not begin the art of representation and a man carry it to perfection. A monkey does not do it at all; he does not begin to do it at all; he does not begin to begin to do it at all. A line of some kind is crossed before the first faint line can begin.

Another distinguished writer, again, in commenting on the cave drawings attributed to the neolithic men of the reindeer period, said that none of their pictures appeared to have any religious purpose; and he seemed almost to infer that they had no religion. I can hardly imagine a thinner thread of argument than this which reconstructs the very inmost moods of the pre-historic mind from the fact that somebody who has scrawled a few sketches on a rock, from what motive we do not know, for what purpose we do not know, acting under what customs or conventions we do not know, may possibly have found it easier to draw reindeer than to draw religion. He may have drawn it because it was his religious symbol. He may have drawn it because it was not his religious symbol. He may have drawn anything except his religious symbol. He may have drawn his real religious symbol somewhere else; or it may have been deliberately destroyed when it was drawn. He may have done or not done half a million things; but in any case it is an amazing leap of logic to infer that he had no religious symbol, or even to infer from his having no religious symbol that he had no religion. Now this particular case happens to illustrate the insecurity of these guesses very clearly. For a little while afterwards, people discovered not only paintings but sculptures of animals in the caves. Some of these were said to be damaged with dints or holes supposed to be the marks of arrows; and the damaged images were conjectured to be the remains of some magic rite of killing the beasts in effigy; while the undamaged images were explained in connection with another magic rite invoking fertility upon the herds. Here again there is something faintly humorous about the scientific habit of having it both ways. If the image is damaged it proves one superstition and if it is undamaged it proves another. Here again there is a rather reckless jumping to conclusions; it has hardly occurred to the speculators that a crowd of hunters imprisoned in winter in a cave might conceivably have aimed at a mark for fun, as a sort of primitive parlour game. But in any case, if it was done out of superstition, what has become of the thesis that it had nothing to do with religion? The truth is that all this guess work has nothing to do with anything. It is not half such a good parlour game as shooting arrows at a carved reindeer, for it is shooting them into the air.

Such speculators rather tend to forget, for instance, that men in the modern world also sometimes make marks in caves. When a crowd of trippers is conducted through the labyrinth of the Marvelous Grotto or the Magic Stalactite Cavern, it has been observed that hieroglyphics spring into sight where they have passed; initials and inscriptions which the learned refuse to refer to any remote date. But the time will come when these inscriptions will really be of remote date. And if the professors of the future are anything like the professors of the present, they will be able to deduce a vast number of very vivid and interesting things from these cave-writings of the twentieth century. If I know anything about the breed, and if they have not fallen away from the full-blooded confidence of their fathers, they will be able to discover the most fascinating facts about us from the initials left in the Magic Grotto by 'Arry and 'Arriet, possibly in the form of two intertwined A's. From this alone they will know (1) That as the letters are rudely chipped with a blunt pocket knife, the twentieth century possessed no delicate graving-tools and was unacquainted with the art of sculpture. (2) That as the letters are capital letters, our civilisation never evolved any small letters or anything like a running hand. (3) That because initial consonants stand together in an unpronounceable fashion, our language was possibly akin to Welsh or more probably of the early Semitic type that ignored vowels. (4) That as the initials of 'Arry and 'Arriet do not in any special fashion profess to be religious symbols, our civilisation possessed no religion. Perhaps the last is about the nearest to the truth; for a civilisation that had religion would have a little more reason.

It is commonly affirmed, again, that religion grew in a very slow and evolutionary manner; and even that it grew not from one cause; but from a combination that might be called a coincidence. Generally speaking, the three chief elements in the combination are, first, the fear of the chief of the tribe (whom Mr. Wells insists on calling, with regrettable familiarity, the Old Man), second, the phenomena of dreams, and third, the sacrificial associations of the harvest and the resurrection symbolised in the growing corn. I may remark in passing that it seems to me very doubtful psychology to refer one living and single spirit to three dead and disconnected causes, if they were merely dead and disconnected causes. Suppose Mr. Wells, in one of his fascinating novels of the future, were to tell us that there would arise among men a new and as yet nameless passion, of which men will dream as they dream of first love, for which they will die as they die for a flag and a fatherland. I think we should be a little puzzled if he told us that this singular sentiment would be a combination of the habit of smoking Woodbines, the increase of the income tax and the pleasure of a motorist in exceeding the speed limit. We could not easily imagine this, because we could not imagine any connection between the three or any common feeling that could include them all. Nor could anyone imagine any connection between corn and dreams and an old chief with a spear, unless there was already a common feeling to include them all. But if there was such a common feeling it could only be the religious feeling; and these things could not be the beginnings of a religious feeling that existed already. I think anybody's common sense will tell him that it is far more likely that this sort of mystical sentiment did exist already; and that in the light of it dreams and kings and corn-fields could appear mystical then, as they can appear mystical now.

For the plain truth is that all this is a trick of making things seem distant and dehumanised, merely by pretending not to understand things that we do understand. It is like saying that prehistoric men had an ugly and uncouth habit of opening their mouths wide at intervals and stuffing strange substances into them, as if we had never heard of eating. It is like saying that the terrible Troglodytes of the Stone Age lifted alternate legs in rotation, as if we never heard of walking. If it were meant to touch the mystical nerve and awaken us to the wonder of walking and eating, it might be a legitimate fancy. As it is here intended to kill the mystical nerve and deaden us to the wonder of religion, it is irrational rubbish. It pretends to find some thing incomprehensible in the feelings that we all comprehend. Who does not find dreams mysterious, and feel that they lie on the dark borderland of being? Who does not feel the death and resurrection of the growing things of the earth as something near to the secret of the universe? Who does not understand that there must always be the savour of something sacred about authority and the solidarity that is the soul of the tribe? If there be any anthropologist who really finds these things remote and impossible to realise, we can say nothing of that scientific gentleman except that he has not got so large and enlightened a mind as a primitive man. To me it seems obvious that nothing but a spiritual sentiment already active could have clothed these separate and diverse things with sanctity. To say that religion came from reverencing a chief or sacrificing at a harvest is to put a highly elaborate cart before a really primitive horse. It is like saying that the impulse to draw pictures came from the contemplation of the pictures of reindeers in the cave. In other words, it is explaining painting by saying that it arose out of the work of painters; or accounting for art by saying that it arose out of art. It is even more like saying that the thing we call poetry arose as the result of certain customs; such as that of an ode being officially composed to celebrate the advent of spring; or that of a young man rising at a regular hour to listen to the skylark and then writing his report on a piece of paper. It is quite true that young men often become poets in the spring; and it is quite true that when once there are poets, no mortal power can restrain them from writing about the skylark But the poems did not exist before the poets. The poetry did not arise out of the poetic forms. In other words, it is hardly an adequate explanation of how a thing appeared for the first time to say it existed already. Similarly, we cannot say that religion arose out of the religious forms, because that is only another way of saying that it only arose when it existed already. It needed a certain sort of mind to see that there was anything mystical about the dreams or the dead, as it needed a particular sort of mind to see that there was any thing poetical about the skylark or the spring. That mind was presumably what we call the human mind, very much as it exists to this day; for mystics still meditate upon death and dreams as poets still write about spring and skylarks. But there is not the faintest hint to suggest that anything short of the human mind we know feels any of these mystical associations at all. A cow in a field seems to derive no lyrical impulse or instruction from her unrivalled opportunities for listening to the skylark. And similarly there is no reason to suppose that live sheep will ever begin to use dead sheep as the basis of a system of elaborate ancestor-worship. It is true that in the spring a young quadruped's fancy may lightly turn to thoughts of love, but no succession of springs has ever led it to turn however lightly to thoughts of literature. And in the same way, while it is true that a dog has dreams, while most other quadrupeds do not seem even to have that, we have waited a long time for the dog to develop his dreams into an elaborate system or religious ceremonial. We have waited so long that we have really ceased to expect it; and we no more look to see a dog apply his dreams to ecclesiastical construction than to see him examine his dreams by the rules of psycho-analysis. It is obvious, in short, that for some reason or other these natural experiences, and even natural excitements, never do pass the line that separates them from creative expression like art and religion, in any creature except man. They never do, they never have, and it is now to all appearance very improbable that they ever will. It is not impossible, in the sense of self-contradictory, that we should see cows fasting from grass every Friday or going on their knees as in the old legend about Christmas Eve. It is not in that sense impossible that cows should contemplate death until they can lift up a sublime psalm of lamentation to the tune the old cow died of. It is not in that sense impossible that they should express their hopes of a heavenly career in a symbolic dance, in honour of the cow that jumped over the moon. It may be that the dog will at last have laid in a sufficient store of dreams to enable him to build a temple to Cerberus as a sort of canine trinity. It may be that his dreams have already begun to turn into visions capable of verbal expression, in some revelation about the Dog Star as the spiritual home for lost dogs. These things are logically possible, in the sense that it is logically difficult to prove the universal negative which we call an impossibility. But all that instinct for the probable, which we call common sense, must long ago have told us that the animals are not to all appearance evolving in that sense; and that, to say the least, we are not likely to have any personal evidence of their passing from the animal experience to the human experiments. But spring and death and even dreams, considered merely as experiences, are their experiences as much as ours. The only possible conclusion is that these experiences, considered as experiences, do not generate anything like a religious sense in any mind except a mind like ours. We come back to the fact of a certain kind of mind that was already alive and alone. It was unique and it could make creeds as it could make cave-drawings. The materials for religion had lain there for countless ages like the materials for everything else; but the power of religion was in the mind. Man could already see in these things the riddles and hints and hopes that he still sees in them. He could not only dream but dream about dreams. He could not only see the dead but see the shadow of death; and was possessed with that mysterious mystification that forever finds death incredible.

It is quite true that we have even these hints chiefly about man when he unmistakably appears as man. We cannot affirm this or anything else about the alleged animal originally connecting man and the brutes. But that is only because he is not an animal but an allegation. We cannot be certain the Pithecanthropus ever worshipped, because we cannot be certain that he ever lived. He is only a vision called up to fill the void that does in fact yawn between the first creatures who were certainly men and any other creatures that are certainly apes or other animals. A few very doubtful fragments are scraped together to suggest such an intermediate creature because it is required by a certain philosophy; but nobody supposes that these are sufficient to establish anything philosophical even in support of that philosophy. A scrap of skull found in Java cannot establish anything about religion or about the absence of religion. If there ever was any such ape-man, he may have exhibited as much ritual in religion as a man or as much simplicity in religion as an ape. He may have been a mythologist or he may have been a myth. It might be interesting to inquire whether this mystical quality appeared in a transition from the ape to the man, if there were really any types of the transition to inquire about. In other words, the missing link might or might not be mystical if he were not missing. But compared with the evidence we have of real human beings, we have no evidence that he was a human being or a half-human being or a being at all. Even the most extreme evolutionists do not attempt to deduce any evolutionary views about the origin of religion from him. Even in trying to prove that religion grew slowly from rude or irrational sources, they begin their proof with the first men who were men. But their own proof only proves that the men who were already men were already mystics. They used the rude and irrational elements as only men and mystics can use them. We come back once more to the simple truth; that at sometime too early for these critics to trace, a transition had occurred to which bones and stones cannot in their nature bear witness; and man became a living soul.

Touching this matter of the origin of religion, the truth is that those who are thus trying to explain it are trying to explain it away. Subconsciously they feel that it looks less formidable when thus lengthened out into a gradual and almost invisible process. But in fact this perspective entirely falsifies the reality of experience. They bring together two things that are totally different, the stray hints of evolutionary origins and the solid and self-evident block of humanity, and try to shift their standpoint till they see them in a single foreshortened line. But it is an optical illusion. Men do not in fact stand related to monkeys or missing links in any such chain as that in which men stand related to men. There may have been intermediate creatures whose faint traces can be found here and there in the huge gap. Of these beings, if they ever existed, it may be true that they were things very unlike men or men very unlike ourselves. But of prehistoric men, such as those called the cave-men or the reindeer men, it is not true in any sense whatever. Prehistoric men of that sort were things exactly like men and men exceedingly like our selves. They only happened to be men about whom we do not know much, for the simple reason that they have left no records or chronicles; but all that we do know about them makes them just as human and ordinary as men in a medieval manor or a Greek city.

Looking from our human standpoint up the long perspective of humanity, we simply recognise this thing as human. If we had to recognise it as animal we should have had to recognise it as abnormal. If we chose to look through the other end of the telescope, as I have done more than once in these speculations, if we chose to project the human figure forward out of an unhuman world, we could only say that one of the animals had obviously gone mad. But seeing the thing from the right end, or rather from the inside, we know it is sanity; and we know that these primitive men were sane. We hail a certain human freemasonry wherever we see it, in savages, in foreigners or in historical characters. For instance, all we can infer from primitive legend, and all we know of barbaric life, supports a certain moral and even mystical idea of which the commonest symbol is clothes. For clothes are very literally vestments and man wears them because he is a priest. It is true that even as an animal he is here different from the animals. Nakedness is not nature to him; it is not his life but rather his death; even in the vulgar sense of his death of cold. But clothes are worn for dignity or decency or decoration where they are not in any way wanted for warmth. It would sometimes appear that they are valued for ornament before they are valued for use. It would almost always appear that they are felt to have some connection with decorum. Conventions of this sort vary a great deal with various times and places; and there are some who cannot get over this reflection, and for whom it seems a sufficient argument for letting all conventions slide. They never tire of repeating, with simple wonder, that dress is different in the Cannibal Islands and in Camden Town; they cannot get any further and throw up the whole idea of decency in despair. They might as well say that because there have been hats of a good many different shapes, and some rather eccentric shapes, therefore hats do not matter or do not exist. They would probably add that there is no such thing as sunstroke or going bald. Men have felt everywhere that certain norms were necessary to fence off and protect certain private things from contempt or coarse misunderstanding; and the keeping of those forms, whatever they were, made for dignity and mutual respect. The fact that they mostly refer, more or less remotely, to the relations of the sexes illustrates the two facts that must be put at the very beginning of the record of the race. The first is the fact that original sin is really original. Not merely in theology but in history it is a thing rooted in the origins. Whatever else men have believed, they have all believed that there is something the matter with mankind This sense of sin has made it impossible to be natural and have no clothes, just as it has made it impossible to be natural and have no laws. But above all it is to be found in that other fact, which is the father and mother of all laws as it is itself founded on a father and mother; the thing that is before all thrones and even all commonwealths.

That fact is the family. Here again we must keep the enormous proportions of a normal thing clear of various modifications and degrees and doubts more or less reasonable, like clouds clinging about a mountain. It may be that what we call the family had to fight its way from or through various anarchies and aberrations; but it certainly survived them and is quite as likely as not to have also preceded them. As we shall see in the case of communism and nomadism, more formless things could and did lie on the flank of societies that had taken a fixed form; but there is nothing to show that the form did not exist before the formlessness. What is vital is that form is more important than formlessness; and that the material called mankind has taken this form. For instance, of the rules revolving round sex, which were recently mentioned, none is more curious than the savage custom commonly called the couvade. That seems like a law out of topsyturvydom; by which the father is treated as if he were the mother. In any case it clearly involves the mystical sense of sex; but many have maintained that it is really a symbolic act by which the father accepts the responsibility of fatherhood. In that case that grotesque antic is really a very solemn act; for it is the foundation of all we call the family and all we know as human society. Some groping in these dark beginnings have said that mankind was once under a matriarchy; I suppose that under a matriarchy it would not be called mankind but womankind. But others have conjectured that what is called matriarchy was simply moral anarchy, in which the mother alone remained fixed because all the fathers were fugitive and irresponsible. Then came the moment when the man decided to guard and guide what he had created. So he became the head of the family, not as a bully with a big club to beat women with, but rather as a respectable person trying to be a responsible person. Now all that might be perfectly true, and might even have been the first family act, and it would still be true that man then for the first time acted like a man, and therefore for the first time became fully a man. But it might quite as well be true that the matriarchy or moral anarchy, or whatever we call it, was only one of the hundred social dissolutions or barbaric backslidings which may have occurred at intervals in prehistoric as they certainly did in historic times. A symbol like the couvade, if it was really such a symbol, may have commemorated the suppression of a heresy rather than the first rise of a religion. We cannot conclude with any certainty about these things, except in their big results in the building of mankind, but we can say in what style the bulk of it and the best of it is built. We can say that the family is the unit of the state; that it is the cell that makes up the formation. Round the family do indeed gather the sanctities that separate men from ants and bees. Decency is the curtain of that tent; liberty is the wall of that city; property is but the family farm; honour is but the family flag. In the practical proportions of human history, we come back to that fundamental of the father and the mother and the child. It has been said already that if this story cannot start with religious assumptions, it must none the less start with some moral or metaphysical assumptions, or no sense can be made of the story of man. And this is a very good instance of that alternative necessity. If we are not of those who begin by invoking a divine Trinity, we must none the less invoke a human Trinity; and see that triangle repeated everywhere in the pattern of the world. For the highest event in history, to which all history looks forward and leads up, is only something that is at once the reversal and the renewal of that triangle. Or rather it is the one triangle superimposed so as to intersect the other, making a sacred pentacle of which, in a mightier sense than that of the magicians, the fiends are afraid. The old Trinity was of father and mother and child and is called the human family. The new is of child and mother and father and has the name of the Holy Family. It is in no way altered except in being entirely reversed; just as the world which is transformed was not in the least different, except in being turned upside-down.

III THE ANTIQUITY OF CIVILISATION

The modern man looking at the most ancient origins has been like a man watching for daybreak in a strange land; and expecting to see that dawn breaking behind bare uplands or solitary peaks. But that dawn is breaking behind the black bulk of great cities long builded and lost for us in the original night; colossal cities like the houses of giants, in which even the carved ornamental animals are taller than the palm-trees; in which the painted portrait can be twelve times the size of the man; with tombs like mountains of man set four-square and pointing to the stars; with winged and bearded bulls standing and staring enormous at the gates of temples; standing still eternally as if a stamp would shake the world. The dawn of history reveals a humanity already civilized. Perhaps it reveals a civilisation already old. And among other more important things, it reveals the folly of most of the generalisations about the previous and unknown period when it was really young. The two first human societies of which we have any reliable and detailed record are Babylon and Egypt. It so happens that these two vast and splendid achievements of the genius of the ancients bear witness against two of the commonest and crudest assumptions of the culture of the moderns. If we want to get rid of half the nonsense about nomads and cave-men and the old man of the forest, we need only look steadily at the two solid and stupendous facts called Egypt and Babylon.

Of course most of these speculators who are talking about primitive men are thinking about modern savages. They prove their progressive evolution by assuming that a great part of the human race has not progressed or evolved; or even changed in any way at all. I do not agree with their theory of change; nor do I agree with their dogma of things unchangeable. I may not believe that civilised man has had so rapid and recent a progress; but I cannot quite understand why uncivilised man should be so mystically immortal and immutable. A somewhat simpler mode of thought and speech seems to me to be needed throughout this inquiry. Modern savages cannot be exactly like primitive man, because they are not primitive. Modern savages are not ancient because they are modern. Something has happened to their race as much as to ours, during the thousands of years of our existence and endurance on the earth. They have had some experiences, and have presumably acted on them if not profited by them. Like the rest of us. They have had some environment, and even some change of environment, and have presumably adapted themselves to it in a proper and decorous evolutionary manner. This would be true even if the experiences were mild or the environment dreary; for there is an effect in mere time when it takes the moral form of monotony. But it has appeared to a good many intelligent and well-informed people quite as probable that the experience of the savages has been that of a decline from civilisation. Most of those who criticise this view do not seem to have any very clear notion of what a decline from civilisation would be like. Heaven help them, it is likely enough that they will soon find out. They seem to be content if cave-men and cannibal islanders have some things in common, such as certain particular implements. But it is obvious on the face of it that any peoples reduced for any reason to a ruder life would have some things in common. If we lost all our firearms we should make bows and arrows; but we should not necessarily resemble in every way the first men who made bows and arrows. It is said that the Russians in their great retreat were so short of armament that they fought with clubs cut in the wood. But a professor of the future would err in supposing that the Russian army of 1916 was a naked Scythian tribe that had never been out of the wood. It is like saying that a man in his second childhood must exactly copy his first. A baby is bald like an old man; but it would be an error for one ignorant of infancy to infer that the baby had a long white beard. Both a baby and an old man walk with difficulty; but he who shall expect the old gentleman to lie on his back, and kick joyfully instead, will be disappointed.

It is therefore absurd to argue that the first pioneers of humanity must have been identical with some of the last and most stagnant leavings of it. There were almost certainly some things, there were probably many things, in which the two were widely different or flatly contrary. An example of the way in which this distinction works, and an example essential to our argument here, is that of the nature and origin of government I have already alluded to Mr. H. G. Wells and the Old Man, with whom he appears to be on such intimate terms. If we considered the cold facts of prehistoric evidence for this portrait of the prehistoric chief of the tribe, we could only excuse it by saying that its brilliant and versatile author simply forgot for a moment that he was supposed to be writing a history, and dreamed he was writing one of his own very wonderful and imaginative romances. At least I cannot imagine how he can possibly know that the prehistoric ruler was called the Old Man or that court etiquette requires it to be spelt with capital letters. He says of the same potentate, 'No one was allowed to touch his spear or to sit in his seat.' I have difficulty in believing that anybody has dug up a prehistoric spear with a prehistoric label, 'Visitors are Requested not to Touch,' or a complete throne with the inscription, 'Reserved for the Old Man.' But it may be presumed that the writer, who can hardly be supposed to be merely making up things out of his own head, was merely taking for granted this very dubious parallel between the prehistoric and the decivilised man. It may be that in certain savage tribes the chief is called the Old Man and nobody is allowed to touch his spear or sit on his seat. It may be that in those cases he is surrounded with superstitious and traditional terrors; and it may be that in those cases, for all I know, he is despotic and tyrannical. But there is not a grain of evidence that primitive government was despotic and tyrannical. It may have been, of course, for it may have been anything or even nothing; it may not have existed at all. But the despotism in certain dingy and decayed tribes in the twentieth century does not prove that the first men were ruled despotically. It does not even suggest it; it does not even begin to hint at it. If there is one fact we really can prove, from the history that we really do know, it is that despotism can be a development, often a late development and very often indeed the end of societies that have been highly democratic. A despotism may almost be defined as a tired democracy. As fatigue falls on a community, the citizens are less inclined for that eternal vigilance which has truly been called the price of liberty; and they prefer to arm only one single sentinel to watch the city while they sleep. It is also true that they sometimes needed him for some sudden and militant act of reform; it is equally true that he often took advantage of being the strong man armed to be a tyrant like some of the Sultans of the East. But I cannot see why the Sultan should have appeared any earlier in history than many other human figures. On the contrary, the strong man armed obviously depends upon the superiority of his armour, and armament of that sort comes with more complex civilisation. One man may kill twenty with a machine-gum; it is obviously less likely that he could do it with a piece of flint. As for the current cant about the strongest man ruling by force and fear, it is simply a nursery fairy-tale about a giant with a hundred hands. Twenty men could hold down the strongest strong man in any society, ancient or modern. Undoubtedly they might admire, in a romantic and poetical sense, the man who was really the strongest; but that is quite a different thing, and is as purely moral and even mystical as the admiration for the purest or the wisest. But the spirit that endures the mere cruelties and caprices of an established despot is the spirit of an ancient and settled and probably stiffened society, not the spirit of a new one. As his name implies, the Old Man is the ruler of an old humanity.

It is far more probable that a primitive society was something like a pure democracy. To this day the comparatively simple agricultural communities are by far the purest democracies. Democracy is a thing which is always breaking down through the complexity of civilisation. Anyone who likes may state it by saying that democracy is the foe of civilisation. But he must remember that some of us really prefer democracy to civilisation, in the sense of preferring democracy to complexity. Anyhow, peasants tilling patches of their own land in a rough equality, and meeting to vote directly under a village tree, are the most truly self-governing of men. It is surely as likely as not that such a simple idea was found in the first condition of even simpler men. Indeed the despotic vision is exaggerated, even if we do not regard the men as men. Even on an evolutionary assumption of the most materialistic sort, there is really no reason why men should not have had at least as much camaraderie as rats or rooks. Leadership of some sort they doubtless had, as have the gregarious animals; but leadership implies no such irrational servility as that attributed to the superstitious subjects of the Old Man. There was doubtless some body corresponding, to use Tennyson's expression, to the many-wintered crow that leads the clanging rookery home. But I fancy that if that venerable fowl began to act after the fashion of some Sultans in ancient and decayed Asia, it would become a very clanging rookery and the many-wintered crow would not see many more winters. It may be remarked, in this connection, but even among animals it would seem that something else is respected more than bestial violence, if it be only the familiarity which in men is called tradition or the experience which in men is called wisdom. I do not know if crows really follow the oldest crow, but if they do they are certainly not following the strongest crow. And I do know, in the human case, that if some ritual of seniority keeps savages reverencing somebody called Old Man, then at least they have not our own servile sentimental weakness for worshipping the Strong Man.

It may be said then that primitive government, like primitive art and religion and everything else, is very imperfectly known or rather guessed at; but that it is at least as good a guess to suggest that it was as popular as a Balkan or Pyrenean village as that it was as capricious and secret as a Turkish divan. Both the mountain democracy and the oriental palace are modern in the sense that they are still there, or are some sort of growth of history; but of the two the palace has much more the look of being an accumulation and a corruption, the village much more the look of being a really unchanged and primitive thing. But my suggestions at this point do not go beyond expressing a wholesome doubt about the current assumption. I think it interesting, for instance, that liberal institutions have been traced even by moderns back to barbarians or undeveloped states, when it happened to be convenient for the support of some race or nation or philosophy. So the Socialists profess that their ideal of communal property existed in very early times. So the Jews are proud of the Jubilees or juster redistributions under their ancient law. So the Teutonists boasted of tracing parliaments and juries and various popular things among the Germanic tribes of the north. So the Celtophiles and those testifying to the wrongs of Ireland have pleaded the more equal justice of the clan system, to which the Irish chiefs bore witness before Strongbow. The strength of the case varies in the different cases; but as there is some case for all of them, I suspect there is some case for the general proposition that popular institutions of some sort were by no means uncommon in early and simple societies. Each of these separate schools were making the admission to prove a particular modern thesis; but taken together they suggest a more ancient and general truth, that there was something more in prehistoric councils than ferocity and fear. Each of these separate theorists had his own axe to grind, but he was willing to use a stone axe; and he manages to suggest that the stone axe might have been as republican as the guillotine.

But the truth is that the curtain rises upon the play already in progress In one sense it is a true paradox that there was history before history. But it is not the irrational paradox implied in prehistoric history; for it is a history we do not know. Very probably it was exceedingly like the history we do know, except in the one detail that we do not know it. It is thus the very opposite of the pretentious prehistoric history, which professes to trace everything in a consistent course from the amoeba to the anthropoid and from the anthropoid to the agnostic. So far from being a question of our knowing all about queer creatures very different from ourselves, they were very probably people very like ourselves, except that we know nothing about them. In other words, our most ancient records only reach back to a time when humanity had long been human, and even long been civilised. The most ancient records we have not only mention but take for granted things like kings and priests and princes and assemblies of the people; they describe communities that are roughly recognisable as communities in our own sense. Some of them are despotic; but we cannot tell that they have always been despotic. Some of them may be already decadent and nearly all are mentioned as if they were old. We do not know what really happened in the world before those records; but the little we do know would leave us anything but astonished if we learnt that it was very much like what happens in this world now. There would be nothing inconsistent or confounding about the discovery that those unknown ages were full of republics collapsing under monarchies and rising again as republics, empires expanding and finding colonies and then losing colonies. Kingdoms combining again into world states and breaking up again into small nationalities, classes selling themselves into slavery and marching out once more into liberty; all that procession of humanity which may or may not be a progress but most assuredly a romance. But the first chapters of the romance have been torn out of the book; and we shall never read them.

It is so also with the more special fancy about evolution and social stability. According to the real records available, barbarism and civilisation were not successive states in the progress of the world. They were conditions that existed side by side, as they still exist side by side. There were civilisations then as there are civilisations now; there are savages now as there were savages then. It is suggested that all men passed through a nomadic stage; but it is certain that there are some who have never passed out of it, and it seems not unlikely that there were some who never passed into it. It is probable that from very primitive times the static tiller of the soil and the wandering shepherd were two distinct types of men; and the chronological rearrangement of them is but a mark of that mania for progressive stages that has largely falsified history. It is suggested that there was a communist stage, in which private property was everywhere unknown, a whole humanity living on the negation of property; but the evidences of this negation are themselves rather negative. Redistributions of property, jubilees, and agrarian laws, occur at various intervals and in various forms; but that humanity inevitably passed through a communist stage seems as doubtful as the parallel proposition that humanity will inevitably return to it. It is chiefly interesting as evidence that the boldest plans for the future invoke the authority of the past; and that even a revolutionary seeks to satisfy himself that he is also a reactionary. There is an amusing parallel example in the case of what is called feminism. In spite of all the pseudo-scientific gossip about marriage by capture and the cave-man beating the cave-woman with a club, it may be noted that as soon as feminism became a fashionable cry, it was insisted that human civilisation in its first stage had been a matriarchy. Apparently it was the cave-woman who carried the club. Anyhow all these ideas are little better than guesses; they have a curious way of following the fortune of modern theories and fads. In any case they are not history in the sense of record; and we may repeat that when it comes to record, the broad truth is that barbarism and civilisation have always dwelt side by side in the world, the civilisation sometimes spreading to absorb the barbarians, sometimes decaying into relative barbarism, and in almost all cases possessing in a more finished form certain ideas and institutions which the barbarians possess in a ruder form; such as government or social authority, the arts and especially the decorative arts, mysteries and taboos of various kinds especially surrounding the matter of sex, and some form of that fundamental thing which is the chief concern of this enquiry; the thing that we call religion.

Now Egypt and Babylon, those two primeval monsters, might in this matter have been specially provided as models. They might almost be called working models to show how these modern theories do not work. The two great truths we know about these two great cultures happen to contradict flatly the two current fallacies which have just been considered. The story of Egypt might have been invented to point the moral that man does not necessarily begin with despotism because he is barbarous, but very often finds his way to despotism because he is civilised. He finds it because he is experienced; or, what is often much the same thing, because he is exhausted And the story of Babylon might have been invented to point the moral that man need not be a nomad or a communist before he becomes a peasant or a citizen, and that such cultures are not always in successive stages but often in contemporary states. Even touching these great civilisations with which our written history begins there is a temptation of course to be too ingenious or too cocksure. We can read the bricks of Babylon in a very different sense from that in which we guess about the Cup and Ring stones; and we do definitely know what is meant by the animals in the Egyptian hieroglyphic as we know nothing of the animal in the neolithic cave. But even here the admirable archeologists who have deciphered line after line of miles of hieroglyphics may be tempted to read too much between the lines; even the real authority on Babylon may forget how fragmentary is his hard-won knowledge; may forget that Babylon has only heaved half a brick at him, though half a brick is better than no cuneiform. But some truths, historic and not prehistoric, dogmatic and not evolutionary, facts and not fancies, do indeed emerge from Egypt and Babylon; and these two truths are among them.

Egypt is a green ribbon along the river edging the dark red desolation of the desert. It is a proverb, and one of vast antiquity, that it is created by the mysterious bounty and almost sinister benevolence of the Nile. When we first hear of Egyptians they are living as in a string of river-side villages, in small and separate but co-operative communities along the bank of the Nile. Where the river branched into the broad Delta there was traditionally the beginning of a somewhat different district or people; but this need not complicate the main truth. These more or less independent though interdependent peoples were considerably civilised already. They had a sort of heraldry; that is, decorative art used for symbolic and social purposes; each sailing the Nile under its own ensign representing some bird or animal. Heraldry involves two things of enormous importance to normal humanity; the combination of the two making that noble thing called co-operation; on which rest all peasantries and peoples that are free. The art of heraldry means independence; an image chosen by the imagination to express the individuality. The science of heraldry means interdependence; an agreement between different bodies to recognise different images; a science of imagery. We have here therefore exactly that compromise of co-operation between free families or groups which is the most normal mode of life for humanity and is particularly apparent wherever men own their own land and live on it. With the very mention of the image of bird and beast the student of mythology will murmur the word 'totem' almost in his sleep. But to my mind much of the trouble arises from his habit of saying such words as if in his sleep. Throughout this rough outline I have made a necessarily inadequate attempt to keep on the inside rather than the outside of such things; to consider them where possible in terms of thought and not merely in terms of terminology. There is very little value in talking about totems unless we have some feeling of what it really felt like to have a totem. Granted that they had totems and we have no totems; was it because they had more fear of animals or more familiarity with animals? Did a man whose totem was a wolf feel like a were-wolf or like a man running away from a were-wolf? Did he feel like Uncle Remus about Brer Wolf or like St. Francis about his brother the wolf, or like Mowgli about his brothers the wolves? Was a totem a thing like the British lion or a thing like the British bull-dog? Was the worship of a totem like the feeling of niggers about Mumbo Jumbo, or of children about Jumbo? I have never read any book of folk-lore, however learned, that gave me any light upon this question, which I think by far the most important one. I will confine myself to repeating that the earliest Egyptian communities had a common understanding about the images that stood for their individual states; and that this amount of communication is prehistoric in the sense that it is already there at the beginning of history. But as history unfolds itself, this question of communication is clearly the main question of these riverside communities. With the need of communication comes the need of a common government and the growing greatness and spreading shadow of the king. The other binding force besides the king, and perhaps older than the king, is the priesthood; and the priesthood has presumably even more to do with these ritual symbols and signals by which men can communicate. And here in Egypt arose probably the primary and certainly the typical invention to which we owe all history, and the whole difference between the historic and the prehistoric: the archetypal script, the art of writing.

The popular pictures of these primeval empires are not half so popular as they might be. There is shed over them the shadow of an exaggerated gloom, more than the normal and even healthy sadness of heathen men. It is part of the same sort of secret pessimism that loves to make primitive man a crawling creature, whose body is filth and whose soul is fear. It comes of course from the fact that men are moved most by their religion; especially when it is irreligion. For them anything primary and elemental must be evil. But it is the curious consequence that while we have been deluged with the wildest experiments in primitive romance, they have all missed the real romance of being primitive. They have described scenes that are wholly imaginary, in which the men of the Stone Age are men of stone like walking statues; in which the Assyrians or Egyptians are as stiff or as painted as their own most archaic art. But none of these makers of imaginary scenes have tried to imagine what it must really have been like to see those things as fresh which we see as familiar. They have not seen a man discovering fire like a child discovering fireworks. They have not seen a man playing with the wonderful invention called the wheel, like a boy playing at putting up a wireless station. They have never put the spirit of youth into their descriptions of the youth of the world. It follows that amid all their primitive or prehistoric fancies there are no jokes. There are not even practical jokes, in connection with the practical inventions. And this is very sharply defined in the particular case of hieroglyphics; for there seems to be serious indication that the whole high human art of scripture or writing began with a joke.

There are some who will learn with regret that it seems to have begun with a pun. The king or the priests or some responsible persons, wishing to send a message up the river in that inconveniently long and narrow territory, hit on the idea of sending it in picture writing, like that of the Red Indian. Like most people who have written picture-writing for fun, he found the words did not always fit. But when the word for taxes sounded rather like the word for pig, he boldly put down a pig as a bad pun and chanced it. So a modern hieroglyphist might represent 'at once' by unscrupulously drawing a hat followed by a series of upright numerals. It was good enough for the Pharaohs and ought to be good enough for him. But it must have been great fun to write or even to read these messages, when writing and reading were really a new thing. And if people must write romances about ancient Egypt (and it seems that neither prayers nor tears nor curses can withhold them from the habit), I suggest that scenes like this would really remind us that the ancient Egyptians were human beings. I suggest that somebody should describe the scene of the great monarch sitting among his priests, and all of them roaring with laughter and bubbling over with suggestions as the royal puns grew more and more wild and indefensible. There might be another scene of almost equal excitement about the decoding of this cipher; the guesses and clues and discoveries having all the popular thrill of a detective story. That is how primitive romance and primitive history really ought to be written. For whatever was the quality of the religious or moral life of remote times, and it was probably much more human than is conventionally supposed, the scientific interest of such a time must have been intense. Words must have been more wonderful than wireless telegraphy; and experiments with common things a series of electric shocks. We are still waiting for somebody to write a lively story of primitive life. The point is in some sense a parenthesis here; but it is connected with the general matter of political development, by the institution which was most active in these first and most fascinating of all the fairy-tales of science.

It is admitted that we owe most of this science to the priests. Modern writers like Mr. Wells cannot be accused of any weakness of sympathy with a pontifical hierarchy; but they agree at least in recognising what pagan priesthoods did for the arts and sciences. Among the more ignorant of the enlightened there was indeed a convention of saying that priests had obstructed progress in all ages; and a politician once told me in a debate that I was resisting modern reforms exactly as some ancient priest probably resisted the discovery of wheels. I pointed out, in reply, that it was far more likely that the ancient priest made the discovery of the wheels. It is overwhelmingly probable that the ancient priest had a great deal to do with the discovery of the art of writing. It is obvious enough in the fact that the very word hieroglyphic is akin to the word hierarchy. The religion of these priests was apparently a more or less tangled polytheism of a type that is more particularly described elsewhere. It passed through a period when it cooperated with the king, another period when it was temporarily destroyed by the king, who happened to be a prince with a private theism of his own, and a third period when it practically destroyed the king and ruled in his stead. But the world has to thank it for many things which it considers common and necessary: and the creators of those common things ought really to have a place among the heroes of humanity. If we were at rest in a real paganism, instead of being restless in a rather irrational reaction from Christianity, we might pay some sort of pagan honour to these nameless makers of mankind. We might have veiled statues of the man who first found fire or the man who first made a boat or the man who first tamed a horse. And if we brought them garlands or sacrifices, there would be more sense in it than in disfiguring our cities with cockney statues of stale politicians and philanthropists. But one of the strange marks of the strength of Christianity is that, since it came, no pagan in our civilisation has been able to be really human.

The point is here, however, that the Egyptian government, whether pontifical or royal, found it more and more necessary to establish communication; and there always went with communication a certain element of coercion. It is not necessarily an indefensible thing that the state grew more despotic as it grew more civilised; it is arguable that it had to grow more despotic in order to grow more civilised. That is the argument for autocracy in every age; and the interest lies in seeing it illustrated in the earliest age. But it is emphatically not true that it was most despotic in the earliest age and grew more liberal in a later age; the practical process of history is exactly the reverse. It is not true that the tribe began in the extreme of terror of the Old Man and his seat and spear; it is probable, at least in Egypt, that the Old Man was rather a New Man armed to attack new conditions. His spear grew longer and longer and his throne rose higher and higher, as Egypt rose into a complex and complete civilisation. That is what I mean by saying that the history of the Egyptian territory is in this the history of the earth; and directly denies the vulgar assumption that terrorism can only come at the beginning and cannot come at the end. We do not know what was the very first condition of the more or less feudal amalgam of land owners, peasants and slaves in the little commonwealths beside the Nile; but it may have been a peasantry of an even more popular sort. What we do know is that it was by experience and education that little commonwealths lose their liberty; that absolute sovereignty is something not merely ancient but rather relatively modern; and it is at the end of the path called progress that men return to the king.

Egypt exhibits, in that brief record of its remotest beginnings, the primary problem of liberty and civilisation. It is the fact that men actually lose variety by complexity. We have not solved the problem properly any more than they did; but it vulgarises the human dignity of the problem itself to suggest that even tyranny has no motive save in tribal terror. And just as the Egyptian example refutes the fallacy about despotism and civilisation, so does the Babylonian example refute the fallacy about civilisation and barbarism. Babylon also we first hear of when it is already civilised; for the simple reason that we cannot hear of anything until it is educated enough to talk. It talks to us in what is called cuneiform; that strange and stiff triangular symbolism that contrasts with the picturesque alphabet of Egypt. However relatively rigid Egyptian art may be, there is always something different from the Babylonian spirit which was too rigid to have any art. There is always a living grace in the lines of the lotus and something of rapidity as well as rigidity in the movement of the arrows and the birds. Perhaps there is something of the restrained but living curve of the river, which makes us in talking of the serpent of old Nile almost think of the Nile as a serpent. Babylon was a civilisation of diagrams rather than of drawings. Mr. W.B. Yeats who has a historical imagination to match his mythological imagination (and indeed the former is impossible without the latter) wrote truly of the men who watched the stars 'from their pedantic Babylon.' The cuneiform was cut upon bricks, of which all their architecture was built up; the bricks were of baked mud and perhaps the material had something in it forbidding the sense of form to develop in sculpture or relief. Theirs was a static but a scientific civilisation, far advanced in the machinery of life and in some ways highly modern. It is said that they had much of the modern cult of the higher spinsterhood and recognised an official class of independent working women. There is perhaps something in that mighty stronghold of hardened mud that suggests the utilitarian activity of a huge hive. But though it was huge it was human; we see many of the same social problems as in ancient Egypt or modern England; and whatever its evils this also was one of the earliest masterpieces of man. It stood, of course, in the triangle formed by the almost legendary rivers of Tigris and Euphrates, and the vast agriculture of its empire, on which its towns depended, was perfected by a highly scientific system of canals. It had by tradition a high intellectual life, though rather philosophic than artistic; and there preside over its primal foundation those figures who have come to stand for the star-gazing wisdom of antiquity; the teachers of Abraham; the Chaldees.

Against this solid society, as against some vast bare wall of brick, there surged age after age the nameless armies of the Nomads. They came out of the deserts where the nomadic life had been lived from the beginning and where it is still lived to-day. It is needless to dwell on the nature of that life; it was obvious enough and even easy enough to follow a herd or a flock which generally found its own grazing-ground and to live on the milk or meat it provided. Nor is there any reason to doubt that this habit of life could give almost every human thing except a home. Many such shepherds or herds men may have talked in the earliest time of all the truths and enigmas of the Book of Job; and of these were Abraham and his children, who have given to the modern world for an endless enigma the almost mono-maniac monotheism of the Jews. But they were a wild people without comprehension of complex social organisation; and a spirit like the wind within them made them wage war on it again and again. The history of Babylonia is largely the history of its defence against the desert hordes; who came on at intervals of a century or two and generally retreated as they came. Some say that an admixture of nomad invasion built at Nineveh the arrogant kingdom of the Assyrians, who carved great monsters upon their temples, bearded bulls with wings like cherubim, and who sent forth many military conquerors who stamped the world as if with such colossal hooves. Assyria was an imperial interlude; but it was an interlude. The main story of all that land is the war between the wandering peoples and the state that was truly static. Presumably in prehistoric times, and certainly in historic times, those wanderers went westward to waste whatever they could find. The last time they came they found Babylon vanished; but that was in historic times and the name of their leader was Mahomet.

Now it is worth while to pause upon that story because, as has been suggested, it directly contradicts the impression still current that nomadism is merely a prehistoric thing and social settlement a comparatively recent thing. There is nothing to show that the Babylonians had ever wandered; there is very little to show that the tribes of the desert ever settled down. Indeed it is probable that this notion of a nomadic stage followed by a static stage has already been abandoned by the sincere and genuine scholars to whose researches we all owe so much. But I am not at issue in this book with sincere and genuine scholars, but with a vast and vague public opinion which has been prematurely spread from certain imperfect investigations, and which has made fashionable a false notion of the whole history of humanity. It is the whole vague notion that a monkey evolved into a man and in the same way a barbarian evolved into a civilised man and therefore at every stage we have to look back to barbarism and forward to civilisation. Unfortunately this notion is in a double sense entirely in the air. It is an atmosphere in which men live rather than a thesis which they defend. Men in that mood are more easily answered by objects than by theories; and it will be well if anyone tempted to make that assumption, in some trivial turn of talk or writing, can be checked for a moment by shutting his eyes and seeing for an instant, vast and vaguely crowded, like a populous precipice, the wonder of the Babylonian wall.

One fact does certainly fall across us like its shadow. Our glimpses of both these early empires show that the first domestic relation had been complicated by something which was less human, but was often regarded as equally domestic. The dark giant called Slavery had been called up like a genius and was labouring on gigantic works of brick and stone. Here again we must not too easily assume that what was backward was barbaric; in the matter of manumission the earlier servitude seems in some ways more liberal than the later; perhaps more liberal than the servitude of the future. To insure food for humanity by forcing part of it to work was after all a very human expedient; which is why it will probably be tried again. But in one sense there is a significance in the old slavery. It stands for one fundamental fact about all antiquity before Christ; something to be assumed from first to last. It is the insignificance of the individual before the State. It was as true of the most democratic City State in Hellas as of any despotism in Babylon. It is one of the signs of this spirit that a whole class of individuals could be insignificant or even invisible. It must be normal because it was needed for what would now be called 'social service.' Somebody said, 'The Man is nothing and the Work is all,' meaning it for a breezy Carlylean commonplace. It was the sinister motto of the heathen Servile State. In that sense there is truth in the traditional vision of vast pillars and pyramids going up under those everlasting skies for ever by the labour of numberless and nameless men, toiling like ants and dying like flies, wiped out by the work of their own hands.

But there are two other reasons for beginning with the two fixed points of Egypt and Babylon. For one thing they are fixed in tradition as the types of antiquity; and history without tradition is dead. Babylon is still the burden of a nursery rhyme, and Egypt (with its enormous population of princesses awaiting reincarnation) is still the topic of an unnecessary number of novels. But a tradition is generally a truth; so long as the tradition is sufficiently popular; even if it is almost vulgar. And there is a significance in this Babylonian and Egyptian element in nursery rhymes and novels; even the news papers, normally so much behind the times, have already got as far as the reign of Tutankhamen. The first reason is full of the common sense of popular legend; it is the simple fact that we do know more of these traditional things than of other contemporary things; and that we always did. All travellers from Herodotus to Lord Carnarvon follow this route. Scientific speculations of to-day do indeed spread out a map of the whole primitive world, with streams of racial emigration or admixture marked in dotted lines everywhere; over spaces which the unscientific medieval map-maker would have been content to call 'Terra incognita,' if he did not fill the inviting blank with a picture of a dragon, to indicate the probable reception given to pilgrims. But these speculations are only speculations at the best; and at the worst the dotted lines can be far more fabulous than the dragon.

There is unfortunately one fallacy here into which it is very easy for men to fall, even those who are most intelligent and perhaps especially those who are most imaginative. It is the fallacy of suppositing that because an idea is greater in the sense of larger, therefore it is greater in the sense of more fundamental and fixed and certain. If a man lives alone in a straw hut in the middle of Thibet, he may be told that he is living in the Chinese Empire; and the Chinese Empire is certainly a splendid and spacious and impressive thing. Or alternatively he may be told that he is living in the British Empire, and be duly impressed. But the curious thing is that in certain mental states he can feel much more certain about the Chinese Empire that he can not see than about the straw hut that he can see. He has some strange magical juggle in his mind, by which his argument begins with the empire though his experience begins with the hut. Sometimes he goes mad and appears to be proving that a straw hut cannot exist in the domains of the Dragon Throne; that it is impossible for such a civilisation as he enjoys to contain such a hovel as he inhabits. But his insanity arises from the intellectual slip of supposing that because China is a large and all-embracing hypothesis, therefore it is something more than a hypothesis. Now modern people are perpetually arguing in this way; and they extend it to things much less real and certain than the Chinese Empire. They seem to forget, for instance, that a man is not even certain of the Solar System as he is certain of the South Downs. The Solar System is a deduction, and doubtless a true deduction; but the point is that it is a very vast and far-reaching deduction and therefore he forgets that it is a deduction at all and treats it as a first principle. He might discover that the whole calculation is a mis-calculation; and the sun and stars and street-lamps would look exactly the same. But he has forgotten that it is a calculation, and is almost ready to contradict the sun if it does not fit into the solar system. If this is a fallacy even in the case of facts pretty well ascertained, such as the Solar System and the Chinese Empire, it is an even more devastating fallacy in connection with theories and other things that are not really ascertained at all. Thus history, especially prehistoric history, has a horrible habit of beginning with certain generalisations about races. I will not describe the disorder and misery this inversion has produced in modern politics. Because the race is vaguely supposed to have produced the nation, men talk as if the nation were something vaguer than the race. Because they have themselves invented a reason to explain a result, they almost deny the result in order to justify the reason. They first treat a Celt as an axiom and then treat an Irishman as an inference. And then they are surprised that a great fighting, roaring Irishman is angry at being treated as an inference. They cannot see that the Irish are Irish whether or no they are Celtic, whether or no there ever were any Celts. And what misleads them once more is the size of the theory; the sense that the fancy is bigger than the fact. A great scattered Celtic race is supposed to contain the Irish, so of course the Irish must depend for their very existence upon it. The same confusion, of course, has eliminated the English and the Germans by swamping them in the Teutonic race; and some tried to prove from the races being at one that the nations could not be at war. But I only give these vulgar and hackneyed examples in passing, as more familiar examples of the fallacy; the matter at issue here is not its application to these modern things but rather to the most ancient things. But the more remote and unrecorded was the racial problem, the more fixed was this curious inverted certainty in the Victorian man of science. To this day it gives a man of those scientific traditions the same sort of shock to question these things, which were only the last inferences when he turned them into first principles. He is still more certain that he is an Aryan even than that he is an Anglo-Saxon, just as he is more certain that he is an Anglo-Saxon than that he is an Englishman. He has never really discovered that he is a European. But he has never doubted that he is an Indo-European. These Victorian theories have shifted a great deal in their shape and scope; but this habit of a rapid hardening of a hypothesis into a theory, and of a theory into an assumption, has hardly yet gone out of fashion. People cannot easily get rid of the mental confusion of feeling that the foundations of history must surely be secure; that the first steps must be safe; that the biggest generalisation must be obvious. But though the contradiction may seem to them a paradox, this is the very contrary of the truth. It is the large thing that is secret and invisible; it is the small thing that is evident and enormous.

Every race on the face of the earth has been the subject of these speculations, and it is impossible even to suggest an outline of the subject. But if we take the European race alone, its history, or rather its prehistory, has undergone many retrospective revolutions in the short period of my own lifetime. It used to be called the Caucasian race; and I read in childhood an account of its collision with the Mongolian race; it was written by Bret Harte and opened with the query 'Or is the

Caucasian played out?' Apparently the Caucasian was played out, for in a very short time he had been turned into the Indo-European man; sometimes, I regret to say, proudly presented as the Indo-Germanic man. It seems that the Hindu and the German have similar words for mother or father; there were other similarities between Sanskrit and various Western tongues; and with that all superficial differences between a Hindu and a German seemed suddenly to disappear. Generally this composite person was more conveniently described as the Aryan, and the really important point was that he had marched westward out of those high lands of India where fragments of his language could still be found. When I read this as a child, I had the fancy that after all the Aryan need not have marched westward and left his language behind him; he might also have marched eastward and taken his language with him. If I were to read it now, I should content myself with confessing my ignorance of the whole matter. But as a matter of fact I have great difficulty in reading it now, because it is not being written now. It looks as if the Aryan is also played out. Anyhow he has not merely changed his name but changed his address; his starting-place and his route of travel. One new theory maintains that our race did not come to its present home from the East but from the South. Some say the Europeans did not come from Asia but from Africa. Some have even had the wild idea that the Europeans came from Europe; or rather that they never left it.

Then there is a certain amount of evidence of a more or less prehistoric pressure from the North, such as that which seems to have brought the Greeks to inherit the Cretan culture and so often brought the Gauls over the hills into the fields in Italy. But I merely mention this example of European ethnology to point out that the learned have pretty well boxed the compass by this time; and that I, who am not one of the learned, cannot pretend for a moment to decide where such doctors disagree. But I can use my own common sense, and I sometimes fancy that theirs is a little rusty from want of use. The first act of common sense is to recognise the difference between a cloud and a mountain. And I will affirm that nobody knows any of these things, in the sense that we all know of the existence of the Pyramids of Egypt.

The truth, it may be repeated, is that what we really see, as distinct from what we may reasonably guess, in this earliest phase of history is darkness covering the earth and great darkness the peoples, with a light or two gleaming here and there on chance patches of humanity; and that two of these flames do burn upon two of these tall primeval towns; upon the high terraces of Babylon and the huge pyramids of the Nile. There are indeed other ancient lights, or lights that may be conjectured to be very ancient, in very remote parts of that vast wilderness of night. Far away to the east there is a high civilisation of vast antiquity in China; there are the remains of civilisations in Mexico and South America and other places, some of them apparently so high in civilisation as to have reached the most refined forms of devil-worship. But the difference lies in the element old tradition; the tradition of these lost cultures has been broken off, and though the tradition of China still lives, it is doubtful whether we know anything about it. Moreover, a man trying to measure the Chinese antiquity has to use Chinese traditions of measurement; and he has a strange sensation of having passed into another world under other laws of time and space. Time is telescoped outwards and centuries assume the slow and stiff movement of aeons; the white man trying to see it as the yellow man sees, feels as if his head were turning round and wonders wildly whether it is growing a pigtail. Any how he cannot take in a scientific sense that queer perspective that leads up to the primeval pagoda of the first of the Sons of Heaven. He is the real antipodes; the only true alternative world to Christendom; and he is after a fashion walking upside down. I have spoken of the medieval map-maker and his dragon; but what medieval traveller, however much interested in monsters, would expect to find a country where a dragon is a benevolent and amiable being? Of the more serious side of Chinese tradition something will be said in another connection; but I am only talking of tradition and the test of antiquity. And I only mention China as an antiquity that is not for us reached by a bridge old tradition; and Babylon and Egypt as antiquities that are. Herodotus is a human being, in a sense in which a Chinaman in a billy-cock hat, sitting opposite to us in a London tea shop, is hardly human. We feel as if we knew what David and Isaiah felt like, in a way in which we never were quite certain what Li Hung Chang felt like. The very sins that snatched away Helen or Bathsheba have passed into a proverb of private human weakness, of pathos and even of pardon. The very virtues of the Chinaman have about them something terrifying. This is the difference made by the destruction or preservation of a continuous historical inheritance; as from ancient Egypt to modern Europe. But when we ask what was that world that we inherit, and why those particular people and places seem to belong to it, we are led to the central fact of civilised history.

That centre was the Mediterranean; which was not so much a piece of water as a world. But it was a world with something of the character of such a water; for it became more and more a place of unification in which the streams of strange and very diverse cultures met. The Nile and the Tiber alike flow into the Mediterranean; so did the Egyptian and the Etrurian alike contribute to a Mediterranean civilisation. The glamour of the great sea spread indeed very far in land and the unity was felt among the Arabs alone in the deserts and the Gauls beyond the northern hills. But the gradual building up of a common culture running round all the coasts of this inner sea is the main business of antiquity. As will be seen, it was sometimes a bad business as well as a good business. In that orbis terrarum or circle of lands there were the extremes of evil and of piety, there were contrasted races and still more contrasted religions. It was the scene of an endless struggle between Asia and Europe from the night of the Persian ships at Salamis to the flight of the Turkish ships at Lepanto. It was the scene, as will be more especially suggested later, of a supreme spiritual struggle between the two types of paganism, confronting each other in the Latin and the Phoenician cities; in the Roman forum and the Punic mart. It was the world of war and peace, the world of good and evil, the world of all that matters most, with all respect to the Aztecs and the Mongols of the Far East, they did not matter as the Mediterranean tradition mattered and still matters. Between it and the Far East there were, of course, interesting cults and conquests of various kinds, more or less in touch with it, and in proportion as they were so intelligible also to us. The Persians came riding in to make an end of Babylon; and we are told in a Greek story how these barbarians learned to draw the bow and tell the truth. Alexander the great Greek marched with his Macedonians into the sunrise and brought back strange birds coloured like the sunrise clouds and strange flowers and jewels from the gardens and treasuries of nameless kings. Islam went eastward into that world and made it partly imaginable to us; precisely because Islam itself was born in that circle of lands that fringed our own ancient and ancestral sea. In the Middle Ages the empire of the Moguls increased its majesty without losing its mystery; the Tartars conquered China and the Chinese apparently took very little notice of them. All these things are interesting in themselves; but it is impossible to shift the centre of gravity to the inland spaces of Asia from the inland sea of Europe. When all is said, if there were nothing in the world but what was said and done and written and built in the lands lying round the Mediterranean, it would still be in all the most vital and valuable things the world in which we live. When that southern culture spread to the north-west it produced many very wonderful things; of which doubtless we ourselves are the most wonderful. When it spread thence to colonies and new countries, it was still the same culture so long as it was culture at all. But round that little sea like a lake were the things themselves, apart from all extensions and echoes and commentaries on the things, the Republic and the Church; the Bible and the heroic epics; Islam and Israel and the memories of the lost empires, Aristotle and the measure of all things. It is because the first light upon this world is really light, the daylight in which we are still walking to-day, and not merely the doubtful visitation of strange stars, that I have begun here with noting where that light first falls on the towered cities of the eastern Mediterranean.

But though Babylon and Egypt have thus a sort of first claim, in the very fact of being familiar and traditional, fascinating riddles to us but also fascinating riddles to our fathers, we must not imagine that they were the only old civilisations on the southern sea; or that all the civilisation was merely Sumerian or Semitic or Coptic, still less merely Asiatic or African. Real research is more and more exalting the ancient civilisation of Europe and especially of what we may still vaguely call the Greeks. It must be understood in the sense that there were Greeks before the Greeks, as in so many of their mythologies there were gods before the gods. The island of Crete was the centre of the civilisation now called Minoan, after the Minos who lingered in ancient legend and whose labyrinth was actually discovered by modern archeology. This elaborate European society, with its harbours and its drainage and its domestic machinery, seems to have gone down before some invasion of its northern neighbours, who made or inherited the Hellas we know in history. But that earlier period did not pass till it had given to the world gifts so great that the world has ever since been striving in vain to repay them, if only by plagiarism.

Somewhere along the Ionian coast opposite Crete and the islands was a town of some sort, probably of the sort that we should call a village or hamlet with a wall. It was called Ilion but it came to be called Troy, and the name will never perish from the earth. A poet who may have been a beggar and a ballad-monger, who may have been unable to read and write, and was described by tradition as a blind, composed a poem about the Greeks going to war with this town to recover the most beautiful woman in the world. That the most beautiful woman in the world lived in that one little town sounds like a legend; that the most beautiful poem in the world was written by somebody who knew of nothing larger than such little towns is a historical fact. It is said that the poem came at the end of the period; that the primitive culture brought it forth in its decay; in which case one would like to have seen that culture in its prime. But anyhow it is true that this, which is our first poem, might very well be our last poem too. It might well be the last word as well as the first word spoken by man about his mortal lot, as seen by merely mortal vision. If the world becomes pagan and perishes, the last man left alive would do well to quote the Iliad and die.

But in this one great human revelation of antiquity there is another element of great historical importance; which has hardly I think been given its proper place in history. The poet has so conceived the poem that his sympathies apparently, and those of his reader certainly, are on the side of the vanquished rather than of the victor. And this is a sentiment which increases in the poetical tradition even as the poetical origin itself recedes. Achilles had some status as a sort of demigod in pagan times; but he disappears altogether in late times. But Hector grows greater as the ages pass, and it is his name that is the name of a Knight of the Round Table and his sword that legend puts into the hand of Roland, laying about him with the weapon of the defeated Hector in the last ruin and splendour of his own defeat. The name anticipates all the defeats through which our race and religion were to pass; that survival of a hundred defeats that is its triumph.

The tale of the end of Troy shall have no ending, for it is lifted up forever into living echoes, immortal as our hopelessness and our hope. Troy standing was a small thing that may have stood nameless for ages. But Troy falling has been caught up in a flame and suspended in an immortal instant of annihilation; and because it was destroyed with fire the fire shall never be destroyed. And as with the city so with the hero; traced in archaic lines in that primeval twilight is found the first figure of the Knight. There is a prophetic coincidence in his title; we have spoken of the word chivalry and how it seems to mingle the horseman with the horse. It is almost anticipated ages before in the thunder of the Homeric hexameter, and that long leaping word with which the Iliad ends. It is that very unity for which we can find no name but the holy centaur of chivalry. But there are other reasons for giving in this glimpse of antiquity the name upon the sacred town. The sanctity of such towns ran like a fire round the coasts and islands of the northern Mediterranean, the high-fenced hamlet for which heroes died. From the smallness of the city came the greatness of the citizen. Hellas with her hundred statues produced nothing statelier than that walking statue; the ideal of the self-commanding man. Hellas of the hundred statues was one legend and literature; and all that labyrinth of little walled nations resounding with the lament of Troy.

A later legend, an afterthought but not an accident, said that stragglers from Troy founded a republic on the Italian shore. It was true in spirit that republican virtue had such a root. A mystery of honour, that was not born of Babylon or the

Egyptian pride, there shone like the shield of Hector, defying Asia and Africa; till the light of a new day was loosened, with the rushing of the eagles and the coming of the name; the name that came like a thunderclap when the world woke to Rome.

IV GOD AND COMPARATIVE RELIGION

I was once escorted over the Roman foundations of an ancient British city by a professor, who said something that seems to me a satire on a good many other professors. Possibly the professor saw the joke, though he maintained an iron gravity, and may or may not have realised that it was a joke against a great deal of what is called comparative religion. I pointed out a sculpture of the head of the sun with the usual halo of rays, but with the difference that the face in the disc, instead of being boyish like Apollo, was bearded like Neptune or Jupiter. 'Yes,' he said with a certain delicate exactitude, 'that is supposed to represent the local god Sul. The best authorities identify Sul with Minerva, but this has been held to show that the identification is not complete.'

That is what we call a powerful understatement. The modern world is madder than any satires on it; long ago Mr. Belloc made his burlesque don say that a bust of Ariadne had been proved by modern research to be a Silenus. But that is not better than the real appearance of Minerva as the Bearded Woman of Mr. Barnum. Only both of them are very like many identifications by 'the best authorities' on comparative religion; and when Catholic creeds are identified with various wild myths, I do not laugh or curse or misbehave myself; I confine myself decorously to saying that the identification is not complete.

In the days of my youth the Religion of Humanity was a term commonly applied to Comtism, the theory of certain rationalists who worshipped corporate mankind as a Supreme Being. Even in the days of my youth, I remarked that there was something slightly odd about despising and dismissing the doctrine of the Trinity as a mystical and even maniacal contradiction; and then asking us to adore a deity who is a hundred million persons in one God, neither confounding the persons nor dividing the substance.

But there is another entity, more or less definable and much more imaginable than the many-headed and monstrous idol of mankind. And it has a much better light to be called, in a reasonable sense, the religion of humanity. Man is not indeed the idol; but man is almost everywhere the idolator. And these multitudinous idolatries of man kind have something about them in many ways more human and sympathetic than modern metaphysical abstractions. If an Asiatic god has three heads and seven arms, there is at least in it an idea of material incarnation bringing an unknown power nearer to us and not farther away. But if our friends Brown, Jones, and Robinson, when out for a Sunday walk, were transformed and amalgamated into an Asiatic idol before our eyes, they would surely seem farther away. If the arms of Brown and the legs of Robinson waved from the same composite body, they would seem to be waving something of a sad farewell. If the heads of an three gentlemen appeared smiling on the same neck, we should hesitate even by what name to address our new and somewhat abnormal friend. In the many-headed and many-handed Oriental idol there is a certain sense of mysteries be coming at least partly intelligible; of formless forces of nature taking some dark but material form, but though this may be true of the multiform god it is not so of the multiform man The human beings be come less human by becoming less separate; we might say less human in being less lonely. The human beings become less intelligible as they become less isolated; we might say with strict truth that the closer they are to us the farther they are away. An Ethical Hymn-book of this humanitarian sort of religion was carefully selected and expurgated on the principle of preserving anything human and eliminating anything divine. One consequence was that a hymn appeared in the amended form of 'Nearer Mankind to Thee, nearer to Thee.' It always suggested to me the sensations of a straphanged during a crush on the Tube. But it is strange and wonderful how far away the souls of men can seem, when their bodies are so near as all that.

The human unity with which I deal here is not to be confounded with this modern industrial monotony and herding, which is rather a congestion than a communion. It is a thing to which human groups left to themselves, and even human individuals left to themselves, have everywhere tended by an instinct that may truly be called human. Like all healthy human things, it has varied very much within the limits of a general character; for that is characteristic of everything belonging to that ancient land of liberty that lies before and around the servile industrial town. Industrialism actually boasts that its products are all of one pattern; that men in Jamaica or Japan can break the same seal and drink the same bad whiskey, that a man at the North Pole and another at the South might recognise the same optimistic level on the same dubious tinned salmon. But wine, the gift of gods to men, can vary with every valley and every vineyard, can turn into a hundred wines without any wine once reminding us of whiskey; and cheeses can change from county to county without forgetting the difference between chalk and cheese. When I am speaking of this thing, therefore, I am speaking of something that doubtless includes very wide differences; nevertheless I will here maintain that it is one thing. I will maintain that most of the modern botheration comes from not realising that it is really one thing. I will advance the thesis that before all talk about comparative religion and the separate religious founders of the world, the first essential is to recognise this thing as a whole, as a thing almost native and normal to the great fellowship that we call mankind. This thing is Paganism, and I propose to show in these pages that it is the one real rival to the Church of Christ.

Comparative religion is very comparative indeed. That is, it is so much a matter of degree and distance and difference that it is only comparatively successful when it tries to compare. When we come to look at it closely we find it comparing things that are really quite incomparable. We are accustomed to see a table or catalogue of the world's great religions in parallel columns, until we fancy they are really parallel. We are accustomed to see the names of the great religious founders all in a row: Christ; Mahomet; Buddha; Confucius. But in truth this is only a trick, another of these optical illusions by which any objects may be put into a particular relation by shifting to a particular point of sight. Those religions and religious founders, or rather those whom we choose to lump together as religions and religious founders, do not really show any common character. The illusion is partly produced by Islam coming immediately after Christianity in the list; as Islam did come after Christianity and was largely an imitation of Christianity. But the other eastern religions, or what we call religions, not only do not resemble the Church but do not resemble each other. When we come to Confucianism at the end of the list, we come to something in a totally different world of thought. To compare the Christian and Confucian religions is like comparing a theist with an English squire or asking whether a man is a believer in immortality or a hundred-per-cent American. Confucianism may be a civilisation but it is not a religion.

In truth the Church is too unique to prove herself unique. For most popular and easy proof is by parallel; and here there is no parallel. It is not easy, therefore, to expose the fallacy by which a false classification is created to swamp a unique thing, when it really is a unique thing. As there is nowhere else exactly the same fact, so there is nowhere else exactly the same fallacy. But I will take the nearest thing I can find to such a solitary social phenomenon, in order to show how it is thus swamped and assimilated. I imagine most of us would agree that there is something unusual and unique about the position of the Jews. There is nothing that is quite in the same sense an international nation; an ancient culture scattered in different countries but still distinct and indestructible. Now this business is like an attempt to make a list of Nomadic Nations in order to soften the strange solitude of the Jew. It would be easy enough to do it, by the same process of putting a plausible approximation first, and then tailing off into totally different things thrown in somehow to make up the list. Thus in the new list of nomadic nations the Jews would be followed by the Gypsies; who at least are really nomadic if they are not really national. Then the professor of the new science of Comparative Nomadics could pass easily on to something different; even if it was very different. He could remark on the wandering adventure of the English who had scattered their colonies over so many seas; and call them nomads. It is quite true that a great many Englishmen seem to be strangely restless in England. It is quite true that not all of them have left their country for their country's good. The moment we mention the wandering empire of the English, we must add the strange exiled empire of the Irish. For it is a curious fact, to be noted in our imperial literature, that the same ubiquity and unrest which is a proof of English enterprise and triumph is a proof of Irish futility and failure. Then the professor of Nomadism would look round thoughtfully and remember that there was great talk recently of German waiters, German barbers, German clerks, Germans naturalising themselves in England and the United States and the South American republics. The Germans would go down as the fifth nomadic race; the words Wanderlust and Folk-Wandering would come in very useful here. For there really have been historians who explained the Crusades by suggesting that the Germans were found wandering (as the police say) in what happened to be the neighbourhood of Palestine. Then the professor, feeling he was now near the end, would make a last leap in desperation. He would recall the fact that the French army has captured nearly every capital in Europe, that it marched across countless conquered lands under Charlemagne or Napoleon; and that would be wanderlust and that would be the note of a nomadic race. Thus he would have his six nomadic nations all compact and complete, and would feel that the Jew was no longer a sort of mysterious and even mystical exception. But people with more common sense would probably realise that he had only extended nomadism by extending the meaning of nomadism, and that he had extended that until it really had no meaning at all. It is quite true that the French soldier has made some of the finest marches in all military history. But it is equally true, and far more self-evident, that if the French peasant is not a rooted reality there is no such thing as a rooted reality in the world; or in other words, if he is a nomad there is nobody who is not a nomad.

Now that is the sort of trick that has been tried in the case of comparative religion and the world's religious founders all standing respectably in a row. It seeks to classify Jesus as the other would classify Jews, by inventing a new class for the purpose and filling up the rest of it with stop-gaps and second-rate copies. I do not mean that these other things are not often great things in their own real character and class. Confucianism and Buddhism are great things, but it is not true to call them Churches; just as the French and English are great peoples, but it is nonsense to call them nomads. There are some points of resemblance between Christendom and its imitation in Islam; for that matter there are some points of resemblance between Jews and Gypsies. But after that the lists are made up of anything that comes to hand; of anything that can be put in the same catalogue without being in the same category.

In this sketch of religious history, with all decent deference to men much more learned than myself, I propose to cut across and disregard this modern method of classification, which I feel sure has falsified the facts of history. I shall here submit an alternative classification of religion or religions, which I believe would be found to cover all the facts and, what is quite as important here, all the fancies. Instead of dividing religion geographically and as it were vertically, into Christian, Moslem, Brahmin, Buddhist, and so on, I would divide it psychologically and in some sense horizontally; into the strata of spiritual elements and influences that could sometimes exist in the same country, or even in the same man. Putting the Church apart for the moment, I should be disposed to divide the natural religion of the mass of mankind under such headings as these: God; the Gods; the Demons; the Philosophers. I believe some such classification will help us to sort out the spiritual experiences of men much more successfully than the conventional business of comparing religions; and that many famous figures will naturally fall into their place in this way who are only forced into their place in the other. As I shall make use of these titles or terms more than once in narrative and allusion, it will be well to define at this stage for what I mean them to stand. And I will begin with the first, the simplest and the most sublime, in this chapter.

In considering the elements of pagan humanity, we must begin by an attempt to describe the indescribable. Many get over the difficulty of describing it by the expedient of denying it, or at least ignoring it; but the whole point of it is that it was something that was never quite eliminated even when it was ignored. They are obsessed by their evolutionary monomania that every great thing grows from a seed, or something smaller than itself. They seem to forget that every seed comes from a tree, or something larger than itself. Now there is very good ground for guessing that religion did not originally come from some detail that was forgotten, because it was too small to be traced. Much more probably it was an idea that was abandoned because it was too large to be managed. There is very good reason to suppose that many people did begin with the simple but overwhelming idea of one God who governs all; and afterwards fell away into such things as demon-worship almost as a sort of secret dissipation. Even the test of savage beliefs, of which the folk-lore students are so fond, is admittedly often found to support such a view. Some of the very rudest savages, primitive in every sense in which anthropologists use the word, the Australian aborigines for instance, are found to have a pure monotheism with a high moral tone. A missionary was preaching to a very wild tribe of polytheists, who had told him all their polytheistic tales, and telling them in return of the existence of the one good God who is a spirit and judges men by spiritual standards. And there was a sudden buzz of excitement among these stolid barbarians, as at somebody who was letting out a secret, and they cried to each other, 'Atahocan! He is speaking of Atahocan!'

Probably it was a point of politeness and even decency among those polytheists not to speak of Atahocan. The name is not perhaps so much adapted as some of our own to direct and solemn religious exhortation but many other social forces are always covering up and confusing such simple ideas. Possibly the old god stood for an old morality found irksome in more expansive moments; possibly intercourse with demons was more fashionable among the best people, as in the modern fashion of Spiritualism. Anyhow, there are any number of similar examples. They all testify to the unmistakable psychology of a thing taken for granted, as distinct from a thing talked about. There is a striking example in a tale taken down word for word from a Red Indian in California which starts out with hearty legendary and literary relish: 'The sun is the father and ruler of the heavens. He is the big chief. The moon is his wife and the stars are their children'; and so on through a most ingenious and complicated story, in the middle of which is a sudden parenthesis saying that the sun and moon have to do something because 'It is ordered that way by the Great Spirit Who lives above the place of all.' That is exactly the attitude of most paganism towards God. He is something assumed and forgotten and remembered by accident; a habit possibly not peculiar to pagans. Sometimes the higher deity is remembered in the higher moral grades and is a sort of mystery. But always, it has been truly said, the savage is talkative about his mythology and taciturn about his religion. The Australian savages, indeed, exhibit a topsyturveydom such as the ancients might have thought truly worthy of the antipodes. The savage who thinks nothing of tossing off such a trifle as a tale of the sun and moon being the halves of a baby chopped in two, or dropping into small-talk about a colossal cosmic cow milked to make the rain, merely in order to be sociable, will then retire to secret caverns sealed against women and white men, temples of terrible initiation where to the thunder of the bull-roarer and the dripping of sacrificial blood, the priest whispers the final secrets, known only to the initiate: that honesty is the best policy, that a little kindness does nobody any harm, that all men are brothers and that there is but one God, the Father Almighty, maker of all things visible and invisible.

In other words, we have here the curiosity of religious history that the savage seems to be parading all the most repulsive and impossible parts of his belief and concealing all the most sensible and creditable parts. But the explanation is that they are not in that sense parts of his belief, or at least not parts of the same sort of belief. The myths are merely tall stories, though as tall as the sky, the water spout, or the tropic rain. The mysteries are true stories, and are taken secretly that they may be taken seriously. Indeed it is only too easy to forget that there is a thrill in theism. A novel in which a number of separate characters all turned out to be the same character would certainly be a sensational novel. It is so with the idea that sun and tree and river are the disguises of one god and not of many. Alas, we also find it only too easy to take Atahocan for granted. But whether he is allowed to fade into a truism or preserved as a sensation by being preserved as a secret, it is clear that he is always either an old truism or an old tradition. There is nothing to show that he is an improved product of the mere mythology and everything to show that he preceded it. He is worshipped by the simplest tribes with no trace of ghosts or grave-offerings, or any of the complications in which Herbert Spencer and Grant Allen sought the origin of the simplest of all ideas. Whatever else there was, there was never as such thing as the Evolution of the Idea of God. The idea was concealed, was avoided, was almost forgotten, was even explained away; but it was never evolved.

There are not a few indications of this change in other places It is implied, for instance, in the fact that even polytheism seems often the combination of several monotheisms. A god will gain only a minor seat on Mount Olympus, when he had owned earth and heaven and all the stars while he lived in his own little valley. Like many a small nation melting in a great empire, he gives up local universality only to come under universal limitation. The very name of Pan suggests that he became a god of the wood when he had been a god of the world. The very name of Jupiter is almost a pagan translation of the words 'Our Father which art in heaven.' As with the Great Father symbolised by the sky, so with the Great Mother whom we still call Mother Earth. Demeter and Ceres and Cybele often seem to be almost capable of taking over the whole business of godhood, so that men should need no other gods. It seems reasonably probable that a good many men did have no other gods but one of these, worshipped as the author of all.

Over some of the most immense and populous tracts of the world such as China, it would seem that the simpler idea of the Great Father has never been very much complicated with rival cults, though it may have in some sense ceased to be a cult itself. The best authorities seem to think that though Confucianism is in one sense agnosticism, it does not directly contradict the old theism, precisely because it has become a rather vague theism. It is one in which God is called Heaven, as in the case of polite persons tempted to swear in drawing-rooms. But Heaven is still overhead, even if it is very far overhead. We have all the impression of a simple truth that has receded, until it was remote without ceasing to be true. And this phrase alone would bring us back to the same idea even in the pagan mythology of the West. There is surely something of this very notion of the withdrawal of some higher power, in all those mysterious and very imaginative myths about the separation of earth and sky. In a hundred forms we are told that heaven and earth were once lovers, or were once at one, when some upstart thing, often some undutiful child, thrust them apart; and the world was built on an abyss; upon a division and a parting. One of its grossest versions was given by Greek civilisation in the myth of Uranus and Saturn. One of its most charming versions was that of some savage niggers, who say that a little pepper-plant grew taller and taller and lifted the whole sky like a lid; a beautiful barbaric vision of daybreak for some of our painters who love that tropical twilight. Of myths, and the highly mythical explanations which the moderns offer of myths, something will be said in another section; for I cannot but think that most mythology is on another and more superficial plane. But in this primeval vision of the rending of one world into two there is surely something more of ultimate ideas. As to what it means, a man will learn far more about it by lying on his back in a field, and merely looking at the sky, than by reading all the libraries even of the most learned and valuable folklore. He will know what is meant by saying that the sky ought to be nearer to us than it is, that perhaps it was once nearer than it is, that it is not a thing merely alien and abysmal but in some fashion sundered from us and saying farewell. There will creep across his mind the curious suggestion that after all, perhaps, the myth-maker was not merely a moon-calf or village idiot thinking he could cut up the clouds like a cake, but had in him something more than it is fashionable to attribute to the Troglodyte; that it is just possible that Thomas Hood was not talking like a Troglodyte when he said that, as time went on, the tree-tops only told him he was further off from heaven than when he was a boy. But anyhow the legend of Uranus the Lord of Heaven dethroned by Saturn the Time Spirit would mean something to the author of that poem. And it would mean, among other things, this banishment of the first fatherhood. There is the idea of God in the very notion that there were gods before the gods. There is an idea of greater simplicity in all the allusions to that more ancient order. The suggestion is supported by the process of propagation we see in historic times. Gods and demigods and heroes breed like herrings before our very eyes and suggest of themselves that the family may have had one founder; mythology grows more and more complicated, and the very complication suggests that at the beginning it was more simple. Even on the external evidence, of the sort called scientific, there is therefore a very good case for the suggestion that man began with monotheism before it developed or degenerated into polytheism. But I am concerned rather with an internal than an external truth; and, as I have already said, the internal truth is almost indescribable. We have to speak of something of which it is the whole point that people did not speak of it; we have not merely to translate from a strange tongue or speech, but from a strange silence.

I suspect an immense implication behind all polytheism and paganism. I suspect we have only a hint of it here and there in these savage creeds or Greek origins. It is not exactly what we mean by the presence of God; in a sense it might more truly be called the absence of God. But absence does not mean non-existence; and a man drinking the toast of absent friends does not mean that from his life all friendship is absent. It is a void but it is not a negation; it is some thing as positive as an empty chair. It would be an exaggeration to say that the pagan saw higher than Olympus an empty throne. It would be nearer the truth to take the gigantic imagery of the Old Testament, in which the prophet saw God from behind; it was as if some immeasurable presence had turned its back on the world. Yet the meaning will again be missed, if it is supposed to be anything so conscious and vivid as the monotheism of Moses and his people. I do not mean that the pagan peoples were in the least overpowered by this idea merely because it is overpowering. On the contrary, it was so large that they all carried it lightly, as we all carry the load of the sky. Gazing at some detail like a bird or a cloud, we can all ignore its awful blue background; we can neglect the sky; and precisely because it bears down upon us with an annihilating force it is felt as nothing. A thing of this kind can only be an impressing and a rather subtle impression; but to me it is a very strong impression made by pagan literature and religion. I repeat that in our special sacramental sense there is, of course, the absence of the presence of God. But there is in a very real sense the presence of the absence of God. We feel it in the unfathomable sadness of pagan poetry; for I doubt if there was ever in all the marvellous manhood of antiquity a man who was happy as St. Francis was happy. We feel it in the legend of a Golden Age and again in the vague implication that the gods themselves are ultimately related to something else, even when that Unknown God has faded into a Fate. Above all we feel it in those immortal moments when the pagan literature seems to return to a more innocent antiquity and speak with a more direct voice, so that no word is worthy of it except our own monotheistic monosyllable. We cannot say anything but 'God' in a sentence like that of Socrates bidding farewell to his judges: 'I go to die and you remain to live; and God alone knows which of us goes the better way.' We can use no other word even for the best moments of Marcus Aurelius: 'Can they say dear city of Cecrops, and canst thou not say dear city of God?' We can use no other word in that mighty line in which Virgil spoke to all who suffer with the veritable cry of a Christian before Christ: 'O you that have borne things more terrible, to this also God shall give an end.'

In short, there is a feeling that there is something higher than the gods; but because it is higher it is also further away. Not yet could even Virgil have read the riddle and the paradox of that other divinity, who is both higher and nearer. For them what was truly divine was very distant, so distant that they dismissed it more and more from their minds. It had less and less to do with the mere mythology of which I shall write later. Yet even in this there was a sort of tacit admission of its intangible purity, when we consider what most of the mythologies like. As the

Jews would not degrade it by images, so the Greeks did not degrade it even by imaginations. When the gods were more and more remembered only by pranks and profligacies, it was relatively a movement of reverence. It was an act of piety to forget God. In other words, there is something in the whole tone of the time suggesting that men had accepted a lower level, and still were half conscious that it was a lower level. It is hard to find words for these things; yet the one really just word stands ready. These men were conscious of the Fall if they were conscious of nothing else; and the same is true of an heathen humanity. Those who have fallen may remember the fall, even when they forget the height. Some such tantalising blank or break in memory is at the back of all pagan sentiment. There is such a thing as the momentary power to remember that we forget. And the most ignorant of humanity know by the very look of earth that they have forgotten heaven. But it remains true that even for these men there were moments, like the memories of childhood, when they heard themselves talking with a simpler language; there were moments when the Roman, like Virgil in the line already quoted, cut his way with a sword-stroke of song out of the tangle of the mythologies, the motley mob of gods and goddesses sank suddenly out of sight and the Sky-Father was alone in the sky.

This latter example is very relevant to the next step in the process. A white light as of a lost morning still lingers on the figure of Jupiter, of Pan or of the elder Apollo; and it may well be, as already noted, that each was once a divinity as solitary as Jehovah or Allah. They lost this lonely universality by a process it is here very necessary to note; a process of amalgamation very like what was afterwards called syncretism. The whole pagan world set itself to build a Pantheon. They admitted more and more gods, gods not only of the Greeks but of the barbarians; gods not only of Europe but of Asia and Africa. The more the merrier, though some of the Asian and African ones were not very merry. They admitted them to equal thrones with their own, sometimes they identified them with their own. They may have regarded it as an enrichment of their religious life; but it meant the final loss of all that we now call religion. It meant that ancient light of simplicity, that had a single source like the sun, finally fades away in a dazzle of conflicting Lights and colours. God is really sacrificed to the Gods; in a very literal sense of the flippant phrase, they have been too many for him.

Polytheism, therefore, was really a sort of pool; in the sense of the pagans having consented to the pooling of their pagan religions. And this point is very important in many controversies ancient and modern. It is regarded as a liberal and enlightened thing to say that the god of the stranger may be as good as our own; and doubtless the pagans thought themselves very liberal and enlightened when they agreed to add to the gods of the city or the hearth some wild and fantastic Dionysus coming down from the mountains or some shaggy and rustic Pan creeping out of the woods. But exactly what it lost by these larger ideas is the largest idea of all. It is the idea of the fatherhood that makes the whole world one. And the converse is also true. Doubtless those more antiquated men of antiquity who clung to their solitary statues and their single sacred names were regarded as superstitious savages benighted and left behind. But these superstitious savages were preserving something that is much more like the cosmic power as conceived by philosophy, or even as conceived by science. This paradox by which the rude reactionary was a sort of prophetic progressive has one consequence very much to the point. In a purely historical sense, and apart from any other controversies in the same connection, it throws a light, a single and a steady light, that shines from the beginning on a little and lonely people. In this paradox, as in some riddle of religion of which the answer was sealed up for centuries, lies the mission and the meaning of the Jews.

It is true in this sense, humanly speaking, that the world owes God to the Jews. It owes that truth to much that is blamed on the Jews, possibly to much that is blameable in the Jews. We have already noted the nomadic position of the Jews amid the other pastoral peoples upon the fringe of the Babylonian Empire, and something of that strange erratic course of theirs blazed across the dark territory of extreme antiquity, as they passed from the seat of Abraham and the shepherd princes into Egypt and doubled back into the Palestinian hills and held them against the Philistines from Crete and fell into captivity in Babylon; and yet again returned to their mountain city by the Zionist policy of the Persian conquerors; and so continued that amazing romance of restlessness of which we have not yet seen the end. But through all their wanderings, and especially through all their early wanderings, they did indeed carry the fate of the world in that wooden tabernacle, that held perhaps a featureless symbol and certainly an invisible god. We may say that one most essential feature was that it was featureless. Much as we may prefer that creative liberty which the Christian culture has declared and by which it has eclipsed even the arts of antiquity, we must not underrate the determining importance at the time of the Hebrew inhibition of images. It is a typical example of one of those limitations that did in fact preserve and perpetuate enlargement, like a wall built round a wide open space. The God who could not have a statue remained a spirit. Nor would his statue in any case have had the disarming dignity and grace of the Greek statues then or the Christian statues afterwards. He was living in a land of monsters. We shall have occasion to consider more fully what those monsters were, Moloch and Dagon and Tanit the terrible goddess. If the deity of Israel had ever had an image, he would have had a phallic image. By merely giving him a body they would have brought in all the worst elements of mythology; all the polygamy of polytheism; the vision of the harem in heaven. This point about the refusal of art is the first example of the limitations which are often adversely criticised, only because the critics themselves are limited. But an even stronger case can be found in the other criticism offered by the same critics. It is often said with a sneer that the God of Israel was only a God of battles, 'a mere barbaric Lord of Hosts' pitted in rivalry against other gods only as their envious foe. Well it is for the world that he was a God of Battles. Well it is for us that he was to all the rest only a rival and a foe. In the ordinary way, it would have been only too easy for them to have achieved the desolate disaster of conceiving him as a friend. It would have been only too easy for them to have seen him stretching out his hands in love and reconciliation, embracing Baal and kissing the painted face of Astarte, feasting in fellowship with the gods; the last god to sell his crown of stars for the Soma of the Indian pantheon or the nectar of Olympus or the mead of Valhalla. It would have been easy enough for his worshippers to follow the enlightened course of Syncretism and the pooling of all the pagan traditions. It is obvious indeed that his followers were always sliding down this easy slope; and it required the almost demoniac energy of certain inspired demagogues, who testified to the divine unity in words that are still like winds of inspiration and ruin. The more we really understand of the ancient conditions that contributed to the final culture of the Faith, the more we shall have a real and even a realistic reverence for the greatness of the Prophets of Israel. As it was, while the whole world melted into this mass of confused mythology, this Deity who is called tribal and narrow, precisely because he was what is called tribal and narrow, preserved the primary religion of all mankind. He was tribal enough to be universal. He was as narrow as the universe. In a word, there was a popular pagan god called Jupiter-Ammon. There was never a god called Jehovah-Ammon. There was never a god called Jehovah-Jupiter. If there had been, there would certainly have been another called Jehovah-Moloch. Long before the liberal and enlightened amalgamators had got so far afield as Jupiter, the image of the Lord of Hosts would have been deformed out of all suggestion of a monotheistic maker and ruler and would have become an idol far worse than any savage fetish; for he might have been as civilised as the gods of Tyre and Carthage. What that civilisation meant we shall consider more fully in the chapter that follows; when we note how the power of demons nearly destroyed Europe and even the heathen health of the world. But the world's destiny would have been distorted still more fatally if monotheism had failed in the Mosaic tradition. I hope in a subsequent section to show that I am not without sympathy with all that health in the heathen world that made its fairy-tales and its fanciful romances of religion. But I hope also to show that these were bound to fail in the long run; and the world would have been lost if it had been unable to return to that great original simplicity of a single authority in all things. That we do preserve something of that primary simplicity that poets and philosophers can still indeed in some sense say an Universal Prayer, that we live in a large and serene world under a sky that stretches paternally over all the peoples of the earth, that philosophy and philanthropy are truisms in a religion of reasonable men, all that we do most truly owe, under heaven, to a secretive and restless nomadic people; who bestowed on men the supreme and serene blessing of a jealous God.

The unique possession was not available or accessible to the pagan world, because it was also the possession of a jealous people. The Jews were unpopular, partly because of this narrowness already noted in the Roman world, partly perhaps because they had already fallen into that habit of merely handling things for exchange instead of working to make them with their hands. It was partly also because polytheism had become a sort of jungle in which solitary monotheism could be lost; but it is strange to realise how completely it really was lost. Apart from more disputed matters, there were things in the tradition of Israel which belong to all humanity now, and might have belonged to all humanity then. They had one of the colossal corner-stones of the world: the Book of Job. It obviously stands over against the Iliad and the Greek tragedies; and even more than they it was an early meeting and parting of poetry and philosophy in the mornings of the world. It is a solemn and uplifting sight to see those two eternal fools, the optimist and the pessimist, destroyed in the dawn of time. And the philosophy really perfects the pagan tragic irony, precisely because it is more monotheistic and therefore more mystical. Indeed the Book of Job avowedly only answers mystery with mystery. Job is comforted with riddles; but he is comforted. Herein is indeed a type, in the sense of a prophecy, of things speaking with authority. For when he who doubts can only say 'I do not understand,' it is true that he who knows can only reply or repeat 'You do not understand.' And under that rebuke there is always a sudden hope in the heart; and the sense of something that would be worth understanding. But this mighty monotheistic poem remained unremarked by the whole world of antiquity, which was thronged with polytheistic poetry. It is a sign of the way in which the Jews stood apart and kept their tradition unshaken and unshared, that they should have kept a thing like the Book of Job out of the whole intellectual world of antiquity. It is as if the Egyptians had modestly concealed the Great Pyramid. But there were other reasons for a cross-purpose and an impasse, characteristic of the whole of the end of paganism. After all, the tradition of Israel had only got hold of one-half of the truth, even if we use the popular paradox and call it the bigger half. I shall try to sketch in the next chapter that love of locality and personality that ran through mythology; here it need only be said that there was a truth in it that could not be let out though it were a lighter and less essential truth. The sorrow of Job had to be joined with the sorrow of Hector; and while the former was the sorrow of the universe the latter was the sorrow of the city; for Hector could only stand pointing to heaven as the pillar of holy Troy. When God speaks out of the whirlwind he may well speak in the wilderness. But the monotheism of the nomad was not enough for all that varied civilisation of fields and fences and walled cities and temples and towns; and the turn of these things also was to come, when the two could be combined in a more definite and domestic religion. Here and there in all that pagan crowd could be found a philosopher whose thought ran of pure theism; but he never had, or supposed that he had, the power to change the customs of the whole populace. Nor is it easy even in such philosophies to find a true definition of this deep business of the relation of polytheism and theism. Perhaps the nearest we can come to striking the note, or giving the thing a name, is in something far away from all that civilisation and more remote from Rome than the isolation of Israel. It is in a saying I once heard from some Hindu tradition; that gods as well as men are only the dreams of Brahma; and will perish when Brahma wakes. There is indeed in such an image something of the soul of Asia which is less sane than the soul of Christendom. We should call it despair, even if they would call it peace. This note of nihilism can be considered later in a fuller comparison between Asia and Europe. It is enough to say here that there is more of disillusion in that idea of a divine awakening than is implied for us in the passage from mythology to religion. But the symbol is very subtle and exact in one respect; that it does suggest the disproportion and even disruption between the very ideas of mythology and religion, the chasm between the two categories. It is really the collapse of comparative religion that there is no comparison between God and the gods. There is no more comparison than there is between a man and the men who walked about in his dreams. Under the next heading some attempt will be made to indicate the twilight of that dream in which the gods walk about like men. But if anyone fancies the contrast of monotheism and polytheism is only a matter of some people having one god and others a few more, for him it will be far nearer the truth to plunge into the elephantine extravagance of Brahmin cosmology; that he may feel a shudder going through the veil of things, the many-handed creators, and the throned and haloed animals and all the network of entangled stars and rulers of the night, as the eyes of Brahma open like dawn upon the death of all.

V MAN AND MYTHOLOGIES

What are here called the Gods might almost alternatively be called the day-dreams. To compare them to dreams is not to deny that dreams can come true. To compare them to travellers' tales is not to deny that they may be true tales, or at least truthful tales. In truth they are the sort of tales the traveller tells to himself. All this mythological business belongs to the poetical part of men. It seems strangely forgotten nowadays that a myth is a work of imagination and therefore a work of art. It needs a poet to make it. It needs a poet to criticise it. There are more poets than non-poets in the world, as is proved by the popular origin of such legends. But for some reason I have never heard explained, it is only the minority of unpoetical people who are allowed to write critical studies of these popular poems. We do not submit a sonnet to a mathematician or a song to a calculating boy; but we do indulge the equally fantastic idea that folk-lore can be treated as a science. Unless these things are appreciated artistically they are not appreciated at all. When the professor is told by the Polynesian that once there was nothing except a great feathered serpent, unless the learned man feels a thrill and a half temptation to wish it were true, he is no judge of such things at all. When he is assured, on the best Red Indian authority, that a primitive hero carried the sun and moon and stars in a box, unless he clasps his hands and almost kicks his legs as a child would at such a charming fancy, he knows nothing about the matter. This test is not nonsensical; primitive children and barbaric children do laugh and kick like other children; and we must have a certain simplicity to repicture the childhood of the world. When Hiawatha was told by his nurse that a warrior threw his grandmother up to the moon, he laughed like any English child told by his nurse that a cow jumped over the moon. The child sees the joke as well as most men, and better than some scientific men. But the ultimate test even of the fantastic is the appropriateness of the inappropriate. And the test must appear merely arbitrary because it is merely artistic. If any student tells me that the infant Hiawatha only laughed out of respect for tribal custom of sacrificing the aged to economical housekeeping, I say he did not. If any scholar tells me that the cow jumped over the moon only because a heifer was sacrificed to Diana, I answer that it did not. It happened because it is obviously the right thing for a cow to jump over the moon. Mythology is a lost art, one of the few arts that really are lost; but it is an art. The horned moon and the horned mooncalf make a harmonious and almost a quiet pattern. And throwing your grandmother into the sky is not good behaviour; but it is perfectly good taste.

Thus scientists seldom understand, as artists understand, that one branch of the beautiful is the ugly. They seldom allow for the legitimate liberty of the grotesque. And they will dismiss a savage myth as merely coarse and clumsy and an evidence of degradation, because it has not all the beauty of the herald Mercury new lighted on a heaven-kissing hill; when it really has the beauty of the Mock Turtle or the Mad Hatter. It is the supreme proof of a man being prosaic that he always insists on poetry being poetical. Sometimes the humour is in the very subject as well as the style of the fable. The Australian aborigines, regarded as the rudest of savages, have a story about a giant frog who had swallowed the sea and all the waters of the world; and who was only forced to spill them by being made to laugh. All the animals with all their antics passed before him and, like Queen Victoria, he was not amused. He collapsed at last before an eel who stood delicately balanced on the tip of its tail, doubtless with a rather desperate dignity. Any amount of fine fantastic literature might be made out of that fable. There is philosophy in that vision of the dry world before the beatific Deluge of laughter. There is imagination in the mountainous monster erupting like an aqueous volcano; there is plenty of fun in the thought of his goggling visage as the pelican or the penguin passed by. Anyhow the frog laughed; but the folk-lore student remains grave.

Moreover, even where the fables are inferior as art, they cannot be properly judged by science; still less properly judged as science. Some myths are very crude and queer like the early drawings of children; but the child is trying to draw. It is none the less an error to treat his drawing as if it were a diagram, or intended to be a diagram. The student cannot make a scientific statement about the savage, because the savage is not making a scientific statement about the world. He is saying something quite different; what might be called the gossip of the gods. We may say, if we like, that it is believed before there is time to examine it. It would be truer to say it is accepted before there is time to believe it.

I confess I doubt the whole theory of the dissemination of myths or (as it commonly is) of one myth. It is true that something in our nature and conditions makes many stories similar; but each of them may be original. One man does not borrow the story from the other man, though he may tell it from the same motive as the other man. It would be easy to apply the whole argument about legend to literature; and turn it into a vulgar monomania of plagiarism. I would undertake to trace a notion like that of the Golden Bough through individual modern novels as easily as through communal and antiquated myths. I would undertake to find something like a bunch of flowers figuring again and again from the fatal bouquet of Becky Sharpe to the spray of roses sent by the Princess of Ruritania. But though these flowers may spring from the same soil, it is not the same faded flower that is flung from hand to hand. Those flowers are always fresh.

The true origin of all the myths has been discovered much too often. There are too many keys to mythology, as there are too many cryptograms in Shakespeare. Everything is phallic; everything is totemistic; everything is seed-time and harvest; everything is ghosts and grave-offerings; everything is the golden bough of sacrifice; everything is the sun and moon; everything is everything. Every folk-lore student who knew a little more than his own monomania, every man of wider reading and critical culture like Andrew Lang, has practically confessed that the bewilderment of these things left his brain spinning. Yet the whole trouble comes from a man trying to look at these stories from the outside, as if they were scientific objects. He has only to look at them from the inside, and ask himself how he would begin a story. A story may start with anything and go anywhere. It may start with a bird without the bird being a totem; it may start with the sun without being a solar myth. It is said there are only ten plots in the world; and there will certainly be common and recurrent elements. Set ten thousand children talking at once, and telling tarradiddles about what they did in the wood, and it will not be hard to find parallels suggesting sun-worship or animal worship. Some of the stories may be pretty and some silly and some perhaps dirty; but they can only be judged as stories. In the modern dialect, they can only be judged aesthetically. It is strange that aesthetics, or mere feeling, which is now allowed to usurp where it has no rights at all, to wreck reason with pragmatism and morals with anarchy, is apparently not allowed to give a purely aesthetic judgement on what is obviously a purely aesthetic question. We may be fanciful about everything except fairy-tales.

Now the first fact is that the most simple people have the most subtle ideas. Everybody ought to know that, for everybody has been a child. Ignorant as a child is, he knows more than he can say and feels not only atmospheres but fine shades. And in this matter there are several fine shades. Nobody understands it who has not had what can only be called the ache of the artist to find some sense and some story in the beautiful things he sees; his hunger for secrets and his anger at any tower or tree escaping with its tale untold. He feels that nothing is perfect unless it is personal. Without that the blind unconscious beauty of the world stands in its garden like a headless statue. One need only be a very minor poet to have wrestled with the tower or the tree until it spoke like a titan or a dryad. It is often said that pagan mythology was a personification of the powers of nature. The phrase is true in a sense, but it is very unsatisfactory; because it implies that the forces are abstractions and the personification is artificial. Myths are not allegories. Natural powers are not in this case abstractions. It is not as if there were a God of Gravitation. There may be a genius of the waterfall; but not of mere falling, even less than of mere water. The impersonation is not of something impersonal. The point is that the personality perfects the water with significance. Father Christmas is not an allegory of snow and holly; he is not merely the stuff called snow afterwards artificially given a human form, like a snow man. He is something that gives a new meaning to the white world and the evergreens, so that snow itself seems to be warm rather than cold. The test therefore is purely imaginative. But imaginative does not mean imaginary. It does not follow that it is all what the moderns call subjective, when they mean false. Every true artist does feel, consciously or unconsciously, that he is touching transcendental truths; that his images are shadows of things seen through the veil. In other words, the natural mystic does know that there is something there; something behind the clouds or within the trees; but he believes that the pursuit of beauty is the way to find it; that imagination is a sort of incantation that can call it up.

Now we do not comprehend this process in ourselves, far less in our most remote fellow-creatures And the danger of these things being classified is that they may seem to be comprehended. A really fine work of folklore, like The Golden Bough, will leave too many readers with the idea, for instance, that this or that story of a giant's or wizard's heart in a casket or a cave only 'means' some stupid and static superstition called 'the external soul.' But we do not know what these things mean, simply because we do not know what we ourselves mean when we are moved by them. Suppose somebody in a story says 'Pluck this flower and a princess will die in a castle beyond the sea,' we do not know why something stirs in the subconsciousness, or why what is impossible seems almost inevitable. Suppose we read 'And in the hour when the king extinguished the candle his ships were wrecked far away on the coast of Hebrides.' We do not know why the imagination has accepted that image before the reason can reject it; or why such correspondences seem really to correspond to something in the soul. Very deep things in our nature, some dim sense of the dependence of great things upon small, some dark suggestion that the things nearest to us stretch far beyond our power, some sacramental feeling of the magic in material substances, and many more emotions past fading out, are in an idea like that of the external soul. The power even in the myths of savages is like the power in the metaphors of poets. The soul of such a metaphor is often very emphatically an external soul. The best critics have remarked that in the best poets the simile is often a picture that seems quite separate from the text. It is as irrelevant as the remote castle to the flower or the Hebridean coast to the candle. Shelley compares the skylark to a young woman on a turret, to a rose embedded in thick foliage, to a series of things that seem to be about as unlike a skylark in the sky as anything we can imagine. I suppose the most potent piece of pure magic in English literature is the much-quoted passage in Keats's Nightingale about the casements opening on the perilous foam. And nobody notices that the image seems to come from nowhere; that it appears abruptly after some almost equally irrelevant remarks about Ruth; and that it has nothing in the world to do with the subject of the poem. If there is one place in the world where nobody could reasonably expect to find a nightingale, it is on a window-sill at the seaside. But it is only in the same sense that nobody would expect to find a giant's heart in a casket under the sea. Now, it would be very dangerous to classify the metaphors of the poets. When Shelley says that the cloud will rise 'like a child from the womb, like a ghost from the tomb,' it would be quite possible to call the first a case of the coarse primitive birth-myth and the second a survival of the ghost-worship which became ancestor-worship. But it is the wrong way of dealing with a cloud; and is liable to leave the learned in the condition of Polonius, only too ready to think it like a weasel, or very like a whale.

Two facts follow from this psychology of day-dreams, which must be kept in mind throughout their development in mythologies and even religions. First, these imaginative impressions are often strictly local. So far from being abstractions turned into allegories, they are often images almost concentrated into idols. The poet feels the mystery of a particular forest; not of the science of afforestation or the department of woods and forests. He worships the peak of a particular mountain, not the abstract idea of altitude. So we find the god is not merely water but often one special river; he may be the sea because the sea is single like a stream; the river that runs round the world. Ultimately doubtless many deities are enlarged into elements; but they are something more than omnipresent. Apollo does not merely dwell wherever the sun shines; his home is on the rock of Delphi. Diana is great enough to be in three places at once, earth and heaven and hell, but greater is Diana of the Ephesians. This localised feeling has its lowest form in the mere fetish or talisman, such as millionaires put on their motor-cars. But it can also harden into something like a high and serious religion, where it is connected with high and serious duties; into the gods of the city or even the gods of the hearth.

The second consequence is this; that in these pagan cults there is every shade of sincerity--and insincerity. In what sense exactly did an Athenian really think he had to sacrifice to Pallas Athena? What scholar is really certain of the answer? In what sense did Dr. Johnson really think that he had to touch all the posts in the street or that he had to collect orange-peel? In what sense does a child really think that he ought to step on every alternate paving-stone? Two things are at least fairly clear. First, in simpler and less self-conscious times these forms could become more solid without really becoming more serious. Day-dreams could be acted in broad daylight, with more liberty of artistic expression; but still perhaps with something of the light step of the somnambulist. Wrap Dr. Johnson in an antique mantle, crown him (by his kind permission) with a garland, and he will move in state under those ancient skies of morning; touching a series of sacred posts carved with the heads of the strange terminal gods, that stand at the limits of the land and of the life of man. Make the child free of the marbles and mosaics of some classic temples to play on a whole floor inlaid with squares of black and white; and he will willingly make this fulfilment of his idle and drifting daydream the clear field for a grave and graceful dance. But the posts and the paving-stones are little more and little less real than they are under modern limits. They are not really much more serious for being taken seriously. They have the sort of sincerity that they always had; the sincerity of art as a symbol that expresses very real spiritualities under the surface of life. But they are only sincere in the same sense as art; not sincere in the same sense as morality. The eccentric's collection of orange-peel may turn to oranges in a Mediterranean festival or to golden apples in a Mediterranean myth. But they are never on the same plane with the difference between giving the orange to a blind beggar and carefully placing the orange-peel so that the beggar may fall and break his leg. Between these two things there is a difference of kind and not of degree. The child does not think it wrong to step on the paving-stone as he thinks it wrong to step on the dog's tail. And it is very certain that whatever jest or sentiment or fancy first set Johnson touching the wooden posts, he never touched wood with any of the feeling with which he stretched out his hands to the timber of that terrible tree, which was the death of God and the life of man.

As already noted, this does not mean that there was no reality or even no religious sentiment in such a mood. As a matter of fact the Catholic Church has taken over with uproarious success the whole of this popular business of giving people local legends and lighter ceremonial movements. In so far as all this sort of paganism was innocent and in touch with nature, there is no reason why it should not be patronised by patron saints as much as by pagan gods. And in any case there are degrees of seriousness in the most natural make-believe. There is all the difference between fancying there are fairies in the wood, which often only means fancying a certain wood as fit for fairies, and really frightening ourselves until we walk a mile rather than pass a house we have told ourselves is haunted. Behind all these things is the fact that beauty and terror are very real things and related to a real spiritual world; and to touch them at all, even in doubt or fancy, is to stir the deep things of the soul. We all understand that and the pagans understood it. The point is that paganism did not really stir the soul except with these doubts and fancies, with the consequence that we to-day can have little beyond doubts and fancies about paganism. All the best critics agree that all the greatest poets, in pagan Hellas for example, had an attitude towards their gods which is quite queer and puzzling to men in the Christian era. There seems to be an admitted conflict between the god and the man; but everybody seems to be doubtful about which is the hero and which is the villain. This doubt does not merely apply to a doubter like Euripides in the Bacchae; it applies to a moderate conservative like Sophocles in the Antigone; or even to a regular Tory and reactionary like Aristophanes in the Frogs. Sometimes it would seem that the Greeks believed above all things in reverence, only they had nobody to revere. But the point of the puzzle is this, that all this vagueness and variation arise from the fact that the whole thing began in fancy and in dreaming; and that there are no rules of architecture for a castle in the clouds.

This is the mighty and branching tree called mythology which ramifies round the whole world, whose remote branches under separate skies bear like coloured birds the costly idols of Asia and the half-baked fetishes of Africa and the fairy kings and princesses of the folk-tales of the forest, and buried amid vines and olives the Lares of the Latins, and carried on the clouds of Olympus the buoyant supremacy of the gods of Greece. These are the myths: and he who has no sympathy with myths has no sympathy with men. But he who has most sympathy with myths will most fully realise that they are not and never were a religion, in the sense that Christianity or even Islam is a religion. They satisfy some of the needs satisfied by a religion; and notably the need for doing certain things at certain dates; the need of the twin ideas of festivity and formality. But though they provide a man with a calendar they do not provide him with a creed. A man did not stand up and say 'I believe in Jupiter and Juno and Neptune,' etc., as he stands up and says 'I believe in God the Father Almighty,' and the rest of the Apostles Creed. Many believed in some and not in others, or more in some and less in others, or only in a very vague poetical sense in any. There was no moment when they were all collected into an orthodox order which men would fight and be tortured to keep intact. Still less did anybody ever say in that fashion: 'I believe in

Odin and Thor and Freya,' for outside Olympus even the Olympian order grows cloudy and chaotic. It seems clear to me that Thor was not a god at all but a hero. Nothing resembling a religion would picture anybody resembling a god as groping like a pigmy in a great cavern, that turned out to be the glove of a giant. That is the glorious ignorance called adventure Thor may have been a great adventurer; but to call him a god is like trying to compare Jehovah with Jack and the Beanstalk. Odin seems to have been a real barbarian chief, possibly of the Dark Ages after Christianity. Polytheism fades away at its fringes into fairy-tales or barbaric memories; it is not a thing like monotheism as held by serious monotheists. Again it does satisfy the need to cry out on some uplifted name or some noble memory in moments that are themselves noble and uplifted; such as the birth of a child or the saving of a city. But the name was so used by many to whom it was only a name. Finally it did satisfy, or rather it partially satisfied, a thing very deep in humanity indeed; the idea of surrendering something as the portion of the unknown powers; of pouring of wine upon the ground, of throwing a ring into the sea; in a word, of sacrifice. It is the wise and worthy idea of not taking our advantage to the full; of putting something in the other balance to ballast our dubious pride, of paying tithes to nature for our land. This deep truth of the danger of insolence, or being too big for our boots, runs through all the great Greek tragedies and makes them great. But it runs side by side with an almost cryptic agnosticism about the real nature of the gods to be propitiated. Where that gesture of surrender is most magnificent, as among the great Greeks, there is really much more idea that the man will be the better for losing the ox than that the god will be the better for getting it. It is said that in its grosser forms there are often actions grotesquely suggestive of the god really eating the sacrifice. But this fact is falsified by the error that I put first in this note on mythology. It is misunderstanding the psychology of day-dreams. A child pretending there is a goblin in a hollow tree will do a crude and material thing, like leaving a piece of cake for him. A poet might do a more dignified and elegant thing, like bringing to the god fruits as well as flowers. But the degree of seriousness in both acts may be the same or it may vary in almost any degree. The crude fancy is no more a creed than the ideal fancy is a creed. Certainly the pagan does not disbelieve like an atheist, any more than he believes like a Christian. He feels the presence of powers about which he guesses and invents. St. Paul said that the Greeks had one altar to an unknown god. But in truth all their gods were unknown gods. And the real break in history did come when St. Paul declared to them whom they had ignorantly worshipped.

The substance of all such paganism may be summarised thus. It is an attempt to reach the divine reality through the imagination alone; in its own field reason does not restrain it at all. It is vital to view of all history that reason is something separate from religion even in the most rational of these civilisations. It is only as an afterthought, when such cults are decadent or on the defensive, that a few Neo-Platonists or a few Brahmins are found trying to rationalise them, and even then only by trying to allegorise them. But in reality the rivers of mythology and philosophy run parallel and do not mingle till they meet in the sea of Christendom. Simple secularists still talk as if the Church had introduced a sort of schism between reason and religion. The truth is that the Church was actually the first thing that ever tried to combine reason and religion. There had never before been any such union of the priests and the philosophers. Mythology, then, sought god through the imagination; or sought truth by means of beauty, in the sense in which beauty includes much of the most grotesque ugliness. But the imagination has its own laws and therefore its own triumphs, which neither logicians nor men of science can understand It remained true to that imaginative instinct through a thousand extravagances, through every crude cosmic pantomime of a pig eating the moon or the world being cut out of a cow, through all the dizzy convolutions and mystic malformations of Asiatic art, through all the stark and staring rigidity of Egyptian and Assyrian portraiture, through every kind of cracked mirror of mad art that seemed to deform the world and displace the sky, it remained true to something about which there can be no argument; something that makes it possible for some artist of some school to stand suddenly still before that particular deformity and say, 'My dream has come true.' Therefore do we all in fact feel that pagan or primitive myths are infinitely suggestive, so long as we are wise enough not to inquire what they suggest. Therefore we all feel what is meant by Prometheus stealing fire from heaven, until some prig of a pessimist or progressive person explains what it means. Therefore we all know the meaning of Jack and the Beanstalk, until we are told. In this sense it is true that it is the ignorant who accept myths, but only because it is the ignorant who appreciate poems. Imagination has its own laws and triumphs; and a tremendous power began to clothe its images, whether images in the mind or in the mud, whether in the bamboo of the South Sea Islands or the marble of the mountains of Hellas. But there was always a trouble in the triumph, which in these pages I have tried to analyse in vain; but perhaps I might in conclusion state it thus.

The crux and crisis is that man found it natural to worship; even natural to worship unnatural things. The posture of the idol might be stiff and strange; but the gesture of the worshipper was generous and beautiful. He not only felt freer when he bent; he actually felt taller when he bowed. Henceforth anything that took away the gesture of worship would stunt and even maim him for ever. Henceforth being merely secular would be a servitude and an inhibition. If man cannot pray he is gagged; if he cannot kneel he is in irons. We therefore feel throughout the whole of paganism a curious double feeling of trust and distrust. When the man makes the gesture of salutation and of sacrifice, when he pours out the libation or lifts up the sword, he knows he is doing a worthy and a virile thing. He knows he is doing one of the things for which a man was made. His imaginative experiment is therefore justified. But precisely because it began with imagination, there is to the end something of mockery in it, and especially in the object of it. This mockery, in the more in tense moments of the intellect, becomes the almost intolerable irony of Greek tragedy. There seems a disproportion between the priest and the altar or between the altar and the god. The priest seems more solemn and almost more sacred than the god. All the order of the temple is solid and sane and satisfactory to certain parts of our nature; except the very centre of it, which seems strangely mutable and dubious, like a dancing flame. It is the first thought round which the whole has been built; and the first thought is still a fancy and almost a frivolity. In that strange place of meeting, the man seems more statuesque than the statue. He himself can stand for ever in the noble and natural attitude of the statue of the Praying Boy. But whatever name be written on the pedestal, whether Zeus or Ammon or Apollo, the god whom he worships is Proteus.

The Praying Boy may be said to express a need rather than to satisfy a need. It is by a normal and necessary action that his hands are lifted; but it is no less a parable that his hands are empty. About the nature of that need there will be more to say; but at this point it may be said that perhaps after all this true instinct, that player and sacrifice are a liberty and an enlargement, refers back to that vast and half-forgotten conception of universal fatherhood, which we have already seen everywhere fading from the morning sky. This is true; and yet it is not all the truth. There remains an indestructible instinct, in the poet as represented by the pagan, that he is not entirely wrong in localising his God. It is something in the soul of poetry if not of piety. And the greatest of poets, when he defined the poet, did not say that he gave us the universe or the absolute or the infinite; but, in his own larger language, a local habitation and a name. No poet is merely a pantheist; those who are counted most pantheistic, like Shelley, start with some local and particular image as the pagans did. After all, Shelley wrote of the skylark because it was a skylark. You could not issue an imperial or international translation of it for use in South America, in which it was changed to an ostrich. So the mythological imagination moves as it were in circles, hovering either to find a place or to return to it. In a word, mythology is a search; it is something that combines a recurrent desire with a recurrent doubt, mixing a most hungry sincerity in the idea of seeking for a place with a most dark and deep and mysterious levity about all the places found. So far could the lonely imagination lead, and we must turn later to the lonely reason. Nowhere along this road did the two ever travel together.

That is where all these things differed from religion or the reality in which these different dimensions met in a sort of solid. They differed from the reality not in what they looked like but in what they were. A picture may look like a landscape; it may look in every detail exactly like a landscape. The only detail in which it differs is that it is not a landscape. The difference is only that which divides a portrait of Queen Elizabeth from Queen Elizabeth. Only in this mythical and mystical world the portrait could exist before the person; and the portrait was therefore more vague and doubtful. But anybody who has felt and fed on the atmosphere of these myths will know what I mean, when I say that in one sense they did not really profess to be realities. The pagans had dreams about realities; and they would have been the first to admit, in their own words, that some came through the gate of ivory and others through the gate of horn. The dreams do indeed tend to be very vivid dreams when they touch on those tender or tragic things, which can really make a sleeper awaken with the sense that his heart has been broken in his sleep. They tend continually to hover over certain passionate themes of meeting and parting, of a life that ends in death or a death that is the beginning of life. Demeter wanders over a stricken world looking for a stolen child; Isis stretches out her arms over the earth in vain to gather the limbs of Osiris; and there is lamentation upon the hills for Atys and through the woods for Adonis. There mingles with all such mourning the mystical and profound sense that death can be a deliverer and an appeasement; that such death gives us a divine blood for a renovating river and that all good is found in gathering the broken body of the god. We may truly call these foreshadowing; so long as we remember that foreshadowings are shadows. And the metaphor of a shadow happens to hit very exactly the truth that is very vital here. For a shadow is a shape; a thing which reproduces shape but not texture. These things were something like the real thing; and to say that they were like is to say that they were different. Saying something is like a dog is another way of saying it is not a dog; and it is in this sense of identity that a myth is not a man. Nobody really thought of Isis as a human being, nobody really thought of Demeter as a historical character, nobody thought of Adonis as the founder of a Church. There was no idea that any one of them had changed the world; but rather that their recurrent death and life bore the sad and beautiful burden of the changelessness of the world. Not one of them was a revolution, save in the sense of the revolution of the sun and moon. Their whole meaning is missed if we do not see that they mean the shadows that we are and the shadows that we pursue. In certain sacrificial and communal aspects they naturally suggest what sort of a god might satisfy them; but they do not profess to be satisfied. Anyone who says they do is a bad judge of poetry.

Those who talk about Pagan Christs have less sympathy with Paganism than with Christianity. Those who call these cults 'religions,' and 'compare' them with the certitude and challenge of the Church have much less appreciation than we have of what made heathenism human, or of why classic literature is still something that hangs in the air like a song. It is no very human tenderness for the hungry to prove that hunger is the same as food. It is no very genial understanding of youth to argue that hope destroys the need for happiness. And it is utterly unreal to argue that these images in the mind, admired entirely in the abstract, were even in the same world with a living man and a living polity that were worshipped because they were concrete. We might as well say that a boy playing at robbers is the same as a man in his first day in the trenches; or that boy's first fancies about 'the not impossible she' are the same as the sacrament of marriage. They are fundamentally different exactly where they are superficially similar; we might almost say they are not the same even when they are the same. They are only different because one is real and the other is not. I do not mean merely that I myself believe that one is true and the other is not. I mean that one was never meant to be true in the same sense as the other. The sense in which it was meant to be true I have tried to suggest vaguely here, but it is undoubtedly very subtle and almost indescribable. It is so subtle that the students who profess to put it up as a rival to our religion miss the whole meaning and purport of their own study. We know better than the scholars, even those of us who are no scholars, what was in that hollow cry that went forth over the dead Adonis and why the Great Mother had a daughter wedded to death. We have entered more deeply than they into the Eleusinian Mysteries and have passed a higher grade, where gate within gate guarded the wisdom of Orpheus. We know the meaning of all the myths. We know the last secret revealed to the perfect initiate. And it is not the voice of a priest or a prophet saying 'These things are.' It is the voice of a dreamer and an idealist crying, 'Why cannot these things be?'

VI THE DEMONS AND THE PHILOSOPHERS

I have dwelt at some little length on this imaginative sort of paganism, which has crowded the world with temples and is everywhere the parent of popular festivity. For the central history of civilisation, as I see it, consists of two further stages before the final stage of Christendom. The first was the struggle between this paganism and something less worthy than itself, and the second the process by which it grew in itself less worthy. In this very varied and often very vague polytheism there was a weakness of original sin. Pagan gods were depicted as tossing men like dice; and indeed they are loaded dice. About sex especially men are born unbalanced; we might almost say men are born mad. They scarcely reach sanity till they reach sanctity. This disproportion dragged down the winged fancies; and filled the end of paganism with a mere filth and litter of spawning gods. But the first point to realise is that this sort of paganism had an early collision with another sort of paganism; and that the issue of that essentially spiritual struggle really determined the history of the world. In order to understand it we must pass to a review of the other kind of paganism. It can be considered much more briefly; indeed there is a very real sense in which the less that is said about it the better. If we have called the first sort of mythology the day-dream, we might very well call the second sort of mythology the nightmare.

Superstition recurs in all ages, and especially in rationalistic ages. I remember defending the religious tradition against a whole luncheon table of distinguished agnostics; and before the end of our conversation every one of them had procured from his pocket, or exhibited on his watch-chain, some charm or talisman from which he admitted that he was never separated. I was the only person present who had neglected to provide himself with a fetish. Superstition recurs in a rationalist age because it rests on something which, if not identical with rationalism, is not unconnected with scepticism. It is at least very closely connected with agnosticism. It rests on something that is really a very human and intelligible sentiment, like the local invocations of the numen in popular paganism. But it is an agnostic sentiment, for it rests on two feelings: first that we do not really know the laws of the universe; and second that they may be very different to all we call reason. Such men realise the real truth that enormous things do often turn upon tiny things. When a whisper comes, from tradition or what not, that one particular tiny thing is the key or clue, something deep and not altogether senseless in human nature tells them that it is not unlikely. This feeling exists in both the forms of paganism here under consideration. But when we come to the second form of it, we find it transformed and filled with another and more terrible spirit.

In dealing with the lighter thing called mythology, I have said little about the most disputable aspect of it; the extent to which such invocation of the spirits of the sea or the elements can indeed call spirits from the vasty deep; or rather, (as the Shakespearean scoffer put it) whether the spirits come when they are called. I believe that I am right in thinking that this problem, practical as it sounds, did not play a dominant part in the poetical business of mythology. But I think it even more obvious, on the evidence, that things of that sort have sometimes appeared, even if they were only appearances. But when we come to the world of superstition, in a more subtle sense, there is a shade of difference; a deepening and a darkening shade. Doubtless most popular superstition is as frivolous as any popular mythology. Men do not believe as a dogma that God would throw a thunderbolt at them for walking under a ladder; more often they amuse themselves with the not very laborious exercise of walking round it. There is no more in it than what I have already adumbrated; a sort of airy agnosticism about the possibilities of so strange a world. But there is another sort of superstition that does definitely look for results; what might be called a realistic superstition. And with that the question of whether spirits do answer or do appear becomes much more serious. As I have said, it seems to me pretty certain that they sometimes do; but about that there is a distinction that has been the beginning of much evil in the world. Whether it be because the Fall has really brought men nearer to less desirable neighbours in the spiritual world, or whether it is merely that the mood of men eager or greedy finds it easier to imagine evil, I believe that the black magic of witchcraft has been much more practical and much less poetical than the white magic of mythology. I fancy the garden of the witch has been kept much more carefully than the woodland of the nymph. I fancy the evil field has even been more fruitful than the good. To start with, some impulse, perhaps a sort of desperate impulse, drove men to the darker powers when dealing with practical problems. There was a sort of secret and perverse feeling that the darker powers would really do things; that they had no nonsense about them. And indeed that popular phase exactly expresses the point. The gods of mere mythology had a great deal of nonsense about them. They had a great deal of good nonsense about them; in the happy and hilarious sense in which we talk of the nonsense of Jabberwocky or the Land where Jumblies live. But the man consulting a demon felt as many a man has felt in consulting a detective, especially a private detective; that it was dirty work but the work would really be done. A man did not exactly go into the wood to meet a nymph; he rather went with the hope of meeting a nymph. It was an adventure rather than an assignation. But the devil really kept his appointments and even in one sense kept his promises; even if a man sometimes wished afterwards, like Macbeth, that he had broken them.

In the accounts given us of many rude or savage races we gather that the cult of demons often came after the cult of deities, and even after the cult of one single and supreme deity. It may be suspected that in almost all such places the higher deity is felt to be too far off for appeal in certain petty matters, and men invoke the spirits because they are in a more literal sense familiar spirits. But with the idea of employing the demons who get things done, a new idea appears more worthy of the demons. It may indeed be truly described as the idea of being worthy of the demons; of making oneself fit for their fastidious and exacting society. Superstition of the lighter sort toys with the idea that some trifle, some small gesture such as throwing the salt, may touch the hidden spring that works the mysterious machinery of the world. And there is after all something in the idea of such an Open Sesame. But with the appeal to lower spirits comes the horrible notion that the gesture must not only be very small but very low; that it must be a monkey trick of an utterly ugly and unworthy sort. Sooner or later a man deliberately sets himself to do the most disgusting thing he can think of. It is felt that the extreme of evil will extort a sort of attention or answer from the evil powers under the surface of the world. This is the meaning of most of the cannibalism in the world. For most cannibalism is not a primitive or even a bestial habit. It is artificial and even artistic, a sort of art for art's sake. Men do not do it because they do not think it horrible; but, on the contrary, because they do think it horrible. They wish, in the most literal sense, to sup on horrors. That is why it is often found that rude races like the Australian natives are not cannibals; while much more refined and intelligent races, like the New Zealand Maories, occasionally are. They are refined and intelligent enough to indulge sometimes in a self-conscious diabolism. But if we could understand their minds, or even really understand their language, we should probably find that they were not acting as ignorant, that is as innocent cannibals. They are not doing it because they do not think it wrong, but precisely because they do think it wrong. They are acting like a Parisian decadent at a Black Mass. But the Black Mass has to hide underground from the presence of the real Mass. In other words, the demons have really been in hiding since the coming of Christ on earth. The cannibalism of the higher barbarians is in hiding from the civilisation of the white man. But before Christendom, and especially outside Europe, this was not always so. In the ancient world the demons often wandered abroad like dragons. They could be positively and publicly enthroned as gods. Their enormous images could be set up in public temples in the centre of populous cities. And all over the world the traces can be found of this striking and solid fact, so curiously overlooked by the moderns who speak of all such evil as primitive and early in evolution, that as a matter of fact some of the very highest civilisations of the world were the very places where the horns of Satan were exalted, not only to the stars but in the face of the sun. Take for example the Aztecs and American Indians of the ancient empires of Mexico and Peru. They were at least as elaborate as Egypt or China and only less lively than that central civilisation which is our own. But those who criticise that central civilisation (which is always their own civilisation) have a curious habit of not merely doing their legitimate duty in condemning its crimes, but of going out of their way to idealise its victims. They always assume that before the advent of Europe there was nothing anywhere but Eden. And Swinburne, in that spirited chorus of the nations in 'Songs before Sunrise,' used an expression about Spain in her South American conquests which always struck me as very strange. He said something about 'her sins and sons through sinless lands dispersed,' and how they 'made accursed the name of man and thrice accursed the name of God.' It may be reasonable enough that he should say the Spaniards were sinful, but why in the world should he say that the South Americans were sinless? Why should he have supposed that continent to be exclusively populated by archangels or saints perfect in heaven? It would be a strong thing to say of the most respectable neighbourhood; but when we come to think of what we really do know of that society the remark is rather funny. We know that the sinless priests of this sinless people worshipped sinless gods, who accepted as the nectar and ambrosia of their sunny paradise nothing but incessant human sacrifice accompanied by horrible torments. We may note also in the mythology of this American civilisation that element of reversal or violence against instinct of which Dante wrote; which runs backwards everywhere through the unnatural religion of the demons. It is notable not only in ethics but in aesthetics. A South American idol was made as ugly as possible, as a Greek image was made as beautiful as possible. They were seeking the secret of power, by working backwards against their own nature and the nature of things. There was always a sort of yearning to carve at last, in gold or granite or the dark red timber of the forests, a face at which the sky itself would break like a cracked mirror.

In any case it is clear enough that the painted and gilded civilisation of tropical America systematically indulged in human sacrifice. It is by no means clear, so far as I know, that the Eskimos ever indulged in human sacrifice. They were not civilised enough. They were too closely imprisoned by the white winter and the endless dark. Chill penury repressed their noble rage and froze the genial current of the soul. It was in brighter days and broader daylight that the noble rage is found unmistakably raging. It was in richer and more instructed lands that the genial current flowed on the altars, to be drunk by great gods wearing goggling and grinning masks and called on in terror or torment by long cacophonous names that sound like laughter in hell. A warmer climate and a more scientific cultivation were needed to bring forth these blooms; to draw up towards the sun the large leaves and flamboyant blossoms that gave their gold and crimson and purple to that garden, which Swinburne compares to the Hesperides. There was at least no doubt about the dragon.

I do not raise in this connection the special controversy about Spain and Mexico; but I may remark in passing that it resembles exactly the question that must in some sense be raised afterwards about Rome and Carthage. In both cases there has been a queer habit among the English of always siding against the Europeans, and representing the rival civilisation, in Swinburne's phrase, as sinless; when its sins were obviously crying or rather screaming to heaven. For Carthage also was a high civilisation, indeed a much more highly civilised civilisation. And Carthage also founded that civilisation on a religion of fear, sending up everywhere the smoke of human sacrifice. Now it is very right to rebuke our own race or religion for falling short of our own standards and ideals. But it is absurd to pretend that they fell lower than the other races and religions that professed the very opposite standards and ideals. There is a very real sense in which the Christian is worse than the heathen, the Spaniard worse than the Red Indian, or even the Roman potentially worse than the Carthaginian. But there is only one sense in which he is worse; and that is not in being positively worse. The Christian is only worse because it is his business to be better.

This inverted imagination produces things of which it is better not to speak. Some of them indeed might almost be named without being known; for they are of that extreme evil which seems innocent to the innocent. They are too inhuman even to be indecent. But without dwelling much longer in these dark corners, it may be noted as not irrelevant here that certain anti-human antagonisms seem to recur in this tradition of black magic. There may be suspected as running through it everywhere, for instance, a mystical hatred of the idea of childhood. People would understand better the popular fury against the witches, if they remembered that the malice most commonly attributed to them was preventing the birth of children. The Hebrew prophets were perpetually protesting against the Hebrew race relapsing into an idolatry that involved such a war upon children; and it is probable enough that this abominable apostasy from the God of Israel has occasionally appeared in Israel since, in the form of what is called ritual murder; not of course by any representative of the religion of Judaism, but by individual and irresponsible diabolists who did happen to be Jews. This sense that the forces of evil especially threaten childhood is found again in the enormous popularity of the Child Martyr of the Middle Ages. Chaucer did but give another version of a very national English legend, when he conceived the wickedest of all possible witches as the dark alien woman watching behind her high lattice and heading, like the babble of a brook down the stony street, the singing of little St. Hugh.

Anyhow the part of such speculations that concerns this story centered especially round that eastern end of the Mediterranean, where the nomads had turned gradually into traders and had begun to trade with the whole world. Indeed in the sense of trade and travel and colonial extension, it already had something like an empire of the whole world. Its purple dye, the emblem of its rich pomp and luxury, had steeped the wares which were sold far away amid the last crags of Cornwall and the sails that entered the silence of tropic seas amid all the mystery of Africa. It might be said truly to have painted the map purple. It was already a world-wide success, when the princes of Tyre would hardly have troubled to notice that one of their princesses had condescended to marry the chief of some tribe called Judah; when the merchants of its African outpost would only have curled their bearded and Semitic lips with a slight smile at the mention of a village called Rome. And indeed no two things could have seemed more distant from each other, not only in space but in Spirit, than the monotheism of the Palestinian tribe and the very virtues of the small Italian republic. There was but one thing between them; and the thing which divided them has united them. Very various and incompatible were the things that could be loved by the consuls of Rome and the prophets of Israel; but they were at one in what they hated. It is very easy in both cases to represent that hatred as something merely hateful. It is easy enough to make a merely harsh and inhuman figure either of Elijah raving above the slaughter of Carmel or Cato thundering against the amnesty of Africa. These men had their limitations and their local passions; but this criticism of them is unimaginative and therefore unreal. It leaves out something, something immense and intermediate, facing east and west and calling up this passion in its eastern and western enemies; and that something is the first subject of this chapter.

The civilisation that centered in Tyre and Sidon was above all things practical. It has left little in the way of art and nothing in the way of poetry. But it prided itself upon being very efficient; and it followed in its philosophy and religion that strange and sometimes secret train of thought which we have already noted in those who look for immediate effects. There is always in such a mentality an idea that there is a short cut to the secret of all success; something that would shock the world by this sort of shameless thoroughness. They believed, in the appropriate modern phrase, in people who delivered the goods. In their dealings with their god Moloch, they themselves were always careful to deliver the goods. It was an interesting transaction, upon which we shall have to touch more than once in the rest of the narrative; it is enough to say here that it involved the theory I have suggested, about a certain attitude towards children. This was what called up against it in simultaneous fury the servant of one God in Palestine and the guardians of all the household gods in Rome This is what challenged two things naturally so much divided by every sort of distance and disunion, whose union was to save the world.

I have called the fourth and final division of the spiritual elements into which I should divide heathen humanity by the name of The Philosophers. I confess that it covers in my mind much that would generally be classified otherwise; and that what are here called philosophies are very often called religions. I believe however that my own description will be found to be much the more realistic and not the less respectful. But we must first take philosophy in its purest and clearest form that we may trace its normal outline; and that is to be found in the world of the purest and clearest outlines, that culture of the Mediterranean of which we have been considering the mythologies and idolatries in the last two chapters.

Polytheism, or that aspect of paganism, was never to the pagan what Catholicism is to the Catholic. It was never a view of the universe satisfying all sides of life; a complete and complex truth with something to say about everything. It was only a satisfaction of one side of the soul of man, even if we call it the religious side; and I think it is truer to call it the imaginative side. But this it did satisfy; in the end it satisfied it to satiety. All that world was a tissue of interwoven tales and cults, and there ran in and out of it, as we have already seen, that black thread among its more blameless colours; the darker paganism that was really diabolism. But we all know that this did not mean that all pagan men thought of nothing but pagan gods. Precisely because mythology only satisfied one mood, they turned in other moods to something totally different. But it is very important to realise that it was totally different. It was too different to be inconsistent. It was so alien that it did not clash. While a mob of people were pouring on a public holiday to the feast of Adonis or the games in honour of Apollo, this or that man would prefer to stop at home and think out a little theory about the nature of things. Sometimes his hobby would even take the form of thinking about the nature of God; or even in that sense about the nature of the gods. But he very seldom thought of pitting his nature of the gods against the gods of nature.

It is necessary to insist on this abstraction in the first student of abstractions. He was not so much antagonistic as absent-minded. His hobby might be the universe; but at first the hobby was as private as if it had been numismatics or playing draughts. And even when his wisdom came to be a public possession, and almost a political situation, it was very seldom on the same plane as the popular and religious institutions. Aristotle, with his colossal common sense, was perhaps the greatest of all philosophers; certainly the most practical of all philosophies But Aristotle would no more have set up the Absolute side by side with the Apollo of Delphi, as a similar or rival religion, than Archimedes would have thought of setting up the lever as a sort of idol or fetish to be substituted for the Palladium of the city. Or we might as well imagine Euclid building an altar to an isosceles triangle, or offering sacrifices to the square of the hypotenuse. The one man meditated on metaphysics as the other man did on mathematics; for the love of truth or for curiosity or for the fun of the thing. But that sort of fun never seems to have interfered very much with the other sort of fun; the fun of dancing or singing to celebrate some rascally romance about Zeus becoming a bull or a swan. It is perhaps the proof of a certain superficiality and even insincerity about the popular polytheism, that men could be philosophers and even sceptics without disturbing it. These thinkers could move the foundations of the world without altering even the outline of that coloured cloud that hung above it in the air.

For the thinkers did move the foundations of the world, even when a curious compromise seemed to prevent them from moving the foundations of the city. The two great philosophers of antiquity do indeed appear to us as defenders of sane and even of sacred ideas; their maxims often read like the answers to sceptical questions too completely answered to be always recorded. Aristotle annihilated a hundred anarchists and nature-worshipping cranks by the fundamental statement that man is a political animal. Plato in some sense anticipated the Catholic realism, as attacked by the heretical nominalism, by insisting on the equally fundamental fact that ideas are realities; that ideas exist just as men exist. Plato however seemed sometimes almost to fancy that ideas exist as men do not exist; or that the men need hardly be considered where they conflict with the ideas. He had something of the social sentiment that we call Fabian in his ideal of fitting the citizen to the city. Like an imaginary head to an ideal hat; and great and glorious as he remains, he has been the Father of all faddists. Aristotle anticipated more fully the sacramental sanity that was to combine the body and the soul of things; for he considered the nature of men as well as the nature of morals, and looked to the eyes as well as to the light. But though these great men were in that sense constructive and conservative, they belonged to a world where thought was free to the point of being fanciful. Many other great intellects did indeed follow them, some exalting an abstract vision of virtue, others following more rationalistically the necessity of the human pursuit of happiness. The former had the name of Stoics; and their name has passed into a proverb for what is indeed one of the main moral ideals of mankind: that of strengthening the mind itself until it is of a texture to resist calamity or even pain. But it is admitted that a great number of the philosophers degenerated into what we still call sophists. They became a sort of professional sceptics who went about asking uncomfortable questions, and were handsomely paid for making themselves a nuisance to normal people. It was perhaps an accidental resemblance to such questioning quacks that was responsible for the unpopularity of the great Socrates; whose death might seem to contradict the suggestion of the permanent truce between the philosophers and the gods. But Socrates did not die as a monotheist who denounced polytheism; certainly not as a prophet who denounced idols. It is clear to anyone reading between the lines that there was some notion, right or wrong, of a purely personal influence affecting morals and perhaps politics The general compromise remained, whether it was that the Greeks thought their myths a joke or that they thought their theories a joke. There was never any collision in which one really destroyed the other, and there was never any combination in which one was really reconciled with the other. They certainly did not work together; if anything the philosopher was a rival of the priest. But both seemed to have accepted a sort of separation of functions and remained parts of the same social system. Another important tradition descends from Pythagoras; who is significant because he stands nearest to the Oriental mystics who must be considered in their turn. He taught a sort of mysticism of mathematics, that number is the ultimate reality; but he also seems to have taught the transmigration of souls like the Brahmins; and to have left to his followers certain traditional tricks of vegetarianism and water-drinking very common among the eastern sages, especially those who figure in fashionable drawing-rooms, like those of the later Roman Empire. But in passing to eastern sages, and the somewhat different atmosphere of the east, we may approach a rather important truth by other path.

One of the great philosophers said that it would be well if philosophers were kings, or kings were philosophers. He spoke as of something too good to be true; but, as a matter of fact, it not unfrequently was true. A certain type, perhaps too little noticed in history, may really be called the royal philosopher. To begin with, apart from actual royalty, it did occasionally become possible for the sage, though he was not what we call a religious founder, to be something like a political founder. And the great example of this, one of the very greatest in the world, will with the very thought of it carry us thousands of miles across the vast spaces of Asia to that very wonderful and in some ways that very wise world of ideas and institutions, which we dismiss somewhat cheaply when we talk of China. Men have served many very strange gods; and trusted themselves loyally to many ideals and even idols. China is a society that has really chosen to believe in intellect. It has taken intellect seriously; and it may be that it stands alone in the world. From a very early age it faced the dilemma of the king and the philosopher by actually appointing a philosopher to advise the king. It made a public institution out of a private individual, who had nothing in the world to do but to be intellectual. It had and has, of course, many other things on the same pattern. It creates all ranks and privileges by public examination; it has nothing that we call an aristocracy; it is a democracy dominated by an intelligensia. But the point here is that it had philosophers to advise kings; and one of those philosophers must have been a great philosopher and a great statesman.

Confucius was not a religious founder or even a religious teacher; possibly not even a religious man. He was not an atheist; he was apparently what we call an agnostic. But the really vital point is that it is utterly irrelevant to talk about his religion at all. It is like talking of theology as the first thing in the story of how Rowland Hill established the postal system or Baden Powell organised the Boy Scouts. Confucius was not there to bring a message from heaven to humanity, but to organise China; and he must have organised it exceedingly well. It follows that he dealt much with morals; but he bound them up strictly with manners. The peculiarity of his scheme and of his country, in which it contrasts with its great pendant the system of Christendom, is that he insisted on perpetuating an external life with all its forms, that outward continuity might preserve internal peace. Anyone who knows how much habit has to do with health, of mind as well as body, will see the truth in his idea. But he will also see that the ancestor-worship and the reverence for the Sacred Emperor were habits and not creeds. It is unfair to the great Confucius to say he was a religious founder. It is even unfair to him to say he was not a religious founder. It is as unfair as going out of one's way to say that Jeremy Bentham was not a Christian martyr.

But there is a class of most interesting cases in which philosophers were kings, and not merely the friends of kings. The combination is not accidental. It has a great deal to do with this rather elusive question of the function of the philosopher. It contains in it some hint of why philosophy and mythology seldom came to an open rupture. It was not only because there was something a little frivolous about the mythology. It was also because there was something a little supercilious about the philosopher. He despised the myths, but he also despised the mob; and thought they suited each other. The pagan philosopher was seldom a man of the people, at any rate in spirit; he was seldom a democrat and often a bitter critic of democracy. He had about him an air of aristocratic and humane leisure; and his part was most easily played by men who happened to be in such a position. It was very easy and natural for a prince or a prominent person to play at being as philosophical as Hamlet or Theseus in the Midsummer Night's Dream. And from very early ages we find ourselves in the presence of these princely intellectuals. In fact, we find one of them in the very first recorded ages of the world; sitting on the primeval throne that looked over ancient Egypt.

The most intense interest of the incident of Akenahten, commonly called the Heretic Pharaoh, lies in the fact that he was the one example, at any rate before Christian times, of one of these royal philosophers who set himself to fight popular mythology in the name of private philosophy. Most of them assumed the attitude of Marcus Aurelius, who is in many ways the model of this sort of monarch and sage. Marcus Aurelius has been blamed for tolerating the pagan amphitheatre or the Christian martyrdoms. But it was characteristic; for this sort of man really thought of popular religion just as he thought of popular circuses. Of him Professor Phillimore has profoundly said 'a great and good man--and he knew it.' The heretic Pharaoh had a philosophy more earnest and perhaps more humble. For there is a corollary to the conception of being too proud to fight. It is that the humble have to do most of the fighting. Anyhow, the Egyptian prince was simple enough to take his own philosophy seriously, and alone among such intellectual princes he affected a sort of coup d'etat; hurling down the high gods of Egypt with one imperial gesture and lifting up for all men, like a blazing mirror of monotheistic truth, the disc of the universal sun. He had other interesting ideas often to be found in such idealists. In the sense in which we speak of a Little Englander he was a Little Egypter. In art he was a realist because he was an idealist; for realism is more impossible than any other ideal. But after all there falls on him something of the shadow of Marcus Aurelius, stalked by the shadow of Professor Phillimore. That is the matter with this noble sort of prince is that he has nowhere quite escaped being something of a prig. Priggishness is so pungent a smell that it clings amid the faded spices even to an Egyptian mummy. That was the matter with the heretic Pharaoh, as with a good many other heretics, was that he probably never paused to ask himself whether there was anything in the popular beliefs and tales of people less educated than himself. And, as already suggested, there was something in them. There was a real human hunger in all that element of feature and locality, that procession of deities like enormous pet animals, in that unwearied watching at certain haunted spots, in all the many wanderings of mythology. Nature may not have the name of Isis; Isis may not be really looking for Osiris. But it is true that Nature is really looking for something; Nature is always looking for the supernatural. Something much more definite was to satisfy that need; but a dignified monarch with a disc of the sun did not satisfy it. The royal experiment failed amid a roaring reaction of popular superstitions, in which the priests rose on the shoulders of the people and ascended the throne of the kings.

The next great example I shall take of the princely sage is Gautama, the great Lord Buddha. I know he is not generally classed merely with the philosophers; but I am more and more convinced from all information that reaches me, that this is the real interpretation of his immense importance. He was by far the greatest and the best of these intellectuals born in the purple. His reaction was perhaps the noblest and most sincere of all the resultant actions of that combination of thinkers and of thrones. For his reaction was renunciation. Marcus Aurelius was content to say, with a refined irony, that even in a palace life could be lived well. The fierier Egyptian king concluded that it could be lived even better after a palace revolution. But the great Gautama was the only one of them who proved he could really do without his palace. One fell back on toleration and the other on revolution. But after all there is something more absolute about abdication. Abdication is perhaps the one really absolute action of an absolute monarch. The Indian prince, reared in Oriental luxury and pomp, deliberately went out and lived the life of a beggar. That is magnificent, but it is not war; that is, it is not necessarily a Crusade in the Christian sense. It does not decide the question of whether the life of a beggar was the life of a saint or the life of a philosopher. It does not decide whether this great man is really to go into the tub of Diogenes or the cave of St. Jerome. Now those who seem to be nearest to the study of Buddha, and certainly those who write most clearly and intelligently about him, convince me for one that he was simply a philosopher who founded a successful school of philosophy, and was turned into a sort of divus or sacred being merely by the more mysterious and unscientific atmosphere of all such traditions in Asia. So that it is necessary to say at this point a word about that invisible yet vivid border-line that we cross in passing from the Mediterranean into the mystery of the East.

Perhaps there are no things out of which we get so little of the truth as the truisms; especially when they are really true. We are all in the habit of saying certain things about Asia, which are true enough but which hardly help us because we do not understand their truth; as that Asia is old or looks to the past or is not progressive. Now it is true that Christendom is more progressive, in a sense that has very little to do with the rather provincial notion of an endless fuss of political improvement. Christendom does believe, for Christianity does believe, that man can eventually get somewhere, here or hereafter, or in various ways according to various doctrines. The world's desire can somehow be satisfied as desires are satisfied, whether by a new life or an old love or some form of positive possession and fulfilment. For the rest, we all know there is a rhythm and not a mere progress in things, that things rise and fall; only with us the rhythm is a fairly free and incalculable rhythm. For most of Asia the rhythm has hardened into a recurrence. It is no longer merely a rather topsy-turvy sort of world; it is a wheel. What has happened to all those highly intelligent and highly civilised peoples is that they have been caught up in a sort of cosmic rotation, of which the hollow hub is really nothing. In that sense the worst part of existence is that it may just as well go on like that forever. That is what we really mean when we say that Asia is old or unprogressive or looking backwards. That is why we see even her curved swords as arcs broken from that blinding wheel; why we see her serpentine ornament as returning everywhere, like a snake that is never slain. It has very little to do with the political varnish of progress; all Asiatics might have top-hats on their heads but if they had this spirit still in their hearts, they would only think the hats would vanish and come round again like the planets; not that running after a hat could lead them to heaven or even to home.

Now when the genius of Buddha arose to deal with the matter, this sort of cosmic sentiment was already common to almost everything in the east. There was indeed the jungle of an extraordinarily extravagant and almost asphyxiating mythology. Nevertheless it is possible to have more sympathy with this popular fruitfulness in folk-lore than with some of the higher pessimism that might have withered it. It must always be remembered, however, when all fair allowances are made, that a great deal of spontaneous eastern imagery really is idolatry; the local and literal worship of an idol. This is probably not true of the ancient Brahminical system, at least as seen by Brahmins. But that phrase alone will remind us of a reality of much greater moment. This great reality is the Caste System of ancient India. It may have had some of the practical advantages of the Guild System of Medieval Europe. But it contrasts not only with that Christian democracy, but with every extreme type of Christian aristocracy, in the fact that it does really conceive the social superiority as a spiritual superiority. This not only divides it fundamentally from the fraternity of Christendom, but leaves it standing like a mighty and terraced mountain of pride between the relatively egalitarian levels both of Islam and of China. But the fixity of this formation through thousands of years is another illustration of that spirit of repetition that has marked time from time immemorial. Now we may also presume the prevalence of another idea which we associate with the Buddhists as interpreted by the Theosophists. As a fact, some of the strictest Buddhists repudiate the idea and still more scornfully repudiate the Theosophists. But whether the idea is in Buddhism, or only in the birthplace of Buddhism, or only in a tradition or a travesty of Buddhism, it is an idea entirely proper to this principle of recurrence. I mean of course the idea of Reincarnation.

But Reincarnation is not really a mystical idea. It is not really a transcendental idea, or in that sense a religious idea. Mysticism conceives something transcending experience; religion seeks glimpses of a better good or a worse evil than experience can give. Reincarnation need only extend experiences in the sense of repeating them. It is no more transcendental for a man to remember what he did in Babylon before he was born than to remember what he did in Brixton before he had a knock on the head. His successive lives need not be any more than human lives, under whatever limitations burden human life. It has nothing to do with seeing God or even conjuring up the devil. In other words, reincarnation as such does not necessarily escape from the wheel of destiny, in some sense it is the wheel of destiny And whether it was something that Buddha founded, or something that Buddha found, or something that Buddha entirely renounced when he found, it is certainly something having the general character of that Asiatic atmosphere in which he had to play his part. And the part he played was that of an intellectual philosopher, with a particular theory about the right intellectual attitude towards it.

I can understand that Buddhists might resent the view that Buddhism is merely a philosophy, if we understand by a philosophy merely an intellectual game such as Greek sophists played, tossing up worlds and catching them like balls. Perhaps a more exact statement would be that Buddha was a man who made a metaphysical discipline; which might even be called a psychological discipline. He proposed a way of escaping from all this recurrent sorrow; and that was simply by getting rid of the delusion that is called desire. It was emphatically not that we should get what we want better by restraining our impatience for part of it, or that we should get it in a better way or in a better world. It was emphatically that we should leave off wanting it. If once a man realised that there is really no reality, that everything, including his soul, is in dissolution at every instant, he would anticipate disappointment and be intangible to change, existing (in so far as he could be said to exist) in a sort of ecstasy of indifference. The Buddhists call this beatitude and we will not stop our story to argue the point; certainly to us it is indistinguishable from despair. I do not see, for instance, why the disappointment of desire should not apply as much to the most benevolent desires as to the most selfish ones. Indeed the Lord of Compassion seems to pity people for living rather than for dying. For the rest, an intelligent Buddhist wrote 'the explanation of popular Chinese and Japanese Buddhism is that it is not Buddhism.' That has doubtless ceased to be a mere philosophy, but only by becoming a mere mythology. One thing is certain; it has never become anything remotely resembling what we call a Church.

It will appear only a jest to say that all religious history has really been a pattern of noughts and crosses. But I do not by noughts mean nothings, but only things that are negative compared with the positive shape or pattern of the other. And though the symbol is of course only a coincidence, it is a coincidence that really does coincide. The mind of Asia can really be represented by a round 0, if not in the sense of a cypher at least of a circle. The great Asiatic symbol of a serpent with its tail in its mouth is really a very perfect image of a certain idea of unity and recurrence that does indeed belong to the Eastern philosophies and religions. It really is a curve that in one sense includes everything, and in another sense comes to nothing. In that sense it does confess, or rather boast, that all argument is an argument in a circle. And though the figure is but a symbol, we can see how sound is the symbolic sense that produces it, the parallel symbol of the Wheel of Buddha generally called the Swastika The cross is a thing at right angles pointing boldly in opposite directions; but the Swastika is the same thing in the very act of returning to the recurrent curve. That crooked cross is in fact a cross turning into a wheel. Before we dismiss even these symbols as if they were arbitrary symbols, we must remember how intense was the imaginative instinct that produced them or selected them both in the east and the west. The cross has become something more than a historical memory; it does convey, almost as by a mathematical diagram, the truth about the real point at issue; the idea of a conflict stretching outwards into eternity. It is true, and even tautological, to say that the cross is the crux of the whole matter.

In other words the cross, in fact as well as figure, does really stand for the idea of breaking out of the circle that is everything and nothing. It does escape from the circular argument by which everything begins and ends in the mind. Since we are still dealing in symbols, it might be put in a parable in the form of that story about St. Francis, which says that the birds departing with his benediction could wing their way into the infinites of the four winds of heaven, their tracks making a vast cross upon the sky; for compared with the freedom of that flight of birds, the very shape of the Swastika is like a kitten chasing its tail. In a more popular allegory, we might say that when St. George thrust his spear into the monster's jaws, he broke in upon the solitude of the self-devouring serpent and gave it something to bite besides its own tail. But while many fancies might be used as figures of the truth, the truth itself is abstract and absolute; though it is not very easy to sum up except by such figures. Christianity does appeal to a solid truth outside itself; to something which is in that sense external as well as eternal. It does declare that things are really there; or in other words that things are really things--In this Christianity is at one with common sense; but all religious history shows that this common sense perishes except where there is Christianity to preserve it.

It cannot otherwise exist, or at least endure, because mere thought does not remain sane. In a sense it becomes too simple to be sane. The temptation of the philosophers is simplicity rather than subtlety. They are always attracted by insane simplifications, as men poised above abysses are fascinated by death and nothingness and the empty air. It needed another kind of philosopher to stand poised upon the pinnacle of the Temple and keep his balance without casting himself down. One of these obvious, these too obvious explanations is that everything is a dream and a delusion and there is nothing outside the ego. Another is that all things recur; another, which is said to be Buddhist and is certainly Oriental, is the idea that what is the matter with us is our creation, in the sense of our coloured differentiation and personality, and that nothing will be well till we are again melted into one unity. By this theory, in short, the Creation was the Fall. It is important historically because it was stored up in the dark heart of Asia and went forth at various times in various forms over the dim borders of Europe. Here we can place the mysterious figure of Manes or Manichaeus, the mystic of inversion, whom we should call a pessimist, parent of many sects and heresies; here, in a higher place, the figure of Zoroaster. He has been popularly identified with another of these too simple explanations; the equality of evil and good, balanced and battling in every atom. He also is of the school of sages that may be called mystics; and from the same mysterious Persian garden came upon ponderous wings Mithras, the unknown god, to trouble the last twilight of Rome.

That circle or disc of the sun set up in the morning of the world by the remote Egyptian has been a mirror and a model for all the philosophers. They have made many things out of it, and sometimes gone mad about it, especially when as in these eastern sages the circle became a wheel going round and round in their heads. But the point about them is that they all think that existence can be represented by a diagram instead of a drawing; and the rude drawings of the childish myth-makers are a sort of crude and spirited protest against that view. They cannot believe that religion is really not a pattern but a picture. Still less can they believe that it is a picture of something that really exists outside our minds. Sometimes the philosophy paints the disc all black and calls himself a pessimist; sometimes he paints it all white and calls himself an optimist; sometimes he divides it exactly into halves of black and white and calls himself a dualist, like those Persian mystics to whom I wish there were space to do justice. None of them could understand a thing that began to draw the proportions just as if they were real proportions, disposed in the living fashion which the mathematical draughtsman would call disproportionate. Like the first artist in the cave, it revealed to incredulous eyes the suggestion of a new purpose in what looked like a wildly crooked pattern; he seemed only to be distorting his diagram, when he began for the first time in all the ages to trace the lines of a form--and of a Face.

VII THE WAR OF THE GODS AND DEMONS

The materialist theory of history, that all politics and ethics are the expression of economics, is a very simple fallacy indeed. It consists simply of confusing the necessary conditions of life with the normal preoccupations of life, that are quite a different thing. It is like saying that because a man can only walk about on two legs, therefore he never walks about except to buy shoes and stockings. Man cannot live without the two props of food and drink, which support him like two legs; but to suggest that they have been the motives of all his movements in history is like saying that the goal of all his military marches or religious pilgrimages must have been the Golden Leg of Miss Kilmansegg or the ideal and perfect leg of Sir Willoughby Patterne. But it is such movements that make up the story of mankind and without them there would practically be no story at all. Cows may be purely economic, in the sense that we cannot see that they do much beyond grazing and seeking better grazing grounds; and that is why a history of cows in twelve volumes would not be very lively reading. Sheep and goats may be pure economists in their external action at least; but that is why the sheep has hardly been a hero of epic wars and empires thought worthy of detailed narration; and even the more active quadruped has not inspired a book for boys called Golden Deeds of Gallant Goats or any similar title. But so far from the movements that make up the story of man being economic, we may say that the story only begins where the motive of the cows and sheep leaves off. It will be hard to maintain that the Crusaders went from their homes into a howling wilderness because cows go from a wilderness to a more comfortable grazing-grounds. It will be hard to maintain that the Arctic explorers went north with the same material motive that made the swallows go south. And if you leave things like all the religious wars and all the merely adventurous explorations out of the human story, it will not only cease to be human at all but cease to be a story at all. The outline of history is made of these decisive curves and angles determined by the will of man. Economic history would not even be history.

But there is a deeper fallacy besides this obvious fact; that men need not live for food merely because they cannot live without food The truth is that the thing most present to the mind of man is not the economic machinery necessary to his existence; but rather that existence itself; the world which he sees when he wakes every morning and the nature of his general position in it. There is something that is nearer to him than livelihood, and that is life. For once that he remembers exactly what work produces his wages and exactly what wages produce his meals, he reflects ten times that it is a fine day or it is a queer world, or wonders whether life is worth living, or wonders whether marriage is a failure, or is pleased and puzzled with his own children, or remembers his own youth, or in any such fashion vaguely reviews the mysterious lot of man. This is true of the majority even of the wage-slaves of our morbid modern industrialism, which by its hideousness and in-humanity has really forced the economic issue to the front. It is immeasurably more true of the multitude of peasants or hunters or fishers who make up the real mass of mankind. Even those dry pedants who think that ethics depend on economics must admit that economics depend on existence. And any number of normal doubts and day-dreams are about existence; not about how we can live, but about why we do. And the proof of it is simple; as simple as suicide. Turn the universe upside down in the mind and you turn all the political economists upside down with it. Suppose that a man wishes to die, and the professor of political economy becomes rather a bore with his elaborate explanations of how he is to live. And all the departures and decisions that make our human past into a story have this character of diverting the direct course of pure economics. As the economist may be excused from calculating the future salary of a suicide, so he may be excused from providing an old age pension for a martyr. As he need not provide for the future of a martyr so he need not provide for the family of a monk. His plan is modified in lesser and varying degrees by a man being a soldier and dying for his own country, by a man being a peasant and specially loving his own land, by a man being more or less affected by any religion that forbids or allows him to do this or that. But all these come back not to an economic calculation about livelihood but to an elemental outlook upon life. They all come back to what a man fundamentally feels, when he looks forth from those strange windows which we call the eyes, upon that strange vision that we call the world.

No wise man will wish to bring more long words into the world. But it may be allowable to say that we need a new thing; which may be called psychological history. I mean the consideration of what things meant in the mind of a man, especially an ordinary man; as distinct from what is defined or deduced merely from official forms or political pronouncements. I have already touched on it in such a case as the totem or indeed any other popular myth. It is not enough to be told that a tom-cat was called a totem; especially when it was not called a totem. We want to know what it felt like. Was it like Whittington's cat or like a witch's cat? Was its real name Pashtl or Puss-in-Boots? That is the sort of thing we need touching the nature of political and social relations. We want to know the real sentiment that was the social bond of many common men, as sane and as selfish as we are. What did soldiers feel when they saw splendid in the sky that strange totem that we call the Golden Eagle of the Legions? What did vassals feel about those other totems the lions or the leopards upon the shield of their lord? So long as we neglect this subjective side of history, which may more simply be called the inside of history, there will always be a certain limitation on that science which can be better transcended by art. So long as the historian cannot do that, fiction will be truer than fact. There will be more reality in a novel; yes, even in a historical novel.

In nothing is this new history needed so much as in the psychology of war. Our history is stiff with official documents, public or private, which tell us nothing of the thing itself. At the worst we only have the official posters, which could not have been spontaneous precisely because they were official. At the best we have only the secret diplomacy, which could not have been popular precisely because it was secret. Upon one or other of these is based the historical judgement about the real reasons that sustained the struggle. Governments fight for colonies or commercial rights; governments fight about harbours or high tariffs; governments fight for a gold mine or a pearl fishery. It seems sufficient to answer that governments do not fight at all. Why do the fighters fight? What is the psychology that sustains the terrible and wonderful thing called a war? Nobody who knows anything of soldiers believes the silly notion of the dons, that millions of men can be ruled by force. If they were all to slack, it would be impossible to punish all the slackers And the least little touch of slacking would lose a whole campaign in half a day. What did men really feel about the policy? If it be said that they accepted the policy from the politician, what did they feel about the politician? If the vassals warred blindly for their prince what did those blind men see in their prince?

There is something we all know which can only be rendered, in an appropriate language, as realpolitik. As a matter of fact, it is an almost insanely unreal politik. It is always stubbornly and stupidly repeating that men fight for material ends, without reflecting for a moment that the material ends are hardly ever material to the men who fight. In any case no man will die for practical politics, just as no man will die for pay. Nero could not hire a hundred Christians to be eaten by lions at a shilling an hour; for men will not be martyred for money. But the vision called up by real politik, or realistic politics, is beyond example crazy and incredible. Does anybody in the world believe that d soldier says, 'My leg is nearly dropping off, but I shall go on till it drops; for after all I shall enjoy all the advantages of my government obtaining a warm-water port in the Gulf of Finland.' Can anybody suppose that a clerk turned conscript says, 'If I am gassed I shall probably die in torments, but it is a comfort to reflect that should I ever decide to become a pearl-diver in the South Seas, that career is now open to me and my countrymen.' Materialist history is the most madly incredible of all histories, or even of all romances. Whatever starts wars, the thing that sustains wars is something in the soul; that is something akin to religion. It is what men feel about life and about death. A man near to death is dealing directly with an absolute; it is nonsense to say he is concerned only with relative and remote complications that death in any case will end. If he is sustained by certain loyalties, they must be loyalties as simple as death. They are generally two ideas, which are only two sides of one idea. The first is the love of something said to be threatened, if it be only vaguely known as home; the second is dislike and defiance of some strange thing that threatens it. The first is far more philosophical than it sounds, though we need not discuss it here. A man does not want his national home destroyed or even changed, because he cannot even remember all the good things that go with it; just as he does not want his house burnt down, because he can hardly count all the things he would miss. Therefore he fights for what sounds like a hazy abstraction, but is really a house. But the negative side of it is quite as noble as well as quite as strong. Men fight hardest when they feel that the foe is at once an old enemy and an eternal stranger, that his atmosphere is alien and antagonistic, as the French feel about the Prussian or the Eastern Christians about the Turk. If we say it is a difference of religion, people will drift into dreary bickerings about sects and dogmas. We will pity them and say it is a difference about death and daylight; a difference that does really come like a dark shadow between our eyes and the day. Men can think of this difference even at the point of death; for it is a difference about the meaning of life.

Men are moved in these things by something far higher and holier than policy; by hatred. When men hung on in the darkest days of the Great War, suffering either in their bodies or in their souls for those they loved, they were long past caring about details of diplomatic objects as motives for their refusal to surrender. Of myself and those I knew best I can answer for the vision that made surrender impossible. It was the vision of the German Emperor's face as he rode into Paris. This is not the sentiment which some of my idealistic friends describe as Love. I am quite content to call it hatred; the hatred of hell and all its works, and to agree that as they do not believe in hell they need not believe in hatred. But in the face of this prevalent prejudice, this long introduction has been unfortunately necessary, to ensure an understanding of what is meant by a religious war. There is a religious war when two worlds meet; that is when two visions of the world meet; or in more modern language when two moral atmospheres meet. What is the one man's breath is the other man's poison; and it is vain to talk of giving a pestilence a place in the sun. And this is what we must understand, even at the expense of digression, if we would see what really happened in the Mediterranean; when right athwart the rising of the Republic on the Tiber, a thing overtopping and disdaining it, dark with all the riddles of Asia and trailing all the tribes and dependencies of imperialism, came Carthage riding on the sea.

The ancient religion of Italy was on the whole that mixture which we have considered under the head of mythology; save that where the Greeks had a natural turn for the mythology, the Latins seem to have had a real turn for religion. Both multiplied gods, yet they sometimes seem to have multiplied them for almost opposite reasons. It would seem sometimes as if the Greek polytheism branched and blossomed upwards like the boughs of a tree, while the Italian polytheism ramified downward like the roots. Perhaps it would be truer to say that the former branches lifted themselves lightly, bearing flowers; while the latter hung down, being heavy with fruit. I mean that the Latins seem to multiply gods to bring them nearer to men, while the Greek gods rose and radiated outwards into the morning sky. What strikes us in the Italian cults is their local and especially their domestic character. We gain the impression of divinities swarming about the house like flies; of deities clustering and clinging like bats about the pillars or building like birds under the eaves. We have a vision of a god of roofs and a god of gate-posts, of a god of doors and even a god of drains. It has been suggested that all mythology was a sort of fairy-tale; but this was a particular sort of fairy-tale which may truly be called a fireside tale, or a nursery-tale; because it was a tale of the interior of the home; like those which make chairs and tables talk like elves. The old household gods of the Italian peasants seem to have been great, clumsy, wooden images, more featureless than the figure-head which Quilp battered with the poker. This religion of the home was very homely. Of course there were other less human elements in the tangle of Italian mythology. There were Greek deities superimposed on the Roman; there were here and there uglier things underneath, experiments in the cruel kind of paganism, like the Arician rite of the priest slaying the slayer. But these things were always potential in paganism; they are certainly not the peculiar character of Latin paganism. The peculiarity of that may be roughly covered by saying that if mythology personified the forces of nature, this mythology personified nature as transformed by the forces of man. It was the god of the corn and not of the grass, of the cattle and not the wild things of the forest; in short the cult was literally a culture; as when we speak of it as agriculture.

With this there was a paradox which is still for many the puzzle or riddle of the Latins. With religion running through every domestic detail like a climbing plant, there went what seems to many the very opposite spirit; the spirit of revolt. Imperialists and reactionaries often involve Rome as the very model of order and obedience; but Rome was the very reverse. The real history of ancient Rome is much more like the history of modern Paris. It might be called in modern language a city built out of barricades. It is said that the gate of Janus was never closed because there was an eternal war without; it is almost as true that there was an eternal revolution within. From the first Plebeian riots to the last Servile Wars, the state that imposed peace on the world was never really at peace. The rulers were themselves rebels.

There is a real relation between this religion in private and this revolution in public life. Stories none the less heroic for being hackneyed remind us that the Republic was founded on a tyrannicide that avenged an insult to a wife; that the Tribunes of the people were re-established after another which avenged an insult to a daughter. The truth is that only men to whom the family is sacred will ever have a standard or a status by which to criticise the state. They alone can appeal to something more holy than the gods of the city; the gods of the hearth. That is why men are mystified in seeing that the same nations that are thought rigid in domesticity are also thought restless in politics, for instance the Irish and the French. It is worth while to dwell on this domestic point because it is an exact example of what is meant here by the inside of history, like the inside of houses. Merely political histories of Rome may be right enough in saying that this or that was a cynical or cruel act of the Roman politicians; but the spirit that lifted Rome from beneath was the spirit of all the Romans; and it is not a cant to call it the ideal of Cincinnatus passing from the senate to the plough. Men of that sort had strengthened their village on every side, had extended its victories already over Italians and even over Greeks, when they found themselves confronted with a war that changed the world. I have called it here the war of the gods and demons.

There was established on the opposite coast of the inland sea a city that bore the name of the New Town. It was already much older, more powerful, and more prosperous than the Italian town; but there still remained about it an atmosphere that made the name not inappropriate. It had been called new because it was a colony like New York or New Zealand. It was an outpost or settlement of the energy and expansion of the great commercial cities of Tyre and Sidon. There was a note of the new countries and colonies about it, a confident and commercial outlook. It was fond of saying things that rang with a certain metallic assurance; as that nobody could wash his hands in the sea without the leave of the New Town. For it depended almost entirely on the greatness of its ships, as did the two great ports and markets from which its people came. It brought from Tyre and Sidon a prodigious talent for trade and considerable experience of travel. It brought other things as well.

In a previous chapter I have hinted at something of the psychology that lies behind a certain type of religion. There was a tendency in those hungry for practical results, apart from poetical results, to call upon spirits of terror and compulsion; to move Acheron in despair of bending the Gods. There is always a sort of dim idea that these darker powers will really do things, with no nonsense about it. In the interior psychology of the Punic peoples this strange sort of pessimistic practicality had grown to great proportions. In the New Town, which the Romans called Carthage, as in the parent cities of Phoenicia, the god who got things done bore the name of Moloch, who was perhaps identical with the other deity whom we know as Baal, the Lord. The Romans did not at first quite know what to call him or what to make of him; they had to go back to the grossest myth of Greek or Roman origins and compare him to Saturn devouring his children. But the worshippers of Moloch were not gross or primitive. They were members of a mature and polished civilisation, abounding in refinements and luxuries; they were probably far more civilised than the Romans. And Moloch was not a myth; or at any rate his meal was not a myth. These highly civilised people really met together to invoke the blessing of heaven on their empire by throwing hundreds of their infants into a large furnace. We can only realise the combination by imagining a number of Manchester merchants with chimney-pot hats and mutton-chop whiskers, going to church every Sunday at eleven o'clock to see a baby roasted alive.

The first stages of the political or commercial quarrel can be followed in far too much detail, precisely because it is merely political or commercial. The Punic Wars looked at one time as if they would never end; and it is not easy to say when they ever began. The Greeks and the Sicilians had already been fighting vaguely on the European side against the African city. Carthage had defeated Greece and conquered Sicily. Carthage had also planted herself firmly in Spain; and between Spain and Sicily the Latin city was contained and would have been crushed; if the Romans had been of the sort to be easily crushed. Yet the interest of the story really consists in the fact that Rome was crushed. If there had not been certain moral elements as well as the material elements, the story would have ended where Carthage certainly thought it had ended. It is common enough to blame Rome for not making peace. But it was a true popular instinct that there could be no peace with that sort of people It is common enough to blame the Roman for his

Delenda est Carthago; Carthage must be destroyed. It is commoner to forget that, to all appearance, Rome itself was destroyed. The sacred savour that hung round Rome for ever, it is too often forgotten, clung to her partly because she had risen suddenly from the dead. Carthage was an aristocracy, as are most of such mercantile states. The pressure of the rich on the poor was impersonal as well as irresistible. For such aristocracies never permit personal government, which is perhaps why this one was jealous of personal talent. But genius can turn up anywhere, even in a governing class. As if to make the world's supreme test as terrible as possible, it was ordained that one of the great houses of Carthage should produce a man who came out of those gilded palaces with all the energy and originality of Napoleon coming from nowhere. At the worst crisis of the war Rome learned that Italy itself, by a military miracle, was invaded from the north. Hannibal, the Grace of Baal as his name ran in his own tongue, had dragged a ponderous chain of armaments over the starry solitudes of the Alps; and pointed southward to the city which he had been pledged by all his dreadful gods to destroy.

Hannibal marched down the road to Rome, and the Romans who rushed to war with him felt as if they were fighting with a magician. Two great armies sank to right and left of him into the swamps of the Trebia; more and more were sucked into the horrible whirlpool of Cannae; more and more went forth only to fall in ruin at his touch. The supreme sign of all disasters, which is treason, turned tribe after tribe against the falling cause of Rome, and still the unconquerable enemy rolled nearer and nearer to the city; and following their great leader the swelling cosmopolitan army of Carthage passed like a pageant of the whole world; the elephants shaking the earth like marching mountains and the gigantic Gauls with their barbaric panoply and the dark Spaniards girt in gold and the brown Numidians on their unbridled desert horses wheeling and darting like hawks, and whole mobs of deserters and mercenaries and miscellaneous peoples; and the grace of Baal went before them.

The Roman augurs and scribes who said in that hour that it brought forth unearthly prodigies, that a child was born with the head of an elephant or that stars fell down like hailstones, had a far more philosophical grasp of what had really happened than the modern historian who can see nothing in it but a success of strategy concluding a rivalry in commerce. Something far different was felt at the time and on the spot, as it is always felt by those who experience a foreign atmosphere entering their own like a fog or a foul savour. It was no mere military defeat, it was certainly no mere mercantile rivalry, that filled the Roman imagination with such hideous omens of nature herself becoming unnatural. It was Moloch upon the mountain of the Latins, looking with his appalling face across the plain; it was Baal who trampled the vineyards with his feet of stone; it was the voice of Tanit the invisible, behind her trailing veils, whispering of the love that is more horrible than hate. The burning of the Italian cornfields, the ruin of the Italian vines, were some thing more than actual; they were allegorical. They were the destruction of domestic and fruitful things, the withering of what was human before that inhumanity that is far beyond the human thing called cruelty. The household gods bowed low in darkness under their lowly roofs; and above them went the demons upon a wind from beyond all walls, blowing the trumpet of the Tramontane. The door of the Alps was broken down; and in no vulgar but a very solemn sense, it was Hell let loose. The war of the gods and demons seemed already to have ended; and the gods were dead. The eagles were lost, the legions were broken; and in Rome nothing remained but honour and the cold courage of despair.

In the whole world one thing still threatened Carthage, and that was Carthage. There still remained the inner working of an element strong in all successful commercial states, and the presence of a spirit that we know. There was still the solid sense and shrewdness of the men who manage big enterprises; there was still the advice of the best financial experts; there was still business government; there was still the broad and sane outlook of practical men of affairs, and in these things could the Romans hope. As the war trailed on to what seemed its tragic end, there grew gradually a faint and strange possibility that even now they might not hope in vain. The plain business men of Carthage, thinking as such men do in terms of living and dying races, saw clearly that Rome was not only dying but dead The war was over; it was obviously hopeless for the Italian city to resist any longer, and inconceivable that anybody should resist when it was hopeless. Under these circumstances, another set of broad, sound business principles remained to be considered. Wars were waged with money, and consequently cost money; perhaps they felt in their hearts, as do so many of their kind, that after all war must be a little wicked because it costs money. The time had now come for peace; and still more for economy. The messages sent by Hannibal from time to time asking for reinforcements were a ridiculous anachronism; there were much more important things to attend to now. It might be true that some consul or other had made a last dash to the Metaurus, had killed Hannibal's brother and flung his head, with Latin fury, into Hannibal's camp; and mad actions of that sort showed how utterly hopeless the Latins felt about their cause. But even excitable Latins could not be so mad as to cling to a lost cause for ever. So argued the best financial experts; and tossed aside more and more letters, full of rather queer alarmist reports. So argued and acted the great Carthaginian Empire. That meaningless prejudice, the curse of commercial states, that stupidity is in some way practical and that genius is in some way futile, led them to starve and abandon that great artist in the school of arms, whom the gods had given them in vain.

Why do men entertain this queer idea that what is sordid must always overthrow what is magnanimous; that there is some dim connection between brains and brutality, or that it does not matter if a man is dull so long as he is also mean? Why do they vaguely think of all chivalry as sentiment and all sentiment as weakness? They do it because they are, like all men, primarily inspired by religion. For them, as for all men, the first fact is their notion of the nature of things; their idea about what world they are living in. And it is their faith that the only ultimate thing is fear and therefore that the very heart of the world is evil. They believe that death is stronger than life, and therefore dead things must be stronger than living things; whether those dead things are gold and iron and machinery or rocks and rivers and forces of nature. It may sound fanciful to say that men we meet at tea-tables or talk to at garden-parties are secretly worshippers of Baal or Moloch. But this sort of commercial mind has its own cosmic vision and it is the vision of Carthage. It has in it the brutal blunder that was the ruin of Carthage. The Punic power fell because there is in this materialism a mad indifference to real thought. By disbelieving in the soul, it comes to disbelieving in the mind. Being too practical to be moral, it denies what every practical soldier calls the moral of an army. It fancies that money will fight when men will no longer fight. So it was with the Punic merchant princes. Their religion was a religion of despair, even when their practical fortunes were hopeful. How could they understand that the Romans could hope even when their fortunes were hopeless? Their religion was a religion of force and fear; how could they understand that men can still despise fear even when they submit to force? Their philosophy of the world had weariness in its very heart; above all they were weary of warfare; how should they understand those who still wage war even when they are weary of it? In a word, how should they understand the mind of Man, who had so long bowed down before mindless things, money and brute force and gods who had the hearts of beasts? They awoke suddenly to the news that the embers they had disdained too much even to tread out were again breaking everywhere into flames; that Hasdrubal was defeated, that Hannibal was outnumbered, that Scipio had carried the war into Spain; that he had carried it into Africa. Before the very gates of the golden city Hannibal fought his last fight for it and lost; and Carthage fell as nothing has fallen since Satan. The name of the New City remains only as a name. There is no stone of it left upon the sand. Another war was indeed waged before the final destruction: but the destruction was final. Only men digging in its deep foundation centuries after found a heap of hundreds of little skeletons, the holy relics of that religion. For Carthage fell because she was faithful to her own philosophy and had followed out to its logical conclusion her own vision of the universe. Moloch had eaten his children.

The gods had risen again, and the demons had been defeated after all. But they had been defeated by the defeated, and almost defeated by the dead. Nobody understands the romance of Rome, and why she rose afterwards to a representative leadership that seemed almost fated and fundamentally natural. Who does not keep in mind the agony of horror and humiliation through which she had continued to testify to the sanity that is the soul of Europe? She came to stand alone in the midst of an empire because she had once stood alone in the midst of a ruin and a waste. After that all men knew in their hearts that she had been representative of mankind, even when she was rejected of men. And there fell on her the shadow from a shining and as yet invisible light and the burden of things to be. It is not for us to guess in what manner or moment the mercy of God might in any case have rescued the world; but it is certain that the struggle which established Christendom would have been very different if there had been an empire of Carthage instead of an empire of Rome. We have to thank the patience of the Punic wars if, in after ages, divine things descended at least upon human things and not inhuman. Europe evolved into its own vices and its own impotence, as will be suggested on another page; but the worst into which it evolved was not like what it had escaped. Can any man in his senses compare the great wooden doll, whom the children expected to eat a little bit of the dinner, with the great idol who would have been expected to eat the children? That is the measure of how far the world went astray, compared with how far it might have gone astray. If the Romans were ruthless, it was in a true sense to an enemy, and certainly not merely a rival. They remembered not trade routes and regulations, but the faces of sneering men; and hated the hateful soul of Carthage. And we owe them something if we never needed to cut down the groves of Venus exactly as men cut down the groves of Baal. We owe it partly to their harshness that our thoughts of our human past are not wholly harsh. If the passage from heathenry to Christianity was a bridge as well as a breach, we owe it to those who kept that heathenry human. If, after all these ages, we are in some sense at peace with paganism, and can think more kindly of our fathers, it is well to remember the things that were and the things that might have been. For this reason alone we can take lightly the load of antiquity and need not shudder at a nymph on a fountain or a cupid on a valentine. Laughter and sadness link us with things long past away and remembered without dishonour; and we can see not altogether without tenderness the twilight sinking around the Sabine farm and hear the household gods rejoice when Catullus comes home to Sirmio. Deleta est Carthago.

VIII THE END OF THE WORLD

I was once sitting on a summer day in a meadow in Kent under the shadow of a little village church, with a rather curious companion with whom I had just been walking through the woods. He was one of a group of eccentrics I had come across in my wanderings who had a new religion called Higher Thought; in which I had been so far initiated as to realise a general atmosphere of loftiness or height, and was hoping at some later and more esoteric stage to discover the beginnings of thought. My companion was the most amusing of them, for however he may have stood towards thought, he was at least very much their superior in experience, having travelled beyond the tropics while they were meditating in the suburbs; though he had been charged with excess in telling travellers' tales. In spite of anything said against him, I preferred him to his companions and willingly went with him through the wood; where I could not but feel that his sunburnt face and fierce tufted eyebrows and pointed beard gave him something of the look of Pan. Then we sat down in the meadow and gazed idly at the tree-tops and the spire of the village church; while the warm afternoon began to mellow into early evening and the song of a speck of a bird was faint far up in the sky and no more than a whisper of breeze soothed rather than stirred the ancient orchards of the garden of England. Then my companion said to me: 'Do you know why the spire of that church goes up like that, I expressed a respectable agnosticism, and he answered in an off-hand way, 'Oh, the same as the obelisks; the Phallic Worship of antiquity.' Then I looked across at him suddenly as he lay there leering above his goatlike beard; and for the moment I thought he was not Pan but the Devil. No mortal words can express the immense, the insane incongruity and unnatural perversion of thought involved in saying such a thing at such a moment and in such a place. For one moment I was in the mood in which men burned witches; and then a sense of absurdity equally enormous seemed to open about me like a dawn. 'Why, of course,' I said after a moment's reflection, 'if it hadn't been for phallic worship, they would have built the spire pointing downwards and standing on its own apex.' I could have sat in that field and laughed for an hour. My friend did not seem offended, for indeed he was never thin-skinned about his scientific discoveries. I had only met him by chance and I never met him again, and I believe he is now dead; but though it has nothing to do with the argument, it may be worth while to mention the name of this adherent of Higher Thought and interpreter of primitive religious origins; or at any rate the name by which he was known. It was Louis de Rougemont.

That insane image of the Kentish church standing on the point of its spire, as in some old rustic, topsy-turvy tale, always comes back into my imagination when I hear these things said about pagan origins; and calls to my aid the laughter of the giants. Then I feel as genially and charitably to all other scientific investigators, higher critics, and authorities on ancient and modern religion, as I do to poor Louis de Rougemont. But the memory of that immense absurdity remains as a sort of measure and check by which to keep sane, not only on the subject of Christian churches, but also on the subject of heathen temples. Now a great many people have talked about heathen origins as the distinguished traveller talked about Christian origins. Indeed a great many modern heathens have been very hard on heathenism. A great many modern humanitarians have been very hard on the real religion of humanity. They have represented it as being everywhere and from the first rooted only in these repulsive arcana; and carrying the character of something utterly shameless and anarchical. Now I do not believe this for a moment. I should never dream of thinking about the whole worship of Apollo what De Rougemont could think about the worship of Christ. I would never admit that there was such an atmosphere in a Greek city as that madman was able to smell in a Kentish village. On the contrary, it is the whole point, even of this final chapter upon the final decay of paganism, to insist once more that the worst sort of paganism had already been defeated by the best sort. It was the best sort of paganism that conquered the gold of Carthage. It was the best sort of paganism that wore the laurels of Rome. It was the best thing the world had yet seen, all things considered and on any large scale, that ruled from the wall of the Grampians to the garden of the Euphrates. It was the best that conquered; it was the best that ruled; and it was the best that began to decay.

Unless this broad truth be grasped, the whole story is seen askew. Pessimism is not in being tired of evil but in being tired of good. Despair does not lie in being weary of suffering, but in being weary of joy. It is when for some reason or other the good things in a society no longer work that the society begins to decline; when its food does not feed, when its cures do not cure, when its blessings refuse to bless. We might almost say that in a society without such good things we should hardly have any test by which to register a decline; that is why some of the static commercial oligarchies like Carthage have rather an air in history of standing and staring like mummies, so dried up and swathed and embalmed that no man knows when they are new or old. But Carthage at any rate was dead, and the worst assault ever made by the demons on mortal society had been defeated. But how much would it matter that the worst was dead if the best was dying?

To begin with, it must be noted that the relation of Rome to Carthage was partially repeated and extended in her relation to nations more normal and more nearly akin to her than Carthage. I am not here concerned to controvert the merely political view that Roman statesmen acted unscrupulously towards Corinth or the Greek cities. But I am concerned to contradict the notion that there was nothing but a hypocritical excuse in the ordinary Roman dislike of Greek cities. I am not presenting these pagans as paladins of chivalry, with a sentiment about nationalism never known until Christian times. But I am presenting them as men with the feelings of men; and those feelings were not a pretence. The truth is that one of the weaknesses in nature-worship and mere mythology had already produced a perversion among the Greeks due to the worst sophistry; the sophistry of simplicity. Just as they became unnatural by worshipping nature, so they actually became unmanly by worshipping man. If Greece led her conqueror, she might have misled her conqueror; but these were things he did originally wish to conquer--ever in himself. It is true that in one sense there was less inhumanity even in Sodom and Gomorrah than in Tyre and Sidon. When we consider the war of the demons on the children, we cannot compare even Greek decadence to Punic devil-worship. But it is not true that the sincere revulsion from either need be merely pharisaical. It is not true to human nature or to common sense. Let any lad who has had the luck to grow up sane and simple in his day-dreams of love hear for the first time of the cult of Ganymede; he will not be merely shocked but sickened. And that first impression, as has been said here so often about first impressions, will be right. Our cynical indifference is an illusion; it is the greatest of all illusions; the illusion of familiarity. It is right to conceive the more or less rustic virtues of the ruck of the original Romans as reacting against the very rumour of it, with complete spontaneity and sincerity. It is right to regard them as reacting, if in a lesser degree, exactly as they did against the cruelty of Carthage. Because it was in a less degree they did not destroy Corinth as they destroyed Carthage. But if their attitude and action was rather destructive, in neither case need their indignation have been mere self-righteousness covering mere selfishness. And if anybody insists that nothing could have operated in either case but reasons of state and commercial conspiracies, we can only tell him that there is something which he does not understand; something which possibly he will never understand; something which, until he does understand, he will never understand the Latins. That something is called democracy. He has probably heard the word a good many times and even used it himself; but he has no notion of what it means. All through the revolutionary history of Rome there was an incessant drive towards democracy; the state and the statesman could do nothing without a considerable backing of democracy; the sort of democracy that never has anything to do with diplomacy. It is precisely because of the presence of Roman democracy that we hear so much about Roman oligarchy. For instance, recent historians have tried to explain the valour and victory of Rome in terms of that detestable and detested usury which was practised by some of the Patricians; as if Curius had conquered the men of the Macedonian phalanx by lending them money; or the consul Nero had negotiated the victory of Metaurus at five per cent. But we realise the usury of the Patricians because of the perpetual revolt of the Plebeians. The rule of the Punic merchant princes had the very soul of usury. But there was never a Punic mob that dared to call them usurers.

Burdened like all mortal things with all mortal sin and weakness, the rise of Rome had really been the rise of normal and especially of popular things; and in nothing more than in the thoroughly normal and profoundly popular hatred of perversion. Now among the Greeks a perversion had become a convention. It is true that it had become so much of a convention, especially a literary convention, that it was sometimes conventionally copied by Roman literary men. But this is one of those complications that always arise out of conventions. It must not obscure our sense of the difference of tone in the two societies as a whole. It is true that Virgil would once in a way take over a theme of Theocritus; but nobody can get the impression that Virgil was particularly fond of that theme. The themes of Virgil were specially and notably the normal themes and nowhere more than in morals; piety and patriotism and the honour of the countryside. And we may well pause upon the name of the poet as we pass into the autumn of antiquity; upon his name who was in so supreme a sense the very voice of autumn of its maturity and its melancholy; of its fruits of fulfilment and its prospect of decay. Nobody who reads even a few lines of Virgil can doubt that he understood what moral sanity means to mankind. Nobody can doubt his feelings when the demons were driven in flight before the household gods. But there are two particular points about him and his work which are particularly important to the main thesis here. The first is that the whole of his great patriotic epic is in a very peculiar sense founded upon the fall of Troy; that is upon an avowed pride in Troy although she had fallen. In tracing to Trojans the foundation of his beloved race and republic, he began what may be called the great Trojan tradition which runs through medieval and modern history. We have already seen the first hint of it in the pathos of Homer about Hector. But Virgil turned it not merely into a literature but into a legend. And it was a legend of the almost divine dignity that belongs to the defeated. This was one of the traditions that did truly prepare the world for the coming of Christianity and especially of Christian chivalry. This is what did help to sustain civilisation through the incessant defeats of the Dark Ages and the barbarian wars; out of which what we call chivalry was born. It is the moral attitude of the man with his back to the wall; and it was the wall of Troy. All through medieval and modern times this version of the virtues in the Homeric conflict can be traced in a hundred ways co-operating with all that was akin to it in Christian sentiment. Our own countrymen, and the men of other countries, loved to claim like Virgil that their own nation was descended from the heroic Trojans. All sorts of people thought it the most superb sort of heraldry to claim to be descended from Hector. Nobody seems to have wanted to be descended from Achilles. The very fact that the Trojan name has become a Christian name, and been scattered to the last limits of Christendom, to Ireland or the Gaelic Highlands, while the Greek name has remained relatively rare and pedantic, is a tribute to the same truth. Indeed it involves a curiosity of language almost in the nature of a joke. The name has been turned into a verb; and the very phrase about hectoring, in the sense of swaggering, suggests the myriads of soldiers who have taken the fallen Trojan for a model. As a matter of fact, nobody in antiquity was less given to hectoring than Hector. But even the bully pretending to be a conqueror took his title from the conquered. That is why the popularisation of the Trojan origin by Virgil has a vital relation to all those elements that have made men say that Virgil was almost a Christian. It is almost as if two great tools or toys of the same timber, the divine and the human, had been in the hands of Providence; and the only thing comparable to the Wooden Cross of Calvary was the Wooden Horse of Troy. So, in some wild allegory, pious in purpose if almost profane in form, the Holy Child might have fought the dragon with a wooden sword and a wooden horse.

The other element in Virgil which is essential to the argument is the particular nature of his relation to mythology; or what may here in a special sense be called folklore, the faiths and fancies of the populace. Everybody knows that his poetry at its most perfect is less concerned with the pomposity of Olympus than with the numina of natural and agricultural life. Everyone knows where Virgil looked for the causes of things. He speaks of finding them not so much in cosmic allegories of Uranus and Chronos; but rather in Pan and the sisterhood of the nymphs and Sylvanus the old man of the forest. He is perhaps most himself in some passages of the Eclogues, in which he has perpetuated for ever the great legend of Arcadia and the shepherds. Here again it is easy enough to miss the point with petty criticism about all the things that happen to separate his literary convention from ours. There is nothing more artificial than the cry of artificiality as directed against the old pastoral poetry. We have entirely missed all that our fathers meant by looking at the externals of what they wrote. People have been so much amused with the mere fact that the china shepherdess was made of china that they have not even asked why she was made at all. They have been so content to consider the Merry Peasant as a figure in an opera that they have not asked even how he came to go to the opera, or how he strayed on to the stage.

In short, one have only to ask why there is a china shepherdess and not a china shopkeeper. Why were not mantelpieces adorned with figures of city merchants in elegant attitudes; of ironmasters wrought in iron or gold speculators in gold? Why did the opera exhibit a Merry Peasant and not a Merry Politician? Why was there not a ballet of bankers, pirouetting upon pointed toes? Because the ancient instinct and humour of humanity have always told them, under whatever conventions, that the conventions of complex cities were less really healthy and happy than the customs of the countryside. So it is with the eternity of the Eclogues. A modern poet did indeed write things called Fleet Street Eclogues, in which poets took the place of the shepherds. But nobody has yet written anything called Wall Street Eclogues, in which millionaires should take the place of the poets. And the reason is that there is a real if only a recurrent yearning for that sort of simplicity; and there is never that sort of yearning for that sort of complexity. The key to the mystery of the Merry Peasant is that the peasant often is merry. Those who do not believe it are simply those who do not know anything about him, and therefore do not know which are his times for merriment. Those who do not believe in the shepherd's feast or song are merely ignorant of the shepherd's calendar. The real shepherd is indeed very different from the ideal shepherd, but that is no reason for forgetting the reality at the root of the ideal. It needs a truth to make a tradition. It needs a tradition to make a convention. Pastoral poetry is certainly often a convention, especially in a social decline. It was in a social decline that Watteau shepherds and shepherdesses lounged about the gardens of Versailles. It was also in a social decline that shepherds and shepherdesses continued to pipe and dance through the most faded imitations of Virgil. But that is no reason for dismissing the dying paganism without ever understanding its life. It is no reason for forgetting that the very word Pagan is the same as the word Peasant. We may say that this art is only artificiality; but it is not a love of the artificial. On the contrary, it is in its very nature only the failure of nature-worship, or the love of the natural.

For the shepherds were dying because their gods were dying. Paganism lived upon poetry; that poetry already considered under the name of mythology. But everywhere, and especially in Italy, it had been a mythology and a poetry rooted in the countryside; and that rustic religion had been largely responsible for the rustic happiness. Only as the whole society grew in age and experience, there began to appear that weakness in all mythology already noted in the chapter under that name. This religion was not quite a religion. In other words, this religion was not quite a reality. It was the young world's riot with images and ideas like a young man's riot with wine or love-making; it was not so much immoral as irresponsible; it had no foresight of the final test of time. Because it was creative to any extent it was credulous to any extent. It belonged to the artistic side of man, yet even considered artistically it had long become overloaded and entangled. The family trees sprung from the seed of Jupiter were a jungle rather than a forest; the claims of the gods and demi-gods seemed like things to be settled rather by a lawyer or a professional herald than by a poet. But it is needless to say that it was not only in the artistic sense that these things had grown more anarchic. There had appeared in more and more flagrant fashion that flower of evil that is really implicit in the very seed of nature-worship, however natural it may seem. I have said that I do not believe that natural worship necessarily begins with this particular passion; I am not of the De Rougemont school of scientific folk-lore. I do not believe that mythology must begin with eroticism. But I do believe that mythology must end in it. I am quite certain that mythology did end in it. Moreover, not only did the poetry grow more immoral, but the immorality grew more indefensible. Greek vices, oriental vices, hints of the old horrors of the Semitic demons began to fill the fancies of decaying Rome, swarming like flies on a dung heap. The psychology of it is really human enough to anyone who will try that experiment of seeing history from the inside There comes an hour in the afternoon when the child is tired of 'pretending'; when he is weary of being a robber or a Red Indian. It is then that he torments the cat. There comes a time in the routine of an ordered civilisation when the man is tired at playing at mythology and pretending that a tree is a maiden or that the moon made love to a man. The effect of this staleness is the same everywhere; it is seen in all drug-taking and dram-drinking and every form of the tendency to increase the dose. Men seek stranger sins or more startling obscenities as stimulants to their jaded sense. They seek after mad oriental religions for the same reason. They try to stab their nerves to life, if it were with the knives of the priests of Baal. They are walking in their sleep and try to wake themselves up with nightmares.

At that stage even of paganism therefore the peasant songs and dances sound fainter and fainter in the forest. For one thing the peasant civilisation was fading, or had already faded from the whole countryside. The Empire at the end was organised more and more on that servile system which generally goes with the boast of organisation, indeed it was almost as senile as the modern schemes for the organisation of industry. It is proverbial that what would once have been a peasantry became a mere populace of the town dependent for bread and circuses; which may again suggest to some a mob dependent upon doles and cinemas. In this as in many other respects the modern return to heathenism has been a return not even to the heathen youth but rather to the heathen old age. But the causes of it were spiritual in both cases; and especially the spirit of paganism had departed with its familiar spirits. The heat had gone out of it with its household gods, who went along with the gods of the garden and the field and the forest. The Old Man of the Forest was too old; he was already dying. It is said truly in a sense that Pan died because Christ was born. It is almost as true in another sense that men knew that Christ was born because Pan was already dead. A void was made by the vanishing of the whole mythology of mankind, which would have asphyxiated like a vacuum if it had not been filled with theology. But the point for the moment is that the mythology could not have lasted like a theology in any case. Theology is thought, whether we agree with it or not. Mythology was never thought, and nobody could really agree with it or disagree with it. It was a mere mood of glamour and when the mood went it could not be recovered. Men not only ceased to believe in the gods, but they realised that they had never believed in them. They had sung their praises; they had danced round their altars. They had played the flute; they had played the fool.

So came the twilight upon Arcady and the last notes of the pipe sound sadly from the beechen grove. In the great Virgilian poems there is already something of the sadness; but the loves and the household gods linger in lovely lines like that which Mr. Belloc took for a test of understanding; incipe parve puer risu cognoscere matrem. But with them as with us, the human family itself began to break down under servile organisation and the herding of the towns. The urban mob became enlightened; that is it lost the mental energy that could create myths. All round the circle of the Mediterranean cities the people mourned for the loss of gods and were consoled with gladiators. And meanwhile something similar was happening to that intellectual aristocracy of antiquity that had been walking about and talking at large ever since Socrates and Pythagoras. They began to betray to the world the fact that they were walking in a circle and saying the same thing over and over again. Philosophy began to be a joke; it also began to be a bore. That unnatural simplification of everything into one system or another, which we have noted as the fault of the philosopher, revealed at once its finality and its futility. Everything was virtue or everything was happiness or everything was fate or everything was good or everything was bad; anyhow, everything was everything and there was no more to be said; so they said it. Everywhere the sages had degenerated into sophists; that is, into hired rhetoricians or askers of riddles. It is one of the symptoms of this that the sage begins to turn not only into a sophist but into a magician. A touch of oriental occultism is very much appreciated in the best houses. As the philosopher is already a society entertainer, he may as well also be a conjurer.

Many moderns have insisted on the smallness of that Mediterranean world; and the wider horizons that might have awaited it with the discovery of the other continents. But this is an illusion, one of the many illusions of materialism. The limits that paganism had reached in Europe were the limits of human existence; at its best it had only reached the same limits anywhere else. The Roman stoics did not need any Chinamen to teach them stoicism. The Pythagoreans did not need any Hindus to teach them about recurrence or the simple life or the beauty of being a vegetarian. In so far as they could get these things from the East, they had already got rather too much of them from the East. The Syncretists were as convinced as Theosophists that all religions are really the same. And how else could they have extended philosophy merely by extending geography? It can hardly be proposed that they should learn a purer religion from the Aztecs or sit at the feet of the Incas of Peru. All the rest of the world was a welter of barbarism. It is essential to recognise that the Roman Empire was recognised as the highest achievement of the human race; and also as the broadest. A dreadful secret seemed to be written as in obscure hieroglyphics across those mighty works of marble and stone, those colossal amphitheatres and aqueducts. Man could do no more.

For it was not the message blazed on the Babylonian wall, that one king was found wanting or his one kingdom given to a stranger. It was no such good news as the news of invasion and conquest. There was nothing left that could conquer Rome; but there was also nothing left that could improve it. It was the strongest thing that was growing weak. It was the best thing that was going to the bad. It is necessary to insist again and again that many civilisations had met in one civilisation of the Mediterranean sea; that it was already universal with a stale and sterile universality. The peoples had pooled their resources and still there was not enough. The empires had gone into partnership and they were still bankrupt. No philosopher who was really philosophical could think anything except that, in that central sea, the wave of the world had risen to its highest, seeming to touch the stars. But the wave was already stooping; for it was only the wave of the world.

That mythology and that philosophy into which paganism has already been analysed had thus both of them been drained most literally to the dregs. If with the multiplication of magic the third department, which we have called the demons, was even increasingly active, it was never anything but destructive. There remains only the fourth element or rather the first; that which had been in a sense forgotten because it was the first. I mean the primary and overpowering yet impalpable impression that the universe after all has one origin and one aim; and because it has an aim must have an author. What became of this great truth in the background of men's minds, at this time, it is perhaps more difficult to determine. Some of the Stoics undoubtedly saw it more and more clearly as the clouds of mythology cleared and thinned away; and great men among them did much even to the last to lay the foundations of a concept of the moral unity of the world. The Jews still held their secret certainty of it jealously behind high fences of exclusiveness; yet it is intensely characteristic of the society and the situation that some fashionable figures, especially fashionable ladies, actually embraced Judaism. But in the case of many others I fancy there entered at this point a new negation. Atheism became really possible in that abnormal time; for atheism is abnormality. It is not merely the denial of a dogma. It is the reversal of a subconscious assumption in the soul; the sense that there is a meaning and a direction in the world it sees. Lucretius, the first evolutionist who endeavoured to substitute Evolution for God, had already dangled before men's eyes his dance of glittering atoms, by which he conceived cosmos as created by chaos. But it was not his strong poetry or his sad philosophy, as I fancy, that made it possible for men to entertain such a vision. It was something in the sense of impotence and despair with which men shook their fists vainly at the stars, as they saw all the best work of humanity sinking slowly and helplessly into a swamp. They could easily believe that even creation itself was not a creation but a perpetual fall, when they saw that the weightiest and worthiest of all human creations was falling by its own weight. They could fancy that all the stars were falling stars; and that the very pillars of their own solemn porticos were bowed under a sort of gradual deluge. To men in that mood there was a reason for atheism that is in some sense reasonable. Mythology might fade and philosophy might stiffen; but if behind these things there was a reality, surely that reality might have sustained things as they sank. There was no God; if there had been a God, surely this was the very moment when He would have moved and saved the world.

The life of the great civilisation went on with dreary industry and even with dreary festivity. It was the end of the world, and the worst of it was that it need never end. A convenient compromise had been made between all the multitudinous myths and religions of the Empire; that each group should worship freely and merely live a sort of official flourish of thanks to the tolerant Emperor, by tossing a little incense to him under his official title of Divus. Naturally there was no difficulty about that; or rather it was a long time before the world realised that there ever had been even a trivial difficulty anywhere. The members of some Eastern sect or secret society or other seemed to have made a scene somewhere; nobody could imagine why. The incident occurred once or twice again and began to arouse irritation out of proportion to its insignificance. It was not exactly what these provincials said; though of course it sounded queer enough. They seemed to be saying that God was dead and that they themselves had seen him die. This might be one of the many manias produced by the despair of the age; only they did not seem particularly despairing. They seem quite unnaturally joyful about it, and gave the reason that the death of God had allowed them to eat him and drink his blood. According to other accounts God was not exactly dead after all; there trailed through the bewildered imagination some sort of fantastic procession of the funeral of God, at which the sun turned black, but which ended with the dead omnipotence breaking out of the tomb and rising again like the sun. But it was not the strange story to which anybody paid any particular attention; people in that world had seen queer religions enough to fill a madhouse. It was something in the tone of the madmen and their type of formation. They were a scratch company of barbarians and slaves and poor and unimportant people; but their formation was military; they moved together and were very absolute about who and what was really a part of their little system; and about what they said. However mildly, there was a ring like iron. Men used to many mythologies and moralities could make no analysis of the mystery, except the curious conjecture that they meant what they said. All attempts to make them see reason in the perfectly simple matter of the Emperor's statue seemed to be spoken to deaf men. It was as if a new meteoric metal had fallen on the earth; it was a difference of substance to the touch. Those who touched their foundation fancied they had struck a rock.

With a strange rapidity, like the changes of a dream, the proportions of things seemed to change in their presence. Before most men knew what had happened, these few men were palpably present. They were important enough to be ignored. People became suddenly silent about them and walked stiffly past them. We see a new scene, in which the world has drawn its skirts away from these men and women and they stand in the centre of a great space like lepers. The scene changes again and the great space where they stand is overhung on every side with a cloud of witnesses, interminable terraces full of faces looking down towards them intently; for strange things are happening to them. New tortures have been invented for the madmen who have brought good news. That sad and weary society seems almost to find a new energy in establishing its first religious persecution. Nobody yet knows very clearly why that level world has thus lost its balance about the people in its midst; but they stand unnaturally still while the arena and the world seem to revolve round them. And there shone on them in that dark hour a light that has never been darkened; a white fire clinging to that group like an unearthly phosphorescence, blazing its track through the twilights of history and confounding every effort to confound it with the mists of mythology and theory; that shaft of light or lightning by which the world itself has struck and isolated and crowned it; by which its own enemies have made it more illustrious and its own critics have made it more inexplicable; the halo of hatred around the Church of God.

PART II ON THE MAN CALLED CHRIST

I THE GOD IN THE CAVE

This sketch of the human story began in a cave; the cave which popular science associates with the cave-man and in which practical discovery has really found archaic drawings of animals. The second half of human history, which was like a new creation of the world, also begins in a cave. There is even a shadow of such a fancy in the fact that animals were again present; for it was a cave used as a stable by the mountaineers of the uplands about Bethlehem; who still drive their cattle into such holes and caverns at night. It was here that a homeless couple had crept underground with the cattle when the doors of the crowded caravanserai had been shut in their faces; and it was here beneath the very feet of the passers-by, in a cellar under the very floor of the world, that Jesus Christ was born. But in that second creation there was indeed something symbolical in the roots of the primeval rock or the horns of the prehistoric herd. God also was a Cave-Man, and had also traced strange shapes of creatures, curiously coloured, upon the wall of the world; but the pictures that he made had come to life.

A mass of legend and literature, which increases and will never end, has repeated and rung the changes on that single paradox; that the hands that had made the sun and stars were too small to reach the huge heads of the cattle. Upon this paradox, we might almost say upon this jest, all the literature of our faith is founded. It is at least like a jest in this, that it is something which the scientific critic cannot see. He laboriously explains the difficulty which we have always defiantly and almost derisively exaggerated; and mildly condemns as improbable something that we have almost madly exalted as incredible; as something that would be much too good to be true, except that it is true. When that contrast between the cosmic creation and the little local infancy has been repeated, reiterated, underlined, emphasised, exulted in, sung, shouted, roared, not to say howled, in a hundred thousand hymns, carols, rhymes, rituals, pictures, poems, and popular sermons, it may be suggested that we hardly need a higher critic to draw our attention to something a little odd about it; especially one of the sort that seems to take a long time to see a joke, even his own joke. But about this contrast and combination of ideas one thing may be said here, because it is relevant to the whole thesis of this book. The sort of modern critic of whom I speak is generally much impressed with the importance of education in life and the importance of psychology in education. That sort of man is never tired of telling us that first impressions fix character by the law of causation; and he will become quite nervous if a child's visual sense is poisoned by the wrong colours on a golliwog or his nervous system prematurely shaken by a cacophonous rattle. Yet he will think us very narrow-minded, if we say that this is exactly why there really is a difference between being brought up as a Christian and being brought up as a Jew or a Moslem or an atheist. The difference is that every Catholic child has learned from pictures, and even every Protestant child from stories, this incredible combination of contrasted ideas as one of the very first impressions on his mind. It is not merely a theological difference. It is a psychological difference which can outlast any theologies. It really is, as that sort of scientist loves to say about anything, incurable. Any agnostic or atheist whose childhood has known a real Christmas has ever afterwards, whether he likes it or not, an association in his mind between two ideas that most of mankind must regard as remote from each other; the idea of a baby and the idea of unknown strength that sustains the stars. His instincts and imagination can still connect them, when his reason can no longer see the need of the connection; for him there will always be some savour of religion about the mere picture of a mother and a baby; some hint of mercy and softening about the mere mention of the dreadful name of God. But the two ideas are not naturally or necessarily combined. They would not be necessarily combined for an ancient Greek or a Chinaman, even for Aristotle or Confucius. It is no more inevitable to connect God with an infant than to connect gravitation with a kitten. It has been created in our minds by Christmas because we are Christians, because we are psychological Christians even when we are not theological ones. In other words, this combination of ideas has emphatically, in the much disputed phrase, altered human nature. There is really a difference between the man who knows it and the man who does not. It may not be a difference of moral worth, for the Moslem or the Jew might be worthier according to his lights; but it is a plain fact about the crossing of two particular lights, the conjunction of two stars in our particular horoscope. Omnipotence and impotence, or divinity and infancy, do definitely make a sort of epigram which a million repetitions cannot turn into a platitude. It is not unreasonable to call it unique. Bethlehem is emphatically a place where extremes meet.

Here begins, it is needless to say, another mighty influence for the humanisation of Christendom. If the world wanted what is called a non-controversial aspect of Christianity, it would probably select Christmas. Yet it is obviously bound up with what is supposed to be a controversial aspect (I could never at any stage of my opinions imagine why); the respect paid to the Blessed Virgin. When I was a boy a more Puritan generation objected to a statue upon my parish church representing the Virgin and Child. After much controversy, they compromised by taking away the Child. One would think that this was even more corrupted with Mariolatry, unless the mother was counted less dangerous when deprived of a sort of weapon. But the practical difficulty is also a parable. You cannot chip away the statue of a mother from all round that of a new-born child. You can not suspend the new-born child in mid-air; indeed you cannot really have a statue of a new-born child at all. Similarly, you cannot suspend the idea of a new-born child in the void or think of him without thinking of his mother. You cannot visit the child without visiting the mother; you cannot in common human life approach the child except through the mother. If we are to think of Christ in this aspect at all, the other idea follows as it is followed in history. We must either leave Christ out of Christmas, or Christmas out of Christ, or we must admit, if only as we admit it in an old picture, that those holy heads are too near together for the haloes not to mingle and cross.

It might be suggested, in a somewhat violent image, that nothing had happened in that fold or crack in the great grey hills except that the whole universe had been turned inside out. I mean that all the eyes of wonder and worship which had been turned outwards to the largest thing were now turned inward to the smallest. The very image will suggest all that multitudinous marvel of converging eyes that makes so much of the coloured Catholic imagery like a peacock's tail. But it is true in a sense that God who had been only a circumference was seen as a centre; and a centre is infinitely small. It is true that the spiritual spiral henceforward works inwards instead of outwards, and in that sense is centripetal and not centrifugal. The faith becomes, in more ways than one, a religion of little things. But its traditions in art and literature and popular fable have quite sufficiently attested, as has been said, this particular paradox of the divine being in the cradle. Perhaps they have not so clearly emphasised the significance of the divine being in the cave. Curiously enough, indeed, tradition has not very clearly emphasised the cave. It is a familiar fact that the Bethlehem scene has been represented in every possible setting of time and country, of landscape and architecture; and it is a wholly happy and admirable fact that men have conceived it as quite different according to their different individual traditions and tastes. But while all have realised that it was a stable, not so many have realised that it was a cave. Some critics have even been so silly as to suppose that there was some contradiction between the stable and the cave; in which case they cannot know much about caves or stables in Palestine. As they see differences that are not there, it is needless to add that they do not see differences that are there. When a well-known critic says, for instance, that Christ being born in a rocky cavern is like Mithras having sprung alive out of a rock, it sounds like a parody upon comparative religion. There is such a thing as the point of a story, even if it is a story in the sense of a lie. And the notion of a hero appearing, like Pallas from the brain of Zeus, mature and without a mother, is obviously the very opposite of the idea of a god being born like an ordinary baby and entirely dependent on a mother. Whichever ideal we might prefer, we should surely see that they are contrary ideals. It is as stupid to connect them because they both contain a substance called stone as to identify the punishment of the Deluge with the baptism in the Jordan because they both contain a substance called water. Whether as a myth or a mystery, Christ was obviously conceived as born in a hole in the rocks primarily because it marked the position of one outcast and homeless. Nevertheless it is true, as I have said, that the cave has not been so commonly or so clearly used as a symbol as the other realities that surrounded the first Christmas.

And the reason for this also refers to the very nature of that new world. It was in a sense the difficulty of a new dimension. Christ was not only born on the level of the world, but even lower than the world. The first act of the divine drama was enacted, not only on no stage set up above the sight-seer, but on a dark and curtained stage sunken out of sight; and that is an idea very difficult to express in most modes of artistic expression. It is the idea of simultaneous happenings on different levels of life. Something like it might have been attempted in the more archaic and decorative medieval art. But the more the artists learned of realism and perspective, the less they could depict at once the angels in the heavens and the shepherds on the hills, and the glory in the darkness that was under the hills. Perhaps it could have been best conveyed by the characteristic expedient of some of the medieval guilds, when they wheeled about the streets a theatre with three stages one above the other, with heaven above the earth and hell under the earth. But in the riddle of Bethlehem it was heaven that was under the earth.

There is in that alone the touch of a revolution, as of the world turned upside down. It would be vain to attempt to say anything adequate, or anything new, about the change which this conception of a deity born like an outcast or even an outlaw had upon the whole conception of law and its duties to the poor and outcast. It is profoundly true to say that after that moment there could be no slaves. There could be and were people bearing that legal title, until the Church was strong enough to weed them out, but there could be no more of the pagan repose in the mere advantage to the state of keeping it a servile state. Individuals became important, in a sense in which no instruments can be important. A man could not be a means to an end, at any rate to any other man's end. All this popular and fraternal element in the story has been rightly attached by tradition to the episode of the Shepherds; the hinds who found themselves talking face to face with the princes of heaven. But there is another aspect of the popular element as represented by the shepherds which has not perhaps been so fully developed; and which is more directly relevant here.

Men of the people, like the shepherds, men of the popular tradition, had everywhere been the makers of the mythologies. It was they who had felt most directly, with least check or chill from philosophy or the corrupt cults of civilisation, the need we have already considered; the images that were adventures of the imagination; the mythology that was a sort of search; the tempting and tantalising hints of something half-human in nature; the dumb significance of seasons and special places. They had best understood that the soul of a landscape is a story and the soul of a story is a personality. But rationalism had already begun to rot away these really irrational though imaginative treasures of the peasant; even as systematic slavery had eaten the peasant out of house and home. Upon all such peasantries everywhere there was descending a dusk and twilight of disappointment, in the hour when these few men discovered what they sought. Everywhere else Arcadia was fading from the forest. Pan was dead and the shepherds were scattered like sheep. And though no man knew it, the hour was near which was to end and to fulfil all things; and though no man heard it, there was one far-off cry in an unknown tongue upon the heaving wilderness of the mountains. The shepherds had found their Shepherd.

And the thing they found was of a kind with the things they sought. The populace had been wrong in many things; but they had not been wrong in believing that holy things could have a habitation and that divinity need not disdain the limits of time and space. And the barbarian who conceived the crudest fancy about the sun being stolen and hidden in a box, or the wildest myth about the god being rescued and his enemy deceived with a stone, was nearer to the secret of the cave and knew more about the crisis of the world, than all those in the circle of cities round the Mediterranean who had become content with cold abstractions or cosmopolitan generalisations; than all those who were spinning thinner and thinner threads of thought out of the transcendentalism of Plato or the orientalism of Pythagoras. The place that the shepherds found was not an academy or an abstract republic, it was not a place of myths allegorised or dissected or explained or explained away. It was a place of dreams come true. Since that hour no mythologies have been made in the world. Mythology is a search.

We all know that the popular presentation of this popular story, in so many miracle plays and carols, has given to the shepherds the costumes, the language, and the landscape of the separate English and European countrysides. We all know that one shepherd will talk in a Somerset dialect or another talk of driving his sheep from Conway towards Clyde. Most of us know by this time how true is that error, how wise, how artistic, how intensely Christian and Catholic is that anachronism. But some who have seen it in these scenes of medieval rusticity have perhaps not seen it in another sort of poetry, which it is sometimes the fashion to call artificial rather than artistic. I fear that many modern critics will see only a faded classicism in the fact that men like Crashaw and Herrick conceived the shepherds of Bethlehem under the form of the shepherds of Virgil. Yet they were profoundly right; and in turning their Bethlehem play into a Latin Eclogue they took up one of the most important links in human history. Virgil, as we have already seen, does stand for all that saner heathenism that had over-thrown the insane heathenism of human sacrifice; but the very fact that even the Virgilian virtues and the sane heathenism were in incurable decay is the whole problem to which the revelation to the shepherds is the solution. If the world had ever had the chance to grow weary of being demoniac, it might have been healed merely by becoming sane. But if it had grown weary even of being sane, what was to happen, except what did happen? Nor is it false to conceive the Arcadian shepherd of the Eclogues as rejoicing in what did happen. One of the Eclogues has even been claimed as a prophecy of what did happen. But it is quite as much in the tone and incidental diction of the great poet that we feel the potential sympathy with the great event; and even in their own human phrases the voices of the Virgilian shepherds might more than once have broken upon more than the tenderness of Italy `Incipe, parve puer, risu cognoscere matrem' They might have found in that strange place all that was best in the last traditions of the Latins; and something better than a wooden idol standing up for ever for the pillar of the human family; a household god. But they and all the other mythologists would be justified in rejoicings that the event had fulfilled not merely the mysticism but the materialism of mythology. Mythology had many sins; but it had not been wrong in being as carnal as the Incarnation. But something of the ancient voice that was supposed to have rung through the graves, it could cry again, 'We have seen, he hath seen us, a visible god.' So the ancient shepherds might have danced, and their feet have been beautiful upon the mountains, rejoicing over the philosophers. But the philosophers had also heard.

It is still a strange story, though an old one, how they came out of orient lands, crowned with the majesty of kings and clothed with something of the mystery of magicians. That truth that is tradition his wisely remembered them almost as unknown quantities, as mysterious as their mysterious and melodious names; Melchior. Caspar, Balthazar. But there came with them all that world of wisdom that had watched the stars in Chaldea and the sun in Persia; and we shall not be wrong if we see in them the same curiosity that moves all the sages. They would stand for the same human ideal if their names had really been Confucius or Pythagoras or Plato. They were those who sought not tales but the truth of things, and since their thirst for truth was itself a thirst for God, they also have had their reward. But even in order to understand that reward, we must understand that for philosophy as much as mythology, that reward was the completion of the incomplete.

Such learned men would doubtless have come, as these learned men did come, to find themselves confirmed in much that was true in their own traditions and right in their own reasoning. Confucius would have found a new foundation for the family in the very reversal of the Holy Family; Buddha would have looked upon a new renunciation, of stars rather than jewels and divinity than royalty. These learned men would still have the right to say, or rather a new right to say, that there was truth in their old teaching. But after all these learned men would have come to learn. They would have come to complete their conceptions with something they had not yet conceived; even to balance their imperfect universe with something they might once have contradicted. Buddha would have come from his impersonal paradise to worship a person. Confucius would have come from his temples of ancestor-worship to worship a child.

We must grasp from the first this character in the new cosmos; that it was larger than the old cosmos. In that sense Christendom is larger than creation; as creation had been before Christ. It included things that had not been there; it also included the things that had been there. The point happens to be well illustrated in this example of Chinese piety, but it would be true of other pagan virtues or pagan beliefs. Nobody can doubt that a reasonable respect for parents is part of a gospel in which God himself was subject in childhood to earthly parents. But the other sense in which the parents were subject to him does introduce an idea that is not Confucian. The infant Christ is not like the infant Confucius; our mysticism conceives him in an immortal infancy. I do not know what Confucius would have done with the Bambino had it come to life in his arms as it did in the arms of St. Francis. But this is true in relation to all the other religions and philosophies; it is the challenge of the Church. The Church contains what the world does not contain. Life itself does not provide as she does for all sides of life. That every other single system is narrow and insufficient compared to this one; that is not a rhetorical boast; it is a real fact and a real dilemma. Where is the Holy child amid the Stoics and the ancestor-worshippers? Where is Our Lady of the Moslems, a woman made for no man and set above all angels? Where is St. Michael of the monks of Buddha, rider and master of the trumpets, guarding for every soldier the honour of the sword? What could St. Thomas Aquinas do with the mythology of Brahminism, he who set forth all the science and rationality and even rationalism of Christianity? Yet even if we compare Aquinas with Aristotle, at the other extreme of reason, we shall find the same sense of something added. Aquinas could understand the most logical parts of Aristotle; it is doubtful if Aristotle could have understood the most mystical parts of Aquinas. Even where we can hardly call the Christian greater, we are forced to call him larger. But it is so to whatever philosophy or heresy or modern movement we may turn. How would Francis the Troubadour have fared among the Calvinists, or for that matter among the Utilitarians of the Manchester School? Yet men like Bossuet and Pascal could be as stern and logical as any Calvinist or Utilitarian. How would St. Joan of Arc, a woman waving on men to war with the sword, have fared among the Quakers or the Doukhabors or the Tolstoyan sect of pacifists? Yet any number of Catholic saints have spent their lives in preaching peace and preventing wars. It is the same with all the modern attempts at Syncretism. They are never able to make something larger than the Creed without leaving something out. I do not mean leaving out something divine but something human; the flag or the inn or the boy's tale of battle or the hedge at the end of the field. The Theosophists build a pantheon; but it is only a pantheon for pantheists. They call a Parliament of Religions as a reunion of all the peoples; but it is only a reunion of all the prigs. Yet exactly such a pantheon had been set up two thousand years before by the shores of the Mediterranean; and Christians were invited to set up the image of Jesus side by side with the image of Jupiter, of Mithras, of Osiris, of Atys, or of Ammon. It was the refusal of the Christians that was the turning-point of history. If the Christians had accepted, they and the whole world would have certainly, in a grotesque but exact metaphor, gone to pot. They would all have been boiled down to one lukewarm liquid in that great pot of cosmopolitan corruption in which all the other myths and mysteries were already melting. It was an awful and an appalling escape. Nobody understands the nature of the Church, or the ringing note of the creed descending from antiquity, who does not realise that the whole world once very nearly died of broadmindedness and the brotherhood of all religions.

Here it is the important point that the Magi, who stand for mysticism and philosophy, are truly conceived as seeking something new and even as finding something unexpected. That tense sense of crisis which still tingles in the Christmas story and even in every Christmas celebration, accentuates the idea of a search and a discovery. The discovery is, in this case, truly a scientific discovery. For the other mystical figures in the miracle play; for the angel and the mother, the shepherds and the soldiers of Herod, there may be aspects both simpler and more supernatural, more elemental or more emotional. But the wise Men must be seeking wisdom, and for them there must be a light also in the intellect. And this is the light; that the Catholic creed is catholic and that nothing else is catholic. The philosophy of the Church is universal. The philosophy of the philosophers was not universal. Had Plato and Pythagoras and Aristotle stood for an instant in the light that came out of that little cave, they would have known that their own light was not universal. It is far from certain, indeed, that they did not know it already. Philosophy also, like mythology, had very much the air of a search. It is the realisation of this truth that gives its traditional majesty and mystery to the figures of the Three Kings; the discovery that religion is broader than philosophy and that this is the broadest of religions, contained within this narrow space. The Magicians were gazing at the strange pentacle with the human triangle reversed; and they have never come to the end of their calculations about it. For it is the paradox of that group in the cave, that while our emotions about it are of childish simplicity, our thoughts about it can branch with a never-ending complexity. And we can never reach the end even of our own ideas about the child who was a father and the mother who was a child.

We might well be content to say that mythology had come with the shepherds and philosophy with the philosophers; and that it only remained for them to combine in the recognisation of religion. But there was a third element that must not be ignored and one which that religion for ever refuses to ignore, in any revel or reconciliation. There was present in the primary scenes of the drama that Enemy that had rotted the legends with lust and frozen theories into atheism, but which answered the direct challenge with something of that more direct method which we have seen in the conscious cult of the demons. In the description of that demon-worship, of the devouring detestation of innocence shown in the works of its witchcraft and the most inhuman of its human sacrifice, I have said less of its incorrect and secret penetration of the saner paganism; the soaking of mythological imagination with sex; the rise of imperial pride into insanity. But both the indirect and the direct influence make themselves felt in the drama of Bethlehem. A ruler under the Roman suzerainty, probably equipped and surrounded with the Roman ornament and order though himself of eastern blood, seems in that hour to have felt stirring within him the spirit of strange things. We all know the story of how Herod, alarmed at some rumour of a mysterious rival, remembered the wild gesture of the capricious despots of Asia and ordered a massacre of suspects of the new generation of the populace. Everyone knows the story; but not everyone has perhaps noted its place in the story of the strange religions of men. Not everybody has seen the significance even of its very contrast with the Corinthian columns and Roman pavement of that conquered and superficially civilised world. Only, as the purpose in his dark spirit began to show and shine in the eyes of the Idumean, a seer might perhaps have seen something like a great grey ghost that looked over his shoulder; have seen behind him filling the dome of night and hovering for the last time over history, that vast and fearful face that was Moloch of the Carthaginians; awaiting his last tribute from a ruler of the races of Shem. The demons also, in that first festival of Christmas, feasted after their own fashion.

Unless we understand the presence of that enemy, we shall not only miss the point of Christianity, but even miss the point of Christmas. Christmas for us in Christendom has become one thing, and in one sense even a simple thing. But like all the truths of that tradition, it is in another sense a very complex thing. Its unique note is the simultaneous striking of many notes; of humility, of gaiety, of gratitude, of mystical fear, but also of vigilance and of drama. It is not only an occasion for the peacemakers any more than for the merry-makers; it is not only a Hindu peace conference any more than it is only a Scandinavian winter feast. There is something defiant in it also; something that makes the abrupt bells at midnight sound like the great guns of a battle that has just been won. All this indescribable thing that we call the Christmas atmosphere only hangs in the air as something like a lingering fragrance or fading vapour from the exultant explosion of that one hour in the Judean hills nearly two thousand years ago. But the savour is still unmistakable, and it is something too subtle or too solitary to be covered by our use of the word peace. By the very nature of the story the rejoicings in the cavern were rejoicings in a fortress or an outlaw's den; properly understood it is not unduly flippant to say they were rejoicings in a dug-out. It is not only true that such a subterranean chamber was a hiding-place from enemies; and that the enemies were already scouring the stony plain that lay above it like a sky. It is not only that the very horse-hoofs of Herod might in that sense have passed like thunder over the sunken head of Christ. It is also that there is in that image a true idea of an outpost, of a piercing through the rock and an entrance into an enemy territory. There is in this buried divinity an idea of undermining the world; of shaking the towers and palaces from below; even as Herod the great king felt that earthquake under him and swayed with his swaying palace.

That is perhaps the mightiest of the mysteries of the cave It is already apparent that though men are said to have looked for hell under the earth, in this case it is rather heaven that is under the earth And there follows in this strange story the idea of an upheaval of heaven. That is the paradox of the whole position; that henceforth the highest thing can only work from below. Royalty can only return to its own by a sort of rebellion. Indeed the Church from its beginnings, and perhaps especially in its beginnings, was not so much a principality as a revolution against the prince of the world. This sense that the world had been conquered by the great usurper, and was in his possession, has been much deplored or derided by those optimists who identify enlightenment with ease. But it was responsible for all that thrill of defiance and a beautiful danger that made the good news seem to be really both good and new. It was in truth against a huge unconscious usurpation that it raised a revolt, and originally so obscure a revolt. Olympus still occupied the sky like a motionless cloud moulded into many mighty forms; philosophy still sat in the high places and even on the thrones of the kings, when Christ was born in the cave and Christianity in the catacombs. In both cases we may remark the same paradox of revolution; the sense of something despised and of something feared The cave in one aspect is only a hole or corner into which the outcasts are swept like rubbish; yet in the other aspect it is a hiding-place of something valuable which the tyrants are seeking like treasure. In one sense they are there because the innkeeper would not even remember them, and in another because the king can never forget them. We have already noted that this paradox appeared also in the treatment of the early Church. It was important while it was still insignificant, and certainly while it was still impotent. It was important solely because it was intolerable; and in that sense it is true to say that it was intolerable because it was intolerant. It was resented, because, in its own still and almost secret way, it had declared war. It had risen out of the ground to wreck the heaven and earth of heathenism. It did not try to destroy all that creation of gold and marble; but it contemplated a world without it. It dared to look right through it as though the gold and marble had been glass. Those who charged the Christians with burning down Rome with firebrands were slanderers; but they were at least far nearer to the nature of Christianity than those among the moderns who tell us that the Christians were a sort of ethical society, being martyred in a languid fashion for telling men they had a duty to their neighbors, and only mildly disliked because they were meek and mild.

Herod had his place, therefore, in the miracle play of Bethlehem because he is the menace to the Church Militant and shows it from the first as under persecution and fighting for its life. For those who think this a discord, it is a discord that sounds simultaneously with the Christmas bells. For those who think the idea of the Crusade is one that spoils the idea of the Cross, we can only say that for them the idea of the Cross is spoiled; the idea of the cross is spoiled quite literally in the cradle. It is not here to the purpose to argue with them on the abstract ethics of fighting; the purpose in this place is merely to sum up the combination of ideas that make up the Christian and Catholic idea, and to note that all of them are already crystallised in the first Christmas story. They are three distinct and commonly contrasted things which are nevertheless one thing; but this is the only thing which can make them one. The first is the human instinct for a heaven that shall be as literal and almost as local as a home. It is the idea pursued by all poets and pagans making myths; that a particular place must be the shrine of the god or the abode of the blest; that fairyland is a land; or that the return of the ghost must be the resurrection of the body. I do not here reason about the refusal of rationalism to satisfy this need. I only say that if the rationalists refuse to satisfy it, the pagans will not be satisfied. This is present in the story of Bethlehem and Jerusalem as it is present in the story of Delos and Delphi; and as it is not present in the whole universe of Lucretius or the whole universe of Herbert Spencer. The second element is a philosophy larger than other philosophies; larger than that of Lucretius and infinitely larger than that of Herbert Spencer. It looks at the world through a hundred windows where the ancient stoic or the modern agnostic only looks through one. It sees life with thousands of eyes belonging to thousands of different sorts of people, where the other is only the individual standpoint of a stoic or an agnostic. It has something for all moods of man, it finds work for all kinds of men, it understands secrets of psychology, it is aware of depths of evil, it is able to distinguish between ideal and unreal marvels and miraculous exceptions, it trains itself in tact about hard cases, all with a multiplicity and subtlety and imagination about the varieties of life which is far beyond the bald or breezy platitudes of most ancient or modern moral philosophy. In a word, there is more in it; it finds more in existence to think about; it gets more out of life. Masses of this material about our many-sided life have been added since the time of St. Thomas Aquinas. But St. Thomas Aquinas alone would have found himself limited in the world of Confucius or of Comte. And the third point is this; that while it is local enough for poetry and larger than any other philosophy, it is also a challenge and a fight. While it is deliberately broadened to embrace every aspect of truth, it is still stiffly embattled against every mode of error. It gets every kind of man to fight for it, it gets every kind of weapon to fight with, it widens its knowledge of the things that are fought for and against with every art of curiosity or sympathy; but it never forgets that it is fighting. It proclaims peace on earth and never forgets why there was war in heaven.

This is the trinity of truths symbolised here by the three types in the old Christmas story; the shepherds and the kings and that other king who warred upon the children. It is simply not true to say that other religions and philosophies are in this respect its rivals. It is not true to say that any one of them combines these characters; it is not true to say that any one of them pretends to combine them. Buddhism may profess to be equally mystical; it does not even profess to be equally military. Islam may profess to be equally military; it does not even profess to be equally metaphysical and subtle. Confucianism may profess to satisfy the need of the philosophers for order and reason; it does not even profess to satisfy the need of the mystics for miracle and sacrament and the consecration of concrete things. There are many evidences of this presence of a spirit at once universal and unique. One will serve here which is the symbol of the subject of this chapter; that no other story, no pagan legend or philosophical anecdote or historical event, does in fact affect any of us with that peculiar and even poignant impression produced on us by the word Bethlehem. No other birth of a god or childhood of a sage seems to us to be Christmas or anything like Christmas. It is either too cold or too frivolous, or too formal and classical, or too simple and savage, or too occult and complicated. Not one of us, whatever his opinions, would ever go to such a scene with the sense that he was going home. He might admire it because it was poetical, or because it was philosophical, or any number of other things in separation; but not because it was itself. The truth is that there is a quite peculiar and individual character about the hold of this story on human nature; it is not in its psychological substance at all like a mere legend or the life of a great man. It does not exactly in the ordinary sense turn our minds to greatness; to those extensions and exaggerations of humanity which are turned into gods and heroes, even by the healthiest sort of hero-worship. It does not exactly work outwards, adventurously, to the wonders to be found at the ends of the earth. It is rather something that surprises us from behind, from the hidden and personal part of our being; like that which can some times take us off our guard in the pathos of small objects or the blind pieties of the poor. It is rather as if a man had found an inner room in the very heart of his own house, which he had never suspected; and seen a light from within. It is as if he found something at the back of his own heart that betrayed him into good. It is not made of what the world would call strong materials; or rather it is made of materials whose strength is in that winged levity with which they brush us and pass. It is all that is in us but a brief tenderness that is there made eternal; all that means no more than a momentary softening that is in some strange fashion become a strengthening and a repose; it is the broken speech and the lost word that are made positive and suspended unbroken; as the strange kings fade into a far country and the mountains resound no more with the feet of the shepherds; and only the night and the cavern lie in fold upon fold over something more human than humanity.

II THE RIDDLES OF THE GOSPEL

To understand the nature of this chapter, it is necessary to recur to the nature of this book. The argument which is meant to be the backbone of the book is of the kind called the reductio ad absurdum. It suggests that the results of assuming the rationalist thesis are more irrational than ours; but to prove it we must assume that thesis. Thus in the first section I often treated man as merely an animal, to show that the effect was more impossible than if he were treated as an angel. In the sense in which it was necessary to treat man merely as an animal, it is necessary to treat Christ merely as a man. I have to suspend my own beliefs, which are much more positive; and assume this limitation even in order to remove it. I must try to imagine what would happen to a man who did really read the story of Christ as the story of a man; and even of a man of whom he had never heard before. And I wish to point out that a really impartial reading of that kind would lead, if not immediately to belief, at least to a bewilderment of which there is really no solution except in belief. In this chapter, for this reason, I shall bring in nothing of the spirit of my own creed; I shall exclude the very style of diction, and even of lettering, which I should think fitting in speaking in my own person. I am speaking as an imaginary heathen human being, honestly, staring at the Gospel story for the first time.

Now it is not at all easy to regard the New Testament as a New Testament. It is not at all easy to realise the good news as new. Both for good and evil familiarity fills us with assumptions and associations; and no man of our civilisation, whatever he thinks of our religion, can really read the thing as if he had never heard of it before. Of course it is in any case utterly unhistorical to talk as if the New Testament were a neatly bound book that had fallen from heaven. It is simply the selection made by the authority of the Church from a mass of early Christian literature. But apart from any such question there is a psychological difficulty in feeling the New Testament as new. There is a psychological difficulty in seeing those well-known words simply as they stand and without going beyond what they intrinsically stand for. And this difficulty must indeed be very great; for the result of it is very curious. The result of it is that most modern critics and most current criticism, even popular criticism, makes a comment that is the exact reverse of the truth. It is so completely the reverse of the truth that one could almost suspect that they had never read the New Testament at all.

We have all heard people say a hundred times over, for they seem never to tire of saying it, that the Jesus of the New Testament is indeed a most merciful and humane lover of humanity, but that the Church has hidden this human character in repellent dogmas and stiffened it with ecclesiastical terrors till it has taken on an inhuman character. This is, I venture to repeat, very nearly the reverse of the truth. The truth is that it is the image of Christ in the churches that is almost entirely mild and merciful. It is the image of Christ in the Gospels that is a good many other things as well. The figure in the Gospels does indeed utter in words of almost heart-breaking beauty his pity for our broken hearts. But they are very far from being the only sort of words that he utters. Nevertheless they are almost the only kind of words that the Church in its popular imagery ever represents him as uttering. That popular imagery is inspired by a perfectly sound popular instinct. The mass of the poor are broken, and the mass of the people are poor, and for the mass of mankind the main thing is to carry the conviction of the incredible compassion of God. But nobody with his eyes open can doubt that it is chiefly this idea of compassion that the popular machinery of the Church does seek to carry. The popular imagery carries a great deal to excess the sentiment of 'Gentle Jesus, meek and mild.' It is the first thing that the outsider feels and criticises in a Pieta or a shrine of the Sacred Heart. As I say, while the art may be insufficient, I am not sure that the instinct is unsound. In any case there is something appalling, something that makes the blood run cold, in the idea of having a statue of Christ in wrath. There is something insupportable even to the imagination in the idea of turning the corner of a street or coming out into the spaces of a marketplace, to meet the petrifying petrifaction of that figure as it turned upon a generation of vipers, or that face as it looked at the face of a hypocrite. The Church can reasonably be justified therefore if she turns the most merciful face or aspect towards men; but it is certainly the most merciful aspect that she does turn. And the point is here that it is very much more specially and exclusively merciful than any impression that could be formed by a man merely reading the New Testament for the first time. A man simply taking the words of the story as they stand would form quite another impression; an impression full of mystery and possibly of inconsistency; but certainly not merely an impression of mildness. It would be intensely interesting; but part of the interest would consist in its leaving a good deal to be guessed at or explained. It is full of sudden gestures evidently significant except that we hardly know what they signify, of enigmatic silences; of ironical replies. The outbreaks of wrath, like storms above our atmosphere, do not seem to break out exactly where we should expect them, but to follow some higher weather-chart of their own. The Peter whom popular Church teaching presents is very rightly the Peter to whom Christ said in forgiveness, 'Feed my lambs.' He is not the Peter upon whom Christ turned as if he were the devil, crying in that obscure wrath, 'Get thee behind me, Satan.' Christ lamented with nothing but love and pity over Jerusalem which was to murder him. We do not know what strange spiritual atmosphere or spiritual insight led him to sink Bethsaida lower in the pit than Sodom. I am putting aside for the moment all questions of doctrinal inferences or expositions, orthodox or otherwise; I am simply imagining the effect on a man's mind if he did really do what these critics are always talking about doing; if he did really read the New Testament without reference to orthodoxy and even without reference to doctrine. He would find a number of things which fit in far less with the current unorthodoxy than they do with the current orthodoxy. He would find, for instance, that if there are any descriptions that deserved to be called realistic, they are precisely the descriptions of the supernatural. If there is one aspect of the New Testament Jesus in which he may be said to present himself eminently as a practical person, it is in the aspect of an exorcist. There is nothing meek and mild, there is nothing even in the ordinary sense mystical, about the tone of the voice that says 'Hold thy peace and come out of him.' It is much more like the tone of a very business-like lion-tamer or a strong-minded doctor dealing with a homicidal maniac. But this is only a side issue for the sake of illustration; I am not now raising these controversies; but considering the case of the imaginary man from the moon to whom the New Testament is new.

Now the first thing to note is that if we take it merely as a human story, it is in some ways a very strange story. I do not refer here to its tremendous and tragic culmination or to any implications involving triumph in that tragedy. I do not refer to what is commonly called the miraculous element; for on that point philosophies vary and modern philosophies very decidedly waver. Indeed the educated Englishman of to-day may be said to have passed from an old fashion, in which he would not believe in any miracles unless they were ancient, and adopted a new fashion in which he will not believe in any miracles unless they are modern. He used to hold that miraculous cures stopped with the first Christians and is now inclined to suspect that they began with the first Christian Scientists. But I refer here rather specially to unmiraculous and even to unnoticed and inconspicuous parts of the story. There are a great many things about it which nobody would have invented, for they are things that nobody has ever made any particular use of; things which if they were remarked at all have remained rather as puzzles. For instance, there is that long stretch of silence in the life of Christ up to the age of thirty. It is of all silences the most immense and imaginatively impressive. But it is not the sort of thing that anybody is particularly likely to invent in order to prove something; and no body so far as I know has ever tried to prove anything in particular from it. It is impressive, but it is only impressive as a fact; there is nothing particularly popular or obvious about it as a fable. The ordinary trend of hero-worship and myth-making is much more likely to say the precise opposite. It is much more likely to say (as I believe some of the gospels rejected by the Church do say) that Jesus displayed a divine precocity and began his mission at a miraculously early age. And there is indeed something strange in the thought that he who of all humanity needed least preparation seems to have had most. Whether it was some mode of the divine humility, or some truth of which we see the shadow of the longer domestic tutelage of the higher creatures of the earth. I do not propose to speculate; I mention it simply as an example of the sort of thing that does in any case give rise to speculations, quite apart from recognised religious speculations. Now the whole story is full of these things. It is not by any means, as baldly presented in print, a story that it is easy to get to the bottom of. It is anything but what these people talk of as a simple Gospel. Relatively speaking, it is the Gospel that has the mysticism and the Church that has the rationalism. As I should put it, of course, it is the Gospel that is the riddle and the Church that is the answer. But whatever be the answer, the Gospel as it stands is almost a book of riddles.

First, a man reading the Gospel sayings would not find platitudes. If he had read even in the most respectful spirit the majority of ancient philosophers and of modern moralists, he would appreciate the unique importance of saying that he did not find platitudes. It is more than can be said even of Plato. It is much more than can be said of Epictetus or Seneca or Marcus Aurelius or Apollonius of Tyana. And it is immeasurably more than can be said of most of the agnostic moralists and the preachers of the ethical societies; with their songs of service and their religion of brotherhood. The morality of most moralists ancient and modern, has been one solid and polished cataract of platitudes flowing for ever and ever. That would certainly not be the impression of the imaginary independent outsider studying the New Testament. He would be conscious of nothing so commonplace and in a sense of nothing so continuous as that stream. He would find a number of strange claims that might sound like the claim to be the brother of the sun and moon; a number of very startling pieces of advice; a number of stunning rebukes; a number of strangely beautiful stories. He would see some very gigantesque figures of speech about the impossibility of threading a needle with a camel or the possibility of throwing a mountain into the sea. He would see a number of very daring simplifications of the difficulties of life; like the advice to shine upon everybody indifferently as does the sunshine or not to worry about the future any more than the birds. He would find on the other hand some passages of almost impenetrable darkness, so far as he is concerned, such as the moral of the parable of the Unjust Steward. Some of these things might strike him as fables and some as truths; but none as truisms. For instance, he would not find the ordinary platitudes in favour of peace. He would find several paradoxes in favour of peace. He would find several ideals of non-resistance, which taken as they stand would be rather too pacific for any pacifist. He would be told in one passage to treat a robber not with passive resistance, but rather with positive and enthusiastic encouragement, if the terms be taken literally; heaping up gifts upon the man who had stolen goods. But he would not find a word of all that obvious rhetoric against war which has filled countless books and odes and orations; not a word about the wickedness of war, the wastefulness of war, the appalling scale of the slaughter in war and all the rest of the familiar frenzy; indeed not a word about war at all. There is nothing that throws any particular light on Christ's attitude towards organised warfare, except that he seems to have been rather fond of Roman soldiers. Indeed it is another perplexity, speaking from the same external and human stand point, that he seems to have got on much better with Romans than he did with Jews. But the question here is a certain tone to be appreciated by merely reading a certain text; and we might give any number of instances of it.

The statement that the meek shall inherit the earth is very far from being a meek statement. I mean it is not meek in the ordinary sense of mild and moderate and inoffensive. To justify it, it would be necessary to go very deep into history and anticipate things undreamed of then and by many unrealised even now; such as the way in which the mystical monks reclaimed the lands which the practical kings had lost. If it was a truth at all, it was because it was a prophecy. But certainly it was not a truth in the sense of a truism. The blessing upon the meek would seem to be a very violent statement; in the sense of doing violence to reason and probability. And with this we come to another important stage in the speculation. As a prophecy it really was fulfilled; but it was only fulfilled long afterwards. The monasteries were the most practical and prosperous estates and experiments in reconstruction after the barbaric deluge; the meek did really inherit the earth. But nobody could have known anything of the sort at the time--unless indeed there was one who knew. Something of the same thing may be said about the incident of Martha and Mary; which has been interpreted in retrospect and from the inside by the mystics of the Christian contemplative life. But it was not at all an obvious view of it; and most moralists, ancient and modern, could be trusted to make a rush for the obvious. What torrents of effortless eloquence would have flowed from them to swell any slight superiority on the part of Martha; what splendid sermons about the Joy of Service and the Gospel of Work and the World Left Better Than We Found It, and generally all the ten thousand platitudes that can be uttered in favour of taking trouble--by people who need take no trouble to utter them. If in Mary the mystic and child of love Christ was guarding the seed of something more subtle, who was likely to understand it at the time? Nobody else could have seen Clare and Catherine and Teresa shining above the little roof at Bethany. It is so in another way with that magnificent menace about bringing into the world a sword to sunder and divide. Nobody could have guessed then either how it could be fulfilled or how it could be justified. Indeed some freethinkers are still so simple as to fall into the trap and be shocked at a phrase so deliberately defiant. They actually complain of the paradox for not being a platitude.

But the point here is that if we could read the Gospel reports as things as new as newspaper reports, they would puzzle us and perhaps terrify us much more than the same things as developed by historical Christianity. For instance, Christ after a clear allusion to the eunuchs of eastern courts, said there would be eunuchs of the kingdom of heaven. If this does not mean the voluntary enthusiasm of virginity, it could only be made to mean something much more unnatural or uncouth. It is the historical religion that humanises it for us by experience of Franciscans or of Sisters of Mercy. The mere statement standing by itself might very well suggest a rather dehumanised atmosphere; the sinister and inhuman silence of the Asiatic harem and divan. This is but one instance out of scores; but the moral is that the Christ of the Gospel might actually seem more strange and terrible than the Christ of the Church.

I am dwelling on the dark or dazzling or defiant or mysterious side of the Gospel words, not because they had not obviously a more obvious and popular side, but because this is the answer to a common criticism on a vital point. The freethinker frequently says that Jesus of Nazareth was a man of his time, even if he was in advance of his time; and that we cannot accept his ethics as final for humanity. The freethinker then goes on to criticise his ethics, saying plausibly enough that men cannot turn the other cheek, or that they must take thought for the morrow, or that the self-denial is too ascetic or the monogamy too severe. But the Zealots and the Legionaries did not turn the other cheek any more than we do, if so much. The Jewish traders and Roman tax-gatherers took thought for the morrow as much as we, if not more. We cannot pretend to be abandoning the morality of the past for one more suited to the present. It is certainly not the morality of another age, but it might be of another world.

In short, we can say that these ideals are impossible in themselves. Exactly what we cannot say is that they are impossible for us. They are rather notably marked by a mysticism which, if it be a sort of madness, would always have struck the same sort of people as mad. Take, for instance, the case of marriage and the relations of the sexes. It might very well have been true that a Galilean teacher taught things natural to a Galilean environment; but it is not. It might rationally be expected that a man in the time of Tiberius would have advanced a view conditioned by the time of Tiberius; but he did not. What he advanced was something quite different; something very difficult; but something no more difficult now than it was then. When, for instance, Mahomet made his polygamous compromise we may reasonably say that it was conditioned by a polygamous society. When he allowed a man four wives he was really doing something suited to the circumstances, which might have been less suited to other circumstances. Nobody will pretend that the four wives were like the four winds, something seemingly a part of the order of nature; nobody will say that the figure four was written for ever in stars upon the sky But neither will anyone say that the figure four is an inconceivable ideal; that it is beyond the power of the mind of man to count up to four; or to count the number of his wives and see whether it amounts to four. It is a practical compromise carrying with it the character of a particular society. If Mahomet had been born in Acton in the nineteenth century, we may well doubt whether he would instantly have filled that suburb with harems of four wives apiece. As he was born in Arabia in the sixth century, he did in his conjugal arrangements suggest the conditions of Arabia in the sixth century. But Christ in his view of marriage does not in the least suggest the conditions of Palestine of the first century. He does not suggest anything at all, except the sacramental view of marriage as developed long afterwards by the Catholic Church. It was quite as difficult for people then as for people now. It was much more puzzling to people then than to people now. Jews and Romans and Greeks did not believe, and did not even understand enough to disbelieve, the mystical idea that the man and the woman had become one sacramental substance. We may think it an incredible or impossible ideal; but we cannot think it any more incredible or impossible than they would have thought it. In other words, whatever else is true, it is not true that the controversy has been altered by time. Whatever else is true, it is emphatically not true that the ideas of Jesus of Nazareth were suitable to his time, but are no longer suitable to our time. Exactly how suitable they we to his time is perhaps suggested in the end of his story.

The same truth might be stated in another way by saying that if the story be regarded as merely human and historical, it is extraordinary how very little there is in the recorded words of Christ that ties him at all to his own time. I do not mean the details of a period, which even a man of the period knows to be passing. I mean the fundamentals which even the wisest man often vaguely assumes to be eternal. For instance, Aristotle was perhaps the wisest and most wide-minded man who ever lived. He founded himself entirely upon fundamentals, which have been generally found to remain rational and solid through all social and historical changes. Still, he lived in a world in which it was thought as natural to have slaves as to have children. And therefore he did permit himself a serious recognition of a difference between slaves and free men. Christ as much as Aristotle lived in a world that took slavery for granted. He did not particularly denounce slavery. He started a movement that could exist in a world with slavery. But he started a movement that could exist in a world without slavery. He never used a phrase that made his philosophy depend even upon the very existence of the social order in which he lived. He spoke as one conscious that everything was ephemeral, including the things that Aristotle thought eternal. By that time the Roman Empire had come to be merely the orbis terrarum, another name for the world. But he never made his morality dependent on the existence of the Roman Empire or even on the existence of the world. 'Heaven and earth shall pass away, but my words shall not pass away.'

The truth is that when critics have spoken of the local limitations of the Galilean, it has always been a case of the local limitations of the critics. He did undoubtedly believe in certain things that one particular modern sect of materialists do not believe. But they were not things particularly peculiar to his time. It would be nearer the truth to say that the denial of them is quite peculiar to our time. Doubtless it would be nearer still to the truth to say merely that a certain solemn social importance, in the minority disbelieving them, is peculiar to our time. He believed, for instance, in evil spirits or in the psychic healing of bodily ills; but not because he was a Galilean born under Augustus. It is absurd to say that a man believed things because he was a Galilean under Augustus when he might have believed the same things if he had been an Egyptian under Tutenkamen or an Indian under Gengis Khan. But with this general question of the philosophy of diabolism or of divine miracles I deal elsewhere. It is enough to say that the materialists have to prove the impossibility of miracles against the testimony of all mankind, not against the prejudices of provincials in North Palestine under the first Roman Emperors. What they have to prove, for the present argument, is the presence in the Gospels of those particular prejudices of those particular provincials. And, humanly speaking, it is astonishing how little they can produce even to make a beginning of proving it.

So it is in this case of the sacrament of marriage. We may not believe in sacraments, as we may not believe in spirits, but it is quite clear that Christ believed in this sacrament in his own way and not in any current or contemporary way. He certainly did not get his argument against divorce from the Mosaic law or the Roman law or the habits of the Palestinian people. It would appear to his critics then exactly what it appears to his critics now; an arbitrary and transcendental dogma coming from nowhere save in the sense that it came from him. I am not at all concerned here to defend that dogma; the point here is that it is just as easy to defend it now as it was to defend it then. It is an ideal altogether outside time; difficult at any period; impossible at no period. In other words, if anyone says it is what might be expected of a man walking about in that place at that period, we can quite fairly answer that it is much more like what might be the mysterious utterance of a being beyond man, if he walked alive among men.

I maintain therefore that a man reading the New Testament frankly and freshly would not get the impression of what is now often meant by a human Christ. The merely human Christ is a made-up figure, a piece of artificial selection, like the merely evolutionary man. Moreover there have been too many of these human Christs found in the same story, just as there have been too many keys to mythology found in the same stories. Three or four separate schools of rationalism have worked over the ground and produced three or four equally rational explanations of his life. The first rational explanation of his life was that he never lived. And this in turn gave an opportunity for three or four different explanations, as that he was a sun-myth or a corn-myth, or any other kind of myth that is also a monomania. Then the idea that he was a divine being who did not exist gave place to the idea that he was a human being who did exist. In my youth it vas the fashion to say that he was merely an ethical teacher in the manner of the Essenes, who had apparently nothing very much to say that Hillel or a hundred other Jews might not have said; as that it is a kindly thing to be kind and an assistance to purification to be pure. Then somebody said he was a madman with a Messianic delusion. Then others said he was indeed an original teacher because he cared about nothing but Socialism; or (as others said) about nothing but Pacifism. Then a more grimly scientific character appeared who said that Jesus would never have been heard of at all except for his prophecies of the end of the world. He was important merely as a Millenarian like Dr. Cumming; and created a provincial scare by announcing the exact date of the crack of doom. Among other variants on the same theme was the theory that he was a spiritual healer and nothing else; a view implied by Christian Science, which has really to expound a Christianity without the Crucifixion in order to explain the curing of Peter's wife's mother or the daughter of a centurion. There is another theory that concentrates entirely on the business of diabolism and what it would call the contemporary superstition about demoniacs, as if Christ, like a young deacon taking his first orders, had got as far as exorcism and never got any further. Now, each of these explanations in itself seems to me singularly inadequate; but taken together they do suggest something of the very mystery which they miss. There must surely have been something not only mysterious but many-sided about Christ if so many smaller Christs can be carved out of him. If the Christian Scientist is satisfied with him as a spiritual healer and the Christian Socialist is satisfied with him as a social reformer, so satisfied that they do not even expect him to be anything else, it looks as if he really covered rather more ground than they could be expected to expect. And it does seem to suggest that there might be more than they fancy in these other mysterious attributes of casting out devils or prophesying doom.

Above all, would not such a new reader of the New Testament stumble over something that would startle him much more than it startles us? I have here more than once attempted the rather impossible task of reversing time and the historic method; and in fancy looking forward to the facts, instead of backward through the memories. So I have imagined the monster that man might have seemed at first to the mere nature around him. We should have a worse shock if we really imagined the nature of Christ named for the first time. What should we feel at the first whisper of a certain suggestion about a certain man? Certainly it is not for us to blame anybody who should find that first wild whisper merely impious and insane. On the contrary, stumbling on that rock of scandal is the first step. Stark staring incredulity is a far more loyal tribute to that truth than a modernist metaphysic that would make it out merely a matter of degree. It were better to rend our robes with a great cry against blasphemy, like Caiaphas in the judgement, or to lay hold of the man as a maniac possessed of devils like the kinsmen and the crowd, rather than to stand stupidly debating fine shades of pantheism in the presence of so catastrophic a claim. There is more of the wisdom that is one with surprise in any simple person, full of the sensitiveness of simplicity, who should expect the grass to wither and the birds to drop dead out of the air, when a strolling carpenter's apprentice said calmly and almost carelessly, like one looking over his shoulder: 'Before Abraham was, I am.'

III THE STRANGEST STORY IN THE WORD

In the last chapter I have deliberately stressed what seems to be nowadays a neglected side of the New Testament story, but nobody will suppose, I imagine, that it is meant to obscure that side that may truly be called human. That Christ was and is the most merciful of judges and the most sympathetic of friends is a fact of considerably more importance in our own private lives than in anybody's historical speculations. But the purpose of this book is to point out that something unique has been swamped in cheap generalisations; and for that purpose it is relevant to insist that even what was most universal was also most original. For instance, we might take a topic which really is sympathetic to the modern mood, as the ascetic vocations recently referred to are not. The exaltation of childhood is something which we do really understand; but it was by no means a thing that was then in that sense understood. If we wanted an example of the originality of the Gospels we could hardly take a stronger or more startling one. Nearly two thousand years afterwards we happen to find ourselves in a mood that does really feel the mystical charm of the child; we express it in romances and regrets about childhood, in Peter Pan or The Child's Garden of verses. And we can say of the words of Christ with so angry an anti-Christian as Swinburne:--

'No sign that ever was given To faithful or faithless eyes Showed ever beyond clouds riven So clear a paradise.

Earth's creeds may be seventy times seven And blood have defiled each creed But if such be the kingdom of heaven It must be heaven indeed.'

But that paradise was not clear until Christianity had gradually cleared it. The pagan world, as such, would not have understood any such thing as a serious suggestion that a child is higher or holier than a man. It would have seemed like the suggestion that a tadpole is higher or holier than a frog. To the merely rationalistic mind, it would sound like saying that a bud must be more beautiful than a flower or that an unripe apple must be better than a ripe one. In other words, this modern feeling is an entirely mystical feeling. It is quite as mystical as the cult of virginity; in fact it is the cult of virginity. But pagan antiquity had much more idea of the holiness of the virgin than of the holiness of the child. For various reasons we have come nowadays to venerate children, perhaps partly because we envy children for still doing what men used to do; such as play simple games and enjoy fairy-tales. Over and above this, however, there is a great deal of real and subtle psychology in our appreciation of childhood; but if we turn it into a modern discovery, we must once more admit that the historical Jesus of Nazareth had already discovered it two thousand years too soon. There was certainly nothing in the world around him to help him to the discovery. Here Christ was indeed human; but more human than a human being was then likely to be. Peter Pan does not belong to the world of Pan but the world of Peter.

Even in the matter of mere literary style, if we suppose ourselves thus sufficiently detached to look at it in that light, there is a curious quality to which no critic seems to have done justice. It had among other things a singular air of piling tower upon tower by the use of the a fortiori; making a pagoda of degrees like the seven heavens. I have already noted that almost inverted imaginative vision which pictured the impossible penance of the Cities of the Plain. There is perhaps nothing so perfect in all language or literature as the use of these three degrees in the parable of the lilies of the field; in which he seems first to take one small flower in his hand and note its simplicity and even its impotence; then suddenly expands it in flamboyant colours into all the palaces and pavilions full of a great name in national legend and national glory; and then, by yet a third overturn, shrivels into nothing once more with a gesture as if flinging it away ``and if God so clothes the grass that today is and tomorrow is cast into the oven--how much more" It is like the building of a good Babel tower by white magic in a moment and in the movement of a hand; a tower heaved suddenly up to heaven on the top of which can be seen afar off, higher than we had fancied possible, the figure of man; lifted by three infinities above all other things, on a starry ladder of light logic and swift imagination. Merely in a literary sense it would be more of a masterpiece than most of the masterpieces in the libraries; yet it seems to have been uttered almost at random while a man might pull a flower. But merely in a literary sense also, this use of the comparative in several degrees has about it a quality which seems to me to hint of much higher things than the modern suggestion of the simple teaching of pastoral or communal ethics. There is nothing that really indicates a subtle and in the true sense a superior mind so much as this power of comparing a lower thing with a higher and yet that higher with a higher still; of thinking on three planes at once. There is nothing that wants the rarest sort of wisdom so much as to see, let us say, that the citizen is higher than the slave and yet that the soul is infinitely higher than the citizen or the city. It is not by any means a faculty that commonly belongs to these simplifiers of the Gospel; those who insist on what they call a simple morality and others call a sentimental morality. It is not at all covered by those who are content to tell everybody to remain at peace. On the contrary, there is a very striking example of it in the apparent inconsistency between Christ's sayings about peace and about a sword. It is precisely this power which perceives that while a good peace is better than a good war, even a good war is better than a bad peace. These far-flung comparisons are nowhere so common as in the Gospels; and to me they suggest something very vast. So a thing solitary and solid, with the added dimension of depth or height, might tower over the flat creatures living only on a plane.

This quality of something that can only be called subtle and superior, something that is capable of long views and even of double meanings, is not noted here merely as a counterblast to the commonplace exaggerations of amiability and mild idealism. It is also to be noted in connection with the more tremendous truth touched upon at the end of the last chapter. For this is the very last character that commonly goes with mere megalomania; especially such steep and staggering megalomania as might be involved in that claim. This quality that can only be called intellectual distinction is not, of course, an evidence of divinity. But it is an evidence of a probable distaste for vulgar and vainglorious claims to divinity. A man of that sort, if he were only a man, would be the last man in the world to suffer from that intoxication by one notion from nowhere in particular, which is the mark of the self-deluding sensationalist in religion. Nor is it even avoided by denying that Christ did make this claim. Of no such man as that, of no other prophet or philosopher of the same intellectual order, would it be even possible to pretend that he had made it. Even if the Church had mistaken his meaning, it would still be true that no other historical tradition except the Church had ever even made the same mistake. Mahomedans did not misunderstand Mahomet and suppose he was Allah. Jews did not misinterpret Moses and identify him with Jehovah. Why was this claim alone exaggerated unless this alone was made. Even if Christianity was one vast universal blunder, it is still a blunder as solitary as the Incarnation.

The purpose of these pages is to fix the falsity of certain vague and vulgar assumptions; and we have here one of the most false. There is a sort of notion in the air everywhere that all the religions are equal because all the religious founders were rivals, that they are all fighting for the same starry crown. It is quite false. The claim to that crown, or anything like that crown, is really so rare as to be unique. Mahomet did not make it any more than Micah or Malachi. Confucius did not make it any more that Plato or Marcus Aurelius. Buddha never said he was Bramah. Zoroaster no more claimed to be Ormuz than to be Ahriman. The truth is that, in the common run of cases, it is just as we should expect it to be, in common sense and certainly in Christian philosophy. It is exactly the other way. Normally speaking, the greater a man is, the less likely he is to make the very greatest claim. Outside the unique case we are considering, the only kind of man who ever does make that kind of claim is a very small man; a secretive or self-centered monomaniac. Nobody can imagine Aristotle claiming to be the father of gods and men, come down from the sky; though we might imagine some insane Roman Emperor like Caligula claiming it for him, or more probably for himself. Nobody can imagine Shakespeare talking as if he were literally divine; though we might imagine some crazy American crank finding it as a cryptogram in Shakespeare's works, or preferably in his own works. It is possible to find here and there human beings who make this supremely superhuman claim. It is possible to find them in lunatic asylums; in padded cells; possibly in strait waistcoats. But what is much more important than their mere materialistic fate in our very materialistic society, under very crude and clumsy laws about lunacy, the type we know as tinged with this, or tending towards it, is a diseased and disproportionate type; narrow yet swollen and morbid to monstrosity. It is by rather an unlucky metaphor that we talk of a madman as cracked; for in a sense he is not cracked enough. He is cramped rather than cracked; there are not enough holes in his head to ventilate it. This impossibility of letting in daylight on a delusion does sometimes cover and conceal a delusion of divinity. It can be found, not among prophets and sages and founders of religions, but only among a low set of lunatics. But this is exactly where the argument becomes intensely interesting; because the argument proves too much. For nobody supposes that Jesus of Nazareth was that sort of person. No modern critic in his five wits thinks that the preacher of the Sermon on the Mount was a horrible half-witted imbecile that might be scrawling stars on the walls of a cell. No atheist or blasphemer believes that the author of the Parable of the Prodigal Son was a monster with one mad idea like a cyclops with one eye. Upon any possible historical criticism, he must be put higher in the scale of human beings than that. Yet by all analogy we have really to put him there or else in the highest place of all.

In, fact, those who can really take it (as I here hypothetically take it) in a quite dry and detached spirit, have here a most curious and interesting human problem. It is so intensely interesting, considered as a human problem, that it is in a spirit quite disinterested, so to speak, that I wish some of them had turned that intricate human problem into something like an intelligible human portrait. If Christ was simply a human character, he really was a highly complex and contradictory human character. For he combined exactly the two things that lie at the two extremes of human variation. He was exactly what the man with a delusion never is; he was wise; he was a good judge. What he said was always unexpected; but it was always unexpectedly magnanimous and often unexpectedly moderate. Take a thing like the point of the parable of the tares and the wheat. It has the quality that unites sanity and subtlety. It has not the simplicity of a madman. It has not even the simplicity of a fanatic. It might be uttered by a philosopher a hundred years old, at the end of a century of Utopias. Nothing could be less like this quality of seeing beyond and all round obvious things, than the condition of the egomaniac with the one sensitive spot on his brain. I really do not see how these two characters could be convincingly combined, except in the astonishing way in which the creed combines them. For until we reach the full acceptance of the fact as a fact, however marvellous, all mere approximations to it are actually further and further away from it. Divinity is great enough to be divine; it is great enough to call itself divine. But as humanity grows greater, it grows less and less likely to do so. God is God, as the Moslems say; but a great man knows he is not God, and the greater he is the better he knows it. That is the paradox; everything that is merely approaching to that point is merely receding from it. Socrates, the wisest man, knows that he knows nothing. A lunatic may think he is omniscience, and a fool may talk as if he were omniscient. But Christ is in another sense omniscient if he not only knows, but knows that he knows.

Even on the purely human and sympathetic side, therefore, the Jesus of the New Testament seems to me to have in a great many ways the note of something superhuman; that is of something human and more than human. But there is another quality running through all his teachings which seems to me neglected in most modern talk about them as teachings; and that is the persistent suggestion that he has not really come to teach. If there is one incident in the record which affects me personally as grandly and gloriously human, it is the incident of giving wine for the wedding-feast. That is really human in the sense in which a whole crowd of prigs, having the appearance of human beings, can hardly be described as human. It rises superior to all superior persons. It is as human as Herrick and as democratic as Dickens. But even in that story there is something else that has that note of things not fully explained; and in a way here very relevant. I mean the first hesitation, not on any ground touching the nature of the miracle, but on that of the propriety of working any miracles at all, at least at that stage; 'my time is not yet come.' What does that mean? At least it certainly meant a general plan or purpose in the mind, with which certain things did or did not fit in. And if we leave out that solitary strategic plan, we not only leave out the point of the story, but the story.

We often hear of Jesus of Nazareth as a wandering teacher, and there is a vital truth in that view in so far as it emphasises an attitude towards luxury and convention which most respectable people would still regard as that of a vagabond. It is expressed in his own great saying about the holes of the foxes and the nests of the birds, and, like many of his great sayings, it is felt as less powerful than it is, through lack of appreciation of that great paradox by which he spoke of his own humanity as in some way collectively and representatively human; calling himself simply the Son of Man; that is, in effect, calling himself simply Man. It is fitting that the New Man or the Second Adam should repeat in so ringing a voice and with so arresting a gesture the great fact which came first in the original story, that man differs from the brutes by everything, even by deficiency; that he is in a sense less normal and even less native; a stranger upon the earth. It is well to speak of his wanderings in this sense and in the sense that he shared the drifting life of the most homeless and hopeless of the poor. It is assuredly well to remember that he would quite certainly have been moved on by the police and almost certainly arrested by the police for having no visible means of subsistence. For our law has in it a turn of humour or touch of fancy which Nero and Herod never happened to think of, that of actually punishing homeless people for not sleeping at home.

But in another sense the word 'wandering' as applied to his life is a little misleading. As a matter of fact, a great many of the pagan sages and not a few of the pagan sophists might truly be described as wandering teachers. In some of them their rambling journeys were not altogether without a parallel in their rambling remarks. Apollonius of Tyana, who figured in some fashionable cults as a sort of ideal philosopher, is represented as rambling as far as the Ganges and Ethiopia, more or less talking all the time. There was actually a school of philosophers called the Peripatetics; and most even of the great philosophers give us a vague impression of having very little to do except to walk and talk. The great conversations which give us our glimpses of the great minds of Socrates or Buddha or even Confucius often seem to be parts of a never-ending picnic; and especially, which is the important point, to have neither beginning nor end. Socrates did indeed find the conversation interrupted by the incident of his execution. But it is the whole point and the whole particular merit, of the position of Socrates that death was only an interruption and an incident. We miss the real moral importance of the great philosopher if we miss that point; that he stares at the executioner with an innocent surprise, and almost an innocent annoyance, at finding anyone so unreasonable as to cut short a little conversation for the elucidation of truth. He is looking for truth and not looking for death. Death is but a stone in the road which can trip him up. His work in life is to wander on the roads of the world and talk about truth for ever. Buddha, on the other hand, did arrest attention by one gesture; it was the gesture of renunciation, and therefore in a sense of denial. But by one dramatic negation he passed into a world of negation that was not dramatic; which he would have been the first to insist was not dramatic. Here again we miss the particular moral importance of the great mystic if we do not see the distinction; that it was his whole point that he had done with drama, which consists of desire and struggle and generally of defeat and disappointment. He passes into peace and lives to instruct others how to pass into it. Henceforth his life is that of the ideal philosopher; certainly a far more really ideal philosopher than Apollonius of Tyana; but still a philosopher in the sense that it is not his business to do anything but rather to explain everything; in his case, we might almost say, mildly and softly to explore everything. For the messages are basically different. Christ said 'Seek first the kingdom, and all these things shall be added unto you.' Buddha said 'Seek first the kingdom, and then you will need none of these things.'

Now compared to these wanderers the life of Jesus went as swift and straight as a thunderbolt. It was above all things dramatic; it did above all things consist in doing something that had to be done. It emphatically would not have been done, if Jesus had walked about the world for ever doing nothing except tell the truth. And even the external movement of it must not be described as a wandering in the sense of forgetting that it was a journey. This is where it was a fulfilment of the myths rather than of the philosophies; it is a journey with a goal and an object, like Jason going to find the Golden Fleece, or Hercules the golden apples of the Hesperides. The gold that he was seeking was death. The primary thing that he was going to do was to die. He was going to do other things equally definite and objective; we might almost say equally external and material. But from first to last the most definite fact is that he is going to die. No two things could possibly be more different than the death of Socrates and the death of Christ. We are meant to feel that the death of Socrates was, from the point of view of his friends at least, a stupid muddle and miscarriage of justice interfering with the flow of a humane and lucid, I had almost said a light philosophy. We are meant to feel that Death was the bride of Christ as Poverty was the bride of St. Francis. We are meant to feel that his life was in that sense a sort of love-affair with death, a romance of the pursuit of the ultimate sacrifice. From the moment when the star goes up like a birthday rocket to the moment when the sun is extinguished like a funeral torch, the whole story moves on wings with the speed and direction of a drama, ending in an act beyond words.

Therefore the story of Christ is the story of a journey, almost in the manner of a military march; certainly in the manner of the quest of a hero moving to his achievement or his doom. It is a story that begins in the paradise of Galilee, a pastoral and peaceful land having really some hint of Eden, and gradually climbs the rising country into the mountains that are nearer to the storm-clouds and the stars, as to a Mountain of Purgatory. He may be met as if straying in strange places, or stopped on the way for discussion or dispute; but his face is set towards the mountain city. That is the meaning of that great culmination when he crested the ridge and stood at the turning of the road and suddenly cried aloud, lamenting over Jerusalem. Some light touch of that lament is in every patriotic poem; or if it is absent, the patriotism stinks with vulgarity. That is the meaning the stirring and startling incident at the gates of the Temple, when the tables were hurled like lumber down the steps, and the rich merchants driven forth with bodily blows; the incident that must be at least as much of a puzzle to the pacifists as any paradox about non resistance can be to any of the militarists. I have compared the quest to the journey of Jason, but we must never forget that in a deeper sense it is rather to be compared to the journey of Ulysses. It was not only a romance of travel but a romance of return; and of the end of a usurpation. No healthy boy reading the story regards the rout of the Ithacan suitors as anything but a happy ending. But there are doubtless some who regard the rout of the Jewish merchants and money changers with that refined repugnance which never fails to move them in the presence of violence, and especially of violence against the well-to-do. The point, here however, is that all these incidents have in them a character of mounting crisis. In other words, these incidents are not incidental. When Apollonius the ideal philosopher is brought before the judgement-seat of Domitian and vanishes by magic, the miracle is entirely incidental. It might have occurred at any time in the wandering life of the Tyanean; indeed, I believe it is doubtful in date as well as in substance. The ideal philosopher merely vanished, and resumed his ideal existence somewhere else for an indefinite period. It is characteristic of the contrast perhaps that Apollonius was supposed to have lived to an almost miraculous old age. Jesus of Nazareth was less prudent in his miracles. When Jesus was brought before the judgement-seat of Pontius Pilate, he did not vanish. It was the crisis and the goal; it was the hour and the power of darkness. It was the supremely supernatural act, of all his miraculous life, that he did not vanish.

Every attempt to amplify that story has diminished it. The task has been attempted by many men of real genius and eloquence as well as by only too many vulgar sentimentalists and self-conscious rhetoricians. The tale has been retold with patronising pathos by elegant sceptics and with fluent enthusiasm by boisterous best-sellers. It will not be retold here. The grinding power of the plain words of the Gospel story is like the power of mill-stones; and those who can read them simply enough will feel as if rocks had been rolled upon them. Criticism is only words about words; and of what use are words about such words as these? What is the use of word-painting about the dark garden filled suddenly with torchlight and furious faces? 'Are you come out with swords and staves as against a robber? All day I sat in your temple teaching, and you took me not.' Can anything be added to the massive and gathered restraint of that irony; like a great wave lifted to the sky and refusing to fall? 'Daughters of Jerusalem, weep not for me but weep for yourselves and for your children.' As the High Priest asked what further need he had of witnesses, we might well ask what further need we have of words. Peter in a panic repudiated him: 'and immediately the cock crew; and Jesus looked upon Peter, and Peter went out and wept bitterly.' Has anyone any further remarks to offer. Just before the murder he prayed for all the murderous race of men, saying, 'They know not what they do'; is there anything to say to that, except that we know as little what we say? Is there any need to repeat and spin out the story of how the tragedy trailed up the Via Dolorosa and how they threw him in haphazard with two thieves in one of the ordinary batches of execution; and how in all that horror and howling wilderness of desertion one voice spoke in homage, a startling voice from the very last place where it was looked for, the gibbet of the criminal; and he said to that nameless ruffian, 'This night shalt thou be with me in Paradise'? Is there anything to put after that but a full stop? Or is anyone prepared to answer adequately that farewell gesture to all flesh which created for his Mother a new Son?

It is more within my powers, and here more immediately to my purpose, to point out that in that scene were symbolically gathered all the human forces that have been vaguely sketched in this story. As kings and philosophers and the popular element had been symbolically present at his birth, so they were more practically concerned in his death; and with that we come face to face with the essential fact to be realised. All the great groups that stood about the Cross represent in one way or another the great historical truth of the time; that the world could not save itself. Man could do no more. Rome and Jerusalem and Athens and everything else were going down like a sea turned into a slow cataract. Externally indeed the ancient world was still at its strongest; it is always at that moment that the inmost weakness begins. But in order to understand that weakness we must repeat what has been said more than once; that it was not the weakness of a thing originally weak. It was emphatically the strength of the world that was turned to weakness and the wisdom of the world that was turned to folly.

In this story of Good Friday it is the best things in the world that are at their worst. That is what really shows us the world at its worst. It was, for instance, the priests of a true monotheism and the soldiers of an international civilisation. Rome, the legend, founded upon fallen Troy and triumphant over fallen Carthage, had stood for a heroism which was the nearest that any pagan ever came to chivalry. Rome had defended the household gods and the human decencies against the ogres of Africa and the hermaphrodite monstrosities of Greece. But in the lightning flash of this incident, we see great Rome, the imperial republic, going downward under her Lucretian doom. Scepticism has eaten away even the confident sanity of the conquerors of the world. He who is enthroned to say what is justice can only ask: 'What is truth?' So in that drama which decided the whole fate of antiquity, one of the central figures is fixed in what seems the reverse of his true role. Rome was almost another name for responsibility. Yet he stands for ever as a sort of rocking statue of the irresponsible. Man could do no more. Even the practical had become the impracticable. Standing between the pillars of his own judgement-seat, a Roman had washed his hands of the world.

There too were the priests of that pure and original truth that was behind all the mythologies like the sky behind the clouds. It was the most important truth in the world; and even that could not save the world. Perhaps there is something overpowering in pure personal theism; like seeing the sun and moon and sky come together to form one staring face. Perhaps the truth is too tremendous when not broken by some intermediaries divine or human; perhaps it is merely too pure and far away. Anyhow it could not save the world; it could not even conquer the world. There were philosophers who held it in its highest and noblest form; but they not only could not convert the world, but they never tried. You could no more fight the jungle of popular mythology with a private opinion than you could clear away a forest with a pocket-knife. The Jewish priests had guarded it jealously in the good and the bad sense. They had kept it as a gigantic secret. As savage heroes might have kept the sun in a box, they kept the Everlasting in the tabernacle. They were proud that they alone could look upon the blinding sun of a single deity; and they did not know that they had themselves gone blind. Since that day their representatives have been like blind men in broad daylight, striking to right and left with their staffs, and cursing the darkness. But there has been that in their monumental monotheism that it has at least remained like a monument, the last thing of its kind, and in a sense motionless in the more restless world which it cannot satisfy. For it is certain that for some reason it cannot satisfy. Since that day it has never been quite enough to say that God is in his heaven and all is right with the world, since the rumour that God had left his heavens to set it right.

And as it was with these powers that were good, or at least had once been good, so it was with the element which was perhaps the best, or which Christ himself seems certainly to have felt as the best. The poor to whom he preached the good news, the common people who heard him gladly, the populace that had made so many popular heroes and demigods in the old pagan world, showed also the weaknesses that were dissolving the world. They suffered the evils often seen in the mob of the city, and especially the mob of the capital, during the decline of a society. The same thing that makes the rural population live on tradition makes the urban population live on rumour. Just as its myths at the best had been irrational, so its likes and dislikes are easily changed by baseless assertion that is arbitrary without being authoritative. Some brigand or other was artificially turned into a picturesque and popular figure and run as a kind of candidate against Christ. In all this we recognise the urban population that we know, with its newspaper scares and scoops. But there was present in this ancient population an evil more peculiar to the ancient world. We have noted it already as the neglect of the individual, even of the individual voting the condemnation and still more of the individual condemned. It was the soul of the hive; a heathen thing. The cry of this spirit also was heard in that hour, 'It is well that one man die for the people.' Yet this spirit in antiquity of devotion to the city and to the state had also been in itself and in its time a noble spirit. It had its poets and its martyrs; men still to be honoured for ever. It was failing through its weakness in not seeing the separate soul of a man, the shrine of all mysticism; but it was only failing as everything else was failing. The mob went along with the Sadducees and the Pharisees, the philosophers and the moralists. It went along with the imperial magistrates and the sacred priests, the scribes and the soldiers, that the one universal human spirit might suffer a universal condemnation; that there might be one deep, unanimous chorus of approval and harmony when Man was rejected of men.

There were solitudes beyond where none shall follow. There were secrets in the inmost and invisible part of that drama that have no symbol in speech; or in any severance of a man from men. Nor is it easy for any words less stark and single-minded than those of the naked narrative even to hint at the horror of exaltation that lifted itself above the hill. Endless expositions have not come to the end of it, or even to the beginning. And if there be any sound that can produce a silence, we may surely be silent about the end and the extremity; when a cry was driven out of that darkness in words dreadfully distinct and dreadfully unintelligible, which man shall never understand in all the eternity they have purchased for him; and for one annihilating instant an abyss that is not for our thoughts had opened even in the unity of the absolute; and God had been forsaken of God.

They took the body down from the cross and one of the few rich men among the first Christians obtained permission to bury it in a rock tomb in his garden; the Romans setting a military guard lest there should be some riot and attempt to recover the body. There was once more a natural symbolism in these natural proceedings; it was well that the tomb should be sealed with all the secrecy of ancient eastern sepulture and guarded by the authority of the Caesars. For in that second cavern the whole of that great and glorious humanity which we call antiquity was gathered up and covered over; and in that place it was buried. It was the end of a very great thing called human history; the history that was merely human. The mythologies and the philosophies were buried there, the gods and the heroes and the sages. In the great Roman phrase, they had lived. But as they could only live, so they could only die; and they were dead.

On the third day the friends of Christ coming at daybreak to the place found the grave empty and the stone rolled away. In varying ways they realised the new wonder; but even they hardly realised that the world had died in the night. What they were looking at was the first day of a new creation, with a new heaven and a new earth; and in a semblance of the gardener God walked again in the garden, in the cool not of the evening but the dawn.

IV THE WITNESS OF THE HERETICS

Christ founded the Church with two great figures of speech; in the final words to the Apostles who received authority to found it. The first was the phrase about founding it on Peter as on a rock; the second was the symbol of the keys. About the meaning of the former there is naturally no doubt in my own case; but it does not directly affect the argument here save in two more secondary aspects. It is yet another example of a thing that could only fully expand and explain itself afterwards, and even long afterwards. And it is yet another example of something the very reverse of simple and self-evident even in the language, in so far as it described a man as a rock when he had much more the appearance of a reed.

But the other image of the keys has an exactitude that has hardly been exactly noticed. The keys have been conspicuous enough in the art and heraldry of Christendom; but not everyone has noted the peculiar aptness of the allegory. We have now reached the point in history where something must be said of the first appearance and activities of the Church in the Roman Empire; and for that brief description nothing could be more perfect than that ancient metaphor. The Early Christian was very precisely a person carrying about a key, or what he said was a key. The whole Christian movement consisted in claiming to possess that key. It was not merely a vague forward movement, which might be better represented by a battering-ram. It was not something that swept along with it similar or dissimilar things, as does a modern social movement. As we shall see in a moment, it rather definitely refused to do so. It definitely asserted that there was a key and that it possessed that key and that no other key was like it; in that sense it was as narrow as you please. Only it happened to be the key that could unlock the prison of the whole world; and let in the white daylight of liberty.

The creed was like a key in three respects; which can be most conveniently summed up under this symbol. First, a key is above all things a thing with a shape It is a thing that depends entirely upon keeping its shape. The Christian creed is above all things the philosophy of shapes and the enemy of shapelessness. That is where it differs from all that formless infinity, Manichean or Buddhist, which makes a sort of pool of night in the dark heart of Asia; the ideal of uncreating all the creatures. That is where it differs also from the analogous vagueness of mere evolutionism, the idea of creatures constantly losing their shape. A man told that his solitary latchkey had been melted down with a million others into a Buddhistic unity would be annoyed. But a man told that his key was gradually growing and sprouting in his pocket, and branching into new wards or complications, would not be more gratified.

Second, the shape of a key is in itself a rather fantastic shape. A savage who did not know it was a key would have the greatest difficulty in guessing what it could possibly be. And it is fantastic because it is in a sense arbitrary. A key is not a matter of abstractions; in that sense a key is not a matter of argument. It either fits the lock or it does not. It is useless for men to stand disputing over it, considered by itself; or reconstructing it on pure principles of geometry or decorative art. It is senseless for a man to say he would like a simple key; it would be far more sensible to do his best with a crowbar. And thirdly, as the key is necessarily a thing with a pattern, so this was one having in some ways a rather elaborate pattern. When people complain of the religion being so early complicated with theology and things of the kind, they forget that the world had not only got into a hole, but had got into a whole maze of holes and corners. The problem itself was a complicated problem; it did not in the ordinary sense merely involve anything so simple as sin. It was also full of secrets, of unexplored and unfathomable fallacies, of unconscious mental diseases, of dangers in all directions. If the faith had faced the world only with the platitudes about peace and simplicity some moralists would confine it to, it would not have had the faintest effect on that luxurious and labyrinthine lunatic asylum. What it did do we must now roughly describe; it is enough to say here that there was undoubtedly much about the key that seemed complex, indeed there was only one thing about it that was simple. It opened the door.

There are certain recognised and accepted statements in this matter which may for brevity and convenience be described as lies. We have all heard people say that Christianity arose in an age of barbarism. They might just as well say that Christian Science arose in an age of barbarism. They may think Christianity was a symptom of social decay, as I think Christian Science a symptom of mental decay. They may think Christianity a superstition that ultimately destroyed a civilisation, as I think Christian Science a superstition capable (if taken seriously) of destroying any number of civilisations. But to say that a Christian of the fourth or fifth centuries was a barbarian living in a barbarous time is exactly like saying that Mrs. Eddy was a Red Indian. And if I allowed my constitutional impatience with Mrs. Eddy to impel me to call her a Red Indian, I should incidentally be telling a lie. We may like or dislike the imperial civilisation of Rome in the fourth century; we may like or dislike the industrial civilisation of America in the nineteenth century; but that they both were what we commonly mean by a civilisation no person of commonsense could deny if he wanted to. This is a very obvious fact but it is also a very fundamental one; and we must make it the foundation of any further description of constructive Christianity in the past. For good or evil, it was pre-eminently the product of a civilised age, perhaps of an over-civilised age. This is the first fact apart from all praise or blame; indeed I am so unfortunate as not to feel that I praise a thing when I compare it to Christian Science. But it is at least desirable to know something of the savour of a society in which we are condemning or praising anything; and the science that connects Mrs. Eddy with tomahawks or the Mater Dolorosa with totems may for our general convenience be eliminated. The dominant fact, not merely about the Christian religion, but about the whole pagan civilisation, was that which has been more than once repeated in these pages. The Mediterranean was a lake in the real sense of a pool; in which a number of different cults or cultures were, as the phrase goes, pooled. Those cities facing each other round the circle of the lake became more and more one cosmopolitan culture. On its legal and military side it was the Roman Empire, but it was very many-sided. It might be called superstitious in the sense that it contained a great number of varied superstitions; but by no possibility can any part of it be called barbarous.

In this level of cosmopolitan culture arose the Christian religion and the Catholic Church; and everything in the story suggests that it was felt to be something new and strange. Those who have tried to suggest that it evolved out of something much milder or more ordinary have found that in this case their evolutionary method is very difficult to apply. They may suggest that Essenes or Ebionites or such things were the seed; but the seed is invisible; the tree appears very rapidly full-grown; and the tree is something totally different. It is certainly a Christmas tree in the sense that it keeps the kindliness and moral beauty of the story of Bethlehem; but it was as ritualistic as the seven-branched candlestick, and the candles it carried were considerably more than were probably permitted by the first prayer-book of Edward the Sixth. It might well be asked, indeed, why any one accepting the Bethlehem tradition should object to golden or gilded ornament since the Magi themselves brought gold, why he should dislike incense in the church since incense was brought even to the stable. But these are controversies that do not concern me here. I am concerned only with the historical fact, more and more admitted by historians, that very early in its history this thing became visible to the civilisation of antiquity; and that already the Church appeared as a Church; with everything that is implied in a Church and much that is disliked in a Church. We will discuss in a moment how far it was like other ritualistic or magical or ascetical mysteries in its own time. It was certainly not in the least like merely ethical and idealistic movements in our time. It had a doctrine; it had a discipline; it had sacraments; it had degrees of initiation, it admitted people and expelled people; it affirmed one dogma with authority and repudiated another with anathemas. If all these things be the marks of Antichrist, the reign of Antichrist followed very rapidly upon Christ.

Those who maintain that Christianity was not a Church but a moral movement of idealists have been forced to push the period of its perversion or disappearance further and further back. A bishop of Rome writes claiming authority in the very lifetime of St. John the Evangelist; and it is described as the first papal aggression. A friend of the Apostles writes of them as men he knew and says they taught him the doctrine of the Sacrament, and Mr. Wells can only murmur that the reaction towards barbaric blood-rites may have happened rather earlier than might be expected. The date of the Fourth Gospel, which at one time was steadily growing later and later, is now steadily growing earlier and earlier; until critics are staggered at the dawning and dreadful possibility that it might be something like what it professes to be. The last limit of an early date for the extinction of true Christianity has probably been found by the latest German professor whose authority is invoked by Dean Inge. This learned scholar says that Pentecost was the occasion for the first founding of an ecclesiastical, dogmatic, and despotic Church utterly alien to the simple ideals of Jesus of Nazareth. This may be called, in a popular as well as a learned sense, the limit. What do professors of this kind imagine that men are made of? Suppose it were a matter of any merely human movement, let us say that of the conscientious objectors. Some say the early Christians were Pacifists; I do not believe it for a moment; but I am quite ready to accept the parallel for the sake of the argument. Tolstoy or some great preacher of peace among peasants has been shot as a mutineer for defying conscription; and a little while afterwards his few followers meet together in an upper room in remembrance of him. They never had any reason for coming together except that common memory; they are men of many kinds with nothing to bind them, except that the greatest event in all their lives was this tragedy of the teacher of universal peace. They are always repeating his words, revolving his problems, trying to imitate his character. The Pacifists meet at their Pentecost and are possessed of a sudden ecstasy of enthusiasm and wild rush of the whirlwind of inspiration, in the course of which they proceed to establish universal Conscription, to increase the Navy Estimates, to insist on everybody going about armed to the teeth and on all the frontiers bristling with artillery; the proceedings concluded with the singing of 'Boys of the Bulldog Breed' and 'Don't let them scrap the British Navy.' That is something like a fair parallel to the theory of these critics; that the transition from their idea of Jesus to their idea of Catholicism could have been made in the little upper room at Pentecost. Surely anybody's commonsense would tell him that enthusiasts who only met through their common enthusiasm for a leader whom they loved, would not instantly rush away to establish everything that he hated. No, if the 'ecclesiastical and dogmatic system' is as old as Pentecost it is as old as Christmas. If we trace it back to such very early Christians we must trace it back to Christ.

We may begin then with these two negations. It is nonsense to say that the Christian faith appeared in a simple age; in the sense of an unlettered and gullible age. It is equally nonsense to say that the Christian faith was a simple thing; in the sense of a vague or childish or merely instinctive thing. Perhaps the only point in which we could possibly say that the Church fitted into the pagan world, is the fact that they were both not only highly civilised but rather complicated. They were both emphatically many-sided; but antiquity was then a many-sided hole, like a hexagonal hole waiting for an equally hexagonal stopper. In that sense only the Church was many-sided enough to fit the world. The six sides of the Mediterranean world faced each other across the sea and waited for something that should look all ways at once. The Church had to be both Roman and Greek and Jewish and African and Asiatic. In the very words of the Apostle of the Gentiles, it was indeed all things to all men. Christianity then was not merely crude and simple and was the very reverse of the growth of a barbaric time. But when we come to the contrary charge, we come to a much more plausible charge. It is very much more tenable that the Faith was but the final phase of the decay of civilisation, in the sense of the excess of civilisation; that this superstition was a sign that Rome was dying, and dying of being much too civilised. That is an argument much better worth considering; and we will proceed to consider it.

At the beginning of this book I ventured on a general summary of it, in a parallel between the rise of humanity out of nature and the rise of Christianity out of history. I pointed out that in both cases what had gone before might imply something coming after; but did not in the least imply what did come after. If a detached mind had seen certain apes it might have deduced more anthropoids; it would not have deduced man or anything within a thousand miles of what man has done. In short, it might have seen Pithecanthropus or the Missing Link looming in the future, if possible almost as dimly and doubtfully as we see him looming in the past. But if it foresaw him appearing it would also foresee him disappearing, and leaving a few faint traces just as he has left a few faint traces; if they are traces. To foresee that Missing Link would not be to foresee Man, or anything like Man. Now this earlier explanation must be kept in mind; because it is an exact parallel to the true view of the Church; and the suggestion of it having evolved naturally out of the Empire in decay.

The truth is that in one sense a man might very well have predicted that the imperial decadence would produce something like Christianity. That is, something a little like and gigantically different. A man might very well have said, for instance, 'Pleasure has been pursued so extravagantly that there will be a reaction into pessimism. Perhaps it will take the form of asceticism; men will mutilate themselves instead of merely hanging themselves.' Or a man might very reasonably have said, 'If we weary of our Greek and Latin gods we shall be hankering after some eastern mystery or other; there will be a fashion in Persians or Hindoos.' Or a man of the world might well have been shrewd enough to say, 'Powerful people are picking up these fads; some day the court will adopt one of them and it may become official.' Or yet another and gloomier prophet might be pardoned for saying, 'The world is going down-hill; dark and barbarous superstitions will return, it does not matter much which. They will all be formless and fugitive like dreams of the night.'

Now it is the intense interest of the case that all these prophecies were really fulfilled; but it was not the Church that fulfilled them. It was the Church that escaped from them, confounded them, and rose above them in triumph. In so far as it was probable that the mere nature of hedonism would produce a mere reaction of asceticism it did produce a mere reaction of asceticism. It was the movement called Manichean and the Church was its mortal enemy. In so far as it would have naturally appeared at that point of history, it did appear; it did also disappear, which was equally natural. The mere pessimist reaction did come with the Manichees and did go with the Manichees But the Church did not come with them or go with them; and she had much more to do with them going than with their coming. Or again, in so far as it was probable that even the growth of scepticism would bring in a fashion of eastern religion, it did bring it in; Mithras came from far beyond Palestine out of the heart of Persia, bringing strange mysteries of the blood of bulls. Certainly there was everything to show that some such fashion would have come in any case but certainly there is nothing in the world to show that it would not have passed away in any case. Certainly an Oriental fad was something eminently fitted to the fourth or fifth century; but that hardly explains it having remained to the twentieth century, and still going strong. In short, in so far as things of the kind might have been expected then, things like Mithraism were experienced then; but it scarcely explains our more recent experiences. And if we were still Mithraists merely because Mithraic head-dresses and other Persian apparatuses might be expected to be all the rage in the days of Domitian, it would almost seem by this time that we must be a little dowdy.

It is the same, as will be suggested in a moment, with the idea of official favouritism. In so far as such favouritism shown towards a fad was something that might have been looked for during the decline and fall of the Roman Empire, it was something that did exist in that Empire and did decline and fall with it. It throws no sort of light on the thing that resolutely refused to decline and fall; that grew steadily while the other was declining and falling; and which even at this moment is going forward with fearless energy, when an other aeon has completed its cycle and another civilisation seems almost ready to fall or to decline.

Now the curious fact is this; that the very heresies which the early Church is blamed for crushing testify to the unfairness for which she is blamed. In so far as something deserved the blame, it was precisely the things that she is blamed for blaming. In so far as something was merely a superstition, she herself condemned that superstition. In so far as something was a mere reaction into barbarism, she herself resisted it because it was a reaction into barbarism. In so far as something was a fad of the fading empire, that died and deserved to die, it was the Church alone that killed it. The Church is reproached for being exactly what the heresy was repressed for being The explanations of the evolutionary historians and higher critics do really explain why Arianism and Gnosticism and Nestorianism were born--and also why they died. They do not explain why the Church was born or why she has refused to die. Above all, they do not explain why she should have made war on the very evils she is supposed to share.

Let us take a few practical examples of the principle; the principle that if there was anything that was really a superstition of the dying empire, it did really die with the dying empire; and certainly was not the same as the very thing that destroyed it. For this purpose we will take in order two or three of the most ordinary explanations of Christian origins among the modern critics of Christianity. Nothing is more common, for instance, than to find such a modern critic writing something like this: 'Christianity was above all a movement of ascetics, a rush into the desert, a refuge in the cloister, a renunciation of all life and happiness; and this was a part of a gloomy and in human reaction against nature itself, a hatred of the body, a horror of the material universe, a sort of universal suicide of the senses and even of the self. It came from an eastern fanaticism like that of the fakirs and was ultimately founded on an eastern pessimism, which seems to feel existence itself as an evil.'

Now the most extraordinary thing about this is that it is all quite true; it is true in every detail except that it happens to be attributed entirely to the wrong person. It is not true of the Church; but it is true of the heretics condemned by the Church. It is as if one were to write a most detailed analysis of the mistakes and misgovernment of the ministers of George the Third, merely with the small inaccuracy that the whole story was told about George Washington; or as if somebody made a list of the crimes of the Bolshevists with no variation except that they were all attributed to the Czar. The early Church was indeed very ascetic in connection with a totally different philosophy; but the philosophy of a war on life and nature as such really did exist in the world, if the critics only knew where to look for it.

What really happened was this. When the Faith first emerged into the world, the very first thing that happened to it was that it was caught in a sort of swarm of mystical and metaphysical sects, mostly out of the East; like one lonely golden bee caught in a swarm of wasps. To the ordinary onlooker, there did not seem to be much difference, or anything beyond a general buzz; indeed in a sense there was not much difference so far as stinging and being stung were concerned. The difference was that only one golden dot in all that whirring gold-dust had the power of going forth to make hives for all humanity; to give the world honey and wax or (as was so finely said in a context too easily forgotten) 'the two noblest things, which are sweetness and light.' The wasps all died that winter; and half the difficulty is that hardly anyone knows anything about them and most people do not know that they ever existed; so that the whole story of that first phase of our religion is lost. Or, to vary the metaphor, when this movement or some other movement pierced the dyke between the east and west and brought more mystical ideas into Europe, it brought with it a whole flood of other mystical ideas besides its own, most of them ascetical and nearly all of them pessimistic. They very nearly flooded and over-whelmed the purely Christian element. They came mostly from that region that was a sort of dim borderland between the eastern philosophies and the eastern mythologies, and which shared with the wilder philosophers that curious crave for making fantastic patterns of the cosmos in the shape of maps and genealogical trees. Those that are supposed to derive from the mysterious Manes are called Manichean; kindred cults are more generally known as Gnostic; they are mostly of a labyrinthine complexity, but the point to insist on is the pessimism; the fact that nearly all in one form or another regarded the creation of the world as the work of an evil spirit. Some of them had that Asiatic atmosphere that surrounds Buddhism; the suggestion that life is a corruption of the purity of being. Some of them suggested a purely spiritual order which had been betrayed by the coarse and clumsy trick of making such toys as the sun and moon and stars. Anyhow all this dark tide out of the metaphysical sea in the midst of Asia poured through the dykes simultaneously with the creed of Christ; but it is the whole point of the story that the two were not the same; that they flowed like oil and water. That creed remained in the shape of a miracle; a river still flowing through the sea. And the proof of the miracle was practical once more; it was merely that while all that sea was salt and bitter with the savour of death, of this one stream in the midst of it a man could drink.

Now that purity was preserved by dogmatic definitions and exclusions. It could not possibly have been preserved by anything else If the Church had not renounced the Manicheans it might have become merely Manichean. If it had not renounced the Gnostics it might have become Gnostic. But by the very fact that it did renounce them it proved that it was not either Gnostic or Manichean. At any rate it proved that something was not either Gnostic or Manichean; and what could it be that condemned them, if it was not the original good news of the runners from Bethlehem and the trumpet of the Resurrection? The early Church was ascetic, but she proved that she was not pessimistic, simply by condemning the pessimists. The creed declared that man was sinful, but it did not declare that life was evil, and it proved it by damning those who did. The condemnation of the early heretics is itself condemned as something crabbed and narrow; but it was in truth the very proof that the Church meant to be brotherly and broad. It proved that the primitive Catholics were specially eager to explain that they did not think man utterly vile; that they did not think life incurably miserable; that they did not think marriage a sin or procreation a tragedy. They were ascetic because asceticism was the only possible purge of the sins of the world; but in the very thunder of their anathemas they affirmed for ever that their asceticism was not to be anti-human or anti-natural; that they did wish to purge the world and not destroy it. And nothing else except those anathemas could possibly have made it clear, amid a confusion which still confuses them with their mortal enemies. Nothing else but dogma could have resisted the riot of imaginative invention with which the pessimists were waging their war against nature; with their Aeons and their Demiurge, their strange Logos and their sinister Sophia. If the Church had not insisted on theology, it would have melted into a mad mythology of the mystics, yet further removed from reason or even from rationalism; and, above all yet further removed from life and from the love of life. Remember that it would have been an inverted mythology, one contradicting everything natural in paganism; a mythology in which Pluto would be above Jupiter and Hades hang higher than Olympus; in which Brahma and all that has the breath of life would be subject to Seeva, shining with the eye of death.

That the early Church was itself full of an ecstatic enthusiasm for renunciation and virginity makes this distinction much more striking and not less so. It makes all the more important the place where the dogma drew the line. A man might crawl about on all fours like a beast because he was an ascetic. He might stand night and day on the top of a pillar and be adored for being an ascetic, but he could not say that the world was a mistake or the marriage state a sin without being a heretic. What was it that thus deliberately disengaged itself from eastern asceticism by sharp definition and fierce refusal, if it was not something with an individuality of its own; and one that was quite different? If the Catholics are to be confused with the Gnostics, we can only say it was not their fault if they are. And it is rather hard that the Catholics should be blamed by the same critics for persecuting the heretics and also for sympathising with the heresy.

The Church was not a Manichean movement if only because it was not a movement at all. It was not even merely an ascetical movement, because it was not a movement at all. It would be nearer the truth to call it the tamer of asceticism than the mere leader or loosener of it. It was a thing having its own theory of asceticism, its own type of asceticism, but most conspicuous at the moment as the moderator of other theories and types. This is the only sense that can be made, for instance, of the story of St. Augustine. As long as he was a mere man of the world, a mere man drifting with his time, he actually was a Manichean. It really was quite modern and fashionable to be a Manichean. But when he became a Catholic, the people he instantly turned on and rent in pieces were the Manicheans. The Catholic way of putting it is that he left off being a pessimist to become an ascetic. But as the pessimists interpreted asceticism, it ought to be said that he left off being an ascetic to become a saint. The war upon life, the denial of nature, were exactly the things he had already found in the heathen world outside the Church, and had to renounce when he entered the Church. The very fact that St Augustine remains a somewhat sterner or sadder figure than St. Francis or St. Teresa only accentuates the dilemma. Face to face with the gravest or even grimmest of Catholics, we can still ask, 'Why did Catholicism make war on Manichees, if Catholicism was Manichean?'

Take another rationalistic explanation of the rise of Christendom. It is common enough to find another critic saying, 'Christianity did not really rise at all; that is, it did not merely rise from below; it was imposed from above. It is an example of the power of the executive, especially in despotic states. The Empire was really an Empire; that is, it was really ruled by the Emperor. One of the Emperors happened to become a Christian. He might just as well have become a Mithraist or a Jew or a Fire-Worshipper; it was common in the decline of the Empire for eminent and educated people to adopt these eccentric eastern cults. But when he adopted it, it became the official religion of the Roman Empire; and when it became the official religion of the Roman Empire, it became as strong, as universal and as invincible as the Roman Empire. It has only remained in the world as a relic of that Empire; or, as many have put it, it is but the ghost of Caesar still hovering over Rome.' This also is a very ordinary line taken in the criticism of orthodoxy, to say that it was only officialism that ever made it orthodoxy. And here again we can call on the heretics to refute it.

The whole great history of the Arian heresy might have been invented to explode this idea. It is a very interesting history often repeated in this connection; and the upshot of it is in that in so far as there ever was a merely official religion, it actually died because it was merely an official religion; and what destroyed it was the real religion. Arius advanced a version of Christianity which moved, more or less vaguely, in the direction of what we should call Unitarianism; though it was not the same, for it gave to Christ a curious intermediary position between the divine and human. The point is that it seemed to many more reasonable and less fanatical; and among these were many of the educated class in a sort of reaction against the first romance of conversion. Arians were a sort of moderates and a sort of modernists. And it was felt that after the first squabbles this was the final form of rationalised religion into which civilisation might well settle down. It was accepted by Divus Caesar himself and became the official orthodoxy; the generals and military princes drawn from the new barbarian powers of the north, full of the future, supported it strongly. But the sequel is still more important. Exactly as a modern man might pass through Unitarianism to complete agnosticism, so the greatest of the Arian emperors ultimately shed the last and thinnest pretense of Christianity; he abandoned ever Arius and returned to Apollo. He was a Caesar of the Caesars; a soldier, a scholar, a man of large ambitions and ideals; another of the philosopher kings. It seemed to him as if at his signal the sun rose again. The oracles began to speak like birds beginning to sing at dawn; paganism was itself again; the gods returned. It seemed the end of that strange interlude of an alien superstition. And indeed it was the end of it, so far as there was a mere interlude of mere superstition. It was the end of it, in so far as it was the fad of an emperor or the fashion of a generation. If there really was something that began with Constantine, then it ended with Julian.

But there was something that did not end. There had arisen in that hour of history, defiant above the democratic tumult of the Councils of the Church, Athanasius against the world. We may pause upon the point at issue; because it is relevant to the whole of this religious history, and the modern world seems to miss the whole point of it. We might put it this way. If there is one question which the enlightened and liberal have the habit of deriding and holding up as a dreadful example of barren dogma and senseless sectarian strife, it is this Athanasian question of the Co-Eternity of the Divine Son. On the other hand, if there is one thing that the same liberals always offer us as a piece of pure and simple Christianity, untroubled by doctrinal disputes, it is the single sentence, 'God is Love.' Yet the two statements are almost identical; at least one is very nearly nonsense without the other. The barren dogma is only the logical way of stating the beautiful sentiment. For if there be a being without beginning, existing before all things, was He loving when there was nothing to be loved? If through that unthinkable eternity He is lonely, what is the meaning of saying He is love? The only justification of such a mystery is the mystical conception that in His own nature there was something analogous to self-expression; something of what begets and beholds what it has begotten. Without some such idea, it is really illogical to complicate the ultimate essence of deity with an idea like love. If the moderns really want a simple religion of love, they must look for it in the Athanasian Creed. The truth is that the trumpet of true Christianity, the challenge of the charities and simplicities of Bethlehem or Christmas Day never rang out more arrestingly and unmistakably than in the defiance of Athanasius to the cold compromise of the Arians. It was emphatically he who really was fighting for a God of Love against a God of colourless and remote cosmic control; the God of the stoics and the agnostics. It was emphatically he who was fighting for the Holy Child against the grey deity of the Pharisees and the Sadducees. He was fighting for that very balance of beautiful interdependence and intimacy, in the very Trinity of the Divine Nature, that draws our hearts to the Trinity of the Holy Family. His dogma, if the phrase be not misunderstood, turns even God into a Holy Family.

That this purely Christian dogma actually for a second time rebelled against the Empire, and actually for a second time refounded the Church in spite of the

Empire, is itself a proof that there was something positive and personal working in the world, other than whatever official faith the Empire chose to adopt. This power utterly destroyed the official faith that the Empire did adopt. It went on its own way as it is going on its own way still. There are any number of other examples in which is repeated precisely the same process we have reviewed in the case of the Manichean and the Arian. A few centuries afterwards, for instance, the Church had to maintain the same Trinity, which is simply the logical side of love, against another appearance of the isolated and simplified deity in the religion of Islam. Yet there are some who cannot see what the Crusaders were fighting for; and some even who talk as if Christianity had never been anything but a form of what they call Hebraism coming in with the decay of Hellenism. Those people must certainly be very much puzzled by the war between the Crescent and the Cross. If Christianity had never been anything but a simpler morality sweeping away polytheism, there is no reason why Christendom should not have been swept into Islam. The truth is that Islam itself was a barbaric reaction against that very humane complexity that is really a Christian character; that idea of balance in the deity, as of balance in the family, that makes that creed a sort of sanity, and that sanity the soul of civilisation. And that is why the Church is from the first a thing holding its own position and point of view, quite apart from the accidents and anarchies of its age. That is why it deals blows impartially right and left, at the pessimism of the Manichean or the optimism of the Pelagian. It was not a Manichean movement because it was not a movement at all. It was not an official fashion because it was not a fashion at all. It was something that could coincide with movements and fashions, could control them and could survive them.

So might rise from their graves the great heresiarchs to confound their comrades of to-day. There is nothing that the critics now affirm that we cannot call on these great witnesses to deny. The modern critic will say lightly enough that Christianity was but a reaction into asceticism and anti-natural spirituality, a dance of fakirs furious against life and love. But Manes the great mystic will answer them from his secret throne and cry, 'These Christians have no right to be called spiritual; these Christians have no title to be called ascetics, they who compromised with the curse of life and all the filth of the family. Through them the earth is still foul with fruit and harvest and polluted with population Theirs was no movement against nature, or my children would have carried it to triumph; but these fools renewed the world when I would have ended it with a gesture.' And another critic will write that the Church was but the shadow of the Empire, the fad of a chance Emperor, and that it remains in Europe only as the ghost of the power of Rome. And Arius the deacon will answer out of the darkness of oblivious 'No, indeed, or the world would have followed my more reasonable religion. For mine went down before demagogues and men defying Caesar; and around my champion was the purple cloak and mine was the glory of the eagles. It was not for lack of these things that I failed. And yet a third modern will maintain that the creed spread only as a sort of panic of hell-fire; men everywhere attempting impossible things in fleeing from incredible vengeance; a nightmare of imaginary remorse; and such an explanation will satisfy many who see something dreadful in the doctrine of orthodoxy. And then there will go up against it the terrible voice of Tertullian, saying, 'And why then was I cast out; and why did soft hearts and heads decide against me when I proclaimed the perdition of all sinners; and what was this power that thwarted me when I threatened all backsliders with hell? For none ever went up that hard road so far as I; and mine was the Credo Quia Impossible.' Then there is the fourth suggestion that there was something of the Semitic secret society in the whole matter; that it was a new invasion of the nomad spirit shaking a kindlier and more comfortable paganism, its cities and its household gods; whereby the jealous monotheistic races could after all establish their jealous God. And Mahomet shall answer out of the whirlwind, the red whirlwind of the desert, 'Who ever served the jealousy of God as I did or left him more lonely in the sky? Who ever paid more honour to Moses and Abraham or won more victories over idols and the images of paganism? And what was this thing that thrust me back with the energy of a thing alive; whose fanaticism could drive me from Sicily and tear up my deep roots out of the rock of Spain? What faith was theirs who thronged in thousands of every class a country crying out that my ruin was the will of God; and what hurled great Godfrey as from a catapult over the wall of Jerusalem, and what brought great Sobieski like a thunderbolt to the gates of Vienna? I think there was more than you fancy in the religion that has so matched itself with mine.'

Those who would suggest that the faith was a fanaticism are doomed to an eternal perplexity. In their account it is bound to appear as fanatical for nothing, and fanatical against everything. It is ascetical and at war with ascetics, Roman and in revolt against Rome, monotheistic and fighting furiously against monotheism; harsh in its condemnation of harshness; a riddle not to be explained even as unreason. And what sort of unreason is it that seems reasonable to millions of educated Europeans through all the revolutions of some sixteen hundred years? People are not amused with a puzzle or a paradox or a mere muddle in the mind for all that time. I know of no explanation except that such a thing is not unreason but reason; that if it is fanatical it is fanatical for reason and fanatical against all the unreasonable things. That is the only explanation I can find of a thing from the first so detached and so confident, condemning things that looked so like itself, refusing help from powers that seemed so essential to its existence, sharing on its human side all the passions of the age, yet always at the supreme moment suddenly rising superior to them, never saying exactly what it was expected to say and never needing to unsay what it had said; I can find no explanation except that, like Pallas from the brain of Jove, it had indeed come forth out of the mind of God, mature and mighty and armed for judgement and for war.

V THE ESCAPE FROM PAGANISM

The modern missionary, with his palm-leaf hat and his umbrella, has become rather a figure of fun. He is chaffed among men of the world for the ease with which he can be eaten by cannibals and the narrow bigotry which makes him regard the cannibal culture as lower than his own. Perhaps the best part of the joke is that the men of the world do not see that the joke is against themselves. It is rather ridiculous to ask a man just about to be boiled in a pot and eaten, at a purely religious feast, why he does not regard all religions as equally friendly and fraternal. But there is a more subtle criticism uttered against the more old-fashioned missionary; to the effect that he generalises too broadly about the heathen and pays too little attention to the difference between Mahomet and Mumbo-Jumbo. There was probably truth in this complaint, especially in the past; but it is my main contention here that the exaggeration is all the other way at present. It is the temptation of the professors to treat mythologies too much as theologies; as things thoroughly thought out are seriously held. It is the temptation of the intellectuals to take much too seriously the fine shades of various schools in the rather irresponsible metaphysics of Asia. Above all it is their temptation to miss the real truth implied in the idea of Aquinas contra Gentiles or Athanasius contra mundum.

If the missionary says, in fact, that he is exceptional in being a Christian, and that the rest of the races and religions can be collectively classified as heathen, he is perfectly right. He may say it in quite the wrong spirit, in which case he is spiritually wrong. But in the cold light of philosophy and history, he is intellectually right. He may not be right minded, but he is right. He may not even have a right to be right, but he is right. The outer world to which he brings his creed really is some thing subject to certain generalisations covering all its varieties, and is not merely a variety of similar creeds. Perhaps it is in any case too much of a temptation to pride or hypocrisy to call it heathenry. Perhaps it could be better simply to call it humanity. But there are certain broad characteristics of what we call humanity while it remains in what we call heathenry. They are not necessarily bad characteristics; some of them are worthy of the respect of Christendom; some of them have been absorbed and transfigured in the substance of Christendom. But they existed before Christendom and they still exist outside Christendom, as certainly as the sea existed before a boat and all round a boat; and they have as strong and as universal and as unmistakable a savour as the sea.

For instance, all real scholars who have studied the Greek and Roman culture say one thing about it. They agree that in the ancient world religion was one thing and philosophy quite another, there was very little effort to rationalise and at the same time to realise a real belief in the gods. There was very little pretense of any such real belief among the philosophers. But neither had the passion or perhaps the power to persecute the others save in particular and peculiar cases; and neither the philosopher in his school nor the priest in his temple seems ever to have seriously contemplated his own concept as covering the world. A priest sacrificing to Artemis in Calydon did not seem to think that people would some day sacrifice to her instead of to Isis beyond the sea; a sage following the vegetarian rule of the Neo-Pythagoreans did not seem to think it would universally prevail and exclude the methods of Epictetus or Epicurus. We may call this liberality if we like; I am not dealing with an argument but describing an atmosphere. All this, I say, is admitted by all scholars; but what neither the learned nor the unlearned have fully realised, perhaps, is that this description is really an exact description of all non-Christian civilisation today; and especially of the great civilisations of the East. Eastern paganism really is much more all of a piece, just as ancient paganism was much more all of a piece, than the modern critics admit. It is a many-coloured Persian Carpet as the other was a varied and tessellated Roman pavement; but the one real crack right across that pavement came from the earthquake of the Crucifixion.

The modern European seeking his religion in Asia is reading his religion into Asia. Religion there is something different; it is both more and less. He is like a man mapping out the sea as land; marking waves as mountains; not understanding the nature of its peculiar permanence. It is perfectly true that Asia has its own dignity and poetry and high civilisation. But it is not in the least true that Asia has its own definite dominions of moral government, where all loyalty is conceived in terms of morality; as when we say that Ireland is Catholic or that New England was Puritan. The map is not marked out in religions, in our sense of churches. The state of mind is far more subtle, more relative, more secretive, more varied and changing, like the colours of the snake. The Moslem is the nearest approach to a militant Christian; and that is precisely because he is a much nearer approach to an envoy from western civilisation. The Moslem in the heart of Asia almost stands for the soul of Europe. And as he stands between them and Europe in the matter of space so he stands between them and Christianity in the matter of time. In that sense the Moslems in Asia are merely like the Nestorians in Asia. Islam, historically speaking, is the greatest of the Eastern heresies. It owed something to the quite isolated and unique individuality of Israel; but it owed more to Byzantium and the theological enthusiasm of Christendom. It owed something even to the Crusades. It owed nothing whatever to Asia. It owed nothing to the atmosphere of the ancient and traditional world of Asia, with its immemorial etiquette and its bottomless or bewildering philosophies. All that ancient and actual Asia felt the entrance of Islam as something foreign and western and warlike, piercing it like a spear.

Even where we might trace in dotted lines the domains of Asiatic religions, we should probably be reading into them something dogmatic and ethical belonging to our own religion. It is as if a European ignorant of the American atmosphere were to suppose that each 'state' was a separate sovereign state as patriotic as France or Poland; or that when a Yankee referred fondly to his 'home town' he meant he had no other nation, like a citizen of ancient Athens or Rome. As he would be reading a particular sort of loyalty into America, so we are reading a particular sort of loyalty into Asia. There are loyalties of other kinds; but not what men in the West mean by being a believer, by trying to be a Christian, by being a good Protestant or a practising Catholic. In the intellectual world it means something far more vague and varied by doubts and speculations. In the moral world it means something far more loose and drifting. A professor of Persian at one of our great universities, so passionate a partisan of the East as practically to profess a contempt for the West, said to a friend of mine: 'You will never understand oriental religions, because you always conceive religion as connected with ethics. This kind has really nothing to do with ethics.' We have most of us known some Masters of the Higher Wisdom, some Pilgrims upon the Path to Power, some eastern esoteric saints and seers, who had really nothing to do with ethics. Something different, something detached and irresponsible, tinges the moral atmosphere of Asia and touches even that of Islam. It was very realistically caught in the atmosphere of Hassan; and a very horrible atmosphere too. It is even more vivid in such glimpses as we get of the genuine and ancient cults of Asia. Deeper than the depths of metaphysics, far down in the abysses of mystical meditations under all that solemn universe of spiritual things, is a secret, an intangible and a terrible levity. It does not really very much matter what one does. Either because they do not believe in a devil, or because they do believe in a destiny, or because experience here is everything and eternal life something totally different, but for some reason they are totally different. I have read somewhere that there were three great friends famous in medieval Persia for their unity of mind. One became the responsible and respected Vizier of the Great King; the second was the poet Omar, pessimist and epicurean, drinking wine in mockery of Mahomet; the third was the Old Man of the Mountain who maddened his people with hashish that they might murder other people with daggers. It does not really much matter what one does.

The Sultan in Hassan would have understood all those three men; indeed he was all those three men. But this sort of universalist cannot have what we call a character; it is what we call a chaos. He cannot choose; he cannot fight; he cannot repent; he cannot hope. He is not in the same sense creating something; for creation means rejection. He is not, in our religious phrase, making his soul. For our doctrine of salvation does really mean a labour like that of a man trying to make a statue beautiful; a victory with wings. For that there must be a final choice, for a man cannot make statues without rejecting stone. And there really is this ultimate unmorality behind the metaphysics of Asia. And the reason is that there has been nothing through all those unthinkable ages to bring the human mind sharply to the point; to tell it that the time has come to choose. The mind has lived too much in eternity. The soul has been too immortal, in the special sense that it ignores the idea of mortal sin. It has had too much of eternity, in the sense that it has not had enough of the hour of death and the day of judgement. It is not crucial enough; in the literal sense that it has not had enough of the cross. That is what we mean when we say that Asia is very old. But strictly speaking Europe is quite as old as Asia; indeed in a sense any place is as old as any other place. What we mean is that Europe has not merely gone on growing older. It has been born again.

Asia is all humanity; as it has worked out its human doom. Asia, in its vast territory, in its varied populations, in its heights of past achievement and its depths of dark speculation, is itself a world; and represents something of what we mean when we speak of the world. It is a cosmos rather than a continent. It is the world as man has made it; and contains many of the most wonderful things that man has made. Therefore Asia stands as the one representative of paganism and the one rival to Christendom. But everywhere else where we get glimpses of that mortal destiny, they suggest stages in the same story. Where Asia trails away into the southern archipelagoes of the savages, or where a darkness full of nameless shapes dwells in the heart of Africa, or where the last survivors of lost races linger in the cold volcano of prehistoric America, it is all the same story; sometimes perhaps later chapters of the same story. It is men entangled in the forest of their own mythology; it is men drowned in the sea of their own metaphysics. Polytheists have grown weary of the wildest of fictions. Monotheists have grown weary of the most wonderful of truths. Diabolists here and there have such a hatred of heaven and earth that they have tried to take refuge in hell. It is the Fall of Man; and it is exactly that fall that was being felt by our own fathers at the first moment of the Roman decline. We also were going down that side road; down that easy slope; following the magnificent procession of the high civilisations of the world.

If the Church had not entered the world then, it seems probable that Europe would be now very much what Asia is now. Something may be allowed for a real difference of race and environment, visible in the ancient as in the modern world. But after all we talk about the changeless East very largely because it has not suffered the great change. Paganism in its last phase showed considerable signs of be coming equally changeless. This would not mean that new schools or sects of philosophy would not arise; as new schools did arise in Antiquity and do arise in Asia. It does not mean that there would be no real mystics or visionaries; as there were mystics in Antiquity and are mystics in Asia. It does not mean that there would be no social codes, as there were codes in Antiquity and are codes in Asia. It does not mean that there could not be good men or happy lives, for God has given all men a conscience and conscience can give all men a kind of peace. But it does mean that the tone and proportion of all these things, and especially the proportion of good and evil things, would be in the unchanged West what they are in the changeless East. And nobody who looks at that changeless East honestly, and with a real sympathy, can believe that there is anything there remotely resembling the challenge and revolution of the Faith.

In short, if classic paganism had lingered until now, a number of things might well have lingered with it; and they would look very like what we call the religions of the East. There would still be Pythagoreans teaching reincarnation, as there are still Hindus teaching reincarnation. There would still be Stoics making a religion out of reason and virtue, as there are still Confucians making a religion out of reason and virtue. There would still be Neo-Platonists studying transcendental truths, the meaning of which was mysterious to other people and disputed even amongst themselves; as the Buddhists still study a transcendentalism mysterious to others and disputed among themselves. There would still be intelligent Apollonians apparently worshipping the sun-god but explaining that they were worshipping the divine principle; just as there are still intelligent Parsees apparently worshipping the sun but explaining that they are worshipping the deity. There would still be wild Dionysians dancing on the mountain as there are still wild Dervishes dancing in the desert. There would still be crowds of people attending the popular feasts of the gods, in pagan Europe as in pagan Asia. There would still be crowds of gods, local and other, for them to worship. And there would still be a great many more people who worshipped them than people who believed in them. Finally there would still be a very large number of people who did worship gods and did believe in gods; and who believed in gods and worshipped gods simply because they were demons. There would still be Levantines secretly sacrificing to Moloch as there are still Thugs secretly sacrificing to Kalee. There would still be a great deal of magic; and a great deal of it would be black magic. There would still be a considerable admiration of Seneca and a considerable imitation of Nero; just as the exalted epigrams of Confucius could coexist with the tortures of China. And over all that tangled forest of traditions growing wild or withering would brood the broad silence of a singular and even nameless mood; but the nearest name of it is nothing. All these things, good and bad, would have an indescribable air of being too old to die.

None of these things occupying Europe in the absence of Christendom would bear the least likeness to Christendom. Since the Pythagorean Metempsychosis would still be there, we might call it the Pythagorean religion as we talk about the Buddhist religion. As the noble maxims of Socrates would still be there, we might call it the Socratic religion as we talk about the Confucian religion. As the popular holiday was still marked by a mythological hymn to Adonis, we might call it the religion of Adonis as we talk about the religion of Juggernaut. As literature would still be based on the Greek mythology, we might call that mythology a religion, as we call the Hindu mythology a religion. We might say that there were so many thousands or millions of people belonging to that religion, in the sense of frequenting such temples or merely living in a land full of such temples. But if we called the last tradition of Pythagoras or the lingering legend of Adonis by the name of a religion, then we must find some other name for the Church of Christ.

If anybody says that philosophic maxims presented through many ages, or mythological temples frequented by many people, are things of the same class and category as the Church, it is enough to answer quite simply that they are not. Nobody thinks they are the same when he sees them in the old civilisation of Greece and Rome; nobody would think they were the same if that civilisation had lasted two thousand years longer and existed at the present day; nobody can in reason think they are the same in the parallel pagan civilisation in the East, as it is at the present day. None of these philosophies or mythologies are anything like a Church; certainly nothing like a Church Militant. And, as I have shown elsewhere, even if this rule were not already proved, the exception would prove the rule. The rule is that pre-Christian or pagan history does not produce a Church Militant; and the exception, or what some would call the exception, is that Islam is at least militant if it is not Church. And that is precisely because Islam is the one religious rival that is not pre-Christian and therefore not in that sense pagan. Islam was a product of Christianity; even if it was a by-product; even if it was a bad product. It was a heresy or parody emulating and therefore imitating the Church. It is no more surprising that Mahomedanism had something of her fighting spirit than that Quakerism had something of her peaceful spirit. After Christianity there are any number of such emulations or extensions. Before it there are none.

The Church Militant is thus unique because it is an army marching to effect a universal deliverance. The bondage from which the world is thus to be delivered is something that is very well symbolised by the state of Asia as by the state of pagan Europe. I do not mean merely their moral or immoral state. The missionary, as a matter of fact, has much more to say for himself than the enlightened imagine even when he says that the heathen are idolatrous and immoral. A touch or two of realistic experience about Eastern religion, even about Moslem religion, will reveal some startling insensibilities in ethics; such as the practical indifference to the line between passion and perversion. It is not prejudice but practical experience which says that Asia is full of demons as well as gods. But the evil I mean is in the mind. And it is in the mind wherever the mind has worked for a long time alone. It is what happens when all dreaming and thinking have come to an end in an emptiness that is at once negation and necessity. It sounds like an anarchy, but it is also a slavery. It is what has been called already the wheel of Asia; all those recurrent arguments about cause and effect or things beginning and ending in the mind, which make it impossible for the soul really to strike out and go anywhere or do anything. And the point is that it is not necessarily peculiar to Asiatics; it would have been true in the end of Europeans--if something had not happened. If the Church Militant had not been a thing marching, all men would have been marking time. If the Church Militant had not endured a discipline, all men would have endured a slavery.

What that universal yet fighting faith brought into the world was hope. Perhaps the one thing common to mythology and philosophy was that both were really sad; in the sense that they had not this hope even if they had touches of faith or charity. We may call Buddhism a faith; though to us it seems more like a doubt. We may call the Lord of Compassion a Lord of Charity, though it seems to us a very pessimist sort of pity. But those who insist most on the antiquity and size of such cults must agree that in all their ages they have not covered all their areas with that sort of practical and pugnacious hope. In Christendom hope has never been absent; rather it has been errant, extravagant, excessively fixed upon fugitive chances. Its perpetual revolution and reconstruction has at least been an evidence of people being in better spirits. Europe did very truly renew its youth like the eagles; just as the eagles of Rome rose again over the legions of Napoleon, or we have seen soaring but yesterday the silver eagle of Poland. But in the Polish case ever revolution always went with religion. Napoleon himself sought a reconciliation with religion. Religion could never be finally separated even from the most hostile of the hopes; simply because it was the very source of the hopefulness. And the cause of this is to be found simply in the religion itself. Those who quarrel about it seldom even consider it in itself. There is neither space nor place for such a full consideration here; but a word may be said to explain a reconciliation that always recurs and still seems to require explanation.

There will be no end to the weary debates about liberalising theology, until people face the fact that the only liberal part of it is really the dogmatic part. If dogma is incredible, it is because it is incredibly liberal. If it is irrational, it can only be in giving us more assurance of freedom than is justified by reason. The obvious example is that essential form of freedom which we call free-will. It is absurd to say that a man shows his liberality in denying his liberty. But it is tenable that he has to affirm a transcendental doctrine in order to affirm his liberty. There is a sense in which we might reasonably say that if man has a primary power of choice, he has in that fact a super-natural power of creation, as if he could raise the dead or give birth to the unbegotten. Possibly in that case a man must be a miracle; and certainly in that case he must be a miracle in order to be a man; and most certainly in order to be a free man. But it is absurd to forbid him to be a free man and do it in the name of a more free religion.

But it is true in twenty other matters. Anybody who believes at all in God must believe in the absolute supremacy of God. But in so far as that supremacy does allow of any degrees that can be called liberal or illiberal, it is self-evident that the illiberal power is the deity of the rationalists and the liberal power is the deity of the dogmatists. Exactly in proportion as you turn monotheism into monism you turn it into despotism. It is precisely the unknown God of the scientist, with his impenetrable purpose and his inevitable and unalterable law, that reminds us of a Prussian autocrat making rigid plans in a remote tent and moving mankind like machinery. It is precisely the God of miracles and of answered prayers who reminds us of a liberal and popular prince, receiving petitions, listening to parliaments and considering the cases of a whole people. I am not now arguing the rationality of this conception in other respects; as a matter of fact it is not, as some suppose, irrational; for there is nothing irrational in the wisest and most well-informed king acting differently according to the action of those he wishes to save. But I am here only noting the general nature of liberality, or of free or enlarged atmosphere of action. And in this respect it is certain that the king can only be what we call magnanimous if he is what some call capricious. It is the Catholic, who has the feeling that his prayers do make a difference, when offered for the living and the dead, who also has the feeling of living like a free citizen in something almost like a constitutional commonwealth. It is the monist who lives under a single iron law who must have the feeling of living like a slave under a sultan. Indeed I believe that the original use of the word suffragium, which we now use in politics for a vote, was that employed in theology about a prayer. The dead in Purgatory were said to have the suffrages of the living. And in this sense, of a sort of right of petition to the supreme ruler, we may truly say that the whole of the Communion of Saints, as well as the whole of the Church Militant, is founded on universal suffrage.

But above all, it is true of the most tremendous issue; of that tragedy which has created the divine comedy of our creed. Nothing short of the extreme and strong and startling doctrine of the divinity of Christ will give that particular effect that can truly stir the popular sense like a trumpet; the idea of the king himself serving in the ranks like a common soldier. By making that figure merely human we make that story much less human. We take away the point of the story which actually pierces humanity; the point of the story which was quite literally the point of a spear. It does not especially humanise the universe to say that good and wise men can die for their opinions; any more than it would be any sort of uproariously popular news in an army that good soldiers may easily get killed. It is no news that King Leonidas is dead any more than that Queen Anne is dead; and men did not wait for Christianity to be men, in the full sense of being heroes. But if we are describing, for the moment, the atmosphere of what is generous and popular and even picturesque, any knowledge of human nature will tell us that no sufferings of the sons of men, or even of the servants of God, strike the same note as the notion of the master suffering instead of his servants. And this is given by the theological and emphatically not by the scientific deity. No mysterious monarch, hidden in his starry pavilion at the base of the cosmic campaign, is in the least like that celestial chivalry of the Captain who carries his five wounds in the front of battle.

What the denouncer of dogma really means is not that dogma is bad; but rather that dogma is too good to be true. That is, he means that dogma is too liberal to be likely. Dogma gives man too much freedom when it permits him to fall. Dogma gives even God too much freedom when it permits him to die. That is what the intelligent sceptics ought to say; and it is not in the least my intention to deny that there is something to be said for it. They mean that the universe is itself a universal prison; that existence itself is a limitation and a control; and it is not for nothing that they call causation a chain. In a word, they mean quite simply that they cannot believe these things; not in the least that they are unworthy of belief. We say not lightly but very literally, that the truth has made us free. They say that it makes us so free that it cannot be the truth. To them it is like believing in fairyland to believe in such freedom as we enjoy. It is like believing in men with wings to entertain the fancy of men with wills. It is like accepting a fable about a squirrel in conversation with a mountain to believe in a man who is free to ask or a God who is free to answer. This is a manly and a rational negation for which I for one shall always show respect. But I decline to show any respect for those who first of all clip the wings and cage the squirrel, rivet the chains and refuse the freedom, close all the doors of the cosmic prison on us with a clang of eternal iron, tell us that our emancipation is a dream and our dungeon a necessity; and then calmly turn round and tell us they have a freer thought and a more liberal theology.

The moral of all this is an old one; that religion is revelation. In other words it is a vision, and a vision received by faith; but it is a vision of reality. The faith consists in a conviction of its reality. That, for example, is the difference between a vision and a day-dream. And that is the difference between religion and mythology. That is the difference between faith and all that fancy-work, quite human and more or less healthy, which we considered under the head of mythology. There is something in the reasonable use of the very word vision that implies two things about it; first that it comes very rarely, possibly that it comes only once; and secondly that it probably comes once and for all. A day-dream may come every day. A day-dream may be different every day. It is something more than the difference between telling ghost-stories and meeting a ghost.

But if it is not a mythology neither is it a philosophy. It is not a philosophy because, being a vision, it is not a pattern but a picture. It is not one of those simplifications which resolve everything into an abstract explanation; as that everything is recurrent; or everything is relative; or everything is inevitable; or everything is illusive. It is not a process but a story. It has proportions, of the sort seen in a picture or a story; it has not the regular repetitions of a pattern or a process; but it replaces them by being convincing as a picture or a story is convincing. In other words, it is exactly, as the phrase goes, like life. For indeed it is life. An example of what is meant here might well be found in the treatment of the problem of evil. It is easy enough to make a plan of life of which the background is black, as the pessimists do; and then admit a speck or two of star-dust more or less accidental, or at least in the literal sense insignificant. And it is easy enough to make another plan on white paper, as the Christian Scientists do, and explain or explain away somehow such dots or smudges as may be difficult to deny. Lastly it is easiest of all perhaps, to say as the dualists do, that life is like a chess-board in which the two are equal, and can as truly be said to consist of white squares on a black board or of black squares on a white board. But every man feels in his heart that none of these three paper plans is like life; that none of these worlds is one in which he can live. Something tells him that the ultimate idea of a world is not bad or even neutral; staring at the sky or the grass or the truths of mathematics or even a new-laid egg, he has a vague feeling like the shadow of that saying of the great Christian philosopher, St. Thomas Aquinas, 'Every existence, as such, is good.' On the other hand, something else tells him that it is unmanly and debased and even diseased to minimise evil to a dot or even a blot. He realises that optimism is morbid. It is if possible even more morbid than pessimism. These vague but healthy feelings, if he followed them out, would result in the idea that evil is in some way an exception but an enormous exception; and ultimately that evil is an invasion or yet more truly a rebellion. He does not think that everything is right or that every thing is wrong, or that everything is equally right and wrong. But he does think that right has a right to be right and therefore a right to be there, and wrong has no right to be wrong and therefore no right to be there. It is the prince of the world; but it is also a usurper. So he will apprehend vaguely what the vision will give to him vividly; no less than all that strange story of treason in heaven and the great desertion by which evil damaged and tried to destroy a cosmos that it could not create. It is a very strange story and its proportions and its lines and colours are as arbitrary and absolute as the artistic composition of a picture. It is a vision which we do in fact symbolise in pictures by titanic limbs and passionate tints of plumage; all that abysmal vision of falling stars and the peacock panoplies of the night. But that strange story has one small advantage over the diagrams. It is like life.

Another example might be found, not in the problem of evil, but in what is called the problem of progress. One of the ablest agnostics of the age once asked me whether I thought mankind grew better or grew worse or remained the same. He was confident that the alternative covered all possibilities. He did not see that it only covered patterns and not pictures; processes and not stories. I asked him whether he thought that Mr. Smith of Golder's Green got better or worse or remained exactly the same between the age of thirty and forty. It then seemed to dawn on him that it would rather depend on Mr. Smith; and how he chose to go on. It had never occurred to him that it might depend on how mankind chose to go on; and that its course was not a straight line or an upward or downward curve, but a track like that of a man across a valley, going where he liked and stopping where he chose, going into a church or falling down in a ditch. The life of man is a story; an adventure story; and in our vision the same is true even of the story of God.

The Catholic faith is the reconciliation because it is the realisation both of mythology and philosophy. It is a story and in that sense one of a hundred stories; only it is a true story. It is a philosophy and in that sense one of a hundred philosophies; only it is a philosophy that is like life. But above all, it is a reconciliation because it is something that can only be called the philosophy of stories. That normal narrative instinct which produced all the fairy tales is something that is neglected by all the philosophies--except one. The Faith is the justification of that popular instinct; the finding of a philosophy for it or the analysis of the philosophy in it. Exactly as a man in an adventure story has to pass various tests to save his life, so the man in this philosophy has to pass several tests and save his soul. In both there is an idea of free will operating under conditions of design; in other words, there is an aim and it is the business of a man to aim at it; we therefore watch to see whether he will hit it. Now this deep and democratic and dramatic instinct is derided and dismissed in all the other philosophies. For all the other philosophies avowedly end where they begin; and it is the definition of a story that it ends differently; that it begins in one place and ends in another. From Buddha and his wheel to Akhen Aten and his disc, from Pythagoras with his abstraction of number to Confucius with his religion of routine, there is not one of them that does not in some way sin against the soul of a story. There is none of them that really grasps this human notion of the tale, the test, the adventure; the ordeal of the free man. Each of them starves the story-telling instinct, so to speak, and does something to spoil human life considered as a romance; either by fatalism (pessimist or optimist) and that destiny that is the death of adventure; or by indifference and that detachment that is the death of drama; or by a fundamental scepticism that dissolves the actors into atoms; or by a materialistic limitation blocking the vista of moral consequences; or a mechanical recurrence making even moral tests monotonous; or a bottomless relativity making even practical tests insecure. There is such a thing as a human story; and there is such a thing as the divine story which is also a human story; but there is no such thing as a Hegelian story or a Monist story or a relativist story or a determinist story; for every story, yes, even a penny dreadful or a cheap novelette, has something in it that belongs to our universe and not theirs. Every short story does truly begin with creation and end with a last judgement.

And that is the reason why the myths and the philosophers were at war until Christ came. That is why the Athenian democracy killed Socrates out of respect for the gods; and why every strolling sophist gave himself the airs of a Socrates whenever he could talk in a superior fashion of the gods; and why the heretic Pharaoh wrecked his huge idols and temples for an abstraction and why the priests could return in triumph and trample his dynasty under foot; and why Buddhism had to divide itself from Brahminism, and why in every age and country outside Christendom there has been a feud for ever between the philosopher and the priest. It is easy enough to say that the philosopher is generally the more rational; it is easier still to forget that the priest is always the more popular. For the priest told the people stories; and the philosopher did not understand the philosophy of stories. It came into the world with the story of Christ.

And this is why it had to be a revelation or vision given from above. Any one who will think of the theory of stories or pictures will easily see the point. The true story of the world must be told by somebody to somebody else. By the very nature of a story it cannot be left to occur to anybody. A story has proportions, variations, surprises, particular dispositions, which cannot be worked out by rule in the abstract, like a sum. We could not deduce whether or no Achilles would give back the body of Hector from a Pythagorean theory of number or recurrence; and we could not infer for ourselves in what way the world would get back the body of Christ, merely from being told that all things go round and round upon the wheel of Buddha. A man might perhaps work out a proposition of Euclid without having heard of Euclid; but he would not work out the precise legend of Eurydice without having heard of Eurydice. At any rate he would not be certain how the story would end and whether Orpheus was ultimately defeated. Still less could he guess the end of our story; or the legend of our Orpheus rising, not defeated from, the dead.

To sum up; the sanity of the world was restored and the soul of man offered salvation by something which did indeed satisfy the two warring tendencies of the past; which had never been satisfied in full and most certainly never satisfied together. It met the mythological search for romance by being a story and the philosophical search for truth by being a true story. That is why the ideal figure had to be a historical character, as nobody had ever felt Adonis or Pan to be a historical character. But that is also why the historical character had to be the ideal figure; and even fulfil many of the functions given to these other ideal figures; why he was at once the sacrifice and the feast, why he could be shown under the emblems of the growing vine or the rising sun. The more deeply we think of the matter the more we shall conclude that, if there be indeed a God, his creation could hardly have reached any other culmination than this granting of a real romance to the world. Otherwise the two sides of the human mind could never have touched at all; and the brain of man would have remained cloven and double; one lobe of it dreaming impossible dreams and the other repeating invariable calculations. The picture-makers would have remained forever painting the portrait of nobody. The sages would have remained for ever adding up numerals that came to nothing. It was that abyss that nothing but an incarnation could cover; a divine embodiment of our dreams; and he stands above that chasm whose name is more than priest and older even than Christendom; Pontifex Maximus, the mightiest maker of a bridge.

But even with that we return to the more specially Christian symbol in the same tradition; the perfect pattern of the keys. This is a historical and not a theological outline, and it is not my duty here to defend in detail that theology, but merely to point out that it could not even be justified in design without being justified in detail--like a key. Beyond the broad suggestion of this chapter I attempt no apologetic about why the creed should be accepted. But in answer to the historical query of why it was accepted and is accepted, I answer for millions of others in my reply; because it fits the lock, because it is like life. It is one among many stories; only it happens to be a true story. It is one among many philosophies; only it happens to be the truth. We accept it; and the ground is solid under our feet and the road is open before us. It does not imprison us in a dream of destiny or a consciousness of the universal delusion. It opens to us not only incredible heavens but what seems to some an equally incredible earth, and makes it credible. This is the sort of truth that is hard to explain because it is a fact; but it is a fact to which we can call witnesses. We are Christians and Catholics not because we worship a key, but because we have passed a door; and felt the wind that is the trumpet of liberty blow over the land of the living.

VI THE FIVE DEATHS OF THE FAITH

It is not the purpose of this book to trace the subsequent history of Christianity, especially the later history of Christianity; which involves controversies of which I hope to write more fully elsewhere. It is devoted only to the suggestion that Christianity, appearing amid heathen humanity, had all the character of a unique thing and even of a supernatural thing. It was not like any of the other things; and the more we study it the less it looks like any of them. But there is a certain rather peculiar character which marked it henceforward even down to the present moment, with a note on which this book may well conclude.

I have said that Asia and the ancient world had an air of being too old to die. Christendom has had the very opposite fate. Christendom has had a series of revolutions and in each one of them Christianity has died. Christianity has died many times and risen again; for it had a God who knew the way out of the grave. But the first extraordinary fact which marks this history is this: that Europe has been turned upside down over and over again; and that at the end of each of these revolutions the same religion has again been found on top. The Faith is always converting the age, not as an old religion but as a new religion. This truth is hidden from many by a convention that is too little noticed. Curiously enough, it is a convention of the sort which those who ignore it claim especially to detect and denounce. They are always telling us that priests and ceremonies are not religion and that religious organisation can be a hollow sham, but they hardly realise how true it is. It is so true that three or four times at least in the history of Christendom the whole soul seemed to have gone out of Christianity; and almost every man in his heart expected its end. This fact is only masked in medieval and other times by that very official religion which such critics pride themselves on seeing through. Christianity remained the official religion of a Renaissance prince or the official religion of an eighteenth-century bishop, just as an ancient mythology remained the official religion of Julius Caesar or the Arian creed long remained the official religion of Julian the Apostate. But there was a difference between the cases of Julius and of Julian; because the Church had begun its strange career. There was no reason why men like Julius should not worship gods like Jupiter for ever in public and laugh at them for ever in private. But when Julian treated Christianity as dead, he found it had come to life again. He also found, incidentally, that there was not the faintest sign of Jupiter ever coming to life again. This case of Julian and the episode of Arianism is but the first of a series of examples that can only be roughly indicated here. Arianism, as has been said, had every human appearance of being the natural way in which that particular superstition of Constantine might be expected to peter out. All the ordinary stages had been passed through; the creed had become a respectable thing, had become a ritual thing, had then been modified into a rational thing; and the rationalists were ready to dissipate the last remains of it, just as they do to-day. When Christianity rose again suddenly and threw them, it was almost as unexpected as Christ rising from the dead. But there are many other examples of the same thing, even about the same time. The rush of missionaries from Ireland, For instance, has all the air of an unexpected onslaught of young men on an old world, and even on a Church that showed signs of growing old. Some of them were martyred on the coast of Cornwall; and the chief authority on Cornish antiquities told me that he did not believe for a moment that they were martyred by heathens but (as he expressed it with some humour) 'by rather slack Christians.'

Now if we were to dip below the surface of history, as it is not in the scope of this argument to do, I suspect that we should find several occasions when Christendom was thus to all appearance hollowed out from within by doubt and indifference, so that only the old Christian shell stood as the pagan shell had stood so long. But the difference is that in every such case, the sons were fanatical for the faith where the fathers had been slack about it. This is obvious in the case of the transition from the Renaissance to the Counter-Reformation. It is obvious in the case of a transition from the eighteenth century to the many Catholic revivals of our own time. But I suspect many other examples which would be worthy of separate studies.

The Faith is not a survival. It is not as if the Druids had managed somehow to survive somewhere for two thousand years. That is what might have happened in Asia or ancient Europe, in that indifference or tolerance in which mythologies and philosophies could live for ever side by side. It has not survived; it has returned again and again in this Western world of rapid change and institutions perpetually perishing. Europe, in the tradition of Rome, was always trying revolution and reconstruction; rebuilding a universal republic. And it always began by rejecting this old stone and ended by making it the head of the corner; by bringing it back from the rubbish-heap to make it the crown of the capitol. Some stones of Stonehenge are standing and some are fallen; and as the stone falleth so shall it lie. There has not been a Druidic renaissance every century or two, with the young Druids crowned with fresh mistletoe, dancing in the sun on Salisbury Plain. Stonehenge has not been rebuilt in every style of architecture from the rude round Norman to the last rococo of the Baroque. The sacred place of the Druids is safe from the vandalism of restoration.

But the Church in the West was not in a world where things were too old to die; but in one in which they were always young enough to get killed. The consequence was that superficially and externally it often did get killed; nay, it sometimes wore out even without getting killed. And there follows a fact I find it somewhat difficult to describe, yet which I believe to be very real and rather important. As a ghost is the shadow of a man, and in that sense the shadow of life, so at intervals there passed across this endless life a sort of shadow of death. It came at the moment when it would have perished had it been perishable. It withered away everything that was perishable. If such animal parallels were worthy of the occasion we might say that the snake shuddered and shed a skin and went on, or even that the cat went into convulsions as it lost only one of its nine-hundred-and-ninety-nine lives. It is truer to say, in a more dignified image, that a clock struck and nothing happened; or that a bell tolled for an execution that was everlastingly postponed.

What was the meaning of all that dim but vast unrest of the twelfth century; when, as it has been so finely said, Julian stirred in his sleep? Why did there appear so strangely early, in the twilight of dawn after the Dark Ages, so deep a scepticism as that involved in urging nominalism against realism? For realism against nominalism was really realism against rationalism, or something more destructive than what we call rationalism. The answer is that just as some might have thought the Church simply a part of the Roman Empire, so others later might have thought the Church only a part of the Dark Ages. The Dark Ages ended as the Empire had ended, and the Church should have departed with them, if she had been also one of the shades of night. It was another of those spectral deaths or simulations of death. I mean that if nominalism had succeeded, it would have been as if Arianism had succeeded, it would have been the beginning of a confession that Christianity had failed. For nominalism is a far more fundamental scepticism than mere atheism. Such was the question that was openly asked as the Dark Ages broadened into that daylight that we call the modern world. But what was the answer? The answer was Aquinas in the chair of Aristotle, taking all knowledge for his province; and tens of thousands of lads down to the lowest ranks of peasant and serf, living in rags and on crusts about the great colleges, to listen to the scholastic philosophy.

What was the meaning of all that whisper of fear that ran round the west under the shadow of Islam, and fills every old romance with incongruous images of Saracen knights swaggering in Norway or the Hebrides? Why were men in the extreme west, such as King John if I remember rightly, accused of being secretly Moslems, as men are accused of being secretly atheists? Why was there that fierce alarm among some of the authorities about the rationalistic Arab version of Aristotle? Authorities are seldom alarmed like that except when it is too late. The answer is that hundreds of people probably believed in their hearts that Islam would conquer Christendom; that Averroes was more rational than Anselm; that the Saracen Culture was really, as it was superficially, a superior culture. Here again we should probably find a whole generation, the older generation, serve doubtful and depressed and weary. The coming of Islam would only have been the coming of Unitarianism a thousand years before its time. To many it may have seemed quite reasonable and quite probable and quite likely to happen. If so, they would have been surprised at what did happen. What did happen was a roar like thunder from thousands and thousands of young men, throwing all their youth into one exultant counter-charge, the Crusades. It was the sons of St. Francis, the Jugglers of God, wandering singing over all the roads of the world; it was the Gothic going up like a flight of arrows; it was the waking of the world. In considering the war of the Albigensians, we come to the breach in the heart of Europe and the landslide of a new philosophy that nearly ended Christendom for ever. In that case the new philosophy was also a very new philosophy; it was pessimism. It was none the less like modern ideas because it was as old as Asia; most modern ideas are. It was the Gnostics returning; but why did the Gnostics return? Because it was the end of an epoch, like the end of the Empire; and should have been the end of the Church. It was Schopenhauer hovering over the future; but it was also Manichaeus rising from the dead; that men might have death and that they might have it more abundantly.

It is rather more obvious in the case of the Renaissance, simply because the period is so much nearer to us and people know so much more about it. But there is more even in that example than most people know. Apart from the particular controversies which I wish to reserve for a separate study, the period was far more chaotic that those controversies commonly imply. When Protestants call Latimer a martyr to Protestantism, and Catholics reply that Campion was a martyr to Catholicism, it is often forgotten that many who perished in such persecutions could only be described as martyrs to atheism or anarchism or even diabolism. That world was almost as wild as our own; the men wandering about in it included the sort of man who says there is no God, the sort of man who says he is himself God, the sort of man who says something that nobody can make head or tail of. If we could have the conversation of the age following the Renaissance, we should probably be shocked by its shameless negations. The remarks attributed to Marlowe are probably pretty typical of the talk in many intellectual taverns. The transition from Pre-Reformation to Post-Reformation Europe was through a void of very yawning questions; yet again in the long run the answer was the same. It was one of those moments when, as Christ walked on the water, so was Christianity walking in the air.

But all these cases are remote in date and could only be proved in detail. We can see the fact much more clearly in the case when the paganism of the Renaissance ended Christianity and Christianity unaccountably began all over again. But we can see it most clearly of all in the case which is close to us and full of manifest and minute evidence; the case of the great decline of religion that began about the time of Voltaire. For indeed it is our own case, and we ourselves have seen the decline of that decline. The two hundred years since Voltaire do not flash past us at a glance like the fourth and fifth centuries or the twelfth and thirteenth centuries. In our own case we can see this oft-repeated process close at hand; we know how completely a society can lose its fundamental religion without abolishing its official religion; we know how men can all become agnostics long before they abolish bishops. And we know that also in this last ending, which really did look to us like the final ending, the incredible thing has happened again; the Faith has a better following among the young men than among the old. When Ibsen spoke of the new generation knocking at the door, he certainly never expected that it would be the church-door.

At least five times, therefore, with the Arian and the Albigensian, with the Humanist sceptic, after Voltaire and after Darwin, the Faith has to all appearance gone to the dogs. In each of these five cases it was the dog that died. How complete was the collapse and how strange the reversal we can only see in detail in the case nearest to our own time.

A thousand things have been said about the Oxford Movement and the parallel French Catholic revival; but few have made us feel the simplest fact about it; that it was a surprise. It was a puzzle as well as a surprise; because it seemed to most people like a river turning backwards from the sea and trying to climb back into the mountains. To have read the literature of the eighteenth and nineteenth centuries is to know that nearly everybody had come to take it for granted that religion was a thing that would continually broaden like a river, till it reached an infinite sea. Some of them expected it to go down in a cataract of catastrophe, most of them expected it to widen into an estuary of equality and moderation; but all of them thought its returning on itself a prodigy as incredible as witchcraft. In other words, most moderate people thought that faith like freedom would be slowly broadened down, and some advanced people thought that it would be very rapidly broadened down, not to say flattened out. All that world of Guizot and Macaulay and the commercial and scientific liberality was perhaps more certain than any men before or since about the direction in which the world is going. People were so certain about the direction that they only differed about the pace. Many anticipated with alarm, and a few with sympathy, a Jacobin revolt that should guillotine the Archbishop of Canterbury or a Chartist riot that should hang the parsons on the lampposts. But it seemed like a convulsion in nature that the Archbishop instead of losing his head should be looking for his mitre; and that instead of diminishing the respect due to parsons we should strengthen it to the respect due to priests. It revolutionised their very vision of revolution; and turned their very topsyturveydom topsyturvey.

In short, the whole world being divided about whether the stream was going slower or faster, became conscious of something vague but vast that was going against the stream. Both in fact and figure there is something deeply disturbing about this, and that for an essential reason. A dead thing can go with the stream, but only a living thing can go against it. A dead dog can be lifted on the leaping water with all the swiftness of a leaping hound; but only a live dog can swim backwards. A paper boat can ride the rising deluge with all the airy arrogance of a fairy ship, but if the fairy ship sails up stream it is really rowed by the fairies. And among the things that merely went with the tide of apparent progress and enlargement there was many a demagogue or sophist whose wild gestures were in truth as lifeless as the movement of a dead dog's limbs wavering in the eddying water; and many a philosophy uncommonly like a paper boat, of the sort that it is not difficult to knock into a cocked hat. But even the truly living and even life-giving things that went with that stream did not thereby prove that they were living or life-giving. It was this other force that was unquestionably and unaccountably alive; the mysterious and unmeasured energy that was thrusting back the river. That was felt to be like the movement of some great monster; and it was none the less clearly a living monster because most people thought it a prehistoric monster. It was none the less an unnatural, an incongruous, and to some a comic upheaval; as if the Great Sea Serpent had suddenly risen out of the Round Pond--unless we consider the Sea Serpent as more likely to live in the Serpentine. This flippant element in the fantasy must not be missed, for it was one of the clearest testimonies to the unexpected nature of the reversal. That age did really feel that a preposterous quality in prehistoric animals belonged also to historic rituals; that mitres and tiaras were like the horns or crests of antediluvian creatures; and that appealing to a Primitive Church was like dressing up as a Primitive Man.

The world is still puzzled by that movement; but most of all because it still moves. I have said something elsewhere of the rather random sort of reproaches that are still directed against it and its much greater consequences; it is enough to say here that the more such critics reproach it the less they explain it. In a sense it is my concern here, if not to explain it, at least to suggest the direction of the explanation; but above all, it is my concern to point out one particular thing about it. And that is that it had all happened before; and even many times before.

To sum up, in so far as it is true that recent centuries have seen an attenuation of Christian doctrine, recent centuries have only seen what the most remote centuries have seen. And even the modern example has only ended as the medieval and pre-medieval examples ended. It is already clear, and grows clearer every day, that it is not going to end in the disappearance of the diminished creed; but rather in the return of those parts of it that had really disappeared. It is going to end as the Arian compromise ended, as the attempts at a compromise with Nominalism and even with Albigensianism ended. But the point to seize in the modern case, as in all the other cases is that what returns is not in that sense a simplified theology; not according to that view a purified theology; it is simply theology. It is that enthusiasm for theological studies that marked the most doctrinal ages; it is the divine science. An old Don with D. D. after his name may have become the typical figure of a bore; but that was because he was himself bored with his theology, not because he was excited about it. It was precisely because he was admittedly more interested in the Latin of Plautus than in the Latin of Augustine, in the Greek of Xenophon than in the Greek of Chrysostom. It was precisely because he was more interested in a dead tradition than in a decidedly living tradition. In short, it was precisely because he was himself a type of the time in which Christian faith was weak. It was not because men would not hail, if they could, the wonderful and almost wild vision of a Doctor of Divinity.

There are people who say they wish Christianity to remain as a spirit. They mean, very literally, that they wish it to remain as a ghost. But it is not going to remain as a ghost. What follows this process of apparent death is not the lingerings of the shade; it is the resurrection of the body. These people are quite prepared to shed pious and reverential tears over the Sepulchre of the Son of Man; what they are not prepared for is the Son of God walking once more upon the hills of morning. These people, and indeed most people, were indeed by this time quite accustomed to the idea that the old Christian candle-light would fade into the light of common day. To many of them it did quite honestly appear like that pale yellow flame of a candle when it is left burning in daylight. It was all the more unexpected, and therefore all the more unmistakable, that the seven branched candle-stick suddenly towered to heaven like a miraculous tree and flamed until the sun turned pale. But other ages have seen the day conquer the candle-light and then the candle-light conquer the day. Again and again, before our time, men have grown content with a diluted doctrine. And again and again there has followed on that dilution, coming as out of the darkness in a crimson cataract, the strength of the red original wine. And we only say once more to-day as has been said many times by our fathers: 'Long years and centuries ago own fathers or the founders of our people drank, as they dreamed, of the blood of God. Long years and centuries have passed since the strength of that giant vintage has been anything but a legend of the age of giants. Centuries ago already is the dark time of the second fermentation, when the wine of Catholicism turned into the vinegar of Calvinism. Long since that bitter drink has been itself diluted; rinsed out and washed away by the waters of oblivion and the wave of the world. Never did we think to taste again even that bitter tang of sincerity and the spirit, still less the richer and the sweeter strength of the purple vineyards in our dreams of the age of gold. Day by day and year by year we have lowered our hopes and lessened our convictions; we have grown more and more used to seeing those vats and vineyards overwhelmed in the water-floods and the last savour and suggestion of that special element fading like a stain of purple upon a sea of grey. We have grown used to dilution, to dissolution, to a watering down that went on for ever. But 'Thou hast kept the good wine until now.'

This is the final fact, and it is the most extraordinary of all. The faith has not only often died but it has often died of old age. It has not only been often killed but it has often died a natural death; in the sense of coming to a natural and necessary end. It is obvious that it has survived the most savage and the most universal persecutions from the shock of the Diocletian fury to the shock of the French Revolution. But it has a more strange and even a more weird tenacity; it has survived not only war but peace. It has not only died often but degenerated often and decayed often; it has survived its own weakness and even its own surrender. We need not repeat what is so obvious about the beauty of the end of Christ in its wedding of youth and death. But this is almost as if Christ had lived to the last possible span, had been a white-haired sage of a hundred and died of natural decay, and then had risen again rejuvenated, with trumpets and the rending of the sky. It was said truly enough that human Christianity in its recurrent weakness was sometimes too much wedded to the powers of the world; but if it was wedded it has very often been widowed. It is a strangely immortal sort of widow. An enemy may have said at one moment that it was but an aspect of the power of the Caesars; and it sounds as strange to-day as to call it an aspect of the Pharaohs. An enemy might say that it was the official faith of feudalism; and it sounds as convincing now as to say that it was bound to perish with the ancient Roman villa. All these things did indeed run their course to its normal end; and there seemed no course for the religion but to end with them. It ended and it began again.

'Heaven and earth shall pass away, but my words shall not pass away.' The civilisation of antiquity was the whole world: and men no more dreamed of its ending than of the ending of daylight. They could not imagine another order unless it were in another world. The civilisation of the world has passed away and those words have not passed away. In the long night of the Dark Ages feudalism was so familiar a thing that no man could imagine himself without a lord: and religion was so woven into that network that no man would have believed they could be torn asunder. Feudalism itself was torn to rags and rotted away in the popular life of the true Middle Ages; and the first and freshest power in that new freedom was the old religion. Feudalism had passed away, and the words did not pass away. The whole medieval order, in many ways so complete and almost cosmic a home for man, wore out gradually in its turn and here at least it was thought that the words would die. They went forth across the radiant abyss of the Renaissance and in fifty years were using all its light and learning for new religious foundations, new apologetics, new saints. It was supposed to have been withered up at last in the dry light of the Age of Reason; it was supposed to have disappeared ultimately in the earthquake of the Age of Revolution. Science explained it away; and it was still there. History disinterred it in the past; and it appeared suddenly in the future. To-day it stands once more in our path; and even as we watch it, it grows.

If our social relations and records retain their continuity, if men really learn to apply reason to the accumulating facts of so crushing a story, it would seem that sooner or later even its enemies will learn from their incessant and interminable disappointments not to look for anything so simple as its death. They may continue to war with it, but it will be as they war with nature; as they war with the landscape, as they war with the skies. 'Heaven and earth shall pass away, but my words shall not pass away.' They will watch for it to stumble; they will watch for it to err; they will no longer watch for it to end. Insensibly, even unconsciously, they will in their own silent anticipations fulfil the relative terms of that astounding prophecy; they will forget to watch for the mere extinction of what has so often been vainly extinguished; and will learn instinctively to look first for the coming of the comet or the freezing of the star.

CONCLUSION - THE SUMMARY OF THIS BOOK

I have taken the liberty once or twice of borrowing the excellent phrase about an Outline of History; though this study of a special truth and a special error can of course claim no sort of comparison with the rich and many-sided encyclopedia of history, for which that name was chosen. And yet there is a certain reason in the reference: and a sense in which the one thing touches and even cuts across the other. For the story of the world as told by Mr. Wells could here only be criticised as an outline. And, strangely enough, it seems to me that it is only wrong as an outline. It is admirable as an accumulation of history; it is splendid as a storehouse or treasure of history; it is a fascinating disquisition on history; it is most attractive as an amplification of history; but it is quite false as an outline of history. The one thing that seems to me quite wrong about it is the outline; the sort of outline that can really be a single line, like that which makes all the difference between a caricature of the profile of Mr. Winston Churchill and of Sir Alfred Mond. In simple and homely language, I mean the things that stick out; the things that make the simplicity of a silhouette. I think the proportions are wrong; the proportions of what is certain as compared with what is uncertain, of what played a great part as compared with what played a smaller part, of what is ordinary and what is extraordinary, of what really lies level with an average and what stands out as an exception.

I do not say it as a small criticism of a great writer, and I have no reason to do so; for in my own much smaller task I feel I have failed in very much the same way. I am very doubtful whether I have conveyed to the reader the main point I meant about the proportions of history, and why I have dwelt so much more on some things than others. I doubt whether I have clearly fulfilled the plan that I set out in the introductory chapter; and for that reason I add these lines as a sort of summary in a concluding chapter. I do believe that the things on which I have insisted are more essential to an outline of history than the things which I have subordinated or dismissed. I do not believe that the past is most truly pictured as a thing in which humanity merely fades away into nature, or civilisation merely fades away into barbarism, or religion fades away into mythology, or our own religion fades away into the religions of the world. In short I do not believe that the best way to produce an outline of history is to rub out the lines. I believe that, of the two, it would be far nearer the truth to tell the tale very simply, like a primitive myth about a man who made the sun and stars or a god who entered the body of a sacred monkey. I will therefore sum up all that has gone before in what seems to me a realistic and reasonably proportioned statement; the short story of mankind.

In the land lit by that neighbouring star, whose blaze is the broad daylight, there are many and very various things motionless and moving. There moves among them a race that is in its relation to others a race of gods. The fact is not lessened but emphasised because it can behave like a race of demons. Its distinction is not an individual illusion, like one bird pluming itself on its own plumes; it is a solid and a many-sided thing. It is demonstrated in the very speculations that have led to its being denied. That men, the gods of this lower world, are linked with it in various ways is true; but it is another aspect of the same truth. That they grow as the grass grows and walk as the beasts walk is a secondary necessity that sharpens the primary distinction. It is like saying that a magician must after all have the appearance of a man; or that even the fairies could not dance without feet. It has lately been the fashion to focus the mind entirely on these mild and subordinate resemblances and to forget the main fact altogether. It is customary to insist that man resembles the other creatures. Yes; and that very resemblance he alone can see. The fish does not trace the fish-bone pattern in the fowls of the air; or the elephant and the emu compare skeletons. Even in the sense in which man is at one with the universe it is an utterly lonely universality. The very sense that he is united with all things is enough to sunder him from all.

Looking around him by this unique light, as lonely as the literal flame that he alone has kindled, this demigod or demon of the visible world makes that world visible. He sees around him a world of a certain style or type. It seems to proceed by certain rules or at least repetitions. He sees a green architecture that builds itself without visible hands; but which builds itself into a very exact plan or pattern, like a design already drawn in the air by an invisible finger. It is not, as is now vaguely suggested, a vague thing. It is not a growth or a groping of blind life. Each seeks an end; a glorious and radiant end, even for every daisy or dandelion we see in looking across the level of a common field. In the very shape of things there is more than green growth; there is the finality of the flower. It is a world of crowns. This impression, whether or no it be an illusion, has so profoundly influenced this race of thinkers and masters of the material world, that the vast majority have been moved to take a certain view of that world. They have concluded, rightly or wrongly, that the world had a plan as the tree seemed to have a plan; and an end and crown like the flower. But so long as the race of thinkers was able to think, it was obvious that the admission of this idea of a plan brought with it another thought more thrilling and even terrible. There was someone else, some strange and unseen being, who had designed these things, if indeed they were designed. There was a stranger who was also a friend; a mysterious benefactor who had been before them and built up the woods and hills for their coming, and had kindled the sunrise against their rising, as a servant kindles a fire. Now this idea of a mind that gives a meaning to the universe has received more and more confirmation within the minds of men, by meditations and experiences much more subtle and searching than any such argument about the external plan of the world. But I am concerned here with keeping the story in its most simple and even concrete terms; and it is enough to say here that most men, including the wisest men, have come to the conclusion that the world has such a final purpose and therefore such a first cause. But most men in some sense separated themselves from the wisest men, when it came to the treatment of that idea. There came into existence two ways of treating that idea, which between them made up most of the religious history of the world. The majority, like the minority, had this strong sense of a second meaning in things; of a strange master who knew the secret of the world. But the majority, the mob or mass of men, naturally tended to treat it rather in the spirit of gossip. The gossip, like all gossip, contained a great deal of truth and falsehood. The world began to tell itself tales about the unknown being or his sons or servants or messengers. Some of the tales may truly be called old wives' tales; as professing only to be very remote memories of the morning of the world; myths about the baby moon or the half-baked mountains. Some of them might more truly be called travellers' tales; as being curious but contemporary tales brought from certain borderlands of experience; such as miraculous cures or those that bring whispers of what has happened to the dead. Many of them are probably true tales; enough of them are probably true to keep a person of real commonsense more or less conscious that there really is something rather marvellous behind the cosmic curtain. But in a sense it is only going by appearances; even if the appearances are called apparitions. It is a matter of appearances--and disappearances. At the most these gods are ghosts; that is, they are glimpses. For most of us they are rather gossip about glimpses. And for the rest, the whole world is full of rumours, most of which are almost avowedly romances. The great majority of the tales about gods and ghosts and the invisible king are told, if not for the sake of the tale, at least for the sake of the topic. They are evidence of the eternal interest of the theme; they are not evidence of anything else, and they are not meant to be. They are mythology or the poetry that is not bound in books--or bound in any other way.

Meanwhile the minority, the sages or thinkers, had withdrawn apart and had taken up an equally congenial trade. They were drawing up plans of the world; of the world which all believed to have a plan. They were trying to set forth the plan seriously and to scale. They were setting their minds directly to the mind that had made the mysterious world; considering what sort of a mind it might be and what its ultimate purpose might be. Some of them made that mind much more impersonal than mankind has generally made it; some simplified it almost to a blank; a few, a very few, doubted it altogether. One or two of the more morbid fancied that it might be evil and an enemy; just one or two of the more degraded in the other class worshipped demons instead of gods. But most of these theorists were theists: and they not only saw a moral plan in nature, but they generally laid down a moral plan for humanity. Most of them were good men who did good work: and they were remembered and reverenced in various ways. They were scribes; any their scriptures became more or less holy scriptures. They were law-givers; and their tradition became not only legal but ceremonial. We may say that they received divine honours, in the sense in which kings and great captains in certain countries often received divine honours. In a word, wherever the other popular spirit, the spirit of legend and gossip could come into play, it surrounded them with the more mystical atmosphere of the myths. Popular poetry turned the sages into saints. But that was all it did. They remained themselves; men never really forgot that they were men, only made into gods in the sense that they were made into heroes. Divine Plato, like Divus Ceasar, was a title and not a dogma. In Asia, where the atmosphere was more mythological, the man was made to look more like a myth, but he remained a man. He remained a man of a certain social class or school of men, receiving and deserving great honour from mankind. It is the order or school of the philosophers; the men who have set themselves seriously to trace the order across any apparent chaos in the vision of life. Instead of living on imaginative rumours and remote traditions and the tail-end of exceptional experiences about the mind and meaning behind the world, they have tried in a sense to project the primary purpose of that mind a priori. They have tried to put on paper a possible plan of the world; almost as if the world were not yet made.

Right in the middle of all these things stands up an enormous exception. It is quite unlike anything else. It is a thing final like the trump of doom, though it is also a piece of good news; or news that seems too good to be true. It is nothing less than the loud assertion that this mysterious maker of the world has visited his world in person. It declares that really and even recently, or right in the middle of historic times, there did walk into the world this original invisible being; about whom the thinkers make theories and the mythologists hand down myths; the Man Who Made the World. That such a higher personality exists behind all things had indeed always been implied by all the best thinkers, as well as by all the most beautiful legends. But nothing of this sort had ever been implied in any of them. It is simply false to say that the other sages and heroes had claimed to be that mysterious master and maker, of whom the world had dreamed and disputed. Not one of them had ever claimed to be anything of the sort. Not one of their sects or schools had even claimed that they had claimed to be anything of the sort. The most that any religious prophet had said was that he was the true servant of such a being. The most that any visionary had ever said was that men might catch glimpses of the glory of that spiritual being; or much more often of lesser spiritual beings. The most that any primitive myth had even suggested was that the Creator was present at the Creation. But that the Creator was present at scenes a little subsequent to the supper-parties of Horace, and talked with tax-collectors and government officials in the detailed daily life of the Roman Empire, and that this fact continued to be firmly asserted by the whole of that great civilisation for more than a thousand years--that is something utterly unlike anything else in nature. It is the one great startling statement that man has made since he spoke his first articulate word, instead of barking like a dog. Its unique character can be used as an argument against it as well as for it. It would be easy to concentrate on it as a case of isolated insanity; but it makes nothing but dust and nonsense of comparative religion.

It came on the world with a wind and rush of running messengers proclaiming that apocalyptic portent, and it is not unduly fanciful to say that they are running still. What puzzles the world, and its wise philosophers and fanciful pagan poets, about the priests and people of the Catholic Church is that they still behave as if they were messengers. A messenger does not dream about what his message might be, or argue about what it probably would be; he delivers it as it is. It is not a theory or a fancy but a fact. It is not relevant to this intentionally rudimentary outline to prove in detail that it is a fact; but merely to point out that these messengers do deal with it as men deal with a fact. All that is condemned in Catholic tradition, authority, and dogmatism and the refusal to retract and modify, are but the natural human attributes of a man with a message relating to a fact. I desire to avoid in this last summary all the controversial complexities that may once more cloud the simple lines of that strange story; which I have already called, in words that are much too weak, the strangest story in the world. I desire merely to mark those main lines and specially to mark where the great line is really to be drawn. The religion of the world, in its right proportions, is not divided into fine shades of mysticism or more or less rational forms of mythology. It is divided by the line between the men who are bringing that message and the men who have not yet heard it, or cannot yet believe it.

But when we translate the terms of that strange tale back into the more concrete and complicated terminology of our time, we find it covered by names and memories of which the very familiarity is a falsification. For instance, when we say that a country contains so many Moslems, we really mean that it contains so many monotheists; and we really mean, by that, that it contains so many men; men with the old average assumption of men--that the invisible ruler remains invisible. They hold it along with the customs of a certain culture and under the simpler laws of a certain law-giver; but so they would if their law-giver were Lycurgus or Solon. They testify to something which is a necessary and noble truth; but was never a new truth. Their creed is not a new colour; it is the neutral and normal tint that is the background of the many-coloured life of man. Mahomet did not, like the Magi, find a new star; he saw through his own particular window a glimpse of the great grey field of the ancient starlight. So when we say that the country contains so many Confucians or Buddhists, we mean it contains so many pagans whose prophets have given them another and rather vaguer version of the invisible power; making it not only invisible but almost impersonal. When we say that they also have temples and idols and priests and periodical festivals, we simply mean that this sort of heathen is enough of a human being to admit the popular element of pomp and pictures and feasts and fairy-tales. We only mean that Pagans have more sense than Puritans. But what the gods are supposed to be, what the priests are commissioned to say, is not a sensational secret like what those running messengers of the Gospel had to say. Nobody else except those messengers has any Gospel; nobody else has any good news; for the simple reason that nobody else has any news.

Those runners gather impetus as they run. Ages afterwards they still speak as if something had just happened. They have not lost the speed and momentum of messengers; they have hardly lost, as it were, the wild eyes of witnesses. In the Catholic Church, which is the cohort of the message, there are still those headlong acts of holiness that speak of something rapid and recent; a self-sacrifice that startles the world like a suicide. But it is not a suicide; it is not pessimistic; it is still as optimistic as St. Francis of the flowers and birds. It is newer in spirit than the newest schools of thought; and it is almost certainly on the eve of new triumphs. For these men serve a mother who seems to grow more beautiful as new generations rise up and call her blessed. We might sometimes fancy that the Church grows younger as the world grows old.

For this is the last proof of the miracle; that something so supernatural should have become so natural. I mean that anything so unique when seen from the outside should only seem universal when seen from the inside. I have not minimised the scale of the miracle, as some of our wilder theologians think it wise to do. Rather have I deliberately dwelt on that incredible interruption, as a blow that broke the very backbone of history. I have great sympathy with the monotheists, the Moslems, or the Jews, to whom it seems a blasphemy; a blasphemy that might shake the world. But it did not shake the world; it steadied the world. That fact, the more we consider it, will seem more solid and more strange. I think it a piece of plain justice to all the unbelievers to insist upon the audacity of the act of faith that is demanded of them. I willingly and warmly agree that it is, in itself, a suggestion at which we might expect even the brain of the believer to reel, when he realised his own belief. But the brain of the believer does not reel; it is the brains of the unbelievers that reel. We can see their brains reeling on every side and into every extravagance of ethics and psychology; into pessimism and the denial of life; into pragmatism and the denial of logic; seeking their omens in nightmares and their canons in contradictions; shrieking for fear at the far-off sight of things beyond good and evil, or whispering of strange stars where two and two make five. Meanwhile this solitary thing that seems at first so outrageous in outline remains solid and sane in substance. It remains the moderator of all these manias; rescuing reason from the Pragmatists exactly as it rescued laughter from the Puritans. I repeat that I have deliberately emphasised its intrinsically defiant and dogmatic character. The mystery is how anything so startling should have remained defiant and dogmatic and yet become perfectly normal and natural. I have admitted freely that, considering the incident in itself, a man who says he is God may be classed with a man who says he is glass. But the man who says he is glass is not a glazier making windows for all the world. He does not remain for after ages as a shining and crystalline figure, in whose light everything is as clear as crystal.

But this madness has remained sane. The madness has remained sane when everything else went mad. The madhouse has been a house to which, age after age, men are continually coming back as to a home. That is the riddle that remains; that anything so abrupt and abnormal should still be found a habitable and hospitable thing. I care not if the sceptic says it is a tall story; I cannot see how so toppling a tower could stand so long without foundation. Still less can I see how it could become, as it has become, the home of man. Had it merely appeared and disappeared, it might possibly have been remembered or explained as the last leap of the rage of illusion, the ultimate myth of the ultimate mood, in which the mind struck the sky and broke. But the mind did not break. It is the one mind that remains unbroken in the break-up of the world. If it were an error, it seems as if the error could hardly have lasted a day. If it were a mere ecstasy, it would seem that such an ecstasy could not endure for an hour. It has endured for nearly two thousand years; and the world within it has been more lucid, more level-headed, more reasonable in its hopes, more healthy in its instincts, more humorous and cheerful in the face of fate and death, than all the world outside. For it was the soul of Christendom that came forth from the incredible Christ; and the soul of it was common sense. Though we dared not look on His face we could look on His fruits; and by His fruits we should know Him. The fruits are solid and the fruitfulness is much more than a metaphor; and nowhere in this sad world are boys happier in apple-trees, or men in more equal chorus singing as they tread the vine, than under the fixed flash of this instant and intolerant enlightenment; the lightning made eternal as the light.

APPENDIX I ON PREHISTORIC MAN

On re-reading these pages I feel that I have tried in many places and with many words, to say something that might be said in one word. In a sense this study is meant to be superficial. That is, it is not meant as a study of the things that need to be studied. It is rather a reminder of the things that are seen so quickly that they are forgotten almost as quickly. Its moral, in a manner of speaking, is that first thoughts are best; so a flash might reveal a landscape; with the Eiffel Tower or the Matterhorn standing up in it as they would never stand up again in the light of common day. I ended the book with an image of everlasting lightning; in a very different sense, alas, this little flash has lasted only too long. But the method has also certain practical disadvantages upon which I think it well to add these two notes. It may seem to simplify too much and to ignore out of ignorance. I feel this especially in the passage about the prehistoric pictures; which is not concerned with all that the learned may learn from prehistoric pictures, but with the single point of what anyone could learn from there being any prehistoric pictures at all. I am conscious that this attempt to express it in terms of innocence may exaggerate even my own ignorance. Without any pretence of scientific research or information, I should be sorry to have it thought that I knew no more than what was needed, in that passage, of the states into which primitive humanity has been divided. I am aware, of course, that the story is elaborately stratified; and that there were many such stages before the Cro-Magnon or any peoples with whom we associate such pictures. Indeed recent studies about the Neanderthal and other races rather tend to repeat the moral that is here most relevant. The notion noted in these pages of something necessarily slow or late in the development of religion, will gain little indeed from these later revelations about the precursors of the reindeer picture-maker. The learned appear to hold that, whether the reindeer picture could be religious or not, the people that lived before it were religious already; burying their dead with the significant signs of mystery and hope. This obviously brings us back to the same argument; an argument that is not approached by any measurement of the earlier man's skull. It is little use here to compare the head of the man with the head of the monkey, if it certainly never came into the head of the monkey to bury another monkey with nuts in his grave to help him towards a heavenly monkey house. Talking of skulls, I am also aware of the story of the Cro-Magnon skull that was much larger and finer than a modern skull. It is a very funny story; because an eminent evolutionist, awakening to a somewhat belated caution, protested against anything being inferred from one specimen. It is the duty of a solitary skull to prove that our fathers were our inferiors. Any solitary skull presuming to prove that they were superior is felt to be suffering from swelled head.

APPENDIX II ON AUTHORITY AND ACCURACY

In this book which is merely meant as a popular criticism of popular fallacies, often indeed of very vulgar errors, I feel that I have sometimes given an impression of scoffing at serious scientific work. It was however the very reverse of my intentions. I am not arguing with the scientist who explains the elephant, but only with the sophist who explains it away. And as a matter of fact the sophist plays to the gallery, as he did in ancient Greece. He appeals to the ignorant, especially when he appeals to the learned. But I never meant my own criticism to be an impertinence to the truly learned. We all owe an infinite debt to the researches, especially the recent researches, of single minded students in these matters; and I have only professed to pick up things here and there from them. I have not loaded my abstract argument with quotations and references, which only make a man look more learned than he is; but in some cases I find that my own loose fashion of allusion is rather misleading about my own meaning. The passage about Chaucer and the Child Martyr is badly expressed; I only mean that the English poet probably had in mind the English saint; of whose story he gives a sort of foreign version. In the same way two statements in the chapter on Mythology follow each other in such a way that it may seem to be suggested that the second story about monotheism refers to the Southern Seas. I may explain that Atahocan belongs not to Australasian but to American savages. So in the chapter called "The Antiquity of Civilisation," which I feel to be the most unsatisfactory, I have given my own impression of the meaning of the development of Egyptian monarchy too much, perhaps, as if it were identical with the facts on which it was formed as given in works like those of Professor J. L Myres. But the confusion was not intentional; still less was there any intention to imply, in the remainder of the chapter, that the anthropological speculations about races are less valuable than they undoubtedly are. My criticism is strictly relative; I may say that the pyramids are plainer than the tracks of the desert; without denying that wiser men than I may see tracks in what is to me the trackless sand.

THE END

ORTHODOXY

PREFACE

This book is meant to be a companion to "Heretics," and to put the positive side in addition to the negative. Many critics complained of the book called "Heretics" because it merely criticised current philosophies without offering any alternative philosophy. This book is an attempt to answer the challenge. It is unavoidably affirmative and therefore unavoidably autobiographical. The writer has been driven back upon somewhat the same difficulty as that which beset Newman in writing his Apologia; he has been forced to be egotistical only in order to be sincere. While everything else may be different the motive in both cases is the same. It is the purpose of the writer to attempt an explanation, not of whether the Christian Faith can be believed, but of how he personally has come to believe it. The book is therefore arranged upon the positive principle of a riddle and its answer. It deals first with all the writer's own solitary and sincere speculations and then with all the startling style in which they were all suddenly satisfied by the Christian Theology. The writer regards it as amounting to a convincing creed. But if it is not that it is at least a repeated and surprising coincidence.

Gilbert K. Chesterton.

I INTRODUCTION IN DEFENCE OF EVERYTHING ELSE

THE only possible excuse for this book is that it is an answer to a challenge. Even a bad shot is dignified when he accepts a duel. When some time ago I published a series of hasty but sincere papers, under the name of "Heretics," several critics for whose intellect I have a warm respect (I may mention specially Mr. G.S.Street) said that it was all very well for me to tell everybody to affirm his cosmic theory, but that I had carefully avoided supporting my precepts with example. "I will begin to worry about my philosophy," said Mr. Street, "when Mr. Chesterton has given us his." It was perhaps an incautious suggestion to make to a person only too ready to write books upon the feeblest provocation. But after all, though Mr. Street has inspired and created this book, he need not read it. If he does read it, he will find that in its pages I have attempted in a vague and personal way, in a set of mental pictures rather than in a series of deductions, to state the philosophy in which I have come to believe. I will not call it my philosophy; for I did not make it. God and humanity made it; and it made me.

I have often had a fancy for writing a romance about an English yachtsman who slightly miscalculated his course and discovered England under the impression that it was a new island in the South Seas. I always find, however, that I am either too busy or too lazy to write this fine work, so I may as well give it away for the purposes of philosophical illustration. There will probably be a general impression that the man who landed (armed to the teeth and talking by signs) to plant the British flag on that barbaric temple which turned out to be the Pavilion at Brighton, felt rather a fool. I am not here concerned to deny that he looked a fool. But if you imagine that he felt a fool, or at any rate that the sense of folly was his sole or his dominant emotion, then you have not studied with sufficient delicacy the rich romantic nature of the hero of this tale. His mistake was really a most enviable mistake; and he knew it, if he was the man I take him for. What could be more delightful than to have in the same few minutes all the fascinating terrors of going abroad combined with all the humane security of coming home again? What could be better than to have all the fun of discovering South Africa without the disgusting necessity of landing there? What could be more glorious than to brace one's self up to discover New South Wales and then realize, with a gush of happy tears, that it was really old South Wales. This at least seems to me the main problem for philosophers, and is in a manner the main problem of this book. How can we contrive to be at once astonished at the world and yet at home in it? How can this queer cosmic town, with its many-legged citizens, with its monstrous and ancient lamps, how can this world give us at once the fascination of a strange town and the comfort and honour of being our own town?

To show that a faith or a philosophy is true from every standpoint would be too big an undertaking even for a much bigger book than this; it is necessary to follow one path of argument; and this is the path that I here propose to follow. I wish to set forth my faith as particularly answering this double spiritual need, the need for that mixture of the familiar and the unfamiliar which Christendom has rightly named romance. For the very word "romance" has in it the mystery and ancient meaning of Rome. Any one setting out to dispute anything ought always to begin by saying what he does not dispute. Beyond stating what he proposes to prove he should always state what he does not propose to prove. The thing I do not propose to prove, the thing I propose to take as common ground between myself and any average reader, is this desirability of an active and imaginative life, picturesque and full of a poetical curiosity, a life such as western man at any rate always seems to have desired. If a man says that extinction is better than existence or blank existence better than variety and adventure, then he is not one of the ordinary people to whom I am talking. If a man prefers nothing I can give him nothing. But nearly all people I have ever met in this western society in which I live would agree to the general proposition that we need this life of practical romance; the combination of something that is strange with something that is secure. We need so to view the world as to combine an idea of wonder and an idea of welcome. We need to be happy in this wonderland without once being merely comfortable. It is THIS achievement of my creed that I shall chiefly pursue in these pages.

But I have a peculiar reason for mentioning the man in a yacht, who discovered England. For I am that man in a yacht. I discovered England. I do not see how this book can avoid being egotistical; and I do not quite see (to tell the truth) how it can avoid being dull. Dulness will, however, free me from the charge which I most lament; the charge of being flippant. Mere light sophistry is the thing that I happen to despise most of all things, and it is perhaps a wholesome fact that this is the thing of which I am generally accused. I know nothing so contemptible as a mere paradox; a mere ingenious defence of the indefensible. If it were true (as has been said) that Mr. Bernard Shaw lived upon paradox, then he ought to be a mere common millionaire; for a man of his mental activity could invent a sophistry every six minutes. It is as easy as lying; because it is lying. The truth is, of course, that Mr. Shaw is cruelly hampered by the fact that he cannot tell any lie unless he thinks it is the truth. I find myself under the same intolerable bondage. I never in my life said anything merely because I thought it funny; though of course, I have had ordinary human vainglory, and may have thought it funny because I had said it. It is one thing to describe an interview with a gorgon or a griffin, a creature who does not exist. It is another thing to discover that the rhinoceros does exist and then take pleasure in the fact that he looks as if he didn't. One searches for truth, but it may be that one pursues instinctively the more extraordinary truths. And I offer this book with the heartiest sentiments to all the jolly people who hate what I write, and regard it (very justly, for all I know), as a piece of poor clowning or a single tiresome joke.

For if this book is a joke it is a joke against me. I am the man who with the utmost daring discovered what had been discovered before. If there is an element of farce in what follows, the farce is at my own expense; for this book explains how I fancied I was the first to set foot in Brighton and then found I was the last. It recounts my elephantine adventures in pursuit of the obvious. No one can think my case more ludicrous than I think it myself; no reader can accuse me here of trying to make a fool of him: I am the fool of this story, and no rebel shall hurl me from my throne. I freely confess all the idiotic ambitions of the end of the nineteenth century. I did, like all other solemn little boys, try to be in advance of the age. Like them I tried to be some ten minutes in advance of the truth. And I found that I was eighteen hundred years behind it. I did strain my voice with a painfully juvenile exaggeration in uttering my truths. And I was punished in the fittest and funniest way, for I have kept my truths: but I have discovered, not that they were not truths, but simply that they were not mine. When I fancied that I stood alone I was really in the ridiculous position of being backed up by all Christendom. It may be, Heaven forgive me, that I did try to be original; but I only succeeded in inventing all by myself an inferior copy of the existing traditions of civilized religion. The man from the yacht thought he was the first to find England; I thought I was the first to find Europe. I did try to found a heresy of my own; and when I had put the last touches to it, I discovered that it was orthodoxy.

It may be that somebody will be entertained by the account of this happy fiasco. It might amuse a friend or an enemy to read how I gradually learnt from the truth of some stray legend or from the falsehood of some dominant philosophy, things that I might have learnt from my catechism—if I had ever learnt it. There may or may not be some entertainment in reading how I found at last in an anarchist club or a Babylonian temple what I might have found in the nearest parish church. If any one is entertained by learning how the flowers of the field or the phrases in an omnibus, the accidents of politics or the pains of youth came together in a certain order to produce a certain conviction of Christian orthodoxy, he may possibly read this book. But there is in everything a reasonable division of labour. I have written the book, and nothing on earth would induce me to read it.

I add one purely pedantic note which comes, as a note naturally should, at the beginning of the book. These essays are concerned only to discuss the actual fact that the central Christian theology (sufficiently summarized in the Apostles' Creed) is the best root of energy and sound ethics. They are not intended to discuss the very fascinating but quite different question of what is the present seat of authority for the proclamation of that creed. When the word "orthodoxy" is used here it means the Apostles' Creed, as understood by everybody calling himself Christian until a very short time ago and the general historic conduct of those who held such a creed. I have been forced by mere space to confine myself to what I have got from this creed; I do not touch the matter much disputed among modern Christians, of where we ourselves got it. This is not an ecclesiastical treatise but a sort of slovenly autobiography. But if any one wants my opinions about the actual nature of the authority, Mr. G.S.Street has only to throw me another challenge, and I will write him another book.

II THE MANIAC

Thoroughly worldly people never understand even the world; they rely altogether on a few cynical maxims which are not true. Once I remember walking with a prosperous publisher, who made a remark which I had often heard before; it is, indeed, almost a motto of the modern world. Yet I had heard it once too often, and I saw suddenly that there was nothing in it. The publisher said of somebody, "That man will get on; he believes in himself." And I remember that as I lifted my head to listen, my eye caught an omnibus on which was written "Hanwell." I said to him, "Shall I tell you where the men are who believe most in themselves? For I can tell you. I know of men who believe in themselves more colossally than Napoleon or Caesar. I know where flames the fixed star of certainty and success. I can guide you to the thrones of the Super-men. The men who really believe in themselves are all in lunatic asylums." He said mildly that there were a good many men after all who believed in themselves and who were not in lunatic asylums. "Yes, there are," I retorted, "and you of all men ought to know them. That drunken poet from whom you would not take a dreary tragedy, he believed in himself. That elderly minister with an epic from whom you were hiding in a back room, he believed in himself. If you consulted your business experience instead of your ugly individualistic philosophy, you would know that believing in himself is one of the commonest signs of a rotter. Actors who can't act believe in themselves; and debtors who won't pay. It would be much truer to say that a man will certainly fail, because he believes in himself. Complete self-confidence is not merely a sin; complete self-confidence is a weakness. Believing utterly in one's self is a hysterical and superstitious belief like believing in Joanna Southcote: the man who has it has `Hanwell' written on his face as plain as it is written on that omnibus." And to all this my friend the publisher made this very deep and effective reply, "Well, if a man is not to believe in himself, in what is he to believe?" After a long pause I replied, "I will go home and write a book in answer to that question." This is the book that I have written in answer to it.

But I think this book may well start where our argument started— in the neighbourhood of the mad-house. Modern masters of science are much impressed with the need of beginning all inquiry with a fact. The ancient masters of religion were quite equally impressed with that necessity. They began with the fact of sin—a fact as practical as potatoes. Whether or no man could be washed in miraculous waters, there was no doubt at any rate that he wanted washing. But certain religious leaders in London, not mere materialists, have begun in our day not to deny the highly disputable water, but to deny the indisputable dirt. Certain new theologians dispute original sin, which is the only part of Christian theology which can really be proved. Some followers of the Reverend R.J.Campbell, in their almost too fastidious spirituality, admit divine sinlessness, which they cannot see even in their dreams. But they essentially deny human sin, which they can see in the street. The strongest saints and the strongest sceptics alike took positive evil as the starting-point of their argument. If it be true (as it certainly is) that a man can feel exquisite happiness in skinning a cat, then the religious philosopher can only draw one of two deductions. He must either deny the existence of God, as all atheists do; or he must deny the present union between God and man, as all Christians do. The new theologians seem to think it a highly rationalistic solution to deny the cat.

In this remarkable situation it is plainly not now possible (with any hope of a universal appeal) to start, as our fathers did, with the fact of sin. This very fact which was to them (and is to me) as plain as a pikestaff, is the very fact that has been specially diluted or denied. But though moderns deny the existence of sin, I do not think that they have yet denied the existence of a lunatic asylum. We all agree still that there is a collapse of the intellect as unmistakable as a falling house. Men deny hell, but not, as yet, Hanwell. For the purpose of our primary argument the one may very well stand where the other stood. I mean that as all thoughts and theories were once judged by whether they tended to make a man lose his soul, so for our present purpose all modern thoughts and theories may be judged by whether they tend to make a man lose his wits.

It is true that some speak lightly and loosely of insanity as in itself attractive. But a moment's thought will show that if disease is beautiful, it is generally some one else's disease. A blind man may be picturesque; but it requires two eyes to see the picture. And similarly even the wildest poetry of insanity can only be enjoyed by the sane. To the insane man his insanity is quite prosaic, because it is quite true. A man who thinks himself a chicken is to himself as ordinary as a chicken. A man who thinks he is a bit of glass is to himself as dull as a bit of glass. It is the homogeneity of his mind which makes him dull, and which makes him mad. It is only because we see the irony of his idea that we think him even amusing; it is only because he does not see the irony of his idea that he is put in Hanwell at all. In short, oddities only strike ordinary people. Oddities do not strike odd people. This is why ordinary people have a much more exciting time; while odd people are always complaining of the dulness of life. This is also why the new novels die so quickly, and why the old fairy tales endure for ever. The old fairy tale makes the hero a normal human boy; it is his adventures that are startling; they startle him because he is normal. But in the modern psychological novel the hero is abnormal; the centre is not central. Hence the fiercest adventures fail to affect him adequately, and the book is monotonous. You can make a story out of a hero among dragons; but not out of a dragon among dragons. The fairy tale discusses what a sane man will do in a mad world. The sober realistic novel of to-day discusses what an essential lunatic will do in a dull world.

Let us begin, then, with the mad-house; from this evil and fantastic inn let us set forth on our intellectual journey. Now, if we are to glance at the philosophy of sanity, the first thing to do in the matter is to blot out one big and common mistake. There is a notion adrift everywhere that imagination, especially mystical imagination, is dangerous to man's mental balance. Poets are commonly spoken of as psychologically unreliable; and generally there is a vague association between wreathing laurels in your hair and sticking straws in it. Facts and history utterly contradict this view. Most of the very great poets have been not only sane, but extremely business-like; and if Shakespeare ever really held horses, it was because he was much the safest man to hold them. Imagination does not breed insanity. Exactly what does breed insanity is reason. Poets do not go mad; but chess-players do. Mathematicians go mad, and cashiers; but creative artists very seldom. I am not, as will be seen, in any sense attacking logic: I only say that this danger does lie in logic, not in imagination. Artistic paternity is as wholesome as physical paternity. Moreover, it is worthy of remark that when a poet really was morbid it was commonly because he had some weak spot of rationality on his brain. Poe, for instance, really was morbid; not because he was poetical, but because he was specially analytical. Even chess was too poetical for him; he disliked chess because it was full of knights and castles, like a poem. He avowedly preferred the black discs of draughts, because they were more like the mere black dots on a diagram. Perhaps the strongest case of all is this: that only one great English poet went mad, Cowper. And he was definitely driven mad by logic, by the ugly and alien logic of predestination. Poetry was not the disease, but the medicine; poetry partly kept him in health. He could sometimes forget the red and thirsty hell to which his hideous necessitarianism dragged him among the wide waters and the white flat lilies of the Ouse. He was damned by John Calvin; he was almost saved by John Gilpin. Everywhere we see that men do not go mad by dreaming. Critics are much madder than poets. Homer is complete and calm enough; it is his critics who tear him into extravagant tatters. Shakespeare is quite himself; it is only some of his critics who have discovered that he was somebody else. And though St. John the Evangelist saw many strange monsters in his vision, he saw no creature so wild as one of his own commentators. The general fact is simple. Poetry is sane because it floats easily in an infinite sea; reason seeks to cross the infinite sea, and so make it finite. The result is mental exhaustion, like the physical exhaustion of Mr. Holbein. To accept everything is an exercise, to understand everything a strain. The poet only desires exaltation and expansion, a world to stretch himself in. The poet only asks to get his head into the heavens. It is the logician who seeks to get the heavens into his head. And it is his head that splits.

It is a small matter, but not irrelevant, that this striking mistake is commonly supported by a striking misquotation. We have all heard people cite the celebrated line of Dryden as "Great genius is to madness near allied." But Dryden did not say that great genius was to madness near allied. Dryden was a great genius himself, and knew better. It would have been hard to find a man more romantic than he, or more sensible. What Dryden said was this, "Great wits are oft to madness near allied"; and that is true. It is the pure promptitude of the intellect that is in peril of a breakdown. Also people might remember of what sort of man Dryden was talking. He was not talking of any unworldly visionary like Vaughan or George Herbert. He was talking of a cynical man of the world, a sceptic, a diplomatist, a great practical politician. Such men are indeed to madness near allied. Their incessant calculation of their own brains and other people's brains is a dangerous trade. It is always perilous to the mind to reckon up the mind. A flippant person has asked why we say, "As mad as a hatter." A more flippant person might answer that a hatter is mad because he has to measure the human head.

And if great reasoners are often maniacal, it is equally true that maniacs are commonly great reasoners. When I was engaged in a controversy with the CLARION on the matter of free will, that able writer Mr. R.B.Suthers said that free will was lunacy, because it meant causeless actions, and the actions of a lunatic would be causeless. I do not dwell here upon the disastrous lapse in determinist logic. Obviously if any actions, even a lunatic's, can be causeless, determinism is done for. If the chain of causation can be broken for a madman, it can be broken for a man. But my purpose is to point out something more practical. It was natural, perhaps, that a modern Marxian Socialist should not know anything about free will. But it was certainly remarkable that a modern Marxian Socialist should not know anything about lunatics. Mr. Suthers evidently did not know anything about lunatics. The last thing that can be said of a lunatic is that his actions are causeless. If any human acts may loosely be called causeless, they are the minor acts of a healthy man; whistling as he walks; slashing the grass with a stick; kicking his heels or rubbing his hands. It is the happy man who does the useless things; the sick man is not strong enough to be idle. It is exactly such careless and causeless actions that the madman could never understand; for the madman (like the determinist) generally sees too much cause in everything. The madman would read a conspiratorial significance into those empty activities. He would think that the lopping of the grass was an attack on private property. He would think that the kicking of the heels was a signal to an accomplice. If the madman could for an instant become careless, he would become sane. Every one who has had the misfortune to talk with people in the heart or on the edge of mental disorder, knows that their most sinister quality is a horrible clarity of detail; a connecting of one thing with another in a map more elaborate than a maze. If you argue with a madman, it is extremely probable that you will get the worst of it; for in many ways his mind moves all the quicker for not being delayed by the things that go with good judgment. He is not hampered by a sense of humour or by charity, or by the dumb certainties of experience. He is the more logical for losing certain sane affections. Indeed, the common phrase for insanity is in this respect a misleading one. The madman is not the man who has lost his reason. The madman is the man who has lost everything except his reason.

The madman's explanation of a thing is always complete, and often in a purely rational sense satisfactory. Or, to speak more strictly, the insane explanation, if not conclusive, is at least unanswerable; this may be observed specially in the two or three commonest kinds of madness. If a man says (for instance) that men have a conspiracy against him, you cannot dispute it except by saying that all the men deny that they are conspirators; which is exactly what conspirators would do. His explanation covers the facts as much as yours. Or if a man says that he is the rightful King of England, it is no complete answer to say that the existing authorities call him mad; for if he were King of England that might be the wisest thing for the existing authorities to do. Or if a man says that he is Jesus Christ, it is no answer to tell him that the world denies his divinity; for the world denied Christ's.

Nevertheless he is wrong. But if we attempt to trace his error in exact terms, we shall not find it quite so easy as we had supposed. Perhaps the nearest we can get to expressing it is to say this: that his mind moves in a perfect but narrow circle. A small circle is quite as infinite as a large circle; but, though it is quite as infinite, it is not so large. In the same way the insane explanation is quite as complete as the sane one, but it is not so large. A bullet is quite as round as the world, but it is not the world. There is such a thing as a narrow universality; there is such a thing as a small and cramped eternity; you may see it in many modern religions. Now, speaking quite externally and empirically, we may say that the strongest and most unmistakable MARK of madness is this combination between a logical completeness and a spiritual contraction. The lunatic's theory explains a large number of things, but it does not explain them in a large way. I mean that if you or I were dealing with a mind that was growing morbid, we should be chiefly concerned not so much to give it arguments as to give it air, to convince it that there was something cleaner and cooler outside the suffocation of a single argument. Suppose, for instance, it were the first case that I took as typical; suppose it were the case of a man who accused everybody of conspiring against him. If we could express our deepest feelings of protest and appeal against this obsession, I suppose we should say something like this: "Oh, I admit that you have your case and have it by heart, and that many things do fit into other things as you say. I admit that your explanation explains a great deal; but what a great deal it leaves out! Are there no other stories in the world except yours; and are all men busy with your business? Suppose we grant the details; perhaps when the man in the street did not seem to see you it was only his cunning; perhaps when the policeman asked you your name it was only because he knew it already. But how much happier you would be if you only knew that these people cared nothing about you! How much larger your life would be if your self could become smaller in it; if you could really look at other men with common curiosity and pleasure; if you could see them walking as they are in their sunny selfishness and their virile indifference! You would begin to be interested in them, because they were not interested in you. You would break out of this tiny and tawdry theatre in which your own little plot is always being played, and you would find yourself under a freer sky, in a street full of splendid strangers." Or suppose it were the second case of madness, that of a man who claims the crown, your impulse would be to answer, "All right! Perhaps you know that you are the King of England; but why do you care? Make one magnificent effort and you will be a human being and look down on all the kings of the earth." Or it might be the third case, of the madman who called himself Christ. If we said what we felt, we should say, "So you are the Creator and Redeemer of the world: but what a small world it must be! What a little heaven you must inhabit, with angels no bigger than butterflies! How sad it must be to be God; and an inadequate God! Is there really no life fuller and no love more marvellous than yours; and is it really in your small and painful pity that all flesh must put its faith? How much happier you would be, how much more of you there would be, if the hammer of a higher God could smash your small cosmos, scattering the stars like spangles, and leave you in the open, free like other men to look up as well as down!"

And it must be remembered that the most purely practical science does take this view of mental evil; it does not seek to argue with it like a heresy but simply to snap it like a spell. Neither modern science nor ancient religion believes in complete free thought. Theology rebukes certain thoughts by calling them blasphemous. Science rebukes certain thoughts by calling them morbid. For example, some religious societies discouraged men more or less from thinking about sex. The new scientific society definitely discourages men from thinking about death; it is a fact, but it is considered a morbid fact. And in dealing with those whose morbidity has a touch of mania, modern science cares far less for pure logic than a dancing Dervish. In these cases it is not enough that the unhappy man should desire truth; he must desire health. Nothing can save him but a blind hunger for normality, like that of a beast. A man cannot think himself out of mental evil; for it is actually the organ of thought that has become diseased, ungovernable, and, as it were, independent. He can only be saved by will or faith. The moment his mere reason moves, it moves in the old circular rut; he will go round and round his logical circle, just as a man in a third-class carriage on the Inner Circle will go round and round the Inner Circle unless he performs the voluntary, vigorous, and mystical act of getting out at Gower Street. Decision is the whole business here; a door must be shut for ever. Every remedy is a desperate remedy. Every cure is a miraculous cure. Curing a madman is not arguing with a philosopher; it is casting out a devil. And however quietly doctors and psychologists may go to work in the matter, their attitude is profoundly intolerant— as intolerant as Bloody Mary. Their attitude is really this: that the man must stop thinking, if he is to go on living. Their counsel is one of intellectual amputation. If thy HEAD offend thee, cut it off; for it is better, not merely to enter the Kingdom of Heaven as a child, but to enter it as an imbecile, rather than with your whole intellect to be cast into hell— or into Hanwell.

Such is the madman of experience; he is commonly a reasoner, frequently a successful reasoner. Doubtless he could be vanquished in mere reason, and the case against him put logically. But it can be put much more precisely in more general and even aesthetic terms. He is in the clean and well-lit prison of one idea: he is sharpened to one painful point. He is without healthy hesitation and healthy complexity. Now, as I explain in the introduction, I have determined in these early chapters to give not so much a diagram of a doctrine as some pictures of a point of view. And I have described at length my vision of the maniac for this reason: that just as I am affected by the maniac, so I am affected by most modern thinkers. That unmistakable mood or note that I hear from Hanwell, I hear also from half the chairs of science and seats of learning to-day; and most of the mad doctors are mad doctors in more senses than one. They all have exactly that combination we have noted: the combination of an expansive and exhaustive reason with a contracted common sense. They are universal only in the sense that they take one thin explanation and carry it very far. But a pattern can stretch for ever and still be a small pattern. They see a chess-board white on black, and if the universe is paved with it, it is still white on black. Like the lunatic, they cannot alter their standpoint; they cannot make a mental effort and suddenly see it black on white.

Take first the more obvious case of materialism. As an explanation of the world, materialism has a sort of insane simplicity. It has just the quality of the madman's argument; we have at once the sense of it covering everything and the sense of it leaving everything out. Contemplate some able and sincere materialist, as, for instance, Mr. McCabe, and you will have exactly this unique sensation. He understands everything, and everything does not seem worth understanding. His cosmos may be complete in every rivet and cog-wheel, but still his cosmos is smaller than our world. Somehow his scheme, like the lucid scheme of the madman, seems unconscious of the alien energies and the large indifference of the earth; it is not thinking of the real things of the earth, of fighting peoples or proud mothers, or first love or fear upon the sea. The earth is so very large, and the cosmos is so very small. The cosmos is about the smallest hole that a man can hide his head in.

It must be understood that I am not now discussing the relation of these creeds to truth; but, for the present, solely their relation to health. Later in the argument I hope to attack the question of objective verity; here I speak only of a phenomenon of psychology. I do not for the present attempt to prove to Haeckel that materialism is untrue, any more than I attempted to prove to the man who thought he was Christ that he was labouring under an error. I merely remark here on the fact that both cases have the same kind of completeness and the same kind of incompleteness. You can explain a man's detention at Hanwell by an indifferent public by saying that it is the crucifixion of a god of whom the world is not worthy. The explanation does explain. Similarly you may explain the order in the universe by saying that all things, even the souls of men, are leaves inevitably unfolding on an utterly unconscious tree— the blind destiny of matter. The explanation does explain, though not, of course, so completely as the madman's. But the point here is that the normal human mind not only objects to both, but feels to both the same objection. Its approximate statement is that if the man in Hanwell is the real God, he is not much of a god. And, similarly, if the cosmos of the materialist is the real cosmos, it is not much of a cosmos. The thing has shrunk. The deity is less divine than many men; and (according to Haeckel) the whole of life is something much more grey, narrow, and trivial than many separate aspects of it. The parts seem greater than the whole.

For we must remember that the materialist philosophy (whether true or not) is certainly much more limiting than any religion. In one sense, of course, all intelligent ideas are narrow. They cannot be broader than themselves. A Christian is only restricted in the same sense that an atheist is restricted. He cannot think Christianity false and continue to be a Christian; and the atheist cannot think atheism false and continue to be an atheist. But as it happens, there is a very special sense in which materialism has more restrictions than spiritualism. Mr. McCabe thinks me a slave because I am not allowed to believe in determinism. I think Mr. McCabe a slave because he is not allowed to believe in fairies. But if we examine the two vetoes we shall see that his is really much more of a pure veto than mine. The Christian is quite free to believe that there is a considerable amount of settled order and inevitable development in the universe. But the materialist is not allowed to admit into his spotless machine the slightest speck of spiritualism or miracle. Poor Mr. McCabe is not allowed to retain even the tiniest imp, though it might be hiding in a pimpernel. The Christian admits that the universe is manifold and even miscellaneous, just as a sane man knows that he is complex. The sane man knows that he has a touch of the beast, a touch of the devil, a touch of the saint, a touch of the citizen. Nay, the really sane man knows that he has a touch of the madman. But the materialist's world is quite simple and solid, just as the madman is quite sure he is sane. The materialist is sure that history has been simply and solely a chain of causation, just as the interesting person before mentioned is quite sure that he is simply and solely a chicken. Materialists and madmen never have doubts.

Spiritual doctrines do not actually limit the mind as do materialistic denials. Even if I believe in immortality I need not think about it. But if I disbelieve in immortality I must not think about it. In the first case the road is open and I can go as far as I like; in the second the road is shut. But the case is even stronger, and the parallel with madness is yet more strange. For it was our case against the exhaustive and logical theory of the lunatic that, right or wrong, it gradually destroyed his humanity. Now it is the charge against the main deductions of the materialist that, right or wrong, they gradually destroy his humanity; I do not mean only kindness, I mean hope, courage, poetry, initiative, all that is human. For instance, when materialism leads men to complete fatalism (as it generally does), it is quite idle to pretend that it is in any sense a liberating force. It is absurd to say that you are especially advancing freedom when you only use free thought to destroy free will. The determinists come to bind, not to loose. They may well call their law the "chain" of causation. It is the worst chain that ever fettered a human being. You may use the language of liberty, if you like, about materialistic teaching, but it is obvious that this is just as inapplicable to it as a whole as the same language when applied to a man locked up in a mad-house. You may say, if you like, that the man is free to think himself a poached egg. But it is surely a more massive and important fact that if he is a poached egg he is not free to eat, drink, sleep, walk, or smoke a cigarette. Similarly you may say, if you like, that the bold determinist speculator is free to disbelieve in the reality of the will. But it is a much more massive and important fact that he is not free to raise, to curse, to thank, to justify, to urge, to punish, to resist temptations, to incite mobs, to make New Year resolutions, to pardon sinners, to rebuke tyrants, or even to say "thank you" for the mustard.

In passing from this subject I may note that there is a queer fallacy to the effect that materialistic fatalism is in some way favourable to mercy, to the abolition of cruel punishments or punishments of any kind. This is startlingly the reverse of the truth. It is quite tenable that the doctrine of necessity makes no difference at all; that it leaves the flogger flogging and the kind friend exhorting as before. But obviously if it stops either of them it stops the kind exhortation. That the sins are inevitable does not prevent punishment; if it prevents anything it prevents persuasion. Determinism is quite as likely to lead to cruelty as it is certain to lead to cowardice. Determinism is not inconsistent with the cruel treatment of criminals. What it is (perhaps) inconsistent with is the generous treatment of criminals; with any appeal to their better feelings or encouragement in their moral struggle. The determinist does not believe in appealing to the will, but he does believe in changing the environment. He must not say to the sinner, "Go and sin no more," because the sinner cannot help it. But he can put him in boiling oil; for boiling oil is an environment. Considered as a figure, therefore, the materialist has the fantastic outline of the figure of the madman. Both take up a position at once unanswerable and intolerable.

Of course it is not only of the materialist that all this is true. The same would apply to the other extreme of speculative logic. There is a sceptic far more terrible than he who believes that everything began in matter. It is possible to meet the sceptic who believes that everything began in himself. He doubts not the existence of angels or devils, but the existence of men and cows. For him his own friends are a mythology made up by himself. He created his own father and his own mother. This horrible fancy has in it something decidedly attractive to the somewhat mystical egoism of our day. That publisher who thought that men would get on if they believed in themselves, those seekers after the Superman who are always looking for him in the looking-glass, those writers who talk about impressing their personalities instead of creating life for the world, all these people have really only an inch between them and this awful emptiness. Then when this kindly world all round the man has been blackened out like a lie; when friends fade into ghosts, and the foundations of the world fail; then when the man, believing in nothing and in no man, is alone in his own nightmare, then the great individualistic motto shall be written over him in avenging irony. The stars will be only dots in the blackness of his own brain; his mother's face will be only a sketch from his own insane pencil on the walls of his cell. But over his cell shall be written, with dreadful truth, "He believes in himself."

All that concerns us here, however, is to note that this panegoistic extreme of thought exhibits the same paradox as the other extreme of materialism. It is equally complete in theory and equally crippling in practice. For the sake of simplicity, it is easier to state the notion by saying that a man can believe that he is always in a dream. Now, obviously there can be no positive proof given to him that he is not in a dream, for the simple reason that no proof can be offered that might not be offered in a dream. But if the man began to burn down London and say that his housekeeper would soon call him to breakfast, we should take him and put him with other logicians in a place which has often been alluded to in the course of this chapter. The man who cannot believe his senses, and the man who cannot believe anything else, are both insane, but their insanity is proved not by any error in their argument, but by the manifest mistake of their whole lives. They have both locked themselves up in two boxes, painted inside with the sun and stars; they are both unable to get out, the one into the health and happiness of heaven, the other even into the health and happiness of the earth. Their position is quite reasonable; nay, in a sense it is infinitely reasonable, just as a threepenny bit is infinitely circular. But there is such a thing as a mean infinity, a base and slavish eternity. It is amusing to notice that many of the moderns, whether sceptics or mystics, have taken as their sign a certain eastern symbol, which is the very symbol of this ultimate nullity. When they wish to represent eternity, they represent it by a serpent with his tail in his mouth. There is a startling sarcasm in the image of that very unsatisfactory meal. The eternity of the material fatalists, the eternity of the eastern pessimists, the eternity of the supercilious theosophists and higher scientists of to-day is, indeed, very well presented by a serpent eating his tail, a degraded animal who destroys even himself.

This chapter is purely practical and is concerned with what actually is the chief mark and element of insanity; we may say in summary that it is reason used without root, reason in the void. The man who begins to think without the proper first principles goes mad; he begins to think at the wrong end. And for the rest of these pages we have to try and discover what is the right end. But we may ask in conclusion, if this be what drives men mad, what is it that keeps them sane? By the end of this book I hope to give a definite, some will think a far too definite, answer. But for the moment it is possible in the same solely practical manner to give a general answer touching what in actual human history keeps men sane. Mysticism keeps men sane. As long as you have mystery you have health; when you destroy mystery you create morbidity. The ordinary man has always been sane because the ordinary man has always been a mystic. He has permitted the twilight. He has always had one foot in earth and the other in fairyland. He has always left himself free to doubt his gods; but (unlike the agnostic of to-day) free also to believe in them. He has always cared more for truth than for consistency. If he saw two truths that seemed to contradict each other, he would take the two truths and the contradiction along with them. His spiritual sight is stereoscopic, like his physical sight: he sees two different pictures at once and yet sees all the better for that. Thus he has always believed that there was such a thing as fate, but such a thing as free will also. Thus he believed that children were indeed the kingdom of heaven, but nevertheless ought to be obedient to the kingdom of earth. He admired youth because it was young and age because it was not. It is exactly this balance of apparent contradictions that has been the whole buoyancy of the healthy man. The whole secret of mysticism is this: that man can understand everything by the help of what he does not understand. The morbid logician seeks to make everything lucid, and succeeds in making everything mysterious. The mystic allows one thing to be mysterious, and everything else becomes lucid. The determinist makes the theory of causation quite clear, and then finds that he cannot say "if you please" to the housemaid. The Christian permits free will to remain a sacred mystery; but because of this his relations with the housemaid become of a sparkling and crystal clearness. He puts the seed of dogma in a central darkness; but it branches forth in all directions with abounding natural health. As we have taken the circle as the symbol of reason and madness, we may very well take the cross as the symbol at once of mystery and of health. Buddhism is centripetal, but Christianity is centrifugal: it breaks out. For the circle is perfect and infinite in its nature; but it is fixed for ever in its size; it can never be larger or smaller. But the cross, though it has at its heart a collision and a contradiction, can extend its four arms for ever without altering its shape. Because it has a paradox in its centre it can grow without changing. The circle returns upon itself and is bound. The cross opens its arms to the four winds; it is a signpost for free travellers.

Symbols alone are of even a cloudy value in speaking of this deep matter; and another symbol from physical nature will express sufficiently well the real place of mysticism before mankind. The one created thing which we cannot look at is the one thing in the light of which we look at everything. Like the sun at noonday, mysticism explains everything else by the blaze of its own victorious invisibility. Detached intellectualism is (in the exact sense of a popular phrase) all moonshine; for it is light without heat, and it is secondary light, reflected from a dead world. But the Greeks were right when they made Apollo the god both of imagination and of sanity; for he was both the patron of poetry and the patron of healing. Of necessary dogmas and a special creed I shall speak later. But that transcendentalism by which all men live has primarily much the position of the sun in the sky. We are conscious of it as of a kind of splendid confusion; it is something both shining and shapeless, at once a blaze and a blur. But the circle of the moon is as clear and unmistakable, as recurrent and inevitable, as the circle of Euclid on a blackboard. For the moon is utterly reasonable; and the moon is the mother of lunatics and has given to them all her name.

III THE SUICIDE OF THOUGHT

The phrases of the street are not only forcible but subtle: for a figure of speech can often get into a crack too small for a definition. Phrases like "put out" or "off colour" might have been coined by Mr. Henry James in an agony of verbal precision. And there is no more subtle truth than that of the everyday phrase about a man having "his heart in the right place." It involves the idea of normal proportion; not only does a certain function exist, but it is rightly related to other functions. Indeed, the negation of this phrase would describe with peculiar accuracy the somewhat morbid mercy and perverse tenderness of the most representative moderns. If, for instance, I had to describe with fairness the character of Mr. Bernard Shaw, I could not express myself more exactly than by saying that he has a heroically large and generous heart; but not a heart in the right place. And this is so of the typical society of our time.

The modern world is not evil; in some ways the modern world is far too good. It is full of wild and wasted virtues. When a religious scheme is shattered (as Christianity was shattered at the Reformation), it is not merely the vices that are let loose. The vices are, indeed, let loose, and they wander and do damage. But the virtues are let loose also; and the virtues wander more wildly, and the virtues do more terrible damage. The modern world is full of the old Christian virtues gone mad. The virtues have gone mad because they have been isolated from each other and are wandering alone. Thus some scientists care for truth; and their truth is pitiless. Thus some humanitarians only care for pity; and their pity (I am sorry to say) is often untruthful. For example, Mr. Blatchford attacks Christianity because he is mad on one Christian virtue: the merely mystical and almost irrational virtue of charity. He has a strange idea that he will make it easier to forgive sins by saying that there are no sins to forgive. Mr. Blatchford is not only an early Christian, he is the only early Christian who ought really to have been eaten by lions. For in his case the pagan accusation is really true: his mercy would mean mere anarchy. He really is the enemy of the human race— because he is so human. As the other extreme, we may take the acrid realist, who has deliberately killed in himself all human pleasure in happy tales or in the healing of the heart. Torquemada tortured people physically for the sake of moral truth. Zola tortured people morally for the sake of physical truth. But in Torquemada's time there was at least a system that could to some extent make righteousness and peace kiss each other. Now they do not even bow. But a much stronger case than these two of truth and pity can be found in the remarkable case of the dislocation of humility.

It is only with one aspect of humility that we are here concerned. Humility was largely meant as a restraint upon the arrogance and infinity of the appetite of man. He was always outstripping his mercies with his own newly invented needs. His very power of enjoyment destroyed half his joys. By asking for pleasure, he lost the chief pleasure; for the chief pleasure is surprise. Hence it became evident that if a man would make his world large, he must be always making himself small. Even the haughty visions, the tall cities, and the toppling pinnacles are the creations of humility. Giants that tread down forests like grass are the creations of humility. Towers that vanish upwards above the loneliest star are the creations of humility. For towers are not tall unless we look up at them; and giants are not giants unless they are larger than we. All this gigantesque imagination, which is, perhaps, the mightiest of the pleasures of man, is at bottom entirely humble. It is impossible without humility to enjoy anything— even pride.

But what we suffer from to-day is humility in the wrong place. Modesty has moved from the organ of ambition. Modesty has settled upon the organ of conviction; where it was never meant to be. A man was meant to be doubtful about himself, but undoubting about the truth; this has been exactly reversed. Nowadays the part of a man that a man does assert is exactly the part he ought not to assert—himself. The part he doubts is exactly the part he ought not to doubt—the Divine Reason. Huxley preached a humility content to learn from Nature. But the new sceptic is so humble that he doubts if he can even learn. Thus we should be wrong if we had said hastily that there is no humility typical of our time. The truth is that there is a real humility typical of our time; but it so happens that it is practically a more poisonous humility than the wildest prostrations of the ascetic. The old humility was a spur that prevented a man from stopping; not a nail in his boot that prevented him from going on. For the old humility made a man doubtful about his efforts, which might make him work harder. But the new humility makes a man doubtful about his aims, which will make him stop working altogether.

At any street corner we may meet a man who utters the frantic and blasphemous statement that he may be wrong. Every day one comes across somebody who says that of course his view may not be the right one. Of course his view must be the right one, or it is not his view. We are on the road to producing a race of men too mentally modest to believe in the multiplication table. We are in danger of seeing philosophers who doubt the law of gravity as being a mere fancy of their own. Scoffers of old time were too proud to be convinced; but these are too humble to be convinced. The meek do inherit the earth; but the modern sceptics are too meek even to claim their inheritance. It is exactly this intellectual helplessness which is our second problem.

The last chapter has been concerned only with a fact of observation: that what peril of morbidity there is for man comes rather from his reason than his imagination. It was not meant to attack the authority of reason; rather it is the ultimate purpose to defend it. For it needs defence. The whole modern world is at war with reason; and the tower already reels.

The sages, it is often said, can see no answer to the riddle of religion. But the trouble with our sages is not that they cannot see the answer; it is that they cannot even see the riddle. They are like children so stupid as to notice nothing paradoxical in the playful assertion that a door is not a door. The modern latitudinarians speak, for instance, about authority in religion not only as if there were no reason in it, but as if there had never been any reason for it. Apart from seeing its philosophical basis, they cannot even see its historical cause. Religious authority has often, doubtless, been oppressive or unreasonable; just as every legal system (and especially our present one) has been callous and full of a cruel apathy. It is rational to attack the police; nay, it is glorious. But the modern critics of religious authority are like men who should attack the police without ever having heard of burglars. For there is a great and possible peril to the human mind: a peril as practical as burglary. Against it religious authority was reared, rightly or wrongly, as a barrier. And against it something certainly must be reared as a barrier, if our race is to avoid ruin.

That peril is that the human intellect is free to destroy itself. Just as one generation could prevent the very existence of the next generation, by all entering a monastery or jumping into the sea, so one set of thinkers can in some degree prevent further thinking by teaching the next generation that there is no validity in any human thought. It is idle to talk always of the alternative of reason and faith. Reason is itself a matter of faith. It is an act of faith to assert that our thoughts have any relation to reality at all. If you are merely a sceptic, you must sooner or later ask yourself the question, "Why should ANYTHING go right; even observation and deduction? Why should not good logic be as misleading as bad logic? They are both movements in the brain of a bewildered ape?" The young sceptic says, "I have a right to think for myself." But the old sceptic, the complete sceptic, says, "I have no right to think for myself. I have no right to think at all."

There is a thought that stops thought. That is the only thought that ought to be stopped. That is the ultimate evil against which all religious authority was aimed. It only appears at the end of decadent ages like our own: and already Mr. H.G.Wells has raised its ruinous banner; he has written a delicate piece of scepticism called "Doubts of the Instrument." In this he questions the brain itself, and endeavours to remove all reality from all his own assertions, past, present, and to come. But it was against this remote ruin that all the military systems in religion were originally ranked and ruled. The creeds and the crusades, the hierarchies and the horrible persecutions were not organized, as is ignorantly said, for the suppression of reason. They were organized for the difficult defence of reason. Man, by a blind instinct, knew that if once things were wildly questioned, reason could be questioned first. The authority of priests to absolve, the authority of popes to define the authority, even of inquisitors to terrify: these were all only dark defences erected round one central authority, more undemonstrable, more supernatural than all—the authority of a man to think. We know now that this is so; we have no excuse for not knowing it. For we can hear scepticism crashing through the old ring of authorities, and at the same moment we can see reason swaying upon her throne. In so far as religion is gone, reason is going. For they are both of the same primary and authoritative kind. They are both methods of proof which cannot themselves be proved. And in the act of destroying the idea of Divine authority we have largely destroyed the idea of that human authority by which we do a long-division sum. With a long and sustained tug we have attempted to pull the mitre off pontifical man; and his head has come off with it.

Lest this should be called loose assertion, it is perhaps desirable, though dull, to run rapidly through the chief modern fashions of thought which have this effect of stopping thought itself. Materialism and the view of everything as a personal illusion have some such effect; for if the mind is mechanical, thought cannot be very exciting, and if the cosmos is unreal, there is nothing to think about. But in these cases the effect is indirect and doubtful. In some cases it is direct and clear; notably in the case of what is generally called evolution.

Evolution is a good example of that modern intelligence which, if it destroys anything, destroys itself. Evolution is either an innocent scientific description of how certain earthly things came about; or, if it is anything more than this, it is an attack upon thought itself. If evolution destroys anything, it does not destroy religion but rationalism. If evolution simply means that a positive thing called an ape turned very slowly into a positive thing called a man, then it is stingless for the most orthodox; for a personal God might just as well do things slowly as quickly, especially if, like the Christian God, he were outside time. But if it means anything more, it means that there is no such thing as an ape to change, and no such thing as a man for him to change into. It means that there is no such thing as a thing. At best, there is only one thing, and that is a flux of everything and anything. This is an attack not upon the faith, but upon the mind; you cannot think if there are no things to think about. You cannot think if you are not separate from the subject of thought. Descartes said, "I think; therefore I am." The philosophic evolutionist reverses and negatives the epigram. He says, "I am not; therefore I cannot think."

Then there is the opposite attack on thought: that urged by Mr. H.G.Wells when he insists that every separate thing is "unique," and there are no categories at all. This also is merely destructive. Thinking means connecting things, and stops if they cannot be connected. It need hardly be said that this scepticism forbidding thought necessarily forbids speech; a man cannot open his mouth without contradicting it. Thus when Mr. Wells says (as he did somewhere), "All chairs are quite different," he utters not merely a misstatement, but a contradiction in terms. If all chairs were quite different, you could not call them "all chairs."

Akin to these is the false theory of progress, which maintains that we alter the test instead of trying to pass the test. We often hear it said, for instance, "What is right in one age is wrong in another." This is quite reasonable, if it means that there is a fixed aim, and that certain methods attain at certain times and not at other times. If women, say, desire to be elegant, it may be that they are improved at one time by growing fatter and at another time by growing thinner. But you cannot say that they are improved by ceasing to wish to be elegant and beginning to wish to be oblong. If the standard changes, how can there be improvement, which implies a standard? Nietzsche started a nonsensical idea that men had once sought as good what we now call evil; if it were so, we could not talk of surpassing or even falling short of them. How can you overtake Jones if you walk in the other direction? You cannot discuss whether one people has succeeded more in being miserable than another succeeded in being happy. It would be like discussing whether Milton was more puritanical than a pig is fat.

It is true that a man (a silly man) might make change itself his object or ideal. But as an ideal, change itself becomes unchangeable. If the change-worshipper wishes to estimate his own progress, he must be sternly loyal to the ideal of change; he must not begin to flirt gaily with the ideal of monotony. Progress itself cannot progress. It is worth remark, in passing, that when Tennyson, in a wild and rather weak manner, welcomed the idea of infinite alteration in society, he instinctively took a metaphor which suggests an imprisoned tedium. He wrote—

"Let the great world spin for ever down the ringing grooves of change."

He thought of change itself as an unchangeable groove; and so it is. Change is about the narrowest and hardest groove that a man can get into.

The main point here, however, is that this idea of a fundamental alteration in the standard is one of the things that make thought about the past or future simply impossible. The theory of a complete change of standards in human history does not merely deprive us of the pleasure of honouring our fathers; it deprives us even of the more modern and aristocratic pleasure of despising them.

This bald summary of the thought-destroying forces of our time would not be complete without some reference to pragmatism; for though I have here used and should everywhere defend the pragmatist method as a preliminary guide to truth, there is an extreme application of it which involves the absence of all truth whatever. My meaning can be put shortly thus. I agree with the pragmatists that apparent objective truth is not the whole matter; that there is an authoritative need to believe the things that are necessary to the human mind. But I say that one of those necessities precisely is a belief in objective truth. The pragmatist tells a man to think what he must think and never mind the Absolute. But precisely one of the things that he must think is the Absolute. This philosophy, indeed, is a kind of verbal paradox. Pragmatism is a matter of human needs; and one of the first of human needs is to be something more than a pragmatist. Extreme pragmatism is just as inhuman as the determinism it so powerfully attacks. The determinist (who, to do him justice, does not pretend to be a human being) makes nonsense of the human sense of actual choice. The pragmatist, who professes to be specially human, makes nonsense of the human sense of actual fact.

To sum up our contention so far, we may say that the most characteristic current philosophies have not only a touch of mania, but a touch of suicidal mania. The mere questioner has knocked his head against the limits of human thought; and cracked it. This is what makes so futile the warnings of the orthodox and the boasts of the advanced about the dangerous boyhood of free thought. What we are looking at is not the boyhood of free thought; it is the old age and ultimate dissolution of free thought. It is vain for bishops and pious bigwigs to discuss what dreadful things will happen if wild scepticism runs its course. It has run its course. It is vain for eloquent atheists to talk of the great truths that will be revealed if once we see free thought begin. We have seen it end. It has no more questions to ask; it has questioned itself. You cannot call up any wilder vision than a city in which men ask themselves if they have any selves. You cannot fancy a more sceptical world than that in which men doubt if there is a world. It might certainly have reached its bankruptcy more quickly and cleanly if it had not been feebly hampered by the application of indefensible laws of blasphemy or by the absurd pretence that modern England is Christian. But it would have reached the bankruptcy anyhow. Militant atheists are still unjustly persecuted; but rather because they are an old minority than because they are a new one. Free thought has exhausted its own freedom. It is weary of its own success. If any eager freethinker now hails philosophic freedom as the dawn, he is only like the man in Mark Twain who came out wrapped in blankets to see the sun rise and was just in time to see it set. If any frightened curate still says that it will be awful if the darkness of free thought should spread, we can only answer him in the high and powerful words of Mr. Belloc, "Do not, I beseech you, be troubled about the increase of forces already in dissolution. You have mistaken the hour of the night: it is already morning." We have no more questions left to ask. We have looked for questions in the darkest corners and on the wildest peaks. We have found all the questions that can be found. It is time we gave up looking for questions and began looking for answers.

But one more word must be added. At the beginning of this preliminary negative sketch I said that our mental ruin has been wrought by wild reason, not by wild imagination. A man does not go mad because he makes a statue a mile high, but he may go mad by thinking it out in square inches. Now, one school of thinkers has seen this and jumped at it as a way of renewing the pagan health of the world. They see that reason destroys; but Will, they say, creates. The ultimate authority, they say, is in will, not in reason. The supreme point is not why a man demands a thing, but the fact that he does demand it. I have no space to trace or expound this philosophy of Will. It came, I suppose, through Nietzsche, who preached something that is called egoism. That, indeed, was simpleminded enough; for Nietzsche denied egoism simply by preaching it. To preach anything is to give it away. First, the egoist calls life a war without mercy, and then he takes the greatest possible trouble to drill his enemies in war. To preach egoism is to practise altruism. But however it began, the view is common enough in current literature. The main defence of these thinkers is that they are not thinkers; they are makers. They say that choice is itself the divine thing. Thus Mr. Bernard Shaw has attacked the old idea that men's acts are to be judged by the standard of the desire of happiness. He says that a man does not act for his happiness, but from his will. He does not say, "Jam will make me happy," but "I want jam." And in all this others follow him with yet greater enthusiasm. Mr. John Davidson, a remarkable poet, is so passionately excited about it that he is obliged to write prose. He publishes a short play with several long prefaces. This is natural enough in Mr. Shaw, for all his plays are prefaces: Mr. Shaw is (I suspect) the only man on earth who has never written any poetry. But that Mr. Davidson (who can write excellent poetry) should write instead laborious metaphysics in defence of this doctrine of will, does show that the doctrine of will has taken hold of men. Even Mr. H.G.Wells has half spoken in its language; saying that one should test acts not like a thinker, but like an artist, saying, "I FEEL this curve is right," or "that line SHALL go thus." They are all excited; and well they may be. For by this doctrine of the divine authority of will, they think they can break out of the doomed fortress of rationalism. They think they can escape.

But they cannot escape. This pure praise of volition ends in the same break up and blank as the mere pursuit of logic. Exactly as complete free thought involves the doubting of thought itself, so the acceptation of mere "willing" really paralyzes the will. Mr. Bernard Shaw has not perceived the real difference between the old utilitarian test of pleasure (clumsy, of course, and easily misstated) and that which he propounds. The real difference between the test of happiness and the test of will is simply that the test of happiness is a test and the other isn't. You can discuss whether a man's act in jumping over a cliff was directed towards happiness; you cannot discuss whether it was derived from will. Of course it was. You can praise an action by saying that it is calculated to bring pleasure or pain to discover truth or to save the soul. But you cannot praise an action because it shows will; for to say that is merely to say that it is an action. By this praise of will you cannot really choose one course as better than another. And yet choosing one course as better than another is the very definition of the will you are praising.

The worship of will is the negation of will. To admire mere choice is to refuse to choose. If Mr. Bernard Shaw comes up to me and says, "Will something," that is tantamount to saying, "I do not mind what you will," and that is tantamount to saying, "I have no will in the matter." You cannot admire will in general, because the essence of will is that it is particular. A brilliant anarchist like Mr. John Davidson feels an irritation against ordinary morality, and therefore he invokes will—will to anything. He only wants humanity to want something. But humanity does want something. It wants ordinary morality. He rebels against the law and tells us to will something or anything. But we have willed something. We have willed the law against which he rebels.

All the will-worshippers, from Nietzsche to Mr. Davidson, are really quite empty of volition. They cannot will, they can hardly wish. And if any one wants a proof of this, it can be found quite easily. It can be found in this fact: that they always talk of will as something that expands and breaks out. But it is quite the opposite. Every act of will is an act of self-limitation. To desire action is to desire limitation. In that sense every act is an act of self-sacrifice. When you choose anything, you reject everything else. That objection, which men of this school used to make to the act of marriage, is really an objection to every act. Every act is an irrevocable selection and exclusion. Just as when you marry one woman you give up all the others, so when you take one course of action you give up all the other courses. If you become King of England, you give up the post of Beadle in Brompton. If you go to Rome, you sacrifice a rich suggestive life in Wimbledon. It is the existence of this negative or limiting side of will that makes most of the talk of the anarchic will-worshippers little better than nonsense. For instance, Mr. John Davidson tells us to have nothing to do with "Thou shalt not"; but it is surely obvious that "Thou shalt not" is only one of the necessary corollaries of "I will." "I will go to the Lord Mayor's Show, and thou shalt not stop me." Anarchism adjures us to be bold creative artists, and care for no laws or limits. But it is impossible to be an artist and not care for laws and limits. Art is limitation; the essence of every picture is the frame. If you draw a giraffe, you must draw him with a long neck. If, in your bold creative way, you hold yourself free to draw a giraffe with a short neck, you will really find that you are not free to draw a giraffe. The moment you step into the world of facts, you step into a world of limits. You can free things from alien or accidental laws, but not from the laws of their own nature. You may, if you like, free a tiger from his bars; but do not free him from his stripes. Do not free a camel of the burden of his hump: you may be freeing him from being a camel. Do not go about as a demagogue, encouraging triangles to break out of the prison of their three sides. If a triangle breaks out of its three sides, its life comes to a lamentable end. Somebody wrote a work called "The Loves of the Triangles"; I never read it, but I am sure that if triangles ever were loved, they were loved for being triangular. This is certainly the case with all artistic creation, which is in some ways the most decisive example of pure will. The artist loves his limitations: they constitute the THING he is doing. The painter is glad that the canvas is flat. The sculptor is glad that the clay is colourless.

In case the point is not clear, an historic example may illustrate it. The French Revolution was really an heroic and decisive thing, because the Jacobins willed something definite and limited. They desired the freedoms of democracy, but also all the vetoes of democracy. They wished to have votes and NOT to have titles. Republicanism had an ascetic side in Franklin or Robespierre as well as an expansive side in Danton or Wilkes. Therefore they have created something with a solid substance and shape, the square social equality and peasant wealth of France. But since then the revolutionary or speculative mind of Europe has been weakened by shrinking from any proposal because of the limits of that proposal. Liberalism has been degraded into liberality. Men have tried to turn "revolutionise" from a transitive to an intransitive verb. The Jacobin could tell you not only the system he would rebel against, but (what was more important) the system he would NOT rebel against, the system he would trust. But the new rebel is a Sceptic, and will not entirely trust anything. He has no loyalty; therefore he can never be really a revolutionist. And the fact that he doubts everything really gets in his way when he wants to denounce anything. For all denunciation implies a moral doctrine of some kind; and the modern revolutionist doubts not only the institution he denounces, but the doctrine by which he denounces it. Thus he writes one book complaining that imperial oppression insults the purity of women, and then he writes another book (about the sex problem) in which he insults it himself. He curses the Sultan because Christian girls lose their virginity, and then curses Mrs. Grundy because they keep it. As a politician, he will cry out that war is a waste of life, and then, as a philosopher, that all life is waste of time. A Russian pessimist will denounce a policeman for killing a peasant, and then prove by the highest philosophical principles that the peasant ought to have killed himself. A man denounces marriage as a lie, and then denounces aristocratic profligates for treating it as a lie. He calls a flag a bauble, and then blames the oppressors of Poland or Ireland because they take away that bauble. The man of this school goes first to a political meeting, where he complains that savages are treated as if they were beasts; then he takes his hat and umbrella and goes on to a scientific meeting, where he proves that they practically are beasts. In short, the modern revolutionist, being an infinite sceptic, is always engaged in undermining his own mines. In his book on politics he attacks men for trampling on morality; in his book on ethics he attacks morality for trampling on men. Therefore the modern man in revolt has become practically useless for all purposes of revolt. By rebelling against everything he has lost his right to rebel against anything.

It may be added that the same blank and bankruptcy can be observed in all fierce and terrible types of literature, especially in satire. Satire may be mad and anarchic, but it presupposes an admitted superiority in certain things over others; it presupposes a standard. When little boys in the street laugh at the fatness of some distinguished journalist, they are unconsciously assuming a standard of Greek sculpture. They are appealing to the marble Apollo. And the curious disappearance of satire from our literature is an instance of the fierce things fading for want of any principle to be fierce about. Nietzsche had some natural talent for sarcasm: he could sneer, though he could not laugh; but there is always something bodiless and without weight in his satire, simply because it has not any mass of common morality behind it. He is himself more preposterous than anything he denounces. But, indeed, Nietzsche will stand very well as the type of the whole of this failure of abstract violence. The softening of the brain which ultimately overtook him was not a physical accident. If Nietzsche had not ended in imbecility, Nietzscheism would end in imbecility. Thinking in isolation and with pride ends in being an idiot. Every man who will not have softening of the heart must at last have softening of the brain.

This last attempt to evade intellectualism ends in intellectualism, and therefore in death. The sortie has failed. The wild worship of lawlessness and the materialist worship of law end in the same void. Nietzsche scales staggering mountains, but he turns up ultimately in Tibet. He sits down beside Tolstoy in the land of nothing and Nirvana. They are both helpless—one because he must not grasp anything, and the other because he must not let go of anything. The Tolstoyan's will is frozen by a Buddhist instinct that all special actions are evil. But the Nietzscheite's will is quite equally frozen by his view that all special actions are good; for if all special actions are good, none of them are special. They stand at the crossroads, and one hates all the roads and the other likes all the roads. The result is—well, some things are not hard to calculate. They stand at the crossroads.

Here I end (thank God) the first and dullest business of this book—the rough review of recent thought. After this I begin to sketch a view of life which may not interest my reader, but which, at any rate, interests me. In front of me, as I close this page, is a pile of modern books that I have been turning over for the purpose—a pile of ingenuity, a pile of futility. By the accident of my present detachment, I can see the inevitable smash of the philosophies of Schopenhauer and Tolstoy, Nietzsche and Shaw, as clearly as an inevitable railway smash could be seen from a balloon. They are all on the road to the emptiness of the asylum. For madness may be defined as using mental activity so as to reach mental helplessness; and they have nearly reached it. He who thinks he is made of glass, thinks to the destruction of thought; for glass cannot think. So he who wills to reject nothing, wills the destruction of will; for will is not only the choice of something, but the rejection of almost everything. And as I turn and tumble over the clever, wonderful, tiresome, and useless modern books, the title of one of them rivets my eye. It is called "Jeanne d'Arc," by Anatole France. I have only glanced at it, but a glance was enough to remind me of Renan's "Vie de Jesus." It has the same strange method of the reverent sceptic. It discredits supernatural stories that have some foundation, simply by telling natural stories that have no foundation. Because we cannot believe in what a saint did, we are to pretend that we know exactly what he felt. But I do not mention either book in order to criticise it, but because the accidental combination of the names called up two startling images of Sanity which blasted all the books before me. Joan of Arc was not stuck at the cross-roads, either by rejecting all the paths like Tolstoy, or by accepting them all like Nietzsche. She chose a path, and went down it like a thunderbolt. Yet Joan, when I came to think of her, had in her all that was true either in Tolstoy or Nietzsche, all that was even tolerable in either of them. I thought of all that is noble in Tolstoy, the pleasure in plain things, especially in plain pity, the actualities of the earth, the reverence for the poor, the dignity of the bowed back. Joan of Arc had all that and with this great addition, that she endured poverty as well as admiring it; whereas Tolstoy is only a typical aristocrat trying to find out its secret. And then I thought of all that was brave and proud and pathetic in poor Nietzsche, and his mutiny against the emptiness and timidity of our time. I thought of his cry for the ecstatic equilibrium of danger, his hunger for the rush of great horses, his cry to arms. Well, Joan of Arc had all that, and again with this difference, that she did not praise fighting, but fought. We KNOW that she was not afraid of an army, while Nietzsche, for all we know, was afraid of a cow. Tolstoy only praised the peasant; she was the peasant. Nietzsche only praised the warrior; she was the warrior. She beat them both at their own antagonistic ideals; she was more gentle than the one, more violent than the other. Yet she was a perfectly practical person who did something, while they are wild speculators who do nothing. It was impossible that the thought should not cross my mind that she and her faith had perhaps some secret of moral unity and utility that has been lost. And with that thought came a larger one, and the colossal figure of her Master had also crossed the theatre of my thoughts. The same modern difficulty which darkened the subject-matter of Anatole France also darkened that of Ernest Renan. Renan also divided his hero's pity from his hero's pugnacity. Renan even represented the righteous anger at Jerusalem as a mere nervous breakdown after the idyllic expectations of Galilee. As if there were any inconsistency between having a love for humanity and having a hatred for inhumanity! Altruists, with thin, weak voices, denounce Christ as an egoist. Egoists (with even thinner and weaker voices) denounce Him as an altruist. In our present atmosphere such cavils are comprehensible enough. The love of a hero is more terrible than the hatred of a tyrant. The hatred of a hero is more generous than the love of a philanthropist. There is a huge and heroic sanity of which moderns can only collect the fragments. There is a giant of whom we see only the lopped arms and legs walking about. They have torn the soul of Christ into silly strips, labelled egoism and altruism, and they are equally puzzled by His insane magnificence and His insane meekness. They have parted His garments among them, and for His vesture they have cast lots; though the coat was without seam woven from the top throughout.

IV THE ETHICS OF ELFLAND

When the business man rebukes the idealism of his office-boy, it is commonly in some such speech as this: "Ah, yes, when one is young, one has these ideals in the abstract and these castles in the air; but in middle age they all break up like clouds, and one comes down to a belief in practical politics, to using the machinery one has and getting on with the world as it is." Thus, at least, venerable and philanthropic old men now in their honoured graves used to talk to me when I was a boy. But since then I have grown up and have discovered that these philanthropic old men were telling lies. What has really happened is exactly the opposite of what they said would happen. They said that I should lose my ideals and begin to believe in the methods of practical politicians. Now, I have not lost my ideals in the least; my faith in fundamentals is exactly what it always was. What I have lost is my old childlike faith in practical politics. I am still as much concerned as ever about the Battle of Armageddon; but I am not so much concerned about the General Election. As a babe I leapt up on my mother's knee at the mere mention of it. No; the vision is always solid and reliable. The vision is always a fact. It is the reality that is often a fraud. As much as I ever did, more than I ever did, I believe in Liberalism. But there was a rosy time of innocence when I believed in Liberals.

I take this instance of one of the enduring faiths because, having now to trace the roots of my personal speculation, this may be counted, I think, as the only positive bias. I was brought up a Liberal, and have always believed in democracy, in the elementary liberal doctrine of a self-governing humanity. If any one finds the phrase vague or threadbare, I can only pause for a moment to explain that the principle of democracy, as I mean it, can be stated in two propositions. The first is this: that the things common to all men are more important than the things peculiar to any men. Ordinary things are more valuable than extraordinary things; nay, they are more extraordinary. Man is something more awful than men; something more strange. The sense of the miracle of humanity itself should be always more vivid to us than any marvels of power, intellect, art, or civilization. The mere man on two legs, as such, should be felt as something more heartbreaking than any music and more startling than any caricature. Death is more tragic even than death by starvation. Having a nose is more comic even than having a Norman nose.

This is the first principle of democracy: that the essential things in men are the things they hold in common, not the things they hold separately. And the second principle is merely this: that the political instinct or desire is one of these things which they hold in common. Falling in love is more poetical than dropping into poetry. The democratic contention is that government (helping to rule the tribe) is a thing like falling in love, and not a thing like dropping into poetry. It is not something analogous to playing the church organ, painting on vellum, discovering the North Pole (that insidious habit), looping the loop, being Astronomer Royal, and so on. For these things we do not wish a man to do at all unless he does them well. It is, on the contrary, a thing analogous to writing one's own love-letters or blowing one's own nose. These things we want a man to do for himself, even if he does them badly. I am not here arguing the truth of any of these conceptions; I know that some moderns are asking to have their wives chosen by scientists, and they may soon be asking, for all I know, to have their noses blown by nurses. I merely say that mankind does recognize these universal human functions, and that democracy classes government among them. In short, the democratic faith is this: that the most terribly important things must be left to ordinary men themselves—the mating of the sexes, the rearing of the young, the laws of the state. This is democracy; and in this I have always believed.

But there is one thing that I have never from my youth up been able to understand. I have never been able to understand where people got the idea that democracy was in some way opposed to tradition. It is obvious that tradition is only democracy extended through time. It is trusting to a consensus of common human voices rather than to some isolated or arbitrary record. The man who quotes some German historian against the tradition of the Catholic Church, for instance, is strictly appealing to aristocracy. He is appealing to the superiority of one expert against the awful authority of a mob. It is quite easy to see why a legend is treated, and ought to be treated, more respectfully than a book of history. The legend is generally made by the majority of people in the village, who are sane. The book is generally written by the one man in the village who is mad. Those who urge against tradition that men in the past were ignorant may go and urge it at the Carlton Club, along with the statement that voters in the slums are ignorant. It will not do for us. If we attach great importance to the opinion of ordinary men in great unanimity when we are dealing with daily matters, there is no reason why we should disregard it when we are dealing with history or fable. Tradition may be defined as an extension of the franchise. Tradition means giving votes to the most obscure of all classes, our ancestors. It is the democracy of the dead. Tradition refuses to submit to the small and arrogant oligarchy of those who merely happen to be walking about. All democrats object to men being disqualified by the accident of birth; tradition objects to their being disqualified by the accident of death. Democracy tells us not to neglect a good man's opinion, even if he is our groom; tradition asks us not to neglect a good man's opinion, even if he is our father. I, at any rate, cannot separate the two ideas of democracy and tradition; it seems evident to me that they are the same idea. We will have the dead at our councils. The ancient Greeks voted by stones; these shall vote by tombstones. It is all quite regular and official, for most tombstones, like most ballot papers, are marked with a cross.

I have first to say, therefore, that if I have had a bias, it was always a bias in favour of democracy, and therefore of tradition. Before we come to any theoretic or logical beginnings I am content to allow for that personal equation; I have always been more inclined to believe the ruck of hard-working people than to believe that special and troublesome literary class to which I belong. I prefer even the fancies and prejudices of the people who see life from the inside to the clearest demonstrations of the people who see life from the outside. I would always trust the old wives' fables against the old maids' facts. As long as wit is mother wit it can be as wild as it pleases.

Now, I have to put together a general position, and I pretend to no training in such things. I propose to do it, therefore, by writing down one after another the three or four fundamental ideas which I have found for myself, pretty much in the way that I found them. Then I shall roughly synthesise them, summing up my personal philosophy or natural religion; then I shall describe my startling discovery that the whole thing had been discovered before. It had been discovered by Christianity. But of these profound persuasions which I have to recount in order, the earliest was concerned with this element of popular tradition. And without the foregoing explanation touching tradition and democracy I could hardly make my mental experience clear. As it is, I do not know whether I can make it clear, but I now propose to try.

My first and last philosophy, that which I believe in with unbroken certainty, I learnt in the nursery. I generally learnt it from a nurse; that is, from the solemn and star-appointed priestess at once of democracy and tradition. The things I believed most then, the things I believe most now, are the things called fairy tales. They seem to me to be the entirely reasonable things. They are not fantasies: compared with them other things are fantastic. Compared with them religion and rationalism are both abnormal, though religion is abnormally right and rationalism abnormally wrong. Fairyland is nothing but the sunny country of common sense. It is not earth that judges heaven, but heaven that judges earth; so for me at least it was not earth that criticised elfland, but elfland that criticised the earth. I knew the magic beanstalk before I had tasted beans; I was sure of the Man in the Moon before I was certain of the moon. This was at one with all popular tradition. Modern minor poets are naturalists, and talk about the bush or the brook; but the singers of the old epics and fables were supernaturalists, and talked about the gods of brook and bush. That is what the moderns mean when they say that the ancients did not "appreciate Nature," because they said that Nature was divine. Old nurses do not tell children about the grass, but about the fairies that dance on the grass; and the old Greeks could not see the trees for the dryads.

But I deal here with what ethic and philosophy come from being fed on fairy tales. If I were describing them in detail I could note many noble and healthy principles that arise from them. There is the chivalrous lesson of "Jack the Giant Killer"; that giants should be killed because they are gigantic. It is a manly mutiny against pride as such. For the rebel is older than all the kingdoms, and the Jacobin has more tradition than the Jacobite. There is the lesson of "Cinderella," which is the same as that of the Magnificat— EXALTAVIT HUMILES. There is the great lesson of "Beauty and the Beast"; that a thing must be loved BEFORE it is loveable. There is the terrible allegory of the "Sleeping Beauty," which tells how the human creature was blessed with all birthday gifts, yet cursed with death; and how death also may perhaps be softened to a sleep. But I am not concerned with any of the separate statutes of elfland, but with the whole spirit of its law, which I learnt before I could speak, and shall retain when I cannot write. I am concerned with a certain way of looking at life, which was created in me by the fairy tales, but has since been meekly ratified by the mere facts.

It might be stated this way. There are certain sequences or developments (cases of one thing following another), which are, in the true sense of the word, reasonable. They are, in the true sense of the word, necessary. Such are mathematical and merely logical sequences. We in fairyland (who are the most reasonable of all creatures) admit that reason and that necessity. For instance, if the Ugly Sisters are older than Cinderella, it is (in an iron and awful sense) NECESSARY that Cinderella is younger than the Ugly Sisters. There is no getting out of it. Haeckel may talk as much fatalism about that fact as he pleases: it really must be. If Jack is the son of a miller, a miller is the father of Jack. Cold reason decrees it from her awful throne: and we in fairyland submit. If the three brothers all ride horses, there are six animals and eighteen legs involved: that is true rationalism, and fairyland is full of it. But as I put my head over the hedge of the elves and began to take notice of the natural world, I observed an extraordinary thing. I observed that learned men in spectacles were talking of the actual things that happened— dawn and death and so on—as if THEY were rational and inevitable. They talked as if the fact that trees bear fruit were just as NECESSARY as the fact that two and one trees make three. But it is not. There is an enormous difference by the test of fairyland; which is the test of the imagination. You cannot IMAGINE two and one not making three. But you can easily imagine trees not growing fruit; you can imagine them growing golden candlesticks or tigers hanging on by the tail. These men in spectacles spoke much of a man named Newton, who was hit by an apple, and who discovered a law. But they could not be got to see the distinction between a true law, a law of reason, and the mere fact of apples falling. If the apple hit Newton's nose, Newton's nose hit the apple. That is a true necessity: because we cannot conceive the one occurring without the other. But we can quite well conceive the apple not falling on his nose; we can fancy it flying ardently through the air to hit some other nose, of which it had a more definite dislike. We have always in our fairy tales kept this sharp distinction between the science of mental relations, in which there really are laws, and the science of physical facts, in which there are no laws, but only weird repetitions. We believe in bodily miracles, but not in mental impossibilities. We believe that a Bean-stalk climbed up to Heaven; but that does not at all confuse our convictions on the philosophical question of how many beans make five.

Here is the peculiar perfection of tone and truth in the nursery tales. The man of science says, "Cut the stalk, and the apple will fall"; but he says it calmly, as if the one idea really led up to the other. The witch in the fairy tale says, "Blow the horn, and the ogre's castle will fall"; but she does not say it as if it were something in which the effect obviously arose out of the cause. Doubtless she has given the advice to many champions, and has seen many castles fall, but she does not lose either her wonder or her reason. She does not muddle her head until it imagines a necessary mental connection between a horn and a falling tower. But the scientific men do muddle their heads, until they imagine a necessary mental connection between an apple leaving the tree and an apple reaching the ground. They do really talk as if they had found not only a set of marvellous facts, but a truth connecting those facts. They do talk as if the connection of two strange things physically connected them philosophically. They feel that because one incomprehensible thing constantly follows another incomprehensible thing the two together somehow make up a comprehensible thing. Two black riddles make a white answer.

In fairyland we avoid the word "law"; but in the land of science they are singularly fond of it. Thus they will call some interesting conjecture about how forgotten folks pronounced the alphabet, Grimm's Law. But Grimm's Law is far less intellectual than Grimm's Fairy Tales. The tales are, at any rate, certainly tales; while the law is not a law. A law implies that we know the nature of the generalisation and enactment; not merely that we have noticed some of the effects. If there is a law that pick-pockets shall go to prison, it implies that there is an imaginable mental connection between the idea of prison and the idea of picking pockets. And we know what the idea is. We can say why we take liberty from a man who takes liberties. But we cannot say why an egg can turn into a chicken any more than we can say why a bear could turn into a fairy prince. As IDEAS, the egg and the chicken are further off from each other than the bear and the prince; for no egg in itself suggests a chicken, whereas some princes do suggest bears. Granted, then, that certain transformations do happen, it is essential that we should regard them in the philosophic manner of fairy tales, not in the unphilosophic manner of science and the "Laws of Nature." When we are asked why eggs turn to birds or fruits fall in autumn, we must answer exactly as the fairy godmother would answer if Cinderella asked her why mice turned to horses or her clothes fell from her at twelve o'clock. We must answer that it is MAGIC. It is not a "law," for we do not understand its general formula. It is not a necessity, for though we can count on it happening practically, we have no right to say that it must always happen. It is no argument for unalterable law (as Huxley fancied) that we count on the ordinary course of things. We do not count on it; we bet on it. We risk the remote possibility of a miracle as we do that of a poisoned pancake or a world-destroying comet. We leave it out of account, not because it is a miracle, and therefore an impossibility, but because it is a miracle, and therefore an exception. All the terms used in the science books, "law," "necessity," "order," "tendency," and so on, are really unintellectual, because they assume an inner synthesis, which we do not possess. The only words that ever satisfied me as describing Nature are the terms used in the fairy books, "charm," "spell," "enchantment." They express the arbitrariness of the fact and its mystery. A tree grows fruit because it is a MAGIC tree. Water runs downhill because it is bewitched. The sun shines because it is bewitched.

I deny altogether that this is fantastic or even mystical. We may have some mysticism later on; but this fairy-tale language about things is simply rational and agnostic. It is the only way I can express in words my clear and definite perception that one thing is quite distinct from another; that there is no logical connection between flying and laying eggs. It is the man who talks about "a law" that he has never seen who is the mystic. Nay, the ordinary scientific man is strictly a sentimentalist. He is a sentimentalist in this essential sense, that he is soaked and swept away by mere associations. He has so often seen birds fly and lay eggs that he feels as if there must be some dreamy, tender connection between the two ideas, whereas there is none. A forlorn lover might be unable to dissociate the moon from lost love; so the materialist is unable to dissociate the moon from the tide. In both cases there is no connection, except that one has seen them together. A sentimentalist might shed tears at the smell of apple-blossom, because, by a dark association of his own, it reminded him of his boyhood. So the materialist professor (though he conceals his tears) is yet a sentimentalist, because, by a dark association of his own, apple-blossoms remind him of apples. But the cool rationalist from fairyland does not see why, in the abstract, the apple tree should not grow crimson tulips; it sometimes does in his country.

This elementary wonder, however, is not a mere fancy derived from the fairy tales; on the contrary, all the fire of the fairy tales is derived from this. Just as we all like love tales because there is an instinct of sex, we all like astonishing tales because they touch the nerve of the ancient instinct of astonishment. This is proved by the fact that when we are very young children we do not need fairy tales: we only need tales. Mere life is interesting enough. A child of seven is excited by being told that Tommy opened a door and saw a dragon. But a child of three is excited by being told that Tommy opened a door. Boys like romantic tales; but babies like realistic tales—because they find them romantic. In fact, a baby is about the only person, I should think, to whom a modern realistic novel could be read without boring him. This proves that even nursery tales only echo an almost pre-natal leap of interest and amazement. These tales say that apples were golden only to refresh the forgotten moment when we found that they were green. They make rivers run with wine only to make us remember, for one wild moment, that they run with water. I have said that this is wholly reasonable and even agnostic. And, indeed, on this point I am all for the higher agnosticism; its better name is Ignorance. We have all read in scientific books, and, indeed, in all romances, the story of the man who has forgotten his name. This man walks about the streets and can see and appreciate everything; only he cannot remember who he is. Well, every man is that man in the story. Every man has forgotten who he is. One may understand the cosmos, but never the ego; the self is more distant than any star. Thou shalt love the Lord thy God; but thou shalt not know thyself. We are all under the same mental calamity; we have all forgotten our names. We have all forgotten what we really are. All that we call common sense and rationality and practicality and positivism only means that for certain dead levels of our life we forget that we have forgotten. All that we call spirit and art and ecstasy only means that for one awful instant we remember that we forget.

But though (like the man without memory in the novel) we walk the streets with a sort of half-witted admiration, still it is admiration. It is admiration in English and not only admiration in Latin. The wonder has a positive element of praise. This is the next milestone to be definitely marked on our road through fairyland. I shall speak in the next chapter about optimists and pessimists in their intellectual aspect, so far as they have one. Here I am only trying to describe the enormous emotions which cannot be described. And the strongest emotion was that life was as precious as it was puzzling. It was an ecstasy because it was an adventure; it was an adventure because it was an opportunity. The goodness of the fairy tale was not affected by the fact that there might be more dragons than princesses; it was good to be in a fairy tale. The test of all happiness is gratitude; and I felt grateful, though I hardly knew to whom. Children are grateful when Santa Claus puts in their stockings gifts of toys or sweets. Could I not be grateful to Santa Claus when he put in my stockings the gift of two miraculous legs? We thank people for birthday presents of cigars and slippers. Can I thank no one for the birthday present of birth?

There were, then, these two first feelings, indefensible and indisputable. The world was a shock, but it was not merely shocking; existence was a surprise, but it was a pleasant surprise. In fact, all my first views were exactly uttered in a riddle that stuck in my brain from boyhood. The question was, "What did the first frog say?" And the answer was, "Lord, how you made me jump!" That says succinctly all that I am saying. God made the frog jump; but the frog prefers jumping. But when these things are settled there enters the second great principle of the fairy philosophy.

Any one can see it who will simply read "Grimm's Fairy Tales" or the fine collections of Mr. Andrew Lang. For the pleasure of pedantry I will call it the Doctrine of Conditional Joy. Touchstone talked of much virtue in an "if"; according to elfin ethics all virtue is in an "if." The note of the fairy utterance always is, "You may live in a palace of gold and sapphire, if you do not say the word `cow'"; or "You may live happily with the King's daughter, if you do not show her an onion." The vision always hangs upon a veto. All the dizzy and colossal things conceded depend upon one small thing withheld. All the wild and whirling things that are let loose depend upon one thing that is forbidden. Mr. W.B.Yeats, in his exquisite and piercing elfin poetry, describes the elves as lawless; they plunge in innocent anarchy on the unbridled horses of the air—

"Ride on the crest of the dishevelled tide, And dance upon the mountains like a flame."

It is a dreadful thing to say that Mr. W.B.Yeats does not understand fairyland. But I do say it. He is an ironical Irishman, full of intellectual reactions. He is not stupid enough to understand fairyland. Fairies prefer people of the yokel type like myself; people who gape and grin and do as they are told. Mr. Yeats reads into elfland all the righteous insurrection of his own race. But the lawlessness of Ireland is a Christian lawlessness, founded on reason and justice. The Fenian is rebelling against something he understands only too well; but the true citizen of fairyland is obeying something that he does not understand at all. In the fairy tale an incomprehensible happiness rests upon an incomprehensible condition. A box is opened, and all evils fly out. A word is forgotten, and cities perish. A lamp is lit, and love flies away. A flower is plucked, and human lives are forfeited. An apple is eaten, and the hope of God is gone.

This is the tone of fairy tales, and it is certainly not lawlessness or even liberty, though men under a mean modern tyranny may think it liberty by comparison. People out of Portland Gaol might think Fleet Street free; but closer study will prove that both fairies and journalists are the slaves of duty. Fairy godmothers seem at least as strict as other godmothers. Cinderella received a coach out of Wonderland and a coachman out of nowhere, but she received a command—which might have come out of Brixton—that she should be back by twelve. Also, she had a glass slipper; and it cannot be a coincidence that glass is so common a substance in folk-lore. This princess lives in a glass castle, that princess on a glass hill; this one sees all things in a mirror; they may all live in glass houses if they will not throw stones. For this thin glitter of glass everywhere is the expression of the fact that the happiness is bright but brittle, like the substance most easily smashed by a housemaid or a cat. And this fairy-tale sentiment also sank into me and became my sentiment towards the whole world. I felt and feel that life itself is as bright as the diamond, but as brittle as the window-pane; and when the heavens were compared to the terrible crystal I can remember a shudder. I was afraid that God would drop the cosmos with a crash.

Remember, however, that to be breakable is not the same as to be perishable. Strike a glass, and it will not endure an instant; simply do not strike it, and it will endure a thousand years. Such, it seemed, was the joy of man, either in elfland or on earth; the happiness depended on NOT DOING SOMETHING which you could at any moment do and which, very often, it was not obvious why you should not do. Now, the point here is that to ME this did not seem unjust. If the miller's third son said to the fairy, "Explain why I must not stand on my head in the fairy palace," the other might fairly reply, "Well, if it comes to that, explain the fairy palace." If Cinderella says, "How is it that I must leave the ball at twelve?" her godmother might answer, "How is it that you are going there till twelve?" If I leave a man in my will ten talking elephants and a hundred winged horses, he cannot complain if the conditions partake of the slight eccentricity of the gift. He must not look a winged horse in the mouth. And it seemed to me that existence was itself so very eccentric a legacy that I could not complain of not understanding the limitations of the vision when I did not understand the vision they limited. The frame was no stranger than the picture. The veto might well be as wild as the vision; it might be as startling as the sun, as elusive as the waters, as fantastic and terrible as the towering trees.

For this reason (we may call it the fairy godmother philosophy) I never could join the young men of my time in feeling what they called the general sentiment of REVOLT. I should have resisted, let us hope, any rules that were evil, and with these and their definition I shall deal in another chapter. But I did not feel disposed to resist any rule merely because it was mysterious. Estates are sometimes held by foolish forms, the breaking of a stick or the payment of a peppercorn: I was willing to hold the huge estate of earth and heaven by any such feudal fantasy. It could not well be wilder than the fact that I was allowed to hold it at all. At this stage I give only one ethical instance to show my meaning. I could never mix in the common murmur of that rising generation against monogamy, because no restriction on sex seemed so odd and unexpected as sex itself. To be allowed, like Endymion, to make love to the moon and then to complain that Jupiter kept his own moons in a harem seemed to me (bred on fairy tales like Endymion's) a vulgar anti-climax. Keeping to one woman is a small price for so much as seeing one woman. To complain that I could only be married once was like complaining that I had only been born once. It was incommensurate with the terrible excitement of which one was talking. It showed, not an exaggerated sensibility to sex, but a curious insensibility to it. A man is a fool who complains that he cannot enter Eden by five gates at once. Polygamy is a lack of the realization of sex; it is like a man plucking five pears in mere absence of mind. The aesthetes touched the last insane limits of language in their eulogy on lovely things. The thistledown made them weep; a burnished beetle brought them to their knees. Yet their emotion never impressed me for an instant, for this reason, that it never occurred to them to pay for their pleasure in any sort of symbolic sacrifice. Men (I felt) might fast forty days for the sake of hearing a blackbird sing. Men might go through fire to find a cowslip. Yet these lovers of beauty could not even keep sober for the blackbird. They would not go through common Christian marriage by way of recompense to the cowslip. Surely one might pay for extraordinary joy in ordinary morals. Oscar Wilde said that sunsets were not valued because we could not pay for sunsets. But Oscar Wilde was wrong; we can pay for sunsets. We can pay for them by not being Oscar Wilde.

Well, I left the fairy tales lying on the floor of the nursery, and I have not found any books so sensible since. I left the nurse guardian of tradition and democracy, and I have not found any modern type so sanely radical or so sanely conservative. But the matter for important comment was here: that when I first went out into the mental atmosphere of the modern world, I found that the modern world was positively opposed on two points to my nurse and to the nursery tales. It has taken me a long time to find out that the modern world is wrong and my nurse was right. The really curious thing was this: that modern thought contradicted this basic creed of my boyhood on its two most essential doctrines. I have explained that the fairy tales founded in me two convictions; first, that this world is a wild and startling place, which might have been quite different, but which is quite delightful; second, that before this wildness and delight one may well be modest and submit to the queerest limitations of so queer a kindness. But I found the whole modern world running like a high tide against both my tendernesses; and the shock of that collision created two sudden and spontaneous sentiments, which I have had ever since and which, crude as they were, have since hardened into convictions.

First, I found the whole modern world talking scientific fatalism; saying that everything is as it must always have been, being unfolded without fault from the beginning. The leaf on the tree is green because it could never have been anything else. Now, the fairy-tale philosopher is glad that the leaf is green precisely because it might have been scarlet. He feels as if it had turned green an instant before he looked at it. He is pleased that snow is white on the strictly reasonable ground that it might have been black. Every colour has in it a bold quality as of choice; the red of garden roses is not only decisive but dramatic, like suddenly spilt blood. He feels that something has been DONE. But the great determinists of the nineteenth century were strongly against this native feeling that something had happened an instant before. In fact, according to them, nothing ever really had happened since the beginning of the world. Nothing ever had happened since existence had happened; and even about the date of that they were not very sure.

The modern world as I found it was solid for modern Calvinism, for the necessity of things being as they are. But when I came to ask them I found they had really no proof of this unavoidable repetition in things except the fact that the things were repeated. Now, the mere repetition made the things to me rather more weird than more rational. It was as if, having seen a curiously shaped nose in the street and dismissed it as an accident, I had then seen six other noses of the same astonishing shape. I should have fancied for a moment that it must be some local secret society. So one elephant having a trunk was odd; but all elephants having trunks looked like a plot. I speak here only of an emotion, and of an emotion at once stubborn and subtle. But the repetition in Nature seemed sometimes to be an excited repetition, like that of an angry schoolmaster saying the same thing over and over again. The grass seemed signalling to me with all its fingers at once; the crowded stars seemed bent upon being understood. The sun would make me see him if he rose a thousand times. The recurrences of the universe rose to the maddening rhythm of an incantation, and I began to see an idea.

All the towering materialism which dominates the modern mind rests ultimately upon one assumption; a false assumption. It is supposed that if a thing goes on repeating itself it is probably dead; a piece of clockwork. People feel that if the universe was personal it would vary; if the sun were alive it would dance. This is a fallacy even in relation to known fact. For the variation in human affairs is generally brought into them, not by life, but by death; by the dying down or breaking off of their strength or desire. A man varies his movements because of some slight element of failure or fatigue. He gets into an omnibus because he is tired of walking; or he walks because he is tired of sitting still. But if his life and joy were so gigantic that he never tired of going to Islington, he might go to Islington as regularly as the Thames goes to Sheerness. The very speed and ecstasy of his life would have the stillness of death. The sun rises every morning. I do not rise every morning; but the variation is due not to my activity, but to my inaction. Now, to put the matter in a popular phrase, it might be true that the sun rises regularly because he never gets tired of rising. His routine might be due, not to a lifelessness, but to a rush of life. The thing I mean can be seen, for instance, in children, when they find some game or joke that they specially enjoy. A child kicks his legs rhythmically through excess, not absence, of life. Because children have abounding vitality, because they are in spirit fierce and free, therefore they want things repeated and unchanged. They always say, "Do it again"; and the grown-up person does it again until he is nearly dead. For grown-up people are not strong enough to exult in monotony. But perhaps God is strong enough to exult in monotony. It is possible that God says every morning, "Do it again" to the sun; and every evening, "Do it again" to the moon. It may not be automatic necessity that makes all daisies alike; it may be that God makes every daisy separately, but has never got tired of making them. It may be that He has the eternal appetite of infancy; for we have sinned and grown old, and our Father is younger than we. The repetition in Nature may not be a mere recurrence; it may be a theatrical ENCORE. Heaven may ENCORE the bird who laid an egg. If the human being conceives and brings forth a human child instead of bringing forth a fish, or a bat, or a griffin, the reason may not be that we are fixed in an animal fate without life or purpose. It may be that our little tragedy has touched the gods, that they admire it from their starry galleries, and that at the end of every human drama man is called again and again before the curtain. Repetition may go on for millions of years, by mere choice, and at any instant it may stop. Man may stand on the earth generation after generation, and yet each birth be his positively last appearance.

This was my first conviction; made by the shock of my childish emotions meeting the modern creed in mid-career. I had always vaguely felt facts to be miracles in the sense that they are wonderful: now I began to think them miracles in the stricter sense that they were WILFUL. I mean that they were, or might be, repeated exercises of some will. In short, I had always believed that the world involved magic: now I thought that perhaps it involved a magician. And this pointed a profound emotion always present and sub-conscious; that this world of ours has some purpose; and if there is a purpose, there is a person. I had always felt life first as a story: and if there is a story there is a story-teller.

But modern thought also hit my second human tradition. It went against the fairy feeling about strict limits and conditions. The one thing it loved to talk about was expansion and largeness. Herbert Spencer would have been greatly annoyed if any one had called him an imperialist, and therefore it is highly regrettable that nobody did. But he was an imperialist of the lowest type. He popularized this contemptible notion that the size of the solar system ought to over-awe the spiritual dogma of man. Why should a man surrender his dignity to the solar system any more than to a whale? If mere size proves that man is not the image of God, then a whale may be the image of God; a somewhat formless image; what one might call an impressionist portrait. It is quite futile to argue that man is small compared to the cosmos; for man was always small compared to the nearest tree. But Herbert Spencer, in his headlong imperialism, would insist that we had in some way been conquered and annexed by the astronomical universe. He spoke about men and their ideals exactly as the most insolent Unionist talks about the Irish and their ideals. He turned mankind into a small nationality. And his evil influence can be seen even in the most spirited and honourable of later scientific authors; notably in the early romances of Mr. H.G.Wells. Many moralists have in an exaggerated way represented the earth as wicked. But Mr. Wells and his school made the heavens wicked. We should lift up our eyes to the stars from whence would come our ruin.

But the expansion of which I speak was much more evil than all this. I have remarked that the materialist, like the madman, is in prison; in the prison of one thought. These people seemed to think it singularly inspiring to keep on saying that the prison was very large. The size of this scientific universe gave one no novelty, no relief. The cosmos went on for ever, but not in its wildest constellation could there be anything really interesting; anything, for instance, such as forgiveness or free will. The grandeur or infinity of the secret of its cosmos added nothing to it. It was like telling a prisoner in Reading gaol that he would be glad to hear that the gaol now covered half the county. The warder would have nothing to show the man except more and more long corridors of stone lit by ghastly lights and empty of all that is human. So these expanders of the universe had nothing to show us except more and more infinite corridors of space lit by ghastly suns and empty of all that is divine.

In fairyland there had been a real law; a law that could be broken, for the definition of a law is something that can be broken. But the machinery of this cosmic prison was something that could not be broken; for we ourselves were only a part of its machinery. We were either unable to do things or we were destined to do them. The idea of the mystical condition quite disappeared; one can neither have the firmness of keeping laws nor the fun of breaking them. The largeness of this universe had nothing of that freshness and airy outbreak which we have praised in the universe of the poet. This modern universe is literally an empire; that is, it was vast, but it is not free. One went into larger and larger windowless rooms, rooms big with Babylonian perspective; but one never found the smallest window or a whisper of outer air.

Their infernal parallels seemed to expand with distance; but for me all good things come to a point, swords for instance. So finding the boast of the big cosmos so unsatisfactory to my emotions I began to argue about it a little; and I soon found that the whole attitude was even shallower than could have been expected. According to these people the cosmos was one thing since it had one unbroken rule. Only (they would say) while it is one thing, it is also the only thing there is. Why, then, should one worry particularly to call it large? There is nothing to compare it with. It would be just as sensible to call it small. A man may say, "I like this vast cosmos, with its throng of stars and its crowd of varied creatures." But if it comes to that why should not a man say, "I like this cosy little cosmos, with its decent number of stars and as neat a provision of live stock as I wish to see"? One is as good as the other; they are both mere sentiments. It is mere sentiment to rejoice that the sun is larger than the earth; it is quite as sane a sentiment to rejoice that the sun is no larger than it is. A man chooses to have an emotion about the largeness of the world; why should he not choose to have an emotion about its smallness?

It happened that I had that emotion. When one is fond of anything one addresses it by diminutives, even if it is an elephant or a life-guardsman. The reason is, that anything, however huge, that can be conceived of as complete, can be conceived of as small. If military moustaches did not suggest a sword or tusks a tail, then the object would be vast because it would be immeasurable. But the moment you can imagine a guardsman you can imagine a small guardsman. The moment you really see an elephant you can call it "Tiny." If you can make a statue of a thing you can make a statuette of it. These people professed that the universe was one coherent thing; but they were not fond of the universe. But I was frightfully fond of the universe and wanted to address it by a diminutive. I often did so; and it never seemed to mind. Actually and in truth I did feel that these dim dogmas of vitality were better expressed by calling the world small than by calling it large. For about infinity there was a sort of carelessness which was the reverse of the fierce and pious care which I felt touching the pricelessness and the peril of life. They showed only a dreary waste; but I felt a sort of sacred thrift. For economy is far more romantic than extravagance. To them stars were an unending income of halfpence; but I felt about the golden sun and the silver moon as a schoolboy feels if he has one sovereign and one shilling.

These subconscious convictions are best hit off by the colour and tone of certain tales. Thus I have said that stories of magic alone can express my sense that life is not only a pleasure but a kind of eccentric privilege. I may express this other feeling of cosmic cosiness by allusion to another book always read in boyhood, "Robinson Crusoe," which I read about this time, and which owes its eternal vivacity to the fact that it celebrates the poetry of limits, nay, even the wild romance of prudence. Crusoe is a man on a small rock with a few comforts just snatched from the sea: the best thing in the book is simply the list of things saved from the wreck. The greatest of poems is an inventory. Every kitchen tool becomes ideal because Crusoe might have dropped it in the sea. It is a good exercise, in empty or ugly hours of the day, to look at anything, the coal-scuttle or the book-case, and think how happy one could be to have brought it out of the sinking ship on to the solitary island. But it is a better exercise still to remember how all things have had this hair-breadth escape: everything has been saved from a wreck. Every man has had one horrible adventure: as a hidden untimely birth he had not been, as infants that never see the light. Men spoke much in my boyhood of restricted or ruined men of genius: and it was common to say that many a man was a Great Might-Have-Been. To me it is a more solid and startling fact that any man in the street is a Great Might-Not-Have-Been.

But I really felt (the fancy may seem foolish) as if all the order and number of things were the romantic remnant of Crusoe's ship. That there are two sexes and one sun, was like the fact that there were two guns and one axe. It was poignantly urgent that none should be lost; but somehow, it was rather fun that none could be added. The trees and the planets seemed like things saved from the wreck: and when I saw the Matterhorn I was glad that it had not been overlooked in the confusion. I felt economical about the stars as if they were sapphires (they are called so in Milton's Eden): I hoarded the hills. For the universe is a single jewel, and while it is a natural cant to talk of a jewel as peerless and priceless, of this jewel it is literally true. This cosmos is indeed without peer and without price: for there cannot be another one.

Thus ends, in unavoidable inadequacy, the attempt to utter the unutterable things. These are my ultimate attitudes towards life; the soils for the seeds of doctrine. These in some dark way I thought before I could write, and felt before I could think: that we may proceed more easily afterwards, I will roughly recapitulate them now. I felt in my bones; first, that this world does not explain itself. It may be a miracle with a supernatural explanation; it may be a conjuring trick, with a natural explanation. But the explanation of the conjuring trick, if it is to satisfy me, will have to be better than the natural explanations I have heard. The thing is magic, true or false. Second, I came to feel as if magic must have a meaning, and meaning must have some one to mean it. There was something personal in the world, as in a work of art; whatever it meant it meant violently. Third, I thought this purpose beautiful in its old design, in spite of its defects, such as dragons. Fourth, that the proper form of thanks to it is some form of humility and restraint: we should thank God for beer and Burgundy by not drinking too much of them. We owed, also, an obedience to whatever made us. And last, and strangest, there had come into my mind a vague and vast impression that in some way all good was a remnant to be stored and held sacred out of some primordial ruin. Man had saved his good as Crusoe saved his goods: he had saved them from a wreck. All this I felt and the age gave me no encouragement to feel it. And all this time I had not even thought of Christian theology.

V THE FLAG OF THE WORLD

When I was a boy there were two curious men running about who were called the optimist and the pessimist. I constantly used the words myself, but I cheerfully confess that I never had any very special idea of what they meant. The only thing which might be considered evident was that they could not mean what they said; for the ordinary verbal explanation was that the optimist thought this world as good as it could be, while the pessimist thought it as bad as it could be. Both these statements being obviously raving nonsense, one had to cast about for other explanations. An optimist could not mean a man who thought everything right and nothing wrong. For that is meaningless; it is like calling everything right and nothing left. Upon the whole, I came to the conclusion that the optimist thought everything good except the pessimist, and that the pessimist thought everything bad, except himself. It would be unfair to omit altogether from the list the mysterious but suggestive definition said to have been given by a little girl, "An optimist is a man who looks after your eyes, and a pessimist is a man who looks after your feet." I am not sure that this is not the best definition of all. There is even a sort of allegorical truth in it. For there might, perhaps, be a profitable distinction drawn between that more dreary thinker who thinks merely of our contact with the earth from moment to moment, and that happier thinker who considers rather our primary power of vision and of choice of road.

But this is a deep mistake in this alternative of the optimist and the pessimist. The assumption of it is that a man criticises this world as if he were house-hunting, as if he were being shown over a new suite of apartments. If a man came to this world from some other world in full possession of his powers he might discuss whether the advantage of midsummer woods made up for the disadvantage of mad dogs, just as a man looking for lodgings might balance the presence of a telephone against the absence of a sea view. But no man is in that position. A man belongs to this world before he begins to ask if it is nice to belong to it. He has fought for the flag, and often won heroic victories for the flag long before he has ever enlisted. To put shortly what seems the essential matter, he has a loyalty long before he has any admiration.

In the last chapter it has been said that the primary feeling that this world is strange and yet attractive is best expressed in fairy tales. The reader may, if he likes, put down the next stage to that bellicose and even jingo literature which commonly comes next in the history of a boy. We all owe much sound morality to the penny dreadfuls. Whatever the reason, it seemed and still seems to me that our attitude towards life can be better expressed in terms of a kind of military loyalty than in terms of criticism and approval. My acceptance of the universe is not optimism, it is more like patriotism. It is a matter of primary loyalty. The world is not a lodging-house at Brighton, which we are to leave because it is miserable. It is the fortress of our family, with the flag flying on the turret, and the more miserable it is the less we should leave it. The point is not that this world is too sad to love or too glad not to love; the point is that when you do love a thing, its gladness is a reason for loving it, and its sadness a reason for loving it more. All optimistic thoughts about England and all pessimistic thoughts about her are alike reasons for the English patriot. Similarly, optimism and pessimism are alike arguments for the cosmic patriot.

Let us suppose we are confronted with a desperate thing—say Pimlico. If we think what is really best for Pimlico we shall find the thread of thought leads to the throne or the mystic and the arbitrary. It is not enough for a man to disapprove of Pimlico: in that case he will merely cut his throat or move to Chelsea. Nor, certainly, is it enough for a man to approve of Pimlico: for then it will remain Pimlico, which would be awful. The only way out of it seems to be for somebody to love Pimlico: to love it with a transcendental tie and without any earthly reason. If there arose a man who loved Pimlico, then Pimlico would rise into ivory towers and golden pinnacles; Pimlico would attire herself as a woman does when she is loved. For decoration is not given to hide horrible things: but to decorate things already adorable. A mother does not give her child a blue bow because he is so ugly without it. A lover does not give a girl a necklace to hide her neck. If men loved Pimlico as mothers love children, arbitrarily, because it is THEIRS, Pimlico in a year or two might be fairer than Florence. Some readers will say that this is a mere fantasy. I answer that this is the actual history of mankind. This, as a fact, is how cities did grow great. Go back to the darkest roots of civilization and you will find them knotted round some sacred stone or encircling some sacred well. People first paid honour to a spot and afterwards gained glory for it. Men did not love Rome because she was great. She was great because they had loved her.

The eighteenth-century theories of the social contract have been exposed to much clumsy criticism in our time; in so far as they meant that there is at the back of all historic government an idea of content and co-operation, they were demonstrably right. But they really were wrong, in so far as they suggested that men had ever aimed at order or ethics directly by a conscious exchange of interests. Morality did not begin by one man saying to another, "I will not hit you if you do not hit me"; there is no trace of such a transaction. There IS a trace of both men having said, "We must not hit each other in the holy place." They gained their morality by guarding their religion. They did not cultivate courage. They fought for the shrine, and found they had become courageous. They did not cultivate cleanliness. They purified themselves for the altar, and found that they were clean. The history of the Jews is the only early document known to most Englishmen, and the facts can be judged sufficiently from that. The Ten Commandments which have been found substantially common to mankind were merely military commands; a code of regimental orders, issued to protect a certain ark across a certain desert. Anarchy was evil because it endangered the sanctity. And only when they made a holy day for God did they find they had made a holiday for men.

If it be granted that this primary devotion to a place or thing is a source of creative energy, we can pass on to a very peculiar fact. Let us reiterate for an instant that the only right optimism is a sort of universal patriotism. What is the matter with the pessimist? I think it can be stated by saying that he is the cosmic anti-patriot. And what is the matter with the anti-patriot? I think it can be stated, without undue bitterness, by saying that he is the candid friend. And what is the matter with the candid friend? There we strike the rock of real life and immutable human nature.

I venture to say that what is bad in the candid friend is simply that he is not candid. He is keeping something back— his own gloomy pleasure in saying unpleasant things. He has a secret desire to hurt, not merely to help. This is certainly, I think, what makes a certain sort of anti-patriot irritating to healthy citizens. I do not speak (of course) of the anti-patriotism which only irritates feverish stockbrokers and gushing actresses; that is only patriotism speaking plainly. A man who says that no patriot should attack the Boer War until it is over is not worth answering intelligently; he is saying that no good son should warn his mother off a cliff until she has fallen over it. But there is an anti-patriot who honestly angers honest men, and the explanation of him is, I think, what I have suggested: he is the uncandid candid friend; the man who says, "I am sorry to say we are ruined," and is not sorry at all. And he may be said, without rhetoric, to be a traitor; for he is using that ugly knowledge which was allowed him to strengthen the army, to discourage people from joining it. Because he is allowed to be pessimistic as a military adviser he is being pessimistic as a recruiting sergeant. Just in the same way the pessimist (who is the cosmic anti-patriot) uses the freedom that life allows to her counsellors to lure away the people from her flag. Granted that he states only facts, it is still essential to know what are his emotions, what is his motive. It may be that twelve hundred men in Tottenham are down with smallpox; but we want to know whether this is stated by some great philosopher who wants to curse the gods, or only by some common clergyman who wants to help the men.

The evil of the pessimist is, then, not that he chastises gods and men, but that he does not love what he chastises—he has not this primary and supernatural loyalty to things. What is the evil of the man commonly called an optimist? Obviously, it is felt that the optimist, wishing to defend the honour of this world, will defend the indefensible. He is the jingo of the universe; he will say, "My cosmos, right or wrong." He will be less inclined to the reform of things; more inclined to a sort of front-bench official answer to all attacks, soothing every one with assurances. He will not wash the world, but whitewash the world. All this (which is true of a type of optimist) leads us to the one really interesting point of psychology, which could not be explained without it.

We say there must be a primal loyalty to life: the only question is, shall it be a natural or a supernatural loyalty? If you like to put it so, shall it be a reasonable or an unreasonable loyalty? Now, the extraordinary thing is that the bad optimism (the whitewashing, the weak defence of everything) comes in with the reasonable optimism. Rational optimism leads to stagnation: it is irrational optimism that leads to reform. Let me explain by using once more the parallel of patriotism. The man who is most likely to ruin the place he loves is exactly the man who loves it with a reason. The man who will improve the place is the man who loves it without a reason. If a man loves some feature of Pimlico (which seems unlikely), he may find himself defending that feature against Pimlico itself. But if he simply loves Pimlico itself, he may lay it waste and turn it into the New Jerusalem. I do not deny that reform may be excessive; I only say that it is the mystic patriot who reforms. Mere jingo self-contentment is commonest among those who have some pedantic reason for their patriotism. The worst jingoes do not love England, but a theory of England. If we love England for being an empire, we may overrate the success with which we rule the Hindoos. But if we love it only for being a nation, we can face all events: for it would be a nation even if the Hindoos ruled us. Thus also only those will permit their patriotism to falsify history whose patriotism depends on history. A man who loves England for being English will not mind how she arose. But a man who loves England for being Anglo-Saxon may go against all facts for his fancy. He may end (like Carlyle and Freeman) by maintaining that the Norman Conquest was a Saxon Conquest. He may end in utter unreason—because he has a reason. A man who loves France for being military will palliate the army of 1870. But a man who loves France for being France will improve the army of 1870. This is exactly what the French have done, and France is a good instance of the working paradox. Nowhere else is patriotism more purely abstract and arbitrary; and nowhere else is reform more drastic and sweeping. The more transcendental is your patriotism, the more practical are your politics.

Perhaps the most everyday instance of this point is in the case of women; and their strange and strong loyalty. Some stupid people started the idea that because women obviously back up their own people through everything, therefore women are blind and do not see anything. They can hardly have known any women. The same women who are ready to defend their men through thick and thin are (in their personal intercourse with the man) almost morbidly lucid about the thinness of his excuses or the thickness of his head. A man's friend likes him but leaves him as he is: his wife loves him and is always trying to turn him into somebody else. Women who are utter mystics in their creed are utter cynics in their criticism. Thackeray expressed this well when he made Pendennis' mother, who worshipped her son as a god, yet assume that he would go wrong as a man. She underrated his virtue, though she overrated his value. The devotee is entirely free to criticise; the fanatic can safely be a sceptic. Love is not blind; that is the last thing that it is. Love is bound; and the more it is bound the less it is blind.

This at least had come to be my position about all that was called optimism, pessimism, and improvement. Before any cosmic act of reform we must have a cosmic oath of allegiance. A man must be interested in life, then he could be disinterested in his views of it. "My son give me thy heart"; the heart must be fixed on the right thing: the moment we have a fixed heart we have a free hand. I must pause to anticipate an obvious criticism. It will be said that a rational person accepts the world as mixed of good and evil with a decent satisfaction and a decent endurance. But this is exactly the attitude which I maintain to be defective. It is, I know, very common in this age; it was perfectly put in those quiet lines of Matthew Arnold which are more piercingly blasphemous than the shrieks of Schopenhauer—

"Enough we live:—and if a life, With large results so little rife, Though bearable, seem hardly worth This pomp of worlds, this pain of birth."

I know this feeling fills our epoch, and I think it freezes our epoch. For our Titanic purposes of faith and revolution, what we need is not the cold acceptance of the world as a compromise, but some way in which we can heartily hate and heartily love it. We do not want joy and anger to neutralize each other and produce a surly contentment; we want a fiercer delight and a fiercer discontent. We have to feel the universe at once as an ogre's castle, to be stormed, and yet as our own cottage, to which we can return at evening.

No one doubts that an ordinary man can get on with this world: but we demand not strength enough to get on with it, but strength enough to get it on. Can he hate it enough to change it, and yet love it enough to think it worth changing? Can he look up at its colossal good without once feeling acquiescence? Can he look up at its colossal evil without once feeling despair? Can he, in short, be at once not only a pessimist and an optimist, but a fanatical pessimist and a fanatical optimist? Is he enough of a pagan to die for the world, and enough of a Christian to die to it? In this combination, I maintain, it is the rational optimist who fails, the irrational optimist who succeeds. He is ready to smash the whole universe for the sake of itself.

I put these things not in their mature logical sequence, but as they came: and this view was cleared and sharpened by an accident of the time. Under the lengthening shadow of Ibsen, an argument arose whether it was not a very nice thing to murder one's self. Grave moderns told us that we must not even say "poor fellow," of a man who had blown his brains out, since he was an enviable person, and had only blown them out because of their exceptional excellence. Mr. William Archer even suggested that in the golden age there would be penny-in-the-slot machines, by which a man could kill himself for a penny. In all this I found myself utterly hostile to many who called themselves liberal and humane. Not only is suicide a sin, it is the sin. It is the ultimate and absolute evil, the refusal to take an interest in existence; the refusal to take the oath of loyalty to life. The man who kills a man, kills a man. The man who kills himself, kills all men; as far as he is concerned he wipes out the world. His act is worse (symbolically considered) than any rape or dynamite outrage. For it destroys all buildings: it insults all women. The thief is satisfied with diamonds; but the suicide is not: that is his crime. He cannot be bribed, even by the blazing stones of the Celestial City. The thief compliments the things he steals, if not the owner of them. But the suicide insults everything on earth by not stealing it. He defiles every flower by refusing to live for its sake. There is not a tiny creature in the cosmos at whom his death is not a sneer. When a man hangs himself on a tree, the leaves might fall off in anger and the birds fly away in fury: for each has received a personal affront. Of course there may be pathetic emotional excuses for the act. There often are for rape, and there almost always are for dynamite. But if it comes to clear ideas and the intelligent meaning of things, then there is much more rational and philosophic truth in the burial at the cross-roads and the stake driven through the body, than in Mr. Archer's suicidal automatic machines. There is a meaning in burying the suicide apart. The man's crime is different from other crimes—for it makes even crimes impossible.

About the same time I read a solemn flippancy by some free thinker: he said that a suicide was only the same as a martyr. The open fallacy of this helped to clear the question. Obviously a suicide is the opposite of a martyr. A martyr is a man who cares so much for something outside him, that he forgets his own personal life. A suicide is a man who cares so little for anything outside him, that he wants to see the last of everything. One wants something to begin: the other wants everything to end. In other words, the martyr is noble, exactly because (however he renounces the world or execrates all humanity) he confesses this ultimate link with life; he sets his heart outside himself: he dies that something may live. The suicide is ignoble because he has not this link with being: he is a mere destroyer; spiritually, he destroys the universe. And then I remembered the stake and the cross-roads, and the queer fact that Christianity had shown this weird harshness to the suicide. For Christianity had shown a wild encouragement of the martyr. Historic Christianity was accused, not entirely without reason, of carrying martyrdom and asceticism to a point, desolate and pessimistic. The early Christian martyrs talked of death with a horrible happiness. They blasphemed the beautiful duties of the body: they smelt the grave afar off like a field of flowers. All this has seemed to many the very poetry of pessimism. Yet there is the stake at the crossroads to show what Christianity thought of the pessimist.

This was the first of the long train of enigmas with which Christianity entered the discussion. And there went with it a peculiarity of which I shall have to speak more markedly, as a note of all Christian notions, but which distinctly began in this one. The Christian attitude to the martyr and the suicide was not what is so often affirmed in modern morals. It was not a matter of degree. It was not that a line must be drawn somewhere, and that the self-slayer in exaltation fell within the line, the self-slayer in sadness just beyond it. The Christian feeling evidently was not merely that the suicide was carrying martyrdom too far. The Christian feeling was furiously for one and furiously against the other: these two things that looked so much alike were at opposite ends of heaven and hell. One man flung away his life; he was so good that his dry bones could heal cities in pestilence. Another man flung away life; he was so bad that his bones would pollute his brethren's. I am not saying this fierceness was right; but why was it so fierce?

Here it was that I first found that my wandering feet were in some beaten track. Christianity had also felt this opposition of the martyr to the suicide: had it perhaps felt it for the same reason? Had Christianity felt what I felt, but could not (and cannot) express—this need for a first loyalty to things, and then for a ruinous reform of things? Then I remembered that it was actually the charge against Christianity that it combined these two things which I was wildly trying to combine. Christianity was accused, at one and the same time, of being too optimistic about the universe and of being too pessimistic about the world. The coincidence made me suddenly stand still.

An imbecile habit has arisen in modern controversy of saying that such and such a creed can be held in one age but cannot be held in another. Some dogma, we are told, was credible in the twelfth century, but is not credible in the twentieth. You might as well say that a certain philosophy can be believed on Mondays, but cannot be believed on Tuesdays. You might as well say of a view of the cosmos that it was suitable to half-past three, but not suitable to half-past four. What a man can believe depends upon his philosophy, not upon the clock or the century. If a man believes in unalterable natural law, he cannot believe in any miracle in any age. If a man believes in a will behind law, he can believe in any miracle in any age. Suppose, for the sake of argument, we are concerned with a case of thaumaturgic healing. A materialist of the twelfth century could not believe it any more than a materialist of the twentieth century. But a Christian Scientist of the twentieth century can believe it as much as a Christian of the twelfth century. It is simply a matter of a man's theory of things. Therefore in dealing with any historical answer, the point is not whether it was given in our time, but whether it was given in answer to our question. And the more I thought about when and how Christianity had come into the world, the more I felt that it had actually come to answer this question.

It is commonly the loose and latitudinarian Christians who pay quite indefensible compliments to Christianity. They talk as if there had never been any piety or pity until Christianity came, a point on which any mediaeval would have been eager to correct them. They represent that the remarkable thing about Christianity was that it was the first to preach simplicity or self-restraint, or inwardness and sincerity. They will think me very narrow (whatever that means) if I say that the remarkable thing about Christianity was that it was the first to preach Christianity. Its peculiarity was that it was peculiar, and simplicity and sincerity are not peculiar, but obvious ideals for all mankind. Christianity was the answer to a riddle, not the last truism uttered after a long talk. Only the other day I saw in an excellent weekly paper of Puritan tone this remark, that Christianity when stripped of its armour of dogma (as who should speak of a man stripped of his armour of bones), turned out to be nothing but the Quaker doctrine of the Inner Light. Now, if I were to say that Christianity came into the world specially to destroy the doctrine of the Inner Light, that would be an exaggeration. But it would be very much nearer to the truth. The last Stoics, like Marcus Aurelius, were exactly the people who did believe in the Inner Light. Their dignity, their weariness, their sad external care for others, their incurable internal care for themselves, were all due to the Inner Light, and existed only by that dismal illumination. Notice that Marcus Aurelius insists, as such introspective moralists always do, upon small things done or undone; it is because he has not hate or love enough to make a moral revolution. He gets up early in the morning, just as our own aristocrats living the Simple Life get up early in the morning; because such altruism is much easier than stopping the games of the amphitheatre or giving the English people back their land. Marcus Aurelius is the most intolerable of human types. He is an unselfish egoist. An unselfish egoist is a man who has pride without the excuse of passion. Of all conceivable forms of enlightenment the worst is what these people call the Inner Light. Of all horrible religions the most horrible is the worship of the god within. Any one who knows any body knows how it would work; any one who knows any one from the Higher Thought Centre knows how it does work. That Jones shall worship the god within him turns out ultimately to mean that Jones shall worship Jones. Let Jones worship the sun or moon, anything rather than the Inner Light; let Jones worship cats or crocodiles, if he can find any in his street, but not the god within. Christianity came into the world firstly in order to assert with violence that a man had not only to look inwards, but to look outwards, to behold with astonishment and enthusiasm a divine company and a divine captain. The only fun of being a Christian was that a man was not left alone with the Inner Light, but definitely recognized an outer light, fair as the sun, clear as the moon, terrible as an army with banners.

All the same, it will be as well if Jones does not worship the sun and moon. If he does, there is a tendency for him to imitate them; to say, that because the sun burns insects alive, he may burn insects alive. He thinks that because the sun gives people sun-stroke, he may give his neighbour measles. He thinks that because the moon is said to drive men mad, he may drive his wife mad. This ugly side of mere external optimism had also shown itself in the ancient world. About the time when the Stoic idealism had begun to show the weaknesses of pessimism, the old nature worship of the ancients had begun to show the enormous weaknesses of optimism. Nature worship is natural enough while the society is young, or, in other words, Pantheism is all right as long as it is the worship of Pan. But Nature has another side which experience and sin are not slow in finding out, and it is no flippancy to say of the god Pan that he soon showed the cloven hoof. The only objection to Natural Religion is that somehow it always becomes unnatural. A man loves Nature in the morning for her innocence and amiability, and at nightfall, if he is loving her still, it is for her darkness and her cruelty. He washes at dawn in clear water as did the Wise Man of the Stoics, yet, somehow at the dark end of the day, he is bathing in hot bull's blood, as did Julian the Apostate. The mere pursuit of health always leads to something unhealthy. Physical nature must not be made the direct object of obedience; it must be enjoyed, not worshipped. Stars and mountains must not be taken seriously. If they are, we end where the pagan nature worship ended. Because the earth is kind, we can imitate all her cruelties. Because sexuality is sane, we can all go mad about sexuality. Mere optimism had reached its insane and appropriate termination. The theory that everything was good had become an orgy of everything that was bad.

On the other side our idealist pessimists were represented by the old remnant of the Stoics. Marcus Aurelius and his friends had really given up the idea of any god in the universe and looked only to the god within. They had no hope of any virtue in nature, and hardly any hope of any virtue in society. They had not enough interest in the outer world really to wreck or revolutionise it. They did not love the city enough to set fire to it. Thus the ancient world was exactly in our own desolate dilemma. The only people who really enjoyed this world were busy breaking it up; and the virtuous people did not care enough about them to knock them down. In this dilemma (the same as ours) Christianity suddenly stepped in and offered a singular answer, which the world eventually accepted as THE answer. It was the answer then, and I think it is the answer now.

This answer was like the slash of a sword; it sundered; it did not in any sense sentimentally unite. Briefly, it divided God from the cosmos. That transcendence and distinctness of the deity which some Christians now want to remove from Christianity, was really the only reason why any one wanted to be a Christian. It was the whole point of the Christian answer to the unhappy pessimist and the still more unhappy optimist. As I am here only concerned with their particular problem, I shall indicate only briefly this great metaphysical suggestion. All descriptions of the creating or sustaining principle in things must be metaphorical, because they must be verbal. Thus the pantheist is forced to speak of God in all things as if he were in a box. Thus the evolutionist has, in his very name, the idea of being unrolled like a carpet. All terms, religious and irreligious, are open to this charge. The only question is whether all terms are useless, or whether one can, with such a phrase, cover a distinct IDEA about the origin of things. I think one can, and so evidently does the evolutionist, or he would not talk about evolution. And the root phrase for all Christian theism was this, that God was a creator, as an artist is a creator. A poet is so separate from his poem that he himself speaks of it as a little thing he has "thrown off." Even in giving it forth he has flung it away. This principle that all creation and procreation is a breaking off is at least as consistent through the cosmos as the evolutionary principle that all growth is a branching out. A woman loses a child even in having a child. All creation is separation. Birth is as solemn a parting as death.

It was the prime philosophic principle of Christianity that this divorce in the divine act of making (such as severs the poet from the poem or the mother from the new-born child) was the true description of the act whereby the absolute energy made the world. According to most philosophers, God in making the world enslaved it. According to Christianity, in making it, He set it free. God had written, not so much a poem, but rather a play; a play he had planned as perfect, but which had necessarily been left to human actors and stage-managers, who had since made a great mess of it. I will discuss the truth of this theorem later. Here I have only to point out with what a startling smoothness it passed the dilemma we have discussed in this chapter. In this way at least one could be both happy and indignant without degrading one's self to be either a pessimist or an optimist. On this system one could fight all the forces of existence without deserting the flag of existence. One could be at peace with the universe and yet be at war with the world. St. George could still fight the dragon, however big the monster bulked in the cosmos, though he were bigger than the mighty cities or bigger than the everlasting hills. If he were as big as the world he could yet be killed in the name of the world. St. George had not to consider any obvious odds or proportions in the scale of things, but only the original secret of their design. He can shake his sword at the dragon, even if it is everything; even if the empty heavens over his head are only the huge arch of its open jaws.

And then followed an experience impossible to describe. It was as if I had been blundering about since my birth with two huge and unmanageable machines, of different shapes and without apparent connection—the world and the Christian tradition. I had found this hole in the world: the fact that one must somehow find a way of loving the world without trusting it; somehow one must love the world without being worldly. I found this projecting feature of Christian theology, like a sort of hard spike, the dogmatic insistence that God was personal, and had made a world separate from Himself. The spike of dogma fitted exactly into the hole in the world—it had evidently been meant to go there— and then the strange thing began to happen. When once these two parts of the two machines had come together, one after another, all the other parts fitted and fell in with an eerie exactitude. I could hear bolt after bolt over all the machinery falling into its place with a kind of click of relief. Having got one part right, all the other parts were repeating that rectitude, as clock after clock strikes noon. Instinct after instinct was answered by doctrine after doctrine. Or, to vary the metaphor, I was like one who had advanced into a hostile country to take one high fortress. And when that fort had fallen the whole country surrendered and turned solid behind me. The whole land was lit up, as it were, back to the first fields of my childhood. All those blind fancies of boyhood which in the fourth chapter I have tried in vain to trace on the darkness, became suddenly transparent and sane. I was right when I felt that roses were red by some sort of choice: it was the divine choice. I was right when I felt that I would almost rather say that grass was the wrong colour than say it must by necessity have been that colour: it might verily have been any other. My sense that happiness hung on the crazy thread of a condition did mean something when all was said: it meant the whole doctrine of the Fall. Even those dim and shapeless monsters of notions which I have not been able to describe, much less defend, stepped quietly into their places like colossal caryatides of the creed. The fancy that the cosmos was not vast and void, but small and cosy, had a fulfilled significance now, for anything that is a work of art must be small in the sight of the artist; to God the stars might be only small and dear, like diamonds. And my haunting instinct that somehow good was not merely a tool to be used, but a relic to be guarded, like the goods from Crusoe's ship— even that had been the wild whisper of something originally wise, for, according to Christianity, we were indeed the survivors of a wreck, the crew of a golden ship that had gone down before the beginning of the world.

But the important matter was this, that it entirely reversed the reason for optimism. And the instant the reversal was made it felt like the abrupt ease when a bone is put back in the socket. I had often called myself an optimist, to avoid the too evident blasphemy of pessimism. But all the optimism of the age had been false and disheartening for this reason, that it had always been trying to prove that we fit in to the world. The Christian optimism is based on the fact that we do NOT fit in to the world. I had tried to be happy by telling myself that man is an animal, like any other which sought its meat from God. But now I really was happy, for I had learnt that man is a monstrosity. I had been right in feeling all things as odd, for I myself was at once worse and better than all things. The optimist's pleasure was prosaic, for it dwelt on the naturalness of everything; the Christian pleasure was poetic, for it dwelt on the unnaturalness of everything in the light of the supernatural. The modern philosopher had told me again and again that I was in the right place, and I had still felt depressed even in acquiescence. But I had heard that I was in the WRONG place, and my soul sang for joy, like a bird in spring. The knowledge found out and illuminated forgotten chambers in the dark house of infancy. I knew now why grass had always seemed to me as queer as the green beard of a giant, and why I could feel homesick at home.

VI THE PARADOXES OF CHRISTIANITY

The real trouble with this world of ours is not that it is an unreasonable world, nor even that it is a reasonable one. The commonest kind of trouble is that it is nearly reasonable, but not quite. Life is not an illogicality; yet it is a trap for logicians. It looks just a little more mathematical and regular than it is; its exactitude is obvious, but its inexactitude is hidden; its wildness lies in wait. I give one coarse instance of what I mean. Suppose some mathematical creature from the moon were to reckon up the human body; he would at once see that the essential thing about it was that it was duplicate. A man is two men, he on the right exactly resembling him on the left. Having noted that there was an arm on the right and one on the left, a leg on the right and one on the left, he might go further and still find on each side the same number of fingers, the same number of toes, twin eyes, twin ears, twin nostrils, and even twin lobes of the brain. At last he would take it as a law; and then, where he found a heart on one side, would deduce that there was another heart on the other. And just then, where he most felt he was right, he would be wrong.

It is this silent swerving from accuracy by an inch that is the uncanny element in everything. It seems a sort of secret treason in the universe. An apple or an orange is round enough to get itself called round, and yet is not round after all. The earth itself is shaped like an orange in order to lure some simple astronomer into calling it a globe. A blade of grass is called after the blade of a sword, because it comes to a point; but it doesn't. Everywhere in things there is this element of the quiet and incalculable. It escapes the rationalists, but it never escapes till the last moment. From the grand curve of our earth it could easily be inferred that every inch of it was thus curved. It would seem rational that as a man has a brain on both sides, he should have a heart on both sides. Yet scientific men are still organizing expeditions to find the North Pole, because they are so fond of flat country. Scientific men are also still organizing expeditions to find a man's heart; and when they try to find it, they generally get on the wrong side of him.

Now, actual insight or inspiration is best tested by whether it guesses these hidden malformations or surprises. If our mathematician from the moon saw the two arms and the two ears, he might deduce the two shoulder-blades and the two halves of the brain. But if he guessed that the man's heart was in the right place, then I should call him something more than a mathematician. Now, this is exactly the claim which I have since come to propound for Christianity. Not merely that it deduces logical truths, but that when it suddenly becomes illogical, it has found, so to speak, an illogical truth. It not only goes right about things, but it goes wrong (if one may say so) exactly where the things go wrong. Its plan suits the secret irregularities, and expects the unexpected. It is simple about the simple truth; but it is stubborn about the subtle truth. It will admit that a man has two hands, it will not admit (though all the Modernists wail to it) the obvious deduction that he has two hearts. It is my only purpose in this chapter to point this out; to show that whenever we feel there is something odd in Christian theology, we shall generally find that there is something odd in the truth.

I have alluded to an unmeaning phrase to the effect that such and such a creed cannot be believed in our age. Of course, anything can be believed in any age. But, oddly enough, there really is a sense in which a creed, if it is believed at all, can be believed more fixedly in a complex society than in a simple one. If a man finds Christianity true in Birmingham, he has actually clearer reasons for faith than if he had found it true in Mercia. For the more complicated seems the coincidence, the less it can be a coincidence. If snowflakes fell in the shape, say, of the heart of Midlothian, it might be an accident. But if snowflakes fell in the exact shape of the maze at Hampton Court, I think one might call it a miracle. It is exactly as of such a miracle that I have since come to feel of the philosophy of Christianity. The complication of our modern world proves the truth of the creed more perfectly than any of the plain problems of the ages of faith. It was in Notting Hill and Battersea that I began to see that Christianity was true. This is why the faith has that elaboration of doctrines and details which so much distresses those who admire Christianity without believing in it. When once one believes in a creed, one is proud of its complexity, as scientists are proud of the complexity of science. It shows how rich it is in discoveries. If it is right at all, it is a compliment to say that it's elaborately right. A stick might fit a hole or a stone a hollow by accident. But a key and a lock are both complex. And if a key fits a lock, you know it is the right key.

But this involved accuracy of the thing makes it very difficult to do what I now have to do, to describe this accumulation of truth. It is very hard for a man to defend anything of which he is entirely convinced. It is comparatively easy when he is only partially convinced. He is partially convinced because he has found this or that proof of the thing, and he can expound it. But a man is not really convinced of a philosophic theory when he finds that something proves it. He is only really convinced when he finds that everything proves it. And the more converging reasons he finds pointing to this conviction, the more bewildered he is if asked suddenly to sum them up. Thus, if one asked an ordinary intelligent man, on the spur of the moment, "Why do you prefer civilization to savagery?" he would look wildly round at object after object, and would only be able to answer vaguely, "Why, there is that bookcase . . . and the coals in the coal-scuttle . . . and pianos . . . and policemen." The whole case for civilization is that the case for it is complex. It has done so many things. But that very multiplicity of proof which ought to make reply overwhelming makes reply impossible.

There is, therefore, about all complete conviction a kind of huge helplessness. The belief is so big that it takes a long time to get it into action. And this hesitation chiefly arises, oddly enough, from an indifference about where one should begin. All roads lead to Rome; which is one reason why many people never get there. In the case of this defence of the Christian conviction I confess that I would as soon begin the argument with one thing as another; I would begin it with a turnip or a taximeter cab. But if I am to be at all careful about making my meaning clear, it will, I think, be wiser to continue the current arguments of the last chapter, which was concerned to urge the first of these mystical coincidences, or rather ratifications. All I had hitherto heard of Christian theology had alienated me from it. I was a pagan at the age of twelve, and a complete agnostic by the age of sixteen; and I cannot understand any one passing the age of seventeen without having asked himself so simple a question. I did, indeed, retain a cloudy reverence for a cosmic deity and a great historical interest in the Founder of Christianity. But I certainly regarded Him as a man; though perhaps I thought that, even in that point, He had an advantage over some of His modern critics. I read the scientific and sceptical literature of my time—all of it, at least, that I could find written in English and lying about; and I read nothing else; I mean I read nothing else on any other note of philosophy. The penny dreadfuls which I also read were indeed in a healthy and heroic tradition of Christianity; but I did not know this at the time. I never read a line of Christian apologetics. I read as little as I can of them now. It was Huxley and Herbert Spencer and Bradlaugh who brought me back to orthodox theology. They sowed in my mind my first wild doubts of doubt. Our grandmothers were quite right when they said that Tom Paine and the free-thinkers unsettled the mind. They do. They unsettled mine horribly. The rationalist made me question whether reason was of any use whatever; and when I had finished Herbert Spencer I had got as far as doubting (for the first time) whether evolution had occurred at all. As I laid down the last of Colonel Ingersoll's atheistic lectures the dreadful thought broke across my mind, "Almost thou persuadest me to be a Christian." I was in a desperate way.

This odd effect of the great agnostics in arousing doubts deeper than their own might be illustrated in many ways. I take only one. As I read and re-read all the non-Christian or anti-Christian accounts of the faith, from Huxley to Bradlaugh, a slow and awful impression grew gradually but graphically upon my mind—the impression that Christianity must be a most extraordinary thing. For not only (as I understood) had Christianity the most flaming vices, but it had apparently a mystical talent for combining vices which seemed inconsistent with each other. It was attacked on all sides and for all contradictory reasons. No sooner had one rationalist demonstrated that it was too far to the east than another demonstrated with equal clearness that it was much too far to the west. No sooner had my indignation died down at its angular and aggressive squareness than I was called up again to notice and condemn its enervating and sensual roundness. In case any reader has not come across the thing I mean, I will give such instances as I remember at random of this self-contradiction in the sceptical attack. I give four or five of them; there are fifty more.

Thus, for instance, I was much moved by the eloquent attack on Christianity as a thing of inhuman gloom; for I thought (and still think) sincere pessimism the unpardonable sin. Insincere pessimism is a social accomplishment, rather agreeable than otherwise; and fortunately nearly all pessimism is insincere. But if Chris-Christianity was, as these people said, a thing purely pessimistic and opposed to life, then I was quite prepared to blow up St. Paul's Cathedral. But the extraordinary thing is this. They did prove to me in Chapter I. (to my complete satisfaction) that Christianity was too pessimistic; and then, in Chapter II., they began to prove to me that it was a great deal too optimistic. One accusation against Christianity was that it prevented men, by morbid tears and terrors, from seeking joy and liberty in the bosom of Nature. But another accusation was that it comforted men with a fictitious providence, and put them in a pink-and-white nursery. One great agnostic asked why Nature was not beautiful enough, and why it was hard to be free. Another great agnostic objected that Christian optimism, "the garment of make-believe woven by pious hands," hid from us the fact that Nature was ugly, and that it was impossible to be free. One rationalist had hardly done calling Christianity a nightmare before another began to call it a fool's paradise. This puzzled me; the charges seemed inconsistent. Christianity could not at once be the black mask on a white world, and also the white mask on a black world. The state of the Christian could not be at once so comfortable that he was a coward to cling to it, and so uncomfortable that he was a fool to stand it. If it falsified human vision it must falsify it one way or another; it could not wear both green and rose-coloured spectacles. I rolled on my tongue with a terrible joy, as did all young men of that time, the taunts which Swinburne hurled at the dreariness of the creed—

"Thou hast conquered, O pale Galilaean, the world has grown gray with Thy breath."

But when I read the same poet's accounts of paganism (as in "Atalanta"), I gathered that the world was, if possible, more gray before the Galilean breathed on it than afterwards. The poet maintained, indeed, in the abstract, that life itself was pitch dark. And yet, somehow, Christianity had darkened it. The very man who denounced Christianity for pessimism was himself a pessimist. I thought there must be something wrong. And it did for one wild moment cross my mind that, perhaps, those might not be the very best judges of the relation of religion to happiness who, by their own account, had neither one nor the other.

It must be understood that I did not conclude hastily that the accusations were false or the accusers fools. I simply deduced that Christianity must be something even weirder and wickeder than they made out. A thing might have these two opposite vices; but it must be a rather queer thing if it did. A man might be too fat in one place and too thin in another; but he would be an odd shape. At this point my thoughts were only of the odd shape of the Christian religion; I did not allege any odd shape in the rationalistic mind.

Here is another case of the same kind. I felt that a strong case against Christianity lay in the charge that there is something timid, monkish, and unmanly about all that is called "Christian," especially in its attitude towards resistance and fighting. The great sceptics of the nineteenth century were largely virile. Bradlaugh in an expansive way, Huxley, in a reticent way, were decidedly men. In comparison, it did seem tenable that there was something weak and over patient about Christian counsels. The Gospel paradox about the other cheek, the fact that priests never fought, a hundred things made plausible the accusation that Christianity was an attempt to make a man too like a sheep. I read it and believed it, and if I had read nothing different, I should have gone on believing it. But I read something very different. I turned the next page in my agnostic manual, and my brain turned up-side down. Now I found that I was to hate Christianity not for fighting too little, but for fighting too much. Christianity, it seemed, was the mother of wars. Christianity had deluged the world with blood. I had got thoroughly angry with the Christian, because he never was angry. And now I was told to be angry with him because his anger had been the most huge and horrible thing in human history; because his anger had soaked the earth and smoked to the sun. The very people who reproached Christianity with the meekness and non-resistance of the monasteries were the very people who reproached it also with the violence and valour of the Crusades. It was the fault of poor old Christianity (somehow or other) both that Edward the Confessor did not fight and that Richard Coeur de Leon did. The Quakers (we were told) were the only characteristic Christians; and yet the massacres of Cromwell and Alva were characteristic Christian crimes. What could it all mean? What was this Christianity which always forbade war and always produced wars? What could be the nature of the thing which one could abuse first because it would not fight, and second because it was always fighting? In what world of riddles was born this monstrous murder and this monstrous meekness? The shape of Christianity grew a queerer shape every instant.

I take a third case; the strangest of all, because it involves the one real objection to the faith. The one real objection to the Christian religion is simply that it is one religion. The world is a big place, full of very different kinds of people. Christianity (it may reasonably be said) is one thing confined to one kind of people; it began in Palestine, it has practically stopped with Europe. I was duly impressed with this argument in my youth, and I was much drawn towards the doctrine often preached in Ethical Societies— I mean the doctrine that there is one great unconscious church of all humanity founded on the omnipresence of the human conscience. Creeds, it was said, divided men; but at least morals united them. The soul might seek the strangest and most remote lands and ages and still find essential ethical common sense. It might find Confucius under Eastern trees, and he would be writing "Thou shalt not steal." It might decipher the darkest hieroglyphic on the most primeval desert, and the meaning when deciphered would be "Little boys should tell the truth." I believed this doctrine of the brotherhood of all men in the possession of a moral sense, and I believe it still—with other things. And I was thoroughly annoyed with Christianity for suggesting (as I supposed) that whole ages and empires of men had utterly escaped this light of justice and reason. But then I found an astonishing thing. I found that the very people who said that mankind was one church from Plato to Emerson were the very people who said that morality had changed altogether, and that what was right in one age was wrong in another. If I asked, say, for an altar, I was told that we needed none, for men our brothers gave us clear oracles and one creed in their universal customs and ideals. But if I mildly pointed out that one of men's universal customs was to have an altar, then my agnostic teachers turned clean round and told me that men had always been in darkness and the superstitions of savages. I found it was their daily taunt against Christianity that it was the light of one people and had left all others to die in the dark. But I also found that it was their special boast for themselves that science and progress were the discovery of one people, and that all other peoples had died in the dark. Their chief insult to Christianity was actually their chief compliment to themselves, and there seemed to be a strange unfairness about all their relative insistence on the two things. When considering some pagan or agnostic, we were to remember that all men had one religion; when considering some mystic or spiritualist, we were only to consider what absurd religions some men had. We could trust the ethics of Epictetus, because ethics had never changed. We must not trust the ethics of Bossuet, because ethics had changed. They changed in two hundred years, but not in two thousand.

This began to be alarming. It looked not so much as if Christianity was bad enough to include any vices, but rather as if any stick was good enough to beat Christianity with. What again could this astonishing thing be like which people were so anxious to contradict, that in doing so they did not mind contradicting themselves? I saw the same thing on every side. I can give no further space to this discussion of it in detail; but lest any one supposes that I have unfairly selected three accidental cases I will run briefly through a few others. Thus, certain sceptics wrote that the great crime of Christianity had been its attack on the family; it had dragged women to the loneliness and contemplation of the cloister, away from their homes and their children. But, then, other sceptics (slightly more advanced) said that the great crime of Christianity was forcing the family and marriage upon us; that it doomed women to the drudgery of their homes and children, and forbade them loneliness and contemplation. The charge was actually reversed. Or, again, certain phrases in the Epistles or the marriage service, were said by the anti-Christians to show contempt for woman's intellect. But I found that the anti-Christians themselves had a contempt for woman's intellect; for it was their great sneer at the Church on the Continent that "only women" went to it. Or again, Christianity was reproached with its naked and hungry habits; with its sackcloth and dried peas. But the next minute Christianity was being reproached with its pomp and its ritualism; its shrines of porphyry and its robes of gold. It was abused for being too plain and for being too coloured. Again Christianity had always been accused of restraining sexuality too much, when Bradlaugh the Malthusian discovered that it restrained it too little. It is often accused in the same breath of prim respectability and of religious extravagance. Between the covers of the same atheistic pamphlet I have found the faith rebuked for its disunion, "One thinks one thing, and one another," and rebuked also for its union, "It is difference of opinion that prevents the world from going to the dogs." In the same conversation a free-thinker, a friend of mine, blamed Christianity for despising Jews, and then despised it himself for being Jewish.

I wished to be quite fair then, and I wish to be quite fair now; and I did not conclude that the attack on Christianity was all wrong. I only concluded that if Christianity was wrong, it was very wrong indeed. Such hostile horrors might be combined in one thing, but that thing must be very strange and solitary. There are men who are misers, and also spendthrifts; but they are rare. There are men sensual and also ascetic; but they are rare. But if this mass of mad contradictions really existed, quakerish and bloodthirsty, too gorgeous and too thread-bare, austere, yet pandering preposterously to the lust of the eye, the enemy of women and their foolish refuge, a solemn pessimist and a silly optimist, if this evil existed, then there was in this evil something quite supreme and unique. For I found in my rationalist teachers no explanation of such exceptional corruption. Christianity (theoretically speaking) was in their eyes only one of the ordinary myths and errors of mortals. THEY gave me no key to this twisted and unnatural badness. Such a paradox of evil rose to the stature of the supernatural. It was, indeed, almost as supernatural as the infallibility of the Pope. An historic institution, which never went right, is really quite as much of a miracle as an institution that cannot go wrong. The only explanation which immediately occurred to my mind was that Christianity did not come from heaven, but from hell. Really, if Jesus of Nazareth was not Christ, He must have been Antichrist.

And then in a quiet hour a strange thought struck me like a still thunderbolt. There had suddenly come into my mind another explanation. Suppose we heard an unknown man spoken of by many men. Suppose we were puzzled to hear that some men said he was too tall and some too short; some objected to his fatness, some lamented his leanness; some thought him too dark, and some too fair. One explanation (as has been already admitted) would be that he might be an odd shape. But there is another explanation. He might be the right shape. Outrageously tall men might feel him to be short. Very short men might feel him to be tall. Old bucks who are growing stout might consider him insufficiently filled out; old beaux who were growing thin might feel that he expanded beyond the narrow lines of elegance. Perhaps Swedes (who have pale hair like tow) called him a dark man, while negroes considered him distinctly blonde. Perhaps (in short) this extraordinary thing is really the ordinary thing; at least the normal thing, the centre. Perhaps, after all, it is Christianity that is sane and all its critics that are mad—in various ways. I tested this idea by asking myself whether there was about any of the accusers anything morbid that might explain the accusation. I was startled to find that this key fitted a lock. For instance, it was certainly odd that the modern world charged Christianity at once with bodily austerity and with artistic pomp. But then it was also odd, very odd, that the modern world itself combined extreme bodily luxury with an extreme absence of artistic pomp. The modern man thought Becket's robes too rich and his meals too poor. But then the modern man was really exceptional in history; no man before ever ate such elaborate dinners in such ugly clothes. The modern man found the church too simple exactly where modern life is too complex; he found the church too gorgeous exactly where modern life is too dingy. The man who disliked the plain fasts and feasts was mad on entrees. The man who disliked vestments wore a pair of preposterous trousers. And surely if there was any insanity involved in the matter at all it was in the trousers, not in the simply falling robe. If there was any insanity at all, it was in the extravagant entrees, not in the bread and wine.

I went over all the cases, and I found the key fitted so far. The fact that Swinburne was irritated at the unhappiness of Christians and yet more irritated at their happiness was easily explained. It was no longer a complication of diseases in Christianity, but a complication of diseases in Swinburne. The restraints of Christians saddened him simply because he was more hedonist than a healthy man should be. The faith of Christians angered him because he was more pessimist than a healthy man should be. In the same way the Malthusians by instinct attacked Christianity; not because there is anything especially anti-Malthusian about Christianity, but because there is something a little anti-human about Malthusianism.

Nevertheless it could not, I felt, be quite true that Christianity was merely sensible and stood in the middle. There was really an element in it of emphasis and even frenzy which had justified the secularists in their superficial criticism. It might be wise, I began more and more to think that it was wise, but it was not merely worldly wise; it was not merely temperate and respectable. Its fierce crusaders and meek saints might balance each other; still, the crusaders were very fierce and the saints were very meek, meek beyond all decency. Now, it was just at this point of the speculation that I remembered my thoughts about the martyr and the suicide. In that matter there had been this combination between two almost insane positions which yet somehow amounted to sanity. This was just such another contradiction; and this I had already found to be true. This was exactly one of the paradoxes in which sceptics found the creed wrong; and in this I had found it right. Madly as Christians might love the martyr or hate the suicide, they never felt these passions more madly than I had felt them long before I dreamed of Christianity. Then the most difficult and interesting part of the mental process opened, and I began to trace this idea darkly through all the enormous thoughts of our theology. The idea was that which I had outlined touching the optimist and the pessimist; that we want not an amalgam or compromise, but both things at the top of their energy; love and wrath both burning. Here I shall only trace it in relation to ethics. But I need not remind the reader that the idea of this combination is indeed central in orthodox theology. For orthodox theology has specially insisted that Christ was not a being apart from God and man, like an elf, nor yet a being half human and half not, like a centaur, but both things at once and both things thoroughly, very man and very God. Now let me trace this notion as I found it.

All sane men can see that sanity is some kind of equilibrium; that one may be mad and eat too much, or mad and eat too little. Some moderns have indeed appeared with vague versions of progress and evolution which seeks to destroy the MESON or balance of Aristotle. They seem to suggest that we are meant to starve progressively, or to go on eating larger and larger breakfasts every morning for ever. But the great truism of the MESON remains for all thinking men, and these people have not upset any balance except their own. But granted that we have all to keep a balance, the real interest comes in with the question of how that balance can be kept. That was the problem which Paganism tried to solve: that was the problem which I think Christianity solved and solved in a very strange way.

Paganism declared that virtue was in a balance; Christianity declared it was in a conflict: the collision of two passions apparently opposite. Of course they were not really inconsistent; but they were such that it was hard to hold simultaneously. Let us follow for a moment the clue of the martyr and the suicide; and take the case of courage. No quality has ever so much addled the brains and tangled the definitions of merely rational sages. Courage is almost a contradiction in terms. It means a strong desire to live taking the form of a readiness to die. "He that will lose his life, the same shall save it," is not a piece of mysticism for saints and heroes. It is a piece of everyday advice for sailors or mountaineers. It might be printed in an Alpine guide or a drill book. This paradox is the whole principle of courage; even of quite earthly or quite brutal courage. A man cut off by the sea may save his life if he will risk it on the precipice.

He can only get away from death by continually stepping within an inch of it. A soldier surrounded by enemies, if he is to cut his way out, needs to combine a strong desire for living with a strange carelessness about dying. He must not merely cling to life, for then he will be a coward, and will not escape. He must not merely wait for death, for then he will be a suicide, and will not escape. He must seek his life in a spirit of furious indifference to it; he must desire life like water and yet drink death like wine. No philosopher, I fancy, has ever expressed this romantic riddle with adequate lucidity, and I certainly have not done so. But Christianity has done more: it has marked the limits of it in the awful graves of the suicide and the hero, showing the distance between him who dies for the sake of living and him who dies for the sake of dying. And it has held up ever since above the European lances the banner of the mystery of chivalry: the Christian courage, which is a disdain of death; not the Chinese courage, which is a disdain of life.

And now I began to find that this duplex passion was the Christian key to ethics everywhere. Everywhere the creed made a moderation out of the still crash of two impetuous emotions. Take, for instance, the matter of modesty, of the balance between mere pride and mere prostration. The average pagan, like the average agnostic, would merely say that he was content with himself, but not insolently self-satisfied, that there were many better and many worse, that his deserts were limited, but he would see that he got them. In short, he would walk with his head in the air; but not necessarily with his nose in the air. This is a manly and rational position, but it is open to the objection we noted against the compromise between optimism and pessimism—the "resignation" of Matthew Arnold. Being a mixture of two things, it is a dilution of two things; neither is present in its full strength or contributes its full colour. This proper pride does not lift the heart like the tongue of trumpets; you cannot go clad in crimson and gold for this. On the other hand, this mild rationalist modesty does not cleanse the soul with fire and make it clear like crystal; it does not (like a strict and searching humility) make a man as a little child, who can sit at the feet of the grass. It does not make him look up and see marvels; for Alice must grow small if she is to be Alice in Wonderland. Thus it loses both the poetry of being proud and the poetry of being humble. Christianity sought by this same strange expedient to save both of them.

It separated the two ideas and then exaggerated them both. In one way Man was to be haughtier than he had ever been before; in another way he was to be humbler than he had ever been before. In so far as I am Man I am the chief of creatures. In so far as I am a man I am the chief of sinners. All humility that had meant pessimism, that had meant man taking a vague or mean view of his whole destiny—all that was to go. We were to hear no more the wail of Ecclesiastes that humanity had no pre-eminence over the brute, or the awful cry of Homer that man was only the saddest of all the beasts of the field. Man was a statue of God walking about the garden. Man had pre-eminence over all the brutes; man was only sad because he was not a beast, but a broken god. The Greek had spoken of men creeping on the earth, as if clinging to it. Now Man was to tread on the earth as if to subdue it. Christianity thus held a thought of the dignity of man that could only be expressed in crowns rayed like the sun and fans of peacock plumage. Yet at the same time it could hold a thought about the abject smallness of man that could only be expressed in fasting and fantastic submission, in the gray ashes of St. Dominic and the white snows of St. Bernard. When one came to think of ONE'S SELF, there was vista and void enough for any amount of bleak abnegation and bitter truth. There the realistic gentleman could let himself go—as long as he let himself go at himself. There was an open playground for the happy pessimist. Let him say anything against himself short of blaspheming the original aim of his being; let him call himself a fool and even a damned fool (though that is Calvinistic); but he must not say that fools are not worth saving. He must not say that a man, QUA man, can be valueless. Here, again in short, Christianity got over the difficulty of combining furious opposites, by keeping them both, and keeping them both furious. The Church was positive on both points. One can hardly think too little of one's self. One can hardly think too much of one's soul.

Take another case: the complicated question of charity, which some highly uncharitable idealists seem to think quite easy. Charity is a paradox, like modesty and courage. Stated baldly, charity certainly means one of two things—pardoning unpardonable acts, or loving unlovable people. But if we ask ourselves (as we did in the case of pride) what a sensible pagan would feel about such a subject, we shall probably be beginning at the bottom of it. A sensible pagan would say that there were some people one could forgive, and some one couldn't: a slave who stole wine could be laughed at; a slave who betrayed his benefactor could be killed, and cursed even after he was killed. In so far as the act was pardonable, the man was pardonable. That again is rational, and even refreshing; but it is a dilution. It leaves no place for a pure horror of injustice, such as that which is a great beauty in the innocent. And it leaves no place for a mere tenderness for men as men, such as is the whole fascination of the charitable. Christianity came in here as before. It came in startlingly with a sword, and clove one thing from another. It divided the crime from the criminal. The criminal we must forgive unto seventy times seven. The crime we must not forgive at all. It was not enough that slaves who stole wine inspired partly anger and partly kindness. We must be much more angry with theft than before, and yet much kinder to thieves than before. There was room for wrath and love to run wild. And the more I considered Christianity, the more I found that while it had established a rule and order, the chief aim of that order was to give room for good things to run wild.

Mental and emotional liberty are not so simple as they look. Really they require almost as careful a balance of laws and conditions as do social and political liberty. The ordinary aesthetic anarchist who sets out to feel everything freely gets knotted at last in a paradox that prevents him feeling at all. He breaks away from home limits to follow poetry. But in ceasing to feel home limits he has ceased to feel the "Odyssey." He is free from national prejudices and outside patriotism. But being outside patriotism he is outside "Henry V." Such a literary man is simply outside all literature: he is more of a prisoner than any bigot. For if there is a wall between you and the world, it makes little difference whether you describe yourself as locked in or as locked out. What we want is not the universality that is outside all normal sentiments; we want the universality that is inside all normal sentiments. It is all the difference between being free from them, as a man is free from a prison, and being free of them as a man is free of a city. I am free from Windsor Castle (that is, I am not forcibly detained there), but I am by no means free of that building. How can man be approximately free of fine emotions, able to swing them in a clear space without breakage or wrong? THIS was the achievement of this Christian paradox of the parallel passions. Granted the primary dogma of the war between divine and diabolic, the revolt and ruin of the world, their optimism and pessimism, as pure poetry, could be loosened like cataracts.

St. Francis, in praising all good, could be a more shouting optimist than Walt Whitman. St. Jerome, in denouncing all evil, could paint the world blacker than Schopenhauer. Both passions were free because both were kept in their place. The optimist could pour out all the praise he liked on the gay music of the march, the golden trumpets, and the purple banners going into battle. But he must not call the fight needless. The pessimist might draw as darkly as he chose the sickening marches or the sanguine wounds. But he must not call the fight hopeless. So it was with all the other moral problems, with pride, with protest, and with compassion. By defining its main doctrine, the Church not only kept seemingly inconsistent things side by side, but, what was more, allowed them to break out in a sort of artistic violence otherwise possible only to anarchists. Meekness grew more dramatic than madness. Historic Christianity rose into a high and strange COUP DE THEATRE of morality—things that are to virtue what the crimes of Nero are to vice. The spirits of indignation and of charity took terrible and attractive forms, ranging from that monkish fierceness that scourged like a dog the first and greatest of the Plantagenets, to the sublime pity of St. Catherine, who, in the official shambles, kissed the bloody head of the criminal. Poetry could be acted as well as composed. This heroic and monumental manner in ethics has entirely vanished with supernatural religion. They, being humble, could parade themselves: but we are too proud to be prominent. Our ethical teachers write reasonably for prison reform; but we are not likely to see Mr. Cadbury, or any eminent philanthropist, go into Reading Gaol and embrace the strangled corpse before it is cast into the quicklime. Our ethical teachers write mildly against the power of millionaires; but we are not likely to see Mr. Rockefeller, or any modern tyrant, publicly whipped in Westminster Abbey.

Thus, the double charges of the secularists, though throwing nothing but darkness and confusion on themselves, throw a real light on the faith. It is true that the historic Church has at once emphasised celibacy and emphasised the family; has at once (if one may put it so) been fiercely for having children and fiercely for not having children. It has kept them side by side like two strong colours, red and white, like the red and white upon the shield of St. George. It has always had a healthy hatred of pink. It hates that combination of two colours which is the feeble expedient of the philosophers. It hates that evolution of black into white which is tantamount to a dirty gray. In fact, the whole theory of the Church on virginity might be symbolized in the statement that white is a colour: not merely the absence of a colour. All that I am urging here can be expressed by saying that Christianity sought in most of these cases to keep two colours coexistent but pure. It is not a mixture like russet or purple; it is rather like a shot silk, for a shot silk is always at right angles, and is in the pattern of the cross.

So it is also, of course, with the contradictory charges of the anti-Christians about submission and slaughter. It IS true that the Church told some men to fight and others not to fight; and it IS true that those who fought were like thunderbolts and those who did not fight were like statues. All this simply means that the Church preferred to use its Supermen and to use its Tolstoyans. There must be SOME good in the life of battle, for so many good men have enjoyed being soldiers. There must be SOME good in the idea of non-resistance, for so many good men seem to enjoy being Quakers. All that the Church did (so far as that goes) was to prevent either of these good things from ousting the other. They existed side by side. The Tolstoyans, having all the scruples of monks, simply became monks. The Quakers became a club instead of becoming a sect. Monks said all that Tolstoy says; they poured out lucid lamentations about the cruelty of battles and the vanity of revenge. But the Tolstoyans are not quite right enough to run the whole world; and in the ages of faith they were not allowed to run it. The world did not lose the last charge of Sir James Douglas or the banner of Joan the Maid. And sometimes this pure gentleness and this pure fierceness met and justified their juncture; the paradox of all the prophets was fulfilled, and, in the soul of St. Louis, the lion lay down with the lamb. But remember that this text is too lightly interpreted. It is constantly assured, especially in our Tolstoyan tendencies, that when the lion lies down with the lamb the lion becomes lamb-like. But that is brutal annexation and imperialism on the part of the lamb. That is simply the lamb absorbing the lion instead of the lion eating the lamb. The real problem is—Can the lion lie down with the lamb and still retain his royal ferocity? THAT is the problem the Church attempted; THAT is the miracle she achieved.

This is what I have called guessing the hidden eccentricities of life. This is knowing that a man's heart is to the left and not in the middle. This is knowing not only that the earth is round, but knowing exactly where it is flat. Christian doctrine detected the oddities of life. It not only discovered the law, but it foresaw the exceptions. Those underrate Christianity who say that it discovered mercy; any one might discover mercy. In fact every one did. But to discover a plan for being merciful and also severe— THAT was to anticipate a strange need of human nature. For no one wants to be forgiven for a big sin as if it were a little one. Any one might say that we should be neither quite miserable nor quite happy. But to find out how far one MAY be quite miserable without making it impossible to be quite happy—that was a discovery in psychology. Any one might say, "Neither swagger nor grovel"; and it would have been a limit. But to say, "Here you can swagger and there you can grovel"—that was an emancipation.

This was the big fact about Christian ethics; the discovery of the new balance. Paganism had been like a pillar of marble, upright because proportioned with symmetry. Christianity was like a huge and ragged and romantic rock, which, though it sways on its pedestal at a touch, yet, because its exaggerated excrescences exactly balance each other, is enthroned there for a thousand years. In a Gothic cathedral the columns were all different, but they were all necessary. Every support seemed an accidental and fantastic support; every buttress was a flying buttress. So in Christendom apparent accidents balanced. Becket wore a hair shirt under his gold and crimson, and there is much to be said for the combination; for Becket got the benefit of the hair shirt while the people in the street got the benefit of the crimson and gold. It is at least better than the manner of the modern millionaire, who has the black and the drab outwardly for others, and the gold next his heart. But the balance was not always in one man's body as in Becket's; the balance was often distributed over the whole body of Christendom. Because a man prayed and fasted on the Northern snows, flowers could be flung at his festival in the Southern cities; and because fanatics drank water on the sands of Syria, men could still drink cider in the orchards of England. This is what makes Christendom at once so much more perplexing and so much more interesting than the Pagan empire; just as Amiens Cathedral is not better but more interesting than the Parthenon. If any one wants a modern proof of all this, let him consider the curious fact that, under Christianity, Europe (while remaining a unity) has broken up into individual nations. Patriotism is a perfect example of this deliberate balancing of one emphasis against another emphasis. The instinct of the Pagan empire would have said, "You shall all be Roman citizens, and grow alike; let the German grow less slow and reverent; the Frenchmen less experimental and swift." But the instinct of Christian Europe says, "Let the German remain slow and reverent, that the Frenchman may the more safely be swift and experimental. We will make an equipoise out of these excesses. The absurdity called Germany shall correct the insanity called France."

Last and most important, it is exactly this which explains what is so inexplicable to all the modern critics of the history of Christianity. I mean the monstrous wars about small points of theology, the earthquakes of emotion about a gesture or a word. It was only a matter of an inch; but an inch is everything when you are balancing. The Church could not afford to swerve a hair's breadth on some things if she was to continue her great and daring experiment of the irregular equilibrium. Once let one idea become less powerful and some other idea would become too powerful. It was no flock of sheep the Christian shepherd was leading, but a herd of bulls and tigers, of terrible ideals and devouring doctrines, each one of them strong enough to turn to a false religion and lay waste the world. Remember that the Church went in specifically for dangerous ideas; she was a lion tamer. The idea of birth through a Holy Spirit, of the death of a divine being, of the forgiveness of sins, or the fulfilment of prophecies, are ideas which, any one can see, need but a touch to turn them into something blasphemous or ferocious. The smallest link was let drop by the artificers of the Mediterranean, and the lion of ancestral pessimism burst his chain in the forgotten forests of the north. Of these theological equalisations I have to speak afterwards. Here it is enough to notice that if some small mistake were made in doctrine, huge blunders might be made in human happiness. A sentence phrased wrong about the nature of symbolism would have broken all the best statues in Europe. A slip in the definitions might stop all the dances; might wither all the Christmas trees or break all the Easter eggs. Doctrines had to be defined within strict limits, even in order that man might enjoy general human liberties. The Church had to be careful, if only that the world might be careless.

This is the thrilling romance of Orthodoxy. People have fallen into a foolish habit of speaking of orthodoxy as something heavy, humdrum, and safe. There never was anything so perilous or so exciting as orthodoxy. It was sanity: and to be sane is more dramatic than to be mad. It was the equilibrium of a man behind madly rushing horses, seeming to stoop this way and to sway that, yet in every attitude having the grace of statuary and the accuracy of arithmetic. The Church in its early days went fierce and fast with any warhorse; yet it is utterly unhistoric to say that she merely went mad along one idea, like a vulgar fanaticism. She swerved to left and right, so exactly as to avoid enormous obstacles. She left on one hand the huge bulk of Arianism, buttressed by all the worldly powers to make Christianity too worldly. The next instant she was swerving to avoid an orientalism, which would have made it too unworldly. The orthodox Church never took the tame course or accepted the conventions; the orthodox Church was never respectable. It would have been easier to have accepted the earthly power of the Arians. It would have been easy, in the Calvinistic seventeenth century, to fall into the bottomless pit of predestination. It is easy to be a madman: it is easy to be a heretic. It is always easy to let the age have its head; the difficult thing is to keep one's own. It is always easy to be a modernist; as it is easy to be a snob. To have fallen into any of those open traps of error and exaggeration which fashion after fashion and sect after sect set along the historic path of Christendom—that would indeed have been simple. It is always simple to fall; there are an infinity of angles at which one falls, only one at which one stands. To have fallen into any one of the fads from Gnosticism to Christian Science would indeed have been obvious and tame. But to have avoided them all has been one whirling adventure; and in my vision the heavenly chariot flies thundering through the ages, the dull heresies sprawling and prostrate, the wild truth reeling but erect.

VII THE ETERNAL REVOLUTION

The following propositions have been urged: First, that some faith in our life is required even to improve it; second, that some dissatisfaction with things as they are is necessary even in order to be satisfied; third, that to have this necessary content and necessary discontent it is not sufficient to have the obvious equilibrium of the Stoic. For mere resignation has neither the gigantic levity of pleasure nor the superb intolerance of pain. There is a vital objection to the advice merely to grin and bear it. The objection is that if you merely bear it, you do not grin. Greek heroes do not grin: but gargoyles do—because they are Christian. And when a Christian is pleased, he is (in the most exact sense) frightfully pleased; his pleasure is frightful. Christ prophesied the whole of Gothic architecture in that hour when nervous and respectable people (such people as now object to barrel organs) objected to the shouting of the gutter-snipes of Jerusalem. He said, "If these were silent, the very stones would cry out." Under the impulse of His spirit arose like a clamorous chorus the facades of the mediaeval cathedrals, thronged with shouting faces and open mouths. The prophecy has fulfilled itself: the very stones cry out.

If these things be conceded, though only for argument, we may take up where we left it the thread of the thought of the natural man, called by the Scotch (with regrettable familiarity), "The Old Man." We can ask the next question so obviously in front of us. Some satisfaction is needed even to make things better. But what do we mean by making things better? Most modern talk on this matter is a mere argument in a circle—that circle which we have already made the symbol of madness and of mere rationalism. Evolution is only good if it produces good; good is only good if it helps evolution. The elephant stands on the tortoise, and the tortoise on the elephant.

Obviously, it will not do to take our ideal from the principle in nature; for the simple reason that (except for some human or divine theory), there is no principle in nature. For instance, the cheap anti-democrat of to-day will tell you solemnly that there is no equality in nature. He is right, but he does not see the logical addendum. There is no equality in nature; also there is no inequality in nature. Inequality, as much as equality, implies a standard of value. To read aristocracy into the anarchy of animals is just as sentimental as to read democracy into it. Both aristocracy and democracy are human ideals: the one saying that all men are valuable, the other that some men are more valuable. But nature does not say that cats are more valuable than mice; nature makes no remark on the subject. She does not even say that the cat is enviable or the mouse pitiable. We think the cat superior because we have (or most of us have) a particular philosophy to the effect that life is better than death. But if the mouse were a German pessimist mouse, he might not think that the cat had beaten him at all. He might think he had beaten the cat by getting to the grave first. Or he might feel that he had actually inflicted frightful punishment on the cat by keeping him alive. Just as a microbe might feel proud of spreading a pestilence, so the pessimistic mouse might exult to think that he was renewing in the cat the torture of conscious existence. It all depends on the philosophy of the mouse. You cannot even say that there is victory or superiority in nature unless you have some doctrine about what things are superior. You cannot even say that the cat scores unless there is a system of scoring. You cannot even say that the cat gets the best of it unless there is some best to be got.

We cannot, then, get the ideal itself from nature, and as we follow here the first and natural speculation, we will leave out (for the present) the idea of getting it from God. We must have our own vision. But the attempts of most moderns to express it are highly vague.

Some fall back simply on the clock: they talk as if mere passage through time brought some superiority; so that even a man of the first mental calibre carelessly uses the phrase that human morality is never up to date. How can anything be up to date?— a date has no character. How can one say that Christmas celebrations are not suitable to the twenty-fifth of a month? What the writer meant, of course, was that the majority is behind his favourite minority—or in front of it. Other vague modern people take refuge in material metaphors; in fact, this is the chief mark of vague modern people. Not daring to define their doctrine of what is good, they use physical figures of speech without stint or shame, and, what is worst of all, seem to think these cheap analogies are exquisitely spiritual and superior to the old morality. Thus they think it intellectual to talk about things being "high." It is at least the reverse of intellectual; it is a mere phrase from a steeple or a weathercock. "Tommy was a good boy" is a pure philosophical statement, worthy of Plato or Aquinas. "Tommy lived the higher life" is a gross metaphor from a ten-foot rule.

This, incidentally, is almost the whole weakness of Nietzsche, whom some are representing as a bold and strong thinker. No one will deny that he was a poetical and suggestive thinker; but he was quite the reverse of strong. He was not at all bold. He never put his own meaning before himself in bald abstract words: as did Aristotle and Calvin, and even Karl Marx, the hard, fearless men of thought. Nietzsche always escaped a question by a physical metaphor, like a cheery minor poet. He said, "beyond good and evil," because he had not the courage to say, "more good than good and evil," or, "more evil than good and evil." Had he faced his thought without metaphors, he would have seen that it was nonsense. So, when he describes his hero, he does not dare to say, "the purer man," or "the happier man," or "the sadder man," for all these are ideas; and ideas are alarming. He says "the upper man," or "over man," a physical metaphor from acrobats or alpine climbers. Nietzsche is truly a very timid thinker. He does not really know in the least what sort of man he wants evolution to produce. And if he does not know, certainly the ordinary evolutionists, who talk about things being "higher," do not know either.

Then again, some people fall back on sheer submission and sitting still. Nature is going to do something some day; nobody knows what, and nobody knows when. We have no reason for acting, and no reason for not acting. If anything happens it is right: if anything is prevented it was wrong. Again, some people try to anticipate nature by doing something, by doing anything. Because we may possibly grow wings they cut off their legs. Yet nature may be trying to make them centipedes for all they know.

Lastly, there is a fourth class of people who take whatever it is that they happen to want, and say that that is the ultimate aim of evolution. And these are the only sensible people. This is the only really healthy way with the word evolution, to work for what you want, and to call THAT evolution. The only intelligible sense that progress or advance can have among men, is that we have a definite vision, and that we wish to make the whole world like that vision. If you like to put it so, the essence of the doctrine is that what we have around us is the mere method and preparation for something that we have to create. This is not a world, but rather the material for a world. God has given us not so much the colours of a picture as the colours of a palette. But he has also given us a subject, a model, a fixed vision. We must be clear about what we want to paint. This adds a further principle to our previous list of principles. We have said we must be fond of this world, even in order to change it. We now add that we must be fond of another world (real or imaginary) in order to have something to change it to.

We need not debate about the mere words evolution or progress: personally I prefer to call it reform. For reform implies form. It implies that we are trying to shape the world in a particular image; to make it something that we see already in our minds. Evolution is a metaphor from mere automatic unrolling. Progress is a metaphor from merely walking along a road—very likely the wrong road. But reform is a metaphor for reasonable and determined men: it means that we see a certain thing out of shape and we mean to put it into shape. And we know what shape.

Now here comes in the whole collapse and huge blunder of our age. We have mixed up two different things, two opposite things. Progress should mean that we are always changing the world to suit the vision. Progress does mean (just now) that we are always changing the vision. It should mean that we are slow but sure in bringing justice and mercy among men: it does mean that we are very swift in doubting the desirability of justice and mercy: a wild page from any Prussian sophist makes men doubt it. Progress should mean that we are always walking towards the New Jerusalem. It does mean that the New Jerusalem is always walking away from us. We are not altering the real to suit the ideal. We are altering the ideal: it is easier.

Silly examples are always simpler; let us suppose a man wanted a particular kind of world; say, a blue world. He would have no cause to complain of the slightness or swiftness of his task; he might toil for a long time at the transformation; he could work away (in every sense) until all was blue. He could have heroic adventures; the putting of the last touches to a blue tiger. He could have fairy dreams; the dawn of a blue moon. But if he worked hard, that high-minded reformer would certainly (from his own point of view) leave the world better and bluer than he found it. If he altered a blade of grass to his favourite colour every day, he would get on slowly. But if he altered his favourite colour every day, he would not get on at all. If, after reading a fresh philosopher, he started to paint everything red or yellow, his work would be thrown away: there would be nothing to show except a few blue tigers walking about, specimens of his early bad manner. This is exactly the position of the average modern thinker. It will be said that this is avowedly a preposterous example. But it is literally the fact of recent history. The great and grave changes in our political civilization all belonged to the early nineteenth century, not to the later. They belonged to the black and white epoch when men believed fixedly in Toryism, in Protestantism, in Calvinism, in Reform, and not unfrequently in Revolution. And whatever each man believed in he hammered at steadily, without scepticism: and there was a time when the Established Church might have fallen, and the House of Lords nearly fell. It was because Radicals were wise enough to be constant and consistent; it was because Radicals were wise enough to be Conservative. But in the existing atmosphere there is not enough time and tradition in Radicalism to pull anything down. There is a great deal of truth in Lord Hugh Cecil's suggestion (made in a fine speech) that the era of change is over, and that ours is an era of conservation and repose. But probably it would pain Lord Hugh Cecil if he realized (what is certainly the case) that ours is only an age of conservation because it is an age of complete unbelief. Let beliefs fade fast and frequently, if you wish institutions to remain the same. The more the life of the mind is unhinged, the more the machinery of matter will be left to itself. The net result of all our political suggestions, Collectivism, Tolstoyanism, Neo-Feudalism, Communism, Anarchy, Scientific Bureaucracy—the plain fruit of all of them is that the Monarchy and the House of Lords will remain. The net result of all the new religions will be that the Church of England will not (for heaven knows how long) be disestablished. It was Karl Marx, Nietzsche, Tolstoy, Cunninghame Grahame, Bernard Shaw and Auberon Herbert, who between them, with bowed gigantic backs, bore up the throne of the Archbishop of Canterbury.

We may say broadly that free thought is the best of all the safeguards against freedom. Managed in a modern style the emancipation of the slave's mind is the best way of preventing the emancipation of the slave. Teach him to worry about whether he wants to be free, and he will not free himself. Again, it may be said that this instance is remote or extreme. But, again, it is exactly true of the men in the streets around us. It is true that the negro slave, being a debased barbarian, will probably have either a human affection of loyalty, or a human affection for liberty. But the man we see every day—the worker in Mr. Gradgrind's factory, the little clerk in Mr. Gradgrind's office—he is too mentally worried to believe in freedom. He is kept quiet with revolutionary literature. He is calmed and kept in his place by a constant succession of wild philosophies. He is a Marxian one day, a Nietzscheite the next day, a Superman (probably) the next day; and a slave every day. The only thing that remains after all the philosophies is the factory. The only man who gains by all the philosophies is Gradgrind. It would be worth his while to keep his commercial helotry supplied with sceptical literature. And now I come to think of it, of course, Gradgrind is famous for giving libraries. He shows his sense. All modern books are on his side. As long as the vision of heaven is always changing, the vision of earth will be exactly the same. No ideal will remain long enough to be realized, or even partly realized. The modern young man will never change his environment; for he will always change his mind.

This, therefore, is our first requirement about the ideal towards which progress is directed; it must be fixed. Whistler used to make many rapid studies of a sitter; it did not matter if he tore up twenty portraits. But it would matter if he looked up twenty times, and each time saw a new person sitting placidly for his portrait. So it does not matter (comparatively speaking) how often humanity fails to imitate its ideal; for then all its old failures are fruitful. But it does frightfully matter how often humanity changes its ideal; for then all its old failures are fruitless. The question therefore becomes this: How can we keep the artist discontented with his pictures while preventing him from being vitally discontented with his art? How can we make a man always dissatisfied with his work, yet always satisfied with working? How can we make sure that the portrait painter will throw the portrait out of window instead of taking the natural and more human course of throwing the sitter out of window?

A strict rule is not only necessary for ruling; it is also necessary for rebelling. This fixed and familiar ideal is necessary to any sort of revolution. Man will sometimes act slowly upon new ideas; but he will only act swiftly upon old ideas. If I am merely to float or fade or evolve, it may be towards something anarchic; but if I am to riot, it must be for something respectable. This is the whole weakness of certain schools of progress and moral evolution. They suggest that there has been a slow movement towards morality, with an imperceptible ethical change in every year or at every instant. There is only one great disadvantage in this theory. It talks of a slow movement towards justice; but it does not permit a swift movement. A man is not allowed to leap up and declare a certain state of things to be intrinsically intolerable. To make the matter clear, it is better to take a specific example. Certain of the idealistic vegetarians, such as Mr. Salt, say that the time has now come for eating no meat; by implication they assume that at one time it was right to eat meat, and they suggest (in words that could be quoted) that some day it may be wrong to eat milk and eggs. I do not discuss here the question of what is justice to animals. I only say that whatever is justice ought, under given conditions, to be prompt justice. If an animal is wronged, we ought to be able to rush to his rescue. But how can we rush if we are, perhaps, in advance of our time? How can we rush to catch a train which may not arrive for a few centuries? How can I denounce a man for skinning cats, if he is only now what I may possibly become in drinking a glass of milk? A splendid and insane Russian sect ran about taking all the cattle out of all the carts. How can I pluck up courage to take the horse out of my hansom-cab, when I do not know whether my evolutionary watch is only a little fast or the cabman's a little slow? Suppose I say to a sweater, "Slavery suited one stage of evolution." And suppose he answers, "And sweating suits this stage of evolution." How can I answer if there is no eternal test? If sweaters can be behind the current morality, why should not philanthropists be in front of it? What on earth is the current morality, except in its literal sense—the morality that is always running away?

Thus we may say that a permanent ideal is as necessary to the innovator as to the conservative; it is necessary whether we wish the king's orders to be promptly executed or whether we only wish the king to be promptly executed. The guillotine has many sins, but to do it justice there is nothing evolutionary about it. The favourite evolutionary argument finds its best answer in the axe. The Evolutionist says, "Where do you draw the line?" the Revolutionist answers, "I draw it HERE: exactly between your head and body." There must at any given moment be an abstract right and wrong if any blow is to be struck; there must be something eternal if there is to be anything sudden. Therefore for all intelligible human purposes, for altering things or for keeping things as they are, for founding a system for ever, as in China, or for altering it every month as in the early French Revolution, it is equally necessary that the vision should be a fixed vision. This is our first requirement.

When I had written this down, I felt once again the presence of something else in the discussion: as a man hears a church bell above the sound of the street. Something seemed to be saying, "My ideal at least is fixed; for it was fixed before the foundations of the world. My vision of perfection assuredly cannot be altered; for it is called Eden. You may alter the place to which you are going; but you cannot alter the place from which you have come. To the orthodox there must always be a case for revolution; for in the hearts of men God has been put under the feet of Satan. In the upper world hell once rebelled against heaven. But in this world heaven is rebelling against hell. For the orthodox there can always be a revolution; for a revolution is a restoration. At any instant you may strike a blow for the perfection which no man has seen since Adam. No unchanging custom, no changing evolution can make the original good any thing but good. Man may have had concubines as long as cows have had horns: still they are not a part of him if they are sinful. Men may have been under oppression ever since fish were under water; still they ought not to be, if oppression is sinful. The chain may seem as natural to the slave, or the paint to the harlot, as does the plume to the bird or the burrow to the fox; still they are not, if they are sinful. I lift my prehistoric legend to defy all your history. Your vision is not merely a fixture: it is a fact." I paused to note the new coincidence of Christianity: but I passed on.

I passed on to the next necessity of any ideal of progress. Some people (as we have said) seem to believe in an automatic and impersonal progress in the nature of things. But it is clear that no political activity can be encouraged by saying that progress is natural and inevitable; that is not a reason for being active, but rather a reason for being lazy. If we are bound to improve, we need not trouble to improve. The pure doctrine of progress is the best of all reasons for not being a progressive. But it is to none of these obvious comments that I wish primarily to call attention.

The only arresting point is this: that if we suppose improvement to be natural, it must be fairly simple. The world might conceivably be working towards one consummation, but hardly towards any particular arrangement of many qualities. To take our original simile: Nature by herself may be growing more blue; that is, a process so simple that it might be impersonal. But Nature cannot be making a careful picture made of many picked colours, unless Nature is personal. If the end of the world were mere darkness or mere light it might come as slowly and inevitably as dusk or dawn. But if the end of the world is to be a piece of elaborate and artistic chiaroscuro, then there must be design in it, either human or divine. The world, through mere time, might grow black like an old picture, or white like an old coat; but if it is turned into a particular piece of black and white art— then there is an artist.

If the distinction be not evident, I give an ordinary instance. We constantly hear a particularly cosmic creed from the modern humanitarians;

I use the word humanitarian in the ordinary sense, as meaning one who upholds the claims of all creatures against those of humanity. They suggest that through the ages we have been growing more and more humane, that is to say, that one after another, groups or sections of beings, slaves, children, women, cows, or what not, have been gradually admitted to mercy or to justice. They say that we once thought it right to eat men (we didn't); but I am not here concerned with their history, which is highly unhistorical. As a fact, anthropophagy is certainly a decadent thing, not a primitive one. It is much more likely that modern men will eat human flesh out of affectation than that primitive man ever ate it out of ignorance. I am here only following the outlines of their argument, which consists in maintaining that man has been progressively more lenient, first to citizens, then to slaves, then to animals, and then (presumably) to plants. I think it wrong to sit on a man. Soon, I shall think it wrong to sit on a horse. Eventually (I suppose) I shall think it wrong to sit on a chair. That is the drive of the argument. And for this argument it can be said that it is possible to talk of it in terms of evolution or inevitable progress. A perpetual tendency to touch fewer and fewer things might—one feels, be a mere brute unconscious tendency, like that of a species to produce fewer and fewer children. This drift may be really evolutionary, because it is stupid.

Darwinism can be used to back up two mad moralities, but it cannot be used to back up a single sane one. The kinship and competition of all living creatures can be used as a reason for being insanely cruel or insanely sentimental; but not for a healthy love of animals. On the evolutionary basis you may be inhumane, or you may be absurdly humane; but you cannot be human. That you and a tiger are one may be a reason for being tender to a tiger. Or it may be a reason for being as cruel as the tiger. It is one way to train the tiger to imitate you, it is a shorter way to imitate the tiger. But in neither case does evolution tell you how to treat a tiger reasonably, that is, to admire his stripes while avoiding his claws.

If you want to treat a tiger reasonably, you must go back to the garden of Eden. For the obstinate reminder continued to recur: only the supernatural has taken a sane view of Nature. The essence of all pantheism, evolutionism, and modern cosmic religion is really in this proposition: that Nature is our mother. Unfortunately, if you regard Nature as a mother, you discover that she is a step-mother. The main point of Christianity was this: that Nature is not our mother: Nature is our sister. We can be proud of her beauty, since we have the same father; but she has no authority over us; we have to admire, but not to imitate. This gives to the typically Christian pleasure in this earth a strange touch of lightness that is almost frivolity. Nature was a solemn mother to the worshippers of Isis and Cybele. Nature was a solemn mother to Wordsworth or to Emerson. But Nature is not solemn to Francis of Assisi or to George Herbert. To St. Francis, Nature is a sister, and even a younger sister: a little, dancing sister, to be laughed at as well as loved.

This, however, is hardly our main point at present; I have admitted it only in order to show how constantly, and as it were accidentally, the key would fit the smallest doors. Our main point is here, that if there be a mere trend of impersonal improvement in Nature, it must presumably be a simple trend towards some simple triumph. One can imagine that some automatic tendency in biology might work for giving us longer and longer noses. But the question is, do we want to have longer and longer noses? I fancy not; I believe that we most of us want to say to our noses, "thus far, and no farther; and here shall thy proud point be stayed:" we require a nose of such length as may ensure an interesting face. But we cannot imagine a mere biological trend towards producing interesting faces; because an interesting face is one particular arrangement of eyes, nose, and mouth, in a most complex relation to each other. Proportion cannot be a drift: it is either an accident or a design. So with the ideal of human morality and its relation to the humanitarians and the anti-humanitarians. It is conceivable that we are going more and more to keep our hands off things: not to drive horses; not to pick flowers. We may eventually be bound not to disturb a man's mind even by argument; not to disturb the sleep of birds even by coughing. The ultimate apotheosis would appear to be that of a man sitting quite still, nor daring to stir for fear of disturbing a fly, nor to eat for fear of incommoding a microbe. To so crude a consummation as that we might perhaps unconsciously drift. But do we want so crude a consummation? Similarly, we might unconsciously evolve along the opposite or Nietzschian line of development—superman crushing superman in one tower of tyrants until the universe is smashed up for fun. But do we want the universe smashed up for fun? Is it not quite clear that what we really hope for is one particular management and proposition of these two things; a certain amount of restraint and respect, a certain amount of energy and mastery? If our life is ever really as beautiful as a fairy-tale, we shall have to remember that all the beauty of a fairy-tale lies in this: that the prince has a wonder which just stops short of being fear. If he is afraid of the giant, there is an end of him; but also if he is not astonished at the giant, there is an end of the fairy-tale. The whole point depends upon his being at once humble enough to wonder, and haughty enough to defy.

So our attitude to the giant of the world must not merely be increasing delicacy or increasing contempt: it must be one particular proportion of the two—which is exactly right. We must have in us enough reverence for all things outside us to make us tread fearfully on the grass. We must also have enough disdain for all things outside us, to make us, on due occasion, spit at the stars. Yet these two things (if we are to be good or happy) must be combined, not in any combination, but in one particular combination. The perfect happiness of men on the earth (if it ever comes) will not be a flat and solid thing, like the satisfaction of animals. It will be an exact and perilous balance; like that of a desperate romance. Man must have just enough faith in himself to have adventures, and just enough doubt of himself to enjoy them.

This, then, is our second requirement for the ideal of progress. First, it must be fixed; second, it must be composite. It must not (if it is to satisfy our souls) be the mere victory of some one thing swallowing up everything else, love or pride or peace or adventure; it must be a definite picture composed of these elements in their best proportion and relation. I am not concerned at this moment to deny that some such good culmination may be, by the constitution of things, reserved for the human race. I only point out that if this composite happiness is fixed for us it must be fixed by some mind; for only a mind can place the exact proportions of a composite happiness. If the beatification of the world is a mere work of nature, then it must be as simple as the freezing of the world, or the burning up of the world. But if the beatification of the world is not a work of nature but a work of art, then it involves an artist. And here again my contemplation was cloven by the ancient voice which said, "I could have told you all this a long time ago. If there is any certain progress it can only be my kind of progress, the progress towards a complete city of virtues and dominations where righteousness and peace contrive to kiss each other. An impersonal force might be leading you to a wilderness of perfect flatness or a peak of perfect height. But only a personal God can possibly be leading you (if, indeed, you are being led) to a city with just streets and architectural proportions, a city in which each of you can contribute exactly the right amount of your own colour to the many coloured coat of Joseph."

Twice again, therefore, Christianity had come in with the exact answer that I required. I had said, "The ideal must be fixed," and the Church had answered, "Mine is literally fixed, for it existed before anything else." I said secondly, "It must be artistically combined, like a picture"; and the Church answered, "Mine is quite literally a picture, for I know who painted it." Then I went on to the third thing, which, as it seemed to me, was needed for an Utopia or goal of progress. And of all the three it is infinitely the hardest to express. Perhaps it might be put thus: that we need watchfulness even in Utopia, lest we fall from Utopia as we fell from Eden.

We have remarked that one reason offered for being a progressive is that things naturally tend to grow better. But the only real reason for being a progressive is that things naturally tend to grow worse. The corruption in things is not only the best argument for being progressive; it is also the only argument against being conservative. The conservative theory would really be quite sweeping and unanswerable if it were not for this one fact. But all conservatism is based upon the idea that if you leave things alone you leave them as they are. But you do not. If you leave a thing alone you leave it to a torrent of change. If you leave a white post alone it will soon be a black post. If you particularly want it to be white you must be always painting it again; that is, you must be always having a revolution. Briefly, if you want the old white post you must have a new white post. But this which is true even of inanimate things is in a quite special and terrible sense true of all human things. An almost unnatural vigilance is really required of the citizen because of the horrible rapidity with which human institutions grow old. It is the custom in passing romance and journalism to talk of men suffering under old tyrannies. But, as a fact, men have almost always suffered under new tyrannies; under tyrannies that had been public liberties hardly twenty years before. Thus England went mad with joy over the patriotic monarchy of Elizabeth; and then (almost immediately afterwards) went mad with rage in the trap of the tyranny of Charles the First. So, again, in France the monarchy became intolerable, not just after it had been tolerated, but just after it had been adored. The son of Louis the well-beloved was Louis the guillotined. So in the same way in England in the nineteenth century the Radical manufacturer was entirely trusted as a mere tribune of the people, until suddenly we heard the cry of the Socialist that he was a tyrant eating the people like bread. So again, we have almost up to the last instant trusted the newspapers as organs of public opinion. Just recently some of us have seen (not slowly, but with a start) that they are obviously nothing of the kind. They are, by the nature of the case, the hobbies of a few rich men. We have not any need to rebel against antiquity; we have to rebel against novelty. It is the new rulers, the capitalist or the editor, who really hold up the modern world. There is no fear that a modern king will attempt to override the constitution; it is more likely that he will ignore the constitution and work behind its back; he will take no advantage of his kingly power; it is more likely that he will take advantage of his kingly powerlessness, of the fact that he is free from criticism and publicity. For the king is the most private person of our time. It will not be necessary for any one to fight again against the proposal of a censorship of the press. We do not need a censorship of the press. We have a censorship by the press.

This startling swiftness with which popular systems turn oppressive is the third fact for which we shall ask our perfect theory of progress to allow. It must always be on the look out for every privilege being abused, for every working right becoming a wrong. In this matter I am entirely on the side of the revolutionists. They are really right to be always suspecting human institutions; they are right not to put their trust in princes nor in any child of man. The chieftain chosen to be the friend of the people becomes the enemy of the people; the newspaper started to tell the truth now exists to prevent the truth being told. Here, I say, I felt that I was really at last on the side of the revolutionary. And then I caught my breath again: for I remembered that I was once again on the side of the orthodox.

Christianity spoke again and said: "I have always maintained that men were naturally backsliders; that human virtue tended of its own nature to rust or to rot; I have always said that human beings as such go wrong, especially happy human beings, especially proud and prosperous human beings. This eternal revolution, this suspicion sustained through centuries, you (being a vague modern) call the doctrine of progress. If you were a philosopher you would call it, as I do, the doctrine of original sin. You may call it the cosmic advance as much as you like; I call it what it is—the Fall."

I have spoken of orthodoxy coming in like a sword; here I confess it came in like a battle-axe. For really (when I came to think of it) Christianity is the only thing left that has any real right to question the power of the well-nurtured or the well-bred. I have listened often enough to Socialists, or even to democrats, saying that the physical conditions of the poor must of necessity make them mentally and morally degraded. I have listened to scientific men (and there are still scientific men not opposed to democracy) saying that if we give the poor healthier conditions vice and wrong will disappear. I have listened to them with a horrible attention, with a hideous fascination. For it was like watching a man energetically sawing from the tree the branch he is sitting on. If these happy democrats could prove their case, they would strike democracy dead. If the poor are thus utterly demoralized, it may or may not be practical to raise them. But it is certainly quite practical to disfranchise them. If the man with a bad bedroom cannot give a good vote, then the first and swiftest deduction is that he shall give no vote. The governing class may not unreasonably say: "It may take us some time to reform his bedroom. But if he is the brute you say, it will take him very little time to ruin our country. Therefore we will take your hint and not give him the chance." It fills me with horrible amusement to observe the way in which the earnest Socialist industriously lays the foundation of all aristocracy, expatiating blandly upon the evident unfitness of the poor to rule. It is like listening to somebody at an evening party apologising for entering without evening dress, and explaining that he had recently been intoxicated, had a personal habit of taking off his clothes in the street, and had, moreover, only just changed from prison uniform. At any moment, one feels, the host might say that really, if it was as bad as that, he need not come in at all. So it is when the ordinary Socialist, with a beaming face, proves that the poor, after their smashing experiences, cannot be really trustworthy. At any moment the rich may say, "Very well, then, we won't trust them," and bang the door in his face. On the basis of Mr. Blatchford's view of heredity and environment, the case for the aristocracy is quite overwhelming. If clean homes and clean air make clean souls, why not give the power (for the present at any rate) to those who undoubtedly have the clean air? If better conditions will make the poor more fit to govern themselves, why should not better conditions already make the rich more fit to govern them? On the ordinary environment argument the matter is fairly manifest. The comfortable class must be merely our vanguard in Utopia.

Is there any answer to the proposition that those who have had the best opportunities will probably be our best guides? Is there any answer to the argument that those who have breathed clean air had better decide for those who have breathed foul? As far as I know, there is only one answer, and that answer is Christianity. Only the Christian Church can offer any rational objection to a complete confidencc in the rich. For she has maintained from the beginning that the danger was not in man's environment, but in man. Further, she has maintained that if we come to talk of a dangerous environment, the most dangerous environment of all is the commodious environment. I know that the most modern manufacture has been really occupied in trying to produce an abnormally large needle. I know that the most recent biologists have been chiefly anxious to discover a very small camel. But if we diminish the camel to his smallest, or open the eye of the needle to its largest—if, in short, we assume the words of Christ to have meant the very least that they could mean, His words must at the very least mean this— that rich men are not very likely to be morally trustworthy. Christianity even when watered down is hot enough to boil all modern society to rags. The mere minimum of the Church would be a deadly ultimatum to the world. For the whole modern world is absolutely based on the assumption, not that the rich are necessary (which is tenable), but that the rich are trustworthy, which (for a Christian) is not tenable. You will hear everlastingly, in all discussions about newspapers, companies, aristocracies, or party politics, this argument that the rich man cannot be bribed. The fact is, of course, that the rich man is bribed; he has been bribed already. That is why he is a rich man. The whole case for Christianity is that a man who is dependent upon the luxuries of this life is a corrupt man, spiritually corrupt, politically corrupt, financially corrupt. There is one thing that Christ and all the Christian saints have said with a sort of savage monotony. They have said simply that to be rich is to be in peculiar danger of moral wreck. It is not demonstrably un-Christian to kill the rich as violators of definable justice. It is not demonstrably un-Christian to crown the rich as convenient rulers of society. It is not certainly un-Christian to rebel against the rich or to submit to the rich. But it is quite certainly un-Christian to trust the rich, to regard the rich as more morally safe than the poor. A Christian may consistently say, "I respect that man's rank, although he takes bribes." But a Christian cannot say, as all modern men are saying at lunch and breakfast, "a man of that rank would not take bribes." For it is a part of Christian dogma that any man in any rank may take bribes. It is a part of Christian dogma; it also happens by a curious coincidence that it is a part of obvious human history. When people say that a man "in that position" would be incorruptible, there is no need to bring Christianity into the discussion. Was Lord Bacon a bootblack? Was the Duke of Marlborough a crossing sweeper? In the best Utopia, I must be prepared for the moral fall of any man in any position at any moment; especially for my fall from my position at this moment.

Much vague and sentimental journalism has been poured out to the effect that Christianity is akin to democracy, and most of it is scarcely strong or clear enough to refute the fact that the two things have often quarrelled. The real ground upon which Christianity and democracy are one is very much deeper. The one specially and peculiarly un-Christian idea is the idea of Carlyle— the idea that the man should rule who feels that he can rule. Whatever else is Christian, this is heathen. If our faith comments on government at all, its comment must be this—that the man should rule who does NOT think that he can rule. Carlyle's hero may say, "I will be king"; but the Christian saint must say "Nolo episcopari." If the great paradox of Christianity means anything, it means this— that we must take the crown in our hands, and go hunting in dry places and dark corners of the earth until we find the one man who feels himself unfit to wear it. Carlyle was quite wrong; we have not got to crown the exceptional man who knows he can rule. Rather we must crown the much more exceptional man who knows he can't.

Now, this is one of the two or three vital defences of working democracy. The mere machinery of voting is not democracy, though at present it is not easy to effect any simpler democratic method. But even the machinery of voting is profoundly Christian in this practical sense—that it is an attempt to get at the opinion of those who would be too modest to offer it. It is a mystical adventure; it is specially trusting those who do not trust themselves. That enigma is strictly peculiar to Christendom. There is nothing really humble about the abnegation of the Buddhist; the mild Hindoo is mild, but he is not meek. But there is something psychologically Christian about the idea of seeking for the opinion of the obscure rather than taking the obvious course of accepting the opinion of the prominent. To say that voting is particularly Christian may seem somewhat curious. To say that canvassing is Christian may seem quite crazy. But canvassing is very Christian in its primary idea. It is encouraging the humble; it is saying to the modest man, "Friend, go up higher." Or if there is some slight defect in canvassing, that is in its perfect and rounded piety, it is only because it may possibly neglect to encourage the modesty of the canvasser.

Aristocracy is not an institution: aristocracy is a sin; generally a very venial one. It is merely the drift or slide of men into a sort of natural pomposity and praise of the powerful, which is the most easy and obvious affair in the world.

It is one of the hundred answers to the fugitive perversion of modern "force" that the promptest and boldest agencies are also the most fragile or full of sensibility. The swiftest things are the softest things. A bird is active, because a bird is soft. A stone is helpless, because a stone is hard. The stone must by its own nature go downwards, because hardness is weakness. The bird can of its nature go upwards, because fragility is force. In perfect force there is a kind of frivolity, an airiness that can maintain itself in the air. Modern investigators of miraculous history have solemnly admitted that a characteristic of the great saints is their power of "levitation." They might go further; a characteristic of the great saints is their power of levity. Angels can fly because they can take themselves lightly. This has been always the instinct of Christendom, and especially the instinct of Christian art. Remember how Fra Angelico represented all his angels, not only as birds, but almost as butterflies. Remember how the most earnest mediaeval art was full of light and fluttering draperies, of quick and capering feet. It was the one thing that the modern Pre-raphaelites could not imitate in the real Pre-raphaelites. Burne-Jones could never recover the deep levity of the Middle Ages. In the old Christian pictures the sky over every figure is like a blue or gold parachute. Every figure seems ready to fly up and float about in the heavens. The tattered cloak of the beggar will bear him up like the rayed plumes of the angels. But the kings in their heavy gold and the proud in their robes of purple will all of their nature sink downwards, for pride cannot rise to levity or levitation. Pride is the downward drag of all things into an easy solemnity. One "settles down" into a sort of selfish seriousness; but one has to rise to a gay self-forgetfulness. A man "falls" into a brown study; he reaches up at a blue sky. Seriousness is not a virtue. It would be a heresy, but a much more sensible heresy, to say that seriousness is a vice. It is really a natural trend or lapse into taking one's self gravely, because it is the easiest thing to do. It is much easier to write a good TIMES leading article than a good joke in PUNCH. For solemnity flows out of men naturally; but laughter is a leap. It is easy to be heavy: hard to be light. Satan fell by the force of gravity.

Now, it is the peculiar honour of Europe since it has been Christian that while it has had aristocracy it has always at the back of its heart treated aristocracy as a weakness—generally as a weakness that must be allowed for. If any one wishes to appreciate this point, let him go outside Christianity into some other philosophical atmosphere. Let him, for instance, compare the classes of Europe with the castes of India. There aristocracy is far more awful, because it is far more intellectual. It is seriously felt that the scale of classes is a scale of spiritual values; that the baker is better than the butcher in an invisible and sacred sense. But no Christianity, not even the most ignorant or perverse, ever suggested that a baronet was better than a butcher in that sacred sense. No Christianity, however ignorant or extravagant, ever suggested that a duke would not be damned. In pagan society there may have been (I do not know) some such serious division between the free man and the slave. But in Christian society we have always thought the gentleman a sort of joke, though I admit that in some great crusades and councils he earned the right to be called a practical joke. But we in Europe never really and at the root of our souls took aristocracy seriously. It is only an occasional non-European alien (such as Dr. Oscar Levy, the only intelligent Nietzscheite) who can even manage for a moment to take aristocracy seriously. It may be a mere patriotic bias, though I do not think so, but it seems to me that the English aristocracy is not only the type, but is the crown and flower of all actual aristocracies; it has all the oligarchical virtues as well as all the defects. It is casual, it is kind, it is courageous in obvious matters; but it has one great merit that overlaps even these. The great and very obvious merit of the English aristocracy is that nobody could possibly take it seriously.

In short, I had spelled out slowly, as usual, the need for an equal law in Utopia; and, as usual, I found that Christianity had been there before me. The whole history of my Utopia has the same amusing sadness. I was always rushing out of my architectural study with plans for a new turret only to find it sitting up there in the sunlight, shining, and a thousand years old. For me, in the ancient and partly in the modern sense, God answered the prayer, "Prevent us, O Lord, in all our doings." Without vanity, I really think there was a moment when I could have invented the marriage vow (as an institution) out of my own head; but I discovered, with a sigh, that it had been invented already. But, since it would be too long a business to show how, fact by fact and inch by inch, my own conception of Utopia was only answered in the New Jerusalem, I will take this one case of the matter of marriage as indicating the converging drift, I may say the converging crash of all the rest.

When the ordinary opponents of Socialism talk about impossibilities and alterations in human nature they always miss an important distinction. In modern ideal conceptions of society there are some desires that are possibly not attainable: but there are some desires that are not desirable. That all men should live in equally beautiful houses is a dream that may or may not be attained. But that all men should live in the same beautiful house is not a dream at all; it is a nightmare. That a man should love all old women is an ideal that may not be attainable. But that a man should regard all old women exactly as he regards his mother is not only an unattainable ideal, but an ideal which ought not to be attained. I do not know if the reader agrees with me in these examples; but I will add the example which has always affected me most. I could never conceive or tolerate any Utopia which did not leave to me the liberty for which I chiefly care, the liberty to bind myself. Complete anarchy would not merely make it impossible to have any discipline or fidelity; it would also make it impossible to have any fun. To take an obvious instance, it would not be worth while to bet if a bet were not binding. The dissolution of all contracts would not only ruin morality but spoil sport. Now betting and such sports are only the stunted and twisted shapes of the original instinct of man for adventure and romance, of which much has been said in these pages. And the perils, rewards, punishments, and fulfilments of an adventure must be real, or the adventure is only a shifting and heartless nightmare. If I bet I must be made to pay, or there is no poetry in betting. If I challenge I must be made to fight, or there is no poetry in challenging. If I vow to be faithful I must be cursed when I am unfaithful, or there is no fun in vowing. You could not even make a fairy tale from the experiences of a man who, when he was swallowed by a whale, might find himself at the top of the Eiffel Tower, or when he was turned into a frog might begin to behave like a flamingo. For the purpose even of the wildest romance results must be real; results must be irrevocable. Christian marriage is the great example of a real and irrevocable result; and that is why it is the chief subject and centre of all our romantic writing. And this is my last instance of the things that I should ask, and ask imperatively, of any social paradise; I should ask to be kept to my bargain, to have my oaths and engagements taken seriously; I should ask Utopia to avenge my honour on myself.

All my modern Utopian friends look at each other rather doubtfully, for their ultimate hope is the dissolution of all special ties. But again I seem to hear, like a kind of echo, an answer from beyond the world. "You will have real obligations, and therefore real adventures when you get to my Utopia. But the hardest obligation and the steepest adventure is to get there."

VIII THE ROMANCE OF ORTHODOXY

It is customary to complain of the bustle and strenuousness of our epoch. But in truth the chief mark of our epoch is a profound laziness and fatigue; and the fact is that the real laziness is the cause of the apparent bustle. Take one quite external case; the streets are noisy with taxicabs and motorcars; but this is not due to human activity but to human repose. There would be less bustle if there were more activity, if people were simply walking about. Our world would be more silent if it were more strenuous. And this which is true of the apparent physical bustle is true also of the apparent bustle of the intellect. Most of the machinery of modern language is labour-saving machinery; and it saves mental labour very much more than it ought. Scientific phrases are used like scientific wheels and piston-rods to make swifter and smoother yet the path of the comfortable. Long words go rattling by us like long railway trains. We know they are carrying thousands who are too tired or too indolent to walk and think for themselves. It is a good exercise to try for once in a way to express any opinion one holds in words of one syllable. If you say "The social utility of the indeterminate sentence is recognized by all criminologists as a part of our sociological evolution towards a more humane and scientific view of punishment," you can go on talking like that for hours with hardly a movement of the gray matter inside your skull. But if you begin "I wish Jones to go to gaol and Brown to say when Jones shall come out," you will discover, with a thrill of horror, that you are obliged to think. The long words are not the hard words, it is the short words that are hard. There is much more metaphysical subtlety in the word "damn" than in the word "degeneration."

But these long comfortable words that save modern people the toil of reasoning have one particular aspect in which they are especially ruinous and confusing. This difficulty occurs when the same long word is used in different connections to mean quite different things. Thus, to take a well-known instance, the word "idealist" has one meaning as a piece of philosophy and quite another as a piece of moral rhetoric. In the same way the scientific materialists have had just reason to complain of people mixing up "materialist" as a term of cosmology with "materialist" as a moral taunt. So, to take a cheaper instance, the man who hates "progressives" in London always calls himself a "progressive" in South Africa.

A confusion quite as unmeaning as this has arisen in connection with the word "liberal" as applied to religion and as applied to politics and society. It is often suggested that all Liberals ought to be freethinkers, because they ought to love everything that is free. You might just as well say that all idealists ought to be

High Churchmen, because they ought to love everything that is high. You might as well say that Low Churchmen ought to like Low Mass, or that Broad Churchmen ought to like broad jokes. The thing is a mere accident of words. In actual modern Europe a freethinker does not mean a man who thinks for himself. It means a man who, having thought for himself, has come to one particular class of conclusions, the material origin of phenomena, the impossibility of miracles, the improbability of personal immortality and so on. And none of these ideas are particularly liberal. Nay, indeed almost all these ideas are definitely illiberal, as it is the purpose of this chapter to show.

In the few following pages I propose to point out as rapidly as possible that on every single one of the matters most strongly insisted on by liberalisers of theology their effect upon social practice would be definitely illiberal. Almost every contemporary proposal to bring freedom into the church is simply a proposal to bring tyranny into the world. For freeing the church now does not even mean freeing it in all directions. It means freeing that peculiar set of dogmas loosely called scientific, dogmas of monism, of pantheism, or of Arianism, or of necessity. And every one of these (and we will take them one by one) can be shown to be the natural ally of oppression. In fact, it is a remarkable circumstance (indeed not so very remarkable when one comes to think of it) that most things are the allies of oppression. There is only one thing that can never go past a certain point in its alliance with oppression—and that is orthodoxy. I may, it is true, twist orthodoxy so as partly to justify a tyrant. But I can easily make up a German philosophy to justify him entirely.

Now let us take in order the innovations that are the notes of the new theology or the modernist church. We concluded the last chapter with the discovery of one of them. The very doctrine which is called the most old-fashioned was found to be the only safeguard of the new democracies of the earth. The doctrine seemingly most unpopular was found to be the only strength of the people. In short, we found that the only logical negation of oligarchy was in the affirmation of original sin. So it is, I maintain, in all the other cases.

I take the most obvious instance first, the case of miracles. For some extraordinary reason, there is a fixed notion that it is more liberal to disbelieve in miracles than to believe in them. Why, I cannot imagine, nor can anybody tell me. For some inconceivable cause a "broad" or "liberal" clergyman always means a man who wishes at least to diminish the number of miracles; it never means a man who wishes to increase that number. It always means a man who is free to disbelieve that Christ came out of His grave; it never means a man who is free to believe that his own aunt came out of her grave. It is common to find trouble in a parish because the parish priest cannot admit that St. Peter walked on water; yet how rarely do we find trouble in a parish because the clergyman says that his father walked on the Serpentine? And this is not because (as the swift secularist debater would immediately retort) miracles cannot be believed in our experience. It is not because "miracles do not happen," as in the dogma which Matthew Arnold recited with simple faith. More supernatural things are ALLEGED to have happened in our time than would have been possible eighty years ago. Men of science believe in such marvels much more than they did: the most perplexing, and even horrible, prodigies of mind and spirit are always being unveiled in modern psychology. Things that the old science at least would frankly have rejected as miracles are hourly being asserted by the new science. The only thing which is still old-fashioned enough to reject miracles is the New Theology. But in truth this notion that it is "free" to deny miracles has nothing to do with the evidence for or against them. It is a lifeless verbal prejudice of which the original life and beginning was not in the freedom of thought, but simply in the dogma of materialism. The man of the nineteenth century did not disbelieve in the Resurrection because his liberal Christianity allowed him to doubt it. He disbelieved in it because his very strict materialism did not allow him to believe it. Tennyson, a very typical nineteenth century man, uttered one of the instinctive truisms of his contemporaries when he said that there was faith in their honest doubt. There was indeed. Those words have a profound and even a horrible truth. In their doubt of miracles there was a faith in a fixed and godless fate; a deep and sincere faith in the incurable routine of the cosmos. The doubts of the agnostic were only the dogmas of the monist.

Of the fact and evidence of the supernatural I will speak afterwards. Here we are only concerned with this clear point; that in so far as the liberal idea of freedom can be said to be on either side in the discussion about miracles, it is obviously on the side of miracles. Reform or (in the only tolerable sense) progress means simply the gradual control of matter by mind. A miracle simply means the swift control of matter by mind. If you wish to feed the people, you may think that feeding them miraculously in the wilderness is impossible—but you cannot think it illiberal. If you really want poor children to go to the seaside, you cannot think it illiberal that they should go there on flying dragons; you can only think it unlikely. A holiday, like Liberalism, only means the liberty of man. A miracle only means the liberty of God. You may conscientiously deny either of them, but you cannot call your denial a triumph of the liberal idea. The Catholic Church believed that man and God both had a sort of spiritual freedom. Calvinism took away the freedom from man, but left it to God. Scientific materialism binds the Creator Himself; it chains up God as the Apocalypse chained the devil. It leaves nothing free in the universe. And those who assist this process are called the "liberal theologians."

This, as I say, is the lightest and most evident case. The assumption that there is something in the doubt of miracles akin to liberality or reform is literally the opposite of the truth. If a man cannot believe in miracles there is an end of the matter; he is not particularly liberal, but he is perfectly honourable and logical, which are much better things. But if he can believe in miracles, he is certainly the more liberal for doing so; because they mean first, the freedom of the soul, and secondly, its control over the tyranny of circumstance. Sometimes this truth is ignored in a singularly naive way, even by the ablest men. For instance, Mr. Bernard Shaw speaks with hearty old-fashioned contempt for the idea of miracles, as if they were a sort of breach of faith on the part of nature: he seems strangely unconscious that miracles are only the final flowers of his own favourite tree, the doctrine of the omnipotence of will. Just in the same way he calls the desire for immortality a paltry selfishness, forgetting that he has just called the desire for life a healthy and heroic selfishness. How can it be noble to wish to make one's life infinite and yet mean to wish to make it immortal? No, if it is desirable that man should triumph over the cruelty of nature or custom, then miracles are certainly desirable; we will discuss afterwards whether they are possible.

But I must pass on to the larger cases of this curious error; the notion that the "liberalising" of religion in some way helps the liberation of the world. The second example of it can be found in the question of pantheism—or rather of a certain modern attitude which is often called immanentism, and which often is Buddhism. But this is so much more difficult a matter that I must approach it with rather more preparation.

The things said most confidently by advanced persons to crowded audiences are generally those quite opposite to the fact; it is actually our truisms that are untrue. Here is a case. There is a phrase of facile liberality uttered again and again at ethical societies and parliaments of religion: "the religions of the earth differ in rites and forms, but they are the same in what they teach." It is false; it is the opposite of the fact. The religions of the earth do not greatly differ in rites and forms; they do greatly differ in what they teach. It is as if a man were to say, "Do not be misled by the fact that the CHURCH TIMES and the FREETHINKER look utterly different, that one is painted on vellum and the other carved on marble, that one is triangular and the other hectagonal; read them and you will see that they say the same thing." The truth is, of course, that they are alike in everything except in the fact that they don't say the same thing. An atheist stockbroker in Surbiton looks exactly like a Swedenborgian stockbroker in Wimbledon. You may walk round and round them and subject them to the most personal and offensive study without seeing anything Swedenborgian in the hat or anything particularly godless in the umbrella. It is exactly in their souls that they are divided. So the truth is that the difficulty of all the creeds of the earth is not as alleged in this cheap maxim: that they agree in meaning, but differ in machinery. It is exactly the opposite. They agree in machinery; almost every great religion on earth works with the same external methods, with priests, scriptures, altars, sworn brotherhoods, special feasts. They agree in the mode of teaching; what they differ about is the thing to be taught. Pagan optimists and Eastern pessimists would both have temples, just as Liberals and Tories would both have newspapers. Creeds that exist to destroy each other both have scriptures, just as armies that exist to destroy each other both have guns.

The great example of this alleged identity of all human religions is the alleged spiritual identity of Buddhism and Christianity. Those who adopt this theory generally avoid the ethics of most other creeds, except, indeed, Confucianism, which they like because it is not a creed. But they are cautious in their praises of Mahommedanism, generally confining themselves to imposing its morality only upon the refreshment of the lower classes. They seldom suggest the Mahommedan view of marriage (for which there is a great deal to be said), and towards

Thugs and fetish worshippers their attitude may even be called cold. But in the case of the great religion of Gautama they feel sincerely a similarity.

Students of popular science, like Mr. Blatchford, are always insisting that Christianity and Buddhism are very much alike, especially Buddhism. This is generally believed, and I believed it myself until I read a book giving the reasons for it. The reasons were of two kinds: resemblances that meant nothing because they were common to all humanity, and resemblances which were not resemblances at all. The author solemnly explained that the two creeds were alike in things in which all creeds are alike, or else he described them as alike in some point in which they are quite obviously different. Thus, as a case of the first class, he said that both Christ and Buddha were called by the divine voice coming out of the sky, as if you would expect the divine voice to come out of the coal-cellar. Or, again, it was gravely urged that these two Eastern teachers, by a singular coincidence, both had to do with the washing of feet. You might as well say that it was a remarkable coincidence that they both had feet to wash. And the other class of similarities were those which simply were not similar. Thus this reconciler of the two religions draws earnest attention to the fact that at certain religious feasts the robe of the Lama is rent in pieces out of respect, and the remnants highly valued. But this is the reverse of a resemblance, for the garments of Christ were not rent in pieces out of respect, but out of derision; and the remnants were not highly valued except for what they would fetch in the rag shops. It is rather like alluding to the obvious connection between the two ceremonies of the sword: when it taps a man's shoulder, and when it cuts off his head. It is not at all similar for the man. These scraps of puerile pedantry would indeed matter little if it were not also true that the alleged philosophical resemblances are also of these two kinds, either proving too much or not proving anything. That Buddhism approves of mercy or of self-restraint is not to say that it is specially like Christianity; it is only to say that it is not utterly unlike all human existence. Buddhists disapprove in theory of cruelty or excess because all sane human beings disapprove in theory of cruelty or excess. But to say that Buddhism and Christianity give the same philosophy of these things is simply false. All humanity does agree that we are in a net of sin. Most of humanity agrees that there is some way out. But as to what is the way out, I do not think that there are two institutions in the universe which contradict each other so flatly as Buddhism and Christianity.

Even when I thought, with most other well-informed, though unscholarly, people, that Buddhism and Christianity were alike, there was one thing about them that always perplexed me; I mean the startling difference in their type of religious art. I do not mean in its technical style of representation, but in the things that it was manifestly meant to represent. No two ideals could be more opposite than a Christian saint in a Gothic cathedral and a Buddhist saint in a Chinese temple. The opposition exists at every point; but perhaps the shortest statement of it is that the Buddhist saint always has his eyes shut, while the Christian saint always has them very wide open. The Buddhist saint has a sleek and harmonious body, but his eyes are heavy and sealed with sleep. The mediaeval saint's body is wasted to its crazy bones, but his eyes are frightfully alive. There cannot be any real community of spirit between forces that produced symbols so different as that. Granted that both images are extravagances, are perversions of the pure creed, it must be a real divergence which could produce such opposite extravagances. The Buddhist is looking with a peculiar intentness inwards. The Christian is staring with a frantic intentness outwards. If we follow that clue steadily we shall find some interesting things.

A short time ago Mrs. Besant, in an interesting essay, announced that there was only one religion in the world, that all faiths were only versions or perversions of it, and that she was quite prepared to say what it was. According to Mrs. Besant this universal Church is simply the universal self. It is the doctrine that we are really all one person; that there are no real walls of individuality between man and man. If I may put it so, she does not tell us to love our neighbours; she tells us to be our neighbours. That is Mrs. Besant's thoughtful and suggestive description of the religion in which all men must find themselves in agreement. And I never heard of any suggestion in my life with which I more violently disagree. I want to love my neighbour not because he is I, but precisely because he is not I. I want to adore the world, not as one likes a looking-glass, because it is one's self, but as one loves a woman, because she is entirely different. If souls are separate love is possible. If souls are united love is obviously impossible. A man may be said loosely to love himself, but he can hardly fall in love with himself, or, if he does, it must be a monotonous courtship. If the world is full of real selves, they can be really unselfish selves. But upon Mrs. Besant's principle the whole cosmos is only one enormously selfish person.

It is just here that Buddhism is on the side of modern pantheism and immanence. And it is just here that Christianity is on the side of humanity and liberty and love. Love desires personality; therefore love desires division. It is the instinct of Christianity to be glad that God has broken the universe into little pieces, because they are living pieces. It is her instinct to say "little children love one another" rather than to tell one large person to love himself. This is the intellectual abyss between Buddhism and Christianity; that for the Buddhist or Theosophist personality is the fall of man, for the Christian it is the purpose of God, the whole point of his cosmic idea. The world-soul of the Theosophists asks man to love it only in order that man may throw himself into it. But the divine centre of Christianity actually threw man out of it in order that he might love it. The oriental deity is like a giant who should have lost his leg or hand and be always seeking to find it; but the Christian power is like some giant who in a strange generosity should cut off his right hand, so that it might of its own accord shake hands with him. We come back to the same tireless note touching the nature of Christianity; all modern philosophies are chains which connect and fetter; Christianity is a sword which separates and sets free. No other philosophy makes God actually rejoice in the separation of the universe into living souls. But according to orthodox Christianity this separation between God and man is sacred, because this is eternal. That a man may love God it is necessary that there should be not only a God to be loved, but a man to love him. All those vague theosophical minds for whom the universe is an immense melting-pot are exactly the minds which shrink instinctively from that earthquake saying of our Gospels, which declare that the Son of God came not with peace but with a sundering sword. The saying rings entirely true even considered as what it obviously is; the statement that any man who preaches real love is bound to beget hate. It is as true of democratic fraternity as a divine love; sham love ends in compromise and common philosophy; but real love has always ended in bloodshed. Yet there is another and yet more awful truth behind the obvious meaning of this utterance of our Lord. According to Himself the Son was a sword separating brother and brother that they should for an aeon hate each other. But the Father also was a sword, which in the black beginning separated brother and brother, so that they should love each other at last.

This is the meaning of that almost insane happiness in the eyes of the mediaeval saint in the picture. This is the meaning of the sealed eyes of the superb Buddhist image. The Christian saint is happy because he has verily been cut off from the world; he is separate from things and is staring at them in astonishment. But why should the Buddhist saint be astonished at things?— since there is really only one thing, and that being impersonal can hardly be astonished at itself. There have been many pantheist poems suggesting wonder, but no really successful ones. The pantheist cannot wonder, for he cannot praise God or praise anything as really distinct from himself. Our immediate business here, however, is with the effect of this Christian admiration (which strikes outwards, towards a deity distinct from the worshipper) upon the general need for ethical activity and social reform. And surely its effect is sufficiently obvious. There is no real possibility of getting out of pantheism, any special impulse to moral action. For pantheism implies in its nature that one thing is as good as another; whereas action implies in its nature that one thing is greatly preferable to another. Swinburne in the high summer of his scepticism tried in vain to wrestle with this difficulty. In "Songs before Sunrise," written under the inspiration of Garibaldi and the revolt of Italy he proclaimed the newer religion and the purer God which should wither up all the priests of the world:

"What doest thou now Looking Godward to cry I am I, thou art thou, I am low, thou art high, I am thou that thou seekest to find him, find thou but thyself, thou art I."

Of which the immediate and evident deduction is that tyrants are as much the sons of God as Garibaldis; and that King Bomba of Naples having, with the utmost success, "found himself" is identical with the ultimate good in all things. The truth is that the western energy that dethrones tyrants has been directly due to the western theology that says "I am I, thou art thou." The same spiritual separation which looked up and saw a good king in the universe looked up and saw a bad king in Naples. The worshippers of Bomba's god dethroned Bomba. The worshippers of Swinburne's god have covered Asia for centuries and have never dethroned a tyrant. The Indian saint may reasonably shut his eyes because he is looking at that which is I and Thou and We and They and It. It is a rational occupation: but it is not true in theory and not true in fact that it helps the Indian to keep an eye on Lord Curzon. That external vigilance which has always been the mark of Christianity (the command that we should WATCH and pray) has expressed itself both in typical western orthodoxy and in typical western politics: but both depend on the idea of a divinity transcendent, different from ourselves, a deity that disappears. Certainly the most sagacious creeds may suggest that we should pursue God into deeper and deeper rings of the labyrinth of our own ego. But only we of Christendom have said that we should hunt God like an eagle upon the mountains: and we have killed all monsters in the chase.

Here again, therefore, we find that in so far as we value democracy and the self-renewing energies of the west, we are much more likely to find them in the old theology than the new. If we want reform, we must adhere to orthodoxy: especially in this matter (so much disputed in the counsels of Mr. R.J.Campbell), the matter of insisting on the immanent or the transcendent deity. By insisting specially on the immanence of God we get introspection, self-isolation, quietism, social indifference—Tibet. By insisting specially on the transcendence of God we get wonder, curiosity, moral and political adventure, righteous indignation—Christendom. Insisting that God is inside man, man is always inside himself. By insisting that God transcends man, man has transcended himself.

If we take any other doctrine that has been called old-fashioned we shall find the case the same. It is the same, for instance, in the deep matter of the Trinity. Unitarians (a sect never to be mentioned without a special respect for their distinguished intellectual dignity and high intellectual honour) are often reformers by the accident that throws so many small sects into such an attitude. But there is nothing in the least liberal or akin to reform in the substitution of pure monotheism for the Trinity. The complex God of the Athanasian Creed may be an enigma for the intellect; but He is far less likely to gather the mystery and cruelty of a Sultan than the lonely god of Omar or Mahomet. The god who is a mere awful unity is not only a king but an Eastern king. The HEART of humanity, especially of European humanity, is certainly much more satisfied by the strange hints and symbols that gather round the Trinitarian idea, the image of a council at which mercy pleads as well as justice, the conception of a sort of liberty and variety existing even in the inmost chamber of the world. For Western religion has always felt keenly the idea "it is not well for man to be alone." The social instinct asserted itself everywhere as when the Eastern idea of hermits was practically expelled by the Western idea of monks. So even asceticism became brotherly; and the Trappists were sociable even when they were silent. If this love of a living complexity be our test, it is certainly healthier to have the Trinitarian religion than the Unitarian. For to us Trinitarians (if I may say it with reverence)—to us God Himself is a society. It is indeed a fathomless mystery of theology, and even if I were theologian enough to deal with it directly, it would not be relevant to do so here. Suffice it to say here that this triple enigma is as comforting as wine and open as an English fireside; that this thing that bewilders the intellect utterly quiets the heart: but out of the desert, from the dry places and the dreadful suns, come the cruel children of the lonely God; the real Unitarians who with scimitar in hand have laid waste the world. For it is not well for God to be alone.

Again, the same is true of that difficult matter of the danger of the soul, which has unsettled so many just minds. To hope for all souls is imperative; and it is quite tenable that their salvation is inevitable. It is tenable, but it is not specially favourable to activity or progress. Our fighting and creative society ought rather to insist on the danger of everybody, on the fact that every man is hanging by a thread or clinging to a precipice. To say that all will be well anyhow is a comprehensible remark: but it cannot be called the blast of a trumpet. Europe ought rather to emphasize possible perdition; and Europe always has emphasized it. Here its highest religion is at one with all its cheapest romances. To the Buddhist or the eastern fatalist existence is a science or a plan, which must end up in a certain way. But to a Christian existence is a STORY, which may end up in any way. In a thrilling novel (that purely Christian product) the hero is not eaten by cannibals; but it is essential to the existence of the thrill that he MIGHT be eaten by cannibals. The hero must (so to speak) be an eatable hero. So Christian morals have always said to the man, not that he would lose his soul, but that he must take care that he didn't. In Christian morals, in short, it is wicked to call a man "damned": but it is strictly religious and philosophic to call him damnable.

All Christianity concentrates on the man at the cross-roads. The vast and shallow philosophies, the huge syntheses of humbug, all talk about ages and evolution and ultimate developments. The true philosophy is concerned with the instant. Will a man take this road or that?—that is the only thing to think about, if you enjoy thinking. The aeons are easy enough to think about, any one can think about them. The instant is really awful: and it is because our religion has intensely felt the instant, that it has in literature dealt much with battle and in theology dealt much with hell. It is full of DANGER, like a boy's book: it is at an immortal crisis. There is a great deal of real similarity between popular fiction and the religion of the western people. If you say that popular fiction is vulgar and tawdry, you only say what the dreary and well-informed say also about the images in the Catholic churches. Life (according to the faith) is very like a serial story in a magazine: life ends with the promise (or menace) "to be continued in our next." Also, with a noble vulgarity, life imitates the serial and leaves off at the exciting moment. For death is distinctly an exciting moment.

But the point is that a story is exciting because it has in it so strong an element of will, of what theology calls free-will. You cannot finish a sum how you like. But you can finish a story how you like. When somebody discovered the Differential Calculus there was only one Differential Calculus he could discover. But when Shakespeare killed Romeo he might have married him to Juliet's old nurse if he had felt inclined. And Christendom has excelled in the narrative romance exactly because it has insisted on the theological free-will. It is a large matter and too much to one side of the road to be discussed adequately here; but this is the real objection to that torrent of modern talk about treating crime as disease, about making a prison merely a hygienic environment like a hospital, of healing sin by slow scientific methods. The fallacy of the whole thing is that evil is a matter of active choice whereas disease is not. If you say that you are going to cure a profligate as you cure an asthmatic, my cheap and obvious answer is, "Produce the people who want to be asthmatics as many people want to be profligates." A man may lie still and be cured of a malady. But he must not lie still if he wants to be cured of a sin; on the contrary, he must get up and jump about violently. The whole point indeed is perfectly expressed in the very word which we use for a man in hospital; "patient" is in the passive mood; "sinner" is in the active. If a man is to be saved from influenza, he may be a patient. But if he is to be saved from forging, he must be not a patient but an IMPATIENT. He must be personally impatient with forgery. All moral reform must start in the active not the passive will.

Here again we reach the same substantial conclusion. In so far as we desire the definite reconstructions and the dangerous revolutions which have distinguished European civilization, we shall not discourage the thought of possible ruin; we shall rather encourage it. If we want, like the Eastern saints, merely to contemplate how right things are, of course we shall only say that they must go right. But if we particularly want to MAKE them go right, we must insist that they may go wrong.

Lastly, this truth is yet again true in the case of the common modern attempts to diminish or to explain away the divinity of Christ. The thing may be true or not; that I shall deal with before I end. But if the divinity is true it is certainly terribly revolutionary. That a good man may have his back to the wall is no more than we knew already; but that God could have his back to the wall is a boast for all insurgents for ever. Christianity is the only religion on earth that has felt that omnipotence made God incomplete. Christianity alone has felt that God, to be wholly God, must have been a rebel as well as a king. Alone of all creeds, Christianity has added courage to the virtues of the Creator. For the only courage worth calling courage must necessarily mean that the soul passes a breaking point—and does not break. In this indeed I approach a matter more dark and awful than it is easy to discuss; and I apologise in advance if any of my phrases fall wrong or seem irreverent touching a matter which the greatest saints and thinkers have justly feared to approach. But in that terrific tale of the Passion there is a distinct emotional suggestion that the author of all things (in some unthinkable way) went not only through agony, but through doubt. It is written, "Thou shalt not tempt the Lord thy God." No; but the Lord thy God may tempt Himself; and it seems as if this was what happened in Gethsemane. In a garden Satan tempted man: and in a garden God tempted God. He passed in some superhuman manner through our human horror of pessimism. When the world shook and the sun was wiped out of heaven, it was not at the crucifixion, but at the cry from the cross: the cry which confessed that God was forsaken of God. And now let the revolutionists choose a creed from all the creeds and a god from all the gods of the world, carefully weighing all the gods of inevitable recurrence and of unalterable power. They will not find another god who has himself been in revolt. Nay, (the matter grows too difficult for human speech,) but let the atheists themselves choose a god. They will find only one divinity who ever uttered their isolation; only one religion in which God seemed for an instant to be an atheist.

These can be called the essentials of the old orthodoxy, of which the chief merit is that it is the natural fountain of revolution and reform; and of which the chief defect is that it is obviously only an abstract assertion. Its main advantage is that it is the most adventurous and manly of all theologies. Its chief disadvantage is simply that it is a theology. It can always be urged against it that it is in its nature arbitrary and in the air. But it is not so high in the air but that great archers spend their whole lives in shooting arrows at it—yes, and their last arrows; there are men who will ruin themselves and ruin their civilization if they may ruin also this old fantastic tale. This is the last and most astounding fact about this faith; that its enemies will use any weapon against it, the swords that cut their own fingers, and the firebrands that burn their own homes. Men who begin to fight the Church for the sake of freedom and humanity end by flinging away freedom and humanity if only they may fight the Church. This is no exaggeration; I could fill a book with the instances of it. Mr. Blatchford set out, as an ordinary Bible-smasher, to prove that Adam was guiltless of sin against God; in manoeuvring so as to maintain this he admitted, as a mere side issue, that all the tyrants, from Nero to King Leopold, were guiltless of any sin against humanity. I know a man who has such a passion for proving that he will have no personal existence after death that he falls back on the position that he has no personal existence now. He invokes Buddhism and says that all souls fade into each other; in order to prove that he cannot go to heaven he proves that he cannot go to Hartlepool. I have known people who protested against religious education with arguments against any education, saying that the child's mind must grow freely or that the old must not teach the young. I have known people who showed that there could be no divine judgment by showing that there can be no human judgment, even for practical purposes. They burned their own corn to set fire to the church; they smashed their own tools to smash it; any stick was good enough to beat it with, though it were the last stick of their own dismembered furniture. We do not admire, we hardly excuse, the fanatic who wrecks this world for love of the other. But what are we to say of the fanatic who wrecks this world out of hatred of the other? He sacrifices the very existence of humanity to the non-existence of God. He offers his victims not to the altar, but merely to assert the idleness of the altar and the emptiness of the throne. He is ready to ruin even that primary ethic by which all things live, for his strange and eternal vengeance upon some one who never lived at all.

And yet the thing hangs in the heavens unhurt. Its opponents only succeed in destroying all that they themselves justly hold dear. They do not destroy orthodoxy; they only destroy political and common courage sense. They do not prove that Adam was not responsible to God; how could they prove it? They only prove (from their premises) that the Czar is not responsible to Russia. They do not prove that Adam should not have been punished by God; they only prove that the nearest sweater should not be punished by men. With their oriental doubts about personality they do not make certain that we shall have no personal life hereafter; they only make certain that we shall not have a very jolly or complete one here. With their paralysing hints of all conclusions coming out wrong they do not tear the book of the Recording Angel; they only make it a little harder to keep the books of Marshall & Snelgrove. Not only is the faith the mother of all worldly energies, but its foes are the fathers of all worldly confusion. The secularists have not wrecked divine things; but the secularists have wrecked secular things, if that is any comfort to them. The Titans did not scale heaven; but they laid waste the world.

IX AUTHORITY AND THE ADVENTURER

The last chapter has been concerned with the contention that orthodoxy is not only (as is often urged) the only safe guardian of morality or order, but is also the only logical guardian of liberty, innovation and advance. If we wish to pull down the prosperous oppressor we cannot do it with the new doctrine of human perfectibility; we can do it with the old doctrine of Original Sin. If we want to uproot inherent cruelties or lift up lost populations we cannot do it with the scientific theory that matter precedes mind; we can do it with the supernatural theory that mind precedes matter. If we wish specially to awaken people to social vigilance and tireless pursuit of practise, we cannot help it much by insisting on the Immanent God and the Inner Light: for these are at best reasons for contentment; we can help it much by insisting on the transcendent God and the flying and escaping gleam; for that means divine discontent. If we wish particularly to assert the idea of a generous balance against that of a dreadful autocracy we shall instinctively be Trinitarian rather than Unitarian. If we desire European civilization to be a raid and a rescue, we shall insist rather that souls are in real peril than that their peril is ultimately unreal. And if we wish to exalt the outcast and the crucified, we shall rather wish to think that a veritable God was crucified, rather than a mere sage or hero. Above all, if we wish to protect the poor we shall be in favour of fixed rules and clear dogmas. The RULES of a club are occasionally in favour of the poor member. The drift of a club is always in favour of the rich one.

And now we come to the crucial question which truly concludes the whole matter. A reasonable agnostic, if he has happened to agree with me so far, may justly turn round and say, "You have found a practical philosophy in the doctrine of the Fall; very well. You have found a side of democracy now dangerously neglected wisely asserted in Original Sin; all right. You have found a truth in the doctrine of hell; I congratulate you. You are convinced that worshippers of a personal God look outwards and are progressive; I congratulate them. But even supposing that those doctrines do include those truths, why cannot you take the truths and leave the doctrines? Granted that all modern society is trusting the rich too much because it does not allow for human weakness; granted that orthodox ages have had a great advantage because (believing in the Fall) they did allow for human weakness, why cannot you simply allow for human weakness without believing in the Fall? If you have discovered that the idea of damnation represents a healthy idea of danger, why can you not simply take the idea of danger and leave the idea of damnation? If you see clearly the kernel of common-sense in the nut of Christian orthodoxy, why cannot you simply take the kernel and leave the nut? Why cannot you (to use that cant phrase of the newspapers which I, as a highly scholarly agnostic, am a little ashamed of using) why cannot you simply take what is good in Christianity, what you can define as valuable, what you can comprehend, and leave all the rest, all the absolute dogmas that are in their nature incomprehensible?" This is the real question; this is the last question; and it is a pleasure to try to answer it.

The first answer is simply to say that I am a rationalist. I like to have some intellectual justification for my intuitions. If I am treating man as a fallen being it is an intellectual convenience to me to believe that he fell; and I find, for some odd psychological reason, that I can deal better with a man's exercise of freewill if I believe that he has got it. But I am in this matter yet more definitely a rationalist. I do not propose to turn this book into one of ordinary Christian apologetics; I should be glad to meet at any other time the enemies of Christianity in that more obvious arena. Here I am only giving an account of my own growth in spiritual certainty. But I may pause to remark that the more I saw of the merely abstract arguments against the Christian cosmology the less I thought of them. I mean that having found the moral atmosphere of the Incarnation to be common sense, I then looked at the established intellectual arguments against the Incarnation and found them to be common nonsense. In case the argument should be thought to suffer from the absence of the ordinary apologetic I will here very briefly summarise my own arguments and conclusions on the purely objective or scientific truth of the matter.

If I am asked, as a purely intellectual question, why I believe in Christianity, I can only answer, "For the same reason that an intelligent agnostic disbelieves in Christianity." I believe in it quite rationally upon the evidence. But the evidence in my case, as in that of the intelligent agnostic, is not really in this or that alleged demonstration; it is in an enormous accumulation of small but unanimous facts. The secularist is not to be blamed because his objections to Christianity are miscellaneous and even scrappy; it is precisely such scrappy evidence that does convince the mind. I mean that a man may well be less convinced of a philosophy from four books, than from one book, one battle, one landscape, and one old friend. The very fact that the things are of different kinds increases the importance of the fact that they all point to one conclusion. Now, the non-Christianity of the average educated man to-day is almost always, to do him justice, made up of these loose but living experiences. I can only say that my evidences for Christianity are of the same vivid but varied kind as his evidences against it. For when I look at these various anti-Christian truths, I simply discover that none of them are true. I discover that the true tide and force of all the facts flows the other way. Let us take cases. Many a sensible modern man must have abandoned Christianity under the pressure of three such converging convictions as these: first, that men, with their shape, structure, and sexuality, are, after all, very much like beasts, a mere variety of the animal kingdom; second, that primeval religion arose in ignorance and fear; third, that priests have blighted societies with bitterness and gloom. Those three anti-Christian arguments are very different; but they are all quite logical and legitimate; and they all converge. The only objection to them (I discover) is that they are all untrue. If you leave off looking at books about beasts and men, if you begin to look at beasts and men then (if you have any humour or imagination, any sense of the frantic or the farcical) you will observe that the startling thing is not how like man is to the brutes, but how unlike he is. It is the monstrous scale of his divergence that requires an explanation. That man and brute are like is, in a sense, a truism; but that being so like they should then be so insanely unlike, that is the shock and the enigma. That an ape has hands is far less interesting to the philosopher than the fact that having hands he does next to nothing with them; does not play knuckle-bones or the violin; does not carve marble or carve mutton. People talk of barbaric architecture and debased art. But elephants do not build colossal temples of ivory even in a rocco-co style; camels do not paint even bad pictures, though equipped with the material of many camel's-hair brushes. Certain modern dreamers say that ants and bees have a society superior to ours. They have, indeed, a civilization; but that very truth only reminds us that it is an inferior civilization. Who ever found an ant-hill decorated with the statues of celebrated ants? Who has seen a bee-hive carved with the images of gorgeous queens of old? No; the chasm between man and other creatures may have a natural explanation, but it is a chasm. We talk of wild animals; but man is the only wild animal. It is man that has broken out. All other animals are tame animals; following the rugged respectability of the tribe or type. All other animals are domestic animals; man alone is ever undomestic, either as a profligate or a monk. So that this first superficial reason for materialism is, if anything, a reason for its opposite; it is exactly where biology leaves off that all religion begins.

It would be the same if I examined the second of the three chance rationalist arguments; the argument that all that we call divine began in some darkness and terror. When I did attempt to examine the foundations of this modern idea I simply found that there were none. Science knows nothing whatever about pre-historic man; for the excellent reason that he is pre-historic. A few professors choose to conjecture that such things as human sacrifice were once innocent and general and that they gradually dwindled; but there is no direct evidence of it, and the small amount of indirect evidence is very much the other way. In the earliest legends we have, such as the tales of Isaac and of Iphigenia, human sacrifice is not introduced as something old, but rather as something new; as a strange and frightful exception darkly demanded by the gods. History says nothing; and legends all say that the earth was kinder in its earliest time. There is no tradition of progress; but the whole human race has a tradition of the Fall. Amusingly enough, indeed, the very dissemination of this idea is used against its authenticity. Learned men literally say that this pre-historic calamity cannot be true because every race of mankind remembers it. I cannot keep pace with these paradoxes.

And if we took the third chance instance, it would be the same; the view that priests darken and embitter the world. I look at the world and simply discover that they don't. Those countries in Europe which are still influenced by priests, are exactly the countries where there is still singing and dancing and coloured dresses and art in the open-air. Catholic doctrine and discipline may be walls; but they are the walls of a playground. Christianity is the only frame which has preserved the pleasure of Paganism. We might fancy some children playing on the flat grassy top of some tall island in the sea. So long as there was a wall round the cliff's edge they could fling themselves into every frantic game and make the place the noisiest of nurseries. But the walls were knocked down, leaving the naked peril of the precipice. They did not fall over; but when their friends returned to them they were all huddled in terror in the centre of the island; and their song had ceased.

Thus these three facts of experience, such facts as go to make an agnostic, are, in this view, turned totally round. I am left saying, "Give me an explanation, first, of the towering eccentricity of man among the brutes; second, of the vast human tradition of some ancient happiness; third, of the partial perpetuation of such pagan joy in the countries of the Catholic Church." One explanation, at any rate, covers all three: the theory that twice was the natural order interrupted by some explosion or revelation such as people now call "psychic." Once Heaven came upon the earth with a power or seal called the image of God, whereby man took command of Nature; and once again (when in empire after empire men had been found wanting) Heaven came to save mankind in the awful shape of a man. This would explain why the mass of men always look backwards; and why the only corner where they in any sense look forwards is the little continent where Christ has His Church. I know it will be said that Japan has become progressive. But how can this be an answer when even in saying "Japan has become progressive," we really only mean, "Japan has become European"? But I wish here not so much to insist on my own explanation as to insist on my original remark. I agree with the ordinary unbelieving man in the street in being guided by three or four odd facts all pointing to something; only when I came to look at the facts I always found they pointed to something else.

I have given an imaginary triad of such ordinary anti-Christian arguments; if that be too narrow a basis I will give on the spur of the moment another. These are the kind of thoughts which in combination create the impression that Christianity is something weak and diseased. First, for instance, that Jesus was a gentle creature, sheepish and unworldly, a mere ineffectual appeal to the world; second, that Christianity arose and flourished in the dark ages of ignorance, and that to these the Church would drag us back; third, that the people still strongly religious or (if you will) superstitious—such people as the Irish—are weak, unpractical, and behind the times. I only mention these ideas to affirm the same thing: that when I looked into them independently I found, not that the conclusions were unphilosophical, but simply that the facts were not facts. Instead of looking at books and pictures about the New Testament I looked at the New Testament. There I found an account, not in the least of a person with his hair parted in the middle or his hands clasped in appeal, but of an extraordinary being with lips of thunder and acts of lurid decision, flinging down tables, casting out devils, passing with the wild secrecy of the wind from mountain isolation to a sort of dreadful demagogy; a being who often acted like an angry god— and always like a god. Christ had even a literary style of his own, not to be found, I think, elsewhere; it consists of an almost furious use of the A FORTIORI. His "how much more" is piled one upon another like castle upon castle in the clouds. The diction used ABOUT Christ has been, and perhaps wisely, sweet and submissive. But the diction used by Christ is quite curiously gigantesque; it is full of camels leaping through needles and mountains hurled into the sea. Morally it is equally terrific; he called himself a sword of slaughter, and told men to buy swords if they sold their coats for them. That he used other even wilder words on the side of non-resistance greatly increases the mystery; but it also, if anything, rather increases the violence. We cannot even explain it by calling such a being insane; for insanity is usually along one consistent channel. The maniac is generally a monomaniac. Here we must remember the difficult definition of Christianity already given; Christianity is a superhuman paradox whereby two opposite passions may blaze beside each other. The one explanation of the Gospel language that does explain it, is that it is the survey of one who from some supernatural height beholds some more startling synthesis.

I take in order the next instance offered: the idea that Christianity belongs to the Dark Ages. Here I did not satisfy myself with reading modern generalisations; I read a little history. And in history I found that Christianity, so far from belonging to the Dark Ages, was the one path across the Dark Ages that was not dark. It was a shining bridge connecting two shining civilizations. If any one says that the faith arose in ignorance and savagery the answer is simple: it didn't. It arose in the Mediterranean civilization in the full summer of the Roman Empire. The world was swarming with sceptics, and pantheism was as plain as the sun, when Constantine nailed the cross to the mast. It is perfectly true that afterwards the ship sank; but it is far more extraordinary that the ship came up again: repainted and glittering, with the cross still at the top. This is the amazing thing the religion did: it turned a sunken ship into a submarine. The ark lived under the load of waters; after being buried under the debris of dynasties and clans, we arose and remembered Rome. If our faith had been a mere fad of the fading empire, fad would have followed fad in the twilight, and if the civilization ever re-emerged (and many such have never re-emerged) it would have been under some new barbaric flag. But the Christian Church was the last life of the old society and was also the first life of the new. She took the people who were forgetting how to make an arch and she taught them to invent the Gothic arch. In a word, the most absurd thing that could be said of the Church is the thing we have all heard said of it. How can we say that the Church wishes to bring us back into the Dark Ages? The Church was the only thing that ever brought us out of them.

I added in this second trinity of objections an idle instance taken from those who feel such people as the Irish to be weakened or made stagnant by superstition. I only added it because this is a peculiar case of a statement of fact that turns out to be a statement of falsehood. It is constantly said of the Irish that they are impractical. But if we refrain for a moment from looking at what is said about them and look at what is DONE about them, we shall see that the Irish are not only practical, but quite painfully successful. The poverty of their country, the minority of their members are simply the conditions under which they were asked to work; but no other group in the British Empire has done so much with such conditions. The Nationalists were the only minority that ever succeeded in twisting the whole British Parliament sharply out of its path. The Irish peasants are the only poor men in these islands who have forced their masters to disgorge. These people, whom we call priest-ridden, are the only Britons who will not be squire-ridden. And when I came to look at the actual Irish character, the case was the same. Irishmen are best at the specially HARD professions—the trades of iron, the lawyer, and the soldier. In all these cases, therefore, I came back to the same conclusion: the sceptic was quite right to go by the facts, only he had not looked at the facts. The sceptic is too credulous; he believes in newspapers or even in encyclopedias. Again the three questions left me with three very antagonistic questions. The average sceptic wanted to know how I explained the namby-pamby note in the Gospel, the connection of the creed with mediaeval darkness and the political impracticability of the Celtic Christians. But I wanted to ask, and to ask with an earnestness amounting to urgency, "What is this incomparable energy which appears first in one walking the earth like a living judgment and this energy which can die with a dying civilization and yet force it to a resurrection from the dead; this energy which last of all can inflame a bankrupt peasantry with so fixed a faith in justice that they get what they ask, while others go empty away; so that the most helpless island of the Empire can actually help itself?"

There is an answer: it is an answer to say that the energy is truly from outside the world; that it is psychic, or at least one of the results of a real psychical disturbance. The highest gratitude and respect are due to the great human civilizations such as the old Egyptian or the existing Chinese. Nevertheless it is no injustice for them to say that only modern Europe has exhibited incessantly a power of self-renewal recurring often at the shortest intervals and descending to the smallest facts of building or costume. All other societies die finally and with dignity. We die daily. We are always being born again with almost indecent obstetrics. It is hardly an exaggeration to say that there is in historic Christendom a sort of unnatural life: it could be explained as a supernatural life. It could be explained as an awful galvanic life working in what would have been a corpse. For our civilization OUGHT to have died, by all parallels, by all sociological probability, in the Ragnorak of the end of Rome. That is the weird inspiration of our estate: you and I have no business to be here at all. We are all REVENANTS; all living Christians are dead pagans walking about. Just as Europe was about to be gathered in silence to Assyria and Babylon, something entered into its body. And Europe has had a strange life—it is not too much to say that it has had the JUMPS— ever since.

I have dealt at length with such typical triads of doubt in order to convey the main contention—that my own case for Christianity is rational; but it is not simple. It is an accumulation of varied facts, like the attitude of the ordinary agnostic. But the ordinary agnostic has got his facts all wrong. He is a non-believer for a multitude of reasons; but they are untrue reasons. He doubts because the Middle Ages were barbaric, but they weren't; because Darwinism is demonstrated, but it isn't; because miracles do not happen, but they do; because monks were lazy, but they were very industrious; because nuns are unhappy, but they are particularly cheerful; because Christian art was sad and pale, but it was picked out in peculiarly bright colours and gay with gold; because modern science is moving away from the supernatural, but it isn't, it is moving towards the supernatural with the rapidity of a railway train.

But among these million facts all flowing one way there is, of course, one question sufficiently solid and separate to be treated briefly, but by itself; I mean the objective occurrence of the supernatural. In another chapter I have indicated the fallacy of the ordinary supposition that the world must be impersonal because it is orderly. A person is just as likely to desire an orderly thing as a disorderly thing. But my own positive conviction that personal creation is more conceivable than material fate, is, I admit, in a sense, undiscussable. I will not call it a faith or an intuition, for those words are mixed up with mere emotion, it is strictly an intellectual conviction; but it is a PRIMARY intellectual conviction like the certainty of self of the good of living. Any one who likes, therefore, may call my belief in God merely mystical; the phrase is not worth fighting about. But my belief that miracles have happened in human history is not a mystical belief at all; I believe in them upon human evidences as I do in the discovery of America. Upon this point there is a simple logical fact that only requires to be stated and cleared up. Somehow or other an extraordinary idea has arisen that the disbelievers in miracles consider them coldly and fairly, while believers in miracles accept them only in connection with some dogma. The fact is quite the other way. The believers in miracles accept them (rightly or wrongly) because they have evidence for them. The disbelievers in miracles deny them (rightly or wrongly) because they have a doctrine against them. The open, obvious, democratic thing is to believe an old apple-woman when she bears testimony to a miracle, just as you believe an old apple-woman when she bears testimony to a murder. The plain, popular course is to trust the peasant's word about the ghost exactly as far as you trust the peasant's word about the landlord. Being a peasant he will probably have a great deal of healthy agnosticism about both. Still you could fill the British Museum with evidence uttered by the peasant, and given in favour of the ghost. If it comes to human testimony there is a choking cataract of human testimony in favour of the supernatural. If you reject it, you can only mean one of two things. You reject the peasant's story about the ghost either because the man is a peasant or because the story is a ghost story. That is, you either deny the main principle of democracy, or you affirm the main principle of materialism— the abstract impossibility of miracle. You have a perfect right to do so; but in that case you are the dogmatist. It is we Christians who accept all actual evidence—it is you rationalists who refuse actual evidence being constrained to do so by your creed. But I am not constrained by any creed in the matter, and looking impartially into certain miracles of mediaeval and modern times, I have come to the conclusion that they occurred. All argument against these plain facts is always argument in a circle. If I say, "Mediaeval documents attest certain miracles as much as they attest certain battles," they answer, "But mediaevals were superstitious"; if I want to know in what they were superstitious, the only ultimate answer is that they believed in the miracles. If I say "a peasant saw a ghost," I am told, "But peasants are so credulous." If I ask, "Why credulous?" the only answer is—that they see ghosts. Iceland is impossible because only stupid sailors have seen it; and the sailors are only stupid because they say they have seen Iceland. It is only fair to add that there is another argument that the unbeliever may rationally use against miracles, though he himself generally forgets to use it.

He may say that there has been in many miraculous stories a notion of spiritual preparation and acceptance: in short, that the miracle could only come to him who believed in it. It may be so, and if it is so how are we to test it? If we are inquiring whether certain results follow faith, it is useless to repeat wearily that (if they happen) they do follow faith. If faith is one of the conditions, those without faith have a most healthy right to laugh. But they have no right to judge. Being a believer may be, if you like, as bad as being drunk; still if we were extracting psychological facts from drunkards, it would be absurd to be always taunting them with having been drunk. Suppose we were investigating whether angry men really saw a red mist before their eyes. Suppose sixty excellent householders swore that when angry they had seen this crimson cloud: surely it would be absurd to answer "Oh, but you admit you were angry at the time." They might reasonably rejoin (in a stentorian chorus), "How the blazes could we discover, without being angry, whether angry people see red?" So the saints and ascetics might rationally reply, "Suppose that the question is whether believers can see visions—even then, if you are interested in visions it is no point to object to believers." You are still arguing in a circle—in that old mad circle with which this book began.

The question of whether miracles ever occur is a question of common sense and of ordinary historical imagination: not of any final physical experiment. One may here surely dismiss that quite brainless piece of pedantry which talks about the need for "scientific conditions" in connection with alleged spiritual phenomena. If we are asking whether a dead soul can communicate with a living it is ludicrous to insist that it shall be under conditions in which no two living souls in their senses would seriously communicate with each other. The fact that ghosts prefer darkness no more disproves the existence of ghosts than the fact that lovers prefer darkness disproves the existence of love. If you choose to say, "I will believe that Miss Brown called her fiance a periwinkle or, any other endearing term, if she will repeat the word before seventeen psychologists," then I shall reply, "Very well, if those are your conditions, you will never get the truth, for she certainly will not say it." It is just as unscientific as it is unphilosophical to be surprised that in an unsympathetic atmosphere certain extraordinary sympathies do not arise. It is as if I said that I could not tell if there was a fog because the air was not clear enough; or as if I insisted on perfect sunlight in order to see a solar eclipse.

As a common-sense conclusion, such as those to which we come about sex or about midnight (well knowing that many details must in their own nature be concealed) I conclude that miracles do happen. I am forced to it by a conspiracy of facts: the fact that the men who encounter elves or angels are not the mystics and the morbid dreamers, but fishermen, farmers, and all men at once coarse and cautious; the fact that we all know men who testify to spiritualistic incidents but are not spiritualists, the fact that science itself admits such things more and more every day. Science will even admit the Ascension if you call it Levitation, and will very likely admit the Resurrection when it has thought of another word for it. I suggest the Regalvanisation. But the strongest of all is the dilemma above mentioned, that these supernatural things are never denied except on the basis either of anti-democracy or of materialist dogmatism—I may say materialist mysticism. The sceptic always takes one of the two positions; either an ordinary man need not be believed, or an extraordinary event must not be believed. For I hope we may dismiss the argument against wonders attempted in the mere recapitulation of frauds, of swindling mediums or trick miracles. That is not an argument at all, good or bad. A false ghost disproves the reality of ghosts exactly as much as a forged banknote disproves the existence of the Bank of England— if anything, it proves its existence.

Given this conviction that the spiritual phenomena do occur (my evidence for which is complex but rational), we then collide with one of the worst mental evils of the age. The greatest disaster of the nineteenth century was this: that men began to use the word "spiritual" as the same as the word "good." They thought that to grow in refinement and uncorporeality was to grow in virtue. When scientific evolution was announced, some feared that it would encourage mere animality. It did worse: it encouraged mere spirituality. It taught men to think that so long as they were passing from the ape they were going to the angel. But you can pass from the ape and go to the devil. A man of genius, very typical of that time of bewilderment, expressed it perfectly. Benjamin Disraeli was right when he said he was on the side of the angels. He was indeed; he was on the side of the fallen angels. He was not on the side of any mere appetite or animal brutality; but he was on the side of all the imperialism of the princes of the abyss; he was on the side of arrogance and mystery, and contempt of all obvious good. Between this sunken pride and the towering humilities of heaven there are, one must suppose, spirits of shapes and sizes. Man, in encountering them, must make much the same mistakes that he makes in encountering any other varied types in any other distant continent. It must be hard at first to know who is supreme and who is subordinate. If a shade arose from the under world, and stared at Piccadilly, that shade would not quite understand the idea of an ordinary closed carriage. He would suppose that the coachman on the box was a triumphant conqueror, dragging behind him a kicking and imprisoned captive. So, if we see spiritual facts for the first time, we may mistake who is uppermost. It is not enough to find the gods; they are obvious; we must find God, the real chief of the gods. We must have a long historic experience in supernatural phenomena— in order to discover which are really natural. In this light I find the history of Christianity, and even of its Hebrew origins, quite practical and clear. It does not trouble me to be told that the Hebrew god was one among many. I know he was, without any research to tell me so. Jehovah and Baal looked equally important, just as the sun and the moon looked the same size. It is only slowly that we learn that the sun is immeasurably our master, and the small moon only our satellite. Believing that there is a world of spirits, I shall walk in it as I do in the world of men, looking for the thing that I like and think good. Just as I should seek in a desert for clean water, or toil at the North Pole to make a comfortable fire, so I shall search the land of void and vision until I find something fresh like water, and comforting like fire; until I find some place in eternity, where I am literally at home. And there is only one such place to be found.

I have now said enough to show (to any one to whom such an explanation is essential) that I have in the ordinary arena of apologetics, a ground of belief. In pure records of experiment (if these be taken democratically without contempt or favour) there is evidence first, that miracles happen, and second that the nobler miracles belong to our tradition. But I will not pretend that this curt discussion is my real reason for accepting Christianity instead of taking the moral good of Christianity as I should take it out of Confucianism.

I have another far more solid and central ground for submitting to it as a faith, instead of merely picking up hints from it as a scheme. And that is this: that the Christian Church in its practical relation to my soul is a living teacher, not a dead one. It not only certainly taught me yesterday, but will almost certainly teach me to-morrow. Once I saw suddenly the meaning of the shape of the cross; some day I may see suddenly the meaning of the shape of the mitre. One fine morning I saw why windows were pointed; some fine morning I may see why priests were shaven. Plato has told you a truth; but Plato is dead. Shakespeare has startled you with an image; but Shakespeare will not startle you with any more. But imagine what it would be to live with such men still living, to know that Plato might break out with an original lecture to-morrow, or that at any moment Shakespeare might shatter everything with a single song. The man who lives in contact with what he believes to be a living Church is a man always expecting to meet Plato and Shakespeare to-morrow at breakfast. He is always expecting to see some truth that he has never seen before. There is one only other parallel to this position; and that is the parallel of the life in which we all began. When your father told you, walking about the garden, that bees stung or that roses smelt sweet, you did not talk of taking the best out of his philosophy. When the bees stung you, you did not call it an entertaining coincidence. When the rose smelt sweet you did not say "My father is a rude, barbaric symbol, enshrining (perhaps unconsciously) the deep delicate truths that flowers smell." No: you believed your father, because you had found him to be a living fountain of facts, a thing that really knew more than you; a thing that would tell you truth to-morrow, as well as to-day. And if this was true of your father, it was even truer of your mother; at least it was true of mine, to whom this book is dedicated. Now, when society is in a rather futile fuss about the subjection of women, will no one say how much every man owes to the tyranny and privilege of women, to the fact that they alone rule education until education becomes futile: for a boy is only sent to be taught at school when it is too late to teach him anything. The real thing has been done already, and thank God it is nearly always done by women. Every man is womanised, merely by being born. They talk of the masculine woman; but every man is a feminised man. And if ever men walk to Westminster to protest against this female privilege, I shall not join their procession.

For I remember with certainty this fixed psychological fact; that the very time when I was most under a woman's authority, I was most full of flame and adventure. Exactly because when my mother said that ants bit they did bite, and because snow did come in winter (as she said); therefore the whole world was to me a fairyland of wonderful fulfilments, and it was like living in some Hebraic age, when prophecy after prophecy came true. I went out as a child into the garden, and it was a terrible place to me, precisely because I had a clue to it: if I had held no clue it would not have been terrible, but tame. A mere unmeaning wilderness is not even impressive. But the garden of childhood was fascinating, exactly because everything had a fixed meaning which could be found out in its turn. Inch by inch I might discover what was the object of the ugly shape called a rake; or form some shadowy conjecture as to why my parents kept a cat.

So, since I have accepted Christendom as a mother and not merely as a chance example, I have found Europe and the world once more like the little garden where I stared at the symbolic shapes of cat and rake; I look at everything with the old elvish ignorance and expectancy. This or that rite or doctrine may look as ugly and extraordinary as a rake; but I have found by experience that such things end somehow in grass and flowers. A clergyman may be apparently as useless as a cat, but he is also as fascinating, for there must be some strange reason for his existence. I give one instance out of a hundred; I have not myself any instinctive kinship with that enthusiasm for physical virginity, which has certainly been a note of historic Christianity. But when I look not at myself but at the world, I perceive that this enthusiasm is not only a note of Christianity, but a note of Paganism, a note of high human nature in many spheres. The Greeks felt virginity when they carved Artemis, the Romans when they robed the vestals, the worst and wildest of the great Elizabethan playwrights clung to the literal purity of a woman as to the central pillar of the world. Above all, the modern world (even while mocking sexual innocence) has flung itself into a generous idolatry of sexual innocence— the great modern worship of children. For any man who loves children will agree that their peculiar beauty is hurt by a hint of physical sex. With all this human experience, allied with the Christian authority, I simply conclude that I am wrong, and the church right; or rather that I am defective, while the church is universal. It takes all sorts to make a church; she does not ask me to be celibate. But the fact that I have no appreciation of the celibates, I accept like the fact that I have no ear for music. The best human experience is against me, as it is on the subject of Bach. Celibacy is one flower in my father's garden, of which I have not been told the sweet or terrible name. But I may be told it any day.

This, therefore, is, in conclusion, my reason for accepting the religion and not merely the scattered and secular truths out of the religion. I do it because the thing has not merely told this truth or that truth, but has revealed itself as a truth-telling thing. All other philosophies say the things that plainly seem to be true; only this philosophy has again and again said the thing that does not seem to be true, but is true. Alone of all creeds it is convincing where it is not attractive; it turns out to be right, like my father in the garden. Theosophists for instance will preach an obviously attractive idea like re-incarnation; but if we wait for its logical results, they are spiritual superciliousness and the cruelty of caste. For if a man is a beggar by his own pre-natal sins, people will tend to despise the beggar. But Christianity preaches an obviously unattractive idea, such as original sin; but when we wait for its results, they are pathos and brotherhood, and a thunder of laughter and pity; for only with original sin we can at once pity the beggar and distrust the king. Men of science offer us health, an obvious benefit; it is only afterwards that we discover that by health, they mean bodily slavery and spiritual tedium. Orthodoxy makes us jump by the sudden brink of hell; it is only afterwards that we realise that jumping was an athletic exercise highly beneficial to our health. It is only afterwards that we realise that this danger is the root of all drama and romance. The strongest argument for the divine grace is simply its ungraciousness. The unpopular parts of Christianity turn out when examined to be the very props of the people. The outer ring of Christianity is a rigid guard of ethical abnegations and professional priests; but inside that inhuman guard you will find the old human life dancing like children, and drinking wine like men; for Christianity is the only frame for pagan freedom. But in the modern philosophy the case is opposite; it is its outer ring that is obviously artistic and emancipated; its despair is within.

And its despair is this, that it does not really believe that there is any meaning in the universe; therefore it cannot hope to find any romance; its romances will have no plots. A man cannot expect any adventures in the land of anarchy. But a man can expect any number of adventures if he goes travelling in the land of authority. One can find no meanings in a jungle of scepticism; but the man will find more and more meanings who walks through a forest of doctrine and design. Here everything has a story tied to its tail, like the tools or pictures in my father's house; for it is my father's house. I end where I began—at the right end. I have entered at last the gate of all good philosophy. I have come into my second childhood.

But this larger and more adventurous Christian universe has one final mark difficult to express; yet as a conclusion of the whole matter I will attempt to express it. All the real argument about religion turns on the question of whether a man who was born upside down can tell when he comes right way up. The primary paradox of Christianity is that the ordinary condition of man is not his sane or sensible condition; that the normal itself is an abnormality. That is the inmost philosophy of the Fall. In Sir Oliver Lodge's interesting new Catechism, the first two questions were: "What are you?" and "What, then, is the meaning of the Fall of Man?" I remember amusing myself by writing my own answers to the questions; but I soon found that they were very broken and agnostic answers. To the question, "What are you?" I could only answer, "God knows." And to the question, "What is meant by the Fall?" I could answer with complete sincerity, "That whatever I am, I am not myself." This is the prime paradox of our religion; something that we have never in any full sense known, is not only better than ourselves, but even more natural to us than ourselves. And there is really no test of this except the merely experimental one with which these pages began, the test of the padded cell and the open door. It is only since I have known orthodoxy that I have known mental emancipation. But, in conclusion, it has one special application to the ultimate idea of joy.

It is said that Paganism is a religion of joy and Christianity of sorrow; it would be just as easy to prove that Paganism is pure sorrow and Christianity pure joy. Such conflicts mean nothing and lead nowhere. Everything human must have in it both joy and sorrow; the only matter of interest is the manner in which the two things are balanced or divided. And the really interesting thing is this, that the pagan was (in the main) happier and happier as he approached the earth, but sadder and sadder as he approached the heavens. The gaiety of the best Paganism, as in the playfulness of Catullus or Theocritus, is, indeed, an eternal gaiety never to be forgotten by a grateful humanity. But it is all a gaiety about the facts of life, not about its origin. To the pagan the small things are as sweet as the small brooks breaking out of the mountain; but the broad things are as bitter as the sea. When the pagan looks at the very core of the cosmos he is struck cold. Behind the gods, who are merely despotic, sit the fates, who are deadly. Nay, the fates are worse than deadly; they are dead. And when rationalists say that the ancient world was more enlightened than the Christian, from their point of view they are right. For when they say "enlightened" they mean darkened with incurable despair. It is profoundly true that the ancient world was more modern than the Christian. The common bond is in the fact that ancients and moderns have both been miserable about existence, about everything, while mediaevals were happy about that at least. I freely grant that the pagans, like the moderns, were only miserable about everything—they were quite jolly about everything else. I concede that the Christians of the Middle Ages were only at peace about everything—they were at war about everything else. But if the question turn on the primary pivot of the cosmos, then there was more cosmic contentment in the narrow and bloody streets of Florence than in the theatre of Athens or the open garden of Epicurus. Giotto lived in a gloomier town than Euripides, but he lived in a gayer universe.

The mass of men have been forced to be gay about the little things, but sad about the big ones. Nevertheless (I offer my last dogma defiantly) it is not native to man to be so. Man is more himself, man is more manlike, when joy is the fundamental thing in him, and grief the superficial. Melancholy should be an innocent interlude, a tender and fugitive frame of mind; praise should be the permanent pulsation of the soul. Pessimism is at best an emotional half-holiday; joy is the uproarious labour by which all things live. Yet, according to the apparent estate of man as seen by the pagan or the agnostic, this primary need of human nature can never be fulfilled. Joy ought to be expansive; but for the agnostic it must be contracted, it must cling to one corner of the world. Grief ought to be a concentration; but for the agnostic its desolation is spread through an unthinkable eternity. This is what I call being born upside down. The sceptic may truly be said to be topsy-turvy; for his feet are dancing upwards in idle ecstasies, while his brain is in the abyss. To the modern man the heavens are actually below the earth. The explanation is simple; he is standing on his head; which is a very weak pedestal to stand on. But when he has found his feet again he knows it. Christianity satisfies suddenly and perfectly man's ancestral instinct for being the right way up; satisfies it supremely in this; that by its creed joy becomes something gigantic and sadness something special and small. The vault above us is not deaf because the universe is an idiot; the silence is not the heartless silence of an endless and aimless world. Rather the silence around us is a small and pitiful stillness like the prompt stillness in a sick-room. We are perhaps permitted tragedy as a sort of merciful comedy: because the frantic energy of divine things would knock us down like a drunken farce. We can take our own tears more lightly than we could take the tremendous levities of the angels. So we sit perhaps in a starry chamber of silence, while the laughter of the heavens is too loud for us to hear.

Joy, which was the small publicity of the pagan, is the gigantic secret of the Christian. And as I close this chaotic volume I open again the strange small book from which all Christianity came; and I am again haunted by a kind of confirmation. The tremendous figure which fills the Gospels towers in this respect, as in every other, above all the thinkers who ever thought themselves tall. His pathos was natural, almost casual. The Stoics, ancient and modern, were proud of concealing their tears. He never concealed His tears; He showed them plainly on His open face at any daily sight, such as the far sight of His native city. Yet He concealed something. Solemn supermen and imperial diplomatists are proud of restraining their anger. He never restrained His anger. He flung furniture down the front steps of the Temple, and asked men how they expected to escape the damnation of Hell. Yet He restrained something. I say it with reverence; there was in that shattering personality a thread that must be called shyness. There was something that He hid from all men when He went up a mountain to pray. There was something that He covered constantly by abrupt silence or impetuous isolation. There was some one thing that was too great for God to show us when He walked upon our earth; and I have sometimes fancied that it was His mirth.

HERETICS

"To My Father"

THE AUTHOR

Gilbert Keith Chesterton was born in London, England on the 29th of May, 1874. Though he considered himself a mere "rollicking journalist," he was actually a prolific and gifted writer in virtually every area of literature. A man of strong opinions and enormously talented at defending them, his exuberant personality nevertheless allowed him to maintain warm friendships with people—such as George Bernard Shaw and H. G. Wells—with whom he vehemently disagreed.

Chesterton had no difficulty standing up for what he believed. He was one of the few journalists to oppose the Boer War. His 1922 "Eugenics and Other Evils" attacked what was at that time the most progressive of all ideas, the idea that the human race could and should breed a superior version of itself. In the Nazi experience, history demonstrated the wisdom of his once "reactionary" views.

His poetry runs the gamut from the comic 1908 "On Running After One's Hat" to dark and serious ballads. During the dark days of 1940, when Britain stood virtually alone against the armed might of Nazi Germany, these lines from his 1911 Ballad of the White Horse were often quoted:

> I tell you naught for your comfort,
> Yea, naught for your desire,
> Save that the sky grows darker yet
> And the sea rises higher.

Though not written for a scholarly audience, his biographies of authors and historical figures like Charles Dickens and St. Francis of Assisi often contain brilliant insights into their subjects. His Father Brown mystery stories, written between 1911 and 1936, are still being read and adapted for television.

His politics fitted with his deep distrust of concentrated wealth and power of any sort. Along with his friend Hilaire Belloc and in books like the 1910 "What's Wrong with the World" he advocated a view called "Distributionism" that was best summed up by his expression that every man ought to be allowed to own "three acres and a cow." Though not known as a political thinker, his political influence has circled the world. Some see in him the father of the "small is beautiful" movement and a newspaper article by him is credited with provoking Gandhi to seek a "genuine" nationalism for India rather than one that imitated the British.

Heretics belongs to yet another area of literature at which Chesterton excelled. A fun-loving and gregarious man, he was nevertheless troubled in his adolescence by thoughts of suicide. In Christianity he found the answers to the dilemmas and paradoxes he saw in life. Other books in that same series include his 1908 Orthodoxy (written in response to attacks on this book) and his 1925 The Everlasting Man. Orthodoxy is also available as electronic text.

Chesterton died on the 14th of June, 1936 in Beaconsfield, Buckinghamshire, England. During his life he published 69 books and at least another ten based on his writings have been published after his death. Many of those books are still in print. Ignatius Press is systematically publishing his collected writings.

I. INTRODUCTORY REMARKS ON THE IMPORTANCE OF ORTHODOXY

Nothing more strangely indicates an enormous and silent evil of modern society than the extraordinary use which is made nowadays of the word "orthodox." In former days the heretic was proud of not being a heretic. It was the kingdoms of the world and the police and the judges who were heretics. He was orthodox. He had no pride in having rebelled against them; they had rebelled against him. The armies with their cruel security, the kings with their cold faces, the decorous processes of State, the reasonable processes of law—all these like sheep had gone astray. The man was proud of being orthodox, was proud of being right. If he stood alone in a howling wilderness he was more than a man; he was a church. He was the centre of the universe; it was round him that the stars swung. All the tortures torn out of forgotten hells could not make him admit that he was heretical. But a few modern phrases have made him boast of it. He says, with a conscious laugh, "I suppose I am very heretical," and looks round for applause. The word "heresy" not only means no longer being wrong; it practically means being clear-headed and courageous. The word "orthodoxy" not only no longer means being right; it practically means being wrong. All this can mean one thing, and one thing only. It means that people care less for whether they are philosophically right. For obviously a man ought to confess himself crazy before he confesses himself heretical. The Bohemian, with a red tie, ought to pique himself on his orthodoxy. The dynamiter, laying a bomb, ought to feel that, whatever else he is, at least he is orthodox.

It is foolish, generally speaking, for a philosopher to set fire to another philosopher in Smithfield Market because they do not agree in their theory of the universe. That was done very frequently in the last decadence of the Middle Ages, and it failed altogether in its object. But there is one thing that is infinitely more absurd and unpractical than burning a man for his philosophy. This is the habit of saying that his philosophy does not matter, and this is done universally in the twentieth century, in the decadence of the great revolutionary period. General theories are everywhere contemned; the doctrine of the Rights of Man is dismissed with the doctrine of the Fall of Man. Atheism itself is too theological for us to-day. Revolution itself is too much of a system; liberty itself is too much of a restraint. We will have no generalizations. Mr. Bernard Shaw has put the view in a perfect epigram: "The golden rule is that there is no golden rule." We are more and more to discuss details in art, politics, literature. A man's opinion on tramcars matters; his opinion on Botticelli matters; his opinion on all things does not matter. He may turn over and explore a million objects, but he must not find that strange object, the universe; for if he does he will have a religion, and be lost. Everything matters—except everything.

Examples are scarcely needed of this total levity on the subject of cosmic philosophy. Examples are scarcely needed to show that, whatever else we think of as affecting practical affairs, we do not think it matters whether a man is a pessimist or an optimist, a Cartesian or a Hegelian, a materialist or a spiritualist. Let me, however, take a random instance. At any innocent tea-table we may easily hear a man say, "Life is not worth living." We regard it as we regard the statement that it is a fine day; nobody thinks that it can possibly have any serious effect on the man or on the world. And yet if that utterance were really believed, the world would stand on its head. Murderers would be given medals for saving men from life; firemen would be denounced for keeping men from death; poisons would be used as medicines; doctors would be called in when people were well; the Royal Humane Society would be rooted out like a horde of assassins. Yet we never speculate as to whether the conversational pessimist will strengthen or disorganize society; for we are convinced that theories do not matter.

This was certainly not the idea of those who introduced our freedom. When the old Liberals removed the gags from all the heresies, their idea was that religious and philosophical discoveries might thus be made. Their view was that cosmic truth was so important that every one ought to bear independent testimony. The modern idea is that cosmic truth is so unimportant that it cannot matter what any one says. The former freed inquiry as men loose a noble hound; the latter frees inquiry as men fling back into the sea a fish unfit for eating. Never has there been so little discussion about the nature of men as now, when, for the first time, any one can discuss it. The old restriction meant that only the orthodox were allowed to discuss religion. Modern liberty means that nobody is allowed to discuss it. Good taste, the last and vilest of human superstitions, has succeeded in silencing us where all the rest have failed. Sixty years ago it was bad taste to be an avowed atheist. Then came the Bradlaughites, the last religious men, the last men who cared about God; but they could not alter it. It is still bad taste to be an avowed atheist. But their agony has achieved just his—that now it is equally bad taste to be an avowed Christian. Emancipation has only locked the saint in the same tower of silence as the heresiarch. Then we talk about Lord Anglesey and the weather, and call it the complete liberty of all the creeds.

But there are some people, nevertheless—and I am one of them—who think that the most practical and important thing about a man is still his view of the universe. We think that for a landlady considering a lodger, it is important to know his income, but still more important to know his philosophy. We think that for a general about to fight an enemy, it is important to know the enemy's numbers, but still more important to know the enemy's philosophy. We think the question is not whether the theory of the cosmos affects matters, but whether in the long run, anything else affects them. In the fifteenth century men cross-examined and tormented a man because he preached some immoral attitude; in the nineteenth century we feted and flattered Oscar Wilde because he preached such an attitude, and then broke his heart in penal servitude because he carried it out. It may be a question which of the two methods was the more cruel; there can be no kind of question which was the more ludicrous. The age of the Inquisition has not at least the disgrace of having produced a society which made an idol of the very same man for preaching the very same things which it made him a convict for practising.

Now, in our time, philosophy or religion, our theory, that is, about ultimate things, has been driven out, more or less simultaneously, from two fields which it used to occupy. General ideals used to dominate literature. They have been driven out by the cry of "art for art's sake." General ideals used to dominate politics. They have been driven out by the cry of "efficiency," which may roughly be translated as "politics for politics' sake." Persistently for the last twenty years the ideals of order or liberty have dwindled in our books; the ambitions of wit and eloquence have dwindled in our parliaments. Literature has purposely become less political; politics have purposely become less literary. General theories of the relation of things have thus been extruded from both; and we are in a position to ask, "What have we gained or lost by this extrusion? Is literature better, is politics better, for having discarded the moralist and the philosopher?"

When everything about a people is for the time growing weak and ineffective, it begins to talk about efficiency. So it is that when a man's body is a wreck he begins, for the first time, to talk about health. Vigorous organisms talk not about their processes, but about their aims. There cannot be any better proof of the physical efficiency of a man than that he talks cheerfully of a journey to the end of the world. And there cannot be any better proof of the practical efficiency of a nation than that it talks constantly of a journey to the end of the world, a journey to the Judgment Day and the New Jerusalem. There can be no stronger sign of a coarse material health than the tendency to run after high and wild ideals; it is in the first exuberance of infancy that we cry for the moon. None of the strong men in the strong ages would have understood what you meant by working for efficiency. Hildebrand would have said that he was working not for efficiency, but for the Catholic Church. Danton would have said that he was working not for efficiency, but for liberty, equality, and fraternity. Even if the ideal of such men were simply the ideal of kicking a man downstairs, they thought of the end like men, not of the process like paralytics. They did not say, "Efficiently elevating my right leg, using, you will notice, the muscles of the thigh and calf, which are in excellent order, I—" Their feeling was quite different. They were so filled with the beautiful vision of the man lying flat at the foot of the staircase that in that ecstasy the rest followed in a flash. In practice, the habit of generalizing and idealizing did not by any means mean worldly weakness. The time of big theories was the time of big results. In the era of sentiment and fine words, at the end of the eighteenth century, men were really robust and effective. The sentimentalists conquered Napoleon. The cynics could not catch De Wet. A hundred years ago our affairs for good or evil were wielded triumphantly by rhetoricians. Now our affairs are hopelessly muddled by strong, silent men. And just as this repudiation of big words and big visions has brought forth a race of small men in politics, so it has brought forth a race of small men in the arts. Our modern politicians claim the colossal license of Caesar and the Superman, claim that they are too practical to be pure and too patriotic to be moral; but the upshot of it all is that a mediocrity is Chancellor of the Exchequer. Our new artistic philosophers call for the same moral license, for a freedom to wreck heaven and earth with their energy; but the upshot of it all is that a mediocrity is Poet Laureate. I do not say that there are no stronger men than these; but will any one say that there are any men stronger than those men of old who were dominated by their philosophy and steeped in their religion? Whether bondage be better than freedom may be discussed. But that their bondage came to more than our freedom it will be difficult for any one to deny.

The theory of the unmorality of art has established itself firmly in the strictly artistic classes. They are free to produce anything they like. They are free to write a "Paradise Lost" in which Satan shall conquer God. They are free to write a "Divine Comedy" in which heaven shall be under the floor of hell. And what have they done? Have they produced in their universality anything grander or more beautiful than the things uttered by the fierce Ghibbeline Catholic, by the rigid Puritan schoolmaster? We know that they have produced only a few roundels. Milton does not merely beat them at his piety, he beats them at their own irreverence. In all their little books of verse you will not find a finer defiance of God than Satan's. Nor will you find the grandeur of paganism felt as that fiery Christian felt it who described Faranata lifting his head as in disdain of hell. And the reason is very obvious. Blasphemy is an artistic effect, because blasphemy depends upon a philosophical conviction. Blasphemy depends upon belief and is fading with it. If any one doubts this, let him sit down seriously and try to think blasphemous thoughts about Thor. I think his family will find him at the end of the day in a state of some exhaustion.

Neither in the world of politics nor that of literature, then, has the rejection of general theories proved a success. It may be that there have been many moonstruck and misleading ideals that have from time to time perplexed mankind. But assuredly there has been no ideal in practice so moonstruck and misleading as the ideal of practicality. Nothing has lost so many opportunities as the opportunism of Lord Rosebery. He is, indeed, a standing symbol of this epoch—the man who is theoretically a practical man, and practically more unpractical than any theorist. Nothing in this universe is so unwise as that kind of worship of worldly wisdom. A man who is perpetually thinking of whether this race or that race is strong, of whether this cause or that cause is promising, is the man who will never believe in anything long enough to make it succeed. The opportunist politician is like a man who should abandon billiards because he was beaten at billiards, and abandon golf because he was beaten at golf. There is nothing which is so weak for working purposes as this enormous importance attached to immediate victory. There is nothing that fails like success.

And having discovered that opportunism does fail, I have been induced to look at it more largely, and in consequence to see that it must fail. I perceive that it is far more practical to begin at the beginning and discuss theories. I see that the men who killed each other about the orthodoxy of the Homoousion were far more sensible than the people who are quarrelling about the Education Act. For the Christian dogmatists were trying to establish a reign of holiness, and trying to get defined, first of all, what was really holy. But our modern educationists are trying to bring about a religious liberty without attempting to settle what is religion or what is liberty. If the old priests forced a statement on mankind, at least they previously took some trouble to make it lucid. It has been left for the modern mobs of Anglicans and Nonconformists to persecute for a doctrine without even stating it.

For these reasons, and for many more, I for one have come to believe in going back to fundamentals. Such is the general idea of this book. I wish to deal with my most distinguished contemporaries, not personally or in a merely literary manner, but in relation to the real body of doctrine which they teach. I am not concerned with Mr. Rudyard Kipling as a vivid artist or a vigorous personality; I am concerned with him as a Heretic—that is to say, a man whose view of things has the hardihood to differ from mine. I am not concerned with Mr. Bernard Shaw as one of the most brilliant and one of the most honest men alive; I am concerned with him as a Heretic—that is to say, a man whose philosophy is quite solid, quite coherent, and quite wrong. I revert to the doctrinal methods of the thirteenth century, inspired by the general hope of getting something done.

Suppose that a great commotion arises in the street about something, let us say a lamp-post, which many influential persons desire to pull down. A grey-clad monk, who is the spirit of the Middle Ages, is approached upon the matter, and begins to say, in the arid manner of the Schoolmen, "Let us first of all consider, my brethren, the value of Light. If Light be in itself good—" At this point he is somewhat excusably knocked down. All the people make a rush for the lamp-post, the lamp-post is down in ten minutes, and they go about congratulating each other on their unmediaeval practicality. But as things go on they do not work out so easily. Some people have pulled the lamp-post down because they wanted the electric light; some because they wanted old iron; some because they wanted darkness, because their deeds were evil. Some thought it not enough of a lamp-post, some too much; some acted because they wanted to smash municipal machinery; some because they wanted to smash something. And there is war in the night, no man knowing whom he strikes. So, gradually and inevitably, to-day, to-morrow, or the next day, there comes back the conviction that the monk was right after all, and that all depends on what is the philosophy of Light. Only what we might have discussed under the gas-lamp, we now must discuss in the dark.

II. ON THE NEGATIVE SPIRIT

Much has been said, and said truly, of the monkish morbidity, of the hysteria which as often gone with the visions of hermits or nuns. But let us never forget that this visionary religion is, in one sense, necessarily more wholesome than our modern and reasonable morality. It is more wholesome for this reason, that it can contemplate the idea of success or triumph in the hopeless fight towards the ethical ideal, in what Stevenson called, with his usual startling felicity, "the lost fight of virtue." A modern morality, on the other hand, can only point with absolute conviction to the horrors that follow breaches of law; its only certainty is a certainty of ill. It can only point to imperfection. It has no perfection to point to. But the monk meditating upon Christ or Buddha has in his mind an image of perfect health, a thing of clear colours and clean air. He may contemplate this ideal wholeness and happiness far more than he ought; he may contemplate it to the neglect of exclusion of essential THINGS he may contemplate it until he has become a dreamer or a driveller; but still it is wholeness and happiness that he is contemplating. He may even go mad; but he is going mad for the love of sanity. But the modern student of ethics, even if he remains sane, remains sane from an insane dread of insanity.

The anchorite rolling on the stones in a frenzy of submission is a healthier person fundamentally than many a sober man in a silk hat who is walking down Cheapside. For many such are good only through a withering knowledge of evil. I am not at this moment claiming for the devotee anything more than this primary advantage, that though he may be making himself personally weak and miserable, he is still fixing his thoughts largely on gigantic strength and happiness, on a strength that has no limits, and a happiness that has no end. Doubtless there are other objections which can be urged without unreason against the influence of gods and visions in morality, whether in the cell or street. But this advantage the mystic morality must always have—it is always jollier. A young man may keep himself from vice by continually thinking of disease. He may keep himself from it also by continually thinking of the Virgin Mary. There may be question about which method is the more reasonable, or even about which is the more efficient. But surely there can be no question about which is the more wholesome.

I remember a pamphlet by that able and sincere secularist, Mr. G. W. Foote, which contained a phrase sharply symbolizing and dividing these two methods. The pamphlet was called BEER AND BIBLE, those two very noble things, all the nobler for a conjunction which Mr. Foote, in his stern old Puritan way, seemed to think sardonic, but which I confess to thinking appropriate and charming. I have not the work by me, but I remember that Mr. Foote dismissed very contemptuously any attempts to deal with the problem of strong drink by religious offices or intercessions, and said that a picture of a drunkard's liver would be more efficacious in the matter of temperance than any prayer or praise. In that picturesque expression, it seems to me, is perfectly embodied the incurable morbidity of modern ethics. In that temple the lights are low, the crowds kneel, the solemn anthems are uplifted. But that upon the altar to which all men kneel is no longer the perfect flesh, the body and substance of the perfect man; it is still flesh, but it is diseased. It is the drunkard's liver of the New Testament that is marred for us, which we take in remembrance of him.

Now, it is this great gap in modern ethics, the absence of vivid pictures of purity and spiritual triumph, which lies at the back of the real objection felt by so many sane men to the realistic literature of the nineteenth century. If any ordinary man ever said that he was horrified by the subjects discussed in Ibsen or Maupassant, or by the plain language in which they are spoken of, that ordinary man was lying. The average conversation of average men throughout the whole of modern civilization in every class or trade is such as Zola would never dream of printing. Nor is the habit of writing thus of these things a new habit. On the contrary, it is the Victorian prudery and silence which is new still, though it is already dying. The tradition of calling a spade a spade starts very early in our literature and comes down very late. But the truth is that the ordinary honest man, whatever vague account he may have given of his feelings, was not either disgusted or even annoyed at the candour of the moderns. What disgusted him, and very justly, was not the presence of a clear realism, but the absence of a clear idealism. Strong and genuine religious sentiment has never had any objection to realism; on the contrary, religion was the realistic thing, the brutal thing, the thing that called names. This is the great difference between some recent developments of Nonconformity and the great Puritanism of the seventeenth century. It was the whole point of the Puritans that they cared nothing for decency. Modern Nonconformist newspapers distinguish themselves by suppressing precisely those nouns and adjectives which the founders of Nonconformity distinguished themselves by flinging at kings and queens. But if it was a chief claim of religion that it spoke plainly about evil, it was the chief claim of all that it spoke plainly about good. The thing which is resented, and, as I think, rightly resented, in that great modern literature of which Ibsen is typical, is that while the eye that can perceive what are the wrong things increases in an uncanny and devouring clarity, the eye which sees what things are right is growing mistier and mistier every moment, till it goes almost blind with doubt. If we compare, let us say, the morality of the DIVINE COMEDY with the morality of Ibsen's GHOSTS, we shall see all that modern ethics have really done. No one, I imagine, will accuse the author of the INFERNO of an Early Victorian prudishness or a Podsnapian optimism. But Dante describes three moral instruments—Heaven, Purgatory, and Hell, the vision of perfection, the vision of improvement, and the vision of failure. Ibsen has only one—Hell. It is often said, and with perfect truth, that no one could read a play like GHOSTS and remain indifferent to the necessity of an ethical self-command. That is quite true, and the same is to be said of the most monstrous and material descriptions of the eternal fire. It is quite certain the realists like Zola do in one sense promote morality—they promote it in the sense in which the hangman promotes it, in the sense in which the devil promotes it. But they only affect that small minority which will accept any virtue of courage. Most healthy people dismiss these moral dangers as they dismiss the possibility of bombs or microbes. Modern realists are indeed Terrorists, like the dynamiters; and they fail just as much in their effort to create a thrill. Both realists and dynamiters are well-meaning people engaged in the task, so obviously ultimately hopeless, of using science to promote morality.

I do not wish the reader to confuse me for a moment with those vague persons who imagine that Ibsen is what they call a pessimist. There are plenty of wholesome people in Ibsen, plenty of good people, plenty of happy people, plenty of examples of men acting wisely and things ending well. That is not my meaning. My meaning is that Ibsen has throughout, and does not disguise, a certain vagueness and a changing attitude as well as a doubting attitude towards what is really wisdom and virtue in this life—a vagueness which contrasts very remarkably with the decisiveness with which he pounces on something which he perceives to be a root of evil, some convention, some deception, some ignorance. We know that the hero of GHOSTS is mad, and we know why he is mad. We do also know that Dr. Stockman is sane; but we do not know why he is sane. Ibsen does not profess to know how virtue and happiness are brought about, in the sense that he professes to know how our modern sexual tragedies are brought about. Falsehood works ruin in THE PILLARS OF SOCIETY, but truth works equal ruin in THE WILD DUCK. There are no cardinal virtues of Ibsenism. There is no ideal man of Ibsen. All this is not only admitted, but vaunted in the most valuable and thoughtful of all the eulogies upon Ibsen, Mr. Bernard Shaw's QUINTESSENCE OF IBSENISM. Mr. Shaw sums up Ibsen's teaching in the phrase, "The golden rule is that there is no golden rule." In his eyes this absence of an enduring and positive ideal, this absence of a permanent key to virtue, is the one great Ibsen merit. I am not discussing now with any fullness whether this is so or not. All I venture to point out, with an increased firmness, is that this omission, good or bad, does leave us face to face with the problem of a human consciousness filled with very definite images of evil, and with no definite image of good. To us light must be henceforward the dark thing—the thing of which we cannot speak. To us, as to Milton's devils in Pandemonium, it is darkness that is visible. The human race, according to religion, fell once, and in falling gained knowledge of good and of evil. Now we have fallen a second time, and only the knowledge of evil remains to us.

A great silent collapse, an enormous unspoken disappointment, has in our time fallen on our Northern civilization. All previous ages have sweated and been crucified in an attempt to realize what is really the right life, what was really the good man. A definite part of the modern world has come beyond question to the conclusion that there is no answer to these questions, that the most that we can do is to set up a few notice-boards at places of obvious danger, to warn men, for instance, against drinking themselves to death, or ignoring the mere existence of their neighbours. Ibsen is the first to return from the baffled hunt to bring us the tidings of great failure.

Every one of the popular modern phrases and ideals is a dodge in order to shirk the problem of what is good. We are fond of talking about "liberty"; that, as we talk of it, is a dodge to avoid discussing what is good. We are fond of talking about "progress"; that is a dodge to avoid discussing what is good. We are fond of talking about "education"; that is a dodge to avoid discussing what is good. The modern man says, "Let us leave all these arbitrary standards and embrace liberty." This is, logically rendered, "Let us not decide what is good, but let it be considered good not to decide it." He says, "Away with your old moral formulae; I am for progress." This, logically stated, means, "Let us not settle what is good; but let us settle whether we are getting more of it." He says, "Neither in religion nor morality, my friend, lie the hopes of the race, but in education." This, clearly expressed, means, "We cannot decide what is good, but let us give it to our children."

Mr. H.G. Wells, that exceedingly clear-sighted man, has pointed out in a recent work that this has happened in connection with economic questions. The old economists, he says, made generalizations, and they were (in Mr. Wells's view) mostly wrong. But the new economists, he says, seem to have lost the power of making any generalizations at all. And they cover this incapacity with a general claim to be, in specific cases, regarded as "experts", a claim "proper enough in a hairdresser or a fashionable physician, but indecent in a philosopher or a man of science." But in spite of the refreshing rationality with which Mr. Wells has indicated this, it must also be said that he himself has fallen into the same enormous modern error. In the opening pages of that excellent book MANKIND IN THE MAKING, he dismisses the ideals of art, religion, abstract morality, and the rest, and says that he is going to consider men in their chief function, the function of parenthood. He is going to discuss life as a "tissue of births." He is not going to ask what will produce satisfactory saints or satisfactory heroes, but what will produce satisfactory fathers and mothers. The whole is set forward so sensibly that it is a few moments at least before the reader realises that it is another example of unconscious shirking. What is the good of begetting a man until we have settled what is the good of being a man? You are merely handing on to him a problem you dare not settle yourself. It is as if a man were asked, "What is the use of a hammer?" and answered, "To make hammers"; and when asked, "And of those hammers, what is the use?" answered, "To make hammers again". Just as such a man would be perpetually putting off the question of the ultimate use of carpentry, so Mr. Wells and all the rest of us are by these phrases successfully putting off the question of the ultimate value of the human life.

The case of the general talk of "progress" is, indeed, an extreme one. As enunciated today, "progress" is simply a comparative of which we have not settled the superlative. We meet every ideal of religion, patriotism, beauty, or brute pleasure with the alternative ideal of progress—that is to say, we meet every proposal of getting something that we know about, with an alternative proposal of getting a great deal more of nobody knows what. Progress, properly understood, has, indeed, a most dignified and legitimate meaning. But as used in opposition to pre-precise moral ideals, it is ludicrous. So far from it being the truth that the ideal of progress is to be set against that of ethical or religious finality, the reverse is the truth. Nobody has any business to use the word "progress" unless he has a definite creed and a cast-iron code of morals. Nobody can be progressive without being doctrinal; I might almost say that nobody can be progressive without being infallible—at any rate, without believing in some infallibility. For progress by its very name indicates a direction; and the moment we are in the least doubtful about the direction, we become in the same degree doubtful about the progress. Never perhaps since the beginning of the world has there been an age that had less right to use the word "progress" than we. In the Catholic twelfth century, in the philosophic eighteenth century, the direction may have been a good or a bad one, men may have differed more or less about how far they went, and in what direction, but about the direction they did in the main agree, and consequently they had the genuine sensation of progress. But it is precisely about the direction that we disagree. Whether the future excellence lies in more law or less law, in more liberty or less liberty; whether property will be finally concentrated or finally cut up; whether sexual passion will reach its sanest in an almost virgin intellectualism or in a full animal freedom; whether we should love everybody with Tolstoy, or spare nobody with Nietzsche;—these are the things about which we are actually fighting most. It is not merely true that the age which has settled least what is progress is this "progressive" age. It is, moreover, true that the people who have settled least what is progress are the most "progressive" people in it. The ordinary mass, the men who have never troubled about progress, might be trusted perhaps to progress. The particular individuals who talk about progress would certainly fly to the four winds of heaven when the pistol-shot started the race. I do not, therefore, say that the word "progress" is unmeaning; I say it is unmeaning without the previous definition of a moral doctrine, and that it can only be applied to groups of persons who hold that doctrine in common. Progress is not an illegitimate word, but it is logically evident that it is illegitimate for us. It is a sacred word, a word which could only rightly be used by rigid believers and in the ages of faith.

III. ON MR. RUDYARD KIPLING AND MAKING THE WORLD SMALL

There is no such thing on earth as an uninteresting subject; the only thing that can exist is an uninterested person. Nothing is more keenly required than a defence of bores. When Byron divided humanity into the bores and bored, he omitted to notice that the higher qualities exist entirely in the bores, the lower qualities in the bored, among whom he counted himself. The bore, by his starry enthusiasm, his solemn happiness, may, in some sense, have proved himself poetical. The bored has certainly proved himself prosaic.

We might, no doubt, find it a nuisance to count all the blades of grass or all the leaves of the trees; but this would not be because of our boldness or gaiety, but because of our lack of boldness and gaiety. The bore would go onward, bold and gay, and find the blades of grass as splendid as the swords of an army. The bore is stronger and more joyous than we are; he is a demigod—nay, he is a god. For it is the gods who do not tire of the iteration of things; to them the nightfall is always new, and the last rose as red as the first.

The sense that everything is poetical is a thing solid and absolute; it is not a mere matter of phraseology or persuasion. It is not merely true, it is ascertainable. Men may be challenged to deny it; men may be challenged to mention anything that is not a matter of poetry. I remember a long time ago a sensible sub-editor coming up to me with a book in his hand, called "Mr. Smith," or "The Smith Family," or some such thing. He said, "Well, you won't get any of your damned mysticism out of this," or words to that effect. I am happy to say that I undeceived him; but the victory was too obvious and easy. In most cases the name is unpoetical, although the fact is poetical. In the case of Smith, the name is so poetical that it must be an arduous and heroic matter for the man to live up to it. The name of Smith is the name of the one trade that even kings respected, it could claim half the glory of that arma virumque which all epics acclaimed. The spirit of the smithy is so close to the spirit of song that it has mixed in a million poems, and every blacksmith is a harmonious blacksmith.

Even the village children feel that in some dim way the smith is poetic, as the grocer and the cobbler are not poetic, when they feast on the dancing sparks and deafening blows in the cavern of that creative violence. The brute repose of Nature, the passionate cunning of man, the strongest of earthly metals, the wierdest of earthly elements, the unconquerable iron subdued by its only conqueror, the wheel and the ploughshare, the sword and the steam-hammer, the arraying of armies and the whole legend of arms, all these things are written, briefly indeed, but quite legibly, on the visiting-card of Mr. Smith. Yet our novelists call their hero "Aylmer Valence," which means nothing, or "Vernon Raymond," which means nothing, when it is in their power to give him this sacred name of Smith—this name made of iron and flame. It would be very natural if a certain hauteur, a certain carriage of the head, a certain curl of the lip, distinguished every one whose name is Smith. Perhaps it does; I trust so. Whoever else are parvenus, the Smiths are not parvenus. From the darkest dawn of history this clan has gone forth to battle; its trophies are on every hand; its name is everywhere; it is older than the nations, and its sign is the Hammer of Thor. But as I also remarked, it is not quite the usual case. It is common enough that common things should be poetical; it is not so common that common names should be poetical. In most cases it is the name that is the obstacle. A great many people talk as if this claim of ours, that all things are poetical, were a mere literary ingenuity, a play on words. Precisely the contrary is true. It is the idea that some things are not poetical which is literary, which is a mere product of words. The word "signal-box" is unpoetical. But the thing signal-box is not unpoetical; it is a place where men, in an agony of vigilance, light blood-red and sea-green fires to keep other men from death. That is the plain, genuine description of what it is; the prose only comes in with what it is called. The word "pillar-box" is unpoetical. But the thing pillar-box is not unpoetical; it is the place to which friends and lovers commit their messages, conscious that when they have done so they are sacred, and not to be touched, not only by others, but even (religious touch!) by themselves. That red turret is one of the last of the temples. Posting a letter and getting married are among the few things left that are entirely romantic; for to be entirely romantic a thing must be irrevocable. We think a pillar-box prosaic, because there is no rhyme to it. We think a pillar-box unpoetical, because we have never seen it in a poem. But the bold fact is entirely on the side of poetry. A signal-box is only called a signal-box; it is a house of life and death. A pillar-box is only called a pillar-box; it is a sanctuary of human words. If you think the name of "Smith" prosaic, it is not because you are practical and sensible; it is because you are too much affected with literary refinements. The name shouts poetry at you. If you think of it otherwise, it is because you are steeped and sodden with verbal reminiscences, because you remember everything in Punch or Comic Cuts about Mr. Smith being drunk or Mr. Smith being henpecked. All these things were given to you poetical. It is only by a long and elaborate process of literary effort that you have made them prosaic.

Now, the first and fairest thing to say about Rudyard Kipling is that he has borne a brilliant part in thus recovering the lost provinces of poetry. He has not been frightened by that brutal materialistic air which clings only to words; he has pierced through to the romantic, imaginative matter of the things themselves. He has perceived the significance and philosophy of steam and of slang. Steam may be, if you like, a dirty by-product of science. Slang may be, if you like, a dirty by-product of language. But at least he has been among the few who saw the divine parentage of these things, and knew that where there is smoke there is fire—that is, that wherever there is the foulest of things, there also is the purest. Above all, he has had something to say, a definite view of things to utter, and that always means that a man is fearless and faces everything. For the moment we have a view of the universe, we possess it.

Now, the message of Rudyard Kipling, that upon which he has really concentrated, is the only thing worth worrying about in him or in any other man. He has often written bad poetry, like Wordsworth. He has often said silly things, like Plato. He has often given way to mere political hysteria, like Gladstone. But no one can reasonably doubt that he means steadily and sincerely to say something, and the only serious question is, What is that which he has tried to say? Perhaps the best way of stating this fairly will be to begin with that element which has been most insisted by himself and by his opponents—I mean his interest in militarism. But when we are seeking for the real merits of a man it is unwise to go to his enemies, and much more foolish to go to himself.

Now, Mr. Kipling is certainly wrong in his worship of militarism, but his opponents are, generally speaking, quite as wrong as he. The evil of militarism is not that it shows certain men to be fierce and haughty and excessively warlike. The evil of militarism is that it shows most men to be tame and timid and excessively peaceable. The professional soldier gains more and more power as the general courage of a community declines. Thus the Pretorian guard became more and more important in Rome as Rome became more and more luxurious and feeble. The military man gains the civil power in proportion as the civilian loses the military virtues. And as it was in ancient Rome so it is in contemporary Europe. There never was a time when nations were more militarist. There never was a time when men were less brave. All ages and all epics have sung of arms and the man; but we have effected simultaneously the deterioration of the man and the fantastic perfection of the arms. Militarism demonstrated the decadence of Rome, and it demonstrates the decadence of Prussia.

And unconsciously Mr. Kipling has proved this, and proved it admirably. For in so far as his work is earnestly understood the military trade does not by any means emerge as the most important or attractive. He has not written so well about soldiers as he has about railway men or bridge builders, or even journalists. The fact is that what attracts Mr. Kipling to militarism is not the idea of courage, but the idea of discipline. There was far more courage to the square mile in the Middle Ages, when no king had a standing army, but every man had a bow or sword. But the fascination of the standing army upon Mr. Kipling is not courage, which scarcely interests him, but discipline, which is, when all is said and done, his primary theme. The modern army is not a miracle of courage; it has not enough opportunities, owing to the cowardice of everybody else. But it is really a miracle of organization, and that is the truly Kiplingite ideal. Kipling's subject is not that valour which properly belongs to war, but that interdependence and efficiency which belongs quite as much to engineers, or sailors, or mules, or railway engines. And thus it is that when he writes of engineers, or sailors, or mules, or steam-engines, he writes at his best. The real poetry, the "true romance" which Mr. Kipling has taught, is the romance of the division of labour and the discipline of all the trades. He sings the arts of peace much more accurately than the arts of war. And his main contention is vital and valuable. Every thing is military in the sense that everything depends upon obedience. There is no perfectly epicurean corner; there is no perfectly irresponsible place. Everywhere men have made the way for us with sweat and submission. We may fling ourselves into a hammock in a fit of divine carelessness. But we are glad that the net-maker did not make the hammock in a fit of divine carelessness. We may jump upon a child's rocking-horse for a joke. But we are glad that the carpenter did not leave the legs of it unglued for a joke. So far from having merely preached that a soldier cleaning his side-arm is to be adored because he is military, Kipling at his best and clearest has preached that the baker baking loaves and the tailor cutting coats is as military as anybody.

Being devoted to this multitudinous vision of duty, Mr. Kipling is naturally a cosmopolitan. He happens to find his examples in the British Empire, but almost any other empire would do as well, or, indeed, any other highly civilized country. That which he admires in the British army he would find even more apparent in the German army; that which he desires in the British police he would find flourishing, in the French police. The ideal of discipline is not the whole of life, but it is spread over the whole of the world. And the worship of it tends to confirm in Mr. Kipling a certain note of worldly wisdom, of the experience of the wanderer, which is one of the genuine charms of his best work.

The great gap in his mind is what may be roughly called the lack of patriotism—that is to say, he lacks altogether the faculty of attaching himself to any cause or community finally and tragically; for all finality must be tragic. He admires England, but he does not love her; for we admire things with reasons, but love them without reasons. He admires England because she is strong, not because she is English. There is no harshness in saying this, for, to do him justice, he avows it with his usual picturesque candour. In a very interesting poem, he says that—

"If England was what England seems"

—that is, weak and inefficient; if England were not what (as he believes) she is—that is, powerful and practical—

"How quick we'd chuck 'er! But she ain't!"

He admits, that is, that his devotion is the result of a criticism, and this is quite enough to put it in another category altogether from the patriotism of the Boers, whom he hounded down in South Africa. In speaking of the really patriotic peoples, such as the Irish, he has some difficulty in keeping a shrill irritation out of his language. The frame of mind which he really describes with beauty and nobility is the frame of mind of the cosmopolitan man who has seen men and cities.

"For to admire and for to see,
For to be'old this world so wide."

He is a perfect master of that light melancholy with which a man looks back on having been the citizen of many communities, of that light melancholy with which a man looks back on having been the lover of many women. He is the philanderer of the nations. But a man may have learnt much about women in flirtations, and still be ignorant of first love; a man may have known as many lands as Ulysses, and still be ignorant of patriotism.

Mr. Rudyard Kipling has asked in a celebrated epigram what they can know of England who know England only. It is a far deeper and sharper question to ask, "What can they know of England who know only the world?" for the world does not include England any more than it includes the Church. The moment we care for anything deeply, the world—that is, all the other miscellaneous interests—becomes our enemy. Christians showed it when they talked of keeping one's self "unspotted from the world;" but lovers talk of it just as much when they talk of the "world well lost." Astronomically speaking, I understand that England is situated on the world; similarly, I suppose that the Church was a part of the world, and even the lovers inhabitants of that orb. But they all felt a certain truth—the truth that the moment you love anything the world becomes your foe. Thus Mr. Kipling does certainly know the world; he is a man of the world, with all the narrowness that belongs to those imprisoned in that planet. He knows England as an intelligent English gentleman knows Venice. He has been to England a great many times; he has stopped there for long visits. But he does not belong to it, or to any place; and the proof of it is this, that he thinks of England as a place. The moment we are rooted in a place, the place vanishes. We live like a tree with the whole strength of the universe.

The globe-trotter lives in a smaller world than the peasant. He is always breathing, an air of locality. London is a place, to be compared to Chicago; Chicago is a place, to be compared to Timbuctoo. But Timbuctoo is not a place, since there, at least, live men who regard it as the universe, and breathe, not an air of locality, but the winds of the world. The man in the saloon steamer has seen all the races of men, and he is thinking of the things that divide men—diet, dress, decorum, rings in the nose as in Africa, or in the ears as in Europe, blue paint among the ancients, or red paint among the modern Britons. The man in the cabbage field has seen nothing at all; but he is thinking of the things that unite men—hunger and babies, and the beauty of women, and the promise or menace of the sky. Mr. Kipling, with all his merits, is the globe-trotter; he has not the patience to become part of anything. So great and genuine a man is not to be accused of a merely cynical cosmopolitanism; still, his cosmopolitanism is his weakness. That weakness is splendidly expressed in one of his finest poems, "The Sestina of the Tramp Royal," in which a man declares that he can endure anything in the way of hunger or horror, but not permanent presence in one place. In this there is certainly danger. The more dead and dry and dusty a thing is the more it travels about; dust is like this and the thistle-down and the High Commissioner in South Africa. Fertile things are somewhat heavier, like the heavy fruit trees on the pregnant mud of the Nile. In the heated idleness of youth we were all rather inclined to quarrel with the implication of that proverb which says that a rolling stone gathers no moss. We were inclined to ask, "Who wants to gather moss, except silly old ladies?" But for all that we begin to perceive that the proverb is right. The rolling stone rolls echoing from rock to rock; but the rolling stone is dead. The moss is silent because the moss is alive.

The truth is that exploration and enlargement make the world smaller. The telegraph and the steamboat make the world smaller. The telescope makes the world smaller; it is only the microscope that makes it larger. Before long the world will be cloven with a war between the telescopists and the microscopists. The first study large things and live in a small world; the second study small things and live in a large world. It is inspiriting without doubt to whizz in a motor-car round the earth, to feel Arabia as a whirl of sand or China as a flash of rice-fields. But Arabia is not a whirl of sand and China is not a flash of rice-fields. They are ancient civilizations with strange virtues buried like treasures. If we wish to understand them it must not be as tourists or inquirers, it must be with the loyalty of children and the great patience of poets. To conquer these places is to lose them. The man standing in his own kitchen-garden, with fairyland opening at the gate, is the man with large ideas. His mind creates distance; the motor-car stupidly destroys it. Moderns think of the earth as a globe, as something one can easily get round, the spirit of a schoolmistress. This is shown in the odd mistake perpetually made about Cecil Rhodes. His enemies say that he may have had large ideas, but he was a bad man. His friends say that he may have been a bad man, but he certainly had large ideas. The truth is that he was not a man essentially bad, he was a man of much geniality and many good intentions, but a man with singularly small views. There is nothing large about painting the map red; it is an innocent game for children. It is just as easy to think in continents as to think in cobble-stones. The difficulty comes in when we seek to know the substance of either of them. Rhodes' prophecies about the Boer resistance are an admirable comment on how the "large ideas" prosper when it is not a question of thinking in continents but of understanding a few two-legged men. And under all this vast illusion of the cosmopolitan planet, with its empires and its Reuter's agency, the real life of man goes on concerned with this tree or that temple, with this harvest or that drinking-song, totally uncomprehended, totally untouched. And it watches from its splendid parochialism, possibly with a smile of amusement, motor-car civilization going its triumphant way, outstripping time, consuming space, seeing all and seeing nothing, roaring on at last to the capture of the solar system, only to find the sun cockney and the stars suburban.

IV. MR. BERNARD SHAW

In the glad old days, before the rise of modern morbidities, when genial old Ibsen filled the world with wholesome joy, and the kindly tales of the forgotten Emile Zola kept our firesides merry and pure, it used to be thought a disadvantage to be misunderstood. It may be doubted whether it is always or even generally a disadvantage. The man who is misunderstood has always this advantage over his enemies, that they do not know his weak point or his plan of campaign. They go out against a bird with nets and against a fish with arrows. There are several modern examples of this situation. Mr. Chamberlain, for instance, is a very good one. He constantly eludes or vanquishes his opponents because his real powers and deficiencies are quite different to those with which he is credited, both by friends and foes. His friends depict him as a strenuous man of action; his opponents depict him as a coarse man of business; when, as a fact, he is neither one nor the other, but an admirable romantic orator and romantic actor. He has one power which is the soul of melodrama—the power of pretending, even when backed by a huge majority, that he has his back to the wall. For all mobs are so far chivalrous that their heroes must make some show of misfortune—that sort of hypocrisy is the homage that strength pays to weakness. He talks foolishly and yet very finely about his own city that has never deserted him. He wears a flaming and fantastic flower, like a decadent minor poet. As for his bluffness and toughness and appeals to common sense, all that is, of course, simply the first trick of rhetoric. He fronts his audiences with the venerable affectation of Mark Antony—

"I am no orator, as Brutus is;
But as you know me all, a plain blunt man."

It is the whole difference between the aim of the orator and the aim of any other artist, such as the poet or the sculptor. The aim of the sculptor is to convince us that he is a sculptor; the aim of the orator, is to convince us that he is not an orator. Once let Mr. Chamberlain be mistaken for a practical man, and his game is won. He has only to compose a theme on empire, and people will say that these plain men say great things on great occasions. He has only to drift in the large loose notions common to all artists of the second rank, and people will say that business men have the biggest ideals after all. All his schemes have ended in smoke; he has touched nothing that he did not confuse. About his figure there is a Celtic pathos; like the Gaels in Matthew Arnold's quotation, "he went forth to battle, but he always fell." He is a mountain of proposals, a mountain of failures; but still a mountain. And a mountain is always romantic.

There is another man in the modern world who might be called the antithesis of Mr. Chamberlain in every point, who is also a standing monument of the advantage of being misunderstood. Mr. Bernard Shaw is always represented by those who disagree with him, and, I fear, also (if such exist) by those who agree with him, as a capering humorist, a dazzling acrobat, a quick-change artist. It is said that he cannot be taken seriously, that he will defend anything or attack anything, that he will do anything to startle and amuse. All this is not only untrue, but it is, glaringly, the opposite of the truth; it is as wild as to say that Dickens had not the boisterous masculinity of Jane Austen. The whole force and triumph of Mr. Bernard Shaw lie in the fact that he is a thoroughly consistent man. So far from his power consisting in jumping through hoops or standing on his head, his power consists in holding his own fortress night and day. He puts the Shaw test rapidly and rigorously to everything that happens in heaven or earth. His standard never varies. The thing which weak-minded revolutionists and weak-minded Conservatives really hate (and fear) in him, is exactly this, that his scales, such as they are, are held even, and that his law, such as it is, is justly enforced. You may attack his principles, as I do; but I do not know of any instance in which you can attack their application. If he dislikes lawlessness, he dislikes the lawlessness of Socialists as much as that of Individualists. If he dislikes the fever of patriotism, he dislikes it in Boers and Irishmen as well as in Englishmen. If he dislikes the vows and bonds of marriage, he dislikes still more the fiercer bonds and wilder vows that are made by lawless love. If he laughs at the authority of priests, he laughs louder at the pomposity of men of science. If he condemns the irresponsibility of faith, he condemns with a sane consistency the equal irresponsibility of art. He has pleased all the bohemians by saying that women are equal to men; but he has infuriated them by suggesting that men are equal to women. He is almost mechanically just; he has something of the terrible quality of a machine. The man who is really wild and whirling, the man who is really fantastic and incalculable, is not Mr. Shaw, but the average Cabinet Minister. It is Sir Michael Hicks-Beach who jumps through hoops. It is Sir Henry Fowler who stands on his head. The solid and respectable statesman of that type does really leap from position to position; he is really ready to defend anything or nothing; he is really not to be taken seriously. I know perfectly well what Mr. Bernard Shaw will be saying thirty years hence; he will be saying what he has always said. If thirty years hence I meet Mr. Shaw, a reverent being with a silver beard sweeping the earth, and say to him, "One can never, of course, make a verbal attack upon a lady," the patriarch will lift his aged hand and fell me to the earth. We know, I say, what Mr. Shaw will be, saying thirty years hence. But is there any one so darkly read in stars and oracles that he will dare to predict what Mr. Asquith will be saying thirty years hence?

The truth is, that it is quite an error to suppose that absence of definite convictions gives the mind freedom and agility. A man who believes something is ready and witty, because he has all his weapons about him. He can apply his test in an instant. The man engaged in conflict with a man like Mr. Bernard Shaw may fancy he has ten faces; similarly a man engaged against a brilliant duellist may fancy that the sword of his foe has turned to ten swords in his hand. But this is not really because the man is playing with ten swords, it is because he is aiming very straight with one. Moreover, a man with a definite belief always appears bizarre, because he does not change with the world; he has climbed into a fixed star, and the earth whizzes below him like a zoetrope. Millions of mild black-coated men call themselves sane and sensible merely because they always catch the fashionable insanity, because they are hurried into madness after madness by the maelstrom of the world.

People accuse Mr. Shaw and many much sillier persons of "proving that black is white." But they never ask whether the current colour-language is always correct. Ordinary sensible phraseology sometimes calls black white, it certainly calls yellow white and green white and reddish-brown white. We call wine "white wine" which is as yellow as a Blue-coat boy's legs. We call grapes "white grapes" which are manifestly pale green. We give to the European, whose complexion is a sort of pink drab, the horrible title of a "white man"—a picture more blood-curdling than any spectre in Poe.

Now, it is undoubtedly true that if a man asked a waiter in a restaurant for a bottle of yellow wine and some greenish-yellow grapes, the waiter would think him mad. It is undoubtedly true that if a Government official, reporting on the Europeans in Burmah, said, "There are only two thousand pinkish men here" he would be accused of cracking jokes, and kicked out of his post. But it is equally obvious that both men would have come to grief through telling the strict truth. That too truthful man in the restaurant; that too truthful man in Burmah, is Mr. Bernard Shaw. He appears eccentric and grotesque because he will not accept the general belief that white is yellow. He has based all his brilliancy and solidity upon the hackneyed, but yet forgotten, fact that truth is stranger than fiction. Truth, of course, must of necessity be stranger than fiction, for we have made fiction to suit ourselves.

So much then a reasonable appreciation will find in Mr. Shaw to be bracing and excellent. He claims to see things as they are; and some things, at any rate, he does see as they are, which the whole of our civilization does not see at all. But in Mr. Shaw's realism there is something lacking, and that thing which is lacking is serious.

Mr. Shaw's old and recognized philosophy was that powerfully presented in "The Quintessence of Ibsenism." It was, in brief, that conservative ideals were bad, not because They were conservative, but because they were ideals. Every ideal prevented men from judging justly the particular case; every moral generalization oppressed the individual; the golden rule was there was no golden rule. And the objection to this is simply that it pretends to free men, but really restrains them from doing the only thing that men want to do. What is the good of telling a community that it has every liberty except the liberty to make laws? The liberty to make laws is what constitutes a free people. And what is the good of telling a man (or a philosopher) that he has every liberty except the liberty to make generalizations. Making generalizations is what makes him a man. In short, when Mr. Shaw forbids men to have strict moral ideals, he is acting like one who should forbid them to have children. The saying that "the golden rule is that there is no golden rule," can, indeed, be simply answered by being turned round. That there is no golden rule is itself a golden rule, or rather it is much worse than a golden rule. It is an iron rule; a fetter on the first movement of a man.

But the sensation connected with Mr. Shaw in recent years has been his sudden development of the religion of the Superman. He who had to all appearance mocked at the faiths in the forgotten past discovered a new god in the unimaginable future. He who had laid all the blame on ideals set up the most impossible of all ideals, the ideal of a new creature. But the truth, nevertheless, is that any one who knows Mr. Shaw's mind adequately, and admires it properly, must have guessed all this long ago.

For the truth is that Mr. Shaw has never seen things as they really are. If he had he would have fallen on his knees before them. He has always had a secret ideal that has withered all the things of this world. He has all the time been silently comparing humanity with something that was not human, with a monster from Mars, with the Wise Man of the Stoics, with the Economic Man of the Fabians, with Julius Caesar, with Siegfried, with the Superman. Now, to have this inner and merciless standard may be a very good thing, or a very bad one, it may be excellent or unfortunate, but it is not seeing things as they are. It is not seeing things as they are to think first of a Briareus with a hundred hands, and then call every man a cripple for only having two. It is not seeing things as they are to start with a vision of Argus with his hundred eyes, and then jeer at every man with two eyes as if he had only one. And it is not seeing things as they are to imagine a demigod of infinite mental clarity, who may or may not appear in the latter days of the earth, and then to see all men as idiots. And this is what Mr. Shaw has always in some degree done. When we really see men as they are, we do not criticise, but worship; and very rightly. For a monster with mysterious eyes and miraculous thumbs, with strange dreams in his skull, and a queer tenderness for this place or that baby, is truly a wonderful and unnerving matter. It is only the quite arbitrary and priggish habit of comparison with something else which makes it possible to be at our ease in front of him. A sentiment of superiority keeps us cool and practical; the mere facts would make, our knees knock under as with religious fear. It is the fact that every instant of conscious life is an unimaginable prodigy. It is the fact that every face in the street has the incredible unexpectedness of a fairy-tale. The thing which prevents a man from realizing this is not any clear-sightedness or experience, it is simply a habit of pedantic and fastidious comparisons between one thing and another. Mr. Shaw, on the practical side perhaps the most humane man alive, is in this sense inhumane. He has even been infected to some extent with the primary intellectual weakness of his new master, Nietzsche, the strange notion that the greater and stronger a man was the more he would despise other things. The greater and stronger a man is the more he would be inclined to prostrate himself before a periwinkle. That Mr. Shaw keeps a lifted head and a contemptuous face before the colossal panorama of empires and civilizations, this does not in itself convince one that he sees things as they are. I should be most effectively convinced that he did if I found him staring with religious astonishment at his own feet. "What are those two beautiful and industrious beings," I can imagine him murmuring to himself, "whom I see everywhere, serving me I know not why? What fairy godmother bade them come trotting out of elfland when I was born? What god of the borderland, what barbaric god of legs, must I propitiate with fire and wine, lest they run away with me?"

The truth is, that all genuine appreciation rests on a certain mystery of humility and almost of darkness. The man who said, "Blessed is he that expecteth nothing, for he shall not be disappointed," put the eulogy quite inadequately and even falsely. The truth "Blessed is he that expecteth nothing, for he shall be gloriously surprised." The man who expects nothing sees redder roses than common men can see, and greener grass, and a more startling sun. Blessed is he that expecteth nothing, for he shall possess the cities and the mountains; blessed is the meek, for he shall inherit the earth. Until we realize that things might not be we cannot realize that things are. Until we see the background of darkness we cannot admire the light as a single and created thing. As soon as we have seen that darkness, all light is lightening, sudden, blinding, and divine. Until we picture nonentity we underrate the victory of God, and can realize none of the trophies of His ancient war. It is one of the million wild jests of truth that we know nothing until we know nothing.

Now this is, I say deliberately, the only defect in the greatness of Mr. Shaw, the only answer to his claim to be a great man, that he is not easily pleased. He is an almost solitary exception to the general and essential maxim, that little things please great minds. And from this absence of that most uproarious of all things, humility, comes incidentally the peculiar insistence on the Superman. After belabouring a great many people for a great many years for being unprogressive, Mr. Shaw has discovered, with characteristic sense, that it is very doubtful whether any existing human being with two legs can be progressive at all. Having come to doubt whether humanity can be combined with progress, most people, easily pleased, would have elected to abandon progress and remain with humanity. Mr. Shaw, not being easily pleased, decides to throw over humanity with all its limitations and go in for progress for its own sake. If man, as we know him, is incapable of the philosophy of progress, Mr. Shaw asks, not for a new kind of philosophy, but for a new kind of man. It is rather as if a nurse had tried a rather bitter food for some years on a baby, and on discovering that it was not suitable, should not throw away the food and ask for a new food, but throw the baby out of window, and ask for a new baby. Mr. Shaw cannot understand that the thing which is valuable and lovable in our eyes is man—the old beer-drinking, creed-making, fighting, failing, sensual, respectable man. And the things that have been founded on this creature immortally remain; the things that have been founded on the fancy of the Superman have died with the dying civilizations which alone have given them birth. When Christ at a symbolic moment was establishing His great society, He chose for its corner-stone neither the brilliant Paul nor the mystic John, but a shuffler, a snob a coward—in a word, a man. And upon this rock He has built His Church, and the gates of Hell have not prevailed against it. All the empires and the kingdoms have failed, because of this inherent and continual weakness, that they were founded by strong men and upon strong men. But this one thing, the historic Christian Church, was founded on a weak man, and for that reason it is indestructible. For no chain is stronger than its weakest link.

V. MR. H. G. WELLS AND THE GIANTS

We ought to see far enough into a hypocrite to see even his sincerity. We ought to be interested in that darkest and most real part of a man in which dwell not the vices that he does not display, but the virtues that he cannot. And the more we approach the problems of human history with this keen and piercing charity, the smaller and smaller space we shall allow to pure hypocrisy of any kind. The hypocrites shall not deceive us into thinking them saints; but neither shall they deceive us into thinking them hypocrites. And an increasing number of cases will crowd into our field of inquiry, cases in which there is really no question of hypocrisy at all, cases in which people were so ingenuous that they seemed absurd, and so absurd that they seemed disingenuous.

There is one striking instance of an unfair charge of hypocrisy. It is always urged against the religious in the past, as a point of inconsistency and duplicity, that they combined a profession of almost crawling humility with a keen struggle for earthly success and considerable triumph in attaining it. It is felt as a piece of humbug, that a man should be very punctilious in calling himself a miserable sinner, and also very punctilious in calling himself King of France. But the truth is that there is no more conscious inconsistency between the humility of a Christian and the rapacity of a Christian than there is between the humility of a lover and the rapacity of a lover. The truth is that there are no things for which men will make such herculean efforts as the things of which they know they are unworthy. There never was a man in love who did not declare that, if he strained every nerve to breaking, he was going to have his desire. And there never was a man in love who did not declare also that he ought not to have it. The whole secret of the practical success of Christendom lies in the Christian humility, however imperfectly fulfilled. For with the removal of all question of merit or payment, the soul is suddenly released for incredible voyages. If we ask a sane man how much he merits, his mind shrinks instinctively and instantaneously. It is doubtful whether he merits six feet of earth. But if you ask him what he can conquer—he can conquer the stars. Thus comes the thing called Romance, a purely Christian product. A man cannot deserve adventures; he cannot earn dragons and hippogriffs. The mediaeval Europe which asserted humility gained Romance; the civilization which gained Romance has gained the habitable globe. How different the Pagan and Stoical feeling was from this has been admirably expressed in a famous quotation. Addison makes the great Stoic say—

"'Tis not in mortals to command success;

But we'll do more, Sempronius, we'll deserve it."

But the spirit of Romance and Christendom, the spirit which is in every lover, the spirit which has bestridden the earth with European adventure, is quite opposite. 'Tis not in mortals to deserve success. But we'll do more, Sempronius; we'll obtain it.

And this gay humility, this holding of ourselves lightly and yet ready for an infinity of unmerited triumphs, this secret is so simple that every one has supposed that it must be something quite sinister and mysterious. Humility is so practical a virtue that men think it must be a vice. Humility is so successful that it is mistaken for pride. It is mistaken for it all the more easily because it generally goes with a certain simple love of splendour which amounts to vanity. Humility will always, by preference, go clad in scarlet and gold; pride is that which refuses to let gold and scarlet impress it or please it too much. In a word, the failure of this virtue actually lies in its success; it is too successful as an investment to be believed in as a virtue. Humility is not merely too good for this world; it is too practical for this world; I had almost said it is too worldly for this world.

The instance most quoted in our day is the thing called the humility of the man of science; and certainly it is a good instance as well as a modern one. Men find it extremely difficult to believe that a man who is obviously uprooting mountains and dividing seas, tearing down temples and stretching out hands to the stars, is really a quiet old gentleman who only asks to be allowed to indulge his harmless old hobby and follow his harmless old nose. When a man splits a grain of sand and the universe is turned upside down in consequence, it is difficult to realize that to the man who did it, the splitting of the grain is the great affair, and the capsizing of the cosmos quite a small one. It is hard to enter into the feelings of a man who regards a new heaven and a new earth in the light of a by-product. But undoubtedly it was to this almost eerie innocence of the intellect that the great men of the great scientific period, which now appears to be closing, owed their enormous power and triumph. If they had brought the heavens down like a house of cards their plea was not even that they had done it on principle; their quite unanswerable plea was that they had done it by accident. Whenever there was in them the least touch of pride in what they had done, there was a good ground for attacking them; but so long as they were wholly humble, they were wholly victorious. There were possible answers to Huxley; there was no answer possible to Darwin. He was convincing because of his unconsciousness; one might almost say because of his dulness. This childlike and prosaic mind is beginning to wane in the world of science. Men of science are beginning to see themselves, as the fine phrase is, in the part; they are beginning to be proud of their humility. They are beginning to be aesthetic, like the rest of the world, beginning to spell truth with a capital T, beginning to talk of the creeds they imagine themselves to have destroyed, of the discoveries that their forbears made. Like the modern English, they are beginning to be soft about their own hardness. They are becoming conscious of their own strength—that is, they are growing weaker. But one purely modern man has emerged in the strictly modern decades who does carry into our world the clear personal simplicity of the old world of science. One man of genius we have who is an artist, but who was a man of science, and who seems to be marked above all things with this great scientific humility. I mean Mr. H. G. Wells. And in his case, as in the others above spoken of, there must be a great preliminary difficulty in convincing the ordinary person that such a virtue is predicable of such a man. Mr. Wells began his literary work with violent visions—visions of the last pangs of this planet; can it be that a man who begins with violent visions is humble? He went on to wilder and wilder stories about carving beasts into men and shooting angels like birds. Is the man who shoots angels and carves beasts into men humble? Since then he has done something bolder than either of these blasphemies; he has prophesied the political future of all men; prophesied it with aggressive authority and a ringing decision of detail. Is the prophet of the future of all men humble? It will indeed be difficult, in the present condition of current thought about such things as pride and humility, to answer the query of how a man can be humble who does such big things and such bold things. For the only answer is the answer which I gave at the beginning of this essay. It is the humble man who does the big things. It is the humble man who does the bold things. It is the humble man who has the sensational sights vouchsafed to him, and this for three obvious reasons: first, that he strains his eyes more than any other men to see them; second, that he is more overwhelmed and uplifted with them when they come; third, that he records them more exactly and sincerely and with less adulteration from his more commonplace and more conceited everyday self. Adventures are to those to whom they are most unexpected—that is, most romantic. Adventures are to the shy: in this sense adventures are to the unadventurous.

Now, this arresting, mental humility in Mr. H. G. Wells may be, like a great many other things that are vital and vivid, difficult to illustrate by examples, but if I were asked for an example of it, I should have no difficulty about which example to begin with. The most interesting thing about Mr. H. G. Wells is that he is the only one of his many brilliant contemporaries who has not stopped growing. One can lie awake at night and hear him grow. Of this growth the most evident manifestation is indeed a gradual change of opinions; but it is no mere change of opinions. It is not a perpetual leaping from one position to another like that of Mr. George Moore. It is a quite continuous advance along a quite solid road in a quite definable direction. But the chief proof that it is not a piece of fickleness and vanity is the fact that it has been upon the whole in advance from more startling opinions to more humdrum opinions. It has been even in some sense an advance from unconventional opinions to conventional opinions. This fact fixes Mr. Wells's honesty and proves him to be no poseur. Mr. Wells once held that the upper classes and the lower classes would be so much differentiated in the future that one class would eat the other. Certainly no paradoxical charlatan who had once found arguments for so startling a view would ever have deserted it except for something yet more startling. Mr. Wells has deserted it in favour of the blameless belief that both classes will be ultimately subordinated or assimilated to a sort of scientific middle class, a class of engineers. He has abandoned the sensational theory with the same honourable gravity and simplicity with which he adopted it.

Then he thought it was true; now he thinks it is not true. He has come to the most dreadful conclusion a literary man can come to, the conclusion that the ordinary view is the right one. It is only the last and wildest kind of courage that can stand on a tower before ten thousand people and tell them that twice two is four.

Mr. H. G. Wells exists at present in a gay and exhilarating progress of conservativism. He is finding out more and more that conventions, though silent, are alive. As good an example as any of this humility and sanity of his may be found in his change of view on the subject of science and marriage. He once held, I believe, the opinion which some singular sociologists still hold, that human creatures could successfully be paired and bred after the manner of dogs or horses. He no longer holds that view. Not only does he no longer hold that view, but he has written about it in "Mankind in the Making" with such smashing sense and humour, that I find it difficult to believe that anybody else can hold it either. It is true that his chief objection to the proposal is that it is physically impossible, which seems to me a very slight objection, and almost negligible compared with the others. The one objection to scientific marriage which is worthy of final attention is simply that such a thing could only be imposed on unthinkable slaves and cowards. I do not know whether the scientific marriage-mongers are right (as they say) or wrong (as Mr. Wells says) in saying that medical supervision would produce strong and healthy men. I am only certain that if it did, the first act of the strong and healthy men would be to smash the medical supervision.

The mistake of all that medical talk lies in the very fact that it connects the idea of health with the idea of care. What has health to do with care? Health has to do with carelessness. In special and abnormal cases it is necessary to have care. When we are peculiarly unhealthy it may be necessary to be careful in order to be healthy. But even then we are only trying to be healthy in order to be careless. If we are doctors we are speaking to exceptionally sick men, and they ought to be told to be careful. But when we are sociologists we are addressing the normal man, we are addressing humanity. And humanity ought to be told to be recklessness itself. For all the fundamental functions of a healthy man ought emphatically to be performed with pleasure and for pleasure; they emphatically ought not to be performed with precaution or for precaution. A man ought to eat because he has a good appetite to satisfy, and emphatically not because he has a body to sustain. A man ought to take exercise not because he is too fat, but because he loves foils or horses or high mountains, and loves them for their own sake. And a man ought to marry because he has fallen in love, and emphatically not because the world requires to be populated. The food will really renovate his tissues as long as he is not thinking about his tissues. The exercise will really get him into training so long as he is thinking about something else. And the marriage will really stand some chance of producing a generous-blooded generation if it had its origin in its own natural and generous excitement. It is the first law of health that our necessities should not be accepted as necessities; they should be accepted as luxuries. Let us, then, be careful about the small things, such as a scratch or a slight illness, or anything that can be managed with care. But in the name of all sanity, let us be careless about the important things, such as marriage, or the fountain of our very life will fail.

Mr. Wells, however, is not quite clear enough of the narrower scientific outlook to see that there are some things which actually ought not to be scientific. He is still slightly affected with the great scientific fallacy; I mean the habit of beginning not with the human soul, which is the first thing a man learns about, but with some such thing as protoplasm, which is about the last. The one defect in his splendid mental equipment is that he does not sufficiently allow for the stuff or material of men. In his new Utopia he says, for instance, that a chief point of the Utopia will be a disbelief in original sin. If he had begun with the human soul—that is, if he had begun on himself—he would have found original sin almost the first thing to be believed in. He would have found, to put the matter shortly, that a permanent possibility of selfishness arises from the mere fact of having a self, and not from any accidents of education or ill-treatment. And the weakness of all Utopias is this, that they take the greatest difficulty of man and assume it to be overcome, and then give an elaborate account of the overcoming of the smaller ones. They first assume that no man will want more than his share, and then are very ingenious in explaining whether his share will be delivered by motor-car or balloon. And an even stronger example of Mr. Wells's indifference to the human psychology can be found in his cosmopolitanism, the abolition in his Utopia of all patriotic boundaries. He says in his innocent way that Utopia must be a world-state, or else people might make war on it. It does not seem to occur to him that, for a good many of us, if it were a world-state we should still make war on it to the end of the world. For if we admit that there must be varieties in art or opinion what sense is there in thinking there will not be varieties in government? The fact is very simple. Unless you are going deliberately to prevent a thing being good, you cannot prevent it being worth fighting for. It is impossible to prevent a possible conflict of civilizations, because it is impossible to prevent a possible conflict between ideals. If there were no longer our modern strife between nations, there would only be a strife between Utopias. For the highest thing does not tend to union only; the highest thing, tends also to differentiation. You can often get men to fight for the union; but you can never prevent them from fighting also for the differentiation. This variety in the highest thing is the meaning of the fierce patriotism, the fierce nationalism of the great European civilization. It is also, incidentally, the meaning of the doctrine of the Trinity.

But I think the main mistake of Mr. Wells's philosophy is a somewhat deeper one, one that he expresses in a very entertaining manner in the introductory part of the new Utopia. His philosophy in some sense amounts to a denial of the possibility of philosophy itself. At least, he maintains that there are no secure and reliable ideas upon which we can rest with a final mental satisfaction. It will be both clearer, however, and more amusing to quote Mr. Wells himself.

He says, "Nothing endures, nothing is precise and certain (except the mind of a pedant).... Being indeed!—there is no being, but a universal becoming of individualities, and Plato turned his back on truth when he turned towards his museum of specific ideals." Mr. Wells says, again, "There is no abiding thing in what we know. We change from weaker to stronger lights, and each more powerful light pierces our hitherto opaque foundations and reveals fresh and different opacities below." Now, when Mr. Wells says things like this, I speak with all respect when I say that he does not observe an evident mental distinction. It cannot be true that there is nothing abiding in what we know. For if that were so we should not know it all and should not call it knowledge. Our mental state may be very different from that of somebody else some thousands of years back; but it cannot be entirely different, or else we should not be conscious of a difference. Mr. Wells must surely realize the first and simplest of the paradoxes that sit by the springs of truth. He must surely see that the fact of two things being different implies that they are similar. The hare and the tortoise may differ in the quality of swiftness, but they must agree in the quality of motion. The swiftest hare cannot be swifter than an isosceles triangle or the idea of pinkness. When we say the hare moves faster, we say that the tortoise moves. And when we say of a thing that it moves, we say, without need of other words, that there are things that do not move. And even in the act of saying that things change, we say that there is something unchangeable.

But certainly the best example of Mr. Wells's fallacy can be found in the example which he himself chooses. It is quite true that we see a dim light which, compared with a darker thing, is light, but which, compared with a stronger light, is darkness. But the quality of light remains the same thing, or else we should not call it a stronger light or recognize it as such. If the character of light were not fixed in the mind, we should be quite as likely to call a denser shadow a stronger light, or vice versa If the character of light became even for an instant unfixed, if it became even by a hair's-breadth doubtful, if, for example, there crept into our idea of light some vague idea of blueness, then in that flash we have become doubtful whether the new light has more light or less. In brief, the progress may be as varying as a cloud, but the direction must be as rigid as a French road. North and South are relative in the sense that I am North of Bournemouth and South of Spitzbergen. But if there be any doubt of the position of the North Pole, there is in equal degree a doubt of whether I am South of Spitzbergen at all. The absolute idea of light may be practically unattainable. We may not be able to procure pure light. We may not be able to get to the North Pole. But because the North Pole is unattainable, it does not follow that it is indefinable. And it is only because the North Pole is not indefinable that we can make a satisfactory map of Brighton and Worthing.

In other words, Plato turned his face to truth but his back on Mr. H. G. Wells, when he turned to his museum of specified ideals. It is precisely here that Plato shows his sense. It is not true that everything changes; the things that change are all the manifest and material things. There is something that does not change; and that is precisely the abstract quality, the invisible idea. Mr. Wells says truly enough, that a thing which we have seen in one connection as dark we may see in another connection as light. But the thing common to both incidents is the mere idea of light—which we have not seen at all. Mr. Wells might grow taller and taller for unending aeons till his head was higher than the loneliest star. I can imagine his writing a good novel about it. In that case he would see the trees first as tall things and then as short things; he would see the clouds first as high and then as low. But there would remain with him through the ages in that starry loneliness the idea of tallness; he would have in the awful spaces for companion and comfort the definite conception that he was growing taller and not (for instance) growing fatter.

And now it comes to my mind that Mr. H. G. Wells actually has written a very delightful romance about men growing as tall as trees; and that here, again, he seems to me to have been a victim of this vague relativism. "The Food of the Gods" is, like Mr. Bernard Shaw's play, in essence a study of the Superman idea. And it lies, I think, even through the veil of a half-pantomimic allegory, open to the same intellectual attack. We cannot be expected to have any regard for a great creature if he does not in any manner conform to our standards. For unless he passes our standard of greatness we cannot even call him great. Nietszche summed up all that is interesting in the Superman idea when he said, "Man is a thing which has to be surpassed." But the very word "surpass" implies the existence of a standard common to us and the thing surpassing us. If the Superman is more manly than men are, of course they will ultimately deify him, even if they happen to kill him first. But if he is simply more supermanly, they may be quite indifferent to him as they would be to another seemingly aimless monstrosity. He must submit to our test even in order to overawe us. Mere force or size even is a standard; but that alone will never make men think a man their superior. Giants, as in the wise old fairy-tales, are vermin. Supermen, if not good men, are vermin.

"The Food of the Gods" is the tale of "Jack the Giant-Killer" told from the point of view of the giant. This has not, I think, been done before in literature; but I have little doubt that the psychological substance of it existed in fact. I have little doubt that the giant whom Jack killed did regard himself as the Superman. It is likely enough that he considered Jack a narrow and parochial person who wished to frustrate a great forward movement of the life-force. If (as not unfrequently was the case) he happened to have two heads, he would point out the elementary maxim which declares them to be better than one. He would enlarge on the subtle modernity of such an equipment, enabling a giant to look at a subject from two points of view, or to correct himself with promptitude. But Jack was the champion of the enduring human standards, of the principle of one man one head and one man one conscience, of the single head and the single heart and the single eye. Jack was quite unimpressed by the question of whether the giant was a particularly gigantic giant. All he wished to know was whether he was a good giant—that is, a giant who was any good to us. What were the giant's religious views; what his views on politics and the duties of the citizen? Was he fond of children—or fond of them only in a dark and sinister sense? To use a fine phrase for emotional sanity, was his heart in the right place? Jack had sometimes to cut him up with a sword in order to find out. The old and correct story of Jack the Giant-Killer is simply the whole story of man; if it were understood we should need no Bibles or histories. But the modern world in particular does not seem to understand it at all. The modern world, like Mr. Wells is on the side of the giants; the safest place, and therefore the meanest and the most prosaic. The modern world, when it praises its little Caesars, talks of being strong and brave: but it does not seem to see the eternal paradox involved in the conjunction of these ideas. The strong cannot be brave. Only the weak can be brave; and yet again, in practice, only those who can be brave can be trusted, in time of doubt, to be strong. The only way in which a giant could really keep himself in training against the inevitable Jack would be by continually fighting other giants ten times as big as himself. That is by ceasing to be a giant and becoming a Jack. Thus that sympathy with the small or the defeated as such, with which we Liberals and Nationalists have been often reproached, is not a useless sentimentalism at all, as Mr. Wells and his friends fancy. It is the first law of practical courage. To be in the weakest camp is to be in the strongest school. Nor can I imagine anything that would do humanity more good than the advent of a race of Supermen, for them to fight like dragons. If the Superman is better than we, of course we need not fight him; but in that case, why not call him the Saint? But if he is merely stronger (whether physically, mentally, or morally stronger, I do not care a farthing), then he ought to have to reckon with us at least for all the strength we have. It we are weaker than he, that is no reason why we should be weaker than ourselves. If we are not tall enough to touch the giant's knees, that is no reason why we should become shorter by falling on our own. But that is at bottom the meaning of all modern hero-worship and celebration of the Strong Man, the Caesar the Superman. That he may be something more than man, we must be something less.

Doubtless there is an older and better hero-worship than this. But the old hero was a being who, like Achilles, was more human than humanity itself. Nietzsche's Superman is cold and friendless. Achilles is so foolishly fond of his friend that he slaughters armies in the agony of his bereavement. Mr. Shaw's sad Caesar says in his desolate pride, "He who has never hoped can never despair." The Man-God of old answers from his awful hill, "Was ever sorrow like unto my sorrow?" A great man is not a man so strong that he feels less than other men; he is a man so strong that he feels more. And when Nietszche says, "A new commandment I give to you, 'be hard,'" he is really saying, "A new commandment I give to you, 'be dead.'" Sensibility is the definition of life.

I recur for a last word to Jack the Giant-Killer. I have dwelt on this matter of Mr. Wells and the giants, not because it is specially prominent in his mind; I know that the Superman does not bulk so large in his cosmos as in that of Mr. Bernard Shaw. I have dwelt on it for the opposite reason; because this heresy of immoral hero-worship has taken, I think, a slighter hold of him, and may perhaps still be prevented from perverting one of the best thinkers of the day. In the course of "The New Utopia" Mr. Wells makes more than one admiring allusion to Mr. W. E. Henley. That clever and unhappy man lived in admiration of a vague violence, and was always going back to rude old tales and rude old ballads, to strong and primitive literatures, to find the praise of strength and the justification of tyranny. But he could not find it. It is not there. The primitive literature is shown in the tale of Jack the Giant-Killer. The strong old literature is all in praise of the weak. The rude old tales are as tender to minorities as any modern political idealist. The rude old ballads are as sentimentally concerned for the under-dog as the Aborigines Protection Society. When men were tough and raw, when they lived amid hard knocks and hard laws, when they knew what fighting really was, they had only two kinds of songs. The first was a rejoicing that the weak had conquered the strong, the second a lamentation that the strong had, for once in a way, conquered the weak. For this defiance of the statu quo, this constant effort to alter the existing balance, this premature challenge to the powerful, is the whole nature and inmost secret of the psychological adventure which is called man. It is his strength to disdain strength. The forlorn hope is not only a real hope, it is the only real hope of mankind. In the coarsest ballads of the greenwood men are admired most when they defy, not only the king, but what is more to the point, the hero. The moment Robin Hood becomes a sort of Superman, that moment the chivalrous chronicler shows us Robin thrashed by a poor tinker whom he thought to thrust aside. And the chivalrous chronicler makes Robin Hood receive the thrashing in a glow of admiration. This magnanimity is not a product of modern humanitarianism; it is not a product of anything to do with peace. This magnanimity is merely one of the lost arts of war. The Henleyites call for a sturdy and fighting England, and they go back to the fierce old stories of the sturdy and fighting English. And the thing that they find written across that fierce old literature everywhere, is "the policy of Majuba."

VI. CHRISTMAS AND THE AESTHETES

The world is round, so round that the schools of optimism and pessimism have been arguing from the beginning whether it is the right way up. The difficulty does not arise so much from the mere fact that good and evil are mingled in roughly equal proportions; it arises chiefly from the fact that men always differ about what parts are good and what evil. Hence the difficulty which besets "undenominational religions." They profess to include what is beautiful in all creeds, but they appear to many to have collected all that is dull in them. All the colours mixed together in purity ought to make a perfect white. Mixed together on any human paint-box, they make a thing like mud, and a thing very like many new religions. Such a blend is often something much worse than any one creed taken separately, even the creed of the Thugs. The error arises from the difficulty of detecting what is really the good part and what is really the bad part of any given religion. And this pathos falls rather heavily on those persons who have the misfortune to think of some religion or other, that the parts commonly counted good are bad, and the parts commonly counted bad are good.

It is tragic to admire and honestly admire a human group, but to admire it in a photographic negative. It is difficult to congratulate all their whites on being black and all their blacks on their whiteness. This will often happen to us in connection with human religions. Take two institutions which bear witness to the religious energy of the nineteenth century. Take the Salvation Army and the philosophy of Auguste Comte.

The usual verdict of educated people on the Salvation Army is expressed in some such words as these: "I have no doubt they do a great deal of good, but they do it in a vulgar and profane style; their aims are excellent, but their methods are wrong." To me, unfortunately, the precise reverse of this appears to be the truth. I do not know whether the aims of the Salvation Army are excellent, but I am quite sure their methods are admirable. Their methods are the methods of all intense and hearty religions; they are popular like all religion, military like all religion, public and sensational like all religion. They are not reverent any more than Roman Catholics are reverent, for reverence in the sad and delicate meaning of the term reverence is a thing only possible to infidels. That beautiful twilight you will find in Euripides, in Renan, in Matthew Arnold; but in men who believe you will not find it—you will find only laughter and war. A man cannot pay that kind of reverence to truth solid as marble; they can only be reverent towards a beautiful lie. And the Salvation Army, though their voice has broken out in a mean environment and an ugly shape, are really the old voice of glad and angry faith, hot as the riots of Dionysus, wild as the gargoyles of Catholicism, not to be mistaken for a philosophy. Professor Huxley, in one of his clever phrases, called the Salvation Army "corybantic Christianity." Huxley was the last and noblest of those Stoics who have never understood the Cross. If he had understood Christianity he would have known that there never has been, and never can be, any Christianity that is not corybantic.

And there is this difference between the matter of aims and the matter of methods, that to judge of the aims of a thing like the Salvation Army is very difficult, to judge of their ritual and atmosphere very easy. No one, perhaps, but a so-sociologist can see whether General Booth's housing scheme is right. But any healthy person can see that banging brass cymbals together must be right. A page of statistics, a plan of model dwellings, anything which is rational, is always difficult for the lay mind. But the thing which is irrational any one can understand. That is why religion came so early into the world and spread so far, while science came so late into the world and has not spread at all. History unanimously attests the fact that it is only mysticism which stands the smallest chance of being understanded of the people. Common sense has to be kept as an esoteric secret in the dark temple of culture. And so while the philanthropy of the Salvationists and its genuineness may be a reasonable matter for the discussion of the doctors, there can be no doubt about the genuineness of their brass bands, for a brass band is purely spiritual, and seeks only to quicken the internal life. The object of philanthropy is to do good; the object of religion is to be good, if only for a moment, amid a crash of brass.

And the same antithesis exists about another modern religion—I mean the religion of Comte, generally known as Positivism, or the worship of humanity. Such men as Mr. Frederic Harrison, that brilliant and chivalrous philosopher, who still, by his mere personality, speaks for the creed, would tell us that he offers us the philosophy of Comte, but not all Comte's fantastic proposals for pontiffs and ceremonials, the new calendar, the new holidays and saints' days. He does not mean that we should dress ourselves up as priests of humanity or let off fireworks because it is Milton's birthday. To the solid English Comtist all this appears, he confesses, to be a little absurd. To me it appears the only sensible part of Comtism. As a philosophy it is unsatisfactory. It is evidently impossible to worship humanity, just as it is impossible to worship the Savile Club; both are excellent institutions to which we may happen to belong. But we perceive clearly that the Savile Club did not make the stars and does not fill the universe. And it is surely unreasonable to attack the doctrine of the Trinity as a piece of bewildering mysticism, and then to ask men to worship a being who is ninety million persons in one God, neither confounding the persons nor dividing the substance.

But if the wisdom of Comte was insufficient, the folly of Comte was wisdom. In an age of dusty modernity, when beauty was thought of as something barbaric and ugliness as something sensible, he alone saw that men must always have the sacredness of mummery. He saw that while the brutes have all the useful things, the things that are truly human are the useless ones. He saw the falsehood of that almost universal notion of to-day, the notion that rites and forms are something artificial, additional, and corrupt. Ritual is really much older than thought; it is much simpler and much wilder than thought. A feeling touching the nature of things does not only make men feel that there are certain proper things to say; it makes them feel that there are certain proper things to do. The more agreeable of these consist of dancing, building temples, and shouting very loud; the less agreeable, of wearing green carnations and burning other philosophers alive. But everywhere the religious dance came before the religious hymn, and man was a ritualist before he could speak. If Comtism had spread the world would have been converted, not by the Comtist philosophy, but by the Comtist calendar. By discouraging what they conceive to be the weakness of their master, the English Positivists have broken the strength of their religion. A man who has faith must be prepared not only to be a martyr, but to be a fool. It is absurd to say that a man is ready to toil and die for his convictions when he is not even ready to wear a wreath round his head for them. I myself, to take a corpus vile, am very certain that I would not read the works of Comte through for any consideration whatever. But I can easily imagine myself with the greatest enthusiasm lighting a bonfire on Darwin Day.

That splendid effort failed, and nothing in the style of it has succeeded. There has been no rationalist festival, no rationalist ecstasy. Men are still in black for the death of God. When Christianity was heavily bombarded in the last century upon no point was it more persistently and brilliantly attacked than upon that of its alleged enmity to human joy. Shelley and Swinburne and all their armies have passed again and again over the ground, but they have not altered it. They have not set up a single new trophy or ensign for the world's merriment to rally to. They have not given a name or a new occasion of gaiety. Mr. Swinburne does not hang up his stocking on the eve of the birthday of Victor Hugo. Mr. William Archer does not sing carols descriptive of the infancy of Ibsen outside people's doors in the snow. In the round of our rational and mournful year one festival remains out of all those ancient gaieties that once covered the whole earth. Christmas remains to remind us of those ages, whether Pagan or Christian, when the many acted poetry instead of the few writing it. In all the winter in our woods there is no tree in glow but the holly.

The strange truth about the matter is told in the very word "holiday." A bank holiday means presumably a day which bankers regard as holy. A half-holiday means, I suppose, a day on which a schoolboy is only partially holy. It is hard to see at first sight why so human a thing as leisure and larkiness should always have a religious origin. Rationally there appears no reason why we should not sing and give each other presents in honour of anything—the birth of Michael Angelo or the opening of Euston Station. But it does not work. As a fact, men only become greedily and gloriously material about something spiritualistic. Take away the Nicene Creed and similar things, and you do some strange wrong to the sellers of sausages. Take away the strange beauty of the saints, and what has remained to us is the far stranger ugliness of Wandsworth. Take away the supernatural, and what remains is the unnatural.

And now I have to touch upon a very sad matter. There are in the modern world an admirable class of persons who really make protest on behalf of that antiqua pulchritudo of which Augustine spoke, who do long for the old feasts and formalities of the childhood of the world. William Morris and his followers showed how much brighter were the dark ages than the age of Manchester. Mr. W. B. Yeats frames his steps in prehistoric dances, but no man knows and joins his voice to forgotten choruses that no one but he can hear. Mr. George Moore collects every fragment of Irish paganism that the forgetfulness of the Catholic Church has left or possibly her wisdom preserved. There are innumerable persons with eye-glasses and green garments who pray for the return of the maypole or the Olympian games. But there is about these people a haunting and alarming something which suggests that it is just possible that they do not keep Christmas. It is painful to regard human nature in such a light, but it seems somehow possible that Mr. George Moore does not wave his spoon and shout when the pudding is set alight. It is even possible that Mr. W. B. Yeats never pulls crackers. If so, where is the sense of all their dreams of festive traditions? Here is a solid and ancient festive tradition still plying a roaring trade in the streets, and they think it vulgar. if this is so, let them be very certain of this, that they are the kind of people who in the time of the maypole would have thought the maypole vulgar; who in the time of the Canterbury pilgrimage would have thought the Canterbury pilgrimage vulgar; who in the time of the Olympian games would have thought the Olympian games vulgar. Nor can there be any reasonable doubt that they were vulgar. Let no man deceive himself; if by vulgarity we mean coarseness of speech, rowdiness of behaviour, gossip, horseplay, and some heavy drinking, vulgarity there always was wherever there was joy, wherever there was faith in the gods. Wherever you have belief you will have hilarity, wherever you have hilarity you will have some dangers. And as creed and mythology produce this gross and vigorous life, so in its turn this gross and vigorous life will always produce creed and mythology. If we ever get the English back on to the English land they will become again a religious people, if all goes well, a superstitious people. The absence from modern life of both the higher and lower forms of faith is largely due to a divorce from nature and the trees and clouds. If we have no more turnip ghosts it is chiefly from the lack of turnips.

VII. OMAR AND THE SACRED VINE

A new morality has burst upon us with some violence in connection with the problem of strong drink; and enthusiasts in the matter range from the man who is violently thrown out at 12.30, to the lady who smashes American bars with an axe. In these discussions it is almost always felt that one very wise and moderate position is to say that wine or such stuff should only be drunk as a medicine. With this I should venture to disagree with a peculiar ferocity. The one genuinely dangerous and immoral way of drinking wine is to drink it as a medicine. And for this reason, If a man drinks wine in order to obtain pleasure, he is trying to obtain something exceptional, something he does not expect every hour of the day, something which, unless he is a little insane, he will not try to get every hour of the day. But if a man drinks wine in order to obtain health, he is trying to get something natural; something, that is, that he ought not to be without; something that he may find it difficult to reconcile himself to being without. The man may not be seduced who has seen the ecstasy of being ecstatic; it is more dazzling to catch a glimpse of the ecstasy of being ordinary. If there were a magic ointment, and we took it to a strong man, and said, "This will enable you to jump off the Monument," doubtless he would jump off the Monument, but he would not jump off the Monument all day long to the delight of the City. But if we took it to a blind man, saying, "This will enable you to see," he would be under a heavier temptation. It would be hard for him not to rub it on his eyes whenever he heard the hoof of a noble horse or the birds singing at daybreak. It is easy to deny one's self festivity; it is difficult to deny one's self normality. Hence comes the fact which every doctor knows, that it is often perilous to give alcohol to the sick even when they need it. I need hardly say that I do not mean that I think the giving of alcohol to the sick for stimulus is necessarily unjustifiable. But I do mean that giving it to the healthy for fun is the proper use of it, and a great deal more consistent with health.

The sound rule in the matter would appear to be like many other sound rules—a paradox. Drink because you are happy, but never because you are miserable. Never drink when you are wretched without it, or you will be like the grey-faced gin-drinker in the slum; but drink when you would be happy without it, and you will be like the laughing peasant of Italy. Never drink because you need it, for this is rational drinking, and the way to death and hell. But drink because you do not need it, for this is irrational drinking, and the ancient health of the world.

For more than thirty years the shadow and glory of a great Eastern figure has lain upon our English literature. Fitzgerald's translation of Omar Khayyam concentrated into an immortal poignancy all the dark and drifting hedonism of our time. Of the literary splendour of that work it would be merely banal to speak; in few other of the books of men has there been anything so combining the gay pugnacity of an epigram with the vague sadness of a song. But of its philosophical, ethical, and religious influence which has been almost as great as its brilliancy, I should like to say a word, and that word, I confess, one of uncompromising hostility. There are a great many things which might be said against the spirit of the Rubaiyat, and against its prodigious influence. But one matter of indictment towers ominously above the rest—a genuine disgrace to it, a genuine calamity to us. This is the terrible blow that this great poem has struck against sociability and the joy of life. Some one called Omar "the sad, glad old Persian." Sad he is; glad he is not, in any sense of the word whatever. He has been a worse foe to gladness than the Puritans.

A pensive and graceful Oriental lies under the rose-tree with his wine-pot and his scroll of poems. It may seem strange that any one's thoughts should, at the moment of regarding him, fly back to the dark bedside where the doctor doles out brandy. It may seem stranger still that they should go back to the grey wastrel shaking with gin in Houndsditch. But a great philosophical unity links the three in an evil bond. Omar Khayyam's wine-bibbing is bad, not because it is wine-bibbing. It is bad, and very bad, because it is medical wine-bibbing. It is the drinking of a man who drinks because he is not happy. His is the wine that shuts out the universe, not the wine that reveals it. It is not poetical drinking, which is joyous and instinctive; it is rational drinking, which is as prosaic as an investment, as unsavoury as a dose of camomile. Whole heavens above it, from the point of view of sentiment, though not of style, rises the splendour of some old English drinking-song—

"Then pass the bowl, my comrades all,
And let the zider vlow."

For this song was caught up by happy men to express the worth of truly worthy things, of brotherhood and garrulity, and the brief and kindly leisure of the poor. Of course, the great part of the more stolid reproaches directed against the Omarite morality are as false and babyish as such reproaches usually are. One critic, whose work I have read, had the incredible foolishness to call Omar an atheist and a materialist. It is almost impossible for an Oriental to be either; the East understands metaphysics too well for that. Of course, the real objection which a philosophical Christian would bring against the religion of Omar, is not that he gives no place to God, it is that he gives too much place to God. His is that terrible theism which can imagine nothing else but deity, and which denies altogether the outlines of human personality and human will.

"The ball no question makes of Ayes or Noes,
But Here or There as strikes the Player goes;
And He that tossed you down into the field,
He knows about it all—he knows—he knows."

A Christian thinker such as Augustine or Dante would object to this because it ignores free-will, which is the valour and dignity of the soul. The quarrel of the highest Christianity with this scepticism is not in the least that the scepticism denies the existence of God; it is that it denies the existence of man.

In this cult of the pessimistic pleasure-seeker the Rubaiyat stands first in our time; but it does not stand alone. Many of the most brilliant intellects of our time have urged us to the same self-conscious snatching at a rare delight. Walter Pater said that we were all under sentence of death, and the only course was to enjoy exquisite moments simply for those moments' sake. The same lesson was taught by the very powerful and very desolate philosophy of Oscar Wilde. It is the carpe diem religion; but the carpe diem religion is not the religion of happy people, but of very unhappy people. Great joy does, not gather the rosebuds while it may; its eyes are fixed on the immortal rose which Dante saw. Great joy has in it the sense of immortality; the very splendour of youth is the sense that it has all space to stretch its legs in. In all great comic literature, in "Tristram Shandy" or "Pickwick", there is this sense of space and incorruptibility; we feel the characters are deathless people in an endless tale.

It is true enough, of course, that a pungent happiness comes chiefly in certain passing moments; but it is not true that we should think of them as passing, or enjoy them simply "for those moments' sake." To do this is to rationalize the happiness, and therefore to destroy it. Happiness is a mystery like religion, and should never be rationalized. Suppose a man experiences a really splendid moment of pleasure. I do not mean something connected with a bit of enamel, I mean something with a violent happiness in it—an almost painful happiness. A man may have, for instance, a moment of ecstasy in first love, or a moment of victory in battle. The lover enjoys the moment, but precisely not for the moment's sake. He enjoys it for the woman's sake, or his own sake. The warrior enjoys the moment, but not for the sake of the moment; he enjoys it for the sake of the flag. The cause which the flag stands for may be foolish and fleeting; the love may be calf-love, and last a week. But the patriot thinks of the flag as eternal; the lover thinks of his love as something that cannot end. These moments are filled with eternity; these moments are joyful because they do not seem momentary. Once look at them as moments after Pater's manner, and they become as cold as Pater and his style. Man cannot love mortal things. He can only love immortal things for an instant.

Pater's mistake is revealed in his most famous phrase. He asks us to burn with a hard, gem-like flame. Flames are never hard and never gem-like—they cannot be handled or arranged. So human emotions are never hard and never gem-like; they are always dangerous, like flames, to touch or even to examine. There is only one way in which our passions can become hard and gem-like, and that is by becoming as cold as gems. No blow then has ever been struck at the natural loves and laughter of men so sterilizing as this carpe diem of the aesthetes. For any kind of pleasure a totally different spirit is required; a certain shyness, a certain indeterminate hope, a certain boyish expectation. Purity and simplicity are essential to passions—yes even to evil passions. Even vice demands a sort of virginity.

Omar's (or Fitzgerald's) effect upon the other world we may let go, his hand upon this world has been heavy and paralyzing. The Puritans, as I have said, are far jollier than he. The new ascetics who follow Thoreau or Tolstoy are much livelier company; for, though the surrender of strong drink and such luxuries may strike us as an idle negation, it may leave a man with innumerable natural pleasures, and, above all, with man's natural power of happiness. Thoreau could enjoy the sunrise without a cup of coffee. If Tolstoy cannot admire marriage, at least he is healthy enough to admire mud. Nature can be enjoyed without even the most natural luxuries. A good bush needs no wine. But neither nature nor wine nor anything else can be enjoyed if we have the wrong attitude towards happiness, and Omar (or Fitzgerald) did have the wrong attitude towards happiness. He and those he has influenced do not see that if we are to be truly gay, we must believe that there is some eternal gaiety in the nature of things. We cannot enjoy thoroughly even a pas-de-quatre at a subscription dance unless we believe that the stars are dancing to the same tune. No one can be really hilarious but the serious man. "Wine," says the Scripture, "maketh glad the heart of man," but only of the man who has a heart. The thing called high spirits is possible only to the spiritual. Ultimately a man cannot rejoice in anything except the nature of things. Ultimately a man can enjoy nothing except religion. Once in the world's history men did believe that the stars were dancing to the tune of their temples, and they danced as men have never danced since. With this old pagan eudaemonism the sage of the Rubaiyat has quite as little to do as he has with any Christian variety. He is no more a Bacchanal than he is a saint. Dionysus and his church was grounded on a serious joie-de-vivre like that of Walt Whitman. Dionysus made wine, not a medicine, but a sacrament. Jesus Christ also made wine, not a medicine, but a sacrament. But Omar makes it, not a sacrament, but a medicine. He feasts because life is not joyful; he revels because he is not glad. "Drink," he says, "for you know not whence you come nor why. Drink, for you know not when you go nor where. Drink, because the stars are cruel and the world as idle as a humming-top. Drink, because there is nothing worth trusting, nothing worth fighting for. Drink, because all things are lapsed in a base equality and an evil peace." So he stands offering us the cup in his hand. And at the high altar of Christianity stands another figure, in whose hand also is the cup of the vine. "Drink" he says "for the whole world is as red as this wine, with the crimson of the love and wrath of God. Drink, for the trumpets are blowing for battle and this is the stirrup-cup. Drink, for this my blood of the new testament that is shed for you. Drink, for I know of whence you come and why. Drink, for I know of when you go and where."

VIII. THE MILDNESS OF THE YELLOW PRESS

There is a great deal of protest made from one quarter or another nowadays against the influence of that new journalism which is associated with the names of Sir Alfred Harmsworth and Mr. Pearson. But almost everybody who attacks it attacks on the ground that it is very sensational, very violent and vulgar and startling. I am speaking in no affected contrariety, but in the simplicity of a genuine personal impression, when I say that this journalism offends as being not sensational or violent enough. The real vice is not that it is startling, but that it is quite insupportably tame. The whole object is to keep carefully along a certain level of the expected and the commonplace; it may be low, but it must take care also to be flat. Never by any chance in it is there any of that real plebeian pungency which can be heard from the ordinary cabman in the ordinary street. We have heard of a certain standard of decorum which demands that things should be funny without being vulgar, but the standard of this decorum demands that if things are vulgar they shall be vulgar without being funny. This journalism does not merely fail to exaggerate life—it positively underrates it; and it has to do so because it is intended for the faint and languid recreation of men whom the fierceness of modern life has fatigued. This press is not the yellow press at all; it is the drab press. Sir Alfred Harmsworth must not address to the tired clerk any observation more witty than the tired clerk might be able to address to Sir Alfred Harmsworth. It must not expose anybody (anybody who is powerful, that is), it must not offend anybody, it must not even please anybody, too much. A general vague idea that in spite of all this, our yellow press is sensational, arises from such external accidents as large type or lurid headlines. It is quite true that these editors print everything they possibly can in large capital letters. But they do this, not because it is startling, but because it is soothing. To people wholly weary or partly drunk in a dimly lighted train, it is a simplification and a comfort to have things presented in this vast and obvious manner. The editors use this gigantic alphabet in dealing with their readers, for exactly the same reason that parents and governesses use a similar gigantic alphabet in teaching children to spell. The nursery authorities do not use an A as big as a horseshoe in order to make the child jump; on the contrary, they use it to put the child at his ease, to make things smoother and more evident. Of the same character is the dim and quiet dame school which Sir Alfred Harmsworth and Mr. Pearson keep. All their sentiments are spelling-book sentiments—that is to say, they are sentiments with which the pupil is already respectfully familiar. All their wildest posters are leaves torn from a copy-book.

Of real sensational journalism, as it exists in France, in Ireland, and in America, we have no trace in this country. When a journalist in Ireland wishes to create a thrill, he creates a thrill worth talking about. He denounces a leading Irish member for corruption, or he charges the whole police system with a wicked and definite conspiracy. When a French journalist desires a frisson there is a frisson; he discovers, let us say, that the President of the Republic has murdered three wives. Our yellow journalists invent quite as unscrupulously as this; their moral condition is, as regards careful veracity, about the same. But it is their mental calibre which happens to be such that they can only invent calm and even reassuring things. The fictitious version of the massacre of the envoys of Pekin was mendacious, but it was not interesting, except to those who had private reasons for terror or sorrow. It was not connected with any bold and suggestive view of the Chinese situation. It revealed only a vague idea that nothing could be impressive except a great deal of blood. Real sensationalism, of which I happen to be very fond, may be either moral or immoral. But even when it is most immoral, it requires moral courage. For it is one of the most dangerous things on earth genuinely to surprise anybody. If you make any sentient creature jump, you render it by no means improbable that it will jump on you. But the leaders of this movement have no moral courage or immoral courage; their whole method consists in saying, with large and elaborate emphasis, the things which everybody else says casually, and without remembering what they have said. When they brace themselves up to attack anything, they never reach the point of attacking anything which is large and real, and would resound with the shock. They do not attack the army as men do in France, or the judges as men do in Ireland, or the democracy itself as men did in England a hundred years ago. They attack something like the War Office—something, that is, which everybody attacks and nobody bothers to defend, something which is an old joke in fourth-rate comic papers. just as a man shows he has a weak voice by straining it to shout, so they show the hopelessly unsensational nature of their minds when they really try to be sensational. With the whole world full of big and dubious institutions, with the whole wickedness of civilization staring them in the face, their idea of being bold and bright is to attack the War Office. They might as well start a campaign against the weather, or form a secret society in order to make jokes about mothers-in-law. Nor is it only from the point of view of particular amateurs of the sensational such as myself, that it is permissible to say, in the words of Cowper's Alexander Selkirk, that "their tameness is shocking to me." The whole modern world is pining for a genuinely sensational journalism. This has been discovered by that very able and honest journalist, Mr. Blatchford, who started his campaign against Christianity, warned on all sides, I believe, that it would ruin his paper, but who continued from an honourable sense of intellectual responsibility. He discovered, however, that while he had undoubtedly shocked his readers, he had also greatly advanced his newspaper. It was bought—first, by all the people who agreed with him and wanted to read it; and secondly, by all the people who disagreed with him, and wanted to write him letters. Those letters were voluminous (I helped, I am glad to say, to swell their volume), and they were generally inserted with a generous fulness. Thus was accidentally discovered (like the steam-engine) the great journalistic maxim—that if an editor can only make people angry enough, they will write half his newspaper for him for nothing.

Some hold that such papers as these are scarcely the proper objects of so serious a consideration; but that can scarcely be maintained from a political or ethical point of view. In this problem of the mildness and tameness of the Harmsworth mind there is mirrored the outlines of a much larger problem which is akin to it.

The Harmsworthian journalist begins with a worship of success and violence, and ends in sheer timidity and mediocrity. But he is not alone in this, nor does he come by this fate merely because he happens personally to be stupid. Every man, however brave, who begins by worshipping violence, must end in mere timidity. Every man, however wise, who begins by worshipping success, must end in mere mediocrity. This strange and paradoxical fate is involved, not in the individual, but in the philosophy, in the point of view. It is not the folly of the man which brings about this necessary fall; it is his wisdom. The worship of success is the only one out of all possible worships of which this is true, that its followers are foredoomed to become slaves and cowards. A man may be a hero for the sake of Mrs. Gallup's ciphers or for the sake of human sacrifice, but not for the sake of success. For obviously a man may choose to fail because he loves Mrs. Gallup or human sacrifice; but he cannot choose to fail because he loves success. When the test of triumph is men's test of everything, they never endure long enough to triumph at all. As long as matters are really hopeful, hope is a mere flattery or platitude; it is only when everything is hopeless that hope begins to be a strength at all. Like all the Christian virtues, it is as unreasonable as it is indispensable.

It was through this fatal paradox in the nature of things that all these modern adventurers come at last to a sort of tedium and acquiescence. They desired strength; and to them to desire strength was to admire strength; to admire strength was simply to admire the statu quo. They thought that he who wished to be strong ought to respect the strong. They did not realize the obvious verity that he who wishes to be strong must despise the strong. They sought to be everything, to have the whole force of the cosmos behind them, to have an energy that would drive the stars. But they did not realize the two great facts—first, that in the attempt to be everything the first and most difficult step is to be something; second, that the moment a man is something, he is essentially defying everything. The lower animals, say the men of science, fought their way up with a blind selfishness. If this be so, the only real moral of it is that our unselfishness, if it is to triumph, must be equally blind. The mammoth did not put his head on one side and wonder whether mammoths were a little out of date. Mammoths were at least as much up to date as that individual mammoth could make them. The great elk did not say, "Cloven hoofs are very much worn now." He polished his own weapons for his own use. But in the reasoning animal there has arisen a more horrible danger, that he may fail through perceiving his own failure. When modern sociologists talk of the necessity of accommodating one's self to the trend of the time, they forget that the trend of the time at its best consists entirely of people who will not accommodate themselves to anything. At its worst it consists of many millions of frightened creatures all accommodating themselves to a trend that is not there. And that is becoming more and more the situation of modern England. Every man speaks of public opinion, and means by public opinion, public opinion minus his opinion. Every man makes his contribution negative under the erroneous impression that the next man's contribution is positive. Every man surrenders his fancy to a general tone which is itself a surrender. And over all the heartless and fatuous unity spreads this new and wearisome and platitudinous press, incapable of invention, incapable of audacity, capable only of a servility all the more contemptible because it is not even a servility to the strong. But all who begin with force and conquest will end in this.

The chief characteristic of the "New journalism" is simply that it is bad journalism. It is beyond all comparison the most shapeless, careless, and colourless work done in our day.

I read yesterday a sentence which should be written in letters of gold and adamant; it is the very motto of the new philosophy of Empire. I found it (as the reader has already eagerly guessed) in Pearson's Magazine, while I was communing (soul to soul) with Mr. C. Arthur Pearson, whose first and suppressed name I am afraid is Chilperic. It occurred in an article on the American Presidential Election. This is the sentence, and every one should read it carefully, and roll it on the tongue, till all the honey be tasted.

"A little sound common sense often goes further with an audience of American working-men than much high-flown argument. A speaker who, as he brought forward his points, hammered nails into a board, won hundreds of votes for his side at the last Presidential Election."

I do not wish to soil this perfect thing with comment; the words of Mercury are harsh after the songs of Apollo. But just think for a moment of the mind, the strange inscrutable mind, of the man who wrote that, of the editor who approved it, of the people who are probably impressed by it, of the incredible American working-man, of whom, for all I know, it may be true. Think what their notion of "common sense" must be! It is delightful to realize that you and I are now able to win thousands of votes should we ever be engaged in a Presidential Election, by doing something of this kind. For I suppose the nails and the board are not essential to the exhibition of "common sense;" there may be variations. We may read—

"A little common sense impresses American working-men more than high-flown argument. A speaker who, as he made his points, pulled buttons off his waistcoat, won thousands of votes for his side." Or, "Sound common sense tells better in America than high-flown argument. Thus Senator Budge, who threw his false teeth in the air every time he made an epigram, won the solid approval of American working-men." Or again, "The sound common sense of a gentleman from Earlswood, who stuck straws in his hair during the progress of his speech, assured the victory of Mr. Roosevelt."

There are many other elements in this article on which I should love to linger. But the matter which I wish to point out is that in that sentence is perfectly revealed the whole truth of what our Chamberlainites, hustlers, bustlers, Empire-builders, and strong, silent men, really mean by "commonsense." They mean knocking, with deafening noise and dramatic effect, meaningless bits of iron into a useless bit of wood. A man goes on to an American platform and behaves like a mountebank fool with a board and a hammer; well, I do not blame him; I might even admire him. He may be a dashing and quite decent strategist. He may be a fine romantic actor, like Burke flinging the dagger on the floor. He may even (for all I know) be a sublime mystic, profoundly impressed with the ancient meaning of the divine trade of the Carpenter, and offering to the people a parable in the form of a ceremony. All I wish to indicate is the abyss of mental confusion in which such wild ritualism can be called "sound common sense." And it is in that abyss of mental confusion, and in that alone, that the new Imperialism lives and moves and has its being. The whole glory and greatness of Mr. Chamberlain consists in this: that if a man hits the right nail on the head nobody cares where he hits it to or what it does. They care about the noise of the hammer, not about the silent drip of the nail. Before and throughout the African war, Mr. Chamberlain was always knocking in nails, with ringing decisiveness. But when we ask, "But what have these nails held together? Where is your carpentry? Where are your contented Outlanders? Where is your free South Africa? Where is your British prestige? What have your nails done?" then what answer is there? We must go back (with an affectionate sigh) to our Pearson for the answer to the question of what the nails have done: "The speaker who hammered nails into a board won thousands of votes."

Now the whole of this passage is admirably characteristic of the new journalism which Mr. Pearson represents, the new journalism which has just purchased the Standard. To take one instance out of hundreds, the incomparable man with the board and nails is described in the Pearson's article as calling out (as he smote the symbolic nail), "Lie number one. Nailed to the Mast! Nailed to the Mast!" In the whole office there was apparently no compositor or office-boy to point out that we speak of lies being nailed to the counter, and not to the mast. Nobody in the office knew that Pearson's Magazine was falling into a stale Irish bull, which must be as old as St. Patrick. This is the real and essential tragedy of the sale of the Standard. It is not merely that journalism is victorious over literature. It is that bad journalism is victorious over good journalism.

It is not that one article which we consider costly and beautiful is being ousted by another kind of article which we consider common or unclean. It is that of the same article a worse quality is preferred to a better. If you like popular journalism (as I do), you will know that Pearson's Magazine is poor and weak popular journalism. You will know it as certainly as you know bad butter. You will know as certainly that it is poor popular journalism as you know that the Strand, in the great days of Sherlock Holmes, was good popular journalism. Mr. Pearson has been a monument of this enormous banality. About everything he says and does there is something infinitely weak-minded. He clamours for home trades and employs foreign ones to print his paper. When this glaring fact is pointed out, he does not say that the thing was an oversight, like a sane man. He cuts it off with scissors, like a child of three. His very cunning is infantile. And like a child of three, he does not cut it quite off. In all human records I doubt if there is such an example of a profound simplicity in deception. This is the sort of intelligence which now sits in the seat of the sane and honourable old Tory journalism. If it were really the triumph of the tropical exuberance of the Yankee press, it would be vulgar, but still tropical. But it is not. We are delivered over to the bramble, and from the meanest of the shrubs comes the fire upon the cedars of Lebanon.

The only question now is how much longer the fiction will endure that journalists of this order represent public opinion. It may be doubted whether any honest and serious Tariff Reformer would for a moment maintain that there was any majority for Tariff Reform in the country comparable to the ludicrous preponderance which money has given it among the great dailies. The only inference is that for purposes of real public opinion the press is now a mere plutocratic oligarchy. Doubtless the public buys the wares of these men, for one reason or another. But there is no more reason to suppose that the public admires their politics than that the public admires the delicate philosophy of Mr. Crosse or the darker and sterner creed of Mr. Blackwell. If these men are merely tradesmen, there is nothing to say except that there are plenty like them in the Battersea Park Road, and many much better. But if they make any sort of attempt to be politicians, we can only point out to them that they are not as yet even good journalists.

IX. THE MOODS OF MR. GEORGE MOORE

Mr. George Moore began his literary career by writing his personal confessions; nor is there any harm in this if he had not continued them for the remainder of his life. He is a man of genuinely forcible mind and of great command over a kind of rhetorical and fugitive conviction which excites and pleases. He is in a perpetual state of temporary honesty. He has admired all the most admirable modern eccentrics until they could stand it no longer. Everything he writes, it is to be fully admitted, has a genuine mental power. His account of his reason for leaving the Roman Catholic Church is possibly the most admirable tribute to that communion which has been written of late years. For the fact of the matter is, that the weakness which has rendered barren the many brilliancies of Mr. Moore is actually that weakness which the Roman Catholic Church is at its best in combating. Mr. Moore hates Catholicism because it breaks up the house of looking-glasses in which he lives. Mr. Moore does not dislike so much being asked to believe in the spiritual existence of miracles or sacraments, but he does fundamentally dislike being asked to believe in the actual existence of other people. Like his master Pater and all the aesthetes, his real quarrel with life is that it is not a dream that can be moulded by the dreamer. It is not the dogma of the reality of the other world that troubles him, but the dogma of the reality of this world.

The truth is that the tradition of Christianity (which is still the only coherent ethic of Europe) rests on two or three paradoxes or mysteries which can easily be impugned in argument and as easily justified in life. One of them, for instance, is the paradox of hope or faith—that the more hopeless is the situation the more hopeful must be the man. Stevenson understood this, and consequently Mr. Moore cannot understand Stevenson. Another is the paradox of charity or chivalry that the weaker a thing is the more it should be respected, that the more indefensible a thing is the more it should appeal to us for a certain kind of defence. Thackeray understood this, and therefore Mr. Moore does not understand Thackeray. Now, one of these very practical and working mysteries in the Christian tradition, and one which the Roman Catholic Church, as I say, has done her best work in singling out, is the conception of the sinfulness of pride. Pride is a weakness in the character; it dries up laughter, it dries up wonder, it dries up chivalry and energy. The Christian tradition understands this; therefore Mr. Moore does not understand the Christian tradition.

For the truth is much stranger even than it appears in the formal doctrine of the sin of pride. It is not only true that humility is a much wiser and more vigorous thing than pride. It is also true that vanity is a much wiser and more vigorous thing than pride. Vanity is social—it is almost a kind of comradeship; pride is solitary and uncivilized. Vanity is active; it desires the applause of infinite multitudes; pride is passive, desiring only the applause of one person, which it already has. Vanity is humorous, and can enjoy the joke even of itself; pride is dull, and cannot even smile. And the whole of this difference is the difference between Stevenson and Mr. George Moore, who, as he informs us, has "brushed Stevenson aside." I do not know where he has been brushed to, but wherever it is I fancy he is having a good time, because he had the wisdom to be vain, and not proud. Stevenson had a windy vanity; Mr. Moore has a dusty egoism. Hence Stevenson could amuse himself as well as us with his vanity; while the richest effects of Mr. Moore's absurdity are hidden from his eyes.

If we compare this solemn folly with the happy folly with which Stevenson belauds his own books and berates his own critics, we shall not find it difficult to guess why it is that Stevenson at least found a final philosophy of some sort to live by, while Mr. Moore is always walking the world looking for a new one. Stevenson had found that the secret of life lies in laughter and humility. Self is the gorgon. Vanity sees it in the mirror of other men and lives. Pride studies it for itself and is turned to stone.

It is necessary to dwell on this defect in Mr. Moore, because it is really the weakness of work which is not without its strength. Mr. Moore's egoism is not merely a moral weakness, it is a very constant and influential aesthetic weakness as well. We should really be much more interested in Mr. Moore if he were not quite so interested in himself. We feel as if we were being shown through a gallery of really fine pictures, into each of which, by some useless and discordant convention, the artist had represented the same figure in the same attitude. "The Grand Canal with a distant view of Mr. Moore," "Effect of Mr. Moore through a Scotch Mist," "Mr. Moore by Firelight," "Ruins of Mr. Moore by Moonlight," and so on, seems to be the endless series. He would no doubt reply that in such a book as this he intended to reveal himself. But the answer is that in such a book as this he does not succeed. One of the thousand objections to the sin of pride lies precisely in this, that self-consciousness of necessity destroys self-revelation. A man who thinks a great deal about himself will try to be many-sided, attempt a theatrical excellence at all points, will try to be an encyclopaedia of culture, and his own real personality will be lost in that false universalism. Thinking about himself will lead to trying to be the universe; trying to be the universe will lead to ceasing to be anything. If, on the other hand, a man is sensible enough to think only about the universe; he will think about it in his own individual way. He will keep virgin the secret of God; he will see the grass as no other man can see it, and look at a sun that no man has ever known. This fact is very practically brought out in Mr. Moore's "Confessions." In reading them we do not feel the presence of a clean-cut personality like that of Thackeray and Matthew Arnold. We only read a number of quite clever and largely conflicting opinions which might be uttered by any clever person, but which we are called upon to admire specifically, because they are uttered by Mr. Moore. He is the only thread that connects Catholicism and

Protestantism, realism and mysticism—he or rather his name. He is profoundly absorbed even in views he no longer holds, and he expects us to be. And he intrudes the capital "I" even where it need not be intruded—even where it weakens the force of a plain statement. Where another man would say, "It is a fine day," Mr. Moore says, "Seen through my temperament, the day appeared fine." Where another man would say "Milton has obviously a fine style," Mr. Moore would say, "As a stylist Milton had always impressed me." The Nemesis of this self-centred spirit is that of being totally ineffectual. Mr. Moore has started many interesting crusades, but he has abandoned them before his disciples could begin. Even when he is on the side of the truth he is as fickle as the children of falsehood. Even when he has found reality he cannot find rest. One Irish quality he has which no Irishman was ever without—pugnacity; and that is certainly a great virtue, especially in the present age. But he has not the tenacity of conviction which goes with the fighting spirit in a man like Bernard Shaw. His weakness of introspection and selfishness in all their glory cannot prevent him fighting; but they will always prevent him winning.

X. ON SANDALS AND SIMPLICITY

The great misfortune of the modern English is not at all that they are more boastful than other people (they are not); it is that they are boastful about those particular things which nobody can boast of without losing them. A Frenchman can be proud of being bold and logical, and still remain bold and logical. A German can be proud of being reflective and orderly, and still remain reflective and orderly. But an Englishman cannot be proud of being simple and direct, and still remain simple and direct. In the matter of these strange virtues, to know them is to kill them. A man may be conscious of being heroic or conscious of being divine, but he cannot (in spite of all the Anglo-Saxon poets) be conscious of being unconscious.

Now, I do not think that it can be honestly denied that some portion of this impossibility attaches to a class very different in their own opinion, at least, to the school of Anglo-Saxonism. I mean that school of the simple life, commonly associated with Tolstoy. If a perpetual talk about one's own robustness leads to being less robust, it is even more true that a perpetual talking about one's own simplicity leads to being less simple. One great complaint, I think, must stand against the modern upholders of the simple life—the simple life in all its varied forms, from vegetarianism to the honourable consistency of the Doukhobors. This complaint against them stands, that they would make us simple in the unimportant things, but complex in the important things. They would make us simple in the things that do not matter—that is, in diet, in costume, in etiquette, in economic system. But they would make us complex in the things that do matter—in philosophy, in loyalty, in spiritual acceptance, and spiritual rejection. It does not so very much matter whether a man eats a grilled tomato or a plain tomato; it does very much matter whether he eats a plain tomato with a grilled mind. The only kind of simplicity worth preserving is the simplicity of the heart, the simplicity which accepts and enjoys. There may be a reasonable doubt as to what system preserves this; there can surely be no doubt that a system of simplicity destroys it. There is more simplicity in the man who eats caviar on impulse than in the man who eats grape-nuts on principle. The chief error of these people is to be found in the very phrase to which they are most attached—"plain living and high thinking." These people do not stand in need of, will not be improved by, plain living and high thinking. They stand in need of the contrary. They would be improved by high living and plain thinking. A little high living (I say, having a full sense of responsibility, a little high living) would teach them the force and meaning of the human festivities, of the banquet that has gone on from the beginning of the world. It would teach them the historic fact that the artificial is, if anything, older than the natural. It would teach them that the loving-cup is as old as any hunger. It would teach them that ritualism is older than any religion. And a little plain thinking would teach them how harsh and fanciful are the mass of their own ethics, how very civilized and very complicated must be the brain of the Tolstoyan who really believes it to be evil to love one's country and wicked to strike a blow.

A man approaches, wearing sandals and simple raiment, a raw tomato held firmly in his right hand, and says, "The affections of family and country alike are hindrances to the fuller development of human love;" but the plain thinker will only answer him, with a wonder not untinged with admiration, "What a great deal of trouble you must have taken in order to feel like that." High living will reject the tomato. Plain thinking will equally decisively reject the idea of the invariable sinfulness of war. High living will convince us that nothing is more materialistic than to despise a pleasure as purely material. And plain thinking will convince us that nothing is more materialistic than to reserve our horror chiefly for material wounds.

The only simplicity that matters is the simplicity of the heart. If that be gone, it can be brought back by no turnips or cellular clothing; but only by tears and terror and the fires that are not quenched. If that remain, it matters very little if a few Early Victorian armchairs remain along with it. Let us put a complex entree into a simple old gentleman; let us not put a simple entree into a complex old gentleman. So long as human society will leave my spiritual inside alone, I will allow it, with a comparative submission, to work its wild will with my physical interior. I will submit to cigars. I will meekly embrace a bottle of Burgundy. I will humble myself to a hansom cab. If only by this means I may preserve to myself the virginity of the spirit, which enjoys with astonishment and fear. I do not say that these are the only methods of preserving it. I incline to the belief that there are others. But I will have nothing to do with simplicity which lacks the fear, the astonishment, and the joy alike. I will have nothing to do with the devilish vision of a child who is too simple to like toys.

The child is, indeed, in these, and many other matters, the best guide. And in nothing is the child so righteously childlike, in nothing does he exhibit more accurately the sounder order of simplicity, than in the fact that he sees everything with a simple pleasure, even the complex things. The false type of naturalness harps always on the distinction between the natural and the artificial. The higher kind of naturalness ignores that distinction. To the child the tree and the lamp-post are as natural and as artificial as each other; or rather, neither of them are natural but both supernatural. For both are splendid and unexplained. The flower with which God crowns the one, and the flame with which Sam the lamplighter crowns the other, are equally of the gold of fairy-tales. In the middle of the wildest fields the most rustic child is, ten to one, playing at steam-engines. And the only spiritual or philosophical objection to steam-engines is not that men pay for them or work at them, or make them very ugly, or even that men are killed by them; but merely that men do not play at them. The evil is that the childish poetry of clockwork does not remain. The wrong is not that engines are too much admired, but that they are not admired enough. The sin is not that engines are mechanical, but that men are mechanical.

In this matter, then, as in all the other matters treated in this book, our main conclusion is that it is a fundamental point of view, a philosophy or religion which is needed, and not any change in habit or social routine. The things we need most for immediate practical purposes are all abstractions. We need a right view of the human lot, a right view of the human society; and if we were living eagerly and angrily in the enthusiasm of those things, we should, ipso facto, be living simply in the genuine and spiritual sense. Desire and danger make every one simple. And to those who talk to us with interfering eloquence about Jaeger and the pores of the skin, and about Plasmon and the coats of the stomach, at them shall only be hurled the words that are hurled at fops and gluttons, "Take no thought what ye shall eat or what ye shall drink, or wherewithal ye shall be clothed. For after all these things do the Gentiles seek. But seek first the kingdom of God and His righteousness, and all these things shall be added unto you." Those amazing words are not only extraordinarily good, practical politics; they are also superlatively good hygiene. The one supreme way of making all those processes go right, the processes of health, and strength, and grace, and beauty, the one and only way of making certain of their accuracy, is to think about something else. If a man is bent on climbing into the seventh heaven, he may be quite easy about the pores of his skin. If he harnesses his waggon to a star, the process will have a most satisfactory effect upon the coats of his stomach. For the thing called "taking thought," the thing for which the best modern word is "rationalizing," is in its nature, inapplicable to all plain and urgent things. Men take thought and ponder rationalistically, touching remote things—things that only theoretically matter, such as the transit of Venus. But only at their peril can men rationalize about so practical a matter as health.

XI SCIENCE AND THE SAVAGES

A permanent disadvantage of the study of folk-lore and kindred subjects is that the man of science can hardly be in the nature of things very frequently a man of the world. He is a student of nature; he is scarcely ever a student of human nature. And even where this difficulty is overcome, and he is in some sense a student of human nature, this is only a very faint beginning of the painful progress towards being human. For the study of primitive race and religion stands apart in one important respect from all, or nearly all, the ordinary scientific studies. A man can understand astronomy only by being an astronomer; he can understand entomology only by being an entomologist (or, perhaps, an insect); but he can understand a great deal of anthropology merely by being a man. He is himself the animal which he studies. Hence arises the fact which strikes the eye everywhere in the records of ethnology and folk-lore—the fact that the same frigid and detached spirit which leads to success in the study of astronomy or botany leads to disaster in the study of mythology or human origins. It is necessary to cease to be a man in order to do justice to a microbe; it is not necessary to cease to be a man in order to do justice to men. That same suppression of sympathies, that same waving away of intuitions or guess-work which make a man preternaturally clever in dealing with the stomach of a spider, will make him preternaturally stupid in dealing with the heart of man. He is making himself inhuman in order to understand humanity. An ignorance of the other world is boasted by many men of science; but in this matter their defect arises, not from ignorance of the other world, but from ignorance of this world. For the secrets about which anthropologists concern themselves can be best learnt, not from books or voyages, but from the ordinary commerce of man with man. The secret of why some savage tribe worships monkeys or the moon is not to be found even by travelling among those savages and taking down their answers in a note-book, although the cleverest man may pursue this course. The answer to the riddle is in England; it is in London; nay, it is in his own heart. When a man has discovered why men in Bond Street wear black hats he will at the same moment have discovered why men in Timbuctoo wear red feathers. The mystery in the heart of some savage war-dance should not be studied in books of scientific travel; it should be studied at a subscription ball. If a man desires to find out the origins of religions, let him not go to the Sandwich Islands; let him go to church. If a man wishes to know the origin of human society, to know what society, philosophically speaking, really is, let him not go into the British Museum; let him go into society.

This total misunderstanding of the real nature of ceremonial gives rise to the most awkward and dehumanized versions of the conduct of men in rude lands or ages. The man of science, not realizing that ceremonial is essentially a thing which is done without a reason, has to find a reason for every sort of ceremonial, and, as might be supposed, the reason is generally a very absurd one—absurd because it originates not in the simple mind of the barbarian, but in the sophisticated mind of the professor. The teamed man will say, for instance, "The natives of Mumbojumbo Land believe that the dead man can eat and will require food upon his journey to the other world. This is attested by the fact that they place food in the grave, and that any family not complying with this rite is the object of the anger of the priests and the tribe." To any one acquainted with humanity this way of talking is topsy-turvy. It is like saying, "The English in the twentieth century believed that a dead man could smell. This is attested by the fact that they always covered his grave with lilies, violets, or other flowers. Some priestly and tribal terrors were evidently attached to the neglect of this action, as we have records of several old ladies who were very much disturbed in mind because their wreaths had not arrived in time for the funeral." It may be of course that savages put food with a dead man because they think that a dead man can eat, or weapons with a dead man because they think that a dead man can fight. But personally I do not believe that they think anything of the kind. I believe they put food or weapons on the dead for the same reason that we put flowers, because it is an exceedingly natural and obvious thing to do. We do not understand, it is true, the emotion which makes us think it obvious and natural; but that is because, like all the important emotions of human existence it is essentially irrational. We do not understand the savage for the same reason that the savage does not understand himself. And the savage does not understand himself for the same reason that we do not understand ourselves either.

The obvious truth is that the moment any matter has passed through the human mind it is finally and for ever spoilt for all purposes of science. It has become a thing incurably mysterious and infinite; this mortal has put on immortality. Even what we call our material desires are spiritual, because they are human. Science can analyse a pork-chop, and say how much of it is phosphorus and how much is protein; but science cannot analyse any man's wish for a pork-chop, and say how much of it is hunger, how much custom, how much nervous fancy, how much a haunting love of the beautiful. The man's desire for the pork-chop remains literally as mystical and ethereal as his desire for heaven. All attempts, therefore, at a science of any human things, at a science of history, a science of folk-lore, a science of sociology, are by their nature not merely hopeless, but crazy. You can no more be certain in economic history that a man's desire for money was merely a desire for money than you can be certain in hagiology that a saint's desire for God was merely a desire for God. And this kind of vagueness in the primary phenomena of the study is an absolutely final blow to anything in the nature of a science. Men can construct a science with very few instruments, or with very plain instruments; but no one on earth could construct a science with unreliable instruments. A man might work out the whole of mathematics with a handful of pebbles, but not with a handful of clay which was always falling apart into new fragments, and falling together into new combinations. A man might measure heaven and earth with a reed, but not with a growing reed.

As one of the enormous follies of folk-lore, let us take the case of the transmigration of stories, and the alleged unity of their source. Story after story the scientific mythologists have cut out of its place in history, and pinned side by side with similar stories in their museum of fables. The process is industrious, it is fascinating, and the whole of it rests on one of the plainest fallacies in the world. That a story has been told all over the place at some time or other, not only does not prove that it never really happened; it does not even faintly indicate or make slightly more probable that it never happened. That a large number of fishermen have falsely asserted that they have caught a pike two feet long, does not in the least affect the question of whether any one ever really did so. That numberless journalists announce a Franco-German war merely for money is no evidence one way or the other upon the dark question of whether such a war ever occurred. Doubtless in a few hundred years the innumerable Franco-German wars that did not happen will have cleared the scientific mind of any belief in the legendary war of '70 which did. But that will be because if folk-lore students remain at all, their nature will be unchanged; and their services to folk-lore will be still as they are at present, greater than they know. For in truth these men do something far more godlike than studying legends; they create them.

There are two kinds of stories which the scientists say cannot be true, because everybody tells them. The first class consists of the stories which are told everywhere, because they are somewhat odd or clever; there is nothing in the world to prevent their having happened to somebody as an adventure any more than there is anything to prevent their having occurred, as they certainly did occur, to somebody as an idea. But they are not likely to have happened to many people. The second class of their "myths" consist of the stories that are told everywhere for the simple reason that they happen everywhere. Of the first class, for instance, we might take such an example as the story of William Tell, now generally ranked among legends upon the sole ground that it is found in the tales of other peoples. Now, it is obvious that this was told everywhere because whether true or fictitious it is what is called "a good story;" it is odd, exciting, and it has a climax. But to suggest that some such eccentric incident can never have happened in the whole history of archery, or that it did not happen to any particular person of whom it is told, is stark impudence. The idea of shooting at a mark attached to some valuable or beloved person is an idea doubtless that might easily have occurred to any inventive poet. But it is also an idea that might easily occur to any boastful archer. It might be one of the fantastic caprices of some story-teller. It might equally well be one of the fantastic caprices of some tyrant. It might occur first in real life and afterwards occur in legends. Or it might just as well occur first in legends and afterwards occur in real life. If no apple has ever been shot off a boy's head from the beginning of the world, it may be done tomorrow morning, and by somebody who has never heard of William Tell.

This type of tale, indeed, may be pretty fairly paralleled with the ordinary anecdote terminating in a repartee or an Irish bull. Such a retort as the famous "je ne vois pas la necessite" we have all seen attributed to Talleyrand, to Voltaire, to Henri Quatre, to an anonymous judge, and so on. But this variety does not in any way make it more likely that the thing was never said at all. It is highly likely that it was really said by somebody unknown. It is highly likely that it was really said by Talleyrand. In any case, it is not any more difficult to believe that the mot might have occurred to a man in conversation than to a man writing memoirs. It might have occurred to any of the men I have mentioned. But there is this point of distinction about it, that it is not likely to have occurred to all of them. And this is where the first class of so-called myth differs from the second to which I have previously referred. For there is a second class of incident found to be common to the stories of five or six heroes, say to Sigurd, to Hercules, to Rustem, to the Cid, and so on. And the peculiarity of this myth is that not only is it highly reasonable to imagine that it really happened to one hero, but it is highly reasonable to imagine that it really happened to all of them. Such a story, for instance, is that of a great man having his strength swayed or thwarted by the mysterious weakness of a woman. The anecdotal story, the story of William Tell, is as I have said, popular, because it is peculiar. But this kind of story, the story of Samson and Delilah of Arthur and Guinevere, is obviously popular because it is not peculiar. It is popular as good, quiet fiction is popular, because it tells the truth about people. If the ruin of Samson by a woman, and the ruin of Hercules by a woman, have a common legendary origin, it is gratifying to know that we can also explain, as a fable, the ruin of Nelson by a woman and the ruin of Parnell by a woman. And, indeed, I have no doubt whatever that, some centuries hence, the students of folk-lore will refuse altogether to believe that Elizabeth Barrett eloped with Robert Browning, and will prove their point up to the hilt by the unquestionable fact that the whole fiction of the period was full of such elopements from end to end.

Possibly the most pathetic of all the delusions of the modern students of primitive belief is the notion they have about the thing they call anthropomorphism. They believe that primitive men attributed phenomena to a god in human form in order to explain them, because his mind in its sullen limitation could not reach any further than his own clownish existence. The thunder was called the voice of a man, the lightning the eyes of a man, because by this explanation they were made more reasonable and comfortable. The final cure for all this kind of philosophy is to walk down a lane at night. Any one who does so will discover very quickly that men pictured something semi-human at the back of all things, not because such a thought was natural, but because it was supernatural; not because it made things more comprehensible, but because it made them a hundred times more incomprehensible and mysterious. For a man walking down a lane at night can see the conspicuous fact that as long as nature keeps to her own course, she has no power with us at all. As long as a tree is a tree, it is a top-heavy monster with a hundred arms, a thousand tongues, and only one leg. But so long as a tree is a tree, it does not frighten us at all. It begins to be something alien, to be something strange, only when it looks like ourselves. When a tree really looks like a man our knees knock under us. And when the whole universe looks like a man we fall on our faces.

XII PAGANISM AND MR. LOWES DICKINSON

Of the New Paganism (or neo-Paganism), as it was preached flamboyantly by Mr. Swinburne or delicately by Walter Pater, there is no necessity to take any very grave account, except as a thing which left behind it incomparable exercises in the English language. The New Paganism is no longer new, and it never at any time bore the smallest resemblance to Paganism. The ideas about the ancient civilization which it has left loose in the public mind are certainly extraordinary enough. The term "pagan" is continually used in fiction and light literature as meaning a man without any religion, whereas a pagan was generally a man with about half a dozen. The pagans, according to this notion, were continually crowning themselves with flowers and dancing about in an irresponsible state, whereas, if there were two things that the best pagan civilization did honestly believe in, they were a rather too rigid dignity and a much too rigid responsibility. Pagans are depicted as above all things inebriate and lawless, whereas they were above all things reasonable and respectable. They are praised as disobedient when they had only one great virtue—civic obedience. They are envied and admired as shamelessly happy when they had only one great sin—despair.

Mr. Lowes Dickinson, the most pregnant and provocative of recent writers on this and similar subjects, is far too solid a man to have fallen into this old error of the mere anarchy of Paganism. In order to make hay of that Hellenic enthusiasm which has as its ideal mere appetite and egotism, it is not necessary to know much philosophy, but merely to know a little Greek. Mr. Lowes Dickinson knows a great deal of philosophy, and also a great deal of Greek, and his error, if error he has, is not that of the crude hedonist. But the contrast which he offers between Christianity and Paganism in the matter of moral ideals—a contrast which he states very ably in a paper called "How long halt ye?" which appeared in the Independent Review—does, I think, contain an error of a deeper kind. According to him, the ideal of Paganism was not, indeed, a mere frenzy of lust and liberty and caprice, but was an ideal of full and satisfied humanity. According to him, the ideal of Christianity was the ideal of asceticism. When I say that I think this idea wholly wrong as a matter of philosophy and history, I am not talking for the moment about any ideal Christianity of my own, or even of any primitive Christianity undefiled by after events. I am not, like so many modern Christian idealists, basing my case upon certain things which Christ said. Neither am I, like so many other Christian idealists, basing my case upon certain things that Christ forgot to say. I take historic Christianity with all its sins upon its head; I take it, as

I would take Jacobinism, or Mormonism, or any other mixed or unpleasing human product, and I say that the meaning of its action was not to be found in asceticism. I say that its point of departure from Paganism was not asceticism. I say that its point of difference with the modern world was not asceticism. I say that St. Simeon Stylites had not his main inspiration in asceticism. I say that the main Christian impulse cannot be described as asceticism, even in the ascetics.

Let me set about making the matter clear. There is one broad fact about the relations of Christianity and Paganism which is so simple that many will smile at it, but which is so important that all moderns forget it. The primary fact about Christianity and Paganism is that one came after the other. Mr. Lowes Dickinson speaks of them as if they were parallel ideals—even speaks as if Paganism were the newer of the two, and the more fitted for a new age. He suggests that the Pagan ideal will be the ultimate good of man; but if that is so, we must at least ask with more curiosity than he allows for, why it was that man actually found his ultimate good on earth under the stars, and threw it away again. It is this extraordinary enigma to which I propose to attempt an answer.

There is only one thing in the modern world that has been face to face with Paganism; there is only one thing in the modern world which in that sense knows anything about Paganism: and that is Christianity. That fact is really the weak point in the whole of that hedonistic neo-Paganism of which I have spoken. All that genuinely remains of the ancient hymns or the ancient dances of Europe, all that has honestly come to us from the festivals of Phoebus or Pan, is to be found in the festivals of the Christian Church. If any one wants to hold the end of a chain which really goes back to the heathen mysteries, he had better take hold of a festoon of flowers at Easter or a string of sausages at Christmas. Everything else in the modern world is of Christian origin, even everything that seems most anti-Christian. The French Revolution is of Christian origin. The newspaper is of Christian origin. The anarchists are of Christian origin. Physical science is of Christian origin. The attack on Christianity is of Christian origin. There is one thing, and one thing only, in existence at the present day which can in any sense accurately be said to be of pagan origin, and that is Christianity.

The real difference between Paganism and Christianity is perfectly summed up in the difference between the pagan, or natural, virtues, and those three virtues of Christianity which the Church of Rome calls virtues of grace. The pagan, or rational, virtues are such things as justice and temperance, and Christianity has adopted them. The three mystical virtues which Christianity has not adopted, but invented, are faith, hope, and charity. Now much easy and foolish Christian rhetoric could easily be poured out upon those three words, but I desire to confine myself to the two facts which are evident about them. The first evident fact (in marked contrast to the delusion of the dancing pagan)—the first evident fact, I say, is that the pagan virtues, such as justice and temperance, are the sad virtues, and that the mystical virtues of faith, hope, and charity are the gay and exuberant virtues. And the second evident fact, which is even more evident, is the fact that the pagan virtues are the reasonable virtues, and that the Christian virtues of faith, hope, and charity are in their essence as unreasonable as they can be.

As the word "unreasonable" is open to misunderstanding, the matter may be more accurately put by saying that each one of these Christian or mystical virtues involves a paradox in its own nature, and that this is not true of any of the typically pagan or rationalist virtues. Justice consists in finding out a certain thing due to a certain man and giving it to him. Temperance consists in finding out the proper limit of a particular indulgence and adhering to that. But charity means pardoning what is unpardonable, or it is no virtue at all. Hope means hoping when things are hopeless, or it is no virtue at all. And faith means believing the incredible, or it is no virtue at all.

It is somewhat amusing, indeed, to notice the difference between the fate of these three paradoxes in the fashion of the modern mind. Charity is a fashionable virtue in our time; it is lit up by the gigantic firelight of Dickens. Hope is a fashionable virtue to-day; our attention has been arrested for it by the sudden and silver trumpet of Stevenson. But faith is unfashionable, and it is customary on every side to cast against it the fact that it is a paradox. Everybody mockingly repeats the famous childish definition that faith is "the power of believing that which we know to be untrue." Yet it is not one atom more paradoxical than hope or charity. Charity is the power of defending that which we know to be indefensible. Hope is the power of being cheerful in circumstances which we know to be desperate. It is true that there is a state of hope which belongs to bright prospects and the morning; but that is not the virtue of hope. The virtue of hope exists only in earthquake and, eclipse. It is true that there is a thing crudely called charity, which means charity to the deserving poor; but charity to the deserving is not charity at all, but justice. It is the undeserving who require it, and the ideal either does not exist at all, or exists wholly for them. For practical purposes it is at the hopeless moment that we require the hopeful man, and the virtue either does not exist at all, or begins to exist at that moment. Exactly at the instant when hope ceases to be reasonable it begins to be useful. Now the old pagan world went perfectly straightforward until it discovered that going straightforward is an enormous mistake. It was nobly and beautifully reasonable, and discovered in its death-pang this lasting and valuable truth, a heritage for the ages, that reasonableness will not do. The pagan age was truly an Eden or golden age, in this essential sense, that it is not to be recovered. And it is not to be recovered in this sense again that, while we are certainly jollier than the pagans, and much more right than the pagans, there is not one of us who can, by the utmost stretch of energy, be so sensible as the pagans. That naked innocence of the intellect cannot be recovered by any man after Christianity; and for this excellent reason, that every man after Christianity knows it to be misleading. Let me take an example, the first that occurs to the mind, of this impossible plainness in the pagan point of view. The greatest tribute to Christianity in the modern world is Tennyson's "Ulysses." The poet reads into the story of Ulysses the conception of an incurable desire to wander. But the real Ulysses does not desire to wander at all. He desires to get home. He displays his heroic and unconquerable qualities in resisting the misfortunes which baulk him; but that is all. There is no love of adventure for its own sake; that is a Christian product. There is no love of Penelope for her own sake;

that is a Christian product. Everything in that old world would appear to have been clean and obvious. A good man was a good man; a bad man was a bad man. For this reason they had no charity; for charity is a reverent agnosticism towards the complexity of the soul. For this reason they had no such thing as the art of fiction, the novel; for the novel is a creation of the mystical idea of charity. For them a pleasant landscape was pleasant, and an unpleasant landscape unpleasant. Hence they had no idea of romance; for romance consists in thinking a thing more delightful because it is dangerous; it is a Christian idea. In a word, we cannot reconstruct or even imagine the beautiful and astonishing pagan world. It was a world in which common sense was really common.

My general meaning touching the three virtues of which I have spoken will now, I hope, be sufficiently clear. They are all three paradoxical, they are all three practical, and they are all three paradoxical because they are practical. it is the stress of ultimate need, and a terrible knowledge of things as they are, which led men to set up these riddles, and to die for them. Whatever may be the meaning of the contradiction, it is the fact that the only kind of hope that is of any use in a battle is a hope that denies arithmetic. Whatever may be the meaning of the contradiction, it is the fact that the only kind of charity which any weak spirit wants, or which any generous spirit feels, is the charity which forgives the sins that are like scarlet. Whatever may be the meaning of faith, it must always mean a certainty about something we cannot prove. Thus, for instance, we believe by faith in the existence of other people.

But there is another Christian virtue, a virtue far more obviously and historically connected with Christianity, which will illustrate even better the connection between paradox and practical necessity. This virtue cannot be questioned in its capacity as a historical symbol; certainly Mr. Lowes Dickinson will not question it. It has been the boast of hundreds of the champions of Christianity. It has been the taunt of hundreds of the opponents of Christianity. It is, in essence, the basis of Mr. Lowes Dickinson's whole distinction between Christianity and Paganism. I mean, of course, the virtue of humility. I admit, of course, most readily, that a great deal of false Eastern humility (that is, of strictly ascetic humility) mixed itself with the main stream of European Christianity. We must not forget that when we speak of Christianity we are speaking of a whole continent for about a thousand years. But of this virtue even more than of the other three, I would maintain the general proposition adopted above. Civilization discovered Christian humility for the same urgent reason that it discovered faith and charity—that is, because Christian civilization had to discover it or die.

The great psychological discovery of Paganism, which turned it into Christianity, can be expressed with some accuracy in one phrase. The pagan set out, with admirable sense, to enjoy himself. By the end of his civilization he had discovered that a man cannot enjoy himself and continue to enjoy anything else. Mr. Lowes Dickinson has pointed out in words too excellent to need any further elucidation, the absurd shallowness of those who imagine that the pagan enjoyed himself only in a materialistic sense. Of course, he enjoyed himself, not only intellectually even, he enjoyed himself morally, he enjoyed himself spiritually. But it was himself that he was enjoying; on the face of it, a very natural thing to do. Now, the psychological discovery is merely this, that whereas it had been supposed that the fullest possible enjoyment is to be found by extending our ego to infinity, the truth is that the fullest possible enjoyment is to be found by reducing our ego to zero.

Humility is the thing which is for ever renewing the earth and the stars. It is humility, and not duty, which preserves the stars from wrong, from the unpardonable wrong of casual resignation; it is through humility that the most ancient heavens for us are fresh and strong. The curse that came before history has laid on us all a tendency to be weary of wonders. If we saw the sun for the first time it would be the most fearful and beautiful of meteors. Now that we see it for the hundredth time we call it, in the hideous and blasphemous phrase of Wordsworth, "the light of common day." We are inclined to increase our claims. We are inclined to demand six suns, to demand a blue sun, to demand a green sun. Humility is perpetually putting us back in the primal darkness. There all light is lightning, startling and instantaneous. Until we understand that original dark, in which we have neither sight nor expectation, we can give no hearty and childlike praise to the splendid sensationalism of things. The terms "pessimism" and "optimism," like most modern terms, are unmeaning. But if they can be used in any vague sense as meaning something, we may say that in this great fact pessimism is the very basis of optimism. The man who destroys himself creates the universe. To the humble man, and to the humble man alone, the sun is really a sun; to the humble man, and to the humble man alone, the sea is really a sea. When he looks at all the faces in the street, he does not only realize that men are alive, he realizes with a dramatic pleasure that they are not dead.

I have not spoken of another aspect of the discovery of humility as a psychological necessity, because it is more commonly insisted on, and is in itself more obvious. But it is equally clear that humility is a permanent necessity as a condition of effort and self-examination. It is one of the deadly fallacies of Jingo politics that a nation is stronger for despising other nations. As a matter of fact, the strongest nations are those, like Prussia or Japan, which began from very mean beginnings, but have not been too proud to sit at the feet of the foreigner and learn everything from him. Almost every obvious and direct victory has been the victory of the plagiarist. This is, indeed, only a very paltry by-product of humility, but it is a product of humility, and, therefore, it is successful. Prussia had no Christian humility in its internal arrangements; hence its internal arrangements were miserable. But it had enough Christian humility slavishly to copy France (even down to Frederick the Great's poetry), and that which it had the humility to copy it had ultimately the honour to conquer. The case of the Japanese is even more obvious; their only Christian and their only beautiful quality is that they have humbled themselves to be exalted. All this aspect of humility, however, as connected with the matter of effort and striving for a standard set above us, I dismiss as having been sufficiently pointed out by almost all idealistic writers.

It may be worth while, however, to point out the interesting disparity in the matter of humility between the modern notion of the strong man and the actual records of strong men. Carlyle objected to the statement that no man could be a hero to his valet. Every sympathy can be extended towards him in the matter if he merely or mainly meant that the phrase was a disparagement of hero-worship. Hero-worship is certainly a generous and human impulse; the hero may be faulty, but the worship can hardly be. It may be that no man would be a hero to his valet. But any man would be a valet to his hero. But in truth both the proverb itself and Carlyle's stricture upon it ignore the most essential matter at issue. The ultimate psychological truth is not that no man is a hero to his valet. The ultimate psychological truth, the foundation of Christianity, is that no man is a hero to himself. Cromwell, according to Carlyle, was a strong man. According to Cromwell, he was a weak one.

The weak point in the whole of Carlyle's case for aristocracy lies, indeed, in his most celebrated phrase. Carlyle said that men were mostly fools. Christianity, with a surer and more reverent realism, says that they are all fools. This doctrine is sometimes called the doctrine of original sin. It may also be described as the doctrine of the equality of men. But the essential point of it is merely this, that whatever primary and far-reaching moral dangers affect any man, affect all men. All men can be criminals, if tempted; all men can be heroes, if inspired. And this doctrine does away altogether with Carlyle's pathetic belief (or any one else's pathetic belief) in "the wise few." There are no wise few. Every aristocracy that has ever existed has behaved, in all essential points, exactly like a small mob. Every oligarchy is merely a knot of men in the street—that is to say, it is very jolly, but not infallible. And no oligarchies in the world's history have ever come off so badly in practical affairs as the very proud oligarchies—the oligarchy of Poland, the oligarchy of Venice. And the armies that have most swiftly and suddenly broken their enemies in pieces have been the religious armies—the Moslem Armies, for instance, or the Puritan Armies. And a religious army may, by its nature, be defined as an army in which every man is taught not to exalt but to abase himself. Many modern Englishmen talk of themselves as the sturdy descendants of their sturdy Puritan fathers. As a fact, they would run away from a cow. If you asked one of their Puritan fathers, if you asked Bunyan, for instance, whether he was sturdy, he would have answered, with tears, that he was as weak as water. And because of this he would have borne tortures. And this virtue of humility, while being practical enough to win battles, will always be paradoxical enough to puzzle pedants. It is at one with the virtue of charity in this respect. Every generous person will admit that the one kind of sin which charity should cover is the sin which is inexcusable. And every generous person will equally agree that the one kind of pride which is wholly damnable is the pride of the man who has something to be proud of. The pride which, proportionally speaking, does not hurt the character, is the pride in things which reflect no credit on the person at all. Thus it does a man no harm to be proud of his country, and comparatively little harm to be proud of his remote ancestors. It does him more harm to be proud of having made money, because in that he has a little more reason for pride. It does him more harm still to be proud of what is nobler than money—intellect. And it does him most harm of all to value himself for the most valuable thing on earth—

goodness. The man who is proud of what is really creditable to him is the Pharisee, the man whom Christ Himself could not forbear to strike.

My objection to Mr. Lowes Dickinson and the reassertors of the pagan ideal is, then, this. I accuse them of ignoring definite human discoveries in the moral world, discoveries as definite, though not as material, as the discovery of the circulation of the blood. We cannot go back to an ideal of reason and sanity. For mankind has discovered that reason does not lead to sanity. We cannot go back to an ideal of pride and enjoyment. For mankind has discovered that pride does not lead to enjoyment. I do not know by what extraordinary mental accident modern writers so constantly connect the idea of progress with the idea of independent thinking. Progress is obviously the antithesis of independent thinking. For under independent or individualistic thinking, every man starts at the beginning, and goes, in all probability, just as far as his father before him. But if there really be anything of the nature of progress, it must mean, above all things, the careful study and assumption of the whole of the past. I accuse Mr. Lowes Dickinson and his school of reaction in the only real sense. If he likes, let him ignore these great historic mysteries—the mystery of charity, the mystery of chivalry, the mystery of faith. If he likes, let him ignore the plough or the printing-press. But if we do revive and pursue the pagan ideal of a simple and rational self-completion we shall end—where Paganism ended. I do not mean that we shall end in destruction. I mean that we shall end in Christianity.

XIII. CELTS AND CELTOPHILES

Science in the modern world has many uses; its chief use, however, is to provide long words to cover the errors of the rich. The word "kleptomania" is a vulgar example of what I mean. It is on a par with that strange theory, always advanced when a wealthy or prominent person is in the dock, that exposure is more of a punishment for the rich than for the poor. Of course, the very reverse is the truth. Exposure is more of a punishment for the poor than for the rich. The richer a man is the easier it is for him to be a tramp. The richer a man is the easier it is for him to be popular and generally respected in the Cannibal Islands. But the poorer a man is the more likely it is that he will have to use his past life whenever he wants to get a bed for the night. Honour is a luxury for aristocrats, but it is a necessity for hall-porters. This is a secondary matter, but it is an example of the general proposition I offer—the proposition that an enormous amount of modern ingenuity is expended on finding defences for the indefensible conduct of the powerful. As I have said above, these defences generally exhibit themselves most emphatically in the form of appeals to physical science. And of all the forms in which science, or pseudo-science, has come to the rescue of the rich and stupid, there is none so singular as the singular invention of the theory of races.

When a wealthy nation like the English discovers the perfectly patent fact that it is making a ludicrous mess of the government of a poorer nation like the Irish, it pauses for a moment in consternation, and then begins to talk about Celts and Teutons. As far as I can understand the theory, the Irish are Celts and the English are Teutons. Of course, the Irish are not Celts any more than the English are Teutons. I have not followed the ethnological discussion with much energy, but the last scientific conclusion which I read inclined on the whole to the summary that the English were mainly Celtic and the Irish mainly Teutonic. But no man alive, with even the glimmering of a real scientific sense, would ever dream of applying the terms "Celtic" or "Teutonic" to either of them in any positive or useful sense.

That sort of thing must be left to people who talk about the Anglo-Saxon race, and extend the expression to America. How much of the blood of the Angles and Saxons (whoever they were) there remains in our mixed British, Roman, German, Dane, Norman, and Picard stock is a matter only interesting to wild antiquaries. And how much of that diluted blood can possibly remain in that roaring whirlpool of America into which a cataract of Swedes, Jews, Germans, Irishmen, and Italians is perpetually pouring, is a matter only interesting to lunatics. It would have been wiser for the English governing class to have called upon some other god.

All other gods, however weak and warring, at least boast of being constant. But science boasts of being in a flux for ever; boasts of being unstable as water.

And England and the English governing class never did call on this absurd deity of race until it seemed, for an instant, that they had no other god to call on. All the most genuine Englishmen in history would have yawned or laughed in your face if you had begun to talk about Anglo-Saxons. If you had attempted to substitute the ideal of race for the ideal of nationality, I really do not like to think what they would have said. I certainly should not like to have been the officer of Nelson who suddenly discovered his French blood on the eve of Trafalgar. I should not like to have been the Norfolk or Suffolk gentleman who had to expound to Admiral Blake by what demonstrable ties of genealogy he was irrevocably bound to the Dutch. The truth of the whole matter is very simple. Nationality exists, and has nothing in the world to do with race. Nationality is a thing like a church or a secret society; it is a product of the human soul and will; it is a spiritual product. And there are men in the modern world who would think anything and do anything rather than admit that anything could be a spiritual product.

A nation, however, as it confronts the modern world, is a purely spiritual product. Sometimes it has been born in independence, like Scotland. Sometimes it has been born in dependence, in subjugation, like Ireland. Sometimes it is a large thing cohering out of many smaller things, like Italy. Sometimes it is a small thing breaking away from larger things, like Poland. But in each and every case its quality is purely spiritual, or, if you will, purely psychological. It is a moment when five men become a sixth man. Every one knows it who has ever founded a club. It is a moment when five places become one place. Every one must know it who has ever had to repel an invasion. Mr. Timothy Healy, the most serious intellect in the present House of Commons, summed up nationality to perfection when he simply called it something for which people will die, As he excellently said in reply to Lord Hugh Cecil, "No one, not even the noble lord, would die for the meridian of Greenwich." And that is the great tribute to its purely psychological character. It is idle to ask why Greenwich should not cohere in this spiritual manner while Athens or Sparta did. It is like asking why a man falls in love with one woman and not with another.

Now, of this great spiritual coherence, independent of external circumstances, or of race, or of any obvious physical thing, Ireland is the most remarkable example. Rome conquered nations, but Ireland has conquered races. The Norman has gone there and become Irish, the Scotchman has gone there and become Irish, the Spaniard has gone there and become Irish, even the bitter soldier of Cromwell has gone there and become Irish. Ireland, which did not exist even politically, has been stronger than all the races that existed scientifically. The purest Germanic blood, the purest Norman blood, the purest blood of the passionate Scotch patriot, has not been so attractive as a nation without a flag. Ireland, unrecognized and oppressed, has easily absorbed races, as such trifles are easily absorbed. She has easily disposed of physical science, as such superstitions are easily disposed of. Nationality in its weakness has been stronger than ethnology in its strength. Five triumphant races have been absorbed, have been defeated by a defeated nationality.

This being the true and strange glory of Ireland, it is impossible to hear without impatience of the attempt so constantly made among her modern sympathizers to talk about Celts and Celticism. Who were the Celts? I defy anybody to say. Who are the Irish? I defy any one to be indifferent, or to pretend not to know. Mr. W. B. Yeats, the great Irish genius who has appeared in our time, shows his own admirable penetration in discarding altogether the argument from a Celtic race. But he does not wholly escape, and his followers hardly ever escape, the general objection to the Celtic argument. The tendency of that argument is to represent the Irish or the Celts as a strange and separate race, as a tribe of eccentrics in the modern world immersed in dim legends and fruitless dreams. Its tendency is to exhibit the Irish as odd, because they see the fairies. Its trend is to make the Irish seem weird and wild because they sing old songs and join in strange dances. But this is quite an error; indeed, it is the opposite of the truth. It is the English who are odd because they do not see the fairies. It is the inhabitants of Kensington who are weird and wild because they do not sing old songs and join in strange dances. In all this the Irish are not in the least strange and separate, are not in the least Celtic, as the word is commonly and popularly used. In all this the Irish are simply an ordinary sensible nation, living the life of any other ordinary and sensible nation which has not been either sodden with smoke or oppressed by money-lenders, or otherwise corrupted with wealth and science. There is nothing Celtic about having legends. It is merely human. The Germans, who are (I suppose) Teutonic, have hundreds of legends, wherever it happens that the Germans are human. There is nothing Celtic about loving poetry; the English loved poetry more, perhaps, than any other people before they came under the shadow of the chimney-pot and the shadow of the chimney-pot hat. It is not Ireland which is mad and mystic; it is Manchester which is mad and mystic, which is incredible, which is a wild exception among human things. Ireland has no need to play the silly game of the science of races; Ireland has no need to pretend to be a tribe of visionaries apart. In the matter of visions, Ireland is more than a nation, it is a model nation.

XIV ON CERTAIN MODERN WRITERS AND THE INSTITUTION OF THE FAMILY

The family may fairly be considered, one would think, an ultimate human institution. Every one would admit that it has been the main cell and central unit of almost all societies hitherto, except, indeed, such societies as that of Lacedaemon, which went in for "efficiency," and has, therefore, perished, and left not a trace behind. Christianity, even enormous as was its revolution, did not alter this ancient and savage sanctity; it merely reversed it. It did not deny the trinity of father, mother, and child. It merely read it backwards, making it run child, mother, father. This it called, not the family, but the Holy Family, for many things are made holy by being turned upside down. But some sages of our own decadence have made a serious attack on the family. They have impugned it, as I think wrongly; and its defenders have defended it, and defended it wrongly. The common defence of the family is that, amid the stress and fickleness of life, it is peaceful, pleasant, and at one. But there is another defence of the family which is possible, and to me evident; this defence is that the family is not peaceful and not pleasant and not at one.

It is not fashionable to say much nowadays of the advantages of the small community. We are told that we must go in for large empires and large ideas. There is one advantage, however, in the small state, the city, or the village, which only the wilfully blind can overlook. The man who lives in a small community lives in a much larger world. He knows much more of the fierce varieties and uncompromising divergences of men. The reason is obvious. In a large community we can choose our companions. In a small community our companions are chosen for us. Thus in all extensive and highly civilized societies groups come into existence founded upon what is called sympathy, and shut out the real world more sharply than the gates of a monastery. There is nothing really narrow about the clan; the thing which is really narrow is the clique. The men of the clan live together because they all wear the same tartan or are all descended from the same sacred cow; but in their souls, by the divine luck of things, there will always be more colours than in any tartan. But the men of the clique live together because they have the same kind of soul, and their narrowness is a narrowness of spiritual coherence and contentment, like that which exists in hell. A big society exists in order to form cliques. A big society is a society for the promotion of narrowness. It is a machinery for the purpose of guarding the solitary and sensitive individual from all experience of the bitter and bracing human compromises. It is, in the most literal sense of the words, a society for the prevention of Christian knowledge.

We can see this change, for instance, in the modern transformation of the thing called a club. When London was smaller, and the parts of London more self-contained and parochial, the club was what it still is in villages, the opposite of what it is now in great cities. Then the club was valued as a place where a man could be sociable. Now the club is valued as a place where a man can be unsociable. The more the enlargement and elaboration of our civilization goes on the more the club ceases to be a place where a man can have a noisy argument, and becomes more and more a place where a man can have what is somewhat fantastically called a quiet chop. Its aim is to make a man comfortable, and to make a man comfortable is to make him the opposite of sociable. Sociability, like all good things, is full of discomforts, dangers, and renunciations. The club tends to produce the most degraded of all combinations—the luxurious anchorite, the man who combines the self-indulgence of Lucullus with the insane loneliness of St. Simeon Stylites.

If we were to-morrow morning snowed up in the street in which we live, we should step suddenly into a much larger and much wilder world than we have ever known. And it is the whole effort of the typically modern person to escape from the street in which he lives. First he invents modern hygiene and goes to Margate. Then he invents modern culture and goes to Florence. Then he invents modern imperialism and goes to Timbuctoo. He goes to the fantastic borders of the earth. He pretends to shoot tigers. He almost rides on a camel. And in all this he is still essentially fleeing from the street in which he was born; and of this flight he is always ready with his own explanation. He says he is fleeing from his street because it is dull; he is lying. He is really fleeing from his street because it is a great deal too exciting. It is exciting because it is exacting; it is exacting because it is alive. He can visit Venice because to him the Venetians are only Venetians; the people in his own street are men. He can stare at the Chinese because for him the Chinese are a passive thing to be stared at; if he stares at the old lady in the next garden, she becomes active. He is forced to flee, in short, from the too stimulating society of his equals—of free men, perverse, personal, deliberately different from himself. The street in Brixton is too glowing and overpowering. He has to soothe and quiet himself among tigers and vultures, camels and crocodiles. These creatures are indeed very different from himself. But they do not put their shape or colour or custom into a decisive intellectual competition with his own. They do not seek to destroy his principles and assert their own; the stranger monsters of the suburban street do seek to do this. The camel does not contort his features into a fine sneer because Mr. Robinson has not got a hump; the cultured gentleman at No. 5 does exhibit a sneer because Robinson has not got a dado. The vulture will not roar with laughter because a man does not fly; but the major at No. 9 will roar with laughter because a man does not smoke. The complaint we commonly have to make of our neighbours is that they will not, as we express it, mind their own business. We do not really mean that they will not mind their own business. If our neighbours did not mind their own business they would be asked abruptly for their rent, and would rapidly cease to be our neighbours. What we really mean when we say that they cannot mind their own business is something much deeper. We do not dislike them because they have so little force and fire that they cannot be interested in themselves. We dislike them because they have so much force and fire that they can be interested in us as well. What we dread about our neighbours, in short, is not the narrowness of their horizon, but their superb tendency to broaden it. And all aversions to ordinary humanity have this general character. They are not aversions to its feebleness (as is pretended), but to its energy. The misanthropes pretend that they despise humanity for its weakness. As a matter of fact, they hate it for its strength.

Of course, this shrinking from the brutal vivacity and brutal variety of common men is a perfectly reasonable and excusable thing as long as it does not pretend to any point of superiority. It is when it calls itself aristocracy or aestheticism or a superiority to the bourgeoisie that its inherent weakness has in justice to be pointed out. Fastidiousness is the most pardonable of vices; but it is the most unpardonable of virtues. Nietzsche, who represents most prominently this pretentious claim of the fastidious, has a description somewhere—a very powerful description in the purely literary sense—of the disgust and disdain which consume him at the sight of the common people with their common faces, their common voices, and their common minds. As I have said, this attitude is almost beautiful if we may regard it as pathetic. Nietzsche's aristocracy has about it all the sacredness that belongs to the weak. When he makes us feel that he cannot endure the innumerable faces, the incessant voices, the overpowering omnipresence which belongs to the mob, he will have the sympathy of anybody who has ever been sick on a steamer or tired in a crowded omnibus. Every man has hated mankind when he was less than a man. Every man has had humanity in his eyes like a blinding fog, humanity in his nostrils like a suffocating smell. But when Nietzsche has the incredible lack of humour and lack of imagination to ask us to believe that his aristocracy is an aristocracy of strong muscles or an aristocracy of strong wills, it is necessary to point out the truth. It is an aristocracy of weak nerves.

We make our friends; we make our enemies; but God makes our next-door neighbour. Hence he comes to us clad in all the careless terrors of nature; he is as strange as the stars, as reckless and indifferent as the rain. He is Man, the most terrible of the beasts. That is why the old religions and the old scriptural language showed so sharp a wisdom when they spoke, not of one's duty towards humanity, but one's duty towards one's neighbour. The duty towards humanity may often take the form of some choice which is personal or even pleasurable. That duty may be a hobby; it may even be a dissipation. We may work in the East End because we are peculiarly fitted to work in the East End, or because we think we are; we may fight for the cause of international peace because we are very fond of fighting. The most monstrous martyrdom, the most repulsive experience, may be the result of choice or a kind of taste. We may be so made as to be particularly fond of lunatics or specially interested in leprosy. We may love negroes because they are black or German Socialists because they are pedantic. But we have to love our neighbour because he is there—a much more alarming reason for a much more serious operation. He is the sample of humanity which is actually given us. Precisely because he may be anybody he is everybody. He is a symbol because he is an accident.

Doubtless men flee from small environments into lands that are very deadly. But this is natural enough; for they are not fleeing from death. They are fleeing from life. And this principle applies to ring within ring of the social system of humanity. It is perfectly reasonable that men should seek for some particular variety of the human type, so long as they are seeking for that variety of the human type, and not for mere human variety. It is quite proper that a British diplomatist should seek the society of Japanese generals, if what he wants is Japanese generals. But if what he wants is people different from himself, he had much better stop at home and discuss religion with the housemaid. It is quite reasonable that the village genius should come up to conquer London if what he wants is to conquer London. But if he wants to conquer something fundamentally and symbolically hostile and also very strong, he had much better remain where he is and have a row with the rector. The man in the suburban street is quite right if he goes to Ramsgate for the sake of Ramsgate—a difficult thing to imagine. But if, as he expresses it, he goes to Ramsgate "for a change," then he would have a much more romantic and even melodramatic change if he jumped over the wall into his neighbours garden. The consequences would be bracing in a sense far beyond the possibilities of Ramsgate hygiene.

Now, exactly as this principle applies to the empire, to the nation within the empire, to the city within the nation, to the street within the city, so it applies to the home within the street. The institution of the family is to be commended for precisely the same reasons that the institution of the nation, or the institution of the city, are in this matter to be commended. It is a good thing for a man to live in a family for the same reason that it is a good thing for a man to be besieged in a city. It is a good thing for a man to live in a family in the same sense that it is a beautiful and delightful thing for a man to be snowed up in a street. They all force him to realize that life is not a thing from outside, but a thing from inside. Above all, they all insist upon the fact that life, if it be a truly stimulating and fascinating life, is a thing which, of its nature, exists in spite of ourselves. The modern writers who have suggested, in a more or less open manner, that the family is a bad institution, have generally confined themselves to suggesting, with much sharpness, bitterness, or pathos, that perhaps the family is not always very congenial. Of course the family is a good institution because it is uncongenial. It is wholesome precisely because it contains so many divergencies and varieties. It is, as the sentimentalists say, like a little kingdom, and, like most other little kingdoms, is generally in a state of something resembling anarchy. It is exactly because our brother George is not interested in our religious difficulties, but is interested in the Trocadero Restaurant, that the family has some of the bracing qualities of the commonwealth. It is precisely because our uncle Henry does not approve of the theatrical ambitions of our sister Sarah that the family is like humanity. The men and women who, for good reasons and bad, revolt against the family, are, for good reasons and bad, simply revolting against mankind. Aunt Elizabeth is unreasonable, like mankind. Papa is excitable, like mankind Our youngest brother is mischievous, like mankind. Grandpapa is stupid, like the world; he is old, like the world.

Those who wish, rightly or wrongly, to step out of all this, do definitely wish to step into a narrower world. They are dismayed and terrified by the largeness and variety of the family. Sarah wishes to find a world wholly consisting of private theatricals; George wishes to think the Trocadero a cosmos. I do not say, for a moment, that the flight to this narrower life may not be the right thing for the individual, any more than I say the same thing about flight into a monastery. But I do say that anything is bad and artificial which tends to make these people succumb to the strange delusion that they are stepping into a world which is actually larger and more varied than their own. The best way that a man could test his readiness to encounter the common variety of mankind would be to climb down a chimney into any house at random, and get on as well as possible with the people inside. And that is essentially what each one of us did on the day that he was born.

This is, indeed, the sublime and special romance of the family. It is romantic because it is a toss-up. It is romantic because it is everything that its enemies call it. It is romantic because it is arbitrary. It is romantic because it is there. So long as you have groups of men chosen rationally, you have some special or sectarian atmosphere. It is when you have groups of men chosen irrationally that you have men. The element of adventure begins to exist; for an adventure is, by its nature, a thing that comes to us. It is a thing that chooses us, not a thing that we choose. Falling in love has been often regarded as the supreme adventure, the supreme romantic accident. In so much as there is in it something outside ourselves, something of a sort of merry fatalism, this is very true. Love does take us and transfigure and torture us. It does break our hearts with an unbearable beauty, like the unbearable beauty of music. But in so far as we have certainly something to do with the matter; in so far as we are in some sense prepared to fall in love and in some sense jump into it; in so far as we do to some extent choose and to some extent even judge—in all this falling in love is not truly romantic, is not truly adventurous at all. In this degree the supreme adventure is not falling in love. The supreme adventure is being born. There we do walk suddenly into a splendid and startling trap. There we do see something of which we have not dreamed before. Our father and mother do lie in wait for us and leap out on us, like brigands from a bush. Our uncle is a surprise. Our aunt is, in the beautiful common expression, a bolt from the blue. When we step into the family, by the act of being born, we do step into a world which is incalculable, into a world which has its own strange laws, into a world which could do without us, into a world that we have not made. In other words, when we step into the family we step into a fairy-tale.

This colour as of a fantastic narrative ought to cling to the family and to our relations with it throughout life. Romance is the deepest thing in life; romance is deeper even than reality. For even if reality could be proved to be misleading, it still could not be proved to be unimportant or unimpressive. Even if the facts are false, they are still very strange. And this strangeness of life, this unexpected and even perverse element of things as they fall out, remains incurably interesting. The circumstances we can regulate may become tame or pessimistic; but the "circumstances over which we have no control" remain god-like to those who, like Mr. Micawber, can call on them and renew their strength. People wonder why the novel is the most popular form of literature; people wonder why it is read more than books of science or books of metaphysics. The reason is very simple; it is merely that the novel is more true than they are. Life may sometimes legitimately appear as a book of science. Life may sometimes appear, and with a much greater legitimacy, as a book of metaphysics. But life is always a novel. Our existence may cease to be a song; it may cease even to be a beautiful lament. Our existence may not be an intelligible justice, or even a recognizable wrong. But our existence is still a story. In the fiery alphabet of every sunset is written, "to be continued in our next." If we have sufficient intellect, we can finish a philosophical and exact deduction, and be certain that we are finishing it right. With the adequate brainpower we could finish any scientific discovery, and be certain that we were finishing it right. But not with the most gigantic intellect could we finish the simplest or silliest story, and be certain that we were finishing it right. That is because a story has behind it, not merely intellect which is partly mechanical, but will, which is in its essence divine. The narrative writer can send his hero to the gallows if he likes in the last chapter but one. He can do it by the same divine caprice whereby he, the author, can go to the gallows himself, and to hell afterwards if he chooses. And the same civilization, the chivalric European civilization which asserted freewill in the thirteenth century, produced the thing called "fiction" in the eighteenth. When Thomas Aquinas asserted the spiritual liberty of man, he created all the bad novels in the circulating libraries.

But in order that life should be a story or romance to us, it is necessary that a great part of it, at any rate, should be settled for us without our permission. If we wish life to be a system, this may be a nuisance; but if we wish it to be a drama, it is an essential. It may often happen, no doubt, that a drama may be written by somebody else which we like very little. But we should like it still less if the author came before the curtain every hour or so, and forced on us the whole trouble of inventing the next act. A man has control over many things in his life; he has control over enough things to be the hero of a novel. But if he had control over everything, there would be so much hero that there would be no novel. And the reason why the lives of the rich are at bottom so tame and uneventful is simply that they can choose the events. They are dull because they are omnipotent. They fail to feel adventures because they can make the adventures. The thing which keeps life romantic and full of fiery possibilities is the existence of these great plain limitations which force all of us to meet the things we do not like or do not expect. It is vain for the supercilious moderns to talk of being in uncongenial surroundings. To be in a romance is to be in uncongenial surroundings. To be born into this earth is to be born into uncongenial surroundings, hence to be born into a romance. Of all these great limitations and frameworks which fashion and create the poetry and variety of life, the family is the most definite and important. Hence it is misunderstood by the moderns, who imagine that romance would exist most perfectly in a complete state of what they call liberty. They think that if a man makes a gesture it would be a startling and romantic matter that the sun should fall from the sky. But the startling and romantic thing about the sun is that it does not fall from the sky. They are seeking under every shape and form a world where there are no limitations—that is, a world where there are no outlines; that is, a world where there are no shapes. There is nothing baser than that infinity. They say they wish to be, as strong as the universe, but they really wish the whole universe as weak as themselves.

XV ON SMART NOVELISTS AND THE SMART SET

In one sense, at any rate, it is more valuable to read bad literature than good literature. Good literature may tell us the mind of one man; but bad literature may tell us the mind of many men. A good novel tells us the truth about its hero; but a bad novel tells us the truth about its author. It does much more than that, it tells us the truth about its readers; and, oddly enough, it tells us this all the more the more cynical and immoral be the motive of its manufacture. The more dishonest a book is as a book the more honest it is as a public document. A sincere novel exhibits the simplicity of one particular man; an insincere novel exhibits the simplicity of mankind. The pedantic decisions and definable readjustments of man may be found in scrolls and statute books and scriptures; but men's basic assumptions and everlasting energies are to be found in penny dreadfuls and halfpenny novelettes. Thus a man, like many men of real culture in our day, might learn from good literature nothing except the power to appreciate good literature. But from bad literature he might learn to govern empires and look over the map of mankind.

There is one rather interesting example of this state of things in which the weaker literature is really the stronger and the stronger the weaker. It is the case of what may be called, for the sake of an approximate description, the literature of aristocracy; or, if you prefer the description, the literature of snobbishness. Now if any one wishes to find a really effective and comprehensible and permanent case for aristocracy well and sincerely stated, let him read, not the modern philosophical conservatives, not even Nietzsche, let him read the Bow Bells Novelettes. Of the case of Nietzsche I am confessedly more doubtful. Nietzsche and the Bow Bells Novelettes have both obviously the same fundamental character; they both worship the tall man with curling moustaches and herculean bodily power, and they both worship him in a manner which is somewhat feminine and hysterical. Even here, however, the Novelette easily maintains its philosophical superiority, because it does attribute to the strong man those virtues which do commonly belong to him, such virtues as laziness and kindliness and a rather reckless benevolence, and a great dislike of hurting the weak. Nietzsche, on the other hand, attributes to the strong man that scorn against weakness which only exists among invalids. It is not, however, of the secondary merits of the great German philosopher, but of the primary merits of the Bow Bells Novelettes, that it is my present affair to speak. The picture of aristocracy in the popular sentimental novelette seems to me very satisfactory as a permanent political and philosophical guide. It may be inaccurate about details such as the title by which a baronet is addressed or the width of a mountain chasm which a baronet can conveniently leap, but it is not a bad description of the general idea and intention of aristocracy as they exist in human affairs. The essential dream of aristocracy is magnificence and valour; and if the Family Herald Supplement sometimes distorts or exaggerates these things, at least, it does not fall short in them. It never errs by making the mountain chasm too narrow or the title of the baronet insufficiently impressive. But above this sane reliable old literature of snobbishness there has arisen in our time another kind of literature of snobbishness which, with its much higher pretensions, seems to me worthy of very much less respect. Incidentally (if that matters), it is much better literature. But it is immeasurably worse philosophy, immeasurably worse ethics and politics, immeasurably worse vital rendering of aristocracy and humanity as they really are. From such books as those of which I wish now to speak we can discover what a clever man can do with the idea of aristocracy. But from the Family Herald Supplement literature we can learn what the idea of aristocracy can do with a man who is not clever. And when we know that we know English history.

This new aristocratic fiction must have caught the attention of everybody who has read the best fiction for the last fifteen years. It is that genuine or alleged literature of the Smart Set which represents that set as distinguished, not only by smart dresses, but by smart sayings. To the bad baronet, to the good baronet, to the romantic and misunderstood baronet who is supposed to be a bad baronet, but is a good baronet, this school has added a conception undreamed of in the former years—the conception of an amusing baronet. The aristocrat is not merely to be taller than mortal men and stronger and handsomer, he is also to be more witty. He is the long man with the short epigram. Many eminent, and deservedly eminent, modern novelists must accept some responsibility for having supported this worst form of snobbishness—an intellectual snobbishness. The talented author of "Dodo" is responsible for having in some sense created the fashion as a fashion. Mr. Hichens, in the "Green Carnation," reaffirmed the strange idea that young noblemen talk well; though his case had some vague biographical foundation, and in consequence an excuse. Mrs. Craigie is considerably guilty in the matter, although, or rather because, she has combined the aristocratic note with a note of some moral and even religious sincerity. When you are saving a man's soul, even in a novel, it is indecent to mention that he is a gentleman. Nor can blame in this matter be altogether removed from a man of much greater ability, and a man who has proved his possession of the highest of human instinct, the romantic instinct—I mean Mr. Anthony Hope. In a galloping, impossible melodrama like "The Prisoner of Zenda," the blood of kings fanned an excellent fantastic thread or theme. But the blood of kings is not a thing that can be taken seriously. And when, for example, Mr. Hope devotes so much serious and sympathetic study to the man called Tristram of Blent, a man who throughout burning boyhood thought of nothing but a silly old estate, we feel even in Mr. Hope the hint of this excessive concern about the oligarchic idea. It is hard for any ordinary person to feel so much interest in a young man whose whole aim is to own the house of Blent at the time when every other young man is owning the stars.

Mr. Hope, however, is a very mild case, and in him there is not only an element of romance, but also a fine element of irony which warns us against taking all this elegance too seriously. Above all, he shows his sense in not making his noblemen so incredibly equipped with impromptu repartee. This habit of insisting on the wit of the wealthier classes is the last and most servile of all the servilities. It is, as I have said, immeasurably more contemptible than the snobbishness of the novelette which describes the nobleman as smiling like an Apollo or riding a mad elephant. These may be exaggerations of beauty and courage, but beauty and courage are the unconscious ideals of aristocrats, even of stupid aristocrats.

The nobleman of the novelette may not be sketched with any very close or conscientious attention to the daily habits of noblemen. But he is something more important than a reality; he is a practical ideal. The gentleman of fiction may not copy the gentleman of real life; but the gentleman of real life is copying the gentleman of fiction. He may not be particularly good-looking, but he would rather be good-looking than anything else; he may not have ridden on a mad elephant, but he rides a pony as far as possible with an air as if he had. And, upon the whole, the upper class not only especially desire these qualities of beauty and courage, but in some degree, at any rate, especially possess them. Thus there is nothing really mean or sycophantic about the popular literature which makes all its marquises seven feet high. It is snobbish, but it is not servile. Its exaggeration is based on an exuberant and honest admiration; its honest admiration is based upon something which is in some degree, at any rate, really there. The English lower classes do not fear the English upper classes in the least; nobody could. They simply and freely and sentimentally worship them. The strength of the aristocracy is not in the aristocracy at all; it is in the slums. It is not in the House of Lords; it is not in the Civil Service; it is not in the Government offices; it is not even in the huge and disproportionate monopoly of the English land. It is in a certain spirit. It is in the fact that when a navvy wishes to praise a man, it comes readily to his tongue to say that he has behaved like a gentleman. From a democratic point of view he might as well say that he had behaved like a viscount. The oligarchic character of the modern English commonwealth does not rest, like many oligarchies, on the cruelty of the rich to the poor. It does not even rest on the kindness of the rich to the poor. It rests on the perennial and unfailing kindness of the poor to the rich.

The snobbishness of bad literature, then, is not servile; but the snobbishness of good literature is servile. The old-fashioned halfpenny romance where the duchesses sparkled with diamonds was not servile; but the new romance where they sparkle with epigrams is servile. For in thus attributing a special and startling degree of intellect and conversational or controversial power to the upper classes, we are attributing something which is not especially their virtue or even especially their aim. We are, in the words of Disraeli (who, being a genius and not a gentleman, has perhaps primarily to answer for the introduction of this method of flattering the gentry), we are performing the essential function of flattery which is flattering the people for the qualities they have not got. Praise may be gigantic and insane without having any quality of flattery so long as it is praise of something that is noticeably in existence. A man may say that a giraffe's head strikes the stars, or that a whale fills the German Ocean, and still be only in a rather excited state about a favourite animal. But when he begins to congratulate the giraffe on his feathers, and the whale on the elegance of his legs, we find ourselves confronted with that social element which we call flattery. The middle and lower orders of London can sincerely, though not perhaps safely, admire the health and grace of the English aristocracy. And this for the very simple reason that the aristocrats are, upon the whole, more healthy and graceful than the poor. But they cannot honestly admire the wit of the aristocrats. And this for the simple reason that the aristocrats are not more witty than the poor, but a very great deal less so. A man does not hear, as in the smart novels, these gems of verbal felicity dropped between diplomatists at dinner. Where he really does hear them is between two omnibus conductors in a block in Holborn. The witty peer whose impromptus fill the books of Mrs. Craigie or Miss Fowler, would, as a matter of fact, be torn to shreds in the art of conversation by the first boot-black he had the misfortune to fall foul of. The poor are merely sentimental, and very excusably sentimental, if they praise the gentleman for having a ready hand and ready money. But they are strictly slaves and sycophants if they praise him for having a ready tongue. For that they have far more themselves.

The element of oligarchical sentiment in these novels, however, has, I think, another and subtler aspect, an aspect more difficult to understand and more worth understanding. The modern gentleman, particularly the modern English gentleman, has become so central and important in these books, and through them in the whole of our current literature and our current mode of thought, that certain qualities of his, whether original or recent, essential or accidental, have altered the quality of our English comedy. In particular, that stoical ideal, absurdly supposed to be the English ideal, has stiffened and chilled us. It is not the English ideal; but it is to some extent the aristocratic ideal; or it may be only the ideal of aristocracy in its autumn or decay. The gentleman is a Stoic because he is a sort of savage, because he is filled with a great elemental fear that some stranger will speak to him. That is why a third-class carriage is a community, while a first-class carriage is a place of wild hermits. But this matter, which is difficult, I may be permitted to approach in a more circuitous way.

The haunting element of ineffectualness which runs through so much of the witty and epigrammatic fiction fashionable during the last eight or ten years, which runs through such works of a real though varying ingenuity as "Dodo," or "Concerning Isabel Carnaby," or even "Some Emotions and a Moral," may be expressed in various ways, but to most of us I think it will ultimately amount to the same thing. This new frivolity is inadequate because there is in it no strong sense of an unuttered joy. The men and women who exchange the repartees may not only be hating each other, but hating even themselves. Any one of them might be bankrupt that day, or sentenced to be shot the next. They are joking, not because they are merry, but because they are not; out of the emptiness of the heart the mouth speaketh. Even when they talk pure nonsense it is a careful nonsense—a nonsense of which they are economical, or, to use the perfect expression of Mr.

W. S. Gilbert in "Patience," it is such "precious nonsense." Even when they become light-headed they do not become light-hearted. All those who have read anything of the rationalism of the moderns know that their Reason is a sad thing. But even their unreason is sad.

The causes of this incapacity are also not very difficult to indicate. The chief of all, of course, is that miserable fear of being sentimental, which is the meanest of all the modern terrors—meaner even than the terror which produces hygiene. Everywhere the robust and uproarious humour has come from the men who were capable not merely of sentimentalism, but a very silly sentimentalism. There has been no humour so robust or uproarious as that of the sentimentalist Steele or the sentimentalist Sterne or the sentimentalist Dickens. These creatures who wept like women were the creatures who laughed like men. It is true that the humour of Micawber is good literature and that the pathos of little Nell is bad. But the kind of man who had the courage to write so badly in the one case is the kind of man who would have the courage to write so well in the other. The same unconsciousness, the same violent innocence, the same gigantesque scale of action which brought the Napoleon of Comedy his Jena brought him also his Moscow. And herein is especially shown the frigid and feeble limitations of our modern wits. They make violent efforts, they make heroic and almost pathetic efforts, but they cannot really write badly. There are moments when we almost think that they are achieving the effect, but our hope shrivels to nothing the moment we compare their little failures with the enormous imbecilities of Byron or Shakespeare.

For a hearty laugh it is necessary to have touched the heart. I do not know why touching the heart should always be connected only with the idea of touching it to compassion or a sense of distress. The heart can be touched to joy and triumph; the heart can be touched to amusement. But all our comedians are tragic comedians. These later fashionable writers are so pessimistic in bone and marrow that they never seem able to imagine the heart having any concern with mirth. When they speak of the heart, they always mean the pangs and disappointments of the emotional life. When they say that a man's heart is in the right place, they mean, apparently, that it is in his boots. Our ethical societies understand fellowship, but they do not understand good fellowship. Similarly, our wits understand talk, but not what Dr. Johnson called a good talk. In order to have, like Dr. Johnson, a good talk, it is emphatically necessary to be, like Dr. Johnson, a good man—to have friendship and honour and an abysmal tenderness. Above all, it is necessary to be openly and indecently humane, to confess with fulness all the primary pities and fears of Adam. Johnson was a clear-headed humorous man, and therefore he did not mind talking seriously about religion. Johnson was a brave man, one of the bravest that ever walked, and therefore he did not mind avowing to any one his consuming fear of death.

The idea that there is something English in the repression of one's feelings is one of those ideas which no Englishman ever heard of until England began to be governed exclusively by Scotchmen, Americans, and Jews. At the best, the idea is a generalization from the Duke of Wellington—who was an Irishman. At the worst, it is a part of that silly Teutonism which knows as little about England as it does about anthropology, but which is always talking about Vikings. As a matter of fact, the Vikings did not repress their feelings in the least. They cried like babies and kissed each other like girls; in short, they acted in that respect like Achilles and all strong heroes the children of the gods. And though the English nationality has probably not much more to do with the Vikings than the French nationality or the Irish nationality, the English have certainly been the children of the Vikings in the matter of tears and kisses. It is not merely true that all the most typically English men of letters, like Shakespeare and Dickens, Richardson and Thackeray, were sentimentalists. It is also true that all the most typically English men of action were sentimentalists, if possible, more sentimental. In the great Elizabethan age, when the English nation was finally hammered out, in the great eighteenth century when the British Empire was being built up everywhere, where in all these times, where was this symbolic stoical Englishman who dresses in drab and black and represses his feelings? Were all the Elizabethan palladins and pirates like that? Were any of them like that? Was Grenville concealing his emotions when he broke wine-glasses to pieces with his teeth and bit them till the blood poured down? Was Essex restraining his excitement when he threw his hat into the sea? Did Raleigh think it sensible to answer the Spanish guns only, as Stevenson says, with a flourish of insulting trumpets? Did Sydney ever miss an opportunity of making a theatrical remark in the whole course of his life and death? Were even the Puritans Stoics? The English Puritans repressed a good deal, but even they were too English to repress their feelings. It was by a great miracle of genius assuredly that Carlyle contrived to admire simultaneously two things so irreconcilably opposed as silence and Oliver Cromwell. Cromwell was the very reverse of a strong, silent man. Cromwell was always talking, when he was not crying. Nobody, I suppose, will accuse the author of "Grace Abounding" of being ashamed of his feelings. Milton, indeed, it might be possible to represent as a Stoic; in some sense he was a Stoic, just as he was a prig and a polygamist and several other unpleasant and heathen things. But when we have passed that great and desolate name, which may really be counted an exception, we find the tradition of English emotionalism immediately resumed and unbrokenly continuous. Whatever may have been the moral beauty of the passions of Etheridge and Dorset, Sedley and Buckingham, they cannot be accused of the fault of fastidiously concealing them. Charles the Second was very popular with the English because, like all the jolly English kings, he displayed his passions. William the Dutchman was very unpopular with the English because, not being an Englishman, he did hide his emotions. He was, in fact, precisely the ideal Englishman of our modern theory; and precisely for that reason all the real Englishmen loathed him like leprosy. With the rise of the great England of the eighteenth century, we find this open and emotional tone still maintained in letters and politics, in arts and in arms. Perhaps the only quality which was possessed in common by the great Fielding, and the great Richardson was that neither of them hid their feelings. Swift, indeed, was hard and logical, because Swift was Irish. And when we pass to the soldiers and the rulers, the patriots and the empire-builders of the eighteenth century, we find, as I have said, that they were, If possible, more romantic than the romancers, more poetical than the poets. Chatham, who showed the world all his strength, showed the House of Commons all his weakness. Wolfe walked about the room with a drawn sword calling himself Caesar and Hannibal, and went to death with poetry in his mouth. Clive was a man of the same type as Cromwell or Bunyan, or, for the matter of that, Johnson—that is, he was a strong, sensible man with a kind of running spring of hysteria and melancholy in him. Like Johnson, he was all the more healthy because he was morbid. The tales of all the admirals and adventurers of that England are full of braggadocio, of sentimentality, of splendid affectation. But it is scarcely necessary to multiply examples of the essentially romantic Englishman when one example towers above them all. Mr. Rudyard Kipling has said complacently of the English, "We do not fall on the neck and kiss when we come together." It is true that this ancient and universal custom has vanished with the modern weakening of England. Sydney would have thought nothing of kissing Spenser. But I willingly concede that Mr. Broderick would not be likely to kiss Mr. Arnold-Foster, if that be any proof of the increased manliness and military greatness of England. But the Englishman who does not show his feelings has not altogether given up the power of seeing something English in the great sea-hero of the Napoleonic war. You cannot break the legend of Nelson. And across the sunset of that glory is written in flaming letters for ever the great English sentiment, "Kiss me, Hardy."

This ideal of self-repression, then, is, whatever else it is, not English. It is, perhaps, somewhat Oriental, it is slightly Prussian, but in the main it does not come, I think, from any racial or national source. It is, as I have said, in some sense aristocratic; it comes not from a people, but from a class. Even aristocracy, I think, was not quite so stoical in the days when it was really strong. But whether this unemotional ideal be the genuine tradition of the gentleman, or only one of the inventions of the modern gentleman (who may be called the decayed gentleman), it certainly has something to do with the unemotional quality in these society novels. From representing aristocrats as people who suppressed their feelings, it has been an easy step to representing aristocrats as people who had no feelings to suppress. Thus the modern oligarchist has made a virtue for the oligarchy of the hardness as well as the brightness of the diamond. Like a sonneteer addressing his lady in the seventeenth century, he seems to use the word "cold" almost as a eulogium, and the word "heartless" as a kind of compliment. Of course, in people so incurably kind-hearted and babyish as are the English gentry, it would be impossible to create anything that can be called positive cruelty; so in these books they exhibit a sort of negative cruelty. They cannot be cruel in acts, but they can be so in words. All this means one thing, and one thing only. It means that the living and invigorating ideal of England must be looked for in the masses; it must be looked for where Dickens found it—Dickens among whose glories it was to be a humorist, to be a sentimentalist, to be an optimist, to be a poor man, to be an Englishman, but the greatest of whose glories was that he saw all mankind in its amazing and tropical luxuriance, and did not even notice the aristocracy; Dickens, the greatest of whose glories was that he could not describe a gentleman.

XVI ON MR. MCCABE AND A DIVINE FRIVOLITY

A critic once remonstrated with me saying, with an air of indignant reasonableness, "If you must make jokes, at least you need not make them on such serious subjects." I replied with a natural simplicity and wonder, "About what other subjects can one make jokes except serious subjects?" It is quite useless to talk about profane jesting. All jesting is in its nature profane, in the sense that it must be the sudden realization that something which thinks itself solemn is not so very solemn after all. If a joke is not a joke about religion or morals, it is a joke about police-magistrates or scientific professors or undergraduates dressed up as Queen Victoria. And people joke about the police-magistrate more than they joke about the Pope, not because the police-magistrate is a more frivolous subject, but, on the contrary, because the police-magistrate is a more serious subject than the Pope. The Bishop of Rome has no jurisdiction in this realm of England; whereas the police-magistrate may bring his solemnity to bear quite suddenly upon us. Men make jokes about old scientific professors, even more than they make them about bishops—not because science is lighter than religion, but because science is always by its nature more solemn and austere than religion. It is not I; it is not even a particular class of journalists or jesters who make jokes about the matters which are of most awful import; it is the whole human race. If there is one thing more than another which any one will admit who has the smallest knowledge of the world, it is that men are always speaking gravely and earnestly and with the utmost possible care about the things that are not important, but always talking frivolously about the things that are. Men talk for hours with the faces of a college of cardinals about things like golf, or tobacco, or waistcoats, or party politics. But all the most grave and dreadful things in the world are the oldest jokes in the world—being married; being hanged.

One gentleman, however, Mr. McCabe, has in this matter made to me something that almost amounts to a personal appeal; and as he happens to be a man for whose sincerity and intellectual virtue I have a high respect, I do not feel inclined to let it pass without some attempt to satisfy my critic in the matter. Mr. McCabe devotes a considerable part of the last essay in the collection called "Christianity and Rationalism on Trial" to an objection, not to my thesis, but to my method, and a very friendly and dignified appeal to me to alter it. I am much inclined to defend myself in this matter out of mere respect for Mr. McCabe, and still more so out of mere respect for the truth which is, I think, in danger by his error, not only in this question, but in others. In order that there may be no injustice done in the matter, I will quote Mr. McCabe himself. "But before I follow Mr. Chesterton in some detail I would make a general observation on his method. He is as serious as I am in his ultimate purpose, and I respect him for that. He knows, as I do, that humanity stands at a solemn parting of the ways. Towards some unknown goal it presses through the ages, impelled by an overmastering desire of happiness. To-day it hesitates, lightheartedly enough, but every serious thinker knows how momentous the decision may be. It is, apparently, deserting the path of religion and entering upon the path of secularism. Will it lose itself in quagmires of sensuality down this new path, and pant and toil through years of civic and industrial anarchy, only to learn it had lost the road, and must return to religion? Or will it find that at last it is leaving the mists and the quagmires behind it; that it is ascending the slope of the hill so long dimly discerned ahead, and making straight for the long-sought Utopia? This is the drama of our time, and every man and every woman should understand it.

"Mr. Chesterton understands it. Further, he gives us credit for understanding it. He has nothing of that paltry meanness or strange density of so many of his colleagues, who put us down as aimless iconoclasts or moral anarchists. He admits that we are waging a thankless war for what we take to be Truth and Progress. He is doing the same. But why, in the name of all that is reasonable, should we, when we are agreed on the momentousness of the issue either way, forthwith desert serious methods of conducting the controversy? Why, when the vital need of our time is to induce men and women to collect their thoughts occasionally, and be men and women—nay, to remember that they are really gods that hold the destinies of humanity on their knees—why should we think that this kaleidoscopic play of phrases is inopportune? The ballets of the Alhambra, and the fireworks of the Crystal Palace, and Mr. Chesterton's Daily News articles, have their place in life. But how a serious social student can think of curing the thoughtlessness of our generation by strained paradoxes; of giving people a sane grasp of social problems by literary sleight-of-hand; of settling important questions by a reckless shower of rocket-metaphors and inaccurate 'facts,' and the substitution of imagination for judgment, I cannot see."

I quote this passage with a particular pleasure, because Mr. McCabe certainly cannot put too strongly the degree to which I give him and his school credit for their complete sincerity and responsibility of philosophical attitude. I am quite certain that they mean every word they say. I also mean every word I say. But why is it that Mr. McCabe has some sort of mysterious hesitation about admitting that I mean every word I say; why is it that he is not quite as certain of my mental responsibility as I am of his mental responsibility? If we attempt to answer the question directly and well, we shall, I think, have come to the root of the matter by the shortest cut.

Mr. McCabe thinks that I am not serious but only funny, because Mr. McCabe thinks that funny is the opposite of serious. Funny is the opposite of not funny, and of nothing else. The question of whether a man expresses himself in a grotesque or laughable phraseology, or in a stately and restrained phraseology, is not a question of motive or of moral state, it is a question of instinctive language and self-expression. Whether a man chooses to tell the truth in long sentences or short jokes is a problem analogous to whether he chooses to tell the truth in French or German. Whether a man preaches his gospel grotesquely or gravely is merely like the question of whether he preaches it in prose or verse. The question of whether Swift was funny in his irony is quite another sort of question to the question of whether Swift was serious in his pessimism. Surely even Mr. McCabe would not maintain that the more funny "Gulliver" is in its method the less it can be sincere in its object. The truth is, as I have said, that in this sense the two qualities of fun and seriousness have nothing whatever to do with each other, they are no more comparable than black and triangular. Mr. Bernard Shaw is funny and sincere. Mr. George Robey is funny and not sincere. Mr. McCabe is sincere and not funny. The average Cabinet Minister is not sincere and not funny.

In short, Mr. McCabe is under the influence of a primary fallacy which I have found very common in men of the clerical type. Numbers of clergymen have from time to time reproached me for making jokes about religion; and they have almost always invoked the authority of that very sensible commandment which says, "Thou shalt not take the name of the Lord thy God in vain." Of course, I pointed out that I was not in any conceivable sense taking the name in vain. To take a thing and make a joke out of it is not to take it in vain. It is, on the contrary, to take it and use it for an uncommonly good object. To use a thing in vain means to use it without use. But a joke may be exceedingly useful; it may contain the whole earthly sense, not to mention the whole heavenly sense, of a situation. And those who find in the Bible the commandment can find in the Bible any number of the jokes. In the same book in which God's name is fenced from being taken in vain, God himself overwhelms Job with a torrent of terrible levities. The same book which says that God's name must not be taken vainly, talks easily and carelessly about God laughing and God winking. Evidently it is not here that we have to look for genuine examples of what is meant by a vain use of the name. And it is not very difficult to see where we have really to look for it. The people (as I tactfully pointed out to them) who really take the name of the Lord in vain are the clergymen themselves. The thing which is fundamentally and really frivolous is not a careless joke. The thing which is fundamentally and really frivolous is a careless solemnity. If Mr. McCabe really wishes to know what sort of guarantee of reality and solidity is afforded by the mere act of what is called talking seriously, let him spend a happy Sunday in going the round of the pulpits. Or, better still, let him drop in at the House of Commons or the House of Lords. Even Mr. McCabe would admit that these men are solemn—more solemn than I am. And even Mr. McCabe, I think, would admit that these men are frivolous—more frivolous than I am. Why should Mr. McCabe be so eloquent about the danger arising from fantastic and paradoxical writers? Why should he be so ardent in desiring grave and verbose writers? There are not so very many fantastic and paradoxical writers. But there are a gigantic number of grave and verbose writers; and it is by the efforts of the grave and verbose writers that everything that Mr. McCabe detests (and everything that I detest, for that matter) is kept in existence and energy. How can it have come about that a man as intelligent as Mr. McCabe can think that paradox and jesting stop the way? It is solemnity that is stopping the way in every department of modern effort. It is his own favourite "serious methods;" it is his own favourite "momentousness;" it is his own favourite "judgment" which stops the way everywhere. Every man who has ever headed a deputation to a minister knows this. Every man who has ever written a letter to the Times knows it. Every rich man who wishes to stop the mouths of the poor talks about "momentousness." Every Cabinet minister who has not got an answer suddenly develops a "judgment." Every sweater who uses vile methods recommends "serious methods." I said a moment ago that sincerity had nothing to do with solemnity, but I confess that I am not so certain that I was right. In the modern world, at any rate, I am not so sure that I was right. In the modern world solemnity is the direct enemy of sincerity. In the modern world sincerity is almost always on one side, and solemnity almost always on the other. The only answer possible to the fierce and glad attack of sincerity is the miserable answer of solemnity. Let Mr. McCabe, or any one else who is much concerned that we should be grave in order to be sincere, simply imagine the scene in some government office in which Mr. Bernard Shaw should head a Socialist deputation to Mr. Austen Chamberlain. On which side would be the solemnity? And on which the sincerity?

I am, indeed, delighted to discover that Mr. McCabe reckons Mr. Shaw along with me in his system of condemnation of frivolity. He said once, I believe, that he always wanted Mr. Shaw to label his paragraphs serious or comic. I do not know which paragraphs of Mr. Shaw are paragraphs to be labelled serious; but surely there can be no doubt that this paragraph of Mr. McCabe's is one to be labelled comic. He also says, in the article I am now discussing, that Mr. Shaw has the reputation of deliberately saying everything which his hearers do not expect him to say. I need not labour the inconclusiveness and weakness of this, because it has already been dealt with in my remarks on Mr. Bernard Shaw. Suffice it to say here that the only serious reason which I can imagine inducing any one person to listen to any other is, that the first person looks to the second person with an ardent faith and a fixed attention, expecting him to say what he does not expect him to say. It may be a paradox, but that is because paradoxes are true. It may not be rational, but that is because rationalism is wrong. But clearly it is quite true that whenever we go to hear a prophet or teacher we may or may not expect wit, we may or may not expect eloquence, but we do expect what we do not expect. We may not expect the true, we may not even expect the wise, but we do expect the unexpected. If we do not expect the unexpected, why do we go there at all? If we expect the expected, why do we not sit at home and expect it by ourselves? If Mr. McCabe means merely this about Mr. Shaw, that he always has some unexpected application of his doctrine to give to those who listen to him, what he says is quite true, and to say it is only to say that Mr. Shaw is an original man. But if he means that Mr. Shaw has ever professed or preached any doctrine but one, and that his own, then what he says is not true. It is not my business to defend Mr. Shaw; as has been seen already, I disagree with him altogether. But I do not mind, on his behalf offering in this matter a flat defiance to all his ordinary opponents, such as Mr. McCabe. I defy Mr. McCabe, or anybody else, to mention one single instance in which Mr. Shaw has, for the sake of wit or novelty, taken up any position which was not directly deducible from the body of his doctrine as elsewhere expressed. I have been, I am happy to say, a tolerably close student of Mr. Shaw's utterances, and I request Mr. McCabe, if he will not believe that I mean anything else, to believe that I mean this challenge.

All this, however, is a parenthesis. The thing with which I am here immediately concerned is Mr. McCabe's appeal to me not to be so frivolous. Let me return to the actual text of that appeal. There are, of course, a great many things that I might say about it in detail. But I may start with saying that Mr. McCabe is in error in supposing that the danger which I anticipate from the disappearance of religion is the increase of sensuality. On the contrary, I should be inclined to anticipate a decrease in sensuality, because I anticipate a decrease in life. I do not think that under modern Western materialism we should have anarchy. I doubt whether we should have enough individual valour and spirit even to have liberty. It is quite an old-fashioned fallacy to suppose that our objection to scepticism is that it removes the discipline from life. Our objection to scepticism is that it removes the motive power. Materialism is not a thing which destroys mere restraint. Materialism itself is the great restraint. The McCabe school advocates a political liberty, but it denies spiritual liberty. That is, it abolishes the laws which could be broken, and substitutes laws that cannot. And that is the real slavery.

The truth is that the scientific civilization in which Mr. McCabe believes has one rather particular defect; it is perpetually tending to destroy that democracy or power of the ordinary man in which Mr. McCabe also believes. Science means specialism, and specialism means oligarchy. If you once establish the habit of trusting particular men to produce particular results in physics or astronomy, you leave the door open for the equally natural demand that you should trust particular men to do particular things in government and the coercing of men. If, you feel it to be reasonable that one beetle should be the only study of one man, and that one man the only student of that one beetle, it is surely a very harmless consequence to go on to say that politics should be the only study of one man, and that one man the only student of politics. As I have pointed out elsewhere in this book, the expert is more aristocratic than the aristocrat, because the aristocrat is only the man who lives well, while the expert is the man who knows better. But if we look at the progress of our scientific civilization we see a gradual increase everywhere of the specialist over the popular function. Once men sang together round a table in chorus; now one man sings alone, for the absurd reason that he can sing better. If scientific civilization goes on (which is most improbable) only one man will laugh, because he can laugh better than the rest.

I do not know that I can express this more shortly than by taking as a text the single sentence of Mr. McCabe, which runs as follows: "The ballets of the Alhambra and the fireworks of the Crystal Palace and Mr. Chesterton's Daily News articles have their places in life." I wish that my articles had as noble a place as either of the other two things mentioned. But let us ask ourselves (in a spirit of love, as Mr. Chadband would say), what are the ballets of the Alhambra? The ballets of the Alhambra are institutions in which a particular selected row of persons in pink go through an operation known as dancing. Now, in all commonwealths dominated by a religion—in the Christian commonwealths of the Middle Ages and in many rude societies—this habit of dancing was a common habit with everybody, and was not necessarily confined to a professional class. A person could dance without being a dancer; a person could dance without being a specialist; a person could dance without being pink. And, in proportion as Mr. McCabe's scientific civilization advances—that is, in proportion as religious civilization (or real civilization) decays—the more and more "well trained," the more and more pink, become the people who do dance, and the more and more numerous become the people who don't. Mr. McCabe may recognize an example of what I mean in the gradual discrediting in society of the ancient European waltz or dance with partners, and the substitution of that horrible and degrading oriental interlude which is known as skirt-dancing. That is the whole essence of decadence, the effacement of five people who do a thing for fun by one person who does it for money. Now it follows, therefore, that when Mr. McCabe says that the ballets of the Alhambra and my articles "have their place in life," it ought to be pointed out to him that he is doing his best to create a world in which dancing, properly speaking, will have no place in life at all. He is, indeed, trying to create a world in which there will be no life for dancing to have a place in. The very fact that Mr. McCabe thinks of dancing as a thing belonging to some hired women at the Alhambra is an illustration of the same principle by which he is able to think of religion as a thing belonging to some hired men in white neckties. Both these things are things which should not be done for us, but by us. If Mr. McCabe were really religious he would be happy. If he were really happy he would dance.

Briefly, we may put the matter in this way. The main point of modern life is not that the Alhambra ballet has its place in life. The main point, the main enormous tragedy of modern life, is that Mr. McCabe has not his place in the Alhambra ballet. The joy of changing and graceful posture, the joy of suiting the swing of music to the swing of limbs, the joy of whirling drapery, the joy of standing on one leg,—all these should belong by rights to Mr. McCabe and to me; in short, to the ordinary healthy citizen. Probably we should not consent to go through these evolutions. But that is because we are miserable moderns and rationalists. We do not merely love ourselves more than we love duty; we actually love ourselves more than we love joy.

When, therefore, Mr. McCabe says that he gives the Alhambra dances (and my articles) their place in life, I think we are justified in pointing out that by the very nature of the case of his philosophy and of his favourite civilization he gives them a very inadequate place. For (if I may pursue the too flattering parallel) Mr. McCabe thinks of the Alhambra and of my articles as two very odd and absurd things, which some special people do (probably for money) in order to amuse him. But if he had ever felt himself the ancient, sublime, elemental, human instinct to dance, he would have discovered that dancing is not a frivolous thing at all, but a very serious thing. He would have discovered that it is the one grave and chaste and decent method of expressing a certain class of emotions. And similarly, if he had ever had, as Mr. Shaw and I have had, the impulse to what he calls paradox, he would have discovered that paradox again is not a frivolous thing, but a very serious thing. He would have found that paradox simply means a certain defiant joy which belongs to belief. I should regard any civilization which was without a universal habit of uproarious dancing as being, from the full human point of view, a defective civilization. And I should regard any mind which had not got the habit in one form or another of uproarious thinking as being, from the full human point of view, a defective mind. It is vain for Mr. McCabe to say that a ballet is a part of him. He should be part of a ballet, or else he is only part of a man. It is in vain for him to say that he is "not quarrelling with the importation of humour into the controversy." He ought himself to be importing humour into every controversy; for unless a man is in part a humorist, he is only in part a man. To sum up the whole matter very simply, if Mr. McCabe asks me why I import frivolity into a discussion of the nature of man, I answer, because frivolity is a part of the nature of man. If he asks me why I introduce what he calls paradoxes into a philosophical problem, I answer, because all philosophical problems tend to become paradoxical. If he objects to my treating of life riotously, I reply that life is a riot. And I say that the Universe as I see it, at any rate, is very much more like the fireworks at the Crystal Palace than it is like his own philosophy. About the whole cosmos there is a tense and secret festivity—like preparations for Guy Fawkes' day. Eternity is the eve of something. I never look up at the stars without feeling that they are the fires of a schoolboy's rocket, fixed in their everlasting fall.

XVII ON THE WIT OF WHISTLER

That capable and ingenious writer, Mr. Arthur Symons, has included in a book of essays recently published, I believe, an apologia for "London Nights," in which he says that morality should be wholly subordinated to art in criticism, and he uses the somewhat singular argument that art or the worship of beauty is the same in all ages, while morality differs in every period and in every respect. He appears to defy his critics or his readers to mention any permanent feature or quality in ethics. This is surely a very curious example of that extravagant bias against morality which makes so many ultra-modern aesthetes as morbid and fanatical as any Eastern hermit. Unquestionably it is a very common phrase of modern intellectualism to say that the morality of one age can be entirely different to the morality of another. And like a great many other phrases of modern intellectualism, it means literally nothing at all. If the two moralities are entirely different, why do you call them both moralities? It is as if a man said, "Camels in various places are totally diverse; some have six legs, some have none, some have scales, some have feathers, some have horns, some have wings, some are green, some are triangular. There is no point which they have in common." The ordinary man of sense would reply, "Then what makes you call them all camels? What do you mean by a camel? How do you know a camel when you see one?" Of course, there is a permanent substance of morality, as much as there is a permanent substance of art; to say that is only to say that morality is morality, and that art is art. An ideal art critic would, no doubt, see the enduring beauty under every school; equally an ideal moralist would see the enduring ethic under every code. But practically some of the best Englishmen that ever lived could see nothing but filth and idolatry in the starry piety of the Brahmin. And it is equally true that practically the greatest group of artists that the world has ever seen, the giants of the Renaissance, could see nothing but barbarism in the ethereal energy of Gothic.

This bias against morality among the modern aesthetes is nothing very much paraded. And yet it is not really a bias against morality; it is a bias against other people's morality. It is generally founded on a very definite moral preference for a certain sort of life, pagan, plausible, humane. The modern aesthete, wishing us to believe that he values beauty more than conduct, reads Mallarme, and drinks absinthe in a tavern. But this is not only his favourite kind of beauty; it is also his favourite kind of conduct. If he really wished us to believe that he cared for beauty only, he ought to go to nothing but Wesleyan school treats, and paint the sunlight in the hair of the Wesleyan babies. He ought to read nothing but very eloquent theological sermons by old-fashioned Presbyterian divines. Here the lack of all possible moral sympathy would prove that his interest was purely verbal or pictorial, as it is; in all the books he reads and writes he clings to the skirts of his own morality and his own immorality. The champion of l'art pour l'art is always denouncing Ruskin for his moralizing. If he were really a champion of l'art pour l'art, he would be always insisting on Ruskin for his style.

The doctrine of the distinction between art and morality owes a great part of its success to art and morality being hopelessly mixed up in the persons and performances of its greatest exponents. Of this lucky contradiction the very incarnation was Whistler. No man ever preached the impersonality of art so well; no man ever preached the impersonality of art so personally. For him pictures had nothing to do with the problems of character; but for all his fiercest admirers his character was, as a matter of fact far more interesting than his pictures. He gloried in standing as an artist apart from right and wrong. But he succeeded by talking from morning till night about his rights and about his wrongs. His talents were many, his virtues, it must be confessed, not many, beyond that kindness to tried friends, on which many of his biographers insist, but which surely is a quality of all sane men, of pirates and pickpockets; beyond this, his outstanding virtues limit themselves chiefly to two admirable ones—courage and an abstract love of good work. Yet I fancy he won at last more by those two virtues than by all his talents. A man must be something of a moralist if he is to preach, even if he is to preach unmorality. Professor Walter Raleigh, in his "In Memoriam: James McNeill Whistler," insists, truly enough, on the strong streak of an eccentric honesty in matters strictly pictorial, which ran through his complex and slightly confused character. "He would destroy any of his works rather than leave a careless or inexpressive touch within the limits of the frame. He would begin again a hundred times over rather than attempt by patching to make his work seem better than it was."

No one will blame Professor Raleigh, who had to read a sort of funeral oration over Whistler at the opening of the Memorial Exhibition, if, finding himself in that position, he confined himself mostly to the merits and the stronger qualities of his subject. We should naturally go to some other type of composition for a proper consideration of the weaknesses of Whistler. But these must never be omitted from our view of him. Indeed, the truth is that it was not so much a question of the weaknesses of Whistler as of the intrinsic and primary weakness of Whistler. He was one of those people who live up to their emotional incomes, who are always taut and tingling with vanity. Hence he had no strength to spare; hence he had no kindness, no geniality; for geniality is almost definable as strength to spare. He had no god-like carelessness; he never forgot himself; his whole life was, to use his own expression, an arrangement. He went in for "the art of living"—a miserable trick. In a word, he was a great artist; but emphatically not a great man. In this connection I must differ strongly with Professor Raleigh upon what is, from a superficial literary point of view, one of his most effective points. He compares Whistler's laughter to the laughter of another man who was a great man as well as a great artist. "His attitude to the public was exactly the attitude taken up by Robert Browning, who suffered as long a period of neglect and mistake, in those lines of 'The Ring and the Book'—

"'Well, British Public, ye who like me not,
(God love you!) and will have your proper laugh
At the dark question; laugh it! I'd laugh first.'

"Mr. Whistler," adds Professor Raleigh, "always laughed first." The truth is, I believe, that Whistler never laughed at all. There was no laughter in his nature; because there was no thoughtlessness and self-abandonment, no humility. I cannot understand anybody reading "The Gentle Art of Making Enemies" and thinking that there is any laughter in the wit. His wit is a torture to him. He twists himself into arabesques of verbal felicity; he is full of a fierce carefulness; he is inspired with the complete seriousness of sincere malice. He hurts himself to hurt his opponent. Browning did laugh, because Browning did not care; Browning did not care, because Browning was a great man. And when Browning said in brackets to the simple, sensible people who did not like his books, "God love you!" he was not sneering in the least. He was laughing—that is to say, he meant exactly what he said.

There are three distinct classes of great satirists who are also great men—that is to say, three classes of men who can laugh at something without losing their souls. The satirist of the first type is the man who, first of all enjoys himself, and then enjoys his enemies. In this sense he loves his enemy, and by a kind of exaggeration of Christianity he loves his enemy the more the more he becomes an enemy. He has a sort of overwhelming and aggressive happiness in his assertion of anger; his curse is as human as a benediction. Of this type of satire the great example is Rabelais. This is the first typical example of satire, the satire which is voluble, which is violent, which is indecent, but which is not malicious. The satire of Whistler was not this. He was never in any of his controversies simply happy; the proof of it is that he never talked absolute nonsense. There is a second type of mind which produces satire with the quality of greatness. That is embodied in the satirist whose passions are released and let go by some intolerable sense of wrong. He is maddened by the sense of men being maddened; his tongue becomes an unruly member, and testifies against all mankind. Such a man was Swift, in whom the saeva indignatio was a bitterness to others, because it was a bitterness to himself. Such a satirist Whistler was not. He did not laugh because he was happy, like Rabelais. But neither did he laugh because he was unhappy, like Swift.

The third type of great satire is that in which he satirist is enabled to rise superior to his victim in the only serious sense which superiority can bear, in that of pitying the sinner and respecting the man even while he satirises both. Such an achievement can be found in a thing like Pope's "Atticus" a poem in which the satirist feels that he is satirising the weaknesses which belong specially to literary genius. Consequently he takes a pleasure in pointing out his enemy's strength before he points out his weakness. That is, perhaps, the highest and most honourable form of satire. That is not the satire of Whistler. He is not full of a great sorrow for the wrong done to human nature; for him the wrong is altogether done to himself.

He was not a great personality, because he thought so much about himself. And the case is stronger even than that. He was sometimes not even a great artist, because he thought so much about art. Any man with a vital knowledge of the human psychology ought to have the most profound suspicion of anybody who claims to be an artist, and talks a great deal about art. Art is a right and human thing, like walking or saying one's prayers; but the moment it begins to be talked about very solemnly, a man may be fairly certain that the thing has come into a congestion and a kind of difficulty.

The artistic temperament is a disease that afflicts amateurs. It is a disease which arises from men not having sufficient power of expression to utter and get rid of the element of art in their being. It is healthful to every sane man to utter the art within him; it is essential to every sane man to get rid of the art within him at all costs. Artists of a large and wholesome vitality get rid of their art easily, as they breathe easily, or perspire easily. But in artists of less force, the thing becomes a pressure, and produces a definite pain, which is called the artistic temperament. Thus, very great artists are able to be ordinary men—men like Shakespeare or Browning. There are many real tragedies of the artistic temperament, tragedies of vanity or violence or fear. But the great tragedy of the artistic temperament is that it cannot produce any art.

Whistler could produce art; and in so far he was a great man. But he could not forget art; and in so far he was only a man with the artistic temperament. There can be no stronger manifestation of the man who is a really great artist than the fact that he can dismiss the subject of art; that he can, upon due occasion, wish art at the bottom of the sea. Similarly, we should always be much more inclined to trust a solicitor who did not talk about conveyancing over the nuts and wine. What we really desire of any man conducting any business is that the full force of an ordinary man should be put into that particular study. We do not desire that the full force of that study should be put into an ordinary man. We do not in the least wish that our particular law-suit should pour its energy into our barrister's games with his children, or rides on his bicycle, or meditations on the morning star. But we do, as a matter of fact, desire that his games with his children, and his rides on his bicycle, and his meditations on the morning star should pour something of their energy into our law-suit. We do desire that if he has gained any especial lung development from the bicycle, or any bright and pleasing metaphors from the morning star, that the should be placed at our disposal in that particular forensic controversy. In a word, we are very glad that he is an ordinary man, since that may help him to be an exceptional lawyer.

Whistler never ceased to be an artist. As Mr. Max Beerbohm pointed out in one of his extraordinarily sensible and sincere critiques, Whistler really regarded Whistler as his greatest work of art. The white lock, the single eyeglass, the remarkable hat—these were much dearer to him than any nocturnes or arrangements that he ever threw off. He could throw off the nocturnes; for some mysterious reason he could not throw off the hat. He never threw off from himself that disproportionate accumulation of aestheticism which is the burden of the amateur.

It need hardly be said that this is the real explanation of the thing which has puzzled so many dilettante critics, the problem of the extreme ordinariness of the behaviour of so many great geniuses in history. Their behaviour was so ordinary that it was not recorded; hence it was so ordinary that it seemed mysterious. Hence people say that Bacon wrote Shakespeare. The modern artistic temperament cannot understand how a man who could write such lyrics as Shakespeare wrote, could be as keen as Shakespeare was on business transactions in a little town in Warwickshire. The explanation is simple enough; it is that Shakespeare had a real lyrical impulse, wrote a real lyric, and so got rid of the impulse and went about his business. Being an artist did not prevent him from being an ordinary man, any more than being a sleeper at night or being a diner at dinner prevented him from being an ordinary man.

All very great teachers and leaders have had this habit of assuming their point of view to be one which was human and casual, one which would readily appeal to every passing man. If a man is genuinely superior to his fellows the first thing that he believes in is the equality of man. We can see this, for instance, in that strange and innocent rationality with which Christ addressed any motley crowd that happened to stand about Him. "What man of you having a hundred sheep, and losing one, would not leave the ninety and nine in the wilderness, and go after that which was lost?" Or, again, "What man of you if his son ask for bread will he give him a stone, or if he ask for a fish will he give him a serpent?" This plainness, this almost prosaic camaraderie, is the note of all very great minds.

To very great minds the things on which men agree are so immeasurably more important than the things on which they differ, that the latter, for all practical purposes, disappear. They have too much in them of an ancient laughter even to endure to discuss the difference between the hats of two men who were both born of a woman, or between the subtly varied cultures of two men who have both to die. The first-rate great man is equal with other men, like Shakespeare. The second-rate great man is on his knees to other men, like Whitman. The third-rate great man is superior to other men, like Whistler.

XVIII THE FALLACY OF THE YOUNG NATION

To say that a man is an idealist is merely to say that he is a man; but, nevertheless, it might be possible to effect some valid distinction between one kind of idealist and another. One possible distinction, for instance, could be effected by saying that humanity is divided into conscious idealists and unconscious idealists. In a similar way, humanity is divided into conscious ritualists and unconscious ritualists. The curious thing is, in that example as in others, that it is the conscious ritualism which is comparatively simple, the unconscious ritual which is really heavy and complicated. The ritual which is comparatively rude and straightforward is the ritual which people call "ritualistic." It consists of plain things like bread and wine and fire, and men falling on their faces. But the ritual which is really complex, and many coloured, and elaborate, and needlessly formal, is the ritual which people enact without knowing it. It consists not of plain things like wine and fire, but of really peculiar, and local, and exceptional, and ingenious things—things like door-mats, and door-knockers, and electric bells, and silk hats, and white ties, and shiny cards, and confetti. The truth is that the modern man scarcely ever gets back to very old and simple things except when he is performing some religious mummery. The modern man can hardly get away from ritual except by entering a ritualistic church. In the case of these old and mystical formalities we can at least say that the ritual is not mere ritual; that the symbols employed are in most cases symbols which belong to a primary human poetry. The most ferocious opponent of the Christian ceremonials must admit that if Catholicism had not instituted the bread and wine, somebody else would most probably have done so. Any one with a poetical instinct will admit that to the ordinary human instinct bread symbolizes something which cannot very easily be symbolized otherwise; that wine, to the ordinary human instinct, symbolizes something which cannot very easily be symbolized otherwise. But white ties in the evening are ritual, and nothing else but ritual. No one would pretend that white ties in the evening are primary and poetical. Nobody would maintain that the ordinary human instinct would in any age or country tend to symbolize the idea of evening by a white necktie. Rather, the ordinary human instinct would, I imagine, tend to symbolize evening by cravats with some of the colours of the sunset, not white neckties, but tawny or crimson neckties—neckties of purple or olive, or some darkened gold. Mr. J. A. Kensit, for example, is under the impression that he is not a ritualist. But the daily life of Mr. J. A. Kensit, like that of any ordinary modern man, is, as a matter of fact, one continual and compressed catalogue of mystical mummery and flummery. To take one instance out of an inevitable hundred: I imagine that Mr. Kensit takes off his hat to a lady; and what can be more solemn and absurd, considered in the abstract, than, symbolizing the existence of the other sex by taking off a portion of your clothing and waving it in the air? This, I repeat, is not a natural and primitive symbol, like fire or food. A man might just as well have to take off his waistcoat to a lady; and if a man, by the social ritual of his civilization, had to take off his waistcoat to a lady, every chivalrous and sensible man would take off his waistcoat to a lady. In short, Mr. Kensit, and those who agree with him, may think, and quite sincerely think, that men give too much incense and ceremonial to their adoration of the other world. But nobody thinks that he can give too much incense and ceremonial to the adoration of this world. All men, then, are ritualists, but are either conscious or unconscious ritualists. The conscious ritualists are generally satisfied with a few very simple and elementary signs; the unconscious ritualists are not satisfied with anything short of the whole of human life, being almost insanely ritualistic. The first is called a ritualist because he invents and remembers one rite; the other is called an anti-ritualist because he obeys and forgets a thousand. And a somewhat similar distinction to this which I have drawn with some unavoidable length, between the conscious ritualist and the unconscious ritualist, exists between the conscious idealist and the unconscious idealist. It is idle to inveigh against cynics and materialists—there are no cynics, there are no materialists. Every man is idealistic; only it so often happens that he has the wrong ideal. Every man is incurably sentimental; but, unfortunately, it is so often a false sentiment. When we talk, for instance, of some unscrupulous commercial figure, and say that he would do anything for money, we use quite an inaccurate expression, and we slander him very much. He would not do anything for money. He would do some things for money; he would sell his soul for money, for instance; and, as Mirabeau humorously said, he would be quite wise "to take money for muck." He would oppress humanity for money; but then it happens that humanity and the soul are not things that he believes in; they are not his ideals. But he has his own dim and delicate ideals; and he would not violate these for money. He would not drink out of the soup-tureen, for money. He would not wear his coat-tails in front, for money. He would not spread a report that he had softening of the brain, for money. In the actual practice of life we find, in the matter of ideals, exactly what we have already found in the matter of ritual. We find that while there is a perfectly genuine danger of fanaticism from the men who have unworldly ideals, the permanent and urgent danger of fanaticism is from the men who have worldly ideals.

People who say that an ideal is a dangerous thing, that it deludes and intoxicates, are perfectly right. But the ideal which intoxicates most is the least idealistic kind of ideal. The ideal which intoxicates least is the very ideal ideal; that sobers us suddenly, as all heights and precipices and great distances do. Granted that it is a great evil to mistake a cloud for a cape; still, the cloud, which can be most easily mistaken for a cape, is the cloud that is nearest the earth. Similarly, we may grant that it may be dangerous to mistake an ideal for something practical. But we shall still point out that, in this respect, the most dangerous ideal of all is the ideal which looks a little practical. It is difficult to attain a high ideal; consequently, it is almost impossible to persuade ourselves that we have attained it. But it is easy to attain a low ideal; consequently, it is easier still to persuade ourselves that we have attained it when we have done nothing of the kind. To take a random example. It might be called a high ambition to wish to be an archangel; the man who entertained such an ideal would very possibly exhibit asceticism, or even frenzy, but not, I think, delusion. He would not think he was an archangel, and go about flapping his hands under the impression that they were wings. But suppose that a sane man had a low ideal; suppose he wished to be a gentleman. Any one who knows the world knows that in nine weeks he would have persuaded himself that he was a gentleman; and this being manifestly not the case, the result will be very real and practical dislocations and calamities in social life. It is not the wild ideals which wreck the practical world; it is the tame ideals.

The matter may, perhaps, be illustrated by a parallel from our modern politics. When men tell us that the old Liberal politicians of the type of Gladstone cared only for ideals, of course, they are talking nonsense—they cared for a great many other things, including votes. And when men tell us that modern politicians of the type of Mr. Chamberlain or, in another way, Lord Rosebery, care only for votes or for material interest, then again they are talking nonsense—these men care for ideals like all other men. But the real distinction which may be drawn is this, that to the older politician the ideal was an ideal, and nothing else. To the new politician his dream is not only a good dream, it is a reality. The old politician would have said, "It would be a good thing if there were a Republican Federation dominating the world." But the modern politician does not say, "It would be a good thing if there were a British Imperialism dominating the world." He says, "It is a good thing that there is a British Imperialism dominating the world;" whereas clearly there is nothing of the kind. The old Liberal would say "There ought to be a good Irish government in Ireland." But the ordinary modern Unionist does not say, "There ought to be a good English government in Ireland." He says, "There is a good English government in Ireland;" which is absurd. In short, the modern politicians seem to think that a man becomes practical merely by making assertions entirely about practical things. Apparently, a delusion does not matter as long as it is a materialistic delusion. Instinctively most of us feel that, as a practical matter, even the contrary is true. I certainly would much rather share my apartments with a gentleman who thought he was God than with a gentleman who thought he was a grasshopper. To be continually haunted by practical images and practical problems, to be constantly thinking of things as actual, as urgent, as in process of completion—these things do not prove a man to be practical; these things, indeed, are among the most ordinary signs of a lunatic. That our modern statesmen are materialistic is nothing against their being also morbid. Seeing angels in a vision may make a man a supernaturalist to excess. But merely seeing snakes in delirium tremens does not make him a naturalist.

And when we come actually to examine the main stock notions of our modern practical politicians, we find that those main stock notions are mainly delusions.

A great many instances might be given of the fact. We might take, for example, the case of that strange class of notions which underlie the word "union," and all the eulogies heaped upon it. Of course, union is no more a good thing in itself than separation is a good thing in itself. To have a party in favour of union and a party in favour of separation is as absurd as to have a party in favour of going upstairs and a party in favour of going downstairs. The question is not whether we go up or down stairs, but where we are going to, and what we are going, for? Union is strength; union is also weakness. It is a good thing to harness two horses to a cart; but it is not a good thing to try and turn two hansom cabs into one four-wheeler. Turning ten nations into one empire may happen to be as feasible as turning ten shillings into one half-sovereign. Also it may happen to be as preposterous as turning ten terriers into one mastiff. The question in all cases is not a question of union or absence of union, but of identity or absence of identity. Owing to certain historical and moral causes, two nations may be so united as upon the whole to help each other. Thus England and Scotland pass their time in paying each other compliments; but their energies and atmospheres run distinct and parallel, and consequently do not clash. Scotland continues to be educated and Calvinistic; England continues to be uneducated and happy. But owing to certain other Moral and certain other political causes, two nations may be so united as only to hamper each other; their lines do clash and do not run parallel. Thus, for instance, England and Ireland are so united that the Irish can sometimes rule England, but can never rule Ireland. The educational systems, including the last Education Act, are here, as in the case of Scotland, a very good test of the matter. The overwhelming majority of Irishmen believe in a strict Catholicism; the overwhelming majority of Englishmen believe in a vague Protestantism. The Irish party in the Parliament of Union is just large enough to prevent the English education being indefinitely Protestant, and just small enough to prevent the Irish education being definitely Catholic. Here we have a state of things which no man in his senses would ever dream of wishing to continue if he had not been bewitched by the sentimentalism of the mere word "union."

This example of union, however, is not the example which I propose to take of the ingrained futility and deception underlying all the assumptions of the modern practical politician. I wish to speak especially of another and much more general delusion. It pervades the minds and speeches of all the practical men of all parties; and it is a childish blunder built upon a single false metaphor. I refer to the universal modern talk about young nations and new nations; about America being young, about New Zealand being new. The whole thing is a trick of words. America is not young, New Zealand is not new. It is a very discussable question whether they are not both much older than England or Ireland.

Of course we may use the metaphor of youth about America or the colonies, if we use it strictly as implying only a recent origin. But if we use it (as we do use it) as implying vigour, or vivacity, or crudity, or inexperience, or hope, or a long life before them or any of the romantic attributes of youth, then it is surely as clear as daylight that we are duped by a stale figure of speech. We can easily see the matter clearly by applying it to any other institution parallel to the institution of an independent nationality. If a club called "The Milk and Soda League" (let us say) was set up yesterday, as I have no doubt it was, then, of course, "The Milk and Soda League" is a young club in the sense that it was set up yesterday, but in no other sense. It may consist entirely of moribund old gentlemen. It may be moribund itself. We may call it a young club, in the light of the fact that it was founded yesterday. We may also call it a very old club in the light of the fact that it will most probably go bankrupt to-morrow. All this appears very obvious when we put it in this form. Any one who adopted the young-community delusion with regard to a bank or a butcher's shop would be sent to an asylum. But the whole modern political notion that America and the colonies must be very vigorous because they are very new, rests upon no better foundation. That America was founded long after England does not make it even in the faintest degree more probable that America will not perish a long time before England. That England existed before her colonies does not make it any the less likely that she will exist after her colonies. And when we look at the actual history of the world, we find that great European nations almost invariably have survived the vitality of their colonies. When we look at the actual history of the world, we find, that if there is a thing that is born old and dies young, it is a colony. The Greek colonies went to pieces long before the Greek civilization. The Spanish colonies have gone to pieces long before the nation of Spain—nor does there seem to be any reason to doubt the possibility or even the probability of the conclusion that the colonial civilization, which owes its origin to England, will be much briefer and much less vigorous than the civilization of England itself. The English nation will still be going the way of all European nations when the Anglo-Saxon race has gone the way of all fads. Now, of course, the interesting question is, have we, in the case of America and the colonies, any real evidence of a moral and intellectual youth as opposed to the indisputable triviality of a merely chronological youth? Consciously or unconsciously, we know that we have no such evidence, and consciously or unconsciously, therefore, we proceed to make it up. Of this pure and placid invention, a good example, for instance, can be found in a recent poem of Mr. Rudyard Kipling's. Speaking of the English people and the South African War Mr. Kipling says that "we fawned on the younger nations for the men that could shoot and ride." Some people considered this sentence insulting. All that I am concerned with at present is the evident fact that it is not true. The colonies provided very useful volunteer troops, but they did not provide the best troops, nor achieve the most successful exploits. The best work in the war on the English side was done, as might have been expected, by the best English regiments. The men who could shoot and ride were not the enthusiastic corn merchants from Melbourne, any more than they were the enthusiastic clerks from Cheapside. The men who could shoot and ride were the men who had been taught to shoot and ride in the discipline of the standing army of a great European power. Of course, the colonials are as brave and athletic as any other average white men. Of course, they acquitted themselves with reasonable credit. All I have here to indicate is that, for the purposes of this theory of the new nation, it is necessary to maintain that the colonial forces were more useful or more heroic than the gunners at Colenso or the

Fighting Fifth. And of this contention there is not, and never has been, one stick or straw of evidence.

A similar attempt is made, and with even less success, to represent the literature of the colonies as something fresh and vigorous and important. The imperialist magazines are constantly springing upon us some genius from Queensland or Canada, through whom we are expected to smell the odours of the bush or the prairie. As a matter of fact, any one who is even slightly interested in literature as such (and I, for one, confess that I am only slightly interested in literature as such), will freely admit that the stories of these geniuses smell of nothing but printer's ink, and that not of first-rate quality. By a great effort of Imperial imagination the generous English people reads into these works a force and a novelty. But the force and the novelty are not in the new writers; the force and the novelty are in the ancient heart of the English. Anybody who studies them impartially will know that the first-rate writers of the colonies are not even particularly novel in their note and atmosphere, are not only not producing a new kind of good literature, but are not even in any particular sense producing a new kind of bad literature. The first-rate writers of the new countries are really almost exactly like the second-rate writers of the old countries. Of course they do feel the mystery of the wilderness, the mystery of the bush, for all simple and honest men feel this in Melbourne, or Margate, or South St. Pancras. But when they write most sincerely and most successfully, it is not with a background of the mystery of the bush, but with a background, expressed or assumed, of our own romantic cockney civilization. What really moves their souls with a kindly terror is not the mystery of the wilderness, but the Mystery of a Hansom Cab.

Of course there are some exceptions to this generalization. The one really arresting exception is Olive Schreiner, and she is quite as certainly an exception that proves the rule. Olive Schreiner is a fierce, brilliant, and realistic novelist; but she is all this precisely because she is not English at all. Her tribal kinship is with the country of Teniers and Maarten Maartens—that is, with a country of realists. Her literary kinship is with the pessimistic fiction of the continent; with the novelists whose very pity is cruel. Olive Schreiner is the one English colonial who is not conventional, for the simple reason that South Africa is the one English colony which is not English, and probably never will be. And, of course, there are individual exceptions in a minor way. I remember in particular some Australian tales by Mr. McIlwain which were really able and effective, and which, for that reason, I suppose, are not presented to the public with blasts of a trumpet. But my general contention if put before any one with a love of letters, will not be disputed if it is understood. It is not the truth that the colonial civilization as a whole is giving us, or shows any signs of giving us, a literature which will startle and renovate our own. It may be a very good thing for us to have an affectionate illusion in the matter; that is quite another affair. The colonies may have given England a new emotion; I only say that they have not given the world a new book.

Touching these English colonies, I do not wish to be misunderstood. I do not say of them or of America that they have not a future, or that they will not be great nations. I merely deny the whole established modern expression about them.

I deny that they are "destined" to a future. I deny that they are "destined" to be great nations. I deny (of course) that any human thing is destined to be anything. All the absurd physical metaphors, such as youth and age, living and dying, are, when applied to nations, but pseudo-scientific attempts to conceal from men the awful liberty of their lonely souls.

In the case of America, indeed, a warning to this effect is instant and essential. America, of course, like every other human thing, can in spiritual sense live or die as much as it chooses. But at the present moment the matter which America has very seriously to consider is not how near it is to its birth and beginning, but how near it may be to its end. It is only a verbal question whether the American civilization is young; it may become a very practical and urgent question whether it is dying. When once we have cast aside, as we inevitably have after a moment's thought, the fanciful physical metaphor involved in the word "youth," what serious evidence have we that America is a fresh force and not a stale one? It has a great many people, like China; it has a great deal of money, like defeated Carthage or dying Venice. It is full of bustle and excitability, like Athens after its ruin, and all the Greek cities in their decline. It is fond of new things; but the old are always fond of new things. Young men read chronicles, but old men read newspapers. It admires strength and good looks; it admires a big and barbaric beauty in its women, for instance; but so did Rome when the Goth was at the gates. All these are things quite compatible with fundamental tedium and decay. There are three main shapes or symbols in which a nation can show itself essentially glad and great—by the heroic in government, by the heroic in arms, and by the heroic in art. Beyond government, which is, as it were, the very shape and body of a nation, the most significant thing about any citizen is his artistic attitude towards a holiday and his moral attitude towards a fight—that is, his way of accepting life and his way of accepting death.

Subjected to these eternal tests, America does not appear by any means as particularly fresh or untouched. She appears with all the weakness and weariness of modern England or of any other Western power. In her politics she has broken up exactly as England has broken up, into a bewildering opportunism and insincerity. In the matter of war and the national attitude towards war, her resemblance to England is even more manifest and melancholy. It may be said with rough accuracy that there are three stages in the life of a strong people. First, it is a small power, and fights small powers. Then it is a great power, and fights great powers. Then it is a great power, and fights small powers, but pretends that they are great powers, in order to rekindle the ashes of its ancient emotion and vanity. After that, the next step is to become a small power itself. England exhibited this symptom of decadence very badly in the war with the Transvaal; but America exhibited it worse in the war with Spain. There was exhibited more sharply and absurdly than anywhere else the ironic contrast between the very careless choice of a strong line and the very careful choice of a weak enemy. America added to all her other late Roman or Byzantine elements the element of the Caracallan triumph, the triumph over nobody.

But when we come to the last test of nationality, the test of art and letters, the case is almost terrible. The English colonies have produced no great artists; and that fact may prove that they are still full of silent possibilities and reserve force. But America has produced great artists. And that fact most certainly proves that she is full of a fine futility and the end of all things. Whatever the American men of genius are, they are not young gods making a young world. Is the art of Whistler a brave, barbaric art, happy and headlong? Does Mr. Henry James infect us with the spirit of a schoolboy? No; the colonies have not spoken, and they are safe. Their silence may be the silence of the unborn. But out of America has come a sweet and startling cry, as unmistakable as the cry of a dying man.

XIX SLUM NOVELISTS AND THE SLUMS

Odd ideas are entertained in our time about the real nature of the doctrine of human fraternity. The real doctrine is something which we do not, with all our modern humanitarianism, very clearly understand, much less very closely practise. There is nothing, for instance, particularly undemocratic about kicking your butler downstairs. It may be wrong, but it is not unfraternal. In a certain sense, the blow or kick may be considered as a confession of equality: you are meeting your butler body to body; you are almost according him the privilege of the duel. There is nothing, undemocratic, though there may be something unreasonable, in expecting a great deal from the butler, and being filled with a kind of frenzy of surprise when he falls short of the divine stature. The thing which is really undemocratic and unfraternal is not to expect the butler to be more or less divine. The thing which is really undemocratic and unfraternal is to say, as so many modern humanitarians say, "Of course one must make allowances for those on a lower plane." All things considered indeed, it may be said, without undue exaggeration, that the really undemocratic and unfraternal thing is the common practice of not kicking the butler downstairs.

It is only because such a vast section of the modern world is out of sympathy with the serious democratic sentiment that this statement will seem to many to be lacking in seriousness. Democracy is not philanthropy; it is not even altruism or social reform. Democracy is not founded on pity for the common man; democracy is founded on reverence for the common man, or, if you will, even on fear of him. It does not champion man because man is so miserable, but because man is so sublime. It does not object so much to the ordinary man being a slave as to his not being a king, for its dream is always the dream of the first Roman republic, a nation of kings.

Next to a genuine republic, the most democratic thing in the world is a hereditary despotism. I mean a despotism in which there is absolutely no trace whatever of any nonsense about intellect or special fitness for the post. Rational despotism—that is, selective despotism—is always a curse to mankind, because with that you have the ordinary man misunderstood and misgoverned by some prig who has no brotherly respect for him at all. But irrational despotism is always democratic, because it is the ordinary man enthroned. The worst form of slavery is that which is called Caesarism, or the choice of some bold or brilliant man as despot because he is suitable. For that means that men choose a representative, not because he represents them, but because he does not. Men trust an ordinary man like George III or William IV. because they are themselves ordinary men and understand him. Men trust an ordinary man because they trust themselves. But men trust a great man because they do not trust themselves. And hence the worship of great men always appears in times of weakness and cowardice; we never hear of great men until the time when all other men are small.

Hereditary despotism is, then, in essence and sentiment democratic because it chooses from mankind at random. If it does not declare that every man may rule, it declares the next most democratic thing; it declares that any man may rule. Hereditary aristocracy is a far worse and more dangerous thing, because the numbers and multiplicity of an aristocracy make it sometimes possible for it to figure as an aristocracy of intellect. Some of its members will presumably have brains, and thus they, at any rate, will be an intellectual aristocracy within the social one. They will rule the aristocracy by virtue of their intellect, and they will rule the country by virtue of their aristocracy. Thus a double falsity will be set up, and millions of the images of God, who, fortunately for their wives and families, are neither gentlemen nor clever men, will be represented by a man like Mr. Balfour or Mr. Wyndham, because he is too gentlemanly to be called merely clever, and just too clever to be called merely a gentleman. But even an hereditary aristocracy may exhibit, by a sort of accident, from time to time some of the basically democratic quality which belongs to a hereditary despotism. It is amusing to think how much conservative ingenuity has been wasted in the defence of the House of Lords by men who were desperately endeavouring to prove that the House of Lords consisted of clever men. There is one really good defence of the House of Lords, though admirers of the peerage are strangely coy about using it; and that is, that the House of Lords, in its full and proper strength, consists of stupid men. It really would be a plausible defence of that otherwise indefensible body to point out that the clever men in the Commons, who owed their power to cleverness, ought in the last resort to be checked by the average man in the Lords, who owed their power to accident. Of course, there would be many answers to such a contention, as, for instance, that the House of Lords is largely no longer a House of Lords, but a House of tradesmen and financiers, or that the bulk of the commonplace nobility do not vote, and so leave the chamber to the prigs and the specialists and the mad old gentlemen with hobbies. But on some occasions the House of Lords, even under all these disadvantages, is in some sense representative. When all the peers flocked together to vote against Mr. Gladstone's second Home Rule Bill, for instance, those who said that the peers represented the English people, were perfectly right. All those dear old men who happened to be born peers were at that moment, and upon that question, the precise counterpart of all the dear old men who happened to be born paupers or middle-class gentlemen. That mob of peers did really represent the English people—that is to say, it was honest, ignorant, vaguely excited, almost unanimous, and obviously wrong. Of course, rational democracy is better as an expression of the public will than the haphazard hereditary method. While we are about having any kind of democracy, let it be rational democracy. But if we are to have any kind of oligarchy, let it be irrational oligarchy. Then at least we shall be ruled by men.

But the thing which is really required for the proper working of democracy is not merely the democratic system, or even the democratic philosophy, but the democratic emotion. The democratic emotion, like most elementary and indispensable things, is a thing difficult to describe at any time. But it is peculiarly difficult to describe it in our enlightened age, for the simple reason that it is peculiarly difficult to find it. It is a certain instinctive attitude which feels the things in which all men agree to be unspeakably important, and all the things in which they differ (such as mere brains) to be almost unspeakably unimportant. The nearest approach to it in our ordinary life would be the promptitude with which we should consider mere humanity in any circumstance of shock or death. We should say, after a somewhat disturbing discovery, "There is a dead man under the sofa." We should not be likely to say, "There is a dead man of considerable personal refinement under the sofa." We should say, "A woman has fallen into the water." We should not say, "A highly educated woman has fallen into the water." Nobody would say, "There are the remains of a clear thinker in your back garden." Nobody would say, "Unless you hurry up and stop him, a man with a very fine ear for music will have jumped off that cliff." But this emotion, which all of us have in connection with such things as birth and death, is to some people native and constant at all ordinary times and in all ordinary places. It was native to St. Francis of Assisi. It was native to Walt Whitman. In this strange and splendid degree it cannot be expected, perhaps, to pervade a whole commonwealth or a whole civilization; but one commonwealth may have it much more than another commonwealth, one civilization much more than another civilization. No community, perhaps, ever had it so much as the early Franciscans. No community, perhaps, ever had it so little as ours.

Everything in our age has, when carefully examined, this fundamentally undemocratic quality. In religion and morals we should admit, in the abstract, that the sins of the educated classes were as great as, or perhaps greater than, the sins of the poor and ignorant. But in practice the great difference between the mediaeval ethics and ours is that ours concentrate attention on the sins which are the sins of the ignorant, and practically deny that the sins which are the sins of the educated are sins at all. We are always talking about the sin of intemperate drinking, because it is quite obvious that the poor have it more than the rich. But we are always denying that there is any such thing as the sin of pride, because it would be quite obvious that the rich have it more than the poor. We are always ready to make a saint or prophet of the educated man who goes into cottages to give a little kindly advice to the uneducated. But the medieval idea of a saint or prophet was something quite different. The mediaeval saint or prophet was an uneducated man who walked into grand houses to give a little kindly advice to the educated. The old tyrants had enough insolence to despoil the poor, but they had not enough insolence to preach to them. It was the gentleman who oppressed the slums; but it was the slums that admonished the gentleman. And just as we are undemocratic in faith and morals, so we are, by the very nature of our attitude in such matters, undemocratic in the tone of our practical politics. It is a sufficient proof that we are not an essentially democratic state that we are always wondering what we shall do with the poor. If we were democrats, we should be wondering what the poor will do with us. With us the governing class is always saying to itself, "What laws shall we make?" In a purely democratic state it would be always saying, "What laws can we obey?" A purely democratic state perhaps there has never been. But even the feudal ages were in practice thus far democratic, that every feudal potentate knew that any laws which he made would in all probability return upon himself. His feathers might be cut off for breaking a sumptuary law. His head might be cut off for high treason. But the modern laws are almost always laws made to affect the governed class, but not the governing. We have public-house licensing laws, but not sumptuary laws. That is to say, we have laws against the festivity and hospitality of the poor, but no laws against the festivity and hospitality of the rich. We have laws against blasphemy—that is, against a kind of coarse and offensive speaking in which nobody but a rough and obscure man would be likely to indulge. But we have no laws against heresy—that is, against the intellectual poisoning of the whole people, in which only a prosperous and prominent man would be likely to be successful. The evil of aristocracy is not that it necessarily leads to the infliction of bad things or the suffering of sad ones; the evil of aristocracy is that it places everything in the hands of a class of people who can always inflict what they can never suffer. Whether what they inflict is, in their intention, good or bad, they become equally frivolous. The case against the governing class of modern England is not in the least that it is selfish; if you like, you may call the English oligarchs too fantastically unselfish. The case against them simply is that when they legislate for all men, they always omit themselves.

We are undemocratic, then, in our religion, as is proved by our efforts to "raise" the poor. We are undemocratic in our government, as is proved by our innocent attempt to govern them well. But above all we are undemocratic in our literature, as is proved by the torrent of novels about the poor and serious studies of the poor which pour from our publishers every month. And the more "modern" the book is the more certain it is to be devoid of democratic sentiment.

A poor man is a man who has not got much money. This may seem a simple and unnecessary description, but in the face of a great mass of modern fact and fiction, it seems very necessary indeed; most of our realists and sociologists talk about a poor man as if he were an octopus or an alligator. There is no more need to study the psychology of poverty than to study the psychology of bad temper, or the psychology of vanity, or the psychology of animal spirits. A man ought to know something of the emotions of an insulted man, not by being insulted, but simply by being a man. And he ought to know something of the emotions of a poor man, not by being poor, but simply by being a man. Therefore, in any writer who is describing poverty, my first objection to him will be that he has studied his subject. A democrat would have imagined it.

A great many hard things have been said about religious slumming and political or social slumming, but surely the most despicable of all is artistic slumming. The religious teacher is at least supposed to be interested in the costermonger because he is a man; the politician is in some dim and perverted sense interested in the costermonger because he is a citizen; it is only the wretched writer who is interested in the costermonger merely because he is a costermonger. Nevertheless, so long as he is merely seeking impressions, or in other words copy, his trade, though dull, is honest. But when he endeavours to represent that he is describing the spiritual core of a costermonger, his dim vices and his delicate virtues, then we must object that his claim is preposterous; we must remind him that he is a journalist and nothing else. He has far less psychological authority even than the foolish missionary. For he is in the literal and derivative sense a journalist, while the missionary is an eternalist. The missionary at least pretends to have a version of the man's lot for all time; the journalist only pretends to have a version of it from day to day. The missionary comes to tell the poor man that he is in the same condition with all men. The journalist comes to tell other people how different the poor man is from everybody else.

If the modern novels about the slums, such as novels of Mr. Arthur Morrison, or the exceedingly able novels of Mr. Somerset Maugham, are intended to be sensational, I can only say that that is a noble and reasonable object, and that they attain it. A sensation, a shock to the imagination, like the contact with cold water, is always a good and exhilarating thing; and, undoubtedly, men will always seek this sensation (among other forms) in the form of the study of the strange antics of remote or alien peoples. In the twelfth century men obtained this sensation by reading about dog-headed men in Africa. In the twentieth century they obtained it by reading about pig-headed Boers in Africa. The men of the twentieth century were certainly, it must be admitted, somewhat the more credulous of the two. For it is not recorded of the men in the twelfth century that they organized a sanguinary crusade solely for the purpose of altering the singular formation of the heads of the Africans. But it may be, and it may even legitimately be, that since all these monsters have faded from the popular mythology, it is necessary to have in our fiction the image of the horrible and hairy East-ender, merely to keep alive in us a fearful and childlike wonder at external peculiarities. But the Middle Ages (with a great deal more common sense than it would now be fashionable to admit) regarded natural history at bottom rather as a kind of joke; they regarded the soul as very important. Hence, while they had a natural history of dog-headed men, they did not profess to have a psychology of dog-headed men. They did not profess to mirror the mind of a dog-headed man, to share his tenderest secrets, or mount with his most celestial musings. They did not write novels about the semi-canine creature, attributing to him all the oldest morbidities and all the newest fads. It is permissible to present men as monsters if we wish to make the reader jump; and to make anybody jump is always a Christian act. But it is not permissible to present men as regarding themselves as monsters, or as making themselves jump. To summarize, our slum fiction is quite defensible as aesthetic fiction; it is not defensible as spiritual fact.

One enormous obstacle stands in the way of its actuality. The men who write it, and the men who read it, are men of the middle classes or the upper classes; at least, of those who are loosely termed the educated classes. Hence, the fact that it is the life as the refined man sees it proves that it cannot be the life as the unrefined man lives it. Rich men write stories about poor men, and describe them as speaking with a coarse, or heavy, or husky enunciation. But if poor men wrote novels about you or me they would describe us as speaking with some absurd shrill and affected voice, such as we only hear from a duchess in a three-act farce. The slum novelist gains his whole effect by the fact that some detail is strange to the reader; but that detail by the nature of the case cannot be strange in itself. It cannot be strange to the soul which he is professing to study. The slum novelist gains his effects by describing the same grey mist as draping the dingy factory and the dingy tavern. But to the man he is supposed to be studying there must be exactly the same difference between the factory and the tavern that there is to a middle-class man between a late night at the office and a supper at Pagani's. The slum novelist is content with pointing out that to the eye of his particular class a pickaxe looks dirty and a pewter pot looks dirty. But the man he is supposed to be studying sees the difference between them exactly as a clerk sees the difference between a ledger and an edition de luxe. The chiaroscuro of the life is inevitably lost; for to us the high lights and the shadows are a light grey. But the high lights and the shadows are not a light grey in that life any more than in any other. The kind of man who could really express the pleasures of the poor would be also the kind of man who could share them. In short, these books are not a record of the psychology of poverty. They are a record of the psychology of wealth and culture when brought in contact with poverty. They are not a description of the state of the slums. They are only a very dark and dreadful description of the state of the slummers. One might give innumerable examples of the essentially unsympathetic and unpopular quality of these realistic writers. But perhaps the simplest and most obvious example with which we could conclude is the mere fact that these writers are realistic. The poor have many other vices, but, at least, they are never realistic. The poor are melodramatic and romantic in grain; the poor all believe in high moral platitudes and copy-book maxims; probably this is the ultimate meaning of the great saying, "Blessed are the poor." Blessed are the poor, for they are always making life, or trying to make life like an Adelphi play. Some innocent educationalists and philanthropists (for even philanthropists can be innocent) have expressed a grave astonishment that the masses prefer shilling shockers to scientific treatises and melodramas to problem plays. The reason is very simple. The realistic story is certainly more artistic than the melodramatic story. If what you desire is deft handling, delicate proportions, a unit of artistic atmosphere, the realistic story has a full advantage over the melodrama. In everything that is light and bright and ornamental the realistic story has a full advantage over the melodrama. But, at least, the melodrama has one indisputable advantage over the realistic story. The melodrama is much more like life. It is much more like man, and especially the poor man. It is very banal and very inartistic when a poor woman at the Adelphi says, "Do you think I will sell my own child?" But poor women in the Battersea High Road do say, "Do you think I will sell my own child?" They say it on every available occasion; you can hear a sort of murmur or babble of it all the way down the street. It is very stale and weak dramatic art (if that is all) when the workman confronts his master and says, "I'm a man." But a workman does say "I'm a man" two or three times every day. In fact, it is tedious, possibly, to hear poor men being melodramatic behind the footlights; but that is because one can always hear them being melodramatic in the street outside. In short, melodrama, if it is dull, is dull because it is too accurate. Somewhat the same problem exists in the case of stories about schoolboys. Mr. Kipling's "Stalky and Co." is much more amusing (if you are talking about amusement) than the late Dean Farrar's "Eric; or, Little by Little." But "Eric" is immeasurably more like real school-life. For real school-life, real boyhood, is full of the things of which Eric is full—priggishness, a crude piety, a silly sin, a weak but continual attempt at the heroic, in a word, melodrama. And if we wish to lay a firm basis for any efforts to help the poor, we must not become realistic and see them from the outside. We must become melodramatic, and see them from the inside. The novelist must not take out his notebook and say, "I am an expert." No; he must imitate the workman in the Adelphi play. He must slap himself on the chest and say, "I am a man."

XX. CONCLUDING REMARKS ON THE IMPORTANCE OF ORTHODOXY

Whether the human mind can advance or not, is a question too little discussed, for nothing can be more dangerous than to found our social philosophy on any theory which is debatable but has not been debated. But if we assume, for the sake of argument, that there has been in the past, or will be in the future, such a thing as a growth or improvement of the human mind itself, there still remains a very sharp objection to be raised against the modern version of that improvement. The vice of the modern notion of mental progress is that it is always something concerned with the breaking of bonds, the effacing of boundaries, the casting away of dogmas. But if there be such a thing as mental growth, it must mean the growth into more and more definite convictions, into more and more dogmas. The human brain is a machine for coming to conclusions; if it cannot come to conclusions it is rusty. When we hear of a man too clever to believe, we are hearing of something having almost the character of a contradiction in terms. It is like hearing of a nail that was too good to hold down a carpet; or a bolt that was too strong to keep a door shut. Man can hardly be defined, after the fashion of Carlyle, as an animal who makes tools; ants and beavers and many other animals make tools, in the sense that they make an apparatus. Man can be defined as an animal that makes dogmas. As he piles doctrine on doctrine and conclusion on conclusion in the formation of some tremendous scheme of philosophy and religion, he is, in the only legitimate sense of which the expression is capable, becoming more and more human. When he drops one doctrine after another in a refined scepticism, when he declines to tie himself to a system, when he says that he has outgrown definitions, when he says that he disbelieves in finality, when, in his own imagination, he sits as God, holding no form of creed but contemplating all, then he is by that very process sinking slowly backwards into the vagueness of the vagrant animals and the unconsciousness of the grass. Trees have no dogmas. Turnips are singularly broad-minded.

If then, I repeat, there is to be mental advance, it must be mental advance in the construction of a definite philosophy of life. And that philosophy of life must be right and the other philosophies wrong. Now of all, or nearly all, the able modern writers whom I have briefly studied in this book, this is especially and pleasingly true, that they do each of them have a constructive and affirmative view, and that they do take it seriously and ask us to take it seriously. There is nothing merely sceptically progressive about Mr. Rudyard Kipling. There is nothing in the least broad minded about Mr. Bernard Shaw. The paganism of Mr. Lowes Dickinson is more grave than any Christianity. Even the opportunism of Mr. H. G. Wells is more dogmatic than the idealism of anybody else. Somebody complained, I think, to Matthew Arnold that he was getting as dogmatic as Carlyle. He replied, "That may be true; but you overlook an obvious difference. I am dogmatic and right, and Carlyle is dogmatic and wrong." The strong humour of the remark ought not to disguise from us its everlasting seriousness and common sense; no man ought to write at all, or even to speak at all, unless he thinks that he is in truth and the other man in error. In similar style, I hold that I am dogmatic and right, while Mr. Shaw is dogmatic and wrong. But my main point, at present, is to notice that the chief among these writers I have discussed do most sanely and courageously offer themselves as dogmatists, as founders of a system. It may be true that the thing in Mr. Shaw most interesting to me, is the fact that Mr. Shaw is wrong. But it is equally true that the thing in Mr. Shaw most interesting to himself, is the fact that Mr. Shaw is right. Mr. Shaw may have none with him but himself; but it is not for himself he cares. It is for the vast and universal church, of which he is the only member.

The two typical men of genius whom I have mentioned here, and with whose names I have begun this book, are very symbolic, if only because they have shown that the fiercest dogmatists can make the best artists. In the fin de siecle atmosphere every one was crying out that literature should be free from all causes and all ethical creeds. Art was to produce only exquisite workmanship, and it was especially the note of those days to demand brilliant plays and brilliant short stories. And when they got them, they got them from a couple of moralists. The best short stories were written by a man trying to preach Imperialism. The best plays were written by a man trying to preach Socialism. All the art of all the artists looked tiny and tedious beside the art which was a byproduct of propaganda.

The reason, indeed, is very simple. A man cannot be wise enough to be a great artist without being wise enough to wish to be a philosopher. A man cannot have the energy to produce good art without having the energy to wish to pass beyond it. A small artist is content with art; a great artist is content with nothing except everything. So we find that when real forces, good or bad, like Kipling and G. B. S., enter our arena, they bring with them not only startling and arresting art, but very startling and arresting dogmas. And they care even more, and desire us to care even more, about their startling and arresting dogmas than about their startling and arresting art. Mr. Shaw is a good dramatist, but what he desires more than anything else to be is a good politician. Mr. Rudyard Kipling is by divine caprice and natural genius an unconventional poet; but what he desires more than anything else to be is a conventional poet. He desires to be the poet of his people, bone of their bone, and flesh of their flesh, understanding their origins, celebrating their destiny. He desires to be Poet Laureate, a most sensible and honourable and public-spirited desire. Having been given by the gods originality—that is, disagreement with others—he desires divinely to agree with them. But the most striking instance of all, more striking, I think, even than either of these, is the instance of Mr. H. G. Wells. He began in a sort of insane infancy of pure art. He began by making a new heaven and a new earth, with the same irresponsible instinct by which men buy a new necktie or button-hole. He began by trifling with the stars and systems in order to make ephemeral anecdotes; he killed the universe for a joke. He has since become more and more serious, and has become, as men inevitably do when they become more and more serious, more and more parochial. He was frivolous about the twilight of the gods; but he is serious about the London omnibus. He was careless in "The Time Machine," for that dealt only with the destiny of all things; but he is careful, and even cautious, in "Mankind in the Making," for that deals with the day after to-morrow. He began with the end of the world, and that was easy. Now he has gone on to the beginning of the world, and that is difficult. But the main result of all this is the same as in the other cases. The men who have really been the bold artists, the realistic artists, the uncompromising artists, are the men who have turned out, after all, to be writing "with a purpose." Suppose that any cool and cynical art-critic, any art-critic fully impressed with the conviction that artists were greatest when they were most purely artistic, suppose that a man who professed ably a humane aestheticism, as did Mr. Max Beerbohm, or a cruel aestheticism, as did Mr. W. E. Henley, had cast his eye over the whole fictional literature which was recent in the year 1895, and had been asked to select the three most vigorous and promising and original artists and artistic works, he would, I think, most certainly have said that for a fine artistic audacity, for a real artistic delicacy, or for a whiff of true novelty in art, the things that stood first were "Soldiers Three," by a Mr. Rudyard Kipling; "Arms and the Man," by a Mr. Bernard Shaw; and "The Time Machine," by a man called Wells. And all these men have shown themselves ingrainedly didactic. You may express the matter if you will by saying that if we want doctrines we go to the great artists. But it is clear from the psychology of the matter that this is not the true statement; the true statement is that when we want any art tolerably brisk and bold we have to go to the doctrinaires.

In concluding this book, therefore, I would ask, first and foremost, that men such as these of whom I have spoken should not be insulted by being taken for artists. No man has any right whatever merely to enjoy the work of Mr. Bernard Shaw; he might as well enjoy the invasion of his country by the French. Mr. Shaw writes either to convince or to enrage us. No man has any business to be a Kiplingite without being a politician, and an Imperialist politician. If a man is first with us, it should be because of what is first with him. If a man convinces us at all, it should be by his convictions. If we hate a poem of Kipling's from political passion, we are hating it for the same reason that the poet loved it; if we dislike him because of his opinions, we are disliking him for the best of all possible reasons. If a man comes into Hyde Park to preach it is permissible to hoot him; but it is discourteous to applaud him as a performing bear. And an artist is only a performing bear compared with the meanest man who fancies he has anything to say.

There is, indeed, one class of modern writers and thinkers who cannot altogether be overlooked in this question, though there is no space here for a lengthy account of them, which, indeed, to confess the truth, would consist chiefly of abuse. I mean those who get over all these abysses and reconcile all these wars by talking about "aspects of truth," by saying that the art of Kipling represents one aspect of the truth, and the art of William Watson another; the art of Mr. Bernard Shaw one aspect of the truth, and the art of Mr. Cunningham Grahame another; the art of Mr. H. G. Wells one aspect, and the art of Mr. Coventry Patmore (say) another. I will only say here that this seems to me an evasion which has not even had the sense to disguise itself ingeniously in words. If we talk of a certain thing being an aspect of truth, it is evident that we claim to know what is truth; just as, if we talk of the hind leg of a dog, we claim to know what is a dog. Unfortunately, the philosopher who talks about aspects of truth generally also asks, "What is truth?" Frequently even he denies the existence of truth, or says it is inconceivable by the human intelligence. How, then, can he recognize its aspects? I should not like to be an artist who brought an architectural sketch to a builder, saying, "This is the south aspect of Sea-View Cottage. Sea-View Cottage, of course, does not exist." I should not even like very much to have to explain, under such circumstances, that Sea-View Cottage might exist, but was unthinkable by the human mind. Nor should I like any better to be the bungling and absurd metaphysician who professed to be able to see everywhere the aspects of a truth that is not there. Of course, it is perfectly obvious that there are truths in Kipling, that there are truths in Shaw or Wells. But the degree to which we can perceive them depends strictly upon how far we have a definite conception inside us of what is truth. It is ludicrous to suppose that the more sceptical we are the more we see good in everything. It is clear that the more we are certain what good is, the more we shall see good in everything.

I plead, then, that we should agree or disagree with these men. I plead that we should agree with them at least in having an abstract belief. But I know that there are current in the modern world many vague objections to having an abstract belief, and I feel that we shall not get any further until we have dealt with some of them. The first objection is easily stated.

A common hesitation in our day touching the use of extreme convictions is a sort of notion that extreme convictions specially upon cosmic matters, have been responsible in the past for the thing which is called bigotry. But a very small amount of direct experience will dissipate this view. In real life the people who are most bigoted are the people who have no convictions at all. The economists of the Manchester school who disagree with Socialism take Socialism seriously. It is the young man in Bond Street, who does not know what socialism means much less whether he agrees with it, who is quite certain that these socialist fellows are making a fuss about nothing. The man who understands the Calvinist philosophy enough to agree with it must understand the Catholic philosophy in order to disagree with it. It is the vague modern who is not at all certain what is right who is most certain that Dante was wrong. The serious opponent of the Latin Church in history, even in the act of showing that it produced great infamies, must know that it produced great saints. It is the hard-headed stockbroker, who knows no history and believes no religion, who is, nevertheless, perfectly convinced that all these priests are knaves. The Salvationist at the Marble Arch may be bigoted, but he is not too bigoted to yearn from a common human kinship after the dandy on church parade. But the dandy on church parade is so bigoted that he does not in the least yearn after the Salvationist at the Marble Arch. Bigotry may be roughly defined as the anger of men who have no opinions. It is the resistance offered to definite ideas by that vague bulk of people whose ideas are indefinite to excess. Bigotry may be called the appalling frenzy of the indifferent. This frenzy of the indifferent is in truth a terrible thing; it has made all monstrous and widely pervading persecutions. In this degree it was not the people who cared who ever persecuted; the people who cared were not sufficiently numerous. It was the people who did not care who filled the world with fire and oppression. It was the hands of the indifferent that lit the faggots; it was the hands of the indifferent that turned the rack. There have come some persecutions out of the pain of a passionate certainty; but these produced, not bigotry, but fanaticism—a very different and a somewhat admirable thing. Bigotry in the main has always been the pervading omnipotence of those who do not care crushing out those who care in darkness and blood.

There are people, however, who dig somewhat deeper than this into the possible evils of dogma. It is felt by many that strong philosophical conviction, while it does not (as they perceive) produce that sluggish and fundamentally frivolous condition which we call bigotry, does produce a certain concentration, exaggeration, and moral impatience, which we may agree to call fanaticism. They say, in brief, that ideas are dangerous things. In politics, for example, it is commonly urged against a man like Mr. Balfour, or against a man like Mr. John Morley, that a wealth of ideas is dangerous. The true doctrine on this point, again, is surely not very difficult to state. Ideas are dangerous, but the man to whom they are least dangerous is the man of ideas. He is acquainted with ideas, and moves among them like a lion-tamer. Ideas are dangerous, but the man to whom they are most dangerous is the man of no ideas. The man of no ideas will find the first idea fly to his head like wine to the head of a teetotaller. It is a common error, I think, among the Radical idealists of my own party and period to suggest that financiers and business men are a danger to the empire because they are so sordid or so materialistic. The truth is that financiers and business men are a danger to the empire because they can be sentimental about any sentiment, and idealistic about any ideal, any ideal that they find lying about. just as a boy who has not known much of women is apt too easily to take a woman for the woman, so these practical men, unaccustomed to causes, are always inclined to think that if a thing is proved to be an ideal it is proved to be the ideal. Many, for example, avowedly followed Cecil Rhodes because he had a vision. They might as well have followed him because he had a nose; a man without some kind of dream of perfection is quite as much of a monstrosity as a noseless man. People say of such a figure, in almost feverish whispers, "He knows his own mind," which is exactly like saying in equally feverish whispers, "He blows his own nose." Human nature simply cannot subsist without a hope and aim of some kind; as the sanity of the Old Testament truly said, where there is no vision the people perisheth. But it is precisely because an ideal is necessary to man that the man without ideals is in permanent danger of fanaticism. There is nothing which is so likely to leave a man open to the sudden and irresistible inroad of an unbalanced vision as the cultivation of business habits. All of us know angular business men who think that the earth is flat, or that Mr. Kruger was at the head of a great military despotism, or that men are graminivorous, or that Bacon wrote Shakespeare. Religious and philosophical beliefs are, indeed, as dangerous as fire, and nothing can take from them that beauty of danger. But there is only one way of really guarding ourselves against the excessive danger of them, and that is to be steeped in philosophy and soaked in religion.

Briefly, then, we dismiss the two opposite dangers of bigotry and fanaticism, bigotry which is a too great vagueness and fanaticism which is a too great concentration. We say that the cure for the bigot is belief; we say that the cure for the idealist is ideas. To know the best theories of existence and to choose the best from them (that is, to the best of our own strong conviction) appears to us the proper way to be neither bigot nor fanatic, but something more firm than a bigot and more terrible than a fanatic, a man with a definite opinion. But that definite opinion must in this view begin with the basic matters of human thought, and these must not be dismissed as irrelevant, as religion, for instance, is too often in our days dismissed as irrelevant. Even if we think religion insoluble, we cannot think it irrelevant. Even if we ourselves have no view of the ultimate verities, we must feel that wherever such a view exists in a man it must be more important than anything else in him. The instant that the thing ceases to be the unknowable, it becomes the indispensable. There can be no doubt, I think, that the idea does exist in our time that there is something narrow or irrelevant or even mean about attacking a man's religion, or arguing from it in matters of politics or ethics. There can be quite as little doubt that such an accusation of narrowness is itself almost grotesquely narrow. To take an example from comparatively current events: we all know that it was not uncommon for a man to be considered a scarecrow of bigotry and obscurantism because he distrusted the Japanese, or lamented the rise of the Japanese, on the ground that the Japanese were Pagans. Nobody would think that there was anything antiquated or fanatical about distrusting a people because of some difference between them and us in practice or political machinery. Nobody would think it bigoted to say of a people, "I distrust their influence because they are Protectionists." No one would think it narrow to say, "I lament their rise because they are Socialists, or Manchester Individualists, or strong believers in militarism and conscription." A difference of opinion about the nature of Parliaments matters very much; but a difference of opinion about the nature of sin does not matter at all. A difference of opinion about the object of taxation matters very much; but a difference of opinion about the object of human existence does not matter at all. We have a right to distrust a man who is in a different kind of municipality; but we have no right to mistrust a man who is in a different kind of cosmos. This sort of enlightenment is surely about the most unenlightened that it is possible to imagine. To recur to the phrase which I employed earlier, this is tantamount to saying that everything is important with the exception of everything. Religion is exactly the thing which cannot be left out—because it includes everything. The most absent-minded person cannot well pack his Gladstone-bag and leave out the bag. We have a general view of existence, whether we like it or not; it alters or, to speak more accurately, it creates and involves everything we say or do, whether we like it or not. If we regard the Cosmos as a dream, we regard the Fiscal Question as a dream. If we regard the Cosmos as a joke, we regard St. Paul's Cathedral as a joke. If everything is bad, then we must believe (if it be possible) that beer is bad; if everything be good, we are forced to the rather fantastic conclusion that scientific philanthropy is good. Every man in the street must hold a metaphysical system, and hold it firmly. The possibility is that he may have held it so firmly and so long as to have forgotten all about its existence.

This latter situation is certainly possible; in fact, it is the situation of the whole modern world. The modern world is filled with men who hold dogmas so strongly that they do not even know that they are dogmas. It may be said even that the modern world, as a corporate body, holds certain dogmas so strongly that it does not know that they are dogmas. It may be thought "dogmatic," for instance, in some circles accounted progressive, to assume the perfection or improvement of man in another world. But it is not thought "dogmatic" to assume the perfection or improvement of man in this world; though that idea of progress is quite as unproved as the idea of immortality, and from a rationalistic point of view quite as improbable. Progress happens to be one of our dogmas, and a dogma means a thing which is not thought dogmatic. Or, again, we see nothing "dogmatic" in the inspiring, but certainly most startling, theory of physical science, that we should collect facts for the sake of facts, even though they seem as useless as sticks and straws. This is a great and suggestive idea, and its utility may, if you will, be proving itself, but its utility is, in the abstract, quite as disputable as the utility of that calling on oracles or consulting shrines which is also said to prove itself. Thus, because we are not in a civilization which believes strongly in oracles or sacred places, we see the full frenzy of those who killed themselves to find the sepulchre of Christ. But being in a civilization which does believe in this dogma of fact for facts' sake, we do not see the full frenzy of those who kill themselves to find the North Pole. I am not speaking of a tenable ultimate utility which is true both of the Crusades and the polar explorations. I mean merely that we do see the superficial and aesthetic singularity, the startling quality, about the idea of men crossing a continent with armies to conquer the place where a man died. But we do not see the aesthetic singularity and startling quality of men dying in agonies to find a place where no man can live—a place only interesting because it is supposed to be the meeting-place of some lines that do not exist.

Let us, then, go upon a long journey and enter on a dreadful search. Let us, at least, dig and seek till we have discovered our own opinions. The dogmas we really hold are far more fantastic, and, perhaps, far more beautiful than we think. In the course of these essays I fear that I have spoken from time to time of rationalists and rationalism, and that in a disparaging sense. Being full of that kindliness which should come at the end of everything, even of a book, I apologize to the rationalists even for calling them rationalists. There are no rationalists. We all believe fairy-tales, and live in them. Some, with a sumptuous literary turn, believe in the existence of the lady clothed with the sun. Some, with a more rustic, elvish instinct, like Mr. McCabe, believe merely in the impossible sun itself. Some hold the undemonstrable dogma of the existence of God; some the equally undemonstrable dogma of the existence of the man next door.

Truths turn into dogmas the instant that they are disputed. Thus every man who utters a doubt defines a religion. And the scepticism of our time does not really destroy the beliefs, rather it creates them; gives them their limits and their plain and defiant shape. We who are Liberals once held Liberalism lightly as a truism. Now it has been disputed, and we hold it fiercely as a faith. We who believe in patriotism once thought patriotism to be reasonable, and thought little more about it. Now we know it to be unreasonable, and know it to be right. We who are Christians never knew the great philosophic common sense which inheres in that mystery until the anti-Christian writers pointed it out to us. The great march of mental destruction will go on. Everything will be denied. Everything will become a creed. It is a reasonable position to deny the stones in the street; it will be a religious dogma to assert them. It is a rational thesis that we are all in a dream; it will be a mystical sanity to say that we are all awake. Fires will be kindled to testify that two and two make four. Swords will be drawn to prove that leaves are green in summer. We shall be left defending, not only the incredible virtues and sanities of human life, but something more incredible still, this huge impossible universe which stares us in the face. We shall fight for visible prodigies as if they were invisible. We shall look on the impossible grass and the skies with a strange courage. We shall be of those who have seen and yet have believed.

THE END

ST FRANCIS OF ASSISI

CHAPTER I THE PROBLEM OF ST. FRANCIS

A sketch of St. Francis of Assisi in modern English may be written in one of three ways. Between these the writer must make his selection; and the third way, which is adopted here, is in some respects the most difficult of all. At least, it would be the most difficult if the other two were not impossible.

First, he may deal with this great and most amazing man as a figure in secular history and a model of social virtues. He may describe this divine demagogue as being, as he probably was, the world's one quite sincere democrat. He may say (what means very little) that St. Francis was in advance of his age. He may say (what is quite true) that St. Francis anticipated all that is most liberal and sympathetic in the modern mood; the love of nature; the love of animals; the sense of social compassion; the sense of the spiritual dangers of prosperity and even of property. All those things that nobody understood before Wordsworth were familiar to St. Francis. All those things that were first discovered by Tolstoy could have been taken for granted by St Francis. He could be presented, not only as a human but a humanitarian hero; indeed as the first hero of humanism. He has been described as a sort of morning star of the Renaissance. And in comparison with all these things, his ascetical theology can be ignored or dismissed as a contempory accident, which was fortunately not a fatal accident. His religion can be regarded as a superstition, but an inevitable superstition, from which not even genius could wholly free itself; in the consideration of which it would be unjust to condemn St. Francis for his self denial or unduly chide him for his chastity. It is quite true that even from so detached a standpoint his stature would still appear heroic. There would still be a great deal to be said about the man who tried to end the Crusades by talking to the Saracens or who interceded with the Emporer for the birds. The writer might describe in a purely historical spirit the whole of the Franciscan inspiration that was felt in the painting of Giotto, in the poetry of Dante, in the miracle plays that made possible the modern drama, and in so many things that are already appreciated by the modern culture. He may try to do it, as others have done, almost without raising any religious question at all. In short, he may try to tell the story of a saint without God; which is like being told to write the life of Nansen and forbidden to mention the North Pole.

Second, he may go to the opposite extreme, and decide, as it were, to be defiantly devotional. He may make the theological enthusiasm as thoroughly the theme as it was the theme of the first Franciscans. He may treat religion as the real thing that it was to the real Francis of Assisi. He can find an austere joy, so to speak, in parading the paradoxes of asceticism and all the topsy-turveydom of humility. He can stamp the whole history with the Stigmata, record fasts like fights against a dragon; till in the vague modern mind St Francis is as dark a figure as St. Dominic. In short, he can produce what many in our world will regard as a sort of photographic negative; the reversal of all lights and shades; what the foolish will find as impenetrable as darkness and even many of the wise will find almost as invisible as if it were written in silver upon white. Such a study of St. Francis would be unintelligible to anyone who does not share his religion, perhaps only partly intelligible to anyone who does not share his vocation. According to degrees of judgement, it will be regarded as something too bad or too good for the world. The only difficulty about doing the thing in this way is that it cannot be done. It would really require a saint to write about the life of a saint. In the present case the objections to such a course are insuperable.

Third, he may try to do what I have tried to do here; and as I have already suggested, the course has peculiar problems of its own. The writer may put himself in the position of the ordinary modern outsider and enquirer; as indeed the present writer is still largely and was once entirely in that position. He may start from the standpoint of a man who already admires St. Francis, but only for those things which such a man finds admirable. In other words he may assume that the reader is at least as enlightened as Renan or Matthew Arnold; but in the light of that enlightenment he may try to illimunate what Renan and Matthew Arnold left dark. He may try to use what is understood to explain what is not understood. He may try to say to the modern English reader: "Here is an historical character which is admittedly attractive to many of us already, by its gaiety, its romantic imagination, its spiritual courtesy and cameraderie, but which also contains elements (evidently equally sincere and emphatic) which seem to you quite remote and repulsive. But after all, this man was a man and not half a dozen men. What seems inconsistency to you did not seem inconsistency to him. Let us see whether we can understand, with the help of the existing understanding, these other things that now seem to be doubly dark, by their intrinsic gloom and their ironic contrast." I do not mean, of course, that I can really reach a psychological completeness in this crude and curt outline. But I mean that this is the only controversial condition that I shall here assume; that I am dealing with the sympathetic outsider. I shall not assume any more or any less agreement than this. A materialist may not care whether the inconsistencies are reconciled or not. A Catholic may not see any inconsistencies to reconcile. But I am here addressing the ordinary common man, sympathetic but sceptical, and I can only rather hazily hope that, by approaching the great saint's story through what is evidently picturesque and popular about it, I may at least leave the reader understanding a little more than he did before of the consistency of a complete character; that by approaching it in this way, we may at least get a glimmering of why the poet who praised his lord the sun, often hid himself in a dark cavern, of why the saint who was so gentle with his Brother the Wolf was so harsh to his Brother the Ass (as he nicknamed his own body), of why the troubadour who said that love set his heart on fire separated himself from women, of why the singer who rejoiced in the strength and gaiety of the fire deliberately rolled himself in the snow, of why the very song which cries with all the passion of a pagan, "Praised be God for our Sister, Mother Earth, which brings forth varied fruits and grass and glowing flowers," ends almost with the words "Praised be God for our Sister, the death of the body."

Renan and Matthew Arnold failed utterly at this test. They were content to follow Francis with their praises until they were stopped by their prejudices; the stubborn prejudices of the sceptic. The moment Francis began to do something they did not understand or did not like, they did not try to understand, still less to like it; they simply turned their backs on the whole business and "walked no more with him." No man will get any further along a path of historical enquiry in that fashion. These skeptics are really driven to drop the whole subject in despair, to leave the most simple and sincere of all historical characters as a mass of contradiction, to be praised on the principle of the curate's egg. Arnold refers to the asceticism of Alverno almost hurriedly, as if it were an unlucky but undeniable blot on the beauty of the story; or rather as if it were a pitiable break-down and bathos at the end of story. Now this is simply to be stone-blind to the whole point of any story. To represent Mount Alverno as the mere collapse of Francis is exactly like representing Mount Calvary as the mere collapse of Christ. Those mountains are mountains, whatever else they are, and it is nonsense to say (like the Red Queen) that they are comparitive hollows or negative holes in the ground. They were quite manifestly meant to be culminations and landmarks. To treat the Stigmata as a sort of scandal, to be touched on tenderly but with pain, is exactly like treating the original five wounds of Jesus Christ as five blots on his character. You may dislike the idea of asceticism; you may dislike equally the idea of martyrdom; for that matter you may have an honest and natural dislike of the whole conception of sacrifice symbolised by the cross. But if it is an intelligent dislike, you will retain the capacity for seeing the point of the story; the story of a martyr or even the story of a monk. You will not be able rationally to read the Gospel and regard the Crucifixion as an afterthought or an anti-climax or an accident in the life of Christ; it is obviously the point of the story like the point of a sword, the sword that pierced the heart of the Mother of God.

And you will not be able rationally to read the story of a man presented as a Mirror of Christ without understanding his final phase as a Man of Sorrows, and at least artistically appreciating the appropriatness of his receiving, in a cloud of mystery and isolation, inflicted by no human hand, the unhealed everlasting wounds that heal the world.

The practical reconciliation of the gaiety and austerity I must leave the story itself to suggest. But since I have mentioned Matthew Arnold and Renan and the rationalistic admirers of St. Francis, I will here give a hint of what it seems to me most advisable for such readers to keep in mind. These distinguished writers found things like the Stigmata a stumbling block because to them a religion was a philosophy. It was an impersonal thing; and it is only the most personal passion that provides here an approximate earthly parallel. A man will not roll in the snow for a stream of tendency by which all things fulfil the law of their being. He will not go without food in the name of something, not ourselves, that makes for righteousness. He will do things like this, or pretty like this, under quite a different impulse. He will do these things when he is in love. The first fact to realise about St Francis is involved with the first fact with which his story starts; that when he said from the first that he was a Troubadour, and said later that he was a Troubadour of a newer and nobler romance, he was not using a mere metaphor, but understood himself much better than the scholars understand him. He was, to the last agonies of asceticism, a Troubadour. He was a Lover. He was a lover of God and he was really and truly a lover of men; possibly a much rarer mystical vocation. A lover of men is very nearly the opposite of a philanthropist; indeed the pedantry of the Greek word carries something like a satire on itself. A philanthropist may be said to love anthropoids. But as St. Francis did not love humanity but men, so he did not love Christianity but Christ. Say, if you think so, that he was a lunatic loving an imaginary person; but an imaginary person, not an imaginary idea. And for the modern reader the clue to the asceticism and all the rest can be found in the stories of lovers when they seemed to be rather like lunatics. Tell it as the tale of one of the Troubadours, and the wild things he would do for his lady, and the whole of the modern puzzle disappears. In such a romance there would be no contradiction between the poet gathering flowers in the sun and enduring a freezing vigil in the snow, between his praising all earthly and bodily beauty and then refusing to eat, and between his glorifying gold and purple and perversely going in rags, between his showing pathetically a hunger for a happy life and a thirst for a heroic death. All these riddles would be easily be resolved in the simplicity of any noble love; only this was so noble a love that nine out of ten men have hardly even heard of it. We shall see later that this parallel of the earthly lover has a very practical relation to the problems of his life, as to his relations with his father and his friends and their families. The modern reader will almost always find that if he could only find this kind of love as a reality, he could feel this kind of extravagance as a romance. But I only note it here as a preliminary point because, though it is very far from being the final truth in the matter, it is the best approach to it. The reader cannot even begin to see the sense of a story that may well seem to him a very wild one, until he understands that to this great mystic his religion was not a thing like a theory but a thing like a love affair. And the only purpose of this prefatory chapter is to explain the limits of the present book; which is only addressed to that part of the modern world which finds in St. Francis a certain modern difficulty; which can admire him yet hardly accept him, or which can appreciate the saint almost without the sanctity. And my only claim even to attempt such a task is that I myself have for so long been in various stages of such a condition. Many thousand things that I now partly comprehend I should have thought utterly incomprehensible, many things I now hold sacred I should have scouted as utterly superstitious, many things that seem to me lucid and enlightened now they are seen from the inside I should honestly have called dark and barbarous seen from the outside, when long ago in those days of boyhood my fancy first caught fire with the glory of Francis of Assisi. I too have lived in Arcady; but even in Arcady I met one walking in a brown habit who loved the woods better than Pan. The figure in the brown habit stands above the hearth in the room where I write, and alone among many such images, at no stage of my pilgrimage has he ever seemed to me a stranger. There is something of a harmony between the hearth and the firelight and my own first pleasure in his words about the brother fire; for he stands far enough back in my memory to mingle with all those more domestic dreams of the first days. Even the fantastic shadows thrown by fire make a sort of shadow pantomine that belongs to the nursery; yet the shadows were even then the shadows of his favourite beast and birds, as he saw them, grotesque but haloed with the love of God. His Brother Wolf and Brother Sheep seemed then almost like the Brer Fox and Brer Rabbit of a more Christian Uncle Remus. I have come slowly to see many more marvellous aspects of such a man, but I have never lost that one. His figure stands on a sort of bridge connecting my boyhood with my conversion to many other things; for the romance of his religion has penetrated even the rationalism of that vague Victorian time. In so far as I have had this experience, I may be able to lead others a little further along that road; but only a very little further. Nobody knows better than I do now that it is a road upon which angels might fear to tread; but though I am certain of failure I am not altogether overcome by fear; for he suffered fools gladly.

CHAPTER II THE WORLD ST. FRANCIS FOUND

The modern innovation which has substituted journalism for history, or for that tradition that is the gossip of history, has had at least one definite effect. It has insured that everybody should only hear the end of every story. Journalists are in the habit of printing above the very last chapters of their serial stories (when the hero and the heroine are just about to embrace in the last chapter, as only an unfathomable perversity prevented them from doing so in the first) the rather misleading words, "You can only begin this story here." But even this is not a complete parallel; for the journals do give some sort of a summary of the story, while they never give anything remotely resembling a summary of the history. Newspapers not only deal with news, but they deal with everything as if it were entirely new. It is exactly in the same fashion that we read that Admiral Bangs has been shot, which is the first intimation we have that he has ever been born.

There is something singularly significant in the use which journalism makes of its stores of biography. It never thinks of publishing the life until it is publishing the death. As it deals with individuals it deals with institutions and ideas. After the Great War our public began to be told of all sorts of nations being emancipated. It had never been told a word about their being enslaved. We were called upon to judge of the justice of settlements, when we had never been allowed to hear of the very existence of the quarrels. People would think it pedantic to talk about the Serbian epics and they prefer to talk about the Yugo-Slavonic international new diplomacy; and they are quite excited about something they call Czecho-Slovakia without apparently having ever heard about Bohemia. Things that are as old as Europe are regarded as more recent than the very latest claims pegged out on the prairies of America. It is very exciting; like the last act of a play to people who have only come into the theatre just before the curtain falls. But it does not conduce exactly to knowing what it is all about. To those content with the mere fact of a pistol-shot or a passionate embrace, such a leisurely manner of patronising the drama may be recommended. To those tormented by a mere intellectual curiosity about who is kissing or killing whom, it is unsatisfactory.

Most modern history, especially in England, suffers from the same imperfection as journalism. At best it only tells half the story of Christendom; and that the second half without the first half. Men for whom reason begins with the Reformation, can never give a complete account of anything, for they have to start with institutions whose origin they can never explain, or generally even imagine. Just as we hear of the admiral being shot but have never heard of his being born, so we all heard a great deal about the dissolution of the monasteries, but we heard next to nothing about the creation of the monasteries. Now this sort of history would be hopelessly insufficient, even for an intelligent man who hated the monasteries. It is hopelessly insufficient in connection with institutions that many intelligent men do in a quite healthy spirit hate. For instance, it is possible that some of us have occasionally seen some mention, by our learned leader-writers, of an obscure institution called the Spanish Inquisition. Well, it really is an obscure institution, according to them and the histories they read. It is obscure because its origin is obscure. Protestant history simply begins with the horrible thing in possession, as the pantomine begins with the demon king in the goblin kitchen. It is likely enough that it was, especially towards the end, a horrible thing that might be haunted by demons; but if we say this was so, we have no notion why it was so. To understand the Spanish Inquisition it would be necessary to discover two things that we have never dreamed of bothering about; what Spain was and what an Inquisition was. The former would bring in the whole great question about the Crusade against the Moors; and by what heroic chivalry a European nation freed itself of an alien domination from Africa. The latter would bring in the whole business of the other Crusade against the Albigensians, and why men loved and hated that nihilistic vision from Asia. Unless we understand that there was in these things originally the rush and romance of a Crusade, we cannot understand how they came to deceive men or drag them on towards evil. The Crusaders doubtless abused their victory, but there was a victory to abuse. And where there is victory there is valour in the field and popularity in the forum. There is some sort of enthusiasm that encourages excesses or covers faults. For instance, I for one have maintained from very early days the responsibility of the English for their atrocious treatment of the Irish. But it would be quite unfair to describe even the devilry of '98 and leave out altogether all mention of the war with Napoleon. It would be unjust to suggest that the English mind was bent on nothing but the death of Emmett, when it was more probably full of the glory of the death of Nelson. Unfortunately '98 was very far from being the last date of such dirty work; and only a few years ago our politicians started trying to rule by random robbing and killing, while gently remonstrating with the Irish for their memory of old unhappy far-off things and battles long ago. But however badly we may think of the Black-and tan business, it would be unjust to forget that most of us were not thinking of Black-and-Tan but of khaki; and that khaki had just then a noble and national connotation covering many things. To write of the war with Ireland and leave out the war against Prussia, and the English sincerity about it, would be unjust to the English. So to talk about the torture-engine as if it had been a hideous toy is unjust to the Spanish. It does not tell sensibly from the start the story of what the Spaniards did, and why. We may concede to our contempories that in any case it is not a story that ends well. We do not insist that in their version it should begin well. What we complain of is that in their version it does not begin at all. They are only in at the death; or even, like Lord Tom Noddy, to late for the hanging. It is quite true that it was more horrible than any hanging; but they only gather, so to speak, the very ashes of the ashes; the fag-end of the faggot.

The case of the Inquisition is here taken at random, for it is one among any number illustrating the same thing; and not because it is especially connected with St. Francis, in whatever sense it may have been connected with St Dominic. It may well be suggested later indeed that St. Francis is unintelligible, just as St. Dominic is unintelligible, unless we do understand something of what the thirteenth century meant by heresy and a crusade. But for the moment I use it as a lesser example for a much larger purpose. It is to point out that to begin the story of St. Francis with the birth of St Francis would be to miss the whole point of the story, or rather not to tell the story at all. And it is to suggest that the modern tail-foremost type of journalistic history perpetually fails us. We learn about reformers without knowing what they had to reform, about rebels without knowing what they rebelled against, of memorials that are not connected with any memory and restorations of things that apparently never existed before. Even at the expense of this chapter appearing disproportionate, it is necessary to say something about the great movements that led up to the entrance of the founder of the Franciscans. It may seem to mean describing a world, or even a universe to describe a man. It will inevitably mean that the world or the universe will be described with a few desperate generalisations in a few abrupt sentences. But so far from its meaning that we shall see a very small figure under so large a sky, it will mean that we must measure the sky before we can begin to measure the towering stature of the man.

And this phrase alone brings me to the preliminary suggestions that seem necessary before even a slight sketch of the life of St. Francis. It is necessary to realise, in however rude and elementary a fashion, into what sort of a world St. Francis entered and what had been the history of that world, at least in so far as it affected him. It is necessary to have, if only in a few sentences, a sort of preface in the form of an Outline of History, if we may borrow the phrase of Mr. Wells. in the case of Mr. Wells himself, it is evident that the distinguished novelist suffered the same disadvantage as if he had been obliged to write a novel of which he hated the hero. To write history and hate Rome, both pagan and papal, is to hate everything that has happened. It comes very nearly to hating humanity on purely humanitarian grounds. To dislike both the priest and the soldier, both the laurels of the warrior and the lilies of the saint, is to suffer a division from the mass of mankind for which not all the dexterities of the finest and most flexible of modern intelligences can compensate. A much wider sympathy is needed for the historical setting of St. Francis, himself both a soldier and a saint. I will therefore conclude this chapter with a few generalisations about the world St. Francis found.

Men will not believe because they will not broaden their minds. As a matter of individual belief, I should of course express it by saying they are not sufficiently catholic to be Catholic. But I am not going to discuss here the doctrinal truths of Christianity, but simply the broad historical fact of Christianity, as it might appear to a really enlightened and imaginative person even if he were not a Christian. What I mean at the moment is that the majority of doubts are made out of details. In the course of random reading a man comes across a pagan custom that strikes him as picturesque or a Christian action that strikes him as cruel; but he does not enlarge his mind sufficiently to see the main truth about pagan custom or the Christian reaction against it. Until we understand, not necessarily in detail, but in their big bulk and proportion that pagan progress and that Christian reaction, we cannot really understand the point of history at which St. Francis appears or what his great popular mission was all about.

Now everybody knows, I imagine, that the twelfth and thirteenth centuries were an awakening of the world. They were a fresh flowering of culture and the creative arts after a long spell of much sterner and even more sterile experience which we call the Dark Ages. They may be called an emancipation; they were certainly an end; an end of what may at least seem a harsher and more inhuman time. But what was it that was ended? From what was it that men were emancipated? That is where there is a real collision and point at issue between the different philosophies of history. On the merely external and secular side, it has been truly said that men awoke from a sleep; but there had been dreams in that sleep of a mystical and sometimes of a monstrous kind. In that rationalistic routine into which most modern historians have fallen, it is considered enough to say that they were emancipated from mere savage superstition and advanced towards mere civilised enlightenment. Now this is the big blunder that stands as a stumbling-block at the very beginning of our story. Anybody who supposes that the Dark Ages were plain darkness and nothing else, and that the dawn of the thirteenth century was plain daylight and nothing else, will not be able to make head or tail of the human story of St. Francis of Assisi. The truth is that the joy of St. Francis and his Jongleurs de Dieu was not merely an awakening. It was something which cannot be understood without understanding their own mystical creed. The end of the Dark Ages was not merely the end of a sleep. It was certainly not merely the end of a superstitious enslavement. It was the end of something belonging to a quite definite but quite different order of ideas.

It was the end of a penance; or, if it be preferred, a purgation. It marked the moment when a certain spiritual expiation had been finally worked out and certain spiritual diseases had been finally expelled from the system. They had been expelled by an era of asceticism, which was the only thing that could have expelled them. Christianity had entered the world to cure the world; and she cured it in the only way in which it could be cured. Viewed merely in an external and experimental fashion, the whole of the high civilisation of antiquity had ended in the learning of a certain lesson; that is, in its conversion to Christianity. But that lesson was a psychological fact as well as a theological faith. That pagan civilization had indeed been a very high civilisation. It would not weaken our thesis, it might even strengthen it, to say that it was the highest that humanity ever reached. It had discovered its still unrivalled arts of poetry and plastic representation; it had discovered its own permanent political ideals; it had discovered its own clear system of logic and language. But above all, it had discovered its own mistake. That mistake was too deep to be ideally defined; the short-hand of it is to call it the mistake of nature-worship. It might almost as truly be called the mistake of being natural; and it was a very natural mistake. The Greeks, the great guides and pioneers of pagan antiquity, started out with the idea of something splendidly obvious and direct; the idea that if a man walked straight ahead on the high road of reason and nature, he would come to no harm; especially if he was, as the Greek was, eminently enlightened and intelligent. We might be so flippant as to say that man was simply to follow his nose, so long as it was a Greek nose. And the case of the Greeks themselves is alone enough to illustrate the strange but certain fatality that attends upon this fallacy. No sooner did the Greeks themselves begin to follow their own noses and their own notion of being natural, than the queerest thing in history seems to have happened to them. It was much too queer to be an easy matter to discuss. It may be remarked that our more repulsive realists never give us the benefit of their realism. Their studies of unsavoury subjects never take note of the testimony they bear to the truths of traditional morality. But if we had the taste for such things, we could cite thousands of such things as part of the case for Christian morals. And an instance of this is found in the fact that nobody has written, in this sense, a real moral history of the Greeks. Nobody has seen the scale or the strangeness of the story. The wisest men in the world set out to be natural; and the most unnatural thing in the world was the very first thing they did. The immediate effect of saluting the sun and the sunny sanity of nature was a perversion spreading like a pestilence. The greatest and even the purest philosophers could not apparently avoid this low sort of lunacy. Why? It would seem simple enough for the people whose poets had conceived Helen of Troy, whose sculptors had carved the Venus of Milo, to remain healthy on the point. The truth is people who worship health cannot remain healthy on the point. When Man goes straight he goes crooked. When he follows his nose he manages somehow to put his nose out of joint, or even to cut off his nose to spite his face; and that in accordance with something much deeper in human nature than nature-worshippers could ever understand. It was the discovery of that deeper thing, humanly speaking, that constituted the conversion to Christianity. There is a bias in a man like the bias on a bowl; and Christianity was the discovery of how to correct the bias and therefore hit the mark. There are many who will smile at the saying; but it is profoundly true to say that the glad good news brought by the Gospel was the news of original sin.

Rome rose at the expense of her Greek teachers largely because she did not entirely consent to be taught these tricks. She had a much more decent tradition; but she ultimately suffered from the same fallacy in her religious tradition; which was necessarily in no small degree the heathen tradition of nature worship. What was the matter with the whole heathen civilisation was that there nothing for the mass of men in the way of mysticism, except that concerned with the mystery of the nameless forces of nature, such as sex and growth and death. In the Roman Empire also, long before the end, we find nature-worship inevitably producing things that are against nature. Cases like that of Nero have passed into a proverb when Sadism sat on a throne brazen in the broad daylight. But the truth I mean is something much more subtle and universal than a conventional catalogue of atrocities. What had happened to the human imagination, as a whole, was that the whole world was coloured by dangerous and rapidly deteriorating passions; by natural passions becoming unnatural passions. Thus the effect of treating sex as only one innocent natural thing was that every other innocent natural thing became soaked and sodden with sex. For sex cannot be admitted to a mere equality among elementary emotions or experiences like eating and sleeping. The moment sex ceases to be a servant it becomes a tyrant. There is something dangerous and disproportionate in its place in human nature, for whatever reason; and it does really need a special purification and dedication. The modern talk about sex being free like any other sense, about the body being beautiful like any tree or flower, is either a description of the Garden of Eden or a piece of thoroughly bad psychology, of which the world grew weary two thousand years ago.

This is not to be confused with mere self-righteous sensationalism about the wickedness of the pagan world. It was not so much that the pagan world was wicked as that it was good enough to realise that its paganism was becoming wicked, or rather it was on the logical high road to wickedness. I mean that there was no future for "natural magic"; to deepen it was only to darken it into black magic. There was no future for it; because in the past it had only been innocent because it was young. We might say it had only been innocent because it was shallow. Pagans were wiser that paganism; that is why the pagans became Christians. Thousands of them had philosophy and family virtues and military honour to hold them up; but by this time the purely popular thing called religion was certainly dragging them down. When this reaction against the evil is allowed for, it is true to repeat that it was an evil that was everywhere. In another and more literal sense its name was Pan.

It was no metaphor to say that these people needed a new heaven and a new earth; for they had really defiled their own earth and even their own heaven. How could their case be met by looking at the sky, when erotic legends were scrawled in stars across it; how could they learn anything from the love of birds and flowers after the sort of love stories that were told of them? It is impossible here to multiply evidences, and one small example may stand for the rest. We know what sort of sentimental associations are called up to us by the phrase "a garden"; and how we think mostly of the memory of melancholy and innocent romances, or quite as often of some gracious maiden lady or kindly old person pottering under a yew hedge, perhaps in sight of a village spire. Then, let anyone who knows a little Latin poetry recall suddenly what would have once stood in place of the sundial or the fountain, obscene and monstrous in the sun; and of what sort was the god of their gardens.

Nothing could purge this obsession but a religion that was literally unearthly. It was no good telling such people to have a natural religion full of stars and flowers; there was not a flower or even a star that had not been stained. They had to go into the desert where they could find no flowers or even into the cavern where they could see no stars. Into that desert and that cavern the highest human intellect entered for some four centuries; and it was the very wisest thing it could do. Nothing but the stark supernatural stood up for its salvation; if God could not save it, certainly the gods could not. The early Church called the gods of paganism devils; and the Early Church was perfectly right. Whatever natural religion may have had to do with their beginnings, nothing but fiends now inhabited those hollow shrines. Pan was nothing but panic. Venus was nothing but venereal vice. I do not mean for a moment, of course, that all the individual pagans were of this character even to the end; but it was as individuals that they differed from it. Nothing distinguishes paganism from Christianity so clearly as the fact that the individual thing called philosophy had little or nothing to do with the social thing called religion. Anyhow it was no good to preach natural religion to people to whom nature had grown as unnatural as any religion. They knew much better than we do what was the matter with them and what sort of demons at once tempted and tormented them; and they wrote across that great space of history the text; "This sort goeth not out but by prayer and fasting."

Now the historical importance of St. Francis and the transition from the twelfth to the thirteenth centuries, lies in the fact that they marked the end of this expiation. Men at the close of the dark Ages may have been rude and unlettered and unlearned in everything but wars with heathen tribes, more barbarous than themselves, but they were clean. They were like children; the first beginnings of their rude arts have all the clean pleasure of children. We have to conceive them in Europe as a whole living under little local governments, feudal in so far as they were a survival of fierce wars with the barbarians, often monastic and carrying a far more friendly and fatherly character, still faintly imperial as far as Rome still ruled as a great legend. But in Italy something had survived more typical of the finer spirit of antiquity; the republic, Italy, was dotted with little states, largely democratic in their ideals, and often filled with real citizens. But the city no longer lay open as under the Roman peace, but was pent in high walls for defence against feudal war and all the citizens had to be soldiers. One of these stood in a steep and striking position on the wooded hills of Umbria; and its name was Assisi. Out of its deep gate under its high turrets was to come the message that was the gospel of the hour, "Your warfare is accomplished, your iniquity is pardoned." But it was out of all these fragmentary things of feudalism and freedom and remains of Roman Law that there were to rise, at the beginning of the thirteenth century, vast and almost universal, the mighty civilisation of the Middle Ages.

It is an exaggeration to attribute it entirely to the inspiration of any one man, even the most original genius of the thirteenth century. Its elementary ethics of fraternity and fair play had never been entirely extinct and Christendom had never been anything less than Christian. The great truisms about justice and pity can be found in the rudest monastic records of the barbaric transition or the stiffest maxims of the Byzantine decline. And early in the eleventh and twelfth centuries a larger moral movement had clearly begun, but what may fairly be said of it is this, that over all those first movements there was still something of that ancient austerity that came from the long penitentiary period. It was the twilight of the morning; but it was still a grey twilight. This may be illustrated by the mere mention of two or three of these reforms before the Franciscan reform. The monastic institution itself, of course, was far older than all these things; indeed it was undoubtedly almost as old as Christianity. Its counsels of perfection had always taken the form of vows of chastity and poverty and obedience. With these unworldly aims it had long ago civilised a great part of the world. The monks had taught people to plough and sow as well as to read and write; indeed they had taught the people nearly everything the people knew. But it may truly be said that the monks were severely practical, in the sense that they not only practical but also severe; though they were generally severe with themselves and practical for other people. All this early monastic movement had long ago settled down and doubtless often deteriorated; but when we come to the first medieval movements this sterner character is still apparent. Three examples may be taken to illustrate the point.

First, the ancient social mould of slavery was already beginning to melt. Not only was the slave turning into a serf, who was practically free as regards his own farm and family life, but many lords were freeing slaves and serfs altogether. This was done under the pressure of the priests; but especially it was done in the spirit of a penance. In one sense, of course, any Catholic society must have an atmosphere of penance; but I am speaking of that sterner spirit of penance which had expiated the excesses of paganism. There was about such restitutions the atmosphere of the death-bed; as many of them were doubtless were examples of death-bed repentance. A very honest atheist with whom I once debated made use of the expression, "Men have only been kept in slavery by the fear of hell." As I pointed out to him, if he had said that men had only been freed from slavery by the fear of hell, he would have at least have been referring to an unquestionable historical fact.

Another example was the sweeping reform of Church discipline by Pope Gregory the Seventh. It really was a reform, undertaken from the highest motives and having the healthiest results; it conducted a searching inquisition against simony or the financial corruption of the clergy; it insisted on a more serious and self-sacrificing ideal for the life of the parish priest. But the very fact that this largely took the form of making universal the obligation of celibacy will strike the note of something which, however noble, would seem to many to be vaguely negative. The third example is in one sense the strongest of all. For the third example was a war; a heroic war and for many of us a holy war; but still having all the stark and terrible responsibilities of war. There is no space here to say all that should be said about the true nature of the Crusades. Everybody knows that in the very darkest hour of the Dark Ages a sort of heresy had sprung up in Arabia and become a new religion of a military but nomadic sort; invoking the name of Mahomet. Intrinsically it had a character found in many heresies from the Moslem to the Monist. It seemed to the heretic a sane simplification of religion; while it seems to a Catholic an insane simplification of religion, because it simplifies all to a single idea and so loses the breadth and balance of Catholicism. Anyhow its objective character was that of a military danger to Christendom and Christendom had struck at the very heart of it, in seeking to reconquer the Holy Places. The great Duke Godfrey and the first Christians who stormed Jerusalem were heroes if there were any in the world; but they were the heroes of a tragedy.

Now I have taken these two or three examples of the earlier medieval movements in order to note about them one general character, which refers back to the penance that followed paganism. There is something in all these movements that is bracing even while it is still bleak, like a wind blowing between the clefts of the mountains. That wind, austere and pure, of which the poet speaks, is really the spirit of the time, for it is the wind of a world that has at last been purified. To anyone who can appreciate atmospheres there is something clear and clean about the atmosphere of this crude and often harsh society. Its very lusts are clean; for they no have longer any smell of perversion. Its very cruelties are clean; they are not the luxurious cruelties of the amphitheatre. They come either of a very simple horror at blasphemy or a very simple fury at an insult. Gradually against this grey background beauty begins to appear, as something really fresh and delicate and above all surprising. Love returning is no longer what was once called platonic but what is still called chivalric love. The flowers and stars are have recovered their first innocence. Fire and water are felt to be worthy to be the brother and sister of a saint. The purge of paganism is complete at last.

For water itself has been washed. Fire itself has been purified as by fire. Water is no longer the water into which slaves were flung to feed the fishes. Fire is no longer that fire through which children were passed to Moloch. Flowers smell no more of the forgotten garlands gathered in the garden of Priapus; stars stand no more as signs of the far frigidity of gods as cold as those cold fires. They are like all new things newly made and awaiting new names, from one who shall come to name them. Neither the universe nor the earth have now any longer the old sinister significance of the world. They await a new reconciliation with man, but they are already capable of being reconciled. Man has stripped from his soul the last rag of nature worship, and can return to nature.

While it was yet twilight a figure appeared silently and suddenly on a little hill above the city, dark against the fading darkness. For it was the end of a long and stern night, a night of vigil, not unvisited by stars. He stood with his hands lifted, as in so many statues and pictures, and about him was a burst of birds singing; and behind him was the break of day.

CHAPTER III FRANCIS THE FIGHTER

According to one tale, which if not true would be none the less typical, the very name of St. Francis was not so much a name as a nickname. There would be something akin to his familiar and popular instinct in the notion that he was nicknamed very much as an ordinary schoolboy might be called "Frenchy" at school. According to this version his name was not Francis at all but John; and his companions called him "Francesco", or "The little Frenchman" because of his passion for the French poetry of the Troubadours. The more probable story is that his mother had him named John when he was born in the absence of his father, who shortly returned from a visit to France, Where his commercial success had filled him with so much enthusiasm for French taste and social usage that he gave his son the new name signifying the Frank or Frenchman. In either case the name had a certain significance, as connecting Francis from the first with what he himself regarded as the romantic fairy land of the Troubadours.

The name of the father was Pietro Bernadone and he was a substantial citizen of the guild of the cloth merchants in the town of Assisi. It is hard to describe the position of such a man without some appreciation of such a guild and even of such a town. It did not exactly correspond to anything that is meant in modern times either by a merchant or a man of business or a tradesman, or anything that exists under the conditions of capitalism. Bernadone may have employed people but he was not an employer; that is; he did not belong to an employing class as distinct from an employed class. The person we definitely hear of his employing is his son Francis; who, one is tempted to guess, was about the last person that any man of business would employ if it were convenient to employ anybody else. He was rich, as a peasant may be rich by the work of his own family; but he evidently expected his own family to work in a way almost as plain as a peasant's. He was a prominent citizen, but he belonged to a social order which existed to prevent him being too prominent to be a citizen. It kept all such people on their own simple level, and no prosperity connoted that escape from drudgery by which in modern times the lad might have seemed to be a lord or a fine gentleman or something other than the cloth merchant's son. This is a rule that is proved even in the exception. Francis was one of those people who are popular with everybody in any case; and his guiless swagger as a Troubadour and leader of French fashions made him a sort of romantic ringleader among the young men of the town. He threw money about both in extravagance and benevolence, in a way native to a man who never, all his life, exactly understood what money was. This moved his mother to mingled exultation and exasperation and she said, as any tradesman's wife might say anywhere: "He is more like a prince than our son." But one of the earliest glimpses we have of him shows him as simply selling bales of cloth from a booth in the market; which his mother may or may not have believed to be one of the habits of princes. This first glimpse of the young man in the market is symbolic in more ways than one. An incident occurred which is perhaps the shortest and sharpest summary that could be given of certain curious things which were a part of his character, long before it was transfigured by transcendental faith. While he was selling velvet and fine embroideries to some solid merchant of the town a beggar came imploring alms; evidently in a somewhat tactless manner. It was a rude and simple society and there were no laws to punish a starving man for expressing his need for food, such as have been established in a more humanitarian age; and the lack of any organised police permitted such persons to pester the wealthy without any great danger. But there was I believe, in many places a local custom of the guild forbidding outsiders to interrupt a fair bargain; and it is possible that some such thing put the mendicant more than normally in the wrong. Francis had all his life a great liking for people who had been put hopelessly in the wrong. On this occasion he seems to have dealt with the double interview with rather a divided mind; certainly with distraction, possibly with irritation. Perhaps he was all the more uneasy because of the almost fastidious standard of manners that came to him quite naturally. All are agreed that politeness flowed from him from the first, like one of the public fountains in such a sunny Italian market place. He might have written among his own poems as his own motto that verse of Mr. Belloc's poem--

"Of Courtesy, it is much less Than courage of heart or holiness Yet in my walks it seems to me That the grace of God is in Courtesy."

Nobody ever doubted that Francis Bernadone had courage of heart, even of the most manly and military sort; and a time was to come when there was quite as little doubt about the holiness and grace of God. But I think that if there was one thing about which he was punctilious, it was punctiliousness. If there was one thing of which so humble a man could be said to be proud, he was proud of good manners. Only behind his perfectly natural urbanity were wider and even wilder possibilities, of which we get the first flash in this trivial incident. Anyhow Francis was evidently torn two ways with the botheration of two talkers, but finished his business with the merchant somehow; and when he had finished it, found the beggar was gone. Francis leapt from his booth, left all the bales of velvet and embroidery behind him apparently unprotected, and went racing across the marketplace like an arrow from the bow. Still running, he threaded the labrynth of the narrow and crooked streets of the little town, looking for his beggar whom he eventually discovered; and loaded the astonished mendicant with money. Then he straightened himself, so to speak, and swore before God that he would never all his life refuse help to a poor man. The sweeping simplicity of this undertaking is extremely characteristic. Never was any man so little afraid of his own promises. His life was one riot of rash vows; of rash vows that turned out right.

CHAPTER III FRANCIS THE FIGHTER

The first biographers of Francis, naturally alive with the great religious revolution that he wrought, equally naturally looked back to his first years chiefly for omens and signs of such a spiritual earthquake. But writing at a greater distance, we shall not decrease that dramatic effect, but rather increase it, if we realise that there was not at this time any external sign of anything particularly mystical about the young man. He had not anything of that early sense of his vocation that has belonged to some of the saints. Over and above his main ambition to win fame as a French poet, he would seem to have most often thought of winning fame as a soldier. He was born kind; he was brave in the normal boyish fashion; but he drew the line in both in kindness and bravery pretty well where most boys would have drawn it; for instance, he had the human horror of leprosy of which few normal people felt any need to be ashamed. He had the love of gay and bright apparel which was inherent in the heraldic taste of medieval times and seems altogether to have been rather a festive figure. If he did not paint the town red, he would probably have preferred to paint it all the colours of the rainbow, as in a medieval picture. But in this story of the young man in gay garments scampering after the vanishing beggar in rags there are certain notes of his natural individuality that must be assumed from first to last.

For instance, there is the spirit of swiftness. In a sense he continued running for the rest of his life, as he ran after the beggar. Because nearly all the errands he ran were errands of mercy, there appeared in his portraiture a mere element of mildness which was true in the truest sense, but is easily misunderstood. A certain precipitancy was the very poise of his soul. This saint should be represented among the other saints as angels were sometimes represented in pictures of angels; with flying feet or with feathers; in the spirit of the text that makes angels winds and messengers a flaming fire. It is a curiosity of language that courage actually means running; and some of our sceptics will no doubt demonstrate that courage really means running away. But his courage was running, in the sense of rushing. With all his gentleness, there was originally something of impatience in his impetuosity. The psychological truth about it illustrates very well the modern muddle about the word "practical." If we mean by what is practical what is most immediately practicable, we merely mean what is easiest. In that sense St. Francis was very impractical, and his ultimate aims were very unworldly. Bit if we mean by practicality a preference for prompt effort and energy over doubt or delay, he was very practical indeed. Some might call him a madman, but he was the very reverse of a dreamer. Nobody would be likely to call him a man of business; but he was very emphatically a man of action. In some of his early experiments he was rather too much of a man of action; he acted too soon and was too practical to be prudent. But at every turn of his extraordinary career we shall find him flinging himself around corners in the most unexpected fashion, as when he flew through the streets after the beggar.

Another element implied in the story, which was already partially a natural instinct, before it became supernatural ideal, was something that had never perhaps been wholly lost in those little republics of medieval Italy. It was something very puzzling to some people; something clearer as a rule to Southerners than to

Northeners, and I think to Catholics than to Protestants; the quite natural assumption of the equality of men. It has nothing necessarily to do with the Franciscan love for men; on the contrary one of its merely practical tests is the equality of the duel. Perhaps a gentleman will never be fully an egalitarian until he can really quarrel with his servant. But it was an antecedant condition of the Franciscan brotherhood; and we feel it in this early and secular incident. Francis, I fancy, felt a real doubt about which he must attend to, the beggar or the merchant; and having attended to the merchant, he turned to attend the beggar; he thought of them as two men. This is a thing much more difficult to describe, in a society from which it is absent, but it was the original basis of the whole business; it was why the popular movement arose in that sort of place and that sort of man. His imaginative magnanimity rose like a tower to starry heights that might well seem dizzy and even crazy; but it was founded on this high table land of human equality.

I have taken this the first among a hundred tales of the youth of St. Francis, and dwelt on its significance a little, because until we have learned to look for the significance there will often seem to be little but a sort of light sentiment in telling the story. St. Francis is not a proper person to be patronised with merely "pretty" stories. There are often any number of them; but they are too often used so as to be a sort of sentimental sediment of the medieval world, instead of being, as the saint emphatically is, a challenge to the modern world. We must take his human development somewhat more seriously; and the next story in which we get a glimpse of it is in a very different setting. But in exactly the same way it opens, as if by accident, certain abysses of the mind and perhaps of the unconscious mind. Francis still looks more or less like an ordinary young man; and it is only when we look at him as an ordinary young man, that we realise what an extraordinary young man he was.

War had broken out between Assisi and Perugia. It is now fashionable to say in a satirical spirit that such wars did not so much break out as to go on idefinitely between the city states of medieval Italy. It will be enough to say here that if one of those medieval wars had really gone on without stopping for a century, it might possibly have come within a remote distance of killing as many people as we kill in a year, in one of our great modern scientific wars between our great modern industrial empires. But the citizens of the medieval republic were certainly under the limitation of only being asked to die for the things with which they had always lived, the house they inhabited, the shrines they venerated and the rulers and representatives they new; and had not the larger vision calling for them to die for the latest rumours about remote colonies as reported in anonymous newspapers. And if we infer from our own experience that war paralyzed civilization, we must at least admit that these warring towns turned out a number of paralytics who go by the names of Dante and Michael Angelo, Ariosto and Titian, Leonardo and Columbus, not to mention Catherine of Siena and the subject of this story. While we lament all this local patriotism as a hubbub of the Dark Ages, it must seem a rather curious fact that about three quarters of the greatest men who ever lived came out of these little towns and were often engaged in these little wars. It remains to be seen what will ultimately come out of our large towns; but there has been no sign of anything of this sort since they became large; and I have sometimes been haunted by a fancy of my youth, that these things will not come till there is a city wall around Clapham and the tocsin is rung at night to arm the citizens of Wimbledon.

Anyhow, the tocsin was rung at Assisi and the citizens armed, and among them was Francis the son of the cloth merchant. He went out to fight with some company of lancers and in some fight or other he and his little band were taken prisoners. To me it seems most probable that there had been some tale of treason or cowardice about the disaster; for we are told that there was one of the captives with whom his fellow-prisoners flatly refused to associate even in prison; and when this happens in such circumstances, it is generally because the military blame for the surrender is thrown on some individual. Anyhow, somebody noted a small but rather curious thing, though it might seem rather negative than positive. Francis, we are told, moved among his captive companions with all his characteristic courtesy and even conviviality, "liberal and hilarious" as somebody said of him, resolved to keep up their spirits and his own. And when he came across the mysterious outcast, traitor or coward or whatever he was called, he simply treated him exactly like all the rest, neither with coldness or compassion, but with the same unaffected gaiety and good fellowship. But if there had been present in that prison someone with a sort of second sight about the truth and trend of spiritual things, he might have known he was in the presence of something new and seemingly almost anarchic; a deep tide driving out to uncharted seas of charity. For in this sense there was really something wanting in Francis of Assisi, something to which he was blind that he might see better and more beautiful things. All those limits in good fellowship and good form, all those landmarks of social life that divide the tolerable and the intolerable, all those social scruples and conventional conditions that are normal and even noble in ordinary men, all those things that hold many decent societies together, could never hold this man at all. He liked as he liked; he seems to have liked everybody, but especially those whom everybody disliked him for liking. Something very vast and universal was already present in that narrow dungeon; and such a seer might have seen in its darkness that red halo of caritas caritatum which marks one saint among saints as well as among men. He might well have heard the first whisper of that wild blessing that afterwards took the form of a blasphemy; "He listens to those whom God himself will not listen".

But though such a seer might have seen such a truth, it is exceedingly doubtful if Francis himself saw it. He had acted out of an unconscious largeness, or in the fine medieval phrase largesse, within himself, something might almost have been lawless if it had not been reaching out to a more divine law; but is doubtful whether he new the law was divine. It is evident that he had not at this time any notion of abandoning the military, still less of adopting the monastic life. It is true that there is not, as pacifists and prigs imagine, the least inconsistency between loving men and fighting them, if we fight them fairly and for a good cause. But it seems to me that there was more than this involved; that the mind of the young man was really running towards a military morality in any case. About this time the first calamity crossed his path in the form of a malady which was to revisit him many times and hamper his headlong career. Sickness made him more serious; but one fancies it would only have made him a more serious soldier, or even more serious about soldiering. And while he was recovering, something rather larger than the little fueds and raids of the Italian towns opened an avenue of adventure and ambition. The crown of Sicily, a considerable centre of controversy at the time, was apparently claimed by a certain Gauthier de Brienne, and the Papal cause to aid which Gauthier was called in aroused enthusiasm among a number of young Assisians, including Francis, who proposed to march into Apulia on the count's behalf; perhaps his French name had something to do with it. For it must never be forgotten that though that world was in one sense a world of little things, it was a world of little things concerned with great things. There was more internationalism in the lands dotted with tiny republics than in the huge homogeneous impenetrable national divisions of to-day. The legal authority of the Assisian magistrates might hardly reach further than a bow-shot from their high embattled city walls. But their sympathies might be with the ride of the Normans through Sicily or the palace of the Troubadours at Toulouse; with the Emperor throned in the German forests or the great Pope dying in the exile of Salerno. Above all, it must be remembered that when the interests of an age are mainly religious they must be universal. Nothing can be more universal than the universe. And there are several things about the religious position at that particular moment which modern people not unnaturally fail to realise. For one thing, modern people naturally think of people so remote as ancient people, and even early people. We feel vaguely that these things happened in the first ages of the Church. The Church was already a good deal more than a thousand years old. That is, the Church was then rather older than France is now, a great deal older than England is now. And she looked old then; almost as old as she does now; possibly older than she does now. The Church looked like great Charlemagne with the long white beard, who had already fought a hundred wars with the heathen, and in the legend was bidden by an angel to go forth and fight once more though he was two thousand years old. The Church had topped her thousand years and turned the corner for the second thousand; she had come through the Dark Ages in which nothing could be done except desperate fighting against the barbarians and the stubborn repitition of the creed. The creed was still being repeated after the victory or escape; but it is not unnatural to suppose that there was something a little monotonous about the repitition. The Church looked old then as now; and there were some who thought her dying as now. In truth orthodoxy was not dead but it may have been dull; it is certain that some people began to think it dull. The Troubadours of the Provencal movement had already begun to take that turn or twist towards Oriental fancies and the paradox of pessimism, which always comes to Europeans as something fresh when their own sanity seems to be something stale. It is likely enough that after all those centuries of hopeless war without and ruthless asceticism within, the official orthodoxy seemed to be something stale. The freshness and freedom of the first Christians seemed then as much as now a lost and almost prehistoric age of gold. Rome was still more rational than anything else; the Church was really wiser but it may well have seemed wearier than the world. There was something more adventurous and alluring, perhaps, about the mad metaphysics that had been blown across out of Asia. Dreams were gathering like dark clouds over the Midi to break in a thunder of anathema and civil war. Only the light lay on the great plain around Rome; but the light was blank and the plain was flat; and there was no stir in the still air and the immemorial silence about the sacred town.

High in the dark house of Assisi Francesco Bernadonne slept and dreamed of arms. There came to him in the darkness a vision splendid with swords, patterned after the cross in the Crusading fashion, of spears and shields and helmets hung in a high armoury, all bearing the sacred sign. When he awoke he accepted the dream as a trumpet bidding him to the battlefield, and rushed out to take horse and arms. He delighted in all the exercises of chivalry; and was evidently an accomplished cavalier and fighting man by the tests of the camp. He would doubtless at any time have preferred a Christian sort of chivalry; but it seems clear that he was also in a mood which thirsted for glory, though in him that glory would always have been identical with honour. He was not without some vision of that wreath of laurel which Ceasar has left for all the Latins. As he rode out to war the great gate in the deep wall of Assisi resounded with his last boast, "I shall come back a great prince."

A little way along the road his sickness rose again and threw him. It seems highly probable, in the light of his impetuous temper, that he had ridden away long before he was fit to move. And in the darkness of this second and fare more desolating interruption, he seems to have had another dream in which a voice said to him, "You have mistaken the meaning of the vision. Return to your own town." And Francis trailed back in his sickness to Assisi, a very dismal and disappointed and perhaps even derided figure, with nothing to do but wait for what should happen next. It was his first descent into a dark ravine that is called the valley of humiliation, which seemed to him very rocky and desolate, but in which he was afterwards to find many flowers.

But he was not only disappointed and humiliated; he was very much puzzled and bewildered. He still firmly believed that his two dreams must have meant something; and he could not imagine what they could possibly mean. It was while he was drifting, one might even say mooning, about the streets of Assisi and the fields outside the city wall, that an incident occurred to him which has not always been immediately connected with the business of the dreams, but which seems to me the obvious culmination of them. He was riding listlessly in some wayside place, apparently in the open country, when he saw a figure coming along the road towards him and halted; for he saw it was a leper. And he knew instantly that his courage was challenged, not as the world challenges, but as one would challenge who knew the secrets of the heart of a man. What he saw advancing was not the banner and spears of Perugia, from which it never occurred to him to shrink; nor the armies that fought for the crown of Sicily, of which he had always thought as a courageous man thinks of mere vulgar danger. Francis Bernadone saw his fear coming up the road towards him; the fear that comes from within and not without; though it stood white and horrible in the sunlight. For once in the long rush of his life his soul must have stood still. Then he sprang from his horse, knowing nothing between stillness and swiftness, and rushed on the leper and threw his arms around him. It was the beginning of a long vocation of ministry among many lepers, for whom he did many services; to this man he gave what money he could and mounted and rode on. We do not know how far he rode, or with what sense of the things around him; but it is said that when he looked back, he could see no figure on the road.

CHAPTER IV FRANCIS THE BUILDER

We have now reached the great break in the life of Francis of Assisi; the point at which something happened to him that must remain greatly dark to most of us, who are ordinary and selfish men whom God has not broken to make anew.

In dealing with this difficult passage, especially for my own purpose of making things moderately easy for the more secular sympathiser, I have hesitated as to the more proper course; and have eventually decided to state first of all what happened, with little more of a hint of what I imagine to have been the meaning of what happened. The fuller meaning may be debated more easily afterwards, when it was unfolded in the full Franciscan life. Anyway, what happened was this. The story very largely revolves around the ruins of the Church of St. Damien, an old shrine in Assisi which was apparently neglected and falling to pieces. Here Francis was in the habit of praying before the crucifix during those dark and aimless days of transition which followed the tragical collapse of all his military ambitions, probably made bitter by some loss of social prestige terrible to his sensitive spirit. As he did so he heard a voice saying to him, "Francis, seest thou not that my house is in ruins? Go and restore it for me."

Francis sprang up and went. To go and do something was one of the driving demands of his nature; probably he had gone and done it before he had at all thoroughly thought out what he had done. In any case what he had done was something very decisive and immediately very disastrous for his singular social career. In the coarse conventional language of the uncomprehending world, he stole. From his own enthusiastic point of view, he extended to his venerable father Peter Bernadone the exquisite excitement and inestimable privilege of assisting, more or less unconsciously, in the rebuilding of St. Damiens Church. In point of fact what he did first was to sell his own horse and then go off and sell several bales of his father's cloth, making the sign of the cross over them to indicate their pious and charitable destination. Peter Bernadone did not see things in this light. Peter Bernadone indeed had not very much light to see by, so far as understanding the genius and temperament of his extraordinary son was concerned. Instead of understanding in what sort of a wind and flame of abstract appetites the lad was living, instead of simply telling him (as the priest practically did later) that he done an indefensible thing with the best intentions, old Bernadone took up the matter in the hardest style; in a legal and literal fashion. He used absolute political powers like a heathen father, and himself put his son under lock and key as a vulgar thief. It would appear that the cry was caught up among many with whom the unlucky Francis had once been popular; and altogether, in his efforts to build up the house of God he had only succeeded in bringing his own house about his ears and lying buried under the ruins. The quarrel dragged drearily through several stages; at one time the wretched young man seems to have disappeared underground, so to speak, into some cavern or cellar where he remained huddled hopelessly in the darkness. Anyhow, it was his blackest moment; the whole world had turned over; the whole world was on top of him.

When he came out, it was only perhaps gradually that anybody grasped that something had happened. He and his father were summoned in the court of the bishop; for Francis had refused the authority of all legal tribunals. The bishop addressed some remarks to him, full of that excellent common sense which the Catholic Church keeps permanently as the background for all the fiery attitudes of her saints. He told Francis that he must unquestionably restore the money to his father; that no blessing could follow a work done by unjust methods; and in short (to put it crudely) if the young fanatic would give back his money to the old fool, the incident would then terminate. There was a new air about Francis. He was no longer crushed, still less crawling, so far as his father was concerned; yet his words do not, I think, indicate either just indignation or wanton insult or anything in the nature of a mere continuation of the quarrel. They are rather remotely akin to the mysterious utterances of his great model, "What have I to do with thee?" or even the terrible "Touch me not."

He stood up before them all and said, "Up to this time I have called Pietro Bernadone father, but now I am the servant of God. Not only the money but everything that can be called his I will restore to my father, even the very clothes he has given me." And he rent off all his garments except one; and they saw that it was a hair-shirt.

He piled the garments in a heap on the floor and threw the money on top of them. Then he turned to the bishop, and received his blessing, like one who turns his back on society; and, according to the account, went out as he was into the cold world. Apparently it was literally a cold world at the moment, and snow was on the ground. A curious detail, very deep in its significance, I fancy, is given in the same account of this great crisis in his life. He went out half-naked in his hair shirt into the winter woods, walking the frozen ground between the frosty trees: a man without a father. He was penniless, he was parentless, he was to all appearances without a trade or a plan or a hope in the world; and as he went under the frosty trees, he burst suddenly into song.

It was apparently noted as remarkable that the language in which he sang was French, or that Provencal which was called for convenience French. It was not his native language; and it was in his native language that he ultimately won fame as a poet; indeed St. Francis is one of the very first of the national poets in the purely national dialects of Europe. But it was the language with which all his most boyish ardours and ambitions had been identified; it was for him pre-eminently the language of romance. That it broke from him in this extraordinary extremity seems to me something at first sight very strange and in the last analysis very significant. What that significance was, or may well have been, I will try to suggest in the subsequent chapter; it is enough to indicate here that the whole philosophy of St. Francis revolved around the idea of a new supernatural light on natural things, which meant the ultimate recovery not the ultimate refusal of natural things. And for the purpose of this purely narrative part of the business, it is enough to record that while he wandered in the winter forest in his hair-shirt, like the very wildest of the hermits, he sang in the tongue of the Troubadours.

Meanwhile the narrative naturally reverts to the problem of the ruined or at least neglected church, which had been the starting point of the saint's innocent crime and beatific punishment. That problem still predominated in his mind and was soon engaging his insatiable activities; but they were activities of a new sort; and he made no more attempts to interfere with commercial ethics of the town of Assisi. There had dawned on him one of those great paradoxes that are also platitudes. He realised that the way to build a church is not to become entangled in bargains and, to him, rather bewildering questions of legal claim. The way to build a church is not to pay for it, certainly not with somebody else's money. The way to build a church is not to pay for it even with your own money. The way to build a church is to build it.

He went about by himself collecting stones. He begged all the people he met to give him stones. In fact he became a new sort of beggar, reversing the parable; a beggar who asks not for bread but stone. Probably, as happened to him again and again throughout his extraordinary existence, the very queerness of the request gave it a sort of popularity; and all sorts of idle and luxurious people fell in with the benevolent project, as they would have done with a bet. He worked with his own hands at the rebuilding of the church, dragging the material like a beast of burden and learning the very last and lowest lessons of toil. A vast number of stories are told about Francis at this as at every other period of his life; but for the purpose here, which is one of simplification, it is best to dwell on this definite re-entrance of the saint into the world by the low gate of physical labour. There does indeed run through the whole of his life a sort of double meaning, like his shadow thrown upon the wall. All his actions had something of the character of an allegory; and it is likely enough that some leaden-witted scientific historian may some day try to prove that he himself was never anything but an allegory. It is true enough in this sense that he was labouring at a double task, and rebuilding something else as well as the church of St. Damien. He was not only discovering the general lesson that his glory was not to be in overthrowing men in battle but in building up the positive and creative monuments of peace. He was truly building up something else, or beginning to build it up; something that has often enough fallen into ruin but has never been past rebuilding; a church that could always be built anew though it had rotted away to its first foundation stone, against which the gates of hell shall not prevail.

The next stage in his progress is probably marked by his transferring the same energies of architectural reconstruction to the little church of St. Mary of the Angels at the Portiuncula. He had already done something of the same kind at a church dedicated to St. Peter; and that quality in his life noted above, which made it seem like a symbolical drama, led many of his most devout biographers to note the numerical symbolism of the three churches. There was at any rate a more historical and practical symbolism about two of them. For the original church of St. Damian afterwards became the seat of his striking experiment of a female order, and of the pure and spiritual romance of St. Clare. And the church of the Portiuncula will remain forever as one of the great historic buildings of the world; for it was here that he gathered the little knot of friends and enthusiasts; it was the home of many homeless men. At this time, however, it is not clear that he had the definite idea of any such monastic developments. How early the plan appeared in his own mind it is of course impossible to say; but on the face of events it first takes the form of a few friends who attached themselves to him one by one because they shared his own passion for simplicity. The account given of the form of their dedication is, however, significant; for it was that of an invocation of the simplification of life as suggested in the New Testament. The adoration of Christ had been a part of the man's passionate nature for a long time past. But the imitation of Christ, as a sort of plan or ordered scheme of life, may in that sense may be said to begin here.

The two men who have the credit, apparently, of having first perceived something of what was happening in the world of the soul were a solid and wealthy citizen named Bernard of Quintaville and a canon from a neighbouring church named Peter. It is the more to their credit because Francis, if one may put it so, was by this time wallowing in poverty and association with lepers and ragged mendicants; and the two were men with much to give up; the one of comforts in the world and the other of ambition in the church. Bernard the rich burgher did quite literally and finally sell all he had and give it to the poor. Peter did even more; for he descended from a chair of spiritual authority, probably when he was already a man of mature years and therefore of fixed mental habits, to follow an extravagant young eccentric whom most people probably regarded as a maniac. What it was which they had caught a glimpse, of which Francis had seen the glory, may be suggested later so far as it can be suggested at all. At this stage we need profess to see no more than all Assisi saw, and that something not altogether unworthy of comment. The citizens of Assisi only saw the camel go in triumph through the eye of the needle and God do impossible things because to him all things were possible; only a priest who rent his robes like the Publican and not like the Pharisee and a rich man who went away joyful, for he had no possessions.

These three strange figures are said to have built themselves a sort of hut or den adjoining the leper hospital. There they talked to each other, in the intervals of drudgery and danger (for it needed ten times more courage to look after a leper than to fight for the crown of Sicily), in the terms of their new life, almost like children talking a secret language. Of these individual elements on their first friendship we can say little with certainty; but it is certain that they remained friends to the end. Bernard of Quintaville occupies in the story something of the position of Sir Bedivere, "first made and latest left of Arthur's knights," for he reappears at the right hand side of the saint on his deathbed and receives some sort of special blessing. But all these things belong to another historical world and were quite remote from the ragged and fantastic trio in their tumble-down hut.

They were not monks except perhaps in the most literal and archaic sense which was identical with hermits. They were, so to speak, three solitaries living together socially, but not as a society. The whole thing seems to have been intensely individual, as seen from the outside doubtless individual to the point of insanity. The stir of something that had in it the promise of a movement or a mission can first be felt as I have said in the affair of the appeal to the New Testament.

It was a sort of sors vigiliana applied to the Bible; a practice not unknown among Protestants though open to their criticism, one would think, as being rather a superstition of pagans. Anyhow it seems almost the opposite of searching the Scriptures to open them at random; but St. Francis certainly opened them at random. According to one story, he merely made the sign of the cross over the volume of the Gospel and opened it at three places reading three texts. The first was the tale of the rich young man whose refusal to sell all his goods was the occasion of the great paradox about the camel and the needle. The second was the commandment to the disciples to take nothing with them on their journey, neither scrip nor staff nor any money. The third was that saying, literally to be called crucial, that the follower of Christ must also carry his cross. There is a somewhat similar story of St. Francis finding one of these texts, almost as accidentally, merely in listening to what happened to be the Gospel of the day. But from the former version at least it would seem that the incident occurred very early indeed in his new life; for it was after this oracle, apparently, that Bernard the first disciple rushed forth and scattered all his goods among the poor. If this be so, it would seem that nothing followed it for the moment except the individual ascetical life with the hut for a hermitage. It must of course have been a rather public sort of hermitage, but it was none the less in a very real sense withdrawn from the world. St. Simeon Stylites on the top of his pillar was in one sense an exceedingly public character; but there was something a little singular in his situation for all that. It must be presumed that most people thought the situation of Francis singular, that some even thought it too singular. There was inevitably indeed in any Catholic society something ultimate and even subconscious that was at least capable of comprehending it better than a pagan or puritan society could comprehend it. But we must not at this stage, I think, exaggerate this potential public sympathy. As has already been suggested, the Church and all its institutions had already the air of being old and settled and sensible things, the monastic institutions amongst the rest. Common sense was commoner in the Middle Ages, I think, than in our own rather jumpy journalistic age; but men like Francis are not common in any age, nor are they to be fully understood merely by the exercise of common sense. The thirteenth century was certainly a progressive period; perhaps the only really progressive period in human history. But it can truly be called progressive precisely because its progress was very orderly. It is really and truly an example of an epoch of reforms without revolutions. But the reforms were not only progressive but very practical; and they were very much to the advantage of highly practical institutions; the towns and the trading guilds and the manual crafts. Now the solid men of town and guild in the time of Francis of Assisi were probably very solid indeed. They were much more economically equal, they were much more justly governed in their own economic environment, than the moderns who struggle madly between starvation and the monopolist prizes of capitalism; but it likely enough that the majority of citizens were as hard-headed as peasants. Certainly the behaviour of the venerable Pietro Bernadone does not indicate a delicate sympathy with the fine and almost fanciful subtleties of the Franciscan spirit. And we cannot measure the beauty and originality of this strange spiritual adventure, unless we have the humour and human sympathy to put into plain words how it would have looked to such an unsympathetic person at the time when it happened. In the next chapter I shall make an attempt, inevitably inadequate, to indicate the inside of the story of the building of the three churches and the little hut. In this chapter I have but outlined it from the outside. And in concluding that chapter I ask the reader to remember and realize what the story really looked like, when thus seen from the outside. Given a critic of rather coarse common sense, with no feeling about the incident except annoyance, and how would the story seem to stand?

A young fool or rascal is caught robbing his father and selling goods which he ought to guard; and the only explanation he will offer is that a loud voice from nowhere spoke in his ear and told him to mend the cracks and holes in a particular wall. He then declared himself naturally independant of all powers corresponding to the police or magistrates, and takes refuge with an amiable bishop who is forced to remonstrate with him and tell him he is wrong. He then proceeds to take off his clothes in public and practically throw them at his father; announcing at the same time that his father is not his father at all. He then runs about the town asking everybody he meets to give him fragments of buildings or building materials, apparently with reference to his old monomania about mending the wall. It may be an excellent thing that cracks should be filled up, but preferably not by somebody who is himself cracked; and architectural restoration like other things is not best performed by builders who, as we should say, have a tile loose. Finally the wretched youth relapses into rags and squalor and practically crawls away into the gutter. That is the spectacle that Francis must have presented to a very large number of his neighbours and friends.

How he lived at all must have seemed to them dubious; but presumably he already begged for bread as he had begged for building materials. But he was always very careful to beg for the blackest or worst bread he could get, for the stalest crusts or something less luxurious than the crumbs which the dogs eat, and which fell from the rich man's table. Thus he probably fared worse than an ordinary beggar; for the beggar would eat the best he could get and the saint ate the worst he could get. In plain fact he was ready to live on refuse; and it was probably something much uglier as an experience than the refined simplicity which vegetarians and water drinkers would call the simple life. As he dealt with the question of food, so he apparently dealt with the question of clothing. He dealt with it, that is, upon the same principle of taking what he could get, and not even the best of what he could get. According to one story he changed clothes with a beggar; and he would doubtless have been content to change them with a scarecrow. In another version he got hold of the rough brown tunic of a peasant, but presumably only because the peasant gave him his very oldest brown tunic, which was probably very old indeed. Most peasants have few changes of clothing to give away; and some peasants are not specially inclined to give them away unless absolutely necessary. It is said that in place of the girdle which he had flung off (perhaps with the more symbolic scorn because it probably carried the purse or wallet by the fashion of the period) he picked up a rope more or less at random, because it was lying near, and tied it round his waist. He undoubtedly meant it as a shabby expedient; rather as the very destitute tramp will sometimes tie his clothes together with a piece of string. He meant to strike the note of collecting his clothes anyway, like rags from a succession of dust bins. Ten years later that make-shift costume was the uniform of five thousand men; and a hundred years later, in that, for a pontifical panoply, they laid great Dante in the grave.

CHAPTER V LE JONGLEUR DE DIEU

Many signs and symbols might yet be used to give a hint of what really happened in the mind of the young poet of Assisi. Indeed they are at once too numerous for selection and yet too slight for satisfaction. But one of them may be adumbrated in this small and apparently accidental fact; that when he and his secular companions carried their pageant of poetry through the town, they called themselves Troubadours. But when he and his spiritual companions came out to do their spiritual work in the world, they were called by their leader the Jongleurs de Dieu.

Nothing has been said here at any length of the great culture of the Troubadours as it appeared in Provence or Languedoc, great as was their influence in history and their influence on St. Francis. Something more May be said of them when we come to summarise his relation to history; it is enough to note here in a few sentences the facts about them that were relevant to him, and especially the particular point now in question, which was the most relevant of all. Everybody knows who the Troubadours were; everybody knows that very early in the Middle Ages, in the twelfth and early thirteenth centuries, there arose a civilisation in Southern France which threatened to rival or eclipse the rising tradition of Paris. Its chief product was a school of poetry, or rather more especially a school of poets. They were primarily love-poets, though they were often also satirists and critics of things in general. Their picturesque posture in history is largely due to the fact that they sang their own poems and often played their own accompaniments, on the light musical instruments of the period; they were minstrels as well as men of letters. Allied to their love-poetry were other institutions of a decorative and fanciful kind concerned with the same theme. There was what was called the "Gay Science," the attempt to reduce to a sort of system the fine shades of flirtation and philandering. There were the things called Courts of Love, in which the same delicate subjects were dealt with legal pomp and pedantry. There is one point in this part of the business that must be remembered in relation to St. Francis. There were manifest moral dangers in all this superb sentimentalism; but it is a mistake to suppose that its only danger of exaggeration was in the direction of sensualism. There was a strain in the southern romance that was actually an excess of spirituality; just as the pessimist heresy it produced was in one sense an excess of spirituality. The love was not always animal; sometimes it was so airy as to be almost allegorical. The reader realises that the lady is the most beautiful being that can possibly exist, only he has occasional doubts as to whether she does exist. Dante owed something to the Troubadours; and the critical debates about his ideal woman are an excellent example of these doubts. We know that Beatrice was not his wife, but we should in any case be equally sure she was not his mistress; and some critics have even suggested that she was nothing at all, so to speak, except his muse. This idea of Beatrice as an allegorical figure is, I believe, unsound; it would seem unsound to any man who has read the Vit Nuova and has been in love. But the very fact that it is possible to suggest it illustrates something abstract and scholastic in these medieval passions. But though they were abstract passions they were very passionate passions. These men could feel almost like lovers, even about allegories and abstractions. It is necessary to realise that St. Francis was talking the true language of a troubadour when he said that he also had a most glorious and gracious lady and that her name was poverty.

But the particular point to be noted here is not concerned so much with the word Troubadour as with the word Jongleur. It is especially concerned with the transition from one to the other; and for this it is necessary to grasp another detail about the poets of the Gay Science. A jongleur was not the same thing as a troubadour, even if the same man were both a troubadour and a jongleur. More often, I believe, they were separate men as well as separate trades. In many cases, apparently the two men would walk the world together like companions in arms, or rather companions in arts. The jongleur was properly a joculator or jester; sometimes he was what we should call a juggler. This is the point, I imagine, of the tale about Taillifer the Jongleur at the Battle of Hastings, who sang the death of Roland while he tossed up his sword and caught it, as a juggler catches balls. Sometimes he may been even a tumbler; like that acrobat in the beautiful legend who was called "The Tumbler of Our Lady," because he turned head over heels and stood on his head before the image of the Blessed Virgin, for which he was nobly thanked and comforted by her and the whole company of heaven. In the ordinary way, we may imagine, the troubadour would exalt the company with earnest and solemn strains of love and then the jongleur would do his turn as a sort as a sort of comic relief. A glorious medieval romance remains to be written about two such companions wandering through the world. At any rate, if there is one place in which the Franciscan spirit can be found outside the true Franciscan story, it is in the tale of the Tumbler of our Lady. And when St. Francis called his followers the Jongleurs de Dieu, he meant something very like the Tumblers of our Lady.

Somewhere in that transition from the ambition of the Troubadour to the antics of the Tumbler is hidden, as under a parable, the truth of St. Francis. Of the two minstrels or entertainers, the jester was presumably the servant or at least the secondary figure. St. Francis really meant what he said when he said he had found the secret of life in being the servant and the secondary figure. There was to be found ultimately in such service a freedom almost amounting to frivolity. It was comparable to the condition of the jongleur because it almost amounted to frivolity. The jester could be free when the knight was rigid; and it was possible to be a jester in the service which is perfect freedom. This parallel of the two poets or minstrels is perhaps the best preliminary and external statement of the Franciscan change of heart, being conceived under an image with which the imagination of the modern world has a certain sympathy. There was, of course, a great deal more than this involved; and we must endeavour however insufficiently to penetrate past the image to the idea. It is so far like the tumblers that it is really to many people a topsy-turvy idea.

Francis, at the time or somewhere about the time when he disappeared into the prison or the dark cavern, underwent a reversal of a certain psychological kind; which was really like the reversal of a complete somersault, in that by coming full circle it came back, or apparently came back, to the same normal posture. It is necessary to use the grotesque simile of an acrobatic antic, because there is hardly any other figure that will make the fact clear. But in the inward sense it was a profound spiritual revolution. The man who went into the cave was not the man who came out again; in that sense he was almost as different as if he were dead, as if he were a ghost or a blessed spirit. And the effects of this on his attitude towards the actual world were really as extravagant as any parallel can make them. He looked at the world as differently from other men as if he had come out of that dark hole walking on his hands.

If we apply this parable of Our Lady's Tumbler to the case, we shall come very near to the point of it. Now it really is a fact that any scene such as a landscape can sometimes be more clearly and freshly seen if it is seen upside down. There have been landscape-painters who adopted the most startling and pantomimic postures in order to look at it for a moment in that fashion. Thus that inverted vision, so much more bright and quaint and arresting, does bear a certain resemblance to the world which a mystic like St. Francis sees every day. But herein is the essential part of the parable. Our Lady's Tumbler did not stand on his head in order to see flowers and trees as a clearer or quainter vision. He did not do so; and it would never have occurred to him to do so. Our Lady's Tumbler stood on his head to please Our Lady. If St. Francis had done the same thing, as he was quite capable of doing, it would originally have been from the same motive; a motive of a purely supernatural thought. It would be after this that his enthusiasm would extend itself and give a sort of halo to the edges of all earthly things. This is why it is not true to represent St. Francis as a mere romantic forerunner of the Renaissance and a revival of natural pleasures for their own sake. The whole point of him was that the secret of recovering the natural pleasures lay in regarding them in the light of a supernatural pleasure. In other words, he repeated in his own person that historic process noted in the introductory chapter; the vigil of asceticism which ends in the vision of a natural world made new. But in the personal case there was even more than this; there were elements that make the parallel of the Jongleur or Tumbler even more appropriate than this.

It may be suspected that in that black cell or cave Francis passed the blackest hours of his life. By nature he was the sort of man who has that vanity which is the opposite of pride; that vanity which is very near to humility. He never despised his fellow creatures and therefore he never despised the opinion of his fellow creatures; including the admiration of his fellow creatures. All that part of his human nature had suffered the heaviest and most crushing blows. It is possible that after his humiliating return from his frustrated military campaign he was called a coward. It is certain that after his quarrel with his father about the bales of cloth he was called a thief. And even those who had sympathised most with him, the priest whose church he had restored, the bishop whose blessing he had received, had evidently treated him with an almost humorous amiability which left only too clear the ultimate conclusion of the matter. He had made a fool of himself. Any man who has been young, who has ridden horses or thought himself ready for a fight, who has fancied himself as a troubadour and accepted the conventions of comradeship, will appreciate the ponderous and crushing weight of that simple phrase. The conversion of St. Francis, like the conversion of St. Paul, involved his being in some sense flung suddenly from a horse; but in a sense it was an even worse fall; for it was a war-horse. Anyhow, there was not a rag of him left that was not ridiculous. Everybody knew that at the best he had made a fool of himself. It was a solid objective fact, like the stones in the road, that he had made a fool of himself. He saw himself as an object, very small and distinct like a fly walking on a clear window pane; and it was unmistakably a fool. And as he stared at the word "fool" written in luminous letters before him, the word itself began to shine and change.

We used to be told in the nursery that if a man were to bore a hole through the centre of the earth and climb continually down and down, there would come a moment at the centre when he would seem to be climbing up and up. I do not know whether this is true. The reason I do not know whether it is true is that I never happened to bore a hole through the centre of the earth, still less to crawl through it. If I do not know what this reversal or inversion feels like, it is because I have never been there. And this also is an allegory. It is certain that the writer, it is even possible that the reader, is an ordinary person who has never been there. We cannot follow St. Francis to that final spiritual overturn in which complete humiliation becomes complete holiness or happiness, because we have never been there. I for one do not profess to follow it any further than that first breaking down of the romantic barricades of boyish vanity, which I have suggested in the last paragraph. And even that paragraph, of course, is merely conjectural, an individual guess at what he may have felt; but he may have felt something quite different. But whatever else it was, it was so far analogous to the story of the man making a tunnel through the earth that it did mean a man going down and down until at some mysterious moment he begins to go up and up. We have never gone up like that because we have never gone down like that; we are obviously incapable of saying that it does not happen; and the more candidly and calmly we read human history, and especially the history of the wisest men, the more we shall come to the conclusion that it does happen. Of the intrinsic internal essence of the experience, I make no pretence of writing at all. But the external effect of it, for the purpose of this narrative, may be expressed by saying that when Francis came forth from his cave of vision, he was wearing the same word "fool" as a feather in his cap; as a crest or even a crown. He would go on being a fool; he would become more and more of a fool; he would be the court fool of the King of Paradise.

This state can only be represented in symbol; but the symbol of inversion is true in another way. If a man saw the world upside down, with all the trees and towers hanging head downwards as in a pool, one effect would be to emphasise the idea of dependence. There is a Latin and literal connection; for the very word dependence only means hanging. It would make vivid the Scriptural text which says that God has hung the world upon nothing. If St. Francis had seen, in one of his strange dreams, the town of Assisi upside down, it need not have differed in a single detail from itself except in being entirely the other way round. But the point is this: that whereas to the normal eye the large masonry of its walls or the massive foundations of its watchtowers and its high citadel would make it seem safer and more permanent, the moment it was turned over the very same weight would make it seem more helpless and more in peril. It is but a symbol; but it happens to fit the psychological fact. St. Francis might love his little town as much as before, or more than before; but the nature of the love would be altered even in being increased. He might see and love every tile on the steep roofs or every bird on the battlements; but he would see them all in a new and divine light of eternal danger and dependence. Instead of being merely proud of his strong city because it could not be moved, he would be thankful to God Almighty that it had not been dropped; he would be thankful to God for not dropping the whole cosmos like a vast crystal to be shattered into falling stars. Perhaps St. Peter saw the world so, when he was crucified head-downwards.

It is commonly in a somewhat cynical sense that men have said, "Blessed is he that expecteth nothing, for he shall not be disappointed." It was in a wholly happy and enthusiastic sense that St. Francis said, "Blessed is he who expecteth nothing, for he shall enjoy everything." It was by this deliberate idea of starting from zero, from the dark nothingness of his own deserts, that he did come to enjoy even earthly things as few people have enjoyed them; and they are in themselves the best working example of the idea. For there is no way in which a man can earn a star or deserve a sunset. But there is more than this involved, and more indeed than is easily to be expressed in words. It is not only true that the less a man thinks of himself, the more he thinks of his good luck and of all the gifts of God. It is also true that he sees more of the things themselves when he sees more of their origin; for their origin is a part of them and indeed the most important part of them. Thus they become more extraordinary by being explained. He has more wonder at them but less fear of them; for a thing is really wonderful when it is significant and not when it is insignificant; and a monster, shapeless or dumb or merely destructive, may be larger than the mountains, but is still in a literal sense insignificant. For a mystic like St. Francis the monsters had a meaning; that is, they had delivered their message. They spoke no longer in an unknown tongue. That is the meaning of all those stories whether legendary or historical, in which he appears as a magician speaking the language of beasts and birds. The mystic will have nothing to do with mere mystery; mere mystery is generally a mystery of iniquity.

The transition from the good man to the saint is a sort of revolution; by which one for whom all things illustrate and illuminate God becomes one for whom God illustrates and illuminates all things. It is rather like the reversal whereby a lover might say at first sight that a lady looked like a flower, and say afterwards that all flowers reminded him of his lady. A saint and a poet standing by the same flower might seem to say the same thing; but indeed though they would both be telling the truth, they would be telling different truths. For one the joy of life is a cause of faith, for the other rather a result of faith. But one effect of the difference is that the sense of a divine dependence, which for the artist is like the brilliant levin-blaze, for the saint is like the broad daylight. Being in some mystical sense on the other side of things, he sees things go forth from the divine as children going forth from a familiar and accepted home, instead of meeting them as they come out, as most of us do, upon the roads of the world. And it is the paradox that by this privilege he is more familiar, more free and fraternal, more carelessly hospitable than we. For us the elements are like heralds who tell us with trumpet and tabard that we are drawing near the city of a great king; but he hails them with an old familiarity that is almost an old frivolity. He calls them his Brother Fire and his Sister Water.

So arises out of this almost nihilistic abyss the noble thing that is called Praise; which no one will ever understand while he identifies it with nature-worship or pantheistic optimism. When we say that a poet praises the whole creation, we commonly mean only that he praises the whole cosmos. But this sort of poet does really praise creation, in the sense of the act of creation. He praises the passage or transition from nonentity to entity; there falls here also the shadow of that arche-typal image of the bridge, which has given to the priest his archaic and mysterious name. The mystic who passes through the moment when there is nothing but God does in some sense behold the beginningless beginnings in which there was really nothing else. He not only appreciates everything but the nothing of which every-thing was made. In a fashion he endures and answers even the earthquake irony of the Book of Job; in some sense he is there when the foundations of the world are laid, with the morning stars singing together and the sons of God shouting for joy. That is but a distant adumbration of the reason why the Franciscan, ragged, penni-less, homeless and apparently hopeless, did indeed come forth singing such songs as might come from the stars of morning; and shouting, a son of God.

This sense of the great gratitude and the sublime dependence was not a phrase or even a sentiment; it is the whole point that this was the very rock of reality. It was not a fancy but a fact; rather it is true that beside it all facts are fancies. That we all depend in every detail, at every instant, as a Christian would say upon God, as even an agnostic would say upon existence and the nature of things, is not an illusion of imagination; on the contrary, it is the fundamental fact which we cover up, as with curtains, with the illusion of ordinary life. That ordinary life is an ad-mirable thing in itself, just as imagination is an admirable thing in itself. But it is much more the ordinary life that is made of imagination than the contemplative life. He who has seen the whole world hanging on a hair of the mercy of God has seen the truth; we might almost say the cold truth. He who has seen the vision of his city upside-down has seen it the right way up.

Rossetti makes the remark somewhere, bitterly but with great truth, that the worst moment for the atheist is when he is really thankful and has nobody to thank. The converse of this proposition is also true; and it is certain that this gratitude produced, in such men as we are here considering, the most purely joyful moments that have been known to man. The great painter boasted that he mixed all his colours with brains, and the great saint may be said to mix all his thoughts with thanks. All goods look better when they look like gifts. In this sense it is certain that the mystical method establishes a very healthy external relation to everything else. But it must always be remembered that everything else has for ever fallen into a second place, in comparison with this simple fact of dependence on the divine reality. In so far as ordinary social relations have in them something that seems solid and self-supporting, some sense of being at once buttressed and cushioned; in so far as they establish sanity in the sense of security and security in the sense of self-sufficiency, the man who has seen the world hanging on a hair does have some difficulty in taking them so seriously as that. In so far as even the secular authorities and hierarchies, even the most natural superiorities and the most necessary subordinations, tend at once to put a man in his place, and to make him sure of his position, the man who has seen the human hierarchy upside down will always have something of a smile for its superiorities. In this sense the direct vision of divine reality does disturb solemnities that are sane enough in themselves. The mystic may have added a cubit to his stature; but he generally loses something of his status. He can no longer take himself for granted, merely because he can verify his own existence in a parish register or a family Bible. Such a man may have something of the appearance of the lunatic who has lost his name while preserving his nature; who straightway forgets what manner of man he was. "Hitherto I have called Pietro Bernardone father; but now I am the servant of God."

All these profound matters must be suggested in short and imperfect phrases; and the shortest statement of one aspect of this illumination is to say that it is the discovery of an infinite debt. It may seem a paradox to say that a man may be transported with joy to discover that he is in debt. But this is only because in commercial cases the creditor does not generally share the transports of joy; especially when the debt is by hypothesis infinite and therefore unrecoverable. But here again the parallel of a natural love-story of the nobler sort disposes of the difficulty in a flash. There the infinite creditor does share the joy of the infinite debtor; for indeed they are both debtors and both creditors. In other words debt and dependence do become pleasures in the presence of unspoilt love; the word is used too loosely and luxuriously in popular simplifications like the present; but here the word is really the key. It is the key of all the problems of Franciscan morality which puzzle the merely modern mind; but above all it is the key of asceticism. It is the highest and holiest of the paradoxes that the man who really knows he cannot pay his debt will be for ever paying it. He will be for ever giving back what he cannot give back, and cannot be expected to give back. He will be always throwing things away into a bottomless pit of unfathomable thanks. Men who think they are too modern to understand this are in fact too mean to understand it; we are most of us too mean to practise it. We are not generous enough to be ascetics; one might almost say not genial enough to be ascetics. A man must have magnanimity of surrender, of which he commonly only catches a glimpse in first love, like a glimpse of our lost Eden. But whether he sees it or not, the truth is in that riddle; that the whole world has, or is, only one good thing; and it is a bad debt.

If ever that rarer sort of romantic love, which was the truth that sustained the Troubadours, falls out of fashion and is treated as fiction, we may see some such misunderstanding as that of the modern world about asceticism. For it seems conceivable that some barbarians might try to destroy chivalry in love, as the barbarians ruling in Berlin destroyed chivalry in war. If that were ever so, we should have the same sort of unintelligent sneers and unimaginative questions. Men will ask what selfish sort of woman it must have been who ruthlessly exacted tribute in the form of flowers, or what an avaricious creature she can have been to demand solid gold in the form of a ring; just as they ask what cruel kind of God can have demanded sacrifice and self-denial. They will have lost the clue to all that lovers have meant by love; and will not understand that it was because the thing was not demanded that it was done. But whether or no any such lesser things will throw a light on the greater, it is utterly useless to study a great thing like the Franciscan movement while remaining in the modern mood that murmurs against gloomy asceticism. The whole point about St. Francis of Assisi is that he certainly was ascetical and he certainly was not gloomy. As soon as ever he had been unhorsed by the glorious humiliation of his vision of dependence on the divine love, he flung himself into fasting and vigil exactly as he had flung himself furiously into battle. He had wheeled his charger clean round, but there was no halt or check in the thundering impetuosity of his charge. There was nothing negative about it; it was not a regimen or a stoical simplicity of life. It was not self-denial merely in the sense of self-control. It was as positive as a passion; it had all the air of being as positive as a pleasure. He devoured fasting as a man devours food. He plunged after poverty as men have dug madly for gold. And it is precisely the positive and passionate quality of this part of his personality that is a challenge to the modern mind in the whole problem of the pursuit of pleasure. There undeniably is the historical fact; and there attached to it is another moral fact almost as undeniable. It is certain that he held on this heroic or unnatural course from the moment when he went forth in his hair-shirt into the winter woods to the moment when he desired even in his death agony to lie bare upon the bare ground, to prove that he had and that he was nothing. And we can say, with almost as deep a certainty, that the stars which passed above that gaunt and wasted corpse stark upon the rocky floor had for once, in all their shining cycles round the world of labouring humanity, looked down upon a happy man.

CHAPTER VI THE LITTLE POOR MAN

From that cavern, that was a furnace of glowing gratitude and humility, there came forth one of the strongest and strangest and most original personalities that human history has known. He was, among other things, emphatically what we call a character; almost as we speak of a character in a good novel or play. He was not only a humanist but a humourist; a humourist especially in the old English sense of a man always in his humour, going his own way and doing what nobody else would have done. The anecdotes about him have a certain biographical quality of which the most familiar example is Dr. Johnson; which belongs in another way to William Blake or to Charles Lamb. The atmosphere can only be defined by a sort of antithesis; the act is always unexpected and never inappropriate. Before the thing is said or done it cannot even be conjectured; but after it is said or done it is felt to be merely characteristic. It is surprisingly and yet inevitably individual. This quality of abrupt fitness and bewildering consistency belongs to St. Francis in a way that marks him out from most men of his time. Men are learning more and more of the solid social virtues of medieval civilisation; but those impressions are still social rather than individual. The medieval world was far ahead of the modern world in its sense of the things in which all men are at one: death and the daylight of reason and the common conscience that holds communities together. Its generalisations were saner and sounder than the mad materialistic theories of to-day; nobody would have tolerated a Schopenhauer scorning life or a Nietzsche living only for scorn. But the modern world is more subtle in its sense of the things in which men are not at one; in the temperamental varieties and differentiations that make up the personal problems of life. All men who can think themselves now realise that the great schoolmen had a type of thought that was wonderfully clear; but it was as it were deliberately colourless. All are now agreed that the greatest art of the age was the art of public buildings; the popular and communal art of architecture. But it was not an age for the art of portrait-painting. Yet the friends of St. Francis have really contrived to leave behind a portrait; something almost resembling a devout and affectionate caricature. There are lines and colours in it that are personal almost to the extent of being perverse, if one can use the word perversity of an inversion that was also a conversion. Even among the saints he has the air of a sort of eccentric, if one may use the word of one whose eccentricity consisted in always turning towards the centre.

Before resuming the narrative of his first adventures, and the building of the great brotherhood which was the beginning of so merciful a revolution, I think it well to complete this imperfect personal portrait here; and having attempted in the last chapter a tentative description of the process, to add in this chapter a few touches to describe the result. I mean by the result the real man as he was after his first formative experiences; the man whom men met walking about on the Italian roads in his brown tunic tied with a rope. For that man, saving the grace of God, is the explanation of all that followed; men acted quite differently according to whether they had met him or not. If we see afterwards a vast tumult, an appeal to the Pope, mobs of men in brown habits besieging the seats of authority, Papal pronouncements, heretical sessions, trial and triumphant survival, the world full of a new movement, the friar a household word in every corner of Europe, and if we ask why all this happened, we can only approximate to any answer to our own question if we can, in some faint and indirect imaginative fashion, hear one human voice or see one human face under a hood. There is no answer except that Francis Bernardone had happened; and we must try in some sense to see what we should have seen if he had happened to us. In other words, after some groping suggestions about his life from the inside, we must again consider it from the outside; as if he were a stranger coming up the road towards us, along the hills of Umbria, between the olives or the vines.

Francis of Assisi was slight in figure with that sort of slightness which, combined with so much vivacity, gives the impression of smallness. He was probably taller than he looked; middle-sized, his biographers say; he was certainly very active and, considering what he went through, must have been tolerably tough. He was of the brownish Southern colouring, with a dark beard thin and pointed such as appears in pictures under the hoods of elves. And his eyes glowed with the fire that fretted him night and day. There is something about the description of all he said and did which suggests that, even more than most Italians, he turned naturally to a passionate pantomime of gestures. If this was so it is equally certain that with him, even more than with most Italians, the gestures were all gestures of politeness or hospitality. And both these facts, the vivacity and the courtesy, are the outward signs of something that mark him out very distinctively from many who might appear to be more of his kind than they really are. It is truly said that Francis of Assisi was on of the founders of the medieval drama, and therefore of the modern drama. He was the very reverse of a theatrical person in the selfish sense; but for all that he was pre-eminently a dramatic person. This side of him can best be suggested by taking what is commonly regarded as a reposeful quality; what is commonly described as a love of nature. We are compelled to use the term; and it is entirely the wrong term.

St. Francis was not a lover of nature. Properly understood, a lover of nature was precisely what he was not. The phrase implies accepting the material universe as a vague environment, a sort of sentimental pantheism. In the romantic period of literature, in the age of Byron and Scott, it was easy enough to imagine that a hermit in the ruins of a chapel (preferably by moonlight) might find peace and a mild pleasure in the harmony of solemn forests and silent stars, while he pondered over some scroll or illuminated volume, about the liturgical nature of which the author was a little vague. In short, the hermit might love nature as a background.

Now for St. Francis nothing was ever in the background. We might say that his mind had no background, except perhaps that divine darkness out of which the divine love had called up every coloured creature one by one. He saw everything as dramatic, distinct from its setting, not all of a piece like a picture but in action like a play. A bird went by him like an arrow; something with a story and a purpose, though it was a purpose of life and not a purpose of death. A bush could stop him like a brigand; and indeed he was as ready to welcome the brigand as the bush.

In a word, we talk about a man who cannot see the wood for the trees. St. Francis was a man who did not want to see the wood for the trees. He wanted to see each tree as a separate and almost a sacred thing, being a child of God and therefore a brother or sister of man. But he did not want to stand against a piece of stage scenery used merely as a background, and inscribed in a general fashion: "Scene; a wood." In this sense we might say that he was too dramatic for the drama. The scenery would have come to life in his comedies; the walls would really have spoken like Snout the Tinker and the trees would really have come walking to Dunsinane. Everything would have been in the foreground; and in that sense in the footlights. Everything would be in every sense a character. This is the quality in which, as a poet, he is the very opposite of a pantheist. He did not call nature his mother; he called a particular donkey his brother or a particular sparrow his sister. If he had called a pelican his aunt or an elephant his uncle as he might possibly have done, e would still have meant that they were particular creatures assigned by their Creator to particular places; not mere expressions of the evolutionary energy of things. That is where his mysticism is so close to the common sense of the child. A child has no difficulty about understanding that God made the dog and the cat; though he is well aware that the making of dogs and cats out of nothing is a mysterious process beyond his own imagination. But no child would understand what you meant if you mixed up the dog and the cat and everything else into one monster with myriad legs and called it nature. The child would resolutely refuse to make head or tail of any such animal. St. Francis was a mystic, but he believed in mysticism and not in mystification. As a mystic he was the mortal enemy of all those mystics who melt away the edges of things and dissolve an entity into its environment. He was a mystic of the daylight and the darkness; but not a mystic of the twilight. He was the very contrary of that sort of oriental visionary who is only a mystic because he is too much of a sceptic to be a materialist. St. Francis was emphatically a realist, using the word realist in its much more real medieval sense. In this matter he really was akin to the best spirit of his age, which had just won its victory over the nominalism of the twelfth century. In this indeed there was something symbolic in the contemporary art and decoration of his period; as in the art of heraldry. The Franciscan birds and beasts were really rather like heraldic birds and beasts; not in the sense of being fabulous animals but in the sense of being treated as if they were facts, clear and positive and unaffected by the illusions of atmosphere and perspective. In that sense he did see a bird sable on a field azure or a sheep argent on a field vert. But the heraldry of humility was richer than the heraldry of pride; for it saw all these things that God had given as something more precious and unique than the blazonry that princes and peers had only given to themselves. Indeed out of the depths of that surrender it rose higher than the highest titles of the feudal age; than the laurel of Ceasar or the Iron Crown of Lombardy. It is an example of extremes that meet, that the Little Poor Man, who had stripped himself of everything and named himself as nothing, took the same title that has been the wild vaunt of the vanity of the gorgeous Asiatic autocrat, and called himself the Brother of the Sun and Moon.

This quality, of something outstanding and even startling in things as St. Francis saw them, is here important as illustrating a character in his own life. As he saw all things dramatically, so he himself was always dramatic. We have to assume throughout, needless to say, that he was a poet and can only be understood as a poet. But he had one poetic privilege denied to most poets. In that respect indeed he might be called the one happy poet among all the unhappy poets of the world. He was a poet whose whole life was a poem. He was not so much a minstrel merely singing his own songs as a dramatist capable of acting the whole of his own play. The things he said were more imaginative than the things he wrote. The things he did were more imaginative than the things he said. His whole course through life was a series of scenes in which he had a sort of perpetual luck in bringing things to a beautiful crisis. To talk about the art of living has come to sound rather artificial than artistic. But St. Francis did in a definite sense make the very act of living an art, though it was an unpremeditated art. Many of his acts will seem grotesque and puzzling to a rationalistic taste. But they were always acts and not explanations; and they always meant what he meant them to mean. The amazing vividness with which he stamped himself on the memory and imagination of mankind is very largely due to the fact that he was seen again and again under such dramatic conditions. From the moment when he rent his robes and flung them at his father's feet to the moment when he stretched himself in death on the bare earth in the pattern of the cross, his life was made up of these unconscious attitudes and unhesitating gestures. It would be easy to fill page after page with examples; but I will here pursue the method found convenient everywhere in this short sketch, and take one typical example, dwelling on it with a little more detail than would be possible in a catalogue, in the hope of making the meaning more clear. The example taken here occurred in the last days of his life, but it refers back in a rather curious fashion to the first; and rounds off the remarkable unity of that romance of religion.

The phrase about his brotherhood with the sun and moon, and with the water and the fire, occurs of course in his famous poem called the Canticle of the Creatures or the Canticle of the Sun. He sang it wandering in the meadows in the sunnier season of his own career, when he was pouring upwards into the sky all the passions of a poet. It is a supremely characteristic work, and much of St. Francis could be reconstructed from that work alone. Though in some ways the thing is as simple and straightforward as a ballad, there is a delicate instinct of differentiation in it. Notice, for instance, the sense of sex in inanimate things, which goes far beyond the arbitrary genders of a grammar. It was not for nothing that he called fire his brother, fierce and gay and strong, and water his sister, pure and clear and inviolate. Remember that St. Francis was neither encumbered nor assisted by all that Greek and Roman polytheism turned into allegory, which has been to European poetry often an inspiration, too often a convention. Whether he gained or lost by his contempt of learning, it never occurred to him to connect Neptune and the nymphs with the water or Vulcan and the Cyclops with the flame. This point exactly illustrates what has already been suggested; that, so far from being a revival of paganism, the Franciscan renascence was a sort of fresh start and first awakening after a forgetfulness of paganism. Certainly it is responsible for a certain freshness in the thing itself. Anyhow St. Francis was, as it were, the founder of a new folk-lore; but he could distinguish his mermaids from his mermen and his witches from his wizards. In short, he had to make his own mythology; but he knew at a glance the goddesses from the gods. This fanciful instinct for the sexes is not the only example of an imaginative instinct of the kind. There is just the same quaint felicity in the fact that he singles out the sun with a slightly more courtly title besides that of brother; a phrase that one king might use of another, corresponding to "Monsieur notre frere." It is like a faint half ironic shadow of the shining primacy that it had held in the pagan heavens. A bishop is said to have complained of a Nonconformist saying Paul instead of Saint Paul; and to have added, "He might at least have called him Mr. Paul." So St. Francis is free of all obligation to cry out in praise or terror on the Lord God Apollo, but in his new nursery heavens, he salutes him as Mr. Sun. Those are the things in which he has a sort of inspired infancy, only to be paralleled in nursery tales. Something of the same hazy but healthy awe makes the story of Br'er Fox and Br'er Rabbit refer respectfully to Mr. Man.

This poem, full of the mirth of youth and the memories of childhood, runs through his whole life like a refrain, and scraps of it turn up continually in the ordinary habit of his talk. Perhaps the last appearance of its special language was in an incident that has always seemed to me intensely impressive, and is at any rate very illustrative of the great manner and gesture of which I speak. Impressions of that kind are a matter of imagination and in that sense of taste. It is idle to argue about them; for it is the whole point of them that they have passed beyond words; and even when they use words, seem to be completed by some ritual movement like a blessing or a blow. So, in a supreme example, there is something far past all exposition, something like the sweeping movement and mighty shadow of a hand, darkening even the darkness of Gethsemane; "Sleep on now, and take your rest..." Yet there are people who have started to paraphrase and expand the story of the Passion.

St. Francis was a dying man. We might say he was an old man, at the time this typical incident occurred; but in fact he was only prematurely old; for he was not fifty when he died, worn out with his fighting and fasting life. But when he came down from the awful asceticism and more awful revelation of Alverno, he was a broken man. As will be apparent when these events are touched on in their turn, it was not only sickness and bodily decay that may well have darkened his life; he had been recently disappointed in his main mission to end the Crusades by the conversion of Islam; he had been still more disappointed by the signs of compromise and a more political or practical spirit in his own order; he had spent his last energies in protest.

At this point he was told that he was going blind. If the faintest hint has been given here of what St. Francis felt about the glory and pageantry of earth and sky, about the heraldic shape and colour and symbolism of birds and beasts and flowers, some notion may be formed of what it meant to him to go blind. Yet the remedy might well have seemed worse than the disease. The remedy, admittedly an uncertain remedy, was to cauterise the eye, and that without any anaesthetic. In other words it was to burn his living eyeballs with a red-hot iron. Many of the tortures of martyrdom, which he envied in martyrology and sought vainly in Syria, can have been no worse. When they took the brand from the furnace, he rose as with an urbane gesture and spoke as to an invisible presence: "Brother Fire, God made you beautiful and strong and useful; I pray you be courteous with me."

If there be any such thing as the art of life, it seems to me that such a moment was one of its masterpieces. Not too many poets has it been given to remember their own poetry at such a moment, still less to live one of their own poems. Even William Blake would have been disconcerted if, while he was re-reading the noble lines, "Tiger, tiger, burning bright," a large live Bengal tiger had put his head in at the window of the cottage in Felpham, evidently with every intention of biting his head off. He might have wavered before politely saluting it, above all by calmly completing the recitation of the poem to the quadruped to whom it was dedicated. Shelley, who wished to be a cloud or a leaf carried before the wind, have been mildly surprised to find himself turning slowly head over heels in midair a thousand feet above the sea. Even Keats, knowing that his hold on life was a frail one, might have been disturbed to discover that the true, the blushful Hippocrene of which he had just partaken freely had indeed contained a drug, which really ensured that he should cease upon the midnight with no pain. For Francis there was no drug; and for Francis there was plenty of pain. But his first thought was one of his first fancies from the songs of his youth. He remembered the time when a flame was a flower, only the most glorious and gaily coloured of the flowers in the garden of God; and when that shining thing returned to him in the shape of an instrument of torture, he hailed it from afar like an old friend, calling it by the nickname which might most truly be called its Christian name.

That is only one incident out of a life of such incidents; and I have selected it partly because it shows what is meant here by that shadow of gesture there is in all his words, the dramatic gesture of the south; and partly because its special reference to courtesy covers the next fact to be noted. The popular instinct of St. Francis, and his perpetual preoccupation with the idea of brotherhood, will be entirely misunderstood if it is understood in the sense of what is often called camaraderie; the backslapping sort of brotherhood. Frequently from the enemies and too frequently from the friends of the democratic ideal, there has come a notion that this note is necessary to that ideal. It is assumed that equality means all men being equally uncivil, whereas it obviously ought to mean all men being equally civil. Such people have forgotten the very meaning and derivation of the word civility, if they do not see that to be uncivil is to be uncivic. But anyhow that was not the equality which Francis of Assisi encouraged; but an equality of the opposite kind; it was a camaraderie actually founded on courtesy.

Even in that fairy borderland of his mere fancies about flowers and animals and even inanimate things, he retained this permanent posture of a sort of deference. A friend of mine said that somebody was the sort of man who apologises to the cat. St. Francis really would have apologised to the cat. When he was about to preach in a wood full of the chatter of birds, he said, with a gentle gesture, "Little sisters, if you have now had your say, it is time that I also should be heard." And all the birds were silent; as I for one can very easily believe. In deference to my special design of making matters intelligible to average modernity, I have treated separately the subject of the miraculous powers that St. Francis most certainly possessed.

But even apart from any miraculous powers, men of that magnetic sort, with that intense interest in animals, often have an extraordinary power over them. St. Francis's power was always exercised with this elaborate politeness. Much of it was doubtless a sort of symbolic joke, a pious pantomime intended to convey the vital distinction in his divine mission, that he not only loved but reverenced God in all his creatures. In this sense he had the air not only of apologising to the cat or to the birds, but of apologising to a chair for sitting on it or to a table for sitting down at it. Any one who had followed him through life merely to laugh at him, as a sort of lovable lunatic, might easily have had an impression as of a lunatic who bowed to every post or took off his hat to every tree. This was all a part of his instinct for imaginative gesture. He taught the world a large part of its lesson by a sort of divine dumb alphabet. But if there was this ceremonial element even in lighter or lesser matters, its significance became far more serious in the serious work of his life, which was an appeal to humanity, or rather to human beings.

I have said that St. Francis deliberately did not see the wood for the trees. It is even more true that he deliberately did not see the mob for the men. What distinguishes this very genuine democrat from any mere demagogue is that he never either deceived or was deceived by the illusion of mass-suggestion. Whatever his taste in monsters, he never saw before him a many-headed beast. He only saw the image of God multiplied but never monotonous. To him a man was always a man and did not disappear in a dense crowd any more than in a desert. He honoured all men; that is, he not only loved but respected them all. What gave him his extraordinary personal power was this; that from the Pope to the beggar, from the sultan of Syria in his pavilion to the ragged robbers crawling out of the wood, there was never a man who looked into those brown burning eyes without being certain that Francis Bernardone was really interested in him; in his own inner individual life from the cradle to the grave; that he himself was being valued and taken seriously, and not merely added to the spoils of some social policy or the names in some clerical document. Now for this particular moral and religious idea there is no external expression except courtesy. Exhortation does not express it, for it is not mere abstract enthusiasm; beneficence does not express it, for it is not mere pity. It can only be conveyed by a certain grand manner which may be called good manners. We may say if we like that St. Francis, in the bare and barren simplicity of his life, had clung to one rag of luxury; the manners of a court.

But whereas in a court there is one king and a hundred courtiers, in this story there was one courtier, moving among a hundred kings. For he treated the whole mob of men as a mob of kings. And this was really and truly the only attitude that will appeal to that part of man to which he wished to appeal. It cannot be done by giving gold or even bread; for it is a proverb that any reveller may fling largesse in mere scorn. It cannot even be done by giving time and attention; for any number of philanthropists and benevolent bureaucrats do such work with a scorn far more cold and horrible in their hearts. No plans or proposals or efficient rearrangements will give back to a broken man his self-respect and sense of speaking with an equal. One gesture will do it.

With that gesture Francis of Assisi moved among men; and it was soon found to have something in it of magic and to act, in a double sense, like a charm. But it must always be conceived as a completely natural gesture; for indeed it was almost a gesture of apology. He must be imagined as moving thus swiftly through the world with a sort of impetuous politeness; almost like the movement of a man who stumbles on one knee half in haste and half in obeisance. The eager face under the brown hood was that of a man always going somewhere, as if he followed as well as watched the flight of the birds. And this sense of motion is indeed the meaning of the whole revolution that he made; for the work that has now to be described was of the nature of an earthquake or a volcano, an explosion that drove outwards with dynamic energy the forces stored up by ten centuries in the monastic fortress or arsenal and scattered all its riches recklessly to the ends of the earth. In a better sense than the antithesis commonly conveys, it is true to say that what St. Benedict had stored St. Francis scattered; but in the world of spiritual things what had been stored into the barns like grain was scattered over the world as seed. The servants of God who had been a besieged garrison became a marching army; the ways of the world were filled as with thunder with the trampling of their feet and far ahead of that ever swelling host went a man singing; as simply he had sung that morning in the winter woods, where he walked alone.

CHAPTER VII THE THREE ORDERS

There is undoubtedly a sense in which two is company and three is none; there is also another sense in which three is company and four is none as is proved by the procession of historic and fictitious figures moving three deep the famous trios like the Three Musketeers or the Three Soldiers of Kipling. But there is yet another and a different sense in which four is company and three is none; if we use the word company in the vaguer sense of a crowd or a mass. With the fourth man enters the shadow of a mob; the group is no longer one of three individuals only conceived individually. That shadow of the fourth man fell across the little hermitage of the Portiuncula when a man named Egidio apparently a poor workman was invited by St. Francis to enter. He mingled without difficulty with the merchant and the canon who had already become the companions of Francis; but with his coming an invisible line was crossed; for it must have been felt by this time that the growth of that small group had become potentially infinite, or at least that its outline had become permanently indefinite. It may have been in the time of that transition that Francis had another of his dreams full of voices; but now the voices were a clamour of the tongues of all nations, Frenchmen and Italians and English and Spanish and Germans, telling of the glory of God each in his own tongue; a new Pentecost and a happier Babel.

Before describing the first steps he took to regularise the growing group, it is well to have a rough grasp of what he conceived that group to be. He did not call his followers monks; and it is not clear, at this time at least, that he even thought of them as monks. He called them by a name which is generally rendered in English as the Friars Minor; but we shall be much closer to the atmosphere of his own mind if we render it almost literally as The Little Brothers. Presumably he was already resolved, indeed, that they should take the three vows of poverty, chastity and obedience which had always been the mark of a monk. But it would seem that he was not so much afraid of the idea of a monk as of the idea of an abbot. He was afraid that the great spiritual magistracies which had given even to their holiest possessors at least a sort of impersonal and corporate pride, would import an element of pomposity that would spoil his extremely and almost extravagantly simple version of the life of humility. But the supreme difference between his discipline and the discipline of the old monastic system was concerned, of course, with the idea that the monks were to become migratory and almost nomadic instead of stationary. They were to mingle with the world; and to this the more old-fashioned monk would naturally reply by asking how they were to mingle with the world without becoming entangled with the world. It was a much more real question than a loose religiosity is likely to realise; but St. Francis had his answer to it, of his own individual sort; and the interest of the problem is in that highly individual answer.

The good Bishop of Assisi expressed a sort of horror at the hard life which the Little Brothers lived at the Portiuncula, without comforts, without possessions, eating anything they could get and sleeping anyhow on the ground. St. Francis answered him with that curious and almost stunning shrewdness which the unworldly can sometimes wield like a club of stone. He said, "if we had any possessions, we should need weapons and laws to defend them." That sentence is the clue to the whole policy that he pursued. It rested upon a real piece of logic; and about that he was never anything but logical. He was ready to own himself wrong about anything else; but he was quite certain he was right about this particular rule. He was only once seen angry; and that was when there was talk of an exception to the rule.

His argument was this: that the dedicated man might go anywhere among any kind of men, even the worst kind of men, so long as there was nothing by which they could hold him. If he had any ties or needs like ordinary men, he would become like ordinary men. St. Francis was the last man in the world to think any the worse of ordinary men for being ordinary. They had more affection and admiration from him than they are ever likely to have again. But for his own particular purpose of stirring up the world to a new spiritual enthusiasm, he saw with a logical clarity that was quite reverse of fanatical or sentimental, that friars must not become like ordinary men; that the salt must not lose its savour even to turn into human nature's daily food. And the difference between a friar and an ordinary man was really that a friar was freer than an ordinary man. It was necessary that he should be free from the cloister; but it was even more important that he should be free from the world. It is perfectly sound common sense to say that there is a sense in which the ordinary man cannot be free from the world; or rather ought not to be free from the world. The feudal world in particular was one labyrinthine system of dependence; but it was not only the feudal world that went to make up the mediaeval world nor the mediaeval world that went to make up the whole world; and the whole world is full of this fact. Family life as much as feudal life is in its nature a system of dependence. Modern trade unions as much as mediaeval guilds are interdependent among themselves even in order to be independent of others. In mediaeval as in modern life, even where these limitations do exist for the sake of liberty, they have in them a considerable element of luck. They are partly the result of circumstances; sometimes the almost unavoidable result of circumstances. So the twelfth century had been the age of vows; and there was something of relative freedom in that feudal gesture of the vow; for no man asks vows from slaves any more than from spades. Still, in practice, a man rode to war in support of the ancient house of the Column or behind the Great Dog of the Stairway largely because had been born in a certain city or countryside. But no man need obey little Francis in the old brown coat unless he chose. Even in his relations with his chosen leader he was in one sense relatively free, compared with the world around him. He was obedient but not dependent. And he was as free as the wind, he was almost wildly free, in his relation to that world around him. The world around him was, as has been noted, a network of feudal and family and other forms of dependence. The whole idea of St. Francis was that the Little Brothers should be like little fishes who could go freely in and out of that net. They could do so precisely because they were small fishes and in that sense even slippery fishes. There was nothing that the world could hold them by; for the world catches us mostly by the fringes of our garments, the futile externals of our lives. One of the Franciscans says later, "A monk should own nothing but his harp"; meaning, I suppose, that he should value nothing but his song, the song with which it was his business as a minstrel to serenade every castle and cottage, the song of the joy of the Creator in his creation and the beauty of the brotherhood of men. In imagining the life of this sort of visionary vagabond, we May already get a glimpse also of the practical side of that asceticism which puzzles those who think themselves practical. A man had to be thin to pass always through the bars and out of the cage; he had to travel light in order to ride so fast and so far. It was the whole calculation, so to speak, of that innocent cunning, that the world was to be outflanked and outwitted by him, and be embarrassed about what to do with him. You could not threaten to starve a man who was ever striving to fast. You could not ruin him and reduce him to beggary, for he was already a beggar. There was a very lukewarm satisfaction even in beating him with a stick, when he only indulged in little leaps and cries of joy because indignity was his only dignity. You could not put his head in a halter without the risk of putting it in a halo.

But one distinction between the old Monks and the new friars counted especially in the matter of practicality and especially of promptitude. The old fraternities with their fixed habitations and enclosed existence had the limitations of ordinary householders. However simply they lived there must be a certain number of cells or a certain number of beds or at least a certain cubic space for a certain number of brothers; their numbers therefore depended on their land and building material. But since a man could become a Franciscan by merely promising to take his chance of eating berries in a lane or begging a crust from a kitchen, of sleeping under a hedge or sitting patiently on a doorstep, there was no economic reason why there should not be any number of such eccentric enthusiasts within any short period of time. It must also be remembered that the whole of this rapid development was full of a certain kind of democratic optimism that really was part of the personal character of St. Francis. His very asceticism was in one sense the height of optimism. He demanded a great deal of human nature not because he despised it but rather because he trusted it. He was expecting a very great deal from the extraordinary men who followed him; but he was also expecting a good deal from the ordinary men to whom he sent them. He asked the laity for food as confidently as he asked the fraternity for fasting. But he counted on the hospitality of humanity because he really did regard every house as the house of a friend. He really did love and honour ordinary men and ordinary things; indeed we may say that he only sent out the extraordinary men to encourage men to be ordinary.

This paradox may be more exactly stated or explained when we come to deal with the very interesting matter of the Third Order, which was designed to assist ordinary men to be ordinary with an extraordinary exultation. The point at issue at present is the audacity and simplicity of the Franciscan plan for quartering its spiritual soldiery upon the population; not by force but by persuasion, and even by the persuasion of impotence. It was an act of confidence and therefore a compliment. It was completely successful. It was an example of something that clung about St. Francis always; a kind of tact that looked like luck because it was as simple and direct as a thunderbolt. There are many examples in his private relations of this sort of tactless tact; this surprise effected by striking at the heart of the matter. It is said that a young friar was suffering from a sort of sulks between morbidity and humility, common enough in youth and hero-worship, in which he had got it into his head that his hero hated or despised him. We can imagine how tactfully social diplomatists would steer clear of scenes and excitements, how cautiously psychologists would watch and handle such delicate cases. Francis suddenly walked up to the young man, who was of course secretive and silent as the grave, and said, "Be not troubled in your thoughts for you are dear to me, and even among the number of those who are most dear. You know that you are worthy of my friendship and society; therefore come to me, in confidence, whensoever you will, and from friendship learn faith." Exactly as he spoke to that morbid boy he spoke to all mankind. He always went to the point; he always seemed at once more right and more simple than the person he was speaking to. He seemed at once to be laying open his guard and yet lunging at the heart. Something in this attitude disarmed the world as it has never been disarmed again. He was better than other men; he was a benefactor of other men; and yet he was not hated. The world came into church by a newer and nearer door; and by friendship it learnt faith.

It was while the little knot of people at the Portiuncula was still small enough to gather in a small room that St. Francis resolved on his first important and even sensational stroke. It is said that there were only twelve Franciscans in the whole world when he decided to march, as it were, on Rome and found a Franciscan order. It would seem that this appeal to remote headquarters was not generally regarded as necessary; possibly something could have been done in a secondary way under the Bishop of Assisi and the local clergy. It would seem even more probable that people thought it somewhat unnecessary to trouble the supreme tribunal of Christendom about what a dozen chance men chose to call themselves. But Francis was obstinate and as it were blind on this point; and his brilliant blindness is exceedingly characteristic of him. A man satisfied with small things, or even in love with small things, he yet never felt quite as we do about the disproportion between small things and large. He never saw things to scale in our sense, but with a dizzy disproportion which makes the mind reel. Sometimes it seems merely out of drawing like a gaily coloured medieval map; and then again it seems to have escaped from everything like a short cut in the fourth dimension. He is said to have made a journey to interview the Emperor, throned among his armies under the eagle of the Holy Roman Empire, to intercede for the lives of certain little birds. He was quite capable of facing fifty emperors to intercede for one bird. He started out with two companions to convert the Mahometan world. He started out with eleven companions to ask the Pope to make a new monastic world.

Innocent III, the great Pope, according to Bonaventura, was walking on the terrace of St. John Lateran, doubtless revolving the great political questions which troubled his reign, when there appeared abruptly before him a person in peasant costume whom he took to be some sort of shepherd. He appears to have got rid of the shepherd with all convenient speed; possibly he formed the opinion that the shepherd was mad. Anyhow he thought no more about it until, says the great Franciscan biographer, he dreamed that night a strange dream. He fancied that he saw the whole huge ancient temple of St. John Lateran, on whose high terraces he had walked so securely, leaning horribly and crooked against the sky as if all its domes and turrets were stooping before an earthquake Then he looked again and saw that a human figure was holding it up like a living caryatid; and the figure was that of the ragged shepherd or peasant from whom he had turned away on the terrace. Whether this be a fact or a figure it is a very true figure of the abrupt simplicity with which Francis won the attention and the favour of Rome. His first friend seems to have been the Cardinal Giovanni di San Paolo who pleaded for the Franciscan idea before a conclave of Cardinals summoned for the purpose. It is interesting to note that the doubts thrown upon it seem to have been chiefly doubts about whether the rule was not too hard for humanity, for the Catholic Church is always on the watch against excessive asceticism and its evils. Probably they meant, especially when they said it was unduly hard, that it was unduly dangerous. For a certain element that can only be called danger is what marks the innovation as compared with older institutions of the kind. In one sense indeed the friar was almost the opposite of the monk. The value of the old monasticism had been that there was not only an ethical but an economic repose. Out of that repose had come the works for which the world will never be sufficiently grateful, the preservation of the classics, the beginning of the Gothic, the schemes of science and philosophies, the illuminated manuscripts and the coloured glass. The whole point of a monk was that his economic affairs were settled for good; he knew where he would get his supper, though it was a very plain supper. But the whole point of a friar was that he did not know where he would get his supper. There was always a possibility that he might get no supper. There was an element of what would be called romance, as of the gipsy or adventurer. But there was also an element of potential tragedy, as of the tramp or the casual labourer. So the Cardinals of the thirteenth century were filled with compassion, seeing a few men entering of their own free will that estate to which the poor of the twentieth century are daily driven by cold coercion and moved on by the police.

Cardinal San Paolo seems to have argued more or less in this manner: it may be a hard life, but after all it is the life apparently described as ideal in the Gospel; make what compromises you think wise or humane about that ideal; but do not commit yourselves to saying that men shall not fulfil that ideal if they can. We shall see the importance of this argument when we come to the whole of that higher aspect of the life of St. Francis which may be called the imitation of Christ. The upshot of the discussion was that the Pope gave his verbal approval to the project and promised a more definite endorsement, if the movement should grow to more considerable proportions. It is probable that Innocent, who was himself a man of no ordinary mentality, had very little doubt that it would do so; anyhow he was not left long in doubt before it did do so. The next passage in the history of the order is simply the story of more and more people flocking to its standard; and as has already been remarked, once it had begun to grow, it could in its nature grow much more quickly than any ordinary society requiring ordinary funds and public buildings. Even the return of the twelve pioneers from their papal audience seems to have been a sort of triumphal procession. In one place in particular, it is said, the whole population of a town, men, women and children, turned out, leaving their work and wealth and homes exactly as they stood and begging to be taken into the army of God on the spot. According to the story, it was on this occasion that St. Francis first foreshadowed his idea of the Third Order which enabled men to share in the movement without leaving the homes and habits of normal humanity. For the moment it is most important to regard this story as one example of the riot of conversion with which he was already filling all the roads of Italy. It was a world of wandering; friars perpetually coming and going in all the highways and byways, seeking to ensure that any man who met one of them by chance should have a spiritual adventure. The first Order of St. Francis had entered history.

This rough outline can only be rounded off here with some description of the Second and Third Orders, though they were founded later and at separate times. The former was an order for women and owed its existence, of course, to the beautiful friendship of St. Francis and St. Clare. There is no story about which even the most sympathetic critics of another creed have been more bewildered and misleading. For there is no story that more clearly turns on that simple test which I have taken as crucial throughout this criticism. I mean that what is the matter with these critics is that they will not believe that a heavenly love can be as real as an earthly love. The moment it is treated as real, like an earthly love, their whole riddle is easily resolved. A girl of seventeen, named Clare and belonging to one of the noble families of Assisi, was filled with an enthusiasm for the conventual life; and Francis helped her to escape from her home and to take up the conventual life. If we like to put it so, he helped her to elope into the cloister, defying her parents as he had defied his father. Indeed the scene had many of the elements of a regular romantic elopement; for she escaped through a hole in the wall, fled through a wood and was received at midnight by the light of torches. Even Mrs. Oliphant, in her fine and delicate study of St. Francis, calls it "an incident which we can hardly record with satisfaction."

Now about that incident I will here only say this. If it had really been a romantic elopement and the girl had become a bride instead of a nun, practically the whole modern world would have made her a heroine. If the action of the Friar towards Clare had been the action of the Friar towards Juliet, everybody would be sympathising with her exactly as they sympathise with Juliet. It is not conclusive to say that Clare was only seventeen. Juliet was only fourteen. Girls married and boys fought in battles at such early ages in mediaeval times; and a girl of seventeen in the thirteenth century was certainly old enough to know her own mind. There cannot be the shadow of a doubt, for any sane person considering subsequent events, that St. Clare did know her own mind. But the point for the moment is that modern romanticism entirely encourages such defiance of parents when it is done in the name of romantic love. For it knows that romantic love is a reality, but it does not know that divine love is a reality. There may have been something to be said for the parents of Clare; there may have been something to be said for Peter Bernardone. So there may have been a great deal to be said for the Montagues or the Capulets; but the modern world does not want it said; and does not say it. The fact is that as soon as we assume for a moment as a hypothesis, what St. Francis and St. Clare assumed all the time as an absolute, that there is a direct divine relation more glorious than any romance, the story of St. Clare's elopement is simply a romance with a happy ending; and St. Francis is the St. George or knight-errant who gave it a happy ending. And seeing that some millions of men and women have lived and died treating this relation as a reality, a man is not much of a philosopher if he cannot even treat it as a hypothesis.

For the rest, we may at least assume that no friend of what is called the emancipation of women will regret the revolt of St. Clare. She did most truly, in the modern jargon, live her own life, the life that she herself wanted to lead, as distinct from the life into which parental commands and conventional arrangements would have forced her. She became the foundress of a great feminine movement which still profoundly affects the world; and her place is with the powerful women of history. It is not clear that she would have been so great or so useful if she had made a runaway match, or even stopped at home and made a mariage de convenance. So much any sensible man may well say considering the matter merely from the outside; and I have no intention of attempting to consider it from the inside. If a man may well doubt whether he is worthy to write a word about St. Francis, he will certainly want words better than his own to speak of the friendship of St. Francis and St. Clare. I have often remarked that the mysteries of this story are best expressed symbolically in certain silent attitudes and actions. And I know no better symbol than that found by the felicity of popular legend, which says that one night the people of Assisi thought the trees and the holy house were on fire, and rushed up to extinguish the conflagration. But they found all quiet within, where St. Francis broke bread with St. Clare at one of their rare meetings, and talked of the love of God. It would be hard to find a more imaginative image, for some sort of utterly pure and disembodied passion, than that red halo round the unconscious figures on the hill; a flame feeding on nothing and setting the very air on fire.

But if the Second Order was the memorial of such an unearthly love, the Third Order was as solid a memorial of a very solid sympathy with earthly loves and earthly lives. The whole of this feature in Catholic life, the lay orders in touch with clerical orders, is very little understood in Protestant countries and very little allowed for in Protestant history. The vision which has been so faintly suggested in these pages has never been confined to monks or even to friars. It has been an inspiration to innumerable crowds of ordinary married men and women; living lives like our own, only entirely different. That morning glory which St. Francis spread over the earth and sky has lingered as a secret sunshine under a multitude of roofs and in a multitude of rooms. In societies like ours nothing is known of such a Franciscan following. Nothing is known of such obscure followers; and if possible less is known of the well-known followers. If we imagine passing us in the street a pageant of the Third Order of St. Francis, the famous figures would surprise us more than the strange ones. For us it would be like the unmasking of some mighty secret society. There rides St. Louis, the great king, lord of the higher justice whose scales hang crooked in favour of the poor. There is Dante crowned with laurel, the poet who in his life of passions sang the praises of the Lady Poverty, whose grey garment is lined with purple and all glorious within. All sorts of great names from the most recent and rationalistic centuries would stand revealed; the great Galvani, for instance, the father of all electricity, the magician who has made so many modern systems of stars and sounds. So various a following would alone be enough to prove that St. Francis had no lack of sympathy with normal men, if the whole of his own life did not prove it.

But in fact his life did prove it, and that possibly in a more subtle sense. There is, I fancy, some truth in the hint of one of his modern biographers, that even his natural passions were singularly normal and even noble, in the sense of turning towards things not unlawful in themselves but only unlawful for him. Nobody ever lived of whom we could less fitly use the word "regret" than Francis of Assisi. Though there was much that was romantic, there was nothing in the least sentimental about his mood. It was not melancholy enough for that. He was of far too swift and rushing a temper to be troubled with doubts and reconsiderations about the race he ran; though he had any amount of self-reproach about not running faster. But it is true, one suspects, that when he wrestled with the devil, as every man must to be worth calling a man, the whispers referred mostly to those healthy instincts that he would have approved for others; they bore no resemblance to that ghastly painted paganism which sent its demoniac courtesans to plague St. Anthony in the desert. If St. Francis had only pleased himself, it would have been with simpler pleasures. He was moved to love rather than lust, and by nothing wilder than wedding bells. It is suggested in that strange story of how he defied the devil by making images in the snow, and crying out that these sufficed him for a wife and family. It is suggested in the saying he used when disclaiming any security from sin, "I may yet have children"; almost as if it was of the children rather than the woman that he dreamed. And this, if it be true, gives a final touch to the truth about his character. There was so much about him of the spirit of the morning, so much that was curiously young and clean, that even what was bad in him was good. As it was said of others that the light in their body was darkness, so it may be said of this luminous spirit that the very shadows in his soul were of light. Evil itself could not come to him save in the form of a forbidden good; and he could only be tempted by a sacrament.

CHAPTER VIII THE MIRROR OF CHRIST

No man who has been given the freedom of the Faith is likely to fall into those hole-and corner extravagances in which later degenerate Franciscans, or rather Fraticelli, sought to concentrate entirely on St. Francis as a second Christ, the creator of a new gospel. In fact any such notion makes nonsense of every motive in the man's life; for no man would reverently magnify what he was meant to rival, or only profess to follow what he existed to supplant. On the contrary, as will appear later, this little study would rather specially insist that it was really the papal sagacity that saved the great Franciscan movement for the whole world and the universal Church, and prevented it from petering out as that sort of stale and second rate sect that is called a new religion. Everything that is written here must be understood not only as distinct from but diametrically opposed to the idolatry of the Fraticelli. The difference between Christ and St. Francis was the difference between the Creator and the creature; and certainly no creature was ever so conscious of that colossal contrast as St. Francis himself. But subject to this understanding, it is perfectly true and it is vitally important that Christ was the pattern on which St. Francis sought to fashion himself; and that at many points their human and historical lives were even curiously coincident; and above all, that compared to most of us at least St. Francis is a most sublime approximation to his Master, and, even in being an intermediary and a reflection, is a splendid and yet a merciful Mirror of Christ. And this truth suggests another, which I think has hardly been noticed; but which happens to be a highly forcible argument for the authority of Christ being continuous in the Catholic Church.

Cardinal Newman wrote in his liveliest controversial work a sentence that might be a model of what we mean by saying that his creed tends to lucidity and logical courage. In speaking of the ease with which truth may be made to look like its own shadow or sham, he said, "And if Antichrist is like Christ, Christ I suppose is like Antichrist." Mere religious sentiment might well be shocked at the end of the sentence; but nobody could object to it except the logician who said that Ceasar and Pompey were very much alike, especially Pompey. It may give a much milder shock if I say here, what most of us have forgotten, that if St. Francis was like Christ, Christ was to that extent like St. Francis. And my present point is that it is really very enlightening to realise that Christ was like St. Francis. What I mean is this; that if men find certain riddles and hard sayings in the story of Galilee, and if they find the answers to those riddles in the story of Assisi, it really does show that a secret has been handed down in one religious tradition and no other. It shows that the casket that was locked in Palestine can be unlocked in Umbria; for the Church is the keeper of the keys.

Now in truth while it has always seemed natural to explain St. Francis in the light of Christ, it has not occurred to many people to explain Christ in the light of St. Francis. Perhaps the word "light" is not here the proper metaphor; but the same truth is admitted in the accepted metaphor of the mirror. St. Francis is the mirror of Christ rather as the moon is the mirror of the sun. The moon is much smaller than the sun, but it is also much nearer to us; and being less vivid it is more visible. Exactly in the same sense St. Francis is nearer to us, and being a mere man like ourselves is in that sense more imaginable. Being necessarily less of a mystery, he does not, for us, so much open his mouth in mysteries. Yet as a matter of fact, many minor things that seem mysteries in the mouth of Christ would seem merely characteristic paradoxes in the mouth of St. Francis. It seems natural to reread the more remote incidents with the help of the more recent ones. It is a truism to say that Christ lived before Christianity; and it follows that as a historical figure. He is a figure in heathen history. I mean that the medium in which He moved was not the medium of Christendom but of the old pagan empire; and from that alone, not to mention the distance of time, it follows that His circumstances are more alien to us than those of an Italian monk such as we might meet even to-day. I suppose the most authoritative commentary can hardly be certain of the current or conventional weight of all His words or phrases; of which of them would then have seemed a common allusion and which a strange fancy. This archaic setting has left many of the sayings standing like hieroglyphics and subject to many and peculiar individual interpretations. Yet it is true of almost any of them that if we simply translate them into the Umbrian dialect of the first Franciscans, they would seem like any other part of the Franciscans story; doubtless in one sense fantastic, but quite familiar. All sorts of critical controversies have revolved round the passage which bids men consider the lilies of the field and copy them in taking no thought for the morrow. The sceptic has alternated between telling us to be true Christians and do it, and explaining that it is impossible to do. When he is a communist as well as an atheist, he is generally doubtful whether to blame us for preaching what is impracticable or for not instantly putting it into practice. I am not going to discuss here the point of ethics and economics; I merely remark that even those who are puzzled at the saying of Christ would hardly pause in accepting it as a saying of St. Francis. Nobody would be surprised to find that he had said, "I beseech you, little brothers, that you be as wise as Brother Daisy and Brother Dandelion; for never do they lie awake thinking of to-morrow, yet they have gold crowns like kings and emperors or like Charlemagne in all his glory." Even more bitterness and bewilderment has arisen about the command to turn the other cheek and to give the coat to the robber who has taken the cloak. It is widely held to imply the wickedness of war among nations about which, in itself, not a word seems to have been said. Taken thus literally and universally, it much more clearly implies the wickedness of all law and government. Yet there are many prosperous peacemakers who are much more shocked at the idea of using the brute force of soldiers against a powerful foreigner than they are at using the brute force of policemen against a poor fellow-citizen. Here again I am content to point out that the paradox becomes perfectly human and probable if addressed by Francis to Franciscans. Nobody would be surprised to read that Brother Juniper did then run after the thief that had stolen his hood, beseeching him to take his gown also; for so St. Francis had commanded him. Nobody would be surprised if St. Francis told a young noble, about to be admitted to his company, that so far from pursuing a brigand to recover his shoes, he ought to pursue him to make him a present of his stockings. We may like or not the atmosphere these things imply; but we know what atmosphere they do imply. We recognise a certain note as natural and clear as the note of a bird; the note of St. Francis. There is in it something of gentle mockery of the very idea of possessions; something of a hope of disarming the enemy by generosity; something of a humorous sense of bewildering the worldly with the unexpected; something of the joy of carrying an enthusiastic conviction to a logical extreme. But anyhow we have no difficulty in recognising it if we have read any of the literature of the Little Brothers and the movement that began in Assisi. It seems reasonable to infer that if it was this spirit that made such strange things possible in Umbria, it was the same spirit that made them possible in Palestine. If we hear the same unmistakable note and sense the same indescribable savour in two things at such a distance from each other, it seems natural to suppose that the case that is more remote from our experience was like the case that is closer to our experience. As the thing is explicable on the assumption that Francis was speaking to Franciscans, it is not an irrational explanation to suggest that Christ also was speaking to some dedicated band that had much the same function as Franciscans. In other words, it seems only natural to hold, as the Catholic Church has held, that these counsels of perfection were part of a particular vocation to astonish and awaken the world. But in any case it is important to note that when we do find these particular features, with their seemingly fantastic fitness, reappearing after more than a thousand years, we find them produced by the same religious system which claims continuity and authority from the scenes in which they first appeared. Any number of philosophies will repeat the platitudes of Christianity. But it is the ancient Church that can again startle the world with the paradoxes of Christianity. Ubi Petrus ibi Franciscus.

But if we understand that it was truly under the inspiration of his divine Master that St. Francis did these merely quaint or eccentric acts of charity, we must understand that it was under the same inspiration that he did acts of self-denial and austerity. It is clear that these more or less playful parables of the love of men were conceived after a close study of the Sermon on the Mount. But it is evident that he made an even closer study of the silent sermon on that other mountain; the mountain that was called Golgotha. Here again he was speaking the strict historical truth, when he said that in fasting or suffering humiliation he was but trying to do something of what Christ did; and here again it seems probable that as the same truth appears at the two ends of a chain of tradition, the tradition has preserved the truth. But the import of this fact at the moment affects the next phase in the personal history of the man himself.

For as it becomes clearer that his great communal scheme is an accomplished fact and past the peril of an early collapse, as it becomes evident that there already is such a thing as an Order of the Friars Minor, this more individual and intense ambition of St. Francis emerges more and more. So soon as he certainly has followers, he does not compare himself with his followers, towards whom he might appear as a master; he compares himself more and more with his Master, towards whom he appears only as a servant. This, it may be said in passing, is one of the moral and even practical conveniences of the ascetical privilege. Every other sort of superiority may be superciliousness. But the saint is never supercilious, for he is always by hypothesis in the presence of a superior. The objection to an aristocracy is that it is a priesthood without a god. But in any case the service to which St. Francis had committed himself was one which, about this time, he conceived more and more in terms of sacrifice and crucifixion. He was full of the sentiment that he had not suffered enough to be worthy even to be a distant follower of his suffering God. And this passage in his history may really be roughly summarized as the Search for Martyrdom.

This was the ultimate idea in the remarkable business of his expedition among the Saracens in Syria. There were indeed other elements in his conception, which are worthy of more intelligent understanding than they have often received. His idea, of course, was to bring the Crusades in a double sense to their end; that is, to reach their conclusion and to achieve their purpose. Only he wished to do it by conversion and not by conquest; that is, by intellectual and not material means. The modern mind is hard to please; and it generally calls the way of Godfrey ferocious and the way of Francis fanatical. That is, it calls any moral method unpractical, when it has just called any practical method immoral. But the idea of St. Francis was far from being a fanatical or necessarily even an unpractical idea; though perhaps he saw the problem as rather too simple, lacking the learning of his great inheritor, Raymond Lully, who understood more but has been quite as little understood. The way he approached the matter was indeed highly personal and peculiar; but that was true of almost everything he did. It was in one way a simple idea, as most of his ideas were simple ideas. But it was not a silly idea; there was a great deal to be said for it and it might have succeeded. It was, of course, simply the idea that it is better to create Christians than to destroy Moslems. If Islam had been converted, the world would have been immeasurably more united and happy; for one thing, three quarters of the wars of modern history would never have taken place. It was not absurd to suppose that this might be effected, without military force, by missionaries who were also martyrs. The Church had conquered Europe in that way and may yet conquer Asia or Africa in that way. But when all this is allowed for, there is still another sense in which St. Francis was not thinking of Martyrdom as a means to an end, but almost as an end in itself; in the sense that to him the supreme end was to come closer to the example of Christ. Through all his plunging and, restless days ran the refrain: I have not suffered enough; I have not sacrificed enough; I am not yet worthy even of the shadow of the crown of thorns. He wandered about the valleys of the world looking for the hill that has the outline of a skull.

A little while before his final departure for the East a vast and triumphant assembly of the whole order had been held near the Portiuncula; and called the Assembly of the Straw Huts, from the manner in which that mighty army encamped in the field. Tradition says that it was on this occasion that St. Francis met St. Dominic for the first and last time. It also says, what is probable enough, that the practical spirit of the Spaniard was almost appalled at the devout irresponsibility of the Italian, who had assembled such a crowd without organising a commissariat. Dominic the Spaniard was, like nearly every Spaniard, a man with the mind of a soldier. His charity took the practical form of provision and preparation. But, apart from the disputes about faith which such incidents open, he probably did not understand in this case the power of mere popularity produced by mere personality. In all his leaps in the dark, Francis had an extraordinary faculty of falling on his feet. The whole countryside came down like a landslide to provide food and drink for this sort of pious picnic. Peasants brought waggons of wine and game; great nobles walked about doing the work of footmen. It was a very real victory for the Franciscan spirit of a reckless faith not only in God but in man. Of course there is much doubt and dispute about the whole story and the whole relation of Francis and Dominic; and the story of the Assembly of the Straw Huts is told from the Franciscan side. But the alleged meeting is worth mentioning, precisely because it was immediately before St. Francis set forth on his bloodless crusade that he is said to have met St. Dominic, who has been so much criticised for lending himself to a more bloody one. There is no space in this little book to explain how St. Francis, as much as St. Dominic, would ultimately have defended the defence of Christian unity by arms. Indeed it would need a large book instead of a little book to develop that point alone from its first principles. For the modern mind is merely a blank about the philosophy of toleration; and the average agnostic of recent times has really had no notion of what he meant by religious liberty and equality. He took his own ethics as self-evident and enforced them; such as decency or the error of the Adamite heresy. Then he was horribly shocked if he heard of anybody else, Moslem or Christian, taking his ethics as self-evident and enforcing them; such as reverence or the error of the Athiest heresy. And then he wound up by taking all this lop-sided illogical deadlock, of the unconscious meeting the unfamiliar, and called it the liberality of his own mind. Medieval men thought that if a social system was founded on a certain idea it must fight for that idea, whether it was as simple as Islam or as carefully balanced as Catholicism. Modern men really think the same thing, as is clear when communists attack their ideas of property. Only they do not think it so clearly, because they have not really thought out their idea of property. But while it is probable that St. Francis would have reluctantly agreed with St. Dominic that war for the truth was right in the last resort, it is certain that St. Dominic did enthusiastically agree with St. Francis that it was far better to prevail by persuasion and enlightenment if it were possible. St. Dominic devoted himself much more to persuading than to persecuting; but there was a difference in the methods simply because there was a difference in the men. About everything St. Francis did there was something that was in a good sense childish, and even in a good sense wilful.

He threw himself into things abruptly, as if they had just occurred to him. He made a dash for his Mediterranean enterprise with something of the air of a schoolboy running away to sea.

In the first act of that attempt he characteristically distinguished himself by becoming the Patron Saint of Stowaways. He never thought of waiting for introductions or bargains or any of the considerable backing that he already had from rich and responsible people. He simply saw a boat and threw himself into it, as he threw himself into everything else. It has all that air of running a race which makes his whole life read like an escapade or even literally an escape. He lay like lumber among the cargo, with one companion whom he had swept with him in his rush; but the voyage was apparently unfortunate and erratic and ended in an enforced return to Italy. Apparently it was after this first false start that the great reunion took place at the Portiuncula, and between this and the final Syrian journey there was also an attempt to meet the Moslem menace by preaching to the Moors in Spain. In Spain indeed several of the first Franciscans had already succeeded gloriously in being martyred. But the great Francis still went about stretching out his arms for such torments and desiring that agony in vain. No one would have said more readily than he that he was probably less like Christ than those others who had already found their Calvary; but the thing remained with him like a secret; the strangest of the sorrows of man.

His later voyage was more successful, so far as arriving at the scene of operations was concerned. He arrived at the headquarters of the Crusade which was in front of the besieged city of Damietta, and went on in his rapid and solitary fashion to seek the headquarters of the Saracens. He succeeded in obtaining an interview with the Sultan; and it was at that interview that he evidently offered, and as some say proceeded, to fling himself into the fire as a divine ordeal, defying the Moslem religious teachers to do the same. It is quite certain that he would have done so at a moment's notice. Indeed throwing himself into the fire was hardly more desperate, in any case, than throwing himself among the weapons and tools of torture of a horde of fanatical Mahometans and asking them to renounce Mahomet. It is said further that the Mahometan muftis showed some coldness towards the proposed competition, and that one of them quietly withdrew while it was under discussion; which would also appear credible. But for whatever reason Francis evidently returned as freely as he came. There may be something in the story of the individual impression produced on the Sultan, which the narrator represents as a sort of secret conversion. There may be something in the suggestion that the holy man was unconsciously protected among half-barbarous Orientals by the halo of sanctity that is supposed in such places to surround an idiot. There is probably as much or more in the more generous explanation of that graceful though capricious courtesy and compassion which mingled with wilder things in the stately Soldans of the type and tradition of Saladin. Finally, there is perhaps something in the suggestion that the tale of St. Francis might be told as a sort of ironic tragedy and comedy called The Man Who Could Not Get Killed. Men liked him too much for himself to let him die for his faith; and the man was received instead of the message. But all these are only converging guesses at a great effort that is hard to judge, because it broke off short like the beginnings of a great bridge that might have united East and West, and remains one of the great might-have-beens of history.

Meanwhile the great movement in Italy was making giant strides. Backed now by papal authority as well as popular enthusiasm, and creating a kind of comradeship among all classes, it had started a riot of reconstruction on all sides of religious and social life; and especially began to express itself in that enthusiasm for building which is the mark of all the resurrections of Western Europe. There had notably been established at Bologna a magnificent mission house of the Friars Minor; and a vast body of them and their sympathisers surrounded it with a chorus of acclamation. Their unanimity had a strange interruption. One man alone in that crowd was seen to turn and suddenly denounce the building as if it had been a Babylonian temple; demanding indignantly since when the Lady Poverty had thus been insulted with the luxury of palaces. It was Francis, a wild figure, returned from his Eastern Crusade; and it was the first and last time that he spoke in wrath to his children.

A word must be said later about this serious division of sentiment and policy, about which many Franciscans, and to some extent Francis himself, parted company with the more moderate policy which ultimately prevailed. At this point we need only note it as another shadow fallen upon his spirit after his disappointment in the desert; and as in some sense the prelude to the next phase of his career, which is the most isolated and the most mysterious. It is true that everything about this episode seems to be covered with some cloud of dispute, even including its date; some writers putting it much earlier in the narrative than this. But whether or no it was chronologically it was certainly logically the culmination of the story, and may best be indicated here. I say indicated for it must be a matter of little more than indication; the thing being a mystery both in the higher moral and the more trivial historical sense. Anyhow the conditions of the affair seem to have been these. Francis and a young companion, in the course of their common wandering, came past a great castle all lighted up with the festivities attending a son of the house receiving the honour of knighthood. This aristocratic mansion, which took its name from Monte Feltro, they entered in their beautiful and casual fashion and began to give their own sort of good news. There were some at least who listened to the saint "as if he had been an angel of God"; among them a gentleman named Orlando of Chiusi, who had great lands in Tuscany and who proceeded to do St. Francis a singular and somewhat picturesque act of courtesy. He gave him a mountain; a thing somewhat unique among the gifts of the world. Presumably the Franciscan rule which forbade a man to accept money had made no detailed provision about accepting mountains. Nor indeed did St. Francis accept it save as he accepted everything, as a temporary convenience rather than a personal possession; but he turned it into a sort of refuge for the eremitical rather than the monastic life; he retired there when he wished for a life of prayer and fasting which he did not ask even his closest friends to follow. This was Alverno of the Apennines, and upon its peak there rests for ever a dark cloud that has a rim or halo of glory.

What it was exactly that happened there may never be known. The matter has been, I believe, a subject of dispute among the most devout students of the saintly life as well as between such students and others of the more secular sort. It may be that St. Francis never spoke to a soul on the subject; it would be highly characteristic, and it is certain in any case that he said very little; I think he is only alleged to have spoken of it to one man. Subject however to such truly sacred doubts, I will confess that to me personally this one solitary and indirect report that has come down to us reads very like the report of something real; of some of those things that are more real than what we call daily realities. Even something as it were double and bewildering about the image seems to carry the impression of an experience shaking the senses; as does the passage in Revelation about the supernatural creatures full of eyes. It would seem that St. Francis beheld the heavens above him occupied by a vast winged being like a seraph spread out like a cross. There seems some mystery about whether the winged figure was itself crucified or in the posture of crucifixion, or whether it merely enclosed in its frame of wings some colossal crucifix. But it seems clear that there was some question of the former impression; for St. Bonaventura distinctly says that St. Francis doubted how a seraph could be crucified, since those awful and ancient principalities were without the infirmity of the Passion. St. Bonaventura suggests that the seeming contradiction may have meant that St. Francis was to be crucified as a spirit since he could not be crucified as a man; but whatever the meaning of the vision, the general idea of it is very vivid and overwhelming. St. Francis saw above him, filling the whole heavens, some vast immemorial unthinkable power, ancient like the Ancient of Days, whose calm men had conceived under the forms of winged bulls or monstrous cherubim, and all that winged wonder was in pain like a wounded bird. This seraphic suffering, it is said, pierced his soul with a sword of grief and pity; it may be inferred that some sort of mounting agony accompanied the ecstasy. Finally after some fashion the apocalypse faded from the sky and the agony within subsided; and silence and the natural air filled the morning twilight and settled slowly in the purple chasms and cleft abysses of the Apennines. The head of the solitary sank, amid all that relaxation and quiet in which time can drift by with the sense of something ended and complete; and as he stared downwards, he saw the marks of nails in his own hands.

CHAPTER IX MIRACLES AND DEATH

The tremendous story of the Stigmata of St. Francis, which was the end of the last chapter, was in some sense the end of his life. In a logical sense, it would have been the end even if it had happened at the beginning. But truer traditions refer it to a later date and suggest that his remaining days on the earth had something about them of the lingering of a shadow. Whether St. Bonaventura was right in his hint that St. Francis saw in that seraphic vision something almost like a vast mirror of his own soul, that could at least suffer like an angel though not like a god, or whether it expressed under an imagery more primitive and colossal than common Christian art the primary paradox of the death of God, it is evident from its traditional consequences that it was meant for a crown and for a seal. It seems to have been after seeing this vision that he began to go blind.

But the incident has another and much less important place in this rough and limited outline. It is the natural occasion for considering briefly and collectively all the facts or fables of another aspect of the life of St. Francis; an aspect which is, I will not say more disputable, but certainly more disputed. I mean all that mass of testimony and tradition that concerns his miraculous powers and supernatural experiences, with which it would have been easy to stud and bejewel every page of the story; only that certain circumstances necessary to the conditions of this narration make it better to gather, somewhat hastily, all such jewels into a heap.

I have here adopted this course in order to make allowance for a prejudice. It is indeed to a great extent a prejudice of the past; a prejudice that is plainly disappearing in days of greater enlightenment, and especially of a greater range of scientific experiment and knowledge. But it is a prejudice that is still tenacious in many of an older generation and still traditional in many of the younger. I mean, of course, what used to be called the belief "that miracles do not happen," as I think Matthew Arnold expressed it, in expressing the standpoint of so many of our Victorian uncles and great-uncles. In other words it was the remains of that sceptical simplification by which some of the philosophers of the early eighteenth century had popularised the impression (for a very short time) that we had discovered the regulations of the cosmos like the works of a clock, of so very simple a clock that it was possible to distinguish almost at a glance what could or could not have happened in human experience. It should be remembered that these real sceptics, of the golden age of scepticism, were quite as scornful of the first fancies of science as of the lingering legends of religion. Voltaire, when he was told that a fossil fish had been found on the peaks of the Alps, laughed openly at the tale and said that some fasting monk or hermit had dropped his fish-bones there; possibly in order to effect another monkish fraud. Everybody knows by this time that science has had its revenge on scepticism. The border between the credible and the incredible has not only become once more as vague as in any barbaric twilight; but the credible is obviously increasing and the incredible shrinking. A man in Voltaire's time did not know what miracle he would next have to throw up. A man in our time does not know what miracle he will next have to swallow.

But long before these things had happened, in those days of my boyhood when I first saw the figure of St. Francis far away in the distance and drawing me even at that distance, in those Victorian days which did seriously separate the virtues from the miracles of the saints---even in those days I could not help feeling vaguely puzzled about how this method could be applied to history. Even then I did not quite understand, and even now I do not quite understand, on what principle one is to pick and choose in the chronicles of the past which seem to be all of a piece. All our knowledge of certain historical periods, and notably of the whole medieval period, rests on certain connected chronicles written by people who are some of them nameless and all of them dead, who cannot in any case be cross-examined and cannot in some cases be corroborated. I have never been quite clear about the nature of the right by which historians accepted masses of detail from them as definitely true, and suddenly denied their truthfulness when one detail was preternatural. I do not complain of their being sceptics; I am puzzled about why the sceptics are not more sceptical. I can understand their saying that these details would never have been included in a chronicle except by lunatics or liars; but in that case the only inference is that the chronicle was written by liars or lunatics. They will write for instance: "Monkish fanaticism found it easy to spread the report that miracles were already being worked at the tomb of Thomas Becket." Why should they not say equally well, "Monkish fanaticism found it easy to spread the slander that four knights from King Henry's court had assassinated Thomas Becket in the cathedral"? They would write something like this: "The credulity of the age readily believed that Joan of Arc had been inspired to point out the Dauphin although he was in disguise." Why should they not write on the same principle: "The credulity of the age was such as to suppose that an obscure peasant girl could get an audience at the court of the Dauphin"? And so, in the present case, when they tell us there is a wild story that St. Francis flung himself into the fire and emerged scathless, upon what precise principle are they forbidden to tell us of a wild story that St. Francis flung himself into the camp of the ferocious Moslems and returned safe? I only ask for information; for I do not see the rationale of the thing myself. I will undertake to say there was not a word written of St. Francis by any contemporary who was himself incapable of believing and telling a miraculous story. Perhaps it is all monkish fables and there never was any St. Francis or any St. Thomas Becket or any Joan of Arc. This is undoubtedly a reductio ad absurdum; but it is a reductio ad absurdum of the view which thought all miracles absurd.

And in abstract logic this method of selection would lead to the wildest absurdities. An intrinsically incredible story could only mean that the authority was unworthy of credit. It could not mean that other parts of his story must be received with complete credulity. If somebody said he had met a man in yellow trousers, who proceeded to jump down his own throat, we should not exactly take our Bible oath or be burned at the stake for the statement that he wore yellow trousers. If somebody claimed to have gone up in a blue balloon and found that the moon was made of green cheese, we should not exactly take an affidavit that the balloon was blue any more than that the moon was green. And the really logical conclusion from throwing doubts on all tales like the miracles of St. Francis was to throw doubts on the existence of men like St. Francis. And there really was a modern moment, a sort of high-water mark of insane scepticism, when this sort of thing was really said or done. People used to go about saying that there was no such person as St. Patrick; which is every bit as much of a human and historical howler as saying there was no such person as St. Francis. There was a time, for instance, when the madness of mythological explanation had dissolved a large part of solid history under the universal and luxuriant warmth and radiance of the Sun-Myth. I believe that that particular sun has already set, but there have been any number of moons and meteors to take its place.

St. Francis, of course, would make a magnificent Sun-Myth. How could anybody miss the chance of being a Sun-Myth when he is actually best known by a song called The Canticle of the Sun? It is needless to point out that the fire in Syria was the dawn in the East and the bleeding wounds in Tuscany the sunset in the West. I could expound this theory at considerable length; only, as so often happens to such fine theorists, another and more promising theory occurs to me. I cannot think how everybody, including myself, can have overlooked the fact that the whole tale of St. Francis is of Totemistic origin. It is unquestionably a tale that simply swarms with totems. The Franciscan woods are as full of them as any Red Indian fable. Francis is made to call himself an ass, because in the original mythos Francis was merely the name given to the real four-footed donkey, afterwards vaguely evolved into a half-human god or hero. And that, no doubt, is why I used to feel that the Brother Wolf and Sister Bird of St. Francis were somehow like the Brer Fox and Sis Cow of Uncle Remus. Some say there is an innocent stage of infancy in which we do really believe that a cow talked or a fox made a tar baby. Anyhow there is an innocent period of intellectual growth in which we do sometimes really believe that St. Patrick was a Sun-Myth or St. Francis a Totem. But for the most of us both those phases of paradise are past.

As I shall suggest in a moment, there is one sense in which we can for practical purposes distinguish between probable and improbable things in such a story. It is not so much a question of cosmic criticism about the nature of the event as of literary criticism about the nature of the story. Some stories are told much more seriously than others. But apart from this, I shall not attempt here any definite differentiation between them. I shall not do so for a practical reason affecting the utility of the proceeding; I mean the fact that in a practical sense the whole of this matter is again in the melting pot, from which many things may emerge moulded into what rationalism would have called monsters. The fixed points of faith and philosophy do indeed remain always the same. Whether a man believes that fire in one case could fail to burn depends on why he thinks it generally does burn. If it burns nine sticks out of ten because it is its nature or doom to do so, then it will burn the tenth stick as well. If it burns nine sticks because it is the will of God that it should, then it might be the will of God that the tenth should be unburned. Nobody can get behind that fundamental difference about the reason of things; and it is as rational for a theist to believe in miracles as for an atheist to disbelieve in them. In other words there is only one intelligent reason why a man does not believe in miracles and that is that he does believe in materialism. But these fixed points of faith and philosophy are things for a theoretical work and have no particular place here. And in the matter of history and biography, which have their place here, nothing is fixed at all. The world is in a welter of the possible and impossible, and nobody knows what will be the next scientific hypothesis to support some ancient superstition. Three-quarters of the miracles attributed to St. Francis would already be explained by psychologists, not indeed as a Catholic explains them, but as a materialist must necessarily refuse to explain them. There is one whole department of the miracles of St. Francis; the miracles of healing. What is the good of a superior sceptic throwing them away as unthinkable, at the moment when faith-healing is already a big booming Yankee business like Barnum's Show? There is another whole department analogous to the tales of Christ "perceiving men's thoughts." What is the use of censoring them and blacking them out because they are marked "miracles," when thought reading is already a parlour game like musical chairs? There is another whole department, to be studied separately if such scientific study were possible, of the well-attested wonders worked from his relics and fragmentary possessions. What is the use of dismissing all that as inconceivable, when even these common psychical parlour tricks turn perpetually upon touching some familiar object or holding in the hand some personal possession? I do not believe, of course, that these tricks are of the same type as the good works of the saint; save perhaps in the sense of Diabolus simius Dei. But it is not a question of what I believe and why, but of what the sceptic disbelieves and why. And the moral for the practical biographer and historian is that he must wait till things settle down a little more, before he claims to disbelieve anything.

This being so he can choose between two courses; and not without some hesitation, I have here chosen between them. The best and boldest course would be to tell the whole story in a straightforward way, miracles and all, as the original historians told it. And to this sane and simple course the new historians will probably have to return. But it must be remembered that this book is avowedly only an introduction to St. Francis or the study of St. Francis. Those who need an introduction are in their nature strangers. With them the object is to get them to listen to St. Francis at all; and in doing so it is perfectly legitimate so to arrange the order of the facts that the familiar come before the unfamiliar and those they can at once understand before those they have a difficulty in understanding. I should only be too thankful if this thin and scratchy sketch contains a line or two that attracts men to study St. Francis for themselves; and if they do study him for themselves, they will soon find that the supernatural part of the story seems quite as natural as the rest. But it was necessary that my outline should be a merely human one, since I was only presenting his claim on all humanity, including sceptical humanity. I therefore adopted the alternative course, of showing first that nobody but a born fool could fail to realise that Francis of Assisi was a very real historical human being; and then summarising briefly in this chapter the superhuman powers that were certainly a part of that history and humanity. It only remains to say a few words about some distinctions that may reasonably be observed in the matter by any man of any views; that he may not confuse the point and climax of the saint's life with the fancies or rumours that were really only the fringes of his reputation.

There is so immense a mass of legends and anecdotes about St. Francis of Assisi, and there are so many admirable compilations that cover nearly all of them, that I have been compelled within these narrow limits to pursue a somewhat narrow policy; that of following one line of explanation and only mentioning one anecdote here or there because it illustrates that explanation. If this is true about all the legends and stories, it is especially true about the miraculous legends and the supernatural stories. If we were to take some stories as they stand, we should receive a rather bewildered impression that the biography contains more supernatural events than natural ones. Now it is clean against Catholic tradition, coincident in so many points with common sense, to suppose that this is really the proportion of these things in practical human life. Moreover, even considered as supernatural or preternatural stories, they obviously fall into certain different classes, not so much by our experience of miracles as by our experience of stories. Some of them have the character of fairy stories in their form even more than their incident. They are obviously tales told by the fire to peasants or the children of peasants, under conditions in which nobody thinks he is propounding a religious doctrine to be received or rejected, but only rounding off a story in the most symmetrical way, according to that sort of decorative scheme or pattern that runs through all fairy stories. Others are obviously in their form most emphatically evidence; that is they are testimony that is truth or lies; and it will be very hard for any judge of human nature to think they are lies.

It is admitted that the story of the Stigmata is not a legend but can only be a lie. I mean that it is certainly not a late legendary accretion added afterwards to the fame of St. Francis; but is something that started almost immediately with his earliest biographers. It is practically necessary to suggest that it was a conspiracy; indeed there has been some disposition to put the fraud upon the unfortunate Elias, whom so many parties have been disposed to treat as a useful universal villain. It has been said, indeed, that these early biographers, St. Bonaventura and Celano and the Three Companions, though they declare that St. Francis received the mystical wounds, do not say that they themselves saw those wounds. I do not think this argument conclusive; because it only arises out of the very nature of the narrative. The Three Companions are not in any case making an affidavit; and therefore none of the admitted parts of their story are in the form of an affidavit. They are writing a chronicle of a comparatively impersonal and very objective description. They do not say, "I saw St. Francis's wounds"; they say, "St. Francis received wounds." But neither do they say, "I saw St. Francis go into the Portiuncula"; they say, "St. Francis went into the Portiuncula." But I still cannot understand why they should be trusted as eye-witnesses about the one fact and not trusted as eye-witnesses about the other. It is all of a piece; it would be a most abrupt and abnormal interruption in their way of telling the story if they suddenly began to curse and to swear, and give their names and addresses, and take their oath that they themselves saw and verified the physical facts in question. It seems to me, therefore, that this particular discussion goes back to the general question I have already mentioned; the question of why these chronicles should be credited at all, if they are credited with abounding in the incredible. But that again will probably be found to revert, in the last resort, to the mere fact that some men cannot believe in miracles because they are materialists. That is logical enough; but they are bound to deny the preternatural as much in the testimony of a modern scientific professor as in that of a medieval monkish chronicler. And there are plenty of professors for them to contradict by this time.

But whatever may be thought of such supernaturalism in the comparatively material and popular sense of supernatural acts, we shall miss the whole point of St. Francis, especially of St. Francis after Alverno, if we do not realise that he was living a supernatural life. And there is more and more of such supernaturalism in his life as he approaches towards his death. This element of the supernatural did not separate him from the natural; for it was the whole point of his position that it united him more perfectly to the natural. It did not make him dismal or dehumanised; for it was the whole meaning of his message that such mysticism makes a man cheerful and humane. But it was the whole point of his position, and it was the whole meaning of his message, that the power that did it was a supernatural power. If this simple distinction were not apparent from the whole of his life, it would be difficult for any one to miss it in reading the account of his death.

In a sense he may be said to have wandered as a dying man, just as he had wandered as a living one. As it became more and more apparent that his health was failing, he seems to have been carried from place to place like a pageant of sickness or almost like a pageant of mortality. He went to Rieti, to Nursia, perhaps to Naples, certainly to Cortona by the lake of Perugia. But there is something profoundly pathetic, and full of great problems, in the fact that at last, as it would seem, his flame of life leapt up and his heart rejoiced when they saw afar off on the Assisian hill the solemn pillars of the Portiuncula. He who had become a vagabond for the sake of a vision, he who had denied himself all sense of place and possession, he whose whole gospel and glory it was to be homeless, received like a Parthian shot from nature, the sting of the sense of home. He also had his maladie du clocher, his sickness of the spire; though his spire was higher than ours. "Never," he cried with the sudden energy of strong spirits in death, "never give up this place. If you would go anywhere or make any pilgrimage, return always to your home, for this is the holy house of God." And the procession passed under the arches of his home; and he lay down on his bed and his brethren gathered round him for the last long vigil. It seems to me no moment for entering into the subsequent disputes about which successors he blessed or in what form and with what significance. In that one mighty moment he blessed us all.

After he had taken farewell of some of his nearest an especially some of his oldest friends, he was lifted at his own request off his own rude bed and laid on the bare ground; as some say clad only in a hair-shirt, as he had first gone forth into the wintry woods from the presence of his father. It was the final assertion of his great fixed idea; of praise and thanks springing to their most towering height out of nakedness and nothing. As he lay there we may be certain that his seared and blinded eyes saw nothing but their object and their origin. We may be sure that the soul, in its last inconceivable isolation, was face to face with nothing less than God Incarnate and Christ Crucified. But for the men standing around him there must have been other thoughts mingling with these; and many memories must have gathered like ghosts in the twilight, as that day wore on and that great darkness descended in which we all lost a friend. For what lay dying there was not Dominic of the Dogs of God, a leader in logical and controversial wars that could be reduced to a plan and handed on like a plan; a master of a machine of democratic discipline by which others could organise themselves. What was passing from the world was a person; a poet; an outlook on life like a light that was never after on sea or land; a thing not to be replaced or repeated while the earth endures. It has been said that there was only one Christian, who died on the cross; it is truer to say in this sense that there was only one Franciscan, whose name was Francis. Huge and happy as was the popular work he left behind him, there was something that he could not leave behind, any more than a landscape painter can leave his eyes in his will. It was an artist in life who was here called to be an artist in death; and he had a better right than Nero, his anti-type, to say Qualis artifex-pereo. For Nero's life was full of posing for the occasion like that of an actor; while the Umbrian's had a natural and continuous grace like that of an athlete. But St. Francis had better things to say and better things to think about, and his thoughts were caught upwards where we cannot follow them, in divine and dizzy heights to which death alone can lift us up.

Round about him stood the brethren in their brown habits, those that had loved him even if they afterwards disputed with each other. There was Bernard, his first friend, and Angelo, who had served as his secretary, and Elias, his successor, whom tradition tried to turn into a sort of Judas, but who seems to have been little worse than an official in the wrong place. His tragedy was that he had a Franciscan habit without a Franciscan heart, or at any rate with a very un-Franciscan head. But though he made a bad Franciscan, he might have made a decent Dominican. Anyhow, there is no reason to doubt that he loved Francis, for ruffians and savages did that. Anyhow he stood among the rest as the hours passed and the shadows lengthened in the house of the Portiuncula; and nobody need think so ill of him as to suppose that his thoughts were then in the tumultuous future, in the ambitions and controversies of his later years.

A man might fancy that the birds must have known when it happened; and made some motion in the evening sky. As they had once, according to the tale, scattered to the four winds of heaven in the pattern of a cross at his signal of dispersion, they might now have written in such dotted lines a more awful augury across the sky. Hidden in the woods perhaps were little cowering creatures never again to be so much noticed and understood; and it has been said that animals are sometimes conscious of things to which man, their spiritual superior, is for the moment blind. We do not know whether any shiver passed through all the thieves and the outcasts and the outlaws, to tell them what had happened to him who never knew the nature of scorn.

But at least in the passages and porches of the Portiuncula there was a sudden stillness, where all the brown figures stood like bronze statues; for the stopping of the great heart that had not broken till it held the world.

CHAPTER X THE TESTAMENT OF ST. FRANCIS

In one sense doubtless it is a sad irony that St. Francis, who all his life had desired all men to agree, should have died amid increasing disagreements. But we must not exaggerate this discord, as some have done, so as to turn it into a mere defeat of all his ideals. There are some who represent his work as having been merely ruined by the wickedness of the world, or what they always assume to be the even greater wickedness of the Church.

This little book is an essay on St. Francis and not on the Franciscan Order, still less on the Catholic Church or the Papacy or the policy pursued towards the extreme Franciscans or the Fraticelli. It is therefore only necessary to note in a very few words what was the general nature of the controversy that raged after the great saint's death, and to some extent troubled the last days of his life. The dominant detail was the interpretation of the vow of poverty, or the refusal of all possessions. Nobody so far as I know ever proposed to interfere with the vow of the individual friar that he would have no individual possessions. Nobody, that is, proposed to interfere with his negation of private property. But some Franciscans, invoking the authority of Francis on their side, went further than this and further I think than anybody else has ever gone. They proposed to abolish not only private property but property. That is, they refused to be corporately responsible for anything at all; for any buildings or stores or tools; they refused to own them collectively even when they used them collectively. It is perfectly true that many, especially among the first supporters of this view, were men of a splendid and selfless spirit, wholly devoted to the great saint's ideal. It is also perfectly true that the Pope and the authorities of the Church did not think this conception was a workable arrangement, and went so far in modifying it as to set aside certain clauses in the great saint's will. But it is not at all easy to see that it was a workable arrangement or even an arrangement at all; for it was really a refusal to arrange anything. Everybody knew of course that Franciscans were communists; but this was not so much being a communist as being an anarchist. Surely upon any argument somebody or something must be answerable for what happened to or in or concerning a number of historic edifices and ordinary goods and chattels. Many idealists of a socialistic sort, notably of the school of Mr. Shaw or Mr. Wells, have treated this dispute as if it were merely a case of the tyranny of wealthy and wicked pontiffs crushing the true Christianity of Christian Socialists. But in truth this extreme ideal was in a sense the very reverse of Socialist, or even social. Precisely the thing which these enthusiasts refused was that social ownership on which Socialism is built; what they primarily refused to do was what Socialists primarily exist to do; to own legally in their corporate capacity. Nor is it true that the tone of the Popes towards the enthusiasts was merely harsh and hostile. The Pope maintained for a long time a compromise which he had specially designed to meet their own conscientious objections, a compromise by which the Papacy itself held the property in a kind of trust for the owners who refused to touch it. The truth is that this incident shows two things which are common enough in Catholic history, but very little understood by the journalistic history of industrial civilisation. It shows that the Saints were sometimes great men when the Popes were small men. But it also shows that great men are sometimes wrong when small men are right. And it will be found, after all, very difficult for any candid and clear-headed outsider to deny that the Pope was right, when he insisted that the world was not made only for Franciscans.

For that was what was behind the quarrel. At the back of this particular practical question there was something much larger and more momentous, the stir and wind of which we can feel as we read the controversy. We might go so far as to put the ultimate truth thus. St. Francis was so great and original a man that he had something in him of what makes the founder of a religion. Many of his followers were more or less ready, in their hearts, to treat him as the founder of a religion. They were willing to let the Franciscan spirit escape from Christendom as the Christian spirit had escaped from Israel. They were willing to let it eclipse Christendom as the Christian spirit had eclipsed Israel. Francis, the fire that ran through the roads of Italy, was to be the beginning of a conflagration in which the old Christian civilisation was to be consumed. That was the point the Pope had to settle; whether Christendom should absorb Francis or Francis Christendom. And he decided rightly, apart from the duties of his place; for the Church could include all that was good in the Franciscans and the Franciscans could not include all that was good in the Church. There is one consideration which, though sufficiently clear in the whole story, has not perhaps been sufficiently noted, especially by those who cannot see the case for a certain Catholic common sense larger even than Franciscan enthusiasm. Yet it arises out of the very merits of the man whom they so rightly admire. Francis of Assisi, as has been said again and again, was a poet; that is, he was a person who could express his personality. Now it is everywhere the mark of this sort of man that his very limitations make him larger. He is what he is, not only by what he has, but in some degree by what he has not. But the limits that make the lines of such a personal portrait cannot be made the limits of all humanity. St. Francis is a very strong example of this quality in the man of genius, that in him even what is negative is positive, because it is part of a character. An excellent example of what I mean may be found in his attitude towards learning and scholarship. He ignored and in some degree discouraged books and book-learning; and from his own point of view and that of his own work in the world he was absolutely right. The whole point of his message was to be so simple that the village idiot could understand it. The whole point of his point of view was that it looked out freshly upon a fresh world, that might have been made that morning. Save for the great primal things, the Creation and the Story of Eden, the first Christmas and the first Easter, the world had no history. But is it desired or desirable that the whole Catholic Church should have no history?

It is perhaps the chief suggestion of this book that St. Francis walked the world like the Pardon of God. I mean that his appearance marked the moment when men could be reconciled not only to God but to nature and, most difficult of all, to themselves. For it marked the moment when all the stale paganism that had poisoned the ancient world was at last worked out of the social system. He opened the gates of the Dark Ages as of a prison of purgatory, where men had cleansed themselves as hermits in the desert or heroes in the barbarian wars. It was in fact his whole function to tell men to start afresh and, in that sense, to tell them to forget. If they were to turn over a new leaf and begin a fresh page with the first large letters of the alphabet, simply drawn and brilliantly coloured in the early mediaeval manner, it was clearly a part of that particular childlike cheerfulness that they should paste down the old page that was all black and bloody with horrid things. For instance, I have already noted that there is not a trace in the poetry of this first Italian poet of all that pagan mythology which lingered long after paganism. The first Italian poet seems the only man in the world who has never even heard of Virgil. This was exactly right for the special sense in which he is the first Italian poet. It is quite right that he should call a nightingale a nightingale, and not have its song spoilt or saddened by the terrible tales of Itylus or Procne. In short, it is really quite right and quite desirable that St. Francis should never have heard of Virgil. But do we really desire that Dante should never have heard of Virgil? Do we really desire that Dante should never have read any pagan mythology? It has been truly said that the use that Dante makes of such fables is altogether part of a deeper orthodoxy; that his huge heathen fragments, his gigantic figures of Minos or of Charon, only give a hint of some enormous natural religion behind all history and from the first foreshadowing the Faith. It is well to have the Sybil as well as David in the Dies Irae. That St. Francis would have burned all the leaves of all the books of the Sybil, in exchange for one fresh leaf from the nearest tree, is perfectly true; and perfectly proper to St. Francis. But it is good to have the Dies Irae as well as the Canticle of the Sun.

By this thesis, in short, the coming of St. Francis was like the birth of a child in a dark house, lifting its doom; a child that grows up unconscious of the tragedy and triumphs over it by his innocence. In him it is necessarily not only innocence but ignorance. It is the essence of the story that he should pluck at the green grass without knowing it grows over a murdered man or climb the apple-tree without knowing it was the gibbet of a suicide. It was such an amnesty and reconciliation that the freshness of the Franciscan spirit brought to all the world. But it does not follow that it ought to impose its ignorance on all the world. And I think it would have tried to impose it on all the world. For some Franciscans it would have seemed right that Franciscan poetry should expel Benedictine prose. For the symbolic child it was quite rational. It was right enough that for such a child the world should be a large new nursery with blank white-washed walls, on which he could draw his own pictures in chalk in the childish fashion, crude in outline and gay in colour; the beginnings of all our art. It was right enough that to him such a nursery should seem the most magnificent mansion of the imagination of man. But in the Church of God are many mansions.

Every heresy has been an effort to narrow the Church. If the Franciscan movement had turned into a new religion, it would after all have been a narrow religion. In so far as it did turn here and there into a heresy, it was a narrow heresy. It did what heresy always does; it set the mood against the mind. The mood was indeed originally the good and glorious mood of the great St. Francis, but it was not the whole mind of God or even of man. And it is a fact that the mood itself degenerated, as the mood turned into a monomania. A sect that came to be called the Fraticelli declared themselves the true sons of St. Francis and broke away from the compromises of Rome in favour of what they would have called the complete programme of Assisi. In a very little while these loose Franciscans began to look as ferocious as Flagellants. They launched new and violent vetoes; they denounced marriage; that is, they denounced mankind. In the name of the most human of saints they declared war upon humanity. They did not perish particularly through being persecuted; many of them were eventually persuaded; and the unpersuadable rump of them that remained remained without producing anything in the least calculated to remind anybody of the real St. Francis. What was the matter with these people was that they were mystics; mystics and nothing else but mystics; mystics and not Catholics; mystics and not Christians; mystics and not men. They rotted away because, in the most exact sense, they would not listen to reason. And St. Francis, however wild and romantic his gyrations might appear to many, always hung on to reason by one invisible and indestructible hair.

The great saint was sane; and with the very sound of the word sanity, as at a deeper chord struck upon a harp, we come back to something that was indeed deeper than everything about him that seemed an almost elvish eccentricity. He was not a mere eccentric because he was always turning towards the centre and heart of the maze; he took the queerest and most zigzag short cuts through the wood, but he was always going home. He was not only far too humble to be an heresiarch, but he was far too human to desire to be an extremist, in the sense of an exile at the ends of the earth. The sense of humour which salts all the stories of his escapades alone prevented him from ever hardening into the solemnity of sectarian self-righteousness. He was by nature ready to admit that he was wrong; and if his followers had on some practical points to admit that he was wrong, they only admitted that he was wrong in order to prove that he was right. For it is they, his real followers, who have really proved that he was right and even in transcending some of his negations have triumphantly extended and interpreted his truth. The Franciscan order did not fossilise or break off short like something of which the true purpose has been frustrated by official tyranny or internal treason. It was this, the central and orthodox trunk of it, that afterwards bore fruit for the world. It counted among its sons Bonaventura, the great mystic, and Bernardino, the popular preacher, who filled Italy with the very beatific buffooneries of a Jongleur de Dieu. It counted Raymond Lully with his strange learning and his large and daring plans for the conversion of the world; a man intensely individual exactly as St. Francis was intensely individual. It counted Roger Bacon, the first naturalist whose experiments with light and water had all the luminous quaintness that belongs to the beginnings of natural history; and whom even the most material scientists have hailed as a father of science. It is not merely true that these were great men who did great work for the world; it is also true that they were a certain kind of men keeping the spirit and savour of a certain kind of man, that we can recognise in them a taste and tang of audacity and simplicity, and know them for the sons of St. Francis.

For that is the full and final spirit in which we should turn to St. Francis; in the spirit of thanks for what he has done. He was above all things a great giver; and he cared chiefly for the best kind of giving which is called thanksgiving. If another great man wrote a grammar of assent, he may well be said to have written a grammar of acceptance; a grammar of gratitude. He understood down to its very depths the theory of thanks; and its depths are a bottomless abyss. He knew that the praise of God stands on its strongest ground when it stands on nothing. He knew that we can best measure the towering miracle of the mere fact of existence if we realise that but for some strange mercy we should not even exist. And something of that larger truth is repeated in a lesser form in our own relations with so mighty a maker of history. He also is a giver of things we could not have even thought of for ourselves; he also is too great for anything but gratitude. From him came a whole awakening of the world and a dawn in which all shapes and colours could be seen anew. The mighty men of genius who made the Christian civilisation that we know appear in history almost as his servants and imitators. Before Dante was, he had given poetry to Italy; before St. Louis ruled, he had risen as the tribune of the poor; and before Giotto had painted the pictures, he had enacted the scenes. That great painter who began the whole human inspiration of European painting had himself gone to St. Francis to be inspired. It is said that when St. Francis staged in his own simple fashion a Nativity Play of Bethlehem, with kings and angels in the stiff and gay mediaeval garments and the golden wigs that stood for haloes, a miracle was wrought full of the Franciscan glory. The Holy Child was a wooden doll or bambino, and it was said that he embraced it and that the image came to life in his arms. He assuredly was not thinking of lesser things; but we may at least say that one thing came to life in his arms; and that was the thing that we call the drama. Save for his intense individual love of song, he did not perhaps himself embody this spirit in any of these arts. He was the spirit that was embodied. He was the spiritual essence and substance that walked the world, before any one had seen these things in visible forms derived from it: a wandering fire as if from nowhere, at which men more material could light both torches and tapers. He was the soul of mediaeval civilisation before it even found a body. Another and quite different stream of spiritual inspiration derives largely from him; all that reforming energy of mediaeval and modern times that goes to the burden of Deus est Deus Pauperum. His abstract ardour for human beings was in a multitude of just mediaeval laws against the pride and cruelty of riches; it is to-day behind much that is loosely called Christian Socialist and can more correctly be called Catholic Democrat. Neither on the artistic nor the social side would anybody pretend that these things would not have existed without him; yet it is strictly true to say that we cannot now imagine them without him; since he has lived and changed the world.

And something of that sense of impotence which was more than half his power will descend on any one who knows what that inspiration has been in history, and can only record it in a series of straggling and meagre sentences. He will know something of what St. Francis meant by the great and good debt that cannot be paid. He will feel at once the desire to have done infinitely more and the futility of having done anything. He will know what it is to stand under such a deluge of a dead man's marvels, and have nothing in return to establish against it; to have nothing to set up under the overhanging, overwhelming arches of such a temple of time and eternity, but this brief candle burnt out so quickly before his shrine.

THE END

ST. THOMAS AQUINAS

INTRODUCTORY NOTE

This book makes no pretence to be anything but a popular sketch of a great historical character who ought to be more popular. Its aim will be achieved, if it leads those who have hardly even heard of St. Thomas Aquinas to read about him in better books. But from this necessary limitation certain consequences follow, which should perhaps be allowed for from the start.

First, it follows that the tale is told very largely to those who are not of the communion of St. Thomas; and who may be interested in him as I might be in Confucius or Mahomet. Yet, on the other hand, the very need of presenting a clean-cut outline involved its cutting into other outlines of thought, among those who may think differently. If I write a sketch of Nelson mainly for foreigners, I may have to explain elaborately many things that all Englishmen know, and possibly cut out, for brevity, many details that many Englishmen would like to know. But, on the other side, it would be difficult to write a very vivid and moving narrative of Nelson, while entirely concealing the fact that he fought with the French. It would be futile to make a sketch of St. Thomas and conceal the fact that he fought with heretics; and yet the fact itself may embarrass the very purpose for which it is employed. I can only express the hope, and indeed the confidence, that those who regard me as the heretic will hardly blame me for expressing my own convictions, and certainly not for expressing my hero's convictions. There is only one point upon which such a question concerns this very simple narrative. It is the conviction, which I have expressed once or twice in the course of it, that the sixteenth-century schism was really a belated revolt of the thirteenth-century pessimists. It was a back-wash of the old Augustinian Puritanism against the Aristotelian liberality. Without that, I could not place my historical figure in history. But the whole is meant only for a rough sketch of a figure in a landscape and not of a landscape with figures.

Second, it follows that in any such simplification I can hardly say much of the philosopher beyond showing that he had a philosophy. I have only, so to speak, given samples of that philosophy. Lastly, it follows that it is practically impossible to deal adequately with the theology. A lady I know picked up a book of selections from St. Thomas with a commentary; and began hopefully to read a section with the innocent heading, "The Simplicity of God." She then laid down the book with a sigh and said, "Well, if that's His simplicity, I wonder what His complexity is like." With all respect to that excellent Thomistic commentary, I have no desire to have this book laid down, at the very first glance, with a similar sigh. I have taken the view that the biography is an introduction to the philosophy, and that the philosophy is an introduction to the theology; and that I can only carry the reader just beyond the first stage of the story.

Third, I have not thought it necessary to notice those critics who, from time to time, desperately play to the gallery by reprinting paragraphs of medieval demonology in the hope of horrifying the modern public merely by an unfamiliar language. I have taken it for granted that educated men know that Aquinas and all his contemporaries, and all his opponents for centuries after, did believe in demons, and similar facts, but I have not thought them worth mentioning here, for the simple reason that they do not help to detach or distinguish the portrait. In all that, there was no disagreement between Protestant or Catholic theologians, for all the hundreds of years during which there was any theology; and St. Thomas is not notable as holding such views, except in holding them rather mildly. I have not discussed such matters, not because I have any reason to conceal them, but because they do not in any way personally concern the one person whom it is here my business to reveal. There is hardly room, even as it is, for such a figure in such a frame.

I ON TWO FRIARS

Let me at once anticipate comment by answering to the name of that notorious character, who rushes in where even the Angels of the Angelic Doctor might fear to tread. Some time ago I wrote a little book of this type and shape on St. Francis of Assisi; and some time after (I know not when or how, as the song says, and certainly not why) I promised to write a book of the same size, or the same smallness on St. Thomas Aquinas. The promise was Franciscan only in its rashness; and the parallel was very far from being Thomistic in its logic. You can make a sketch of St. Francis: you could only make a plan of St. Thomas, like the plan of a labyrinthine city. And yet in a sense he would fit into a much larger or a much smaller book. What we really know of his life might be pretty fairly dealt with in a few pages; for he did not, like St. Francis, disappear in a shower of personal anecdotes and popular legends. What we know, or could know, or may eventually have the luck to learn, of his work, will probably fill even more libraries in the future than it has filled in the past. It was allowable to sketch St. Francis in an outline; but with St. Thomas everything depends on the filling up of the outline. It was even medieval in a manner to illuminate a miniature of the Poverello, whose very title is a diminutive. But to make a digest, in the tabloid manner, of the Dumb Ox of Sicily passes all digestive experiments in the matter of an ox in a tea-cup. But we must hope it is possible to make an outline of biography, now that anybody seems capable of writing an outline of history or an outline of anything. Only in the present case the outline is rather an outsize. The gown that could contain the colossal friar is not kept in stock.

I have said that these can only be portraits in outline. But the concrete contrast is here so striking, that even if we actually saw the two human figures in outline, coming over the hill in their friar's gowns, we should find that contrast even comic. It would be like seeing, even afar off, the silhouettes of Don Quixote and Sancho Panza, or of Falstaff and Master Slender. St. Francis was a lean and lively little man; thin as a thread and vibrant as a bowstring; and in his motions like an arrow from the bow. All his life was a series of plunges and scampers; darting after the beggar, dashing naked into the woods, tossing himself into the strange ship, hurling himself into the Sultan tent and offering to hurl himself into the fire. In appearance he must have been like a thin brown skeleton autumn leaf dancing eternally before the wind; but in truth it was he that was the wind.

St. Thomas was a huge heavy bull of a man, fat and slow and quiet; very mild and magnanimous but not very sociable; shy, even apart from the humility of holiness; and abstracted, even apart from his occasional and carefully concealed experiences of trance or ecstasy. St. Francis was so fiery and even fidgety that the ecclesiastics, before whom he appeared quite suddenly, thought he was a madman. St. Thomas was so stolid that the scholars, in the schools which he attended regularly, thought he was a dunce. Indeed, he was the sort of schoolboy, not unknown, who would much rather be thought a dunce than have his own dreams invaded, by more active or animated dunces. This external contrast extends to almost every point in the two personalities. It was the paradox of St. Francis that while he was passionately fond of poems, he was rather distrustful of books. It was the outstanding fact about St. Thomas that he loved books and lived on books; that he lived the very life of the clerk or scholar in The Canterbury Tales, who would rather have a hundred books of Aristotle and his philosophy than any wealth the world could give him. When asked for what he thanked God most, he answered simply, "I have understood every page I ever read." St. Francis was very vivid in his poems and rather vague in his documents; St. Thomas devoted his whole life to documenting whole systems of Pagan and Christian literature; and occasionally wrote a hymn like a man taking a holiday. They saw the same problem from different angles, of simplicity and subtlety; St. Francis thought it would be enough to pour out his heart to the Mohammedans, to persuade them not to worship Mahound. St. Thomas bothered his head with every hair-splitting distinction and deduction, about the Absolute or the Accident, merely to prevent them from misunderstanding Aristotle. St. Francis was the son of a shopkeeper, or middle class trader; and while his whole life was a revolt against the mercantile life of his father, he retained none the less, something of the quickness and social adaptability which makes the market hum like a hive. In the common phrase, fond as he was of green fields, he did not let the grass grow under his feet. He was what American millionaires and gangsters call a live wire. It is typical of the mechanistic moderns that, even when they try to imagine a live thing, they can only think of a mechanical metaphor from a dead thing. There is such a thing as a live worm; but there is no such thing as a live wire. St. Francis would have heartily agreed that he was a worm; but he was a very live worm. Greatest of all foes to the go-getting ideal, he had certainly abandoned getting, but he was still going. St. Thomas, on the other hand, came out of a world where he might have enjoyed leisure, and he remained one of those men whose labour has something of the placidity of leisure. He was a hard worker, but nobody could possibly mistake him for a hustler. He had something indefinable about him, which marks those who work when they need not work. For he was by birth a gentleman of a great house, and such repose can remain as a habit, when it is no longer a motive. But in him it was expressed only in its most amiable elements; for instance, there was possibly something of it in his effortless courtesy and patience. Every saint is a man before he is a saint; and a saint may be made of every sort or kind of man; and most of us will choose between these different types according to our different tastes. But I will confess that, while the romantic glory of St. Francis has lost nothing of its glamour for me, I have in later years grown to feel almost as much affection, or in some aspects even more, for this man who unconsciously inhabited a large heart and a large head, like one inheriting a large house, and exercised there an equally generous if rather more absent-minded hospitality. There are moments when St. Francis, the most unworldly man who ever walked the world, is almost too efficient for me.

St. Thomas Aquinas has recently reappeared, in the current culture of the colleges and the salons, in a way that would have been quite startling even ten years ago. And the mood that has concentrated on him is doubtless very different from that which popularised St. Francis quite twenty years ago.

The Saint is a medicine because he is an antidote. Indeed that is why the saint is often a martyr; he is mistaken for a poison because he is an antidote. He will generally be found restoring the world to sanity by exaggerating whatever the world neglects, which is by no means always the same element in every age. Yet each generation seeks its saint by instinct; and he is not what the people want, but rather what the people need. This is surely the very much mistaken meaning of those words to the first saints, "Ye are the salt of the earth," which caused the Ex-Kaiser to remark with all solemnity that his beefy Germans were the salt of the earth; meaning thereby merely that they were the earth's beefiest and therefore best. But salt seasons and preserves beef, not because it is like beef; but because it is very unlike it. Christ did not tell his apostles that they were only the excellent people, or the only excellent people, but that they were the exceptional people; the permanently incongruous and incompatible people; and the text about the salt of the earth is really as sharp and shrewd and tart as the taste of salt. It is because they were the exceptional people, that they must not lose their exceptional quality. "If salt lose its savour, wherewith shall it be salted?" is a much more pointed question than any mere lament over the price of the best beef. If the world grows too worldly, it can be rebuked by the Church; but if the Church grows too worldly, it cannot be adequately rebuked for worldliness by the world.

Therefore it is the paradox of history that each generation is converted by the saint who contradicts it most. St. Francis had a curious and almost uncanny attraction for the Victorians; for the nineteenth century English who seemed superficially to be most complacent about their commerce and their common sense. Not only a rather complacent Englishman like Matthew Arnold, but even the English Liberals whom he criticised for their complacency, began slowly to discover the mystery of the Middle Ages through the strange story told in feathers and flames in the hagiographical pictures of Giotto. There was something in the story of St. Francis that pierced through all those English qualities which are most famous and fatuous, to all those English qualities which are most hidden and human: the secret softness of heart; the poetical vagueness of mind; the love of landscape and of animals. St. Francis of Assisi was the only medieval Catholic who really became popular in England on his own merits. It was largely because of a subconscious feeling that the modern world had neglected those particular merits. The English middle classes found their only missionary in the figure, which of all types in the world they most despised; an Italian beggar.

So, as the nineteenth century clutched at the Franciscan romance, precisely because it had neglected romance, so the twentieth century is already clutching at the Thomist rational theology, because it has neglected reason. In a world that was too stolid, Christianity returned in the form of a vagabond; in a world that has grown a great deal too wild, Christianity has returned in the form of a teacher of logic. In the world of Herbert Spencer men wanted a cure for indigestion; in the world of Einstein they want a cure for vertigo. In the first case, they dimly perceived the fact that it was after a long fast that St. Francis sang the Song of the Sun and the praise of the fruitful earth. In the second case, they already dimly perceived that, even if they only want to understand Einstein, it is necessary first to understand the use of the understanding. They begin to see that, as the eighteenth century thought itself the age of reason, and the nineteenth century thought itself the age of common sense, the twentieth century cannot as yet even manage to think itself anything but the age of uncommon nonsense. In those conditions the world needs a saint; but above all, it needs a philosopher. And these two cases do show that the world, to do it justice, has an instinct for what it needs. The earth was really very flat, for those Victorians who most vigorously repeated that it was round, and Alverno of the Stigmata stood up as a single mountain in the plain. But the earth is an earthquake, a ceaseless and apparently endless earthquake, for the moderns for whom Newton has been scrapped along with Ptolemy. And for them there is something more steep and even incredible than a mountain; a piece of really solid ground; the level of the level-headed man. Thus in our time the two saints have appealed to two generations, an age of romantics and an age of sceptics; yet in their own age they were doing the same work; a work that has changed the world.

Again, it may be said truly that the comparison is idle, and does not fit in well even as a fancy; since the men were not properly even of the same generation or the same historic moment. If two friars are to be presented as a pair of Heavenly Twins, the obvious comparison is between St. Francis and St. Dominic. The relations of St. Francis and St. Thomas were, at nearest, those of uncle and nephew; and my fanciful excursus may appear only a highly profane version of "Tommy make room for your uncle." For if St. Francis and St. Dominic were the great twin brethren, Thomas was obviously the first great son of St. Dominic, as was his friend Bonaventure of St. Francis. Nevertheless, I have a reason (indeed two reasons) for taking as a text the accident of two title-pages; and putting St. Thomas beside St. Francis, instead of pairing him off with Bonaventure the Franciscan. It is because the comparison, remote and perverse as it may seem, is really a sort of short cut to the heart of history; and brings us by the most rapid route to the real question of the life and work of St. Thomas Aquinas. For most people now have a rough but picturesque picture in their minds of the life and work of St. Francis of Assisi. And the shortest way of telling the other story is to say that, while the two men were thus a contrast in almost every feature, they were really doing the same thing. One of them was doing it in the world of the mind and the other in the world of the worldly. But it was the same great medieval movement; still but little understood. In a constructive sense, it was more important than the Reformation. Nay, in a constructive sense, it was the Reformation.

About this medieval movement there are two facts that must first be emphasised. They are not, of course, contrary facts, but they are perhaps answers to contrary fallacies. First, in spite of all that was once said about superstition, the Dark Ages and the sterility of Scholasticism, it was in every sense a movement of enlargement, always moving towards greater light and even greater liberty. Second, in spite of all that was said later on about progress and the Renaissance and forerunners of modern thought, it was almost entirely a movement of orthodox theological enthusiasm, unfolded from within. It was not a compromise with the world, or a surrender to heathens or heretics, or even a mere borrowing of external aids, even when it did borrow them. In so far as it did reach out to the light of common day, it was like the action of a plant which by its own force thrusts out its leaves into the sun; not like the action of one who merely lets daylight into a prison.

In short, it was what is technically called a Development in doctrine. But there seems to be a queer ignorance, not only about the technical, but the natural meaning of the word Development. The critics of Catholic theology seem to suppose that it is not so much an evolution as an evasion; that it is at best an adaptation. They fancy that its very success is the success of surrender. But that is not the natural meaning of the word Development. When we talk of a child being well-developed, we mean that he has grown bigger and stronger with his own strength; not that he is padded with borrowed pillows or walks on stilts to make him look taller. When we say that a puppy develops into a dog, we do not mean that his growth is a gradual compromise with a cat; we mean that he becomes more doggy and not less. Development is the expansion of all the possibilities and implications of a doctrine, as there is time to distinguish them and draw them out; and the point here is that the enlargement of medieval theology was simply the full comprehension of that theology. And it is of primary importance to realise this fact first, about the time of the great Dominican and the first Franciscan, because their tendency, humanistic and naturalistic in a hundred ways, was truly the development of the supreme doctrine, which was also the dogma of all dogmas. It is in this that the popular poetry of St. Francis and the almost rationalistic prose of St. Thomas appear most vividly as part of the same movement. There are both great growths of Catholic development, depending upon external things only as every living and growing thing depends on them; that is, it digests and transforms them, but continues in its own image and not in theirs. A Buddhist or a Communist might dream of two things which simultaneously eat each other, as the perfect form of unification. But it is not so with living things. St. Francis was content to call himself the Troubadour of God; but not content with the God of the Troubadours. St. Thomas did not reconcile Christ to Aristotle; he reconciled Aristotle to Christ.

Yes; in spite of the contrasts that are as conspicuous and even comic as the comparison between the fat man and the thin man, the tall man and the short; in spite of the contrast between the vagabond and the student, between the apprentice and the aristocrat, between the book-hater and the book-lover, between the wildest of all missionaries and the mildest of all professors, the great fact of medieval history is that these two great men were doing the same great work; one in the study and the other in the street. They were not bringing something new into Christianity, in the sense of something heathen or heretical into Christianity; on the contrary, they were bringing Christianity into Christendom. But they were bringing it back against the pressure of certain historic tendencies, which had hardened into habits in many great schools and authorities in the Christian Church; and they were using tools and weapons which seemed to many people to be associated with heresy or heathenry. St. Francis used Nature much as St. Thomas used Aristotle; and to some they seemed to be using a Pagan goddess and a Pagan sage. What they were really doing, and especially what St. Thomas was really doing, will form the main matter of these pages; but it is convenient to be able to compare him from the first with a more popular saint; because we may thus sum up the substance of it in the most popular way. Perhaps it would sound too paradoxical to say that these two saints saved us from Spirituality; a dreadful doom. Perhaps it may be misunderstood if I say that St. Francis, for all his love of animals, saved us from being Buddhists; and that St. Thomas, for all his love of Greek philosophy, saved us from being Platonists. But it is best to say the truth in its simplest form; that they both reaffirmed the Incarnation, by bringing God back to earth.

This analogy, which may seem rather remote, is really perhaps the best practical preface to the philosophy of St. Thomas. As we shall have to consider more closely later on, the purely spiritual or mystical side of Catholicism had very much got the upper hand in the first Catholic centuries; through the genius of Augustine, who had been a Platonist, and perhaps never ceased to be a Platonist; through the transcendentalism of the supposed work of the Areopagite; through the Oriental trend of the later Empire and something Asiatic about the almost pontifical kinghood of Byzantium; all these things weighed down what we should now roughly call the Western element; though it has as good a right to be called the Christian element; since its common sense is but the holy familiarity of the word made flesh. Anyhow, it must suffice for the moment to say that theologians had somewhat stiffened into a sort of Platonic pride in the possession of intangible and untranslatable truths within; as if no part of their wisdom had any root anywhere in the real world. Now the first thing that Aquinas did, though by no means the last, was to say to these pure transcendentalists something substantially like this.

"Far be it from a poor friar to deny that you have these dazzling diamonds in your head, all designed in the most perfect mathematical shapes and shining with a purely celestial light; all there, almost before you begin to think, let alone to see or hear or feel. But I am not ashamed to say that I find my reason fed by my senses; that I owe a great deal of what I think to what I see and smell and taste and handle; and that so far as my reason is concerned, I feel obliged to treat all this reality as real. To be brief, in all humility, I do not believe that God meant Man to exercise only that peculiar, uplifted and abstracted sort of intellect which you are so fortunate as to possess: but I believe that there is a middle field of facts which are given by the senses to be the subject matter of the reason; and that in that field the reason has a right to rule, as the representative of God in Man. It is true that all this is lower than the angels; but it is higher than the animals, and all the actual material objects Man finds around him. True, man also can be an object; and even a deplorable object. But what man has done man may do; and if an antiquated old heathen called Aristotle can help me to do it I will thank him in all humility."

Thus began what is commonly called the appeal to Aquinas and Aristotle. It might be called the appeal to Reason and the Authority of the Senses. And it will be obvious that there is a sort of popular parallel to it in the fact that St. Francis did not only listen for the angels, but also listened to the birds. And before we come to those aspects of St. Thomas that were very severely intellectual, we may note that in him as in St. Francis there is a preliminary practical element which is rather moral; a sort of good and straightforward humility; and a readiness in the man to regard even himself in some ways as an animal; as St. Francis compared his body to a donkey. It may be said that the contrast holds everywhere, even in zoological metaphor, and that if St. Francis was like that common or garden donkey who carried Christ into Jerusalem, St. Thomas, who was actually compared to an ox, rather resembled that Apocalyptic monster of almost Assyrian mystery; the winged bull. But again, we must not let all that can be contrasted eclipse what was common; or forget that neither of them would have been too proud to wait as patiently as the ox and ass in the stable of Bethlehem.

There were of course, as we shall soon see, many other much more curious and complicated ideas in the philosophy of St. Thomas; besides this primary idea of a central common sense that is nourished by the five senses. But at this stage, the point of the story is not only that this was a Thomist doctrine, but that it is a truly and eminently Christian doctrine. For upon this point modern writers write a great deal of nonsense; and show more than their normal ingenuity in missing the point. Having assumed without argument, at the start, that all emancipation must lead men away from religion and towards irreligion, they have just blankly and blindly forgotten what is the outstanding feature of the religion itself.

It will not be possible to conceal much longer from anybody the fact that St. Thomas Aquinas was one of the great liberators of the human intellect. The sectarians of the seventeenth and eighteenth centuries were essentially obscurantists, and they guarded an obscurantist legend that the Schoolman was an obscurantist. This was wearing thin even in the nineteenth century; it will be impossible in the twentieth. It has nothing to do with the truth of their theology or his; but only with the truth of historical proportion, which begins to reappear as quarrels begin to die down. Simply as one of the facts that bulk big in history, it is true to say that Thomas was a very great man who reconciled religion with reason, who expanded it towards experimental science, who insisted that the senses were the windows of the soul and that the reason had a divine right to feed upon facts, and that it was the business of the Faith to digest the strong meat of the toughest and most practical of pagan philosophies. It is a fact, like the military strategy of Napoleon, that Aquinas was thus fighting for all that is liberal and enlightened, as compared with his rivals, or for that matter his successors and supplanters. Those who, for other reasons, honestly accept the final effect of the Reformation will none the less face the fact, that it was the Schoolman who was the Reformer; and that the later Reformers were by comparison reactionaries. I use the word not as a reproach from my own stand-point, but as a fact from the ordinary modern progressive standpoint. For instance, they riveted the mind back to the literal sufficiency of the Hebrew Scriptures; when St. Thomas had already spoken of the Spirit giving grace to the Greek philosophies. He insisted on the social duty of works; they only on the spiritual duty of faith. It was the very life of the Thomist teaching that Reason can be trusted: it was the very life of Lutheran teaching that Reason is utterly untrustworthy.

Now when this fact is found to be a fact, the danger is that all the unstable opposition will suddenly slide to the opposite extreme. Those who up to that moment have been abusing the Schoolman as a dogmatist will begin to admire the Schoolman as a Modernist who diluted dogma. They will hastily begin to adorn his statue with all the faded garlands of progress, to present him as a man in advance of his age, which is always supposed to mean in agreement with our age; and to load him with the unprovoked imputation of having produced the modern mind. They will discover his attraction, and somewhat hastily assume that he was like themselves, because he was attractive. Up to a point this is pardonable enough; up to a point it has already happened in the case of St. Francis. But it would not go beyond a certain point in the case of St. Francis. Nobody, not even a Freethinker like Renan or Matthew Arnold, would pretend that St. Francis was anything but a devout Christian, or had any other original motive except the imitation of Christ. Yet St. Francis also had that liberating and humanising effect upon religion; though perhaps rather on the imagination than the intellect. But nobody says that St. Francis was loosening the Christian code, when he was obviously tightening it; like the rope round his friar's frock. Nobody says he merely opened the gates to sceptical science, or sold the pass to heathen humanism, or looked forward only to the Renaissance or met the Rationalists half way. No biographer pretends that St. Francis, when he is reported to have opened the Gospels at random and read the great texts about Poverty, really only opened the Aeneid and practised the Sors Virgiliana out of respect for heathen letters and learning. No historian will pretend that St. Francis wrote The Canticle of the Sun in close imitation of a Homeric Hymn to Apollo or loved birds because he had carefully learned all the tricks of the Roman Augurs.

In short, most people, Christian or heathen, would now agree that the Franciscan sentiment was primarily a Christian sentiment, unfolded from within, out of an innocent (or, if you will, ignorant) faith in the Christian religion itself. Nobody, as I have said, says that St. Francis drew his primary inspiration from Ovid. It would be every bit as false to say that Aquinas drew his primary inspiration from Aristotle. The whole lesson of his life, especially of his early life, the whole story of his childhood and choice of a career, shows that he was supremely and directly devotional; and that he passionately loved the Catholic worship long before he found he had to fight for it. But there is also a special and clinching instance of this which once more connects St. Thomas with St. Francis. It seems to be strangely forgotten that both these saints were in actual fact imitating a Master, who was not Aristotle let alone Ovid, when they sanctified the senses or the simple things of nature; when St. Francis walked humbly among the beasts or St. Thomas debated courteously among the Gentiles.

Those who miss this, miss the point of the religion, even if it be a superstition; nay, they miss the very point they would call most superstitious. I mean the whole staggering story of the God-Man in the Gospels. A few even miss it touching St. Francis and his unmixed and unlearned appeal to the Gospels. They will talk of the readiness of St. Francis to learn from the flowers or the birds as something that can only point onward to the Pagan Renaissance. Whereas the fact stares them in the face; first, that it points backwards to the New Testament, and second that it points forward, if it points to anything, to the Aristotelian realism of the Summa of St. Thomas Aquinas. They vaguely imagine that anybody who is humanising divinity must be paganising divinity without seeing that the humanising of divinity is actually the strongest and starkest and most incredible dogma in the Creed. St. Francis was becoming more like Christ, and not merely more like Buddha, when he considered the lilies of the field or the fowls of the air; and St. Thomas was becoming more of a Christian, and not merely more of an Aristotelian, when he insisted that God and the image of God had come in contact through matter with a material world. These saints were, in the most exact sense of the term, Humanists; because they were insisting on the immense importance of the human being in the theological scheme of things. But they were not Humanists marching along a path of progress that leads to Modernism and general scepticism; for in their very Humanism they were affirming a dogma now often regarded as the most superstitious Superhumanism. They were strengthening that staggering doctrine of Incarnation, which the sceptics find it hardest to believe. There cannot be a stiffer piece of Christian divinity than the divinity of Christ.

This is a point that is here very much to the point; that these men became more orthodox, when they became more rational or natural. Only by being thus orthodox could they be thus rational and natural. In other words, what may really be called a liberal theology was unfolded from within, from out of the original mysteries of Catholicism. But that liberality had nothing to do with liberalism; in fact it cannot even now coexist with liberalism[1]. The matter is so cogent, that I will take one or two special ideas of St. Thomas to illustrate what I mean. Without anticipating the elementary sketch of Thomism that must be made later, the following points may be noted here.

For instance, it was a very special idea of St. Thomas that Man is to be studied in his whole manhood; that a man is not a man without his body, just as he is not a man without his soul. A corpse is not a man; but also a ghost is not a man. The earlier school of Augustine and even of Anselm had rather neglected this, treating the soul as the only necessary treasure, wrapped for a time in a negligible napkin.

---

[1] I use the word liberalism here in the strictly limited theological sense, in which Newman and other theologians use it. In its popular political sense, as I point out later, St. Thomas rather tended to be a Liberal, especially for his time.

Even here they were less orthodox in being more spiritual. They sometimes hovered on the edge of those Eastern deserts that stretch away to the land of transmigration where the essential soul may pass through a hundred unessential bodies; reincarnated even in the bodies of beasts or birds. St. Thomas stood up stoutly for the fact that a man's body is his body as his mind is his mind; and that he can only be a balance and union of the two. Now this is in some ways a naturalistic notion, very near to the modern respect for material things; a praise of the body that might be sung by Walt Whitman or justified by D. H. Lawrence: a thing that might be called Humanism or even claimed by Modernism. In fact, it may be Materialism; but it is the flat contrary of Modernism. It is bound up, in the modern view, with the most monstrous, the most material, and therefore the most miraculous of miracles. It is specially connected with the most startling sort of dogma, which the Modernist can least accept; the Resurrection of the Body.

Or again, his argument for Revelation is quite rationalistic; and on the other side, decidedly democratic and popular. His argument for Revelation is not in the least an argument against Reason. On the contrary, he seems inclined to admit that truth could be reached by a rational process, if only it were rational enough; and also long enough. Indeed, something in his character, which I have called elsewhere optimism, and for which I know no other approximate term, led him rather to exaggerate the extent to which all men would ultimately listen to reason. In his controversies, he always assumes that they will listen to reason. That is, he does emphatically believe that men can be convinced by argument; when they reach the end of the argument. Only his common sense also told him that the argument never ends. I might convince a man that matter as the origin of Mind is quite meaningless, if he and I were very fond of each other and fought each other every night for forty years. But long before he was convinced on his deathbed, a thousand other materialists could have been born, and nobody can explain everything to everybody. St. Thomas takes the view that the souls of all the ordinary hard-working and simple-minded people are quite as important as the souls of thinkers and truth-seekers; and he asks how all these people are possibly to find time for the amount of reasoning that is needed to find truth. The whole tone of the passage shows both a respect for scientific enquiry and a strong sympathy with the average man. His argument for Revelation is not an argument against Reason; but it is an argument for Revelation. The conclusion he draws from it is that men must receive the highest moral truths in a miraculous manner; or most men would not receive them at all. His arguments are rational and natural; but his own deduction is all for the supernatural; and, as is common in the case of his argument, it is not easy to find any deduction except his own deduction. And when we come to that, we find it is something as simple as St. Francis himself could desire; the message from heaven; the story that is told out of the sky; the fairytale that is really true.

It is plainer still in more popular problems like Free Will. If St. Thomas stands for one thing more than another, it is what may be called subordinate sovereignties or autonomies. He was, if the flippancy may be used, a strong Home Ruler. We might even say he was always defending the independence of dependent things. He insisted that such a thing could have its own rights in its own region. It was his attitude to the Home Rule of the reason and even the senses; "Daughter am I in my father's house; but mistress in my own." And in exactly this sense he emphasised a certain dignity in Man, which was sometimes rather swallowed up in the purely theistic generalisations about God. Nobody would say he wanted to divide Man from God; but he did want to distinguish Man from God. In this strong sense of human dignity and liberty there is much that can be and is appreciated now as a noble humanistic liberality. But let us not forget that its upshot was that very Free Will, or moral responsibility of Man, which so many modern liberals would deny. Upon this sublime and perilous liberty hang heaven and hell, and all the mysterious drama of the soul. It is distinction and not division; but a man can divide himself from God, which, in a certain aspect, is the greatest distinction of all.

Again, though it is a more metaphysical matter, which must be mentioned later, and then only too slightly, it is the same with the old philosophical dispute about the Many and the One. Are things so different that they can never be classified; or so unified that they can never be distinguished? Without pretending to answer such questions here, we may say broadly that St. Thomas comes down definitely on the side of Variety, as a thing that is real as well as Unity. In this, and questions akin to this, he often departs from the great Greek philosophers who were sometimes his models; and entirely departs from the great Oriental philosophers who are in some sense his rivals. He seems fairly certain that the difference between chalk and cheese, or pigs and pelicans, is not a mere illusion, or dazzle of our bewildered mind blinded by a single light; but is pretty much what we all feel it to be. It may be said that this is mere common sense; the common sense that pigs are pigs; to that extent related to the earthbound Aristotelian common sense; to a human and even a heathen common sense. But note that here again the extremes of earth and heaven meet. It is also connected with the dogmatic Christian idea of the Creation; of a Creator who created pigs, as distinct from a Cosmos that merely evolved them.

In all these cases we see repeated the point stated at the start. The Thomist movement in metaphysics, like the Franciscan movement in morals and manners, was an enlargement and a liberation, it was emphatically a growth of Christian theology from within; it was emphatically not a shrinking of Christian theology under heathen or even human influences. The Franciscan was free to be a friar, instead of being bound to be a monk. But he was more of a Christian, more of a Catholic, even more of an ascetic. So the Thomist was free to be an Aristotelian, instead of being bound to be an Augustinian. But he was even more of a theologian; more of an orthodox theologian; more of a dogmatist, in having recovered through Aristotle the most defiant of all dogmas, the wedding of God with Man and therefore with Matter. Nobody can understand the greatness of the thirteenth century, who does not realise that it was a great growth of new things produced by a living thing. In that sense it was really bolder and freer than what we call the Renaissance, which was a resurrection of old things discovered in a dead thing. In that sense medievalism was not a Renascence, but rather a Nascence. It did not model its temples upon the tombs, or call up dead gods from Hades. It made an architecture as new as modern engineering; indeed it still remains the most modern architecture. Only it was followed at the Renaissance by a more antiquated architecture. In that sense the Renaissance might be called the Relapse. Whatever may be said of the Gothic and the Gospel according to St. Thomas, they were not a Relapse. It was a new thrust like the titanic thrust of Gothic engineering; and its strength was in a God who makes all things new.

In a word, St. Thomas was making Christendom more Christian in making it more Aristotelian. This is not a paradox but a plain truism, which can only be missed by those who may know what is meant by an Aristotelian, but have simply forgotten what is meant by a Christian. As compared with a Jew, a Moslem, a Buddhist, a Deist, or most obvious alternatives, a Christian means a man who believes that deity or sanctity has attached to matter or entered the world of the senses. Some modern writers, missing this simple point, have even talked as if the acceptance of Aristotle was a sort of concession to the Arabs; like a Modernist vicar making a concession to the Agnostics. They might as well say that the Crusades were a concession to the Arabs as say that Aquinas rescuing Aristotle from Averrhoes was a concession to the Arabs. The Crusaders wanted to recover the place where the body of Christ had been, because they believed, rightly or wrongly, that it was a Christian place. St. Thomas wanted to recover what was in essence the body of Christ itself; the sanctified body of the Son of Man which had become a miraculous medium between heaven and earth. And he wanted the body, and all its senses, because he believed, rightly or wrongly, that it was a Christian thing. It might be a humbler or homelier thing than the Platonic mind; that is why it was Christian. St. Thomas was, if you will, taking the lower road when he walked in the steps of Aristotle. So was God, when He worked in the workshop of Joseph.

Lastly, these two great men were not only united to each other but separated from most of their comrades and contemporaries by the very revolutionary character of their own revolution. In 1215, Dominic Guzman, the Castilian, founded an Order very similar to that of Francis; and, by a most curious coincidence of history, at almost exactly the same moment as Francis. It was directed primarily to preaching the Catholic philosophy to the Albigensian heretics; whose own philosophy was one of the many forms of that Manicheanism with which this story is much concerned. It had its roots in the remote mysticism and moral detachment of the East; and it was therefore inevitable that the Dominicans should be rather more a brotherhood of philosophers, where the Franciscans were by comparison a brotherhood of poets. For this and other reasons, St. Dominic and his followers are little known or understood in modern England; they were involved eventually in a religious war which followed on a theological argument; and there was something in the atmosphere of our country, during the last century or so, which made the theological argument even more incomprehensible than the religious war. The ultimate effect is in some ways curious; because St. Dominic, even more than St. Francis, was marked by that intellectual independence, and strict standard of virtue and veracity, which Protestant cultures are wont to regard as specially

Protestant. It was of him that the tale was told, and would certainly have been told more widely among us if it had been told of a Puritan, that the Pope pointed to his gorgeous Papal Palace and said, "Peter can no longer say `Silver and gold have I none'"; and the Spanish friar answered, "No, and neither can he now say, `Rise and walk.'"

Thus there is another way in which the popular story of St. Francis can be a sort of bridge between the modern and medieval world. And it is based on that very fact already mentioned: that St. Francis and St. Dominic stand together in history as having done the same work, and yet are divided in English popular tradition in the most strange and startling way. In their own lands they are like Heavenly Twins, irradiating the same light from heaven, seeming sometimes to be two saints in one halo, as another order depicted Holy Poverty as two knights on one horse. In the legends of our own land, they are about as much united as St. George and the Dragon. Dominic is still conceived as an Inquisitor devising thumbscrews; while Francis is already accepted as a humanitarian deploring mousetraps. It seems, for instance, quite natural to us, and full of the same associations of flowers and starry fancies, that the name of Francis should belong to Francis Thompson. But I fancy it would seem less natural to call him Dominic Thompson; or find that a man, with a long record of popular sympathies and practical tenderness to the poor, could bear such a name as Dominic Plater. It would sound as if he had been called Torquemada Thompson.

Now there must be something wrong behind this contradiction; turning those who were allies at home into antagonists abroad. On any other question, the fact would be apparent to common sense. Suppose English Liberals or Free-Traders found that, in remote parts of China, it was generally held that Cobden was a cruel monster but Bright a stainless saint. They would think there was a mistake somewhere. Suppose that American Evangelicals learned that in France or Italy, or other civilizations impenetrable by Moody and Sankey, there was a popular belief that Moody was an angel but Sankey a devil; they would guess that there must be a muddle somewhere. Some other later accidental distinction must have cut across the main course of a historical tendency. These parallels are not so fantastic as they may sound. Cobden and Bright have actually been called "child-torturers", in anger at their alleged callousness about the evils amended by the Factory Acts; and some would call the Moody and Sankey sermon on Hell a hellish exhibition. All that is a matter of opinion; but both men held the same sort of opinion, and there must be a blunder in an opinion that separates them so completely. And of course there is a complete blunder in the legend about St. Dominic. Those who know anything about St. Dominic know that he was a missionary and not a militant persecutor; that his contribution to religion was the Rosary and not the Rack; that his whole career is meaningless, unless we understand that his famous victories were victories of persuasion and not persecution. He did believe in the justification of persecution; in the sense that the secular arm could repress religious disorders. So did everybody else believe in persecution; and none more than the elegant blasphemer, Frederick II who believed in nothing else. Some say he was the first to burn heretics; but anyhow, he thought it was one of his imperial privileges and duties to persecute heretics. But to talk as if Dominic did nothing but persecute heretics, is like blaming Father Matthew, who persuaded millions of drunkards to take a temperance pledge, because the accepted law sometimes allowed a drunkard to be arrested by a policeman. It is to miss the whole point; which is that this particular man had a genius for conversion, quite apart from compulsion. The real difference between Francis and Dominic, which is no discredit to either of them, is that Dominic did happen to be confronted with a huge campaign for the conversion of heretics, while Francis had only the more subtle task of the conversion of human beings. It is an old story that, while we may need somebody like Dominic to convert the heathen to Christianity, we are in even greater need of somebody like Francis, to convert the Christians to Christianity. Still, we must not lose sight of St. Dominic's special problem, which was that of dealing with a whole population, kingdoms and cities and countrysides, that had drifted from the Faith and solidified into strange and abnormal new religions. That he did win back masses of men so deceived, merely by talking and preaching, remains an enormous triumph worthy of a colossal trophy. St. Francis is called humane because he tried to convert Saracens and failed; St. Dominic is called bigoted and besotted because he tried to convert Albigensians and succeeded. But we happen to be in a curious nook or corner of the hills of history, from which we can see Assisi and the Umbrian hills, but are out of sight of the vast battle-field of the Southern Crusade; the miracle of Muret and the greater miracle of Dominic, when the roots of the Pyrenees and the shores of the Mediterranean saw defeated the Asiatic despair.

But there is an earlier and more essential link between Dominic and Francis, which is more to the immediate purpose of this book. They were in later times bracketed in glory because they were in their own time bracketed in infamy; or at least in unpopularity. For they did the most unpopular thing that men can do; they started a popular movement. A man who dares to make a direct appeal to the populace always makes a long series of enemies-- beginning with the populace. In proportion as the poor begin to understand that he means to help and not hurt them, the solid classes above begin to close in, resolved to hinder and not help. The rich, and even the learned, sometimes feel not unreasonably that the thing will change the world, not only in its worldliness or its worldly wisdom, but to some extent perhaps in its real wisdom. Such a feeling was not unnatural in this case; when we consider, for instance, St. Francis's really reckless attitude about rejecting books and scholarship; or the tendency that the Friars afterwards showed to appeal to the Pope in contempt of local bishops and ecclesiastical officers. In short, St. Dominic and St. Francis created a Revolution, quite as popular and unpopular as the French Revolution. But it is very hard today to feel that even the French Revolution was as fresh as it really was. The Marseillaise once sounded like the human voice of the volcano or the dance-tune of the earthquake, and the kings of the earth trembled, some fearing that the heavens might fall; some fearing far more that justice might be done. The Marseillaise is played today at diplomatic dinner-parties, where smiling monarchs meet beaming millionaires, and is rather less revolutionary than "Home Sweet Home." Also, it is highly pertinent to recall, the modern revolutionists would now call the revolt of the French Jacobins insufficient, just as they would call the revolt of the Friars insufficient. They would say that neither went far enough; but many, in their own day, thought they went very much too far. In the case of the Friars, the higher orders of the State, and to some extent even of the Church, were profoundly shocked at such a loosening of wild popular preachers among the people. It is not at all easy for us to feel that distant events were thus disconcerting and even disreputable. Revolutions turn into institutions; revolts that renew the youth of old societies in their turn grow old; and the past, which was full of new things, of splits and innovations and insurrections, seems to us a single texture of tradition.

But if we wish for one fact that will make vivid this shock of change and challenge, and show how raw and ragged, how almost rowdy in its reckless novelty, how much of the gutter and how remote from refined life, this experiment of the Friars did really seem to many in its own day, there is here a very relevant fact to reveal it. It shows how much a settled and already ancient Christendom did feel it as something like the end of an age; and how the very roads of the earth seem to shake under the feet of the new and nameless army; the march of the Beggars. A mystic nursery rhyme suggests the atmosphere of such a crisis: "Hark, hark, the dogs do bark; the Beggars are coming to town." There were many towns that almost fortified themselves against them and many watchdogs of property and rank did really bark, and hark loudly, when those Beggars went by; but louder was the singing of the Beggars who sang their Canticle to the Sun, and louder the baying of the Hounds of Heaven; the Domini canes of the medieval pun; the Dogs of God. And if we would measure how real and rending seemed that revolution, what a break with the past, we can see it in the first and most extraordinary event in the life of St. Thomas Aquinas.

--/--

II THE RUNAWAY ABBOT

Thomas Aquinas, in a strange and rather symbolic manner, sprang out of the very centre of the civilised world of his time; the central knot or coil of the powers then controlling Christendom. He was closely connected with all of them; even with some of them that might well be described as destroying Christendom. The whole religious quarrel, the whole international quarrel, was for him, a family quarrel. He was born in the purple, almost literally on the hem of the imperial purple; for his own cousin was the Holy Roman Emperor. He could have quartered half the kingdoms of Europe on his shield-- if he had not thrown away the shield. He was Italian and French and German and in every way European. On one side, he inherited from the energy that made the episode of the Normans, whose strange organising raids rang and rattled like flights of arrows in the corners of Europe and the ends of the earth; one flight of them following Duke William far northward through the blinding snows to Chester; another treading in Greek and Punic footsteps through the island of Sicily to the gates of Syracuse. Another bond of blood bound him to the great Emperors of the Rhine and Danube who claimed to wear the crown of Charlemagne; Red Barbarossa, who sleeps under the rushing river, was his great uncle, and Frederick II, the Wonder of the World, his second cousin, and yet he held by a hundred more intimate ties to the lively inner life, the local vivacity, the little walled nations and the thousand shrines of Italy. While inheriting this physical kinship with the Emperor, he maintained far more firmly his spiritual kinship with the Pope. He understood the meaning of Rome, and in what sense it was still ruling the world; and was not likely to think that the German Emperors of his times any more than the Greek Emperors of a previous time, would be able to be really Roman in defiance of Rome. To this cosmopolitan comprehensiveness in his inherited position, he afterwards added many things of his own, that made for mutual understanding among the peoples, and gave him something of the character of an ambassador and interpreter. He travelled a great deal; he was not only well known in Paris and the German universities, but he almost certainly visited England; probably he went to Oxford and London; and it has been said that we may be treading in the footsteps of him and his Dominican companions, whenever we go down by the river to the railway-station that still bears the name of Black-friars. But the truth applies to the travels of his mind as well as his body. He studied the literature even of the opponents of Christianity much more carefully and impartially than was then the fashion; he really tried to understand the Arabian Aristotelianism of the Moslems; and wrote a highly humane and reasonable treatise on the problem of the treatment of the Jews. He always attempted to look at everything from the inside; but he was certainly lucky in having been born in the inside of the state system and the high politics of his day. What he thought of them may perhaps be inferred from the next passage in his history.

St. Thomas might thus stand very well for the International Man, to borrow the title of a modern book. But it is only fair to remember that he lived in the International Age; in a world that was international in a sense not to be suggested in any modern book, or by any modern man. If I remember right, the modern candidate for the post of International Man was Cobden, who was an almost abnormally national man, a narrowly national man; a very fine type, but one which can hardly be imagined except as moving between Midhurst and Manchester. He had an international policy and he indulged in international travel; but if he always remained a national person, it was because he remained a normal person; that is normal to the nineteenth century. But it was not so in the thirteenth century. There a man of international influence, like Cobden, could be also almost a man of international nationality. The names of nations and cities and places of origin did not connote that deep division that is the mark of the modern world. Aquinas as a student was nicknamed the ox of Sicily, though his birthplace was near Naples; but this did not prevent the city of Paris regarding him as simply and solidly as a Parisian, because he had been a glory of the Sorbonne, that it proposed to bury his bones when he was dead. Or take a more obvious contrast with modern times. Consider what is meant in most modern talk by a German Professor. And then realise that the greatest of all German Professors, Albertus Magnus, was himself one of the glories of the University of Paris; and it was in Paris that Aquinas supported him. Think of the modern German Professor being famous throughout Europe for his popularity when lecturing in Paris.

Thus, if there was war in Christendom, it was international war in the special sense in which we speak of international peace. It was not the war of two nations; but the war of two internationalisms: of two World States: the Catholic Church and the Holy Roman Empire. The political crisis in Christendom affected the life of Aquinas at the start in one sharp disaster, and afterwards in many indirect ways. It had many elements; the Crusades; the embers of the Albigensian pessimism over which St. Dominic had triumphed in argument and Simon de Montfort in arms; the dubious experiment of an Inquisition which started from it; and many other things. But, broadly speaking, it is the period of the great duel between the Popes and the Emperors, that is the German Emperors who called themselves Holy Roman Emperors, the House of Hohenstaufen. The particular period of the life of Aquinas, however, is entirely overshadowed by the particular Emperor who was himself more an Italian than a German; the brilliant Frederick II who was called the Wonder of the World. It may be reminded, in passing, that Latin was the most living of languages at this time, and we often feel a certain weakness in the necessary translation. For I seem to have read somewhere that the word used was stronger than the Wonder of the World; that his medieval title was Stupor Mundi, which is more exactly the Stupefaction of the World. Something of the sort may be noted later of philosophical language, and the weakness of translating a word like Ens by a word like Being. But for the moment the parenthesis has another application; for it might well be said that Frederick did indeed stupefy the world; that there was something stunning and blinding about the blows he struck at religion, as in that blow which almost begins the biography of Thomas Aquinas. He may also be called stupefying in another sense; in that his very brilliancy has made some of his modern admirers very stupid.

For Frederick II is the first figure, and that a rather fierce and ominous figure, who rides across the scene of his cousin's birth and boyhood: a scene of wild fighting and of fire. And it may be allowable to pause for a parenthesis upon his name, for two particular reasons: first that his romantic reputation, even among modern historians, covers and partly conceals the true background of the times and second that the tradition in question directly involves the whole status of St. Thomas Aquinas. The nineteenth century view, still so strangely called the modern view by many moderns, touching such a man as Frederick II was well summed up by some solid Victorian, I think by Macaulay; Frederick was "a statesman in an age of Crusaders; a philosopher in an age of monks." It may be noted that the antithesis invokes the assumption that a Crusader cannot easily be a statesman; and that a monk cannot easily be a philosopher. Yet, to take only that special instance, it would be easy to point out that the cases of two famous men in the age of Frederick II would alone be strong enough to upset both the assumption and the antithesis. St. Louis, though a Crusader and even an unsuccessful Crusader, was really a far more successful statesman than Frederick II. By the test of practical politics, he popularised, solidified and sanctified the most powerful government in Europe, the order and concentration of the French Monarchy; the single dynasty that steadily increased its strength for five hundred years up to the glories of the Grand Siecle whereas Frederick went down in ruin before the Papacy and the Republics and a vast combination of priests and peoples. The Holy Roman Empire he wished to found was an ideal rather in the sense of a dream; it was certainly never a fact like the square and solid State which the French statesman did found. Or, to take another example from the next generation, one of the most strictly practical statesmen in history, our own Edward I, was also a Crusader.

The other half of the antithesis is even more false and here even more relevant. Frederick II was not a philosopher in the age of monks. He was a gentleman dabbling in philosophy in the age of the monk Thomas Aquinas. He was doubtless an intelligent and even brilliant gentleman; but if he did leave any notes on the nature of Being and Becoming, or the precise sense in which realities can be relative to Reality, I do not imagine those notes are now exciting undergraduates at Oxford or literary men in Paris, let alone the little groups of Thomists who have already sprung up even in New York and Chicago. It is no disrespect to the Emperor to say that he certainly was not a philosopher in the sense in which Thomas Aquinas was a philosopher, let alone so great or so universal or so permanent a philosopher. And Thomas Aquinas lived in that very age of monks, and in that very world of monks, which Macaulay talks of as if it were incapable of producing philosophy.

We need not dwell on the causes of this Victorian prejudice, which some still think so well advanced. It arose mainly from one narrow or insular notion; that no man could possibly be building up the best of the modern world, if he went with the main movement of the medieval world. These Victorians thought that only the heretic had ever helped humanity; only the man who nearly wrecked medieval civilisation could be of any use in constructing modern civilisation. Hence came a score of comic fables; as that the cathedrals must have been built by a secret society of Freemasons; or that the epic of Dante must be a cryptogram referring to the political hopes of Garibaldi. But the generalisation is not in its nature probable and it is not in fact true. This medieval period was rather specially the period of communal or corporate thinking, and in some matters it was really rather larger than the individualistic modern thinking. This could be proved in a flash from the mere fact of the use of the word 'statesman.' To a man of Macaulay's period, a statesman always meant a man who maintained the more narrow national interests of his own state against other states, as Richelieu maintained those of France, or Chatham of England, or Bismarck of Prussia. But if a man actually wanted to defend all these states, to combine all these states, to make a living brotherhood of all these states, to resist some outer peril as from the Mongolian millions--then that poor devil, of course, could not really be called a statesman. He was only a Crusader.

In this way it is but fair to Frederick II to say that he was a Crusader; if he was also rather like an Anti-Crusader. Certainly he was an international statesman. Indeed he was a particular type, which may be called an international soldier. The international soldier is always very much disliked by internationalists. They dislike Charlemagne and Charles V and Napoleon; and everybody who tried to create the World State for which they cry aloud day and night. But Frederick is more dubious and less doubted; he was supposed to be the head of the Holy Roman Empire; and accused of wanting to be the head of a very Unholy Roman Empire. But even if he were Antichrist, he would still be a witness to the unity of Christendom.

Nevertheless, there is a queer quality in that time; which, while it was international was also internal and intimate. War, in the wide modern sense, is possible, not because more men disagree, but because more men agree. Under the peculiarly modern coercions, such as Compulsory Education and Conscription, there are such very large peaceful areas, that they can all agree upon War. In that age men disagreed even about war; and peace might break out anywhere. Peace was interrupted by feuds and feuds by pardons. Individuality wound in and out of a maze; spiritual extremes were walled up with one another in one little walled town; and we see the great soul of Dante divided, a cloven flame; loving and hating his own city. This individual complexity is intensely vivid in the particular story we have here to tell, in a very rough outline. If anyone wishes to know what is meant by saying that action was more individual, and indeed incalculable, he may well note some of the stages in the story of the great feudal house of Aquino, which had its castle not far from Naples. In the mere hasty anecdote we have now to tell, we shall note in succession five or six stages of this sort. Landulf of Aquino, a heavy feudal fighter typical of the times, rode in armour behind the imperial banners, and attacked a monastery, because the Emperor regarded the monastery as a fortress held for his enemy the Pope. Later, we shall see the same feudal Lord sent his own son to the same monastery; probably on the friendly advice of the same Pope. Later still, another of his sons, entirely on his own, rebelled against the Emperor, and went over to the armies of the Pope. For this he was executed by the Emperor, with promptitude and despatch. I wish we knew more about that brother of Thomas Aquinas who risked and lost his life to support the cause of the Pope which was in all human essentials the cause of the People. He may not have been a saint; but he must have had some qualities of a martyr. Meanwhile, two other brothers, still ardent and active apparently in the service of the Emperor who killed the third brother, themselves proceeded to kidnap another brother, because they did not approve of his sympathy with the new social movements in religion. That is the sort of tangle in which this one distinguished medieval family found itself. It was not a war of nations, but it was a rather widespread family quarrel.

The reason for dwelling here, however, upon the position of the Emperor Frederick, as a type of his time, in his culture and his violence, in his concern for philosophy and his quarrel with religion, is not merely concerned with these things. He may here be the first figure that crosses the stage, because one of his very typical actions precipitated the first action, or obstinate inaction, which began the personal adventures of Thomas Aquinas in this world. The story also illustrates the extraordinary tangle in which a family like that of the Count of Aquino found itself; being at once so close to the Church and so much at odds with it. For Frederick II, in the course of these remarkable manoeuvres, military and political, which ranged from burning heretics to allying himself with Saracens, made a swoop as of a predatory eagle (and the Imperial eagle was rather predatory) upon a very large and wealthy monastery; the Benedictine Abbey of Monte Cassino; and stormed and sacked the place.

Some miles from the monastery of Monte Cassino stood a great crag or cliff, standing up like a pillar of the Apennines. It was crowned with a castle that bore the name of The Dry Rock, and was the eyrie in which the eaglets of the Aquino branch of the Imperial family were nursed to fly. Here lived Count Landulf of Aquino, who was the father of Thomas Aquinas and some seven other sons. In military affairs he doubtless rode with his family, in the feudal manner; and apparently had something to do with the destruction of the monastery. But it was typical of the tangle of the time, that Count Landulf seems afterwards to have thought that it would be a tactful and delicate act to put in his son Thomas as Abbot of the monastery. This would be of the nature of a graceful apology to the Church, and also, it would appear, the solution of a family difficulty.

For it had been long apparent to Count Landulf that nothing could be done with his seventh son Thomas, except to make him an Abbot or something of that kind. Born in 1226, he had from childhood a mysterious objection to becoming a predatory eagle, or even to taking an ordinary interest in falconry or tilting or any other gentlemanly pursuits. He was a large and heavy and quiet boy, and phenomenally silent, scarcely opening his mouth except to say suddenly to his schoolmaster in an explosive manner, "What is God?" The answer is not recorded but it is probable that the asker went on worrying out answers for himself. The only place for a person of this kind was the Church and presumably the cloister; and so far as that went, there was no particular difficulty. It was easy enough for a man in Count Landulf's position to arrange with some monastery for his son to be received there; and in this particular case he thought it would be a good idea if he were received in some official capacity, that would be worthy of his worldly rank. So everything was smoothly arranged for Thomas Aquinas becoming a monk, which would seem to be what he himself wanted; and sooner or later becoming Abbot of Monte Cassino. And then the curious thing happened.

In so far as we may follow rather dim and disputed events, it would seem that the young Thomas Aquinas walked into his father's castle one day and calmly announced that he had become one of the Begging Friars, of the new order founded by Dominic the Spaniard; much as the eldest son of the squire might go home and airily inform the family that he had married a gypsy; or the heir of a Tory Duke state that he was walking tomorrow with the Hunger Marchers organised by alleged Communists. By this, as has been noted already, we may pretty well measure the abyss between the old monasticism and the new, and the earthquake of the Dominican and Franciscan revolution. Thomas had appeared to wish to be a Monk; and the gates were silently opened to him and the long avenues of the abbey, the very carpet, so to speak, laid for him up to the throne of the mitred abbot. He said he wished to be a Friar, and his family flew at him like wild beasts; his brothers pursued him along the public roads, half-rent his friar's frock from his back and finally locked him up in a tower like a lunatic.

It is not very easy to trace the course of this furious family quarrel, and how it eventually spent itself against the tenacity of the young Friar; according to some stories, his mother's disapproval was short-lived and she went over to his side; but it was not only his relatives that were embroiled. We might say that the central governing class of Europe, which partly consisted of his family, were in a turmoil over the deplorable youth; even the Pope was asked for tactful intervention, and it was at one time proposed that Thomas should be allowed to wear the Dominican habit while acting as Abbot in the Benedictine Abbey. To many this would seem a tactful compromise; but it did not commend itself to the narrow medieval mind of Thomas Aquinas. He indicated sharply that he wished to be a Dominican in the Dominican Order, and not at a fancy-dress ball; and the diplomatic proposal appears to have been dropped.

Thomas of Aquino wanted to be a Friar. It was a staggering fact to his contemporaries; and it is rather an intriguing fact even to us; for this desire, limited literally and strictly to this statement, was the one practical thing to which his will was clamped with adamantine obstinacy till his death. He would not be an Abbot; he would not be a Monk; he would not even be a Prior or ruler in his own fraternity; he would not be a prominent or important Friar; he would be a Friar. It is as if

Napoleon had insisted on remaining a private soldier all his life. Something in this heavy, quiet, cultivated, rather academic gentleman would not be satisfied till he was, by fixed authoritative proclamation and official pronouncement, established and appointed to be a Beggar. It is all the more interesting because, while he did more than his duty a thousand times over, he was not at all like a Beggar; nor at all likely to be a good Beggar. He had nothing of the native vagabond about him, as had his great precursors; he was not born with something of the wandering minstrel, like St. Francis; or something of the tramping missionary, like St. Dominic. But he insisted upon putting himself under military orders, to do these things at the will of another, if required. He may be compared with some of the more magnanimous aristocrats who have enrolled themselves in revolutionary armies; or some of the best of the poets and scholars who volunteered as private soldiers in the Great War. Something in the courage and consistency of Dominic and Francis had challenged his deep sense of justice; and while remaining a very reasonable person, and even a diplomatic one, he never let anything shake the iron immobility of this one decision of his youth; nor was he to be turned from his tall and towering ambition to take the lowest place.

The first effect of his decision, as we have seen, was much more stimulating and even startling. The General of the Dominicans, under whom Thomas had enrolled himself, was probably well aware of the diplomatic attempts to dislodge him and the worldly difficulties of resisting them. His expedient was to take his young follower out of Italy altogether; bidding him proceed with a few other friars to Paris. There was something prophetic even about this first progress of the travelling teacher of the nations; for Paris was indeed destined to be in some sense the goal of his spiritual journey; since it was there that he was to deliver both his great defence of the Friars and his great defiance to the antagonists of Aristotle. But this his first journey to Paris was destined to be broken off very short indeed. The friars had reached a turn of the road by a wayside fountain, a little way north of Rome, when they were overtaken by a wild cavalcade of captors, who seized on Thomas like brigands, but who were in fact only rather needlessly agitated brothers. He had a large number of brothers: perhaps only two were here involved. Indeed he was the seventh; and friends of Birth Control may lament that this philosopher was needlessly added to the noble line of ruffians who kidnapped him. It was an odd affair altogether. There is something quaint and picturesque in the idea of kidnapping a begging friar, who might in a sense be called a runaway abbot. There is a comic and tragic tangle in the motives and purposes of such a trio of strange kinsmen. There is a sort of Christian cross-purposes in the contrast between the feverish illusion of the importance of things, always marking men who are called practical; and the much more practical pertinacity of the man who is called theoretical.

Thus at least did those three strange brethren stagger or trail along their tragic road, tied together, as it were, like criminal and constable; only that the criminals were making the arrest. So their figures are seen for an instant against the horizon of history; brothers as sinister as any since Cain and Abel. For this queer outrage in the great family of Aquino does really stand out symbolically, as representing something that will forever make the Middle Ages a mystery and a bewilderment; capable of sharply contrasted interpretations like darkness and light. For in two of those men there raged, we might say screamed, a savage pride of blood and blazonry of arms, though they were princes of the most refined world of their time, which would seem more suitable to a tribe dancing round a totem. For the moment they had forgotten everything except the name of a family, that is narrower than a tribe, and far narrower than a nation. And the third figure of that trio, born of the same mother and perhaps visibly one with the others in face or form, had a conception of brotherhood broader than most modern democracy, for it was not national but international; a faith in mercy and modesty far deeper than any mere mildness of manners in the modern world; and a drastic oath of poverty, which would now be counted quite a mad exaggeration of the revolt against plutocracy and pride. Out of the same Italian castle came two savages and one sage; or one saint more pacific than most modern sages. That is the double aspect confusing a hundred controversies. That is what makes the riddle of the medieval age; that it was not one age but two ages. We look into the moods of some men, and it might be the Stone Age; we look into the minds of other men, and they might be living in the Golden Age; in the most modern sort of Utopia. There were always good men and bad men; but in this time good men who were subtle lived with bad men who were simple. They lived in the same family; they were brought up in the same nursery; and they came out to struggle, as the brothers of Aquino struggled by the wayside, when they dragged the new friar along the road and shut him up in the castle on the hill.

When his relations tried to despoil him of his friar's frock he seems to have laid about them in the fighting manner of his fathers, and it would seem successfully, since this attempt was abandoned. He accepted the imprisonment itself with his customary composure, and probably did not mind very much whether he was left to philosophise in a dungeon or in a cell. Indeed there is something in the way the whole tale is told, which suggests that through a great part of that strange abduction, he had been carried about like a lumbering stone statue. Only one tale told of his captivity shows him merely in anger; and that shows him angrier than he ever was before or after. It struck the imagination of his own time for more important reasons; but it has an interest that is psychological as well as moral. For once in his life, for the first time and the last, Thomas of Aquino was really hors de lui; riding a storm outside that tower of intellect and contemplation in which he commonly lived. And that was when his brothers introduced into his room some specially gorgeous and painted courtesan, with the idea of surprising him by a sudden temptation, or at least involving him in a scandal. His anger was justified, even by less strict moral standards than his own; for the meanness was even worse than the foulness of the expedient. Even on the lowest grounds, he knew his brothers knew, and they knew that he knew, that it was an insult to him as a gentleman to suppose that he would break his pledge upon so base a provocation; and he had behind him a far more terrible sensibility; all that huge ambition of humility which was to him the voice of God out of heaven. In this one flash alone we see that huge unwieldy figure in an attitude of activity, or even animation; and he was very animated indeed. He sprang from his seat and snatched a brand out of the fire, and stood brandishing it like a flaming sword. The woman not unnaturally shrieked and fled, which was all that he wanted; but it is quaint to think of what she must have thought of that madman of monstrous stature juggling with flames and apparently threatening to burn down the house. All he did, however, was to stride after her to the door and bang and bar it behind her; and then, with a sort of impulse of violent ritual, he rammed the burning brand into the door, blackening and blistering it with one big black sign of the cross. Then he returned, and dropped it again into the fire; and sat down on that seat of sedentary scholarship, that chair of philosophy, that secret throne of contemplation, from which he never rose again.

--/--

III THE ARISTOTELIAN REVOLUTION

Albert, the Swabian, rightly called the Great, was the founder of modern science. He did more than any other man to prepare that process, which has turned the alchemist into the chemist, and the astrologer into the astronomer. It is odd that, having been in his time, in this sense almost the first astronomer, he now lingers in legend almost as the last astrologer. Serious historians are abandoning the absurd notion that the mediaeval Church persecuted all scientists as wizards. It is very nearly the opposite of the truth. The world sometimes persecuted them as wizards, and sometimes ran after them as wizards; the sort of pursuing that is the reverse of persecuting. The Church alone regarded them really and solely as scientists. Many an enquiring cleric was charged with mere magic in making his lenses and mirrors; he was charged by his rude and rustic neighbours; and would probably have been charged in exactly the same way if they had been Pagan neighbours or Puritan neighbours or Seventh-Day Adventist neighbours. But even then he stood a better chance when judged by the Papacy, than if he had been merely lynched by the laity. The Catholic Pontiff did not denounce Albertus Magnus as a magician. It was the half-heathen tribes of the north who admired him as a magician. It is the half-heathen tribes of the industrial towns today, the readers of cheap dream-books, and quack pamphlets, and newspaper prophets, who still admire him as an astrologer. It is admitted that the range of his recorded knowledge, of strictly material and mechanical facts, was amazing in a man of his time. It is true that, in most other cases, there was a certain limitation to the data of medieval science; but this certainly had nothing to do with medieval religion. For the data of Aristotle, and the great Greek civilisation, were in many ways more limited still. But it is not really so much a question of access to the facts, as of attitude to the facts. Most of the Schoolmen, if informed by the only informants they had that a unicorn has one horn or a salamander lives in the fire, still used it more as an illustration of logic than an incident of life. What they really said was, "If a Unicorn has one horn, two unicorns have as many horns as one cow." And that is not one inch the less a fact because the unicorn is a fable. But with Albertus in medieval times, as with Aristotle in ancient times, there did begin something like the idea of emphasising the question: "But does the unicorn only have one horn or the salamander a fire instead of a fireside?" Doubtless when the social and geographical limits of medieval life began to allow them to search the fire for salamanders or the desert for unicorns, they had to modify many of their scientific ideas. A fact which will expose them to the very proper scorn of a generation of scientists which has just discovered that Newton is nonsense, that space is limited, and that there is no such thing as an atom.

This great German, known in his most famous period as a professor in Paris, was previously for some time professor at Cologne. In that beautiful Roman city, there gathered round him in thousands the lovers of that extraordinary life; the student life of the Middle Ages. They came together in great groups called Nations; and the fact illustrates very well the difference between medieval nationalism and modern nationalism. For although there might any morning be a brawl between the Spanish students and the Scottish students, or between the Flemish and the French, and swords flash or stones fly on the most purely patriotic principles, the fact remains that they had all come to the same school to learn the same philosophy. And though that might not prevent the starting of a quarrel, it might have a great deal to do with the ending of it. Before these motley groups of men from the ends of the earth, the father of science unrolled his scroll of strange wisdom; of sun and comet, of fish and bird. He was an Aristotelian developing, as it were, the one experimental hint of Aristotle; and in this he was entirely original. He cared less to be original about the deeper matters of men and morals; about which he was content to hand on a decent and Christianised Aristotelianism; he was even in a sense ready to compromise upon the merely metaphysical issue of the Nominalists and the Realists. He would never have maintained alone the great war that was coming, for a balanced and humanised Christianity; but when it came, he was entirely on its side. He was called the Universal Doctor, because of the range of his scientific studies; yet he was in truth a specialist. The popular legend is never quite wrong; if a man of science is a magician, he was a magician. And the man of science has always been much more of a magician than the priest; since he would "control the elements" rather than submit to the Spirit who is more elementary than the elements.

Among the students thronging into the lecture-rooms there was one student, conspicuous by his tall and bulky figure, and completely failing or refusing to be conspicuous for anything else. He was so dumb in the debates that his fellows began to assume an American significance in the word dumbness; for in that land it is a synonym for dullness. It is clear that, before long, even his imposing stature began to have only the ignominious immensity of the big boy left behind in the lowest form. He was called the Dumb Ox. He was the object, not merely of mockery, but of pity. One good-natured student pitied him so much as to try to help him with his lessons, going over the elements of logic like an alphabet in a horn-book. The dunce thanked him with pathetic politeness; and the philanthropist went on swimmingly, till he came to a passage about which he was himself a little doubtful; about which, in point of fact, he was wrong. Whereupon the dunce, with every appearance of embarrassment and disturbance, pointed out a possible solution which happened to be right. The benevolent student was left staring, as at a monster, at this mysterious lump of ignorance and intelligence; and strange whispers began to run round the schools.

A regular religious biographer of Thomas Aquinas (who, needless to say, was the dunce in question) has said that by the end of this interview "his love of truth overcame his humility"; which, properly understood, is precisely true. But it does not, in the secondary psychological and social sense, describe all the welter of elements that went on within that massive head. All the relatively few anecdotes about Aquinas have a very peculiar vividness if we visualise the type of man; and this is an excellent example. Amid those elements was something of the difficulty which the generalising intellect has in adapting itself suddenly to a tiny detail of daily life; there was something of the shyness of really well-bred people about showing off; there was something even, perhaps, of that queer paralysis, and temptation to prefer even misunderstandings to long explanations, which led Sir James Barrie, in his amusing sketch, to allow himself to be saddled with a Brother Henry he never possessed, rather than exert himself to put in a word of warning. These other elements doubtless worked with the very extraordinary humility of this very extraordinary man; but another element worked with his equally unquestionable "love of truth" in bringing the misunderstanding to an end. It is an element that must never be left out of the make-up of St. Thomas. However dreamy or distracted or immersed in theories he might be, he had any amount of Common Sense; and by the time it came, not only to being taught, but to being taught wrong, there was something in him that said sharply, "Oh, this has got to stop!"

It seems probable that it was Albertus Magnus himself, the lecturer and learned teacher of all these youths, who first suspected something of the kind. He gave Thomas small jobs to do, of annotation or exposition; he persuaded him to banish his bashfulness so as to take part in at least one debate. He was a very shrewd old man and had studied the habits of other animals besides the salamander and the unicorn. He had studied many specimens of the most monstrous of all monstrosities; that is called Man. He knew the signs and marks of the sort of man, who is in an innocent way something of a monster among men. He was too good a schoolmaster not to know that the dunce is not always a dunce. He learned with amusement that this dunce had been nicknamed the Dumb Ox by his schoolfellows. All that is natural enough; but it does not take away the savour of something rather strange and symbolic, about the extraordinary emphasis with which he spoke at last. For Aquinas was still generally known only as one obscure and obstinately unresponsive pupil, among many more brilliant and promising pupils, when the great Albert broke silence with his famous cry and prophecy; "You call him a Dumb Ox; I tell you this Dumb Ox shall bellow so loud that his bellowings will fill the world."

To Albertus Magnus, as to Aristotle or Augustine or any number of other and older teachers, St. Thomas was always ready, with the hearty sort of humility, to give thanks for all his thinking. None the less, his own thinking was an advance on Albertus and the other Aristotelians, just as it was an advance on Augustine and the Augustinians. Albert had drawn attention to the direct study of natural facts, if only through fables like the unicorn and the salamander but the monster called Man awaited a much more subtle and flexible vivi-section. The two men, however, became close friends and their friendship counts for a great deal in this central fight of the Middle Ages. For, as we shall see, the rehabilitation of Aristotle was a revolution almost as revolutionary as the exaltation of Dominic and Francis; and St. Thomas was destined to play a striking part in both.

It will be realised that the Aquino family had ultimately abandoned its avenging pursuit of its ugly duckling; who, as a black friar, should perhaps be called its black sheep. Of that escape some picturesque stories are told. The black sheep generally profits at last by quarrels among the white sheep of a family. They begin by quarrelling with him, but they end by quarrelling with each other. There is a rather confusing account concerning which members of his family came over to his side, while he was still imprisoned in the tower. But it is a fact that he was very fond of his sisters, and therefore probably not a fable that it was they who engineered his escape. According to the story, they rigged up a rope to the top of the tower, attached to a big basket, and it must have been rather a big basket if he was indeed lowered in this fashion from his prison, and escaped into the world. Anyhow, he did escape by energy, external or internal. But it was only an individual energy. The world was still pursuing and persecuting the Friars, quite as much as when they fled along the road to Rome. Thomas Aquinas had the good fortune to gather under the shadow of the one great outstanding Friar, whose respectability it was difficult to dispute, the learned and orthodox Albertus; but even he and his were soon troubled by the growing storm that threatened the new popular movements in the Church. Albertus was summoned to Paris, to receive the degree of a Doctor; but everyone knew that every move in that game had the character of a challenge. He made only the request, which probably looked like an eccentric request, that he should take his Dumb Ox with him. They set out, like ordinary Friars or religious vagabonds; they slept in such monasteries as they could find; and finally in the monastery of St. James in Paris, where Thomas met another Friar who was also another friend.

Perhaps under the shadow of the storm that menaced all Friars, Bonaventure, the Franciscan, grew into so great a friendship with Thomas the Dominican, that their contemporaries compared them to David and Jonathan. The point is of some interest; because it would be quite easy to represent the Franciscan and the Dominican as flatly contradicting each other. The Franciscan may be represented as the Father of all the Mystics; and the Mystics can be represented as men who maintain that the final fruition or joy of the soul is rather a sensation than a thought. The motto of the Mystics has always been, "Taste and see." Now St. Thomas also began by saying, "Taste and see"; but he said it of the first rudimentary impressions of the human animal. It might well be maintained that the Franciscan puts Taste last and the Dominican puts it first. It might be said that the Thomist begins with something solid like the taste of an apple, and afterwards deduces a divine life for the intellect; while the Mystic exhausts the intellect first, and says finally that the sense of God is something like the taste of an apple. A common enemy might claim that St. Thomas begins with the taste of fruit and St. Bonaventure ends with the taste of fruit. But they are both right; if I may say so, it is a privilege of people who contradict each other in their cosmos to be both right. The Mystic is right in saying that the relation of God and Man is essentially a love-story; the pattern and type of all love-stories. The Dominican rationalist is equally right in saying that the intellect is at home in the topmost heavens; and that the appetite for truth may outlast and even devour all the duller appetites of man.

At the moment Aquinas and Bonaventure were encouraged in the possibility that they were both right; by the almost universal agreement that they were both wrong. It was in any case a time of wild disturbance, and, as is common in such times, those who were trying to put things right were most vigorously accused of putting things wrong. Nobody knew who would win in that welter; Islam, or the Manichees of the Midi; or the two-faced and mocking Emperor; or the Crusades; or the old Orders of Christendom. But some men had a very vivid feeling that everything was breaking up; and that all the recent experiments or excesses were part of the same social dissolution; and there were two things that such men regarded as signs of ruin; one was the awful apparition of Aristotle out of the East, a sort of Greek god supported by Arabian worshippers; and the other was the new freedom of the Friars. It was the opening of the monastery and the scattering of the monks to wander over the world. The general feeling that they wandered like sparks from a furnace hitherto contained; the furnace of the abnormal love of God: the sense that they would utterly unbalance the common people with the counsels of perfection; that they would drift into being demagogues; all this finally burst out in a famous book called The Perils of the Latter Times, by a furious reactionary, William de St. Amour. It challenged the French King and the Pope, so that they established an enquiry. And Aquinas and Bonaventure, the two incongruous friends, with their respectively topsy-turvy universes, went up to Rome together, to defend the freedom of the Friars.

Thomas Aquinas defended the great vow of his youth, for freedom and for the poor; and it was probably the topmost moment of his generally triumphant career; for he turned back the whole backward movement of his time. Responsible authorities have said that, but for him, the whole great popular movement of the Friars might have been destroyed. With this popular victory the shy and awkward student finally becomes a historical character and a public man. After that, he was identified with the Mendicant Orders. But while St. Thomas may be said to have made his name in the defence of the Mendicant Orders against the reactionaries, who took the same view of them as his own family had taken, there is generally a difference between a man making his name and a man really doing his work. The work of Thomas Aquinas was yet to come; but less shrewd observers than he could already see that it was coming. Broadly speaking, the danger was the danger of the orthodox, or those who too easily identify the old order with the orthodox, forcing a final and conclusive condemnation of Aristotle. There had already been rash and random condemnations to that effect, issued here and there, and the pressure of the narrower Augustinians upon the Pope and the principal judges became daily more pressing. The peril had appeared, not unnaturally, because of the historical and geographical accident of the Moslem proximity to the culture of Byzantium. The Arabs had got hold of the Greek manuscripts before the Latins who were the true heirs of the Greeks. And Moslems, though not very orthodox Moslems, were turning Aristotle into a pantheist philosophy still less acceptable to orthodox Christians. This second controversy, however, requires more explanation than the first. As is remarked on an introductory page, most modern people do know that St. Francis at least was a liberator of large sympathies; that, whatever their positive view of medievalism, the Friars were in a relative sense a popular movement, pointing to greater fraternity and freedom; and a very little further information would inform them that this was every bit as true of the Dominican as of the Franciscan Friars. Nobody now is particularly likely to start up in defence of feudal abbots or fixed and stationary monks, against such impudent innovators as St. Francis and St. Thomas. We may therefore be allowed to summarise briefly the great debate about the Friars, though it shook all Christendom in its day. But the greater debate about Aristotle presents a greater difficulty; because there are modern misconceptions about it which can only be approached with a little more elaboration.

Perhaps there is really no such thing as a Revolution recorded in history. What happened was always a Counter-Revolution. Men were always rebelling against the last rebels; or even repenting of the last rebellion. This could be seen in the most casual contemporary fashions, if the fashionable mind had not fallen into the habit of seeing the very latest rebel as rebelling against all ages at once. The Modern Girl with the lipstick and the cocktail is as much a rebel against the Woman's Rights Woman of the '80's, with her stiff stick-up collars and strict teetotalism, as the latter was a rebel against the Early Victorian lady of the languid waltz tunes and the album full of quotations from Byron; or as the last, again, was a rebel against a Puritan mother to whom the waltz was a wild orgy and Byron the Bolshevist of his age. Trace even the Puritan mother back through history and she represents a rebellion against the Cavalier laxity of the English Church, which was at first a rebel against the Catholic civilisation, which had been a rebel against the Pagan civilisation. Nobody but a lunatic could pretend that these things were a progress; for they obviously go first one way and then the other. But whichever is right, one thing is certainly wrong; and that is the modern habit of looking at them only from the modern end. For that is only to see the end of the tale; they rebel against they know not what, because it arose they know not when; intent only on its ending, they are ignorant of its beginning; and therefore of its very being. The difference between the smaller cases and the larger, is that in the latter there is really so huge a human upheaval that men start from it like men in a new world; and that very novelty enables them to go on very long; and generally to go on too long. It is because these things start with a vigorous revolt that the intellectual impetus lasts long enough to make them seem like a survival. An excellent example of this is the real story of the revival and the neglect of Aristotle. By the end of the medieval time, Aristotelianism did eventually grow stale. Only a very fresh and successful novelty ever gets quite so stale as that.

When the moderns, drawing the blackest curtain of obscurantism that ever obscured history, decided that nothing mattered much before the Renaissance and the Reformation, they instantly began their modern career by falling into a big blunder. It was the blunder about Platonism. They found, hanging about the courts of the swaggering princes of the sixteenth century (which was as far back in history as they were allowed to go) certain anti-clerical artists and scholars who said they were bored with Aristotle and were supposed to be secretly indulging in Plato. The moderns, utterly ignorant of the whole story of the medievals, instantly fell into the trap. They assumed that Aristotle was some crabbed antiquity and tyranny from the black back of the Dark Ages, and that Plato was an entirely new Pagan pleasure never yet tasted by Christian men. Father Knox has shown in what a startling state of innocence is the mind of Mr. H. L. Mencken, for instance, upon this point. In fact, of course, the story is exactly the other way round. If anything, it was Platonism that was the old orthodoxy. It was Aristotelianism that was the very modern revolution. And the leader of that modern revolution was the man who is the subject of this book.

The truth is that the historical Catholic Church began by being Platonist; by being rather too Platonist. Platonism was in that golden Greek air that was breathed by the first great Greek theologians. The Christian Fathers were much more like the Neo-Platonists than were the scholars of the Renaissance; who were only Neo-Neo-Platonists. For Chrysostom or Basil it was as ordinary and normal to think in terms of the Logos, or the Wisdom which is the aim of philosophers, as it is to any men of any religion today to talk about social problems or progress or the economic crisis throughout the world. St. Augustine followed a natural mental evolution when he was a Platonist before he was a Manichean, and a Manichean before he was a Christian. And it was exactly in that last association that the first faint hint, of the danger of being too Platonist, may be seen.

From the Renaissance to the nineteenth century, the Moderns have had an almost monstrous love of the Ancients. In considering medieval life, they could never regard the Christians as anything but the pupils of the Pagans; of Plato in ideas, or Aristotle in reason and science. It was not so. On some points, even from the most monotonously modern standpoint, Catholicism was centuries ahead of Platonism or Aristotelianism. We can see it still, for instance, in the tiresome tenacity of Astrology. On that matter the philosophers were all in favour of superstition; and the saints and all such superstitious people were against superstition. But even the great saints found it difficult to get disentangled from this superstition. Two points were always put by those suspicious of the Aristotelianism of Aquinas; and they sound to us now very quaint and comic, taken together. One was the view that the stars are personal beings, governing our lives: the other the great general theory that men have one mind between them; a view obviously opposed to immortality; that is, to individuality. Both linger among the Moderns: so strong is still the tyranny of the Ancients. Astrology sprawls over the Sunday papers, and the other doctrine has its hundredth form in what is called Communism: or the Soul of the Hive.

For on one preliminary point, this position must not be misunderstood. When we praise the practical value of the Aristotelian Revolution, and the originality of Aquinas in leading it, we do not mean that the Scholastic philosophers before him had not been philosophers, or had not been highly philosophical, or had not been in touch with ancient philosophy. In so far as there was ever a bad break in philosophical history, it was not before St. Thomas, or at the beginning of medieval history; it was after St. Thomas and at the beginning of modern history. The great intellectual tradition that comes down to us from Pythagoras and Plato was never interrupted or lost through such trifles as the sack of Rome, the triumph of Attila or all the barbarian invasions of the Dark Ages. It was only lost after the introduction of printing, the discovery of America, the founding of the Royal Society and all the enlightenment of the Renaissance and the modern world. It was there, if anywhere, that there was lost or impatiently snapped the long thin delicate thread that had descended from distant antiquity; the thread of that unusual human hobby; the habit of thinking. This is proved by the fact that the printed books of this later period largely had to wait for the eighteenth century, or the end of the seventeenth century, to find even the names of the new philosophers; who were at the best a new kind of philosophers. But the decline of the Empire, the Dark Ages and the early Middle Ages, though too much tempted to neglect what was opposed to Platonic philosophy, had never neglected philosophy. In that sense St. Thomas, like most other very original men, has a long and clear pedigree. He himself is constantly referring back to the authorities from St. Augustine to St. Anselm, and from St. Anselm to St. Albert, and even when he differs, he also defers.

A very learned Anglican once said to me, not perhaps without a touch of tartness, "I can't understand why everybody talks as if Thomas Aquinas were the beginning of the Scholastic philosophy. I could understand their saying he was the end of it." Whether or no the comment was meant to be tart, we may be sure that the reply of St. Thomas would have been perfectly urbane. And indeed it would be easy to answer with a certain placidity, that in his Thomist language the end of a thing does not mean its destruction, but its fulfilment. No Thomist will complain, if Thomism is the end of our philosophy, in the sense in which God is the end of our existence. For that does not mean that we cease to exist, but that we become as perennial as the philosophia perennis. Putting this claim on one side, however, it is important to remember that my distinguished interlocutor was perfectly right, in that there had been whole dynasties of doctrinal philosophers before Aquinas, leading up to the day of the great revolt of the Aristotelians. Nor was even that revolt a thing entirely abrupt and unforeseen. An able writer in the Dublin Review not long ago pointed out that in some respects the whole nature of metaphysics had advanced a long way since Aristotle, by the time it came to Aquinas. And that it is no disrespect to the primitive and gigantic genius of the Stagirite to say that in some respects he was really but a rude and rough founder of philosophy, compared with some of the subsequent subtleties of medievalism; that the Greek gave a few grand hints which the Scholastics developed into the most delicate fine shades. This may be an overstatement, but there is a truth in it. Anyhow, it is certain that even in Aristotelian philosophy, let alone Platonic philosophy, there was already a tradition of highly intelligent interpretation. If that delicacy afterwards degenerated into hair-splitting, it was none the less delicate hair-splitting; and work requiring very scientific tools.

What made the Aristotelian Revolution really revolutionary was the fact that it was really religious. It is the fact, so fundamental that I thought it well to lay it down in the first few pages of this book; that the revolt was largely a revolt of the most Christian elements in Christendom. St. Thomas, every bit as much as St. Francis, felt subconsciously that the hold of his people was slipping on the solid Catholic doctrine and discipline, worn smooth by more than a thousand years of routine; and that the Faith needed to be shown under a new light and dealt with from another angle. But he had no motive except the desire to make it popular for the salvation of the people. It was true, broadly speaking, that for some time past it had been too Platonist to be popular. It needed something like the shrewd and homely touch of Aristotle to turn it again into a religion of common sense. Both the motive and the method are illustrated in the war of Aquinas against the Augustinians.

First, it must be remembered that the Greek influence continued to flow from the Greek Empire; or at least from the centre of the Roman Empire which was in the Greek city of Byzantium, and no longer in Rome. That influence was Byzantine in every good and bad sense; like Byzantine art, it was severe and mathematical and a little terrible; like Byzantine etiquette, it was Oriental and faintly decadent. We owe to the learning of Mr. Christopher Dawson much enlightenment upon the way in which Byzantium slowly stiffened into a sort of Asiatic theocracy, more like that which served the Sacred Emperor in China. But even the unlearned can see the difference, in the way in which Eastern Christianity flattened everything, as it flattened the faces of the images into icons. It became a thing of patterns rather than pictures; and it made definite and destructive war upon statues. Thus we see, strangely enough, that the East was the land of the Cross and the West was the land of the Crucifix. The Greeks were being dehumanised by a radiant symbol, while the Goths were being humanised by an instrument of torture. Only the West made realistic pictures of the greatest of all the tales out of the East. Hence the Greek element in Christian theology tended more and more to be a sort of dried up Platonism; a thing of diagrams and abstractions; to the last indeed noble abstractions, but not sufficiently touched by that great thing that is by definition almost the opposite of abstraction: Incarnation. Their Logos was the Word; but not the Word made Flesh. In a thousand very subtle ways, often escaping doctrinal definition, this spirit spread over the world of Christendom from the place where the Sacred Emperor sat under his golden mosaics; and the flat pavement of the Roman Empire was at last a sort of smooth pathway for Mahomet. For Islam was the ultimate fulfilment of the Iconoclasts. Long before that, however, there was this tendency to make the Cross merely decorative like the Crescent; to make it a pattern like the Greek key or the Wheel of Buddha. But there is something passive about such a world of patterns, and the Greek Key does not open any door, while the Wheel of Buddha always moves round and never moves on.

Partly through these negative influences, partly through a necessary and noble asceticism which sought to emulate the awful standard of the martyrs, the earlier Christian ages had been excessively anti-corporeal and too near the danger-line of Manichean mysticism. But there was far less danger in the fact that the saints macerated the body than in the fact that the sages neglected it. Granted all the grandeur of Augustine's contribution to Christianity, there was in a sense a more subtle danger in Augustine the Platonist than even in Augustine the Manichee. There came from it a mood which unconsciously committed the heresy of dividing the substance of the Trinity. It thought of God too exclusively as a Spirit who purifies or a Saviour who redeems; and too little as a Creator who creates. That is why men like Aquinas thought it right to correct Plato by an appeal to Aristotle; Aristotle who took things as he found them, just as Aquinas accepted things as God created them. In all the work of St. Thomas the world of positive creation is perpetually present. Humanly speaking, it was he who saved the human element in Christian theology, if he used for convenience certain elements in heathen philosophy. Only, as has already been urged, the human element is also the Christian one.

The panic upon the Aristotelian peril, that had passed across the high places of the Church, was probably a dry wind from the desert. It was really filled rather with fear of Mahomet than fear of Aristotle. And this was ironic, because there was really much more difficulty in reconciling Aristotle with Mahomet than in reconciling him with Christ. Islam is essentially a simple creed for simple men; and nobody can ever really turn pantheism into a simple creed. It is at once too abstract and too complicated. There are simple believers in a personal God; and there are atheists more simple-minded than any believers in a personal God. But few can, in mere simplicity, accept a godless universe as a god. And while the Moslem, as compared with the Christian, had perhaps a less human God, he had if possible a more personal God. The will of Allah was very much of a will, and could not be turned into a stream of tendency. On all that cosmic and abstract side the Catholic was more accommodating than the Moslem--up to a point. The Catholic could admit at least that Aristotle was right about the impersonal elements of a personal God. Hence, we may say broadly of the Moslem philosophers, that those who became good philosophers became bad Moslems. It is not altogether unnatural that many bishops and doctors feared that the Thomists might become good philosophers and bad Christians. But there were also many, of the strict school of Plato and Augustine, who stoutly denied that they were even good philosophers. Between those rather incongruous passions, the love of Plato and the fear of Mahomet, there was a moment when the prospects of any Aristotelian culture in Christendom looked very dark indeed. Anathema after anathema was thundered from high places; and under the shadow of the persecution, as so often happens, it seemed for a moment that barely one or two figures stood alone in the storm-swept area. They were both in the black and white of the Dominicans; for Albertus and Aquinas stood firm.

In that sort of combat there is always confusion; and majorities change into minorities and back again, as if by magic. It is always difficult to date the turn of the tide, which seems to be a welter of eddies; the very dates seeming to overlap and confuse the crisis. But the change, from the moment when the two Dominicans stood alone to the moment when the whole Church at last wheeled into line with them, may perhaps be found at about the moment when they were practically brought before a hostile but a not unjust judge. Stephen Tempier, the Bishop of Paris, was apparently a rather fine specimen of the old fanatical Churchman, who thought that admiring Aristotle was a weakness likely to be followed by adoring Apollo. He was also, by a piece of bad luck, one of the old social conservatives, who had intensely resented the popular revolution of the Preaching Friars. But he was an honest man; and Thomas Aquinas never asked for anything but permission to address honest men. All around him there were other Aristotelian revolutionaries of a much more dubious sort. There was Siger, the sophist from Brabant, who learned all his Aristotelianism from the Arabs; and had an ingenious theory about how an Arabian agnostic could also be a Christian. There were a thousand young men of the sort that had shouted for Abelard; full of the youth of the thirteenth century and drunken with the Greek wine of Stagira. Over against them, lowering and implacable, was the old Puritan party of the Augustinians; only too delighted to class the rationalistic Albert and Thomas with equivocal Moslem metaphysicians.

It would seem that the triumph of Thomas was really a personal triumph. He withdrew not a single one of his propositions; though it is said that the reactionary Bishop did condemn some of them after his death. On the whole, however, Aquinas convinced most of his critics that he was quite as good a Catholic as they were. There was a sequel of squabbles between the Religious Orders, following upon this controversial crisis. But it is probably true to say that the fact, that a man like Aquinas had managed even partially to satisfy a man like Tempier, was the end of the essential quarrel. What was already familiar to the few became familiar to the many; that an Aristotelian could really be a Christian. Another fact assisted in the common conversion. It rather curiously resembles the story of the translation of the Bible; and the alleged Catholic suppression of the Bible. Behind the scenes, where the Pope was much more tolerant than the Paris Bishop, the friends of Aquinas had been hard at work producing a new translation of Aristotle. It demonstrated that in many ways the heretical translation had been a very heretical translation. With the final consummation of this work, we may say that the great Greek philosophy entered finally into the system of Christendom. The process has been half humourously described as the Baptism of Aristotle.

We have all heard of the humility of the man of science; of many who were very genuinely humble; and of some who were very proud of their humility. It will be the somewhat too recurrent burden of this brief study that Thomas Aquinas really did have the humility of the man of science; as a special variant of the humility of the saint. It is true that he did not himself contribute anything concrete in the experiment or detail of physical science; in this, it may be said, he even lagged behind the last generation, and was far less of an experimental scientist than his tutor Albertus Magnus. But for all that, he was historically a great friend to the freedom of science. The principles he laid down, properly understood, are perhaps the best that can be produced for protecting science from mere obscurantist persecution. For instance, in the matter of the inspiration of Scripture, he fixed first on the obvious fact, which was forgotten by four furious centuries of sectarian battle, that the meaning of Scripture is very far from self-evident and that we must often interpret it in the light of other truths. If a literal interpretation is really and flatly contradicted by an obvious fact, why then we can only say that the literal interpretation must be a false interpretation. But the fact must really be an obvious fact. And unfortunately, nineteenth century scientists were just as ready to jump to the conclusion that any guess about nature was an obvious fact, as were seventeenth-century sectarians to jump to the conclusion that any guess about Scripture was the obvious explanation. Thus, private theories about what the Bible ought to mean, and premature theories about what the world ought to mean, have met in loud and widely advertised controversy, especially in the Victorian time; and this clumsy collision of two very impatient forms of ignorance was known as the quarrel of Science and Religion.

But St. Thomas had the scientific humility in this very vivid and special sense; that he was ready to take the lowest place; for the examination of the lowest things. He did not, like a modern specialist, study the worm as if it were the world; but he was willing to begin to study the reality of the world in the reality of the worm. His Aristotelianism simply meant that the study of the humblest fact will lead to the study of the highest truth. That for him the process was logical and not biological, was concerned with philosophy rather than science, does not alter the essential idea that he believed in beginning at the bottom of the ladder. But he also gave, by his view of Scripture and Science, and other questions, a sort of charter for pioneers more purely practical than himself. He practically said that if they could really prove their practical discoveries, the traditional interpretation of Scripture must give way before those discoveries. He could hardly, as the common phrase goes, say fairer than that. If the matter had been left to him, and men like him, there never would have been any quarrel between Science and Religion. He did his very best to map out two provinces for them, and to trace a just frontier between them.

It is often cheerfully remarked that Christianity has failed, by which is meant that it has never had that sweeping, imperial and imposed supremacy, which has belonged to each of the great revolutions, every one of which has subsequently failed. There was never a moment when men could say that every man was a Christian; as they might say for several months that every man was a Royalist or a Republican or a Communist. But if sane historians want to understand the sense in which the Christian character has succeeded, they could not find a better case than the massive moral pressure of a man like St. Thomas, in support of the buried rationalism of the heathens, which had as yet only been dug up for the amusement of the heretics. It was, quite strictly and exactly, because a new kind of man was conducting rational enquiry in a new kind of way, that men forgot the curse that had fallen on the temples of the dead demons and the palaces of the dead despots; forgot even the new fury out of Arabia against which they were fighting for their lives; because the man who was asking them to return to sense, or to return to their senses, was not a sophist but a saint. Aristotle had described the magnanimous man, who is great and knows that he is great. But Aristotle would never have recovered his own greatness, but for the miracle that created the more magnanimous man; who is great and knows that he is small.

There is a certain historical importance in what some would call the heaviness of the style employed. It carries a curious impression of candour, which really did have, I think, a considerable effect upon contemporaries. The saint has sometimes been called a sceptic. The truth is that he was very largely tolerated as a sceptic because he was obviously a saint. When he seemed to stand up as a stubborn Aristotelian, hardly distinguishable from the Arabian heretics, I do seriously believe that what protected him was very largely the prodigious power of his simplicity and his obvious goodness and love of truth. Those who went out against the haughty confidence of the heretics were stopped and brought up all standing, against a sort of huge humility which was like a mountain: or perhaps like that immense valley that is the mould of a mountain. Allowing for all medieval conventions, we can feel that with the other innovators, this was not always so. The others, from Abelard down to Siger of Brabant, have never quite lost, in the long process of history, a faint air of showing off. Nobody could feel for a moment that Thomas Aquinas was showing off. The very dullness of diction, of which some complain, was enormously convincing. He could have given wit as well as wisdom; but he was so prodigiously in earnest that he gave his wisdom without his wit.

After the hour of triumph came the moment of peril. It is always so with alliances, and especially because Aquinas was fighting on two fronts. His main business was to defend the Faith against the abuse of Aristotle; and he boldly did it by supporting the use of Aristotle. He knew perfectly well that armies of atheists and anarchists were roaring applause in the background at his Aristotelian victory over all he held most dear. Nevertheless, it was never the existence of atheists, any more than Arabs or Aristotelian pagans, that disturbed the extraordinary controversial composure of Thomas Aquinas. The real peril that followed on the victory he had won for Aristotle was vividly presented in the curious case of Siger of Brabant; and it is well worth study, for anyone who would begin to comprehend the strange history of Christendom. It is marked by one rather queer quality; which has always been the unique note of the Faith, though it is not noticed by its modern enemies, and rarely by its modern friends. It is the fact symbolised in the legend of Antichrist, who was the double of Christ; in the profound proverb that the Devil is the ape of God. It is the fact that falsehood is never so false as when it is very nearly true. It is when the stab comes near the nerve of truth, that the Christian conscience cries out in pain. And Siger of Brabant, following on some of the Arabian Aristotelians, advanced a theory which most modern newspaper readers would instantly have declared to be the same as the theory of St. Thomas. That was what finally roused St. Thomas to his last and most emphatic protest. He had won his battle for a wider scope of philosophy and science; he had cleared the ground for a general understanding about faith and enquiry; an understanding that has generally been observed among Catholics, and certainly never deserted without disaster. It was the idea that the scientist should go on exploring and experimenting freely, so long as he did not claim an infallibility and finality which it was against his own principles to claim. Meanwhile the Church should go on developing and defining, about supernatural things, so long as she did not claim a right to alter the deposit of faith, which it was against her own principles to claim. And when he had said this, Siger of Brabant got up and said something so horribly like it, and so horribly unlike, that (like the Antichrist) he might have deceived the very elect.

Siger of Brabant said this: the Church must be right theologically, but she can be wrong scientifically. There are two truths; the truth of the supernatural world, and the truth of the natural world, which contradicts the supernatural world. While we are being naturalists, we can suppose that Christianity is all nonsense; but then, when we remember that we are Christians, we must admit that Christianity is true even if it is nonsense. In other words, Siger of Brabant split the human head in two, like the blow in an old legend of battle; and declared that a man has two minds, with one of which he must entirely believe and with the other may utterly disbelieve. To many this would at least seem like a parody of Thomism. As a fact, it was the assassination of Thomism. It was not two ways of finding the same truth; it was an untruthful way of pretending that there are two truths. And it is extraordinarily interesting to note that this is the one occasion when the Dumb Ox really came out like a wild bull. When he stood up to answer Siger of Brabant, he was altogether transfigured, and the very style of his sentences, which is a thing like the tone of a man's voice, is suddenly altered. He had never been angry with any of the enemies who disagreed with him. But these enemies had attempted the worst treachery: they had made him agree with them.

Those who complain that theologians draw fine distinctions could hardly find a better example of their own folly. In fact, a fine distinction can be a flat contradiction. It was notably so in this case. St. Thomas was willing to allow the one truth to be approached by two paths, precisely because he was sure there was only one truth. Because the Faith was the one truth, nothing discovered in nature could ultimately contradict the Faith. Because the Faith was the one truth, nothing really deduced from the Faith could ultimately contradict the facts. It was in truth a curiously daring confidence in the reality of his religion: and though some may linger to dispute it, it has been justified. The scientific facts, which were supposed to contradict the Faith in the nineteenth century, are nearly all of them regarded as unscientific fictions in the twentieth century. Even the materialists have fled from materialism; and those who lectured us about determinism in psychology are already talking about indeterminism in matter. But whether his confidence was right or wrong, it was specially and supremely a confidence that there is one truth which cannot contradict itself. And this last group of enemies suddenly sprang up, to tell him they entirely agreed with him in saying that there are two contradictory truths. Truth, in the medieval phrase, carried two faces under one hood; and these double-faced sophists practically dared to suggest that it was the Dominican hood.

So, in his last battle and for the first time, he fought as with a battle-axe. There is a ring in the words altogether beyond the almost impersonal patience he maintained in debate with so many enemies. "Behold our refutation of the error. It is not based on documents of faith, but on the reasons and statements of the philosophers themselves. If then anyone there be who, boastfully taking pride in his supposed wisdom, wishes to challenge what we have written, let him not do it in some corner nor before children who are powerless to decide on such difficult matters. Let him reply openly if he dare. He shall find me then confronting him, and not only my negligible self, but many another whose study is truth. We shall do battle with his errors or bring a cure to his ignorance."

The Dumb Ox is bellowing now; like one at bay and yet terrible and towering over all the baying pack. We have already noted why, in this one quarrel with Siger of Brabant, Thomas Aquinas let loose such thunders of purely moral passion; it was because the whole work of his life was being betrayed behind his back, by those who had used his victories over the reactionaries. The point at the moment is that this is perhaps his one moment of personal passion, save for a single flash in the troubles of his youth: and he is once more fighting his enemies with a firebrand. And yet, even in this isolated apocalypse of anger, there is one phrase that may be commended for all time to men who are angry with much less cause. If there is one sentence that could be carved in marble, as representing the calmest and most enduring rationality of his unique intelligence, it is a sentence which came pouring out with all the rest of this molten lava. If there is one phrase that stands before history as typical of Thomas Aquinas, it is that phrase about his own argument: "It is not based on documents of faith, but on the reasons and statements of the philosophers themselves." Would that all Orthodox doctors in deliberation were as reasonable as Aquinas in anger! Would that all Christian apologists would remember that maxim; and write it up in large letters on the wall, before they nail any theses there. At the top of his fury, Thomas Aquinas understands, what so many defenders of orthodoxy will not understand. It is no good to tell an atheist that he is an atheist; or to charge a denier of immortality with the infamy of denying it; or to imagine that one can force an opponent to admit he is wrong, by proving that he is wrong on somebody else's principles, but not on his own. After the great example of St. Thomas, the principle stands, or ought always to have stood established; that we must either not argue with a man at all, or we must argue on his grounds and not ours. We may do other things instead of arguing, according to our views of what actions are morally permissible; but if we argue we must argue "On the reasons and statements of the philosophers themselves." This is the common sense in a saying attributed to a friend of St. Thomas, the great St. Louis, King of France, which shallow people quote as a sample of fanaticism; the sense of which is, that I must either argue with an infidel as a real philosopher can argue, or else "thrust a sword through his body as far as it will go." A real philosopher (even of the opposite school) will be the first to agree that St. Louis was entirely philosophical.

So, in the last great controversial crisis of his theological campaign, Thomas Aquinas contrived to give his friends and enemies not only a lesson in theology, but a lesson in controversy. But it was in fact his last controversy. He had been a man with a huge controversial appetite, a thing that exists in some men and not others, in saints and in sinners. But after this great and victorious duel with Siger of Brabant, he was suddenly overwhelmed with a desire for silence and repose. He said one strange thing about this mood of his to a friend, which will fall into its more appropriate place elsewhere. He fell back on the extreme simplicities of his monastic round and seemed to desire nothing but a sort of permanent retreat. A request came to him from the Pope that he should set out upon some further mission of diplomacy or disputation; and he made ready to obey. But before he had gone many miles on the journey, he was dead.

--/--

IV A MEDITATION ON THE MANICHEES

There is one casual anecdote about St. Thomas Aquinas which illuminates him like a lightning-flash, not only without but within. For it not only shows him as a character, and even as a comedy character, and shows the colours of his period and social background; but also, as if for an instant, makes a transparency of his mind. It is a trivial incident which occurred one day, when he was reluctantly dragged from his work, and we might almost say from his play. For both were for him found in the unusual hobby of thinking, which is for some men a thing much more intoxicating than mere drinking. He had declined any number of society invitations, to the courts of kings and princes, not because he was unfriendly, for he was not; but because he was always glowing within with the really gigantic plans of exposition and argument which filled his life. On one occasion, however, he was invited to the court of King Louis IX of France, more famous as the great St. Louis; and for some reason or other, the Dominican authorities of his Order told him to accept; so he immediately did so, being an obedient friar even in his sleep; or rather in his permanent trance of reflection.

It is a real case against conventional hagiography that it sometimes tends to make all saints seem to be the same. Whereas in fact no men are more different than saints; not even murderers. And there could hardly be a more complete contrast, given the essentials of holiness, than between St. Thomas and St. Louis. St. Louis was born a knight and a king; but he was one of those men in whom a certain simplicity, combined with courage and activity, makes it natural, and in a sense easy, to fulfil directly and promptly any duty or office, however official. He was a man in whom holiness and healthiness had no quarrel; and their issue was in action. He did not go in for thinking much, in the sense of theorising much. But, even in theory, he had that sort of presence of mind, which belongs to the rare and really practical man when he has to think. He never said the wrong thing; and he was orthodox by instinct. In the old pagan proverb about kings being philosophers or philosophers kings, there was a certain miscalculation, connected with a mystery that only Christianity could reveal. For while it is possible for a king to wish much to be a saint, it is not possible for a saint to wish very much to be a king. A good man will hardly be always dreaming of being a great monarch; but, such is the liberality of the Church, that she cannot forbid even a great monarch to dream of being a good man. But Louis was a straight-forward soldierly sort of person who did not particularly mind being a king, any more than he would have minded being a captain or a sergeant or any other rank in his army.

Now a man like St. Thomas would definitely dislike being a king, or being entangled with the pomp and politics of kings; not only his humility, but a sort of subconscious fastidiousness and fine dislike of futility, often found in leisurely and learned men with large minds, would really have prevented him making contact with the complexity of court life. Also, he was anxious all his life to keep out of politics; and there was no political symbol more striking, or in a sense more challenging, at that moment, than the power of the King in Paris.

Paris was truly at that time an aurora borealis; a Sunrise in the North. We must realise that lands much nearer to Rome had rotted with paganism and pessimism and Oriental influences of which the most respectable was that of Mahound. Provence and all the South had been full of a fever of nihilism or negative mysticism, and from Northern France had come the spears and swords that swept away the unchristian thing. In Northern France also sprang up that splendour of building that shines like swords and spears: the first spires of the Gothic. We talk now of grey Gothic buildings; but they must have been very different when they went up white and gleaming into the northern skies, partly picked out with gold and bright colours; a new flight of architecture, as startling as flying-ships. The new Paris ultimately left behind by St. Louis must have been a thing white like lilies and splendid as the oriflamme. It was the beginning of the great new thing: the nation of France, which was to pierce and overpower the old quarrel of Pope and Emperor in the lands from which Thomas came. But Thomas came very unwillingly, and, if we may say it of so kindly a man, rather sulkily. As he entered Paris. they showed him from the hill that splendour of new spires beginning, and somebody said something like, "How grand it must be to own all this." And Thomas Aquinas only muttered, "I would rather have that Chrysostom MS. I can't get hold of."

Somehow they steered that reluctant bulk of reflection to a seat in the royal banquet hall; and all that we know of Thomas tells us that he was perfectly courteous to those who spoke to him, but spoke little, and was soon forgotten in the most brilliant and noisy clatter in the world: the noise of French talking. What the Frenchmen were talking about we do not know; but they forgot all about the large fat Italian in their midst, and it seems only too possible that he forgot all about them. Sudden silences will occur even in French conversation; and in one of these the interruption came. There had long been no word or motion in that huge heap of black and white weeds, like motley in mourning, which marked him as a mendicant friar out of the streets, and contrasted with all the colours and patterns and quarterings of that first and freshest dawn of chivalry and heraldry. The triangular shields and pennons and pointed spears, the triangular swords of the Crusade, the pointed windows and the conical hoods, repeated everywhere that fresh French medieval spirit that did, in every sense, come to the point. But the colours of the coats were gay and varied, with little to rebuke their richness; for St. Louis, who had himself a special quality of coming to the point, had said to his courtiers, "Vanity should be avoided; but every man should dress well, in the manner of his rank, that his wife may the more easily love him."

And then suddenly the goblets leapt and rattled on the board and the great table shook, for the friar had brought down his huge fist like a club of stone, with a crash that startled everyone like an explosion; and had cried out in a strong voice, but like a man in the grip of a dream, "And that will settle the Manichees!"

The palace of a king, even when it is the palace of a saint, has it conventions. A shock thrilled through the court, and every one felt as if the fat friar from Italy had thrown a plate at King Louis, or knocked his crown sideways. They all looked timidly at the terrible seat, that was for a thousand years the throne of the Capets: and many there were presumably prepared to pitch the big black-robed beggarman out of the window. But St. Louis, simple as he seemed, was no mere medieval fountain of honour or even fountain of mercy but also the fountain of two eternal rivers: the irony and the courtesy of France. And he turned to his secretaries, asking them in a low voice to take their tablets round to the seat of the absent-minded controversialist, and take a note of the argument that had just occurred to him; because it must be a very good one and he might forget it. I have paused upon this anecdote, first, as has been said, because it is the one which gives us the most vivid snapshot of a great medieval character; indeed of two great medieval characters. But it also specially fitted to be taken as a type or a turning-point, because of the glimpse it gives of the man's main preoccupation; and the sort of thing that might have been found in his thoughts, if they had been thus surprised at any moment by a philosophical eavesdropper or through a psychological keyhole. It was not for nothing that he was still brooding, even in the white court of St. Louis, upon the dark cloud of the Manichees.

This book is meant only to be the sketch of a man; but it must at least lightly touch, later on, upon a method and a meaning; or what our journalism has an annoying way of calling a message. A few very inadequate pages must be given to the man in relation to his theology and his philosophy; but the thing of which I mean to speak here is something at once more general and more personal even than his philosophy. I have therefore introduced it here, before we come to anything like technical talk about his philosophy. It was something that might alternatively be called his moral attitude, or his temperamental predisposition, or the purpose of his life so far as social and human effects were concerned: for he knew better than most of us that there is but one purpose in this life, and it is one that is beyond this life. But if we wanted to put in a picturesque and simplified form what he wanted for the world, and what was his work in history, apart from theoretical and theological definitions, we might well say that it really was to strike a blow and settle the Manichees.

The full meaning of this may not be apparent to those who do not study theological history and perhaps even less apparent to those who do. Indeed it may seem equally irrelevant to the history and the theology. In history St. Dominic and Simon de Montfort between them had already pretty well settled the Manichees. And in theology of course an encyclopaedic doctor like Aquinas dealt with a thousand other heresies besides the Manichean heresy. Nevertheless, it does represent his main position and the turn he gave to the whole history of Christendom.

I think it well to interpose this chapter, though its scope may seem more vague than the rest; because there is a sort of big blunder about St. Thomas and his creed, which is an obstacle for most modern people in even beginning to understand them. It arises roughly thus. St. Thomas, like other monks, and especially other saints, lived a life of renunciation and austerity; his fasts, for instance, being in marked contrast to the luxury in which he might have lived if he chose. This element stands high in his religion, as a manner of asserting the will against the power of nature, of thanking the Redeemer by partially sharing his sufferings, of making a man ready for anything as a missionary or martyr, and similar ideals. These happen to be rare in the modern industrial society of the West, outside his communion; and it is therefore assumed that they are the whole meaning of that communion. Because it is uncommon for an alderman to fast for forty days, or a politician to take a Trappist vow of silence, or a man about town to live a life of strict celibacy, the average outsider is convinced, not only that Catholicism is nothing except asceticism, but that asceticism is nothing except pessimism. He is so obliging as to explain to Catholics why they hold this heroic virtue in respect; and is ever ready to point out that the philosophy behind it is an Oriental hatred of anything connected with Nature, and a purely Schopenhauerian disgust with the Will to Live. I read in a "high-class" review of Miss Rebecca West's book on St. Augustine, the astounding statement that the Catholic Church regards sex as having the nature of sin. How marriage can be a sacrament if sex is a sin, or why it is the Catholics who are in favour of birth and their foes who are in favour of birth-control, I will leave the critic to worry out for himself. My concern is not with that part of the argument; but with another.

The ordinary modern critic, seeing this ascetic ideal in an authoritative Church, and not seeing it in most other inhabitants of Brixton or Brighton, is apt to say, "This is the result of Authority; it would be better to have Religion without Authority." But in truth, a wider experience outside Brixton or Brighton would reveal the mistake. It is rare to find a fasting alderman or a Trappist politician, but it is still more rare to see nuns suspended in the air on hooks or spikes; it is unusual for a Catholic Evidence Guild orator in Hyde Park to begin his speech by gashing himself all over with knives; a stranger calling at an ordinary presbytery will seldom find the parish priest lying on the floor with a fire lighted on his chest and scorching him while he utters spiritual ejaculations. Yet all these things are done all over Asia, for instance, by voluntary enthusiasts acting solely on the great impulse of Religion; of Religion, in their case, not commonly imposed by any immediate Authority; and certainly not imposed by this particular Authority. In short, a real knowledge of mankind will tell anybody that Religion is a very terrible thing; that it is truly a raging fire, and that Authority is often quite as much needed to restrain it as to impose it. Asceticism, or the war with the appetites, is itself an appetite. It can never be eliminated from among the strange ambitions of Man. But it can be kept in some reasonable control; and it is indulged in much saner proportion under Catholic Authority than in Pagan or Puritan anarchy. Meanwhile, the whole of this ideal, though an essential part of Catholic idealism when it is understood, is in some ways entirely a side issue. It is not the primary principle of Catholic philosophy; it is only a particular deduction from Catholic ethics. And when we begin to talk about primary philosophy, we realise the full and flat contradiction between the monk fasting and the fakir hanging himself on hooks.

Now nobody will begin to understand the Thomist philosophy, or indeed the Catholic philosophy, who does not realise that the primary and fundamental part of it is entirely the praise of Life, the praise of Being, the praise of God as the Creator of the World. Everything else follows a long way after that, being conditioned by various complications like the Fall or the vocation of heroes. The trouble occurs because the Catholic mind moves upon two planes; that of the Creation and that of the Fall. The nearest parallel is, for instance, that of England invaded; there might be strict martial law in Kent because the enemy had landed in Kent, and relative liberty in Hereford; but this would nor affect the affection of an English patriot for Hereford or Kent, and strategic caution in Kent would not affect the love of Kent. For the love of England would remain, both of the parts to be redeemed by discipline and the parts to be enjoyed in liberty. Any extreme of Catholic asceticism is a wise, or unwise, precaution against the evil of the Fall; it is never a doubt about the good of the Creation. And that is where it really does differ, nor only from the rather excessive eccentricity of the gentleman who hangs himself on hooks, but from the whole cosmic theory which is the hook on which he hangs. In the case of many Oriental religions, it really is true that the asceticism is pessimism; that the ascetic tortures himself to death out of an abstract hatred of life; that he does not merely mean to control Nature as he should, but to contradict Nature as much as he can. And though it takes a milder form than hooks in millions of the religious populations of Asia, it is a fact far too little realised, that the dogma of the denial of life does really rule as a first principal on so vast a scale. One historic form it took was that great enemy of Christianity from its beginnings: the Manichees.

What is called the Manichean philosophy has had many forms; indeed it has attacked what is immortal and immutable with a very curious kind of immortal mutability. It is like the legend of the magician who turns himself into a snake or a cloud; and the whole has that nameless note of irresponsibility, which belongs to much of the metaphysics and morals of Asia, from which the Manichean mystery came. But it is always in one way or another a notion that nature is evil; or that evil is at least rooted in nature. The essential point is that as evil has roots in nature, so it has rights in nature. Wrong has as much right to exist as right. As already stated this notion took many forms. Sometimes it was a dualism, which made evil an equal partner with good; so that neither could be called an usurper. More often it was a general idea that demons had made the material world, and if there were any good spirits, they were concerned only with the spiritual world. Later, again, it took the form of Calvinism, which held that God had indeed made the world, but in a special sense, made the evil as well as the good: had made an evil will as well as an evil world. On this view, if a man chooses to damn his soul alive, he is not thwarting God's will but rather fulfilling it. In these two forms, of the early Gnosticism and the later Calvinism, we see the superficial variety and fundamental unity of Manicheanism. The old Manicheans taught that Satan originated the whole work of creation commonly attributed to God. The new

Calvinists taught that God originates the whole work of damnation commonly attributed to Satan. One looked back to the first day when a devil acted like a god, the other looked forward to a last day when a god acted like a devil. But both had the idea that the creator of the earth was primarily the creator of the evil, whether we call him a devil or a god.

Since there are a good many Manicheans among the Moderns, as we may remark in a moment, some may agree with this view, some may be puzzled about it, some may only be puzzled about why we should object to it. To understand the medieval controversy, a word must be said of the Catholic doctrine, which is as modern as it is medieval. That "God looked on all things and saw that they were good" contains a subtlety which the popular pessimist cannot follow, or is too hasty to notice. It is the thesis that there are no bad things, but only bad uses of things. If you will, there are no bad things but only bad thoughts; and especially bad intentions. Only Calvinists can really believe that hell is paved with good intentions. That is exactly the one thing it cannot be paved with. But it is possible to have bad intentions about good things; and good things, like the world and the flesh have been twisted by a bad intention called the devil. But he cannot make things bad; they remain as on the first day of creation. The work of heaven alone was material; the making of a material world. The work of hell is entirely spiritual.

This error then had many forms; but especially, like nearly every error, it had two forms, a fiercer one which was outside the Church and attacking the Church, and a subtler one, which was inside the Church and corrupting the Church. There has never been a time when the Church was not torn between that invasion and that treason. It was so, for instance, in the Victorian time, Darwinian "competition", in commerce or race conflict, was every bit as brazen an atheist assault, in the nineteenth century, as the Bolshevist No-God movement in the twentieth century. To brag of brute prosperity, to admire the most muddly millionaires who had cornered wheat by a trick, to talk about the "unfit" (in imitation of the scientific thinker who would finish them off because he cannot even finish his own sentence-- unfit for what?)--all that is as simply and openly Anti-Christian as the Black Mass. Yet some weak and worldly Catholics did use this cant in defence of Capitalism, in their first rather feeble resistance to Socialism. At least they did until the great Encyclical of the Pope on the Rights of Labour put a stop to all their nonsense. The evil is always both within and without the Church; but in a wilder form outside and a milder form inside. So it was, again, in the seventeenth century, when there was Calvinism outside and Jansenism inside. And so it was in the thirteenth century, when the obvious danger outside was in the revolution of the Albigensians; but the potential danger inside was in the very traditionalism of the Augustinians. For the Augustinians derived only from Augustine, and Augustine derived partly from Plato, and Plato was right, but not quite right. It is a mathematical fact that if a line be not perfectly directed towards a point, it will actually go further away from it as it comes nearer to it. After a thousand years of extension, the miscalculation of Platonism had come very near to Manicheanism.

Popular errors are nearly always right. They nearly always refer to some ultimate reality, about which those who correct them are themselves incorrect. It is a very queer thing that "Platonic Love" has come to mean for the un-lettered something rather purer and cleaner than it means for the learned. Yet even those who realise the great Greek evil may well realise that perversity often comes out of the wrong sort of purity. Now it was the inmost lie of the Manichees that they identified purity with sterility. It is singularly contrasted with the language of St. Thomas, which always connects purity with fruitfulness; whether it be natural or supernatural. And, queerly enough, as I have said, there does remain a sort of reality in the vulgar colloquialism that the affair between Sam and Susan is "quite Platonic." It is true that, quite apart from the local perversion, there was in Plato a sort of idea that people would be better without their bodies: that their heads might fly off and meet in the sky in merely intellectual marriage, like cherubs in a picture. The ultimate phase of this "Platonic" philosophy was what inflamed poor D. H. Lawrence into talking nonsense, and he was probably unaware that the Catholic doctrine of marriage would say much of what he said, without talking nonsense. Anyhow, it is historically important to see that Platonic love did somewhat distort both human and divine love, in the theory of the early theologians. Many medieval men, who would indignantly deny the Albigensian doctrine of sterility, were yet in an emotional mood to abandon the body in despair; and some of them to abandon everything in despair.

In truth, this vividly illuminates the provincial stupidity of those who object to what they call "creeds and dogmas." It was precisely the creed and dogma that saved the sanity of the world. These people generally propose an alternative religion of intuition and feeling. If, in the really Dark Ages, there had been a religion of feeling, it would have been a religion of black and suicidal feeling. It was the rigid creed that resisted the rush of suicidal feeling. The critics of asceticism are probably right in supposing that many a Western hermit did feel rather like an Eastern fakir. But he could not really think like an Eastern fakir; because he was an orthodox Catholic. And what kept his thought in touch with healthier and more humanistic thought was simply and solely the Dogma. He could not deny that a good God had created the normal and natural world; he could not say that the devil had made the world; because he was not a Manichee. A thousand enthusiasts for celibacy, in the day of the great rush to the desert or the cloister, might have called marriage a sin, if they had only considered their individual ideals, in the modern manner, and their own immediate feelings about marriage. Fortunately, they had to accept the Authority of the Church, which had definitely said that marriage was not a sin. A modern emotional religion might at any moment have turned Catholicism into Manicheanism. But when Religion would have maddened men, Theology kept them sane.

In this sense St. Thomas stands up simply as the great orthodox theologian, who reminded men of the creed of Creation, when many of them were still in the mood of mere destruction. It is futile for the critics of medievalism to quote a hundred medieval phrases that may be supposed to sound like mere pessimism, if they will not understand the central fact; that medieval men did not care about being medieval and did not accept the authority of a mood, because it was melancholy, but did care very much about orthodoxy, which is not a mood. It was because St. Thomas could prove that his glorification of the Creator and His creative joy was more orthodox than any atmospheric pessimism, that he dominated the Church and the world, which accepted that truth as a test. But when this immense and impersonal importance is allowed for, we may agree that there was a personal element as well. Like most of the great religious teachers, he was fitted individually for the task that God had given him to do. We can if we like call that talent instinctive; we can even descend to calling it temperamental.

Anybody trying to popularise a medieval philosopher must use language that is very modern and very unphilosophical. Nor is this a sneer at modernity; it arises from the moderns having dealt so much in moods and emotions, especially in the arts, that they have developed a large but loose vocabulary, which deals more with atmosphere than with actual attitude or position. As noted elsewhere, even the modern philosophers are more like the modern poets; in giving an individual tinge even to truth, and often looking at all life through different coloured spectacles. To say that Schopenhauer had the blues, or that William James had a rather rosier outlook, would often convey more than calling the one a Pessimist or the other a Pragmatist. This modern moodiness has its value, though the moderns overrate it; just as medieval logic had its value, though it was overrated in the later Middle Ages. But the point is that to explain the medievals to the moderns, we must often use this modern language of mood. Otherwise the character will be missed, through certain prejudices and ignorances about all such medieval characters. Now there is something that lies all over the work of St. Thomas Aquinas like a great light: which is something quite primary and perhaps unconscious with him, which he would perhaps have passed over as an irrelevant personal quality; and which can now only be expressed by a rather cheap journalistic term, which he would probably have thought quite senseless.

Nevertheless, the only working word for that atmosphere is Optimism. I know that the word is now even more degraded in the twentieth century than it was in the nineteenth century. Men talked lately of being Optimists about the issue of War; they talk now of being Optimists about the revival of Trade; they may talk tomorrow of being Optimists about the International Ping-pong Tournament. But men in the Victorian time did mean a little more than that, when they used the word Optimist of Browning or Stevenson or Walt Whitman. And in a rather larger and more luminous sense than in the case of these men, the term was basically true of Thomas Aquinas. He did, with a most solid and colossal conviction, believe in Life: and in something like what Stevenson called the great theorem of the livableness of life. It breathes somehow in his very first phrases about the reality of Being. If the morbid Renaissance intellectual is supposed to say, "To be or not to be-- that is the question," then the massive medieval doctor does most certainly reply in a voice of thunder, "To be--that is the answer." The point is important; many not unnaturally talk of the Renaissance as the time when certain men began to believe in Life. The truth is that it was the time when a few men, for the first time, began to disbelieve in Life. The medievals had put many restrictions, and some excessive restrictions, upon the universal human hunger and even fury for Life. Those restrictions had often been expressed in fanatical and rabid terms; the terms of those resisting a great natural force; the force of men who desired to live. Never until modern thought began, did they really have to fight with men who desired to die. That horror had threatened them in Asiatic Albigensianism, but it never became normal to them--until now.

But this fact becomes very vivid indeed, when we compare the greatest of Christian philosophers with the only men who were anything like his equals, or capable of being his rivals. They were people with whom he did not directly dispute; most of them he had never seen; some of them he had never heard of. Plato and Augustine were the only two with whom he could confer as he did with Bonaventure or even Averrhoes. But we must look elsewhere for his real rivals, and the only real rivals of the Catholic theory. They are the heads of great heathen systems; some of them very ancient, some very modern, like Buddha on the one hand or Nietzsche on the other. It is when we see his gigantic figure against this vast and cosmic background, that we realise, first, that he was the only optimist theologian, and second, that Catholicism is the only optimist theology. Something milder and more amiable may be made out of the deliquescence of theology, and the mixture of the creed with everything that contradicts it; but among consistent cosmic creeds, this is the only one that is entirely on the side of Life.

Comparative religion has indeed allowed us to compare religions-- and to contrast them. Fifty years ago, it set out to prove that all religions were much the same; generally proving, alternately, that they were all equally worthy and that they were all equally worthless. Since then this scientific process has suddenly begun to be scientific, and discovered the depths of the chasms as well as the heights of the hills. It is indeed an excellent improvement that sincerely religious people should respect each other. But respect has discovered difference, where contempt knew only indifference. The more we really appreciate the noble revulsion and renunciation of Buddha, the more we see that intellectually it was the converse and almost the contrary of the salvation of the world by Christ. The Christian would escape from the world into the universe: the Buddhist wishes to escape from the universe even more than from the world. One would uncreate himself; the other would return to his Creation: to his Creator. Indeed it was so genuinely the converse of the idea of the Cross as the Tree of Life, that there is some excuse for setting up the two things side by side, as if they were of equal significance. They are in one sense parallel and equal; as a mound and a hollow, as a valley and a hill. There is a sense in which that sublime despair is the only alternative to that divine audacity. It is even true that the truly spiritual and intellectual man sees it as a sort of dilemma; a very hard and terrible choice. There is little else on earth that can compare with these for completeness. And he who will not climb the mountain of Christ does indeed fall into the abyss of Buddha.

The same is true, in a less lucid and dignified fashion, of most other alternatives of heathen humanity; nearly all are sucked back into that whirlpool of recurrence which all the ancients knew. Nearly all return to the one idea of returning. That is what Buddha described so darkly as the Sorrowful Wheel. It is true that the sort of recurrence which Buddha described as the Sorrowful Wheel, poor Nietzsche actually managed to describe as the Joyful Wisdom. I can only say that if bare repetition was his idea of Joyful Wisdom, I should be curious to know what was his idea of Sorrowful Wisdom. But as a fact, in the case of Nietzsche, this did not belong to the moment of his breaking out, but to the moment of his breaking down. It came at the end of his life, when he was near to mental collapse; and it is really quite contrary to his earlier and finer inspirations of wild freedom or fresh and creative innovation. Once at least he had tried to break out; but he also was only broken-- on the wheel.

Alone upon the earth, and lifted and liberated from all the wheels and whirlpools of the earth, stands up the faith of St. Thomas; weighted and balanced indeed with more than Oriental metaphysics and more than Pagan pomp and pageantry; but vitally and vividly alone in declaring that life is a living story, with a great beginning and a great close; rooted in the primeval joy of God and finding its fruition in the final happiness of humanity; opening with the colossal chorus in which the sons of God shouted for joy, and ending in that mystical comradeship, shown in a shadowy fashion in those ancient words that move like an archaic dance; "For His delight is with the sons of men."

It is the fate of this sketch to be sketchy about philosophy, scanty or rather empty about theology, and to achieve little more than a decent silence on the subject of sanctity. And yet it must none the less be the recurrent burden of this little book, to which it must return with some monotony, that in this story the philosophy did depend on the theology, and the theology did depend on the sanctity. In other words, it must repeat the first fact, which was emphasised in the first chapter: that this great intellectual creation was a Christian and Catholic creation and cannot be understood as anything else. It was Aquinas who baptised Aristotle, when Aristotle could not have baptised Aquinas; it was a purely Christian miracle which raised the great Pagan from the dead. And this is proved in three ways (as St. Thomas himself might say), which it will be well to summarise as a sort of summary of this book.

First, in the life of St. Thomas, it is proved in the fact that only his huge and solid orthodoxy could have supported so many things which then seemed to be unorthodox. Charity covers a multitude of sins; and in that sense orthodoxy covers a multitude of heresies; or things which are hastily mistaken for heresies. It was precisely because his personal Catholicism was so convincing, that his impersonal Aristotelianism was given the benefit of the doubt. He did not smell of the faggot because he did smell of the firebrand; of the firebrand he had so instantly and instinctively snatched up, under a real assault on essential Catholic ethics. A typically cynical modern phrase refers to the man who is so good that he is good for nothing. St. Thomas was so good that he was good for everything; that his warrant held good for what others considered the most wild and daring speculations, ending in the worship of nothing. Whether or no he baptised Aristotle, he was truly the godfather of Aristotle, he was his sponsor; he swore that the old Greek would do no harm; and the whole world trusted his word.

Second, in the philosophy of St. Thomas, it is proved by the fact that everything depended on the new Christian motive for the study of facts, as distinct from truths. The Thomist philosophy began with the lowest roots of thought, the senses and the truisms of the reason; and a Pagan sage might have scorned such things, as he scorned the servile arts. But the materialism, which is merely cynicism in a Pagan, can be Christian humility in a Christian. St. Thomas was willing to begin by recording the facts and sensations of the material world, just as he would have been willing to begin by washing up the plates and dishes in the monastery. The point of his Aristotelianism was that even if common sense about concrete things really was a sort of servile labour, he must not be ashamed to be servus servorum Dei. Among heathens the mere sceptic might become the mere cynic; Diogenes in his tub had always a touch of the tub-thumper; but even the dirt of the cynics was dignified into dust and ashes among the saints. If we miss that, we miss the whole meaning of the greatest revolution in history. There was a new motive for beginning with the most material, and even with the meanest things.

Third, in the theology of St. Thomas, it is proved by the tremendous truth that supports all that theology; or any other Christian theology. There really was a new reason for regarding the senses, and the sensations of the body, and the experiences of the common man, with a reverence at which great Aristotle would have stared, and no man in the ancient world could have begun to understand. The Body was no longer what it was when Plato and Porphyry and the old mystics had left it for dead. It had hung upon a gibbet. It had risen from a tomb. It was no longer possible for the soul to despise the senses, which had been the organs of something that was more than man. Plato might despise the flesh; but God had not despised it. The senses had truly become sanctified; as they are blessed one by one at a Catholic baptism. "Seeing is believing" was no longer the platitude of a mere idiot, or common individual, as in Plato's world; it was mixed up with real conditions of real belief. Those revolving mirrors that send messages to the brain of man, that light that breaks upon the brain, these had truly revealed to God himself the path to Bethany or the light on the high rock of Jerusalem. These ears that resound with common noises had reported also to the secret knowledge of God the noise of the crowd that strewed palms and the crowd that cried for Crucifixion. After the Incarnation had become the idea that is central in our civilisation, it was inevitable that there should be a return to materialism, in the sense of the serious value of matter and the making of the body. When once Christ had risen, it was inevitable that Aristotle should rise again.

Those are three real reasons, and very sufficient reasons, for the general support given by the saint to a solid and objective philosophy. And yet there was something else, very vast and vague, to which I have tried to give a faint expression by the interposition of this chapter. It is difficult to express it fully, without the awful peril of being popular, or what the Modernists quite wrongly imagine to be popular; in short, passing from religion to religiosity. But there is a general tone and temper of Aquinas, which it is as difficult to avoid as daylight in a great house of windows. It is that positive position of his mind, which is filled and soaked as with sunshine with the warmth of the wonder of created things. There is a certain private audacity, in his communion, by which men add to their private names the tremendous titles of the Trinity and the Redemption; so that some nun may be called "of the Holy Ghost"; or a man bear such a burden as the title of St. John of the Cross. In this sense, the man we study may specially be called St. Thomas of the Creator. The Arabs have a phrase about the hundred names of God; but they also inherit the tradition of a tremendous name unspeakable because it expresses Being itself, dumb and yet dreadful as an instant inaudible shout; the proclamation of the Absolute. And perhaps no other man ever came so near to calling the Creator by His own name, which can only be written I Am.

--/--

V THE REAL LIFE OF ST. THOMAS

At this point, even so crude and external a sketch of a great saint involves the necessity of writing something that cannot fit in with the rest; the one thing which it is important to write and impossible to write. A saint may be any kind of man, with an additional quality that is at once unique and universal. We might even say that the one thing which separates a saint from ordinary men is his readiness to be one with ordinary men. In this sense the word ordinary must be understood in its native and noble meaning; which is connected with the word order. A saint is long past any desire for distinction; he is the only sort of superior man who has never been a superior person. But all this arises from a great central fact, which he does not condescend to call a privilege, but which is in its very nature a sort of privacy; and in that sense almost a form of private property. As with all sound private property, it is enough for him that he has it, he does not desire to limit the number of people who have it. He is always trying to hide it, out of a sort of celestial good manners; and Thomas Aquinas tried to hide it more than most. To reach it, in so far as we can reach it, it will be best to begin with the upper strata; and reach what was in the inside from what was most conspicuous on the outside.

The appearance or bodily presence of St. Thomas Aquinas is really easier to resurrect than that of many who lived before the age of portrait painting. It has been said that in his bodily being or bearing there was little of the Italian; but this is at the best, I fancy an unconscious comparison between St. Thomas and St. Francis; and at worst, only a comparison between him and the hasty legend of vivacious organ-grinders and incendiary ice-cream men. Not all Italians are vivacious organ-grinders, and very few Italians are like St. Francis. A nation is never a type, but it is nearly always a tangle of two or three roughly recognizable types. St. Thomas was of a certain type, which is not so much common in Italy, as common to uncommon Italians.

His bulk made it easy to regard him humorously as the sort of walking wine-barrel, common in the comedies of many nations: he joked about it himself. It may be that he, and not some irritated partisan of the Augustinian or Arabian parties, was responsible for the sublime exaggeration that a crescent was cut out of the dinner-table to allow him to sit down. It is quite certain that it was an exaggeration; and that his stature was more remarked than his stoutness; but, above all, that his head was quite powerful enough to dominate his body. And his head was of a very real and recognisable type, to judge by the traditional portraits and the personal descriptions. It was that sort of head with the heavy chin and jaws, the

Roman nose and the big rather bald brow, which, in spite of its fullness, gives also a curious concave impression of hollows here and there, like caverns of thought. Napoleon carried that head upon a short body. Mussolini carries it today, upon a rather taller but equally active one. It can be seen in the busts of several Roman Emperors, and occasionally above the shabby shirt-front of an Italian waiter; but he is generally a head waiter. So unmistakable is the type, that I cannot but think that the most vivid villain of light fiction, in the Victorian shocker called 'The Woman in White', was really sketched by Wilkie Collins from an actual Italian Count; he is so complete a contrast to the conventional skinny, swarthy and gesticulating villain whom the Victorians commonly presented as an Italian Count. Count Fosco, it may be remembered (I hope) by some, was a calm, corpulent, colossal gentleman, whose head was exactly like a bust of Napoleon of heroic size. He may have been a melodramatic villain; but he was a tolerably convincing Italian--of that kind. If we recall his tranquil manner, and the excellent common sense of his everyday external words and actions, we shall probably have a merely material image of the type of Thomas Aquinas; given only the slight effort of faith required to imagine Count Fosco turned suddenly into a saint.

The pictures of St. Thomas, though many of them were painted long after his death, are all obviously pictures of the same man. He rears himself defiantly, with the Napoleonic head and the dark bulk of body, in Raphael's "Dispute About the Sacrament." A portrait by Ghirlandajo emphasises a point which specially reveals what may be called the neglected Italian quality in the man. It also emphasises points that are very important in the mystic and the philosopher. It is universally attested that Aquinas was what is commonly called an absent-minded man. That type has often been rendered in painting, humorous or serious; but almost always in one of two or three conventional ways. Sometimes the expression of the eyes is merely vacant, as if absent-mindedness did really mean a permanent absence of mind. Sometimes it is rendered more respectfully as a wistful expression, as of one yearning for something afar off, that he cannot see and can only faintly desire. Look at the eyes in Ghirlandajo's portrait of St. Thomas; and you will see a sharp difference. While the eyes are indeed completely torn away from the immediate surroundings, so that the pot of flowers above the philosopher's head might fall on it without attracting his attention, they are not in the least wistful, let alone vacant. There is kindled in them a fire of instant inner excitement; they are vivid and very Italian eyes. The man is thinking about something; and something that has reached a crisis; not about nothing or about anything; or, what is almost worse, about everything. There must have been that smouldering vigilance in his eyes, the moment before he smote the table and startled the banquet hall of the King.

Of the personal habits that go with the personal physique, we have also a few convincing and confirming impressions. When he was not sitting still, reading a book, he walked round and round the cloisters and walked fast and even furiously, a very characteristic action of men who fight their battles in the mind. Whenever he was interrupted he was very polite and more apologetic than the apologizer. But there was that about him, which suggested that he was rather happier when he was not interrupted. He was ready to stop his truly Peripatetic tramp: but we feel that when he resumed it, he walked all the faster.

All this suggests that his superficial abstraction, that which the world saw, was of a certain kind. It will be well to understand the quality, for there are several kinds of absence of mind, including that of some pretentious poets and intellectuals, in whom the mind has never been noticeably present. There is the abstraction of the contemplative, whether he is the true sort of Christian contemplative, who is contemplating Something, or the wrong sort of Oriental contemplative, who is contemplating Nothing. Obviously St. Thomas was not a Buddhist mystic; but I do not think his fits of abstraction were even those of a Christian mystic. If he had trances of true Christian mysticism, he took jolly good care that they should not occur at other people's dinner-tables. I think he had the sort of bemused fit, which really belongs to the practical man rather than the entirely mystical man. He uses the recognised distinction between the active life and the contemplative life, but in the cases concerned here, I think even his contemplative life was an active life. It had nothing to do with his higher life, in the sense of ultimate sanctity. It rather reminds us that Napoleon would fall into a fit of apparent boredom at the Opera, and afterwards confess that he was thinking how he could get three army corps at Frankfurt to combine with two army corps at Cologne. So, in the case of Aquinas, if his daydreams were dreams, they were dreams of the day; and dreams of the day of battle. If he talked to himself, it was because he was arguing with somebody else. We can put it another way, by saying that his daydreams, like the dreams of a dog, were dreams of hunting; of pursuing the error as well as pursuing the truth; of following all the twists and turns of evasive falsehood, and tracking it at last to its lair in hell. He would have been the first to admit that the erroneous thinker would probably be more surprised to learn where his thought came from, than anybody else to discover where it went to. But this notion of pursuing he certainly had, and it was the beginning of a thousand mistakes and misunderstandings that pursuing is called in Latin Persecution. Nobody had less than he had of what is commonly called the temper of a persecutor; but he had the quality which in desperate times is often driven to persecute; and that is simply the sense that everything lives somewhere, and nothing dies unless it dies in its own home. That he did sometimes, in this sense, urge in dreams the shadowy chase even in broad daylight, is quite true. But he was an active dreamer, if not what is commonly called a man of action; and in that chase he was truly to be counted among the domini canes; and surely the mightiest and most magnanimous of the Hounds of Heaven.

There may be many who do not understand the nature even of this sort of abstraction. But then, unfortunately, there are many who do not understand the nature of any sort or argument. Indeed, I think there are fewer people now alive who understand argument than there were twenty or thirty years ago; and St. Thomas might have preferred the society of the atheists of the early nineteenth century to that of the blank sceptics of the early twentieth. Anyhow, one of the real disadvantages of the great and glorious sport, that is called argument, is its inordinate length. If you argue honestly, as St. Thomas always did, you will find that the subject sometimes seems as if it would never end. He was strongly conscious of this fact, as appears in many places; for instance his argument that most men must have a revealed religion, because they have not time to argue. No time, that is, to argue fairly. There is always time to argue unfairly; not least in a time like ours. Being himself resolved to argue, to argue honestly, to answer everybody, to deal with everything, he produced books enough to sink a ship or stock a library; though he died in comparatively early middle age. Probably he could not have done it at all, if he had not been thinking even when he was not writing; but above all thinking combatively. This, in his case, certainly did not mean bitterly or spitefully or uncharitably; but it did mean combatively. As a matter of fact, it is generally the man who is not ready to argue, who is ready to sneer. That is why, in recent literature, there has been so little argument and so much sneering.

We have noted that there are barely one or two occasions on which St. Thomas indulged in a denunciation. There is not a single occasion on which he indulged in a sneer. His curiously simple character, his lucid but laborious intellect, could not be better summed up than by saying that he did not know how to sneer. He was in a double sense an intellectual aristocrat: but he was never an intellectual snob. He never troubled at all whether those to whom he talked were more or less of the sort whom the world thinks worth talking to: and it was apparent by the impression of his contemporaries that those who received the ordinary scraps of his wit or wisdom were quite as likely to be nobodies as somebodies, or even quite as likely to be noodles as clever people. He was interested in the souls of all his fellow creatures, but not in classifying the minds of any of them; in a sense it was too personal and in another sense too arrogant for his particular mind and temper. He was very much interested in the subject he was talking about; and may sometimes have talked for a long time, though he was probably silent for a much longer time. But he had all the unconscious contempt which the really intelligent have for an intelligentsia.

Like most men concerned with the common problems of men, he seems to have had a considerable correspondence; considering that correspondence was so much more difficult in his time. We have records of a great many cases in which complete strangers wrote to ask him questions, and sometimes rather ridiculous questions. To all of these he replied with a characteristic mixture of patience and that sort of rationality, which in some rational people tends to be impatience. Somebody, for instance, asked him whether the names of all the blessed were written on a scroll exhibited in heaven. He wrote back with untiring calm; "So far as I can see, this is not the case; but there is no harm in saying so."

I have remarked on the portrait of St. Thomas by an Italian painter, which shows him alert even in abstraction; and only silent as if about to speak. Pictures in that great tradition are generally full of small touches that show a very large imagination. I mean the sort of imagination on which Ruskin remarked, when he saw that in Tintoretto's sunlit scene of the Crucifixion the face of Christ is dark and undecipherable; but the halo round his head unexpectedly faint and grey like the colour of ashes. It would be hard to put more powerfully the idea of Divinity itself in eclipse. There is a touch, which it may be fanciful to find equally significant, in the portrait of Thomas Aquinas. The artist, having given so much vividness and vigilance to the eyes, may have felt that he stressed too much the merely combative concentration of the saint; but anyhow for some reason he has blazoned upon his breast a rather curious emblem, as if it were some third symbolic and cyclopean eye. At least it is no normal Christian sign; but something more like the disk of the sun such as held the face of a heathen god; but the face itself is dark and occult, and only the rays breaking from it are a ring of fire. I do not know whether any traditional meaning has been attached to this; but its imaginative meaning is strangely apt. That secret sun, dark with excess of light, or not showing its light save in the enlightenment of others, might well be the exact emblem of that inner and ideal life of the saint, which was not only hidden by his external words and actions, but even hidden by his merely outward and automatic silences and fits of reflection. In short, this spiritual detachment is not to be confused with his common habit of brooding or falling into a brown study. He was a man entirely careless of all casual criticism of his casual demeanour; as are many men built on a big masculine model and unconsciously inheriting a certain social splendour and largesse. But about his real life of sanctity he was intensely secretive. Such secrecy has indeed generally gone with sanctity; for the saint has an unfathomable horror of playing the Pharisee. But in Thomas Aquinas it was even more sensitive, and what many in the world would call morbid. He did not mind being caught wool-gathering over the wine-cups of the King's banquet; for that was merely upon a point of controversy. But when there was some question of his having seen St. Paul in a vision, he was in an agony of alarm lest it should be discussed; and the story remains somewhat uncertain in consequence. Needless to say, his followers and admirers were as eager to collect these strictly miraculous stories as he was eager to conceal them; and one or two seem to be preserved with a fairly solid setting of evidence. But there are certainly fewer of them, known to the world, than in the case of many saints equally sincere and even equally modest, but more preoccupied with zeal and less sensitive about publicity.

The truth is that about all such things, in life and death, there is a sort of enormous quiet hanging about St. Thomas. He was one of those large things who take up little room. There was naturally a certain stir about his miracles after his death; and about his burial at the time when the University of Paris wished to bury him. I do not know in detail the long history of the other plans of sepulture, which have ultimately ended with his sacred bones lying in the church of St. Sernin in Toulouse: at the very base of the battle-fields where his Dominicans had warred down the pestilence of pessimism from the East. But somehow, it is not easy to think of his shrine as the scene of the more jolly, rowdy and vulgar devotion either in its medieval or modern form. He was very far from being a Puritan, in the true sense; he made a provision for a holiday and banquet for his young friends, which has quite a convivial sound. The trend of his writing especially for his time, is reasonable in its recognition of physical life; and he goes out of his way to say that men must vary their lives with jokes and even with pranks. But for all that, we cannot somehow see his personality as a sort of magnet for mobs: or the road to the tomb of St. Thomas at Toulouse having always been a long street of taverns like that to the tomb of St. Thomas at Canterbury. I think he rather disliked noise; there is a legend that he disliked thunderstorms; but it is contradicted by the fact that in an actual shipwreck he was supremely calm. However that may be, and it probably concerned his health, in some ways sensitive, he certainly was very calm. We have a feeling that we should gradually grow conscious of his presence; as of an immense background.

Here, if this slight sketch could be worthy of its subject, there should stand forth something of that stupendous certitude, in the presence of which all his libraries of philosophy, and even theology, were but a litter of pamphlets. It is certain that this thing was in him from the first, in the form of conviction, long before it could possibly have even begun to take the form of controversy. It was very vivid in his childhood; and his were exactly the circumstances in which the anecdotes of the nursery and the playground are likely enough to have been really preserved. He had from the first that full and final test of truly orthodox Catholicity; the impetuous, impatient intolerant passion for the poor; and even that readiness to be rather a nuisance to the rich, out of a hunger to feed the hungry. This can have had nothing to do with the intellectualism of which he was afterwards accused; still less with any habit of dialectic. It would seem unlikely that at the age of six he had any ambition to answer Averrhoes or that he knew what Effective Causality is; or even that he had worked out, as he did in later life, the whole theory by which a man's love of himself is Sincere and Constant and Indulgent; and that this should be transferred intact (if possible) to his love of his neighbour. At this early age he did not understand all this. He only did it. But all the atmosphere of his actions carries a sort of conviction with it. It is beautifully typical for instance, of that sort of aristocratic menage, that his parents seem to have objected mildly, if at all, to his handing out things to beggars and tramps; but it was intensely disliked by the upper servants.

Still, if we take the thing as seriously as all childish things should be taken, we may learn something from that mysterious state of innocence, which is the first and best spring of all our later indignations. We may begin to understand why it was that there grew steadily with his growing mind, a great and very solitary mind, an ambition that was the inversion of all the things about him. We shall guess what had continuously swelled within him, whether in protest or prophecy or prayer for deliverance, before he startled his family by flinging away not only the trappings of nobility, but all forms of ambition, even ecclesiastical ambition. His childhood may contain the hint of that first stride of his manhood, from the house onto the highway; and his proclamation that he also would be a Beggar.

There is another case of a sort of second glimpse or sequel, in which an incident well known in the external sense gives us also a glimpse of the internal. After the affair of the firebrand, and the woman who tempted him in the tower, it is said that he had a dream; in which two angels girded him with a cord of fire, a thing of terrible pain and yet giving a terrible strength; and he awoke with a great cry in the darkness. This also has something very vivid about it, under the circumstances; and probably contains truths that will be some day better understood, when priests and doctors have learned to talk to each other without the stale etiquette of nineteenth-century negations. It would be easy to analyse the dream, as the very nineteenth-century doctor did in Armadale, resolving it into the details of the past days; the cord from his struggle against being stripped of his Friar's frock; the thread of fire running through the tapestries of the night, from the firebrand he had snatched from the fireside. But even in Armadale the dream was fulfilled mystically as well, and the dream of St. Thomas was fulfilled very mystically indeed. For he did in fact remain remarkably untroubled on that side of his human nature after the incident; though it is likely enough that the incident had caused an upheaval of his normal humanity, which produced a dream stronger than a nightmare. This is no place to analyse the psychological fact, which puzzles Non-Catholics so much: of the way in which priests do manage to be celibate without ceasing to be virile. Anyhow, it seems probable that in this matter he was less troubled than most. This has nothing to do with true virtue, which is of the will; saints as holy as he have rolled themselves in brambles to distract the pressure of passion; but he never needed much in the way of a counter-irritant; for the simple reason that in this way, as in most ways, he was not very often irritated. Much must remain unexplained, as part of the mysteries of grace; but there is probably some truth in the psychological idea of "sublimation"; that is the lifting of a lower energy to higher ends; so that appetite almost faded in the furnace of his intellectual energy. Between supernatural and natural causes, it is probable that he never knew or suffered greatly on this side of his mind.

There are moments when the most orthodox reader is tempted to hate the hagiographer as much as he loves the holy man. The holy man always conceals his holiness; that is the one invariable rule. And the hagiographer sometimes seems like a persecutor trying to frustrate the holy man; a spy or eavesdropper hardly more respectful than an American interviewer. I admit that these sentiments are fastidious and one-sided, and I will now proceed to prove my penitence by mentioning one or two of the incidents that could only have come to common knowledge in this deplorable way.

It seems certain that he did live a sort of secondary and mysterious life; the divine double of what is called a double life. Somebody seems to have caught a glimpse of the sort of solitary miracle which modern psychic people call Levitation; and he must surely have either been a liar or a literal witness, for there could have been no doubts or degrees about such a prodigy happening to such a person: it must have been like seeing one of the huge pillars of the church suspended like a cloud. Nobody knows, I imagine, what spiritual storm of exaltation or agony produces this convulsion in matter or space; but the thing does almost certainly occur. Even in the case of ordinary Spiritualist mediums, for whatever reason, the evidence is very difficult to refute. But probably the most representative revelation of this side of his life may be found in the celebrated story of the miracle of the crucifix; when in the stillness of the church of St. Dominic in Naples, a voice spoke from the carven Christ, and told the kneeling Friar that he had written rightly, and offered him the choice of a reward among all the things of the world.

Not all, I think, have appreciated the point of this particular story as applied to this particular saint. It is an old story, in so far as it is simply the offer made to a devotee of solitude or simplicity, of the pick of all the prizes of life. The hermit, true or false, the fakir, the fanatic or the cynic, Stylites on his column or Diogenes in his tub, can all be pictured as tempted by the powers of the earth, of the air or of the heavens, with the offer of the best of everything; and replying that they want nothing. In the Greek cynic or stoic it really meant the mere negative; that he wanted nothing. In the Oriental mystic or fanatic, it sometimes meant a sort of positive negative; that he wanted Nothing; that Nothing was really what he wanted. Sometimes it expressed a noble independence, and the twin virtues of antiquity, the love of liberty and the hatred of luxury. Sometimes it only expressed a self-sufficiency that is the very opposite of sanctity. But even the stories of real saints, of this sort, do not quite cover the case of St. Thomas. He was not a person who wanted nothing; and he was a person who was enormously interested in everything. His answer is not so inevitable or simple as some may suppose. As compared with many other saints, and many other philosophers, he was avid in his acceptance of Things; in his hunger and thirst for Things. It was his special spiritual thesis that there really are things; and not only the Thing; that the Many existed as well as the One. I do not mean things to eat or drink or wear, though he never denied to these their place in the noble hierarchy of Being; but rather things to think about, and especially things to prove, to experience and to know. Nobody supposes that Thomas Aquinas, when offered by God his choice among all the gifts of God, would ask for a thousand pounds, or the Crown of Sicily, or a present of rare Greek wine. But he might have asked for things that he really wanted: and he was a man who could want things; as he wanted the lost manuscript of St. Chrysostom. He might have asked for the solution of an old difficulty; or the secret of a new science; or a flash of the inconceivable intuitive mind of the angels, or any one of a thousand things that would really have satisfied his broad and virile appetite for the very vastness and variety of the universe. The point is that for him, when the voice spoke from between the outstretched arms of the Crucified, those arms were truly opened wide, and opening most gloriously the gates of all the worlds; they were arms pointing to the east and to the west, to the ends of the earth and the very extremes of existence. They were truly spread out with a gesture of omnipotent generosity; the Creator himself offering Creation itself; with all its millionfold mystery of separate beings, and the triumphal chorus of the creatures. That is the blazing background of multitudinous Being that gives the particular strength, and even a sort of surprise, to the answer of St. Thomas, when he lifted at last his head and spoke with, and for, that almost blasphemous audacity which is one with the humility of his religion; "I will have Thyself."

Or, to add the crowning and crushing irony to this story, so uniquely Christian for those who can really understand it, there are some who feel that the audacity is softened by insisting that he said, "Only Thyself."

Of these miracles, in the strictly miraculous sense, there are not so many as in the lives of less immediately influential saints; but they are probably pretty well authenticated; for he was a well-known public man in a prominent position, and, what is even more convenient for him, he had any number of highly incensed enemies, who could be trusted to sift his claims. There is at least one miracle of healing; that of a woman who touched his gown; and several incidents that may be variants of the story of the crucifix at Naples. One of these stories, however, has a further importance as bringing us to another section of his more private, personal or even emotional religious life; the section that expressed itself in poetry. When he was stationed at Paris, the other Doctors of the Sorbonne put before him a problem about the nature of the mystical change in the elements of the Blessed Sacrament, and he proceeded to write, in his customary manner, a very careful and elaborately lucid statement of his own solution. Needless to say he felt with hearty simplicity the heavy responsibility and gravity of such a judicial decision; and not unnaturally seems to have worried about it more than he commonly did over his work. He sought for guidance in more than usually prolonged prayer and intercession; and finally, with one of those few but striking bodily gestures that mark the turning points of his life, he threw down his thesis at the foot of the crucifix on the altar, and left it lying there; as if awaiting judgment. Then he turned and came down the altar steps and buried himself once more in prayer; but the other Friars, it is said, were watching; and well they might be. For they declared afterwards that the figure of Christ had come down from the cross before their mortal eyes; and stood upon the scroll, saying "Thomas, thou hast written well concerning the Sacrament of My Body." It was after this vision that the incident is said to have happened, of his being born up miraculously in mid-air.

An acute observer said of Thomas Aquinas in his own time, "He could alone restore all philosophy, if it had been burnt by fire." That is what is meant by saying that he was an original man, a creative mind; that he could have made his own cosmos out of stones and straws, even without the manuscripts of Aristotle or Augustine. But there is here a not uncommon confusion, between the thing in which a man is most original and that in which he is most interested; or between the thing that he does best and the thing that he loves most. Because St. Thomas was a unique and striking philosopher, it is almost unavoidable that this book should be merely, or mainly, a sketch of his philosophy. It cannot be, and does not pretend to be, a sketch of his theology. But this is because the theology of a saint is simply the theism of a saint; or rather the theism of all saints. It is less individual, but it is much more intense. It is concerned with the common origin; but it is hardly an occasion for originality. Thus we are forced to think first of Thomas as the maker of the Thomist philosophy; as we think first of Christopher Columbus as the discoverer of America, though he may have been quite sincere in his pious hope to convert the Khan of Tartary; or of James Watt as the discoverer of the steam-engine, though he may have been a devout fire-worshipper, or a sincere Scottish Calvinist, or all kinds of curious things. Anyhow, it is but natural that Augustine and Aquinas, Bonaventure and Duns Scotus, all the doctors and the saints, should draw nearer to each other as they approach the divine units in things; and that there should in that sense be less difference between them in theology than in philosophy. It is true that, in some matters, the critics of Aquinas thought his philosophy had unduly affected his theology. This is especially so, touching the charge that he made the state of Beatitude too intellectual, conceiving it as the satisfaction of the love of truth; rather than specially as the truth of love. It is true that the mystics and the men of the Franciscan school, dwelt more lovingly on the admitted supremacy of love. But it was mostly a matter of emphasis; perhaps tinged faintly by temperament, possibly (to suggest something which is easier to feel than to explain), in the case of St. Thomas, a shadowy influence of a sort of shyness. Whether the supreme ecstasy is more affectional than intellectual is no very deadly matter of quarrel among men who believe it is both, but do not profess even to imagine the actual experience of either. But I have a sort of feeling that, even if St. Thomas had thought it was as emotional as St. Bonaventure did, he would never have been so emotional about it. It would always have embarrassed him to write about love at such length.

The one exception permitted to him was the rare but remarkable output of his poetry. All sanctity is secrecy; and his sacred poetry was really a secretion; like the pearl in a very tightly closed oyster. He may have written more of it than we know; but part of it came into public use through the particular circumstance of his being asked to compose the office for the Feast of Corpus Christi: a festival first established after the controversy to which he had contributed, in the scroll that he laid on the altar. It does certainly reveal an entirely different side of his genius; and it certainly was genius. As a rule, he was an eminently practical prose writer; some would say a very prosaic prose writer. He maintained controversy with an eye on only two qualities; clarity and courtesy. And he maintained these because they were entirely practical qualities; affecting the probabilities of conversion. But the composer of the Corpus Christi service was not merely what even the wild and woolly would call a poet; he was what the most fastidious would call an artist. His double function rather recalls the double activity of some great Renaissance craftsman, like Michelangelo or Leonardo da Vinci, who would work on the outer wall, planning and building the fortifications of the city; and then retire into the inner chamber to carve or model some cup or casket for a reliquary. The Corpus Christi Office is like some old musical instrument, quaintly and carefully inlaid with many coloured stones and metals; the author has gathered remote texts about pasture and fruition like rare herbs; there is a notable lack of the loud and obvious in the harmony; and the whole is strung with two strong Latin lyrics. Father John O'Connor has translated them with an almost miraculous aptitude; but a good translator will be the first to agree that no translation is good; or, at any rate, good enough. How are we to find eight short English words which actually stand for "Sumit unus, sumunt mille; quantum isti, tantum ille"? How is anybody really to render the sound of the "Pange Lingua", when the very first syllable has a clang like the clash of cymbals?

There was one other channel, besides that of poetry, and it was that of private affections, by which this large and shy man could show that he had really as much Caritas as St. Francis; and certainly as much as any Franciscan theologian. Bonaventure was not likely to think that Thomas was lacking in the love of God, and certainly he was never lacking in the love of Bonaventure. He felt for his whole family a steady, we might say a stubborn tenderness; and, considering how his family treated him, this would seem to call not only for charity, but for his characteristic virtue of patience. Towards the end of his life, he seems to have leaned especially on his love of one of the brethren, a Friar named Reginald, who received from him some strange and rather startling confidences, of the kind that he very seldom gave even to his friends. It was to Reginald that he gave that last and rather extraordinary hint, which was the end of his controversial career, and practically of his earthly life; a hint that history has never been able to explain.

He had returned victorious from his last combat with Siger of Brabant; returned and retired. This particular quarrel was the one point, as we may say, in which his outer and his inner life had crossed and coincided; he realised how he had longed from childhood to call up all allies in the battle for Christ; how he had only long afterwards called up Aristotle as an ally; and now in that last nightmare of sophistry, he had for the first time truly realised that some might really wish Christ to go down before Aristotle. He never recovered from the shock. He won his battle, because he was the best brain of his time, but he could not forget such an inversion of the whole idea and purpose of his life. He was the sort of man who hates hating people. He had not been used to hating even their hateful ideas, beyond a certain point. But in the abyss of anarchy opened by Siger's sophistry of the Double Mind of Man, he had seen the possibility of the perishing of all idea of religion, and even of all idea of truth. Brief and fragmentary as are the phrases that record it, we can gather that he came back with a sort of horror of that outer world, in which there blew such wild winds of doctrine, and a longing for the inner world which any Catholic can share, and in which the saint is not cut off from simple men. He resumed the strict routine of religion, and for some time said nothing to anybody. And then something happened (it is said while he was celebrating Mass) the nature of which will never be known among mortal men.

His friend Reginald asked him to return also to his equally regular habits of reading and writing, and following the controversies of the hour. He said with a singular emphasis, "I can write no more." There seems to have been a silence; after which Reginald again ventured to approach the subject; and Thomas answered him with even greater vigour, "I can write no more. I have seen things which make all my writings like straw."

In 1274, when Aquinas was nearly fifty, the Pope, rejoicing in the recent victory over the Arabian sophists, sent word to him, asking him to come to a Council on these controversial matters, to be held at Lyons. He rose in automatic obedience, as a soldier rises; but we may fancy that there was something in his eyes that told those around him that obedience to the outer command would not in fact frustrate obedience to some more mysterious inner command; a signal that only he had seen. He set out with his friend on the journey, proposing to rest for the night with his sister, to whom he was deeply devoted; and when he came into her house he was stricken down with some unnamed malady. We need not discuss the doubtful medical problems. It is true that he had always been one of those men, healthy in the main, who are overthrown by small illnesses; it is equally true that there is no very clear account of this particular illness. He was eventually taken to a monastery at Fossanuova; and his strange end came upon him with great strides. It may be worth remarking, for those who think that he thought too little of the emotional or romantic side of religious truth, that he asked to have The Song of

Solomon read through to him from beginning to end. The feelings of the men about him must have been mingled and rather indescribable; and certainly quite different from his own. He confessed his sins and he received his God; and we may be sure that the great philosopher had entirely forgotten philosophy. But it was not entirely so with those who had loved him, or even those who merely lived in his time. The elements of the narrative are so few, yet so essential, that we have a strong sense in reading the story of the two emotional sides of the event. Those men must have known that a great mind was still labouring like a great mill in the midst of them. They must have felt that, for that moment, the inside of the monastery was larger than the outside. It must have resembled the case of some mighty modern engine, shaking the ramshackle building in which it is for the moment enclosed. For truly that machine was made of the wheels of all the worlds; and revolved like that cosmos of concentric spheres which, whatever its fate in the face of changing science, must always be something of a symbol for philosophy; the depth of double and triple transparencies more mysterious than darkness; the sevenfold, the terrible crystal. In the world of that mind there was a wheel of angels, and a wheel of planets, and a wheel of plants or of animals; but there was also a just and intelligible order of all earthly things, a sane authority and a self-respecting liberty, and a hundred answers to a hundred questions in the complexity of ethics or economics. But there must have been a moment, when men knew that the thunderous mill of thought had stopped suddenly; and that after the shock of stillness that wheel would shake the world no more; that there was nothing now within that hollow house but a great hill of clay; and the confessor, who had been with him in the inner chamber, ran forth as if in fear, and whispered that his confession had been that of a child of five.

--/--

VI THE APPROACH TO THOMISM

The fact that Thomism is the philosophy of common sense is itself a matter of common sense. Yet it wants a word of explanation, because we have so long taken such matters in a very uncommon sense. For good or evil, Europe since the Reformation, and most especially England since the Reformation, has been in a peculiar sense the home of paradox. I mean in the very peculiar sense that paradox was at home, and that men were at home with it. The most familiar example is the English boasting that they are practical because they are not logical. To an ancient Greek or a Chinaman this would seem exactly like saying that London clerks excel in adding up their ledgers, because they are not accurate in their arithmetic. But the point is not that it is a paradox; it is that parodoxy has become orthodoxy; that men repose in a paradox as placidly as in a platitude. It is not that the practical man stands on his head, which may sometimes be a stimulating if startling gymnastic; it is that he rests on his head; and even sleeps on his head. This is an important point, because the use of paradox is to awaken the mind. Take a good paradox, like that of Oliver Wendell Holmes: "Give us the luxuries of life and we will dispense with the necessities." It is amusing and therefore arresting; it has a fine air of defiance; it contains a real if romantic truth. It is all part of the fun that it is stated almost in the form of a contradiction in terms. But most people would agree that there would be considerable danger in basing the whole social system on the notion that necessities are not necessary; as some have based the whole British Constitution on the notion that nonsense will always work out as common sense. Yet even here, it might be said that the invidious example has spread, and that the modern industrial system does really say, "Give us luxuries like coal-tar soap, and we will dispense with necessities like corn."

So much is familiar; but what is not even now realised is that not only the practical politics, but the abstract philosophies of the modern world have had this queer twist. Since the modern world began in the sixteenth century, nobody's system of philosophy has really corresponded to everybody's sense of reality: to what, if left to themselves, common men would call common sense. Each started with a paradox: a peculiar point of view demanding the sacrifice of what they would call a sane point of view. That is the one thing common to Hobbes and Hegel, to Kant and Bergson, to Berkeley and William James. A man had to believe something that no normal man would believe, if it were suddenly propounded to his simplicity; as that law is above right, or right is outside reason, or things are only as we think them, or everything is relative to a reality that is not there. The modern philosopher claims, like a sort of confidence man, that if once we will grant him this, the rest will be easy; he will straighten out the world, if once he is allowed to give this one twist to the mind.

It will be understood that in these matters I speak as a fool; or, as our democratic cousins would say, a moron; anyhow as a man in the street; and the only object of this chapter is to show that the Thomist philosophy is nearer than most philosophies to the mind of the man in the street. I am not, like Father D'Arcy, whose admirable book on St. Thomas has illuminated many problems for me, a trained philosopher, acquainted with the technique of the trade. But I hope Father D'Arcy will forgive me if I take one example from his book, which exactly illustrates what I mean. He, being a trained philosopher, is naturally trained to put up with philosophers. Also, being a trained priest, he is naturally accustomed, not only to suffer fools gladly, but (what is sometimes even harder) to suffer clever people gladly. Above all, his wide reading in metaphysics has made him patient with clever people when they indulge in folly. The consequence is that he can write calmly and even blandly sentences like these. "A certain likeness can be detected between the aim and method of St. Thomas and those of Hegel. There are, however, also remarkable differences. For St. Thomas it is impossible that contradictories should exist together, and again reality and intelligibility correspond, but a thing must first be, to be intelligible."

Let the man in the street be forgiven, if he adds that the "remarkable difference" seems to him to be that St. Thomas was sane and Hegel was mad. The moron refuses to admit that Hegel can both exist and not exist; or that it can be possible to understand Hegel, if there is no Hegel to understand. Yet Father D'Arcy mentions this Hegelian paradox as if it were all in the day's work; and of course it is, if the work is reading all the modern philosophers as searchingly and sympathetically as he has done. And this is what I mean saying that all modern philosophy starts with a stumbling-block. It is surely not too much to say that there seems to be a twist, in saying that contraries are not incompatible; or that a thing can "be" intelligible and not as yet "be" at all.

Against all this the philosophy of St. Thomas stands founded on the universal common conviction that eggs are eggs. The Hegelian may say that an egg is really a hen, because it is a part of an endless process of Becoming; the Berkeleian may hold that poached eggs only exist as a dream exists; since it is quite as easy to call the dream the cause of the eggs as the eggs the cause of the dream; the Pragmatist may believe that we get the best out of scrambled eggs by forgetting that they ever were eggs, and only remembering the scramble. But no pupil of St. Thomas needs to addle his brains in order adequately to addle his eggs; to put his head at any peculiar angle in looking at eggs, or squinting at eggs, or winking the other eye in order to see a new simplification of eggs. The Thomist stands in the broad daylight of the brotherhood of men, in their common consciousness that eggs are not hens or dreams or mere practical assumptions; but things attested by the Authority of the Senses, which is from God.

Thus, even those who appreciate the metaphysical depth of Thomism in other matters have expressed surprise that he does not deal at all with what many now think the main metaphysical question; whether we can prove that the primary act of recognition of any reality is real. The answer is that St. Thomas recognised instantly, what so many modern sceptics have begun to suspect rather laboriously; that a man must either answer that question in the affirmative, or else never answer any question, never ask any question, never even exist intellectually, to answer or to ask. I suppose it is true in a sense that a man can be a fundamental sceptic, but he cannot be anything else: certainly not even a defender of fundamental scepticism. If a man feels that all the movements of his own mind are meaningless, then his mind is meaningless, and he is meaningless; and it does not mean anything to attempt to discover his meaning. Most fundamental sceptics appear to survive, because they are not consistently sceptical and not at all fundamental. They will first deny everything and then admit something, if for the sake of argument--or often rather of attack without argument. I saw an almost startling example of this essential frivolity in a professor of final scepticism, in a paper the other day. A man wrote to say that he accepted nothing but Solipsism, and added that he had often wondered it was not a more common philosophy. Now Solipsism simply means that a man believes in his own existence, but not in anybody or anything else. And it never struck this simple sophist, that if his philosophy was true, there obviously were no other philosophers to profess it.

To this question "Is there anything?" St. Thomas begins by answering "Yes"; if he began by answering "No", it would not be the beginning, but the end. That is what some of us call common sense. Either there is no philosophy, no philosophers, no thinkers, no thought, no anything; or else there is a real bridge between the mind and reality. But he is actually less exacting than many thinkers, much less so than most rationalist and materialist thinkers, as to what that first step involves; he is content, as we shall see, to say that it involves the recognition of Ens or Being as something definitely beyond ourselves. Ens is Ens: Eggs are eggs, and it is not tenable that all eggs were found in a mare's nest.

Needless to say, I am not so silly as to suggest that all the writings of St. Thomas are simple and straightforward; in the sense of being easy to understand. There are passages I do not in the least understand myself; there are passages that puzzle much more learned and logical philosophers than I am; there are passages about which the greatest Thomists still differ and dispute. But that is a question of a thing being hard to read or understand: not hard to accept when understood. That is a mere matter of "The Cat sat on the Mat" being written in Chinese characters: or "Mary had a Little Lamb" in Egyptian hieroglyphics. The only point I am stressing here is that Aquinas is almost always on the side of simplicity, and supports the ordinary man's acceptance of ordinary truisms. For instance, one of the most obscure passages, in my very inadequate judgment, is that in which he explains how the mind is certain of an external object and not merely of an impression of that object; and yet apparently reaches it through a concept, though not merely through an impression. But the only point here is that he does explain that the mind is certain of an external object. It is enough for this purpose that his conclusion is what is called the conclusion of common sense; that it is his purpose to justify common sense; even though he justifies it in a passage which happens to be one of rather uncommon subtlety. The problem of later philosophers is that their conclusion is as dark as their demonstration; or that they bring out a result of which the result is chaos.

Unfortunately, between the man in the street and the Angel of the Schools, there stands at this moment a very high brick wall, with spikes on the top, separating two men who in many ways stand for the same thing. The wall is almost a historical accident; at least it was built a very long time ago, for reasons that need not affect the needs of normal men today; least of all the greatest need of normal men; which is for a normal philosophy. The first difficulty is merely a difference of form; not in the medieval but in the modern sense. There is first a simple obstacle of language; there is then a rather more subtle obstacle of logical method. But the language itself counts for a great deal; even when it is translated, it is still a foreign language; and it is, like other foreign languages, very often translated wrong. As with every other literature from another age or country, it carried with it an atmosphere which is beyond the mere translation of words, as they are translated in a traveller's phrase-book. For instance, the whole system of St. Thomas hangs on one huge and yet simple idea; which does actually cover everything there is, and even everything that could possibly be. He represents this cosmic conception by the word Ens; and anybody who can read any Latin at all, however rudely, feels it to be the apt and fitting word; exactly as he feels it in a French word in a piece of good French prose. It ought to be a matter of logic; but it is also a matter of language.

Unfortunately there is no satisfying translation of the word Ens. The difficulty is rather verbal than logical, but it is practical. I mean that when the translator says in English 'being', we are aware of a rather different atmosphere. Atmosphere ought not to affect these absolutes of the intellect; but it does. The new psychologists, who are almost eagerly at war with reason, never tire of telling us that the very terms we use are coloured by our subconsciousness, with something we meant to exclude from our consciousness. And one need not be so idealistically irrational as a modern psychologist, in order to admit that the very shape and sound of words do make a difference, even in the baldest prose, as they do in the most beautiful poetry. We cannot quite prevent the imagination from remembering irrelevant associations even in the abstract sciences like mathematics. Jones Minimus, hustled from history to geometry, may for an instant connect the Angles of the isosceles triangle with the Angles of the Anglo-Saxon Chronicle; and even the mature mathematician, if he is as mad as the psychoanalyst hopes, may have in the roots of his subconscious mind something material in his idea of a root. Now it unfortunately happens that the word 'being', as it comes to a modern Englishman, through modern associations, has a sort of hazy atmosphere that is not in the short and sharp Latin word. Perhaps it reminds him of fantastic professors in fiction, who wave their hands and say, "Thus do we mount to the ineffable heights of pure and radiant Being:" or, worse still, of actual professors in real life, who say, "All Being is Becoming; and is but the evolution of Not-Being by the law of its Being." Perhaps it only reminds him of romantic rhapsodies in old love stories; "Beautiful and adorable being, light and breath of my very being". Anyhow it has a wild and woolly sort of sound; as if only very vague people used it; or as if it might mean all sorts of different things.

Now the Latin word Ens has a sound like the English word End. It is final and even abrupt; it is nothing except itself. There was once a silly gibe against Scholastics like Aquinas, that they discussed whether angels could stand on the point of a needle. It is at least certain that this first word of Aquinas is as sharp as the point of a pin. For that also is, in an almost ideal sense, an End. But when we say that St. Thomas Aquinas is concerned fundamentally with the idea of Being, we must not admit any of the cloudier generalisations that we may have grown used to, or even grown tired of, in the sort of idealistic writing that is rather rhetoric than philosophy. Rhetoric is a very fine thing in its place, as a medieval scholar would have willingly agreed, as he taught it along with logic in the schools; but St. Thomas Aquinas himself is not at all rhetorical. Perhaps he is hardly even sufficiently rhetorical. There are any number of purple patches in Augustine; but there are no purple patches in Aquinas. He did on certain definite occasions drop into poetry; but he very seldom dropped into oratory. And so little was he in touch with some modern tendencies, that whenever he did write poetry, he actually put it into poems. There is another side to this, to be noted later. He very specially possessed the philosophy that inspires poetry; as he did so largely inspire Dante's poetry. And poetry without philosophy has only inspiration, or, in vulgar language, only wind. He had, so to speak, the imagination without the imagery. And even this is perhaps too sweeping. There is an image of his, that is true poetry as well as true philosophy; about the tree of life bowing down with a huge humility, because of the very load of its living fruitfulness; a thing Dante might have described so as to overwhelm us with the tremendous twilight and almost drug us with the divine fruit. But normally, we may say that his words are brief even when his books are long. I have taken the example of the word Ens, precisely because it is one of the cases in which Latin is plainer than plain English. And his style, unlike that of St. Augustine and many Catholic Doctors, is always a penny plain rather than twopence coloured. It is often difficult to understand, simply because the subjects are so difficult that hardly any mind, except one like his own, can fully understand them. But he never darkens it by using words without knowledge, or even more legitimately, by using words belonging only to imagination or intuition. So far as his method is concerned, he is perhaps the one real Rationalist among all the children of men.

This brings us to the other difficulty; that of logical method. I have never understood why there is supposed to be something crabbed or antique about a syllogism; still less can I understand what anybody means by talking as if induction had somehow taken the place of deduction. The whole point of deduction is that true premises produce a true conclusion. What is called induction seems simply to mean collecting a larger number of true premises, or perhaps, in some physical matters, taking rather more trouble to see that they are true. It may be a fact that a modern man can get more out of a great many premises, concerning microbes or asteroids than a medieval man could get out of a very few premises about salamanders and unicorns. But the process of deduction from the data is the same for the modern mind as for the medieval mind; and what is pompously called induction is simply collecting more of the data. And Aristotle or Aquinas, or anybody in his five wits, would of course agree that the conclusion could only be true if the premises were true; and that the more true premises there were the better. It was the misfortune of medieval culture that there were not enough true premises, owing to the rather ruder conditions of travel or experiment. But however perfect were the conditions of travel or experiment, they could only produce premises; it would still be necessary to deduce conclusions. But many modern people talk as if what they call induction were some magic way of reaching a conclusion, without using any of those horrid old syllogisms. But induction does not lead us to a conclusion. Induction only leads us to a deduction. Unless the last three syllogistic steps are all right, the conclusion is all wrong. Thus, the great nineteenth century men of science, whom I was brought up to revere ("accepting the conclusions of science", it was always called), went out and closely inspected the air and the earth, the chemicals and the gases, doubtless more closely than Aristotle or Aquinas, and then came back and embodied their final conclusion in a syllogism. "All matter is made of microscopic little knobs which are indivisible. My body is made of matter. Therefore my body is made of microscopic little knobs which are indivisible." They were not wrong in the form of their reasoning; because it is the only way to reason. In this world there is nothing except a syllogism--and a fallacy. But of course these modern men knew, as the medieval men knew, that their conclusions would not be true unless their premises were true. And that is where the trouble began. For the men of science, or their sons and nephews, went out and took another look at the knobby nature of matter; and were surprised to find that it was not knobby at all. So they came back and completed the process with their syllogism; "All matter is made of whirling protons and electrons. My body is made of matter. Therefore my body is made of whirling protons and electrons." And that again is a good syllogism; though they may have to look at matter once or twice more, before we know whether it is a true premise and a true conclusion. But in the final process of truth there is nothing else except a good syllogism. The only other thing is a bad syllogism; as in the familiar fashionable shape; "All matter is made of protons and electrons. I should very much like to think that mind is much the same as matter. So I will announce, through the microphone or the megaphone, that my mind is made of protons and electrons." But that is not induction; it is only a very bad blunder in deduction. That is not another or new way of thinking; it is only ceasing to think.

What is really meant, and what is much more reasonable, is that the old syllogists sometimes set out the syllogism at length; and certainly that is not always necessary. A man can run down the three steps much more quickly than that; but a man cannot run down the three steps if they are not there. If he does, he will break his neck, as if he walked out of a fourth-story window. The truth about this false antithesis of induction and deduction is simply this; that as premises or data accumulated, the emphasis and detail was shifted to them, from the final deduction to which they lead. But they did lead to a final deduction; or else they led to nothing. The logician had so much to say about electrons or microbes that he dwelt most on these data and shortened or assumed his ultimate syllogism. But if he reasoned rightly, however rapidly, he reasoned syllogistically.

As a matter of fact, Aquinas does not usually argue in syllogisms; though he always argues syllogistically. I mean he does not set out all the steps of the logic in each case; the legend that he does so is part of that loose and largely unverified legend of the Renaissance; that the Schoolmen were all crabbed and mechanical medieval bores. But he does argue with a certain austerity, and disdain of ornament, which may make him seem monotonous to anyone specially seeking the modern forms of wit or fancy. But all this has nothing to do with the question asked at the beginning of this chapter and needing to be answered at the end of it; the question of what he is arguing for. In that respect it can be repeated, most emphatically, that he is arguing for common sense. He is arguing for a common sense which would even now commend itself to most of the common people. He is arguing for the popular proverbs that seeing is believing; that the proof of the pudding is in the eating; that a man cannot jump down his own throat or deny the fact of his own existence. He often maintains the view by the use of abstractions; but the abstractions are no more abstract than Energy or Evolution or Space-Time; and they do not land us, as the others often do, in hopeless contradictions about common life. The Pragmatist sets out to be practical, but his practicality turns out to be entirely theoretical. The Thomist begins by being theoretical, but his theory turns out to be entirely practical. That is why a great part of the world is returning to it today.

Finally, there is some real difficulty in the fact of a foreign language; apart from the ordinary fact of the Latin language. Modern philosophical terminology is not always exactly identical with plain English; and medieval philosophical terminology is not at all identical even with modern philosophical terminology. It is not really very difficult to learn the meaning of the main terms; but their medieval meaning is sometimes the exact opposite of their modern meaning. The obvious example is in the pivotal word "form". We say nowadays, "I wrote a formal apology to the Dean", or "The proceedings when we wound up the Tip-Cat Club were purely formal." But we mean that they were purely fictitious; and St. Thomas, had he been a member of the Tip-Cat Club, would have meant just the opposite. He would have meant that the proceedings dealt with the very heart and soul and secret of the whole being of the Tip-Cat Club; and that the apology to the Dean was so essentially apologetic that it tore the very heart out in tears of true contrition. For "formal" in Thomist language means actual, or possessing the real decisive quality that makes a thing itself. Roughly when he describes a thing as made out of Form and Matter, he very rightly recognises that Matter is the more mysterious and indefinite and featureless element; and that what stamps anything with its own identity is its Form. Matter, so to speak, is not so much the solid as the liquid or gaseous thing in the cosmos: and in this most modern scientists are beginning to agree with him. But the form is the fact; it is that which makes a brick a brick, and a bust a bust, and not the shapeless and trampled clay of which either may be made. The stone that broke a statuette, in some Gothic niche, might have been itself a statuette; and under chemical analysis, the statuette is only a stone. But such a chemical analysis is entirely false as a philosophical analysis. The reality, the thing that makes the two things real, is in the idea of the image and in the idea of the image-breaker. This is only a passing example of the mere idiom of the Thomist terminology; but it is not a bad prefatory specimen of the truth of Thomist thought. Every artist knows that the form is not superficial but fundamental; that the form is the foundation. Every sculptor knows that the form of the statue is not the outside of the statue, but rather the inside of the statue; even in the sense of the inside of the sculptor. Every poet knows that the sonnet-form is not only the form of the poem; but the poem. No modern critic who does not understand what the medieval Schoolman meant by form can meet the Schoolman as an intellectual equal.

--/--

VII THE PERMANENT PHILOSOPHY

It is a pity that the word Anthropology has been degraded to the study of Anthropoids. It is now incurably associated with squabbles between prehistoric professors (in more senses than one) about whether a chip of stone is the tooth of a man or an ape; sometimes settled as in that famous case, when it was found to be the tooth of a pig. It is very right that there should be a purely physical science of such things; but the name commonly used might well, by analogy, have been dedicated to things not only wider and deeper, but rather more relevant. Just as, in America, the new Humanists have pointed out to the old Humanitarians that their humanitarianism has been largely concentrated on things that are not specially human, such as physical conditions, appetites, economic needs, environment and so on-- so in practice those who are called Anthropologists have to narrow their minds to the materialistic things that are not notably anthropic. They have to hunt through history and pre-history something which emphatically is not Homo Sapiens, but is always in fact regarded as Simius Insipiens. Homo Sapiens can only be considered in relation to Sapientia and only a book like that of St. Thomas is really devoted to the intrinsic idea of Sapientia. In short, there ought to be a real study called Anthropology corresponding to Theology. In this sense St. Thomas Aquinas, perhaps more than he is anything else, is a great anthropologist.

I apologise for the opening words of this chapter to all those excellent and eminent men of science, who are engaged in the real study of humanity in its relation to biology. But I rather fancy that they will be the last to deny that there has been a somewhat disproportionate disposition, in popular science, to turn the study of human beings into the study of savages. And savagery is not history; it is either the beginning of history or the end of it. I suspect that the greatest scientists would agree that only too many professors have thus been lost in the bush or the jungle; professors who wanted to study anthropology and never got any further than anthropophagy. But I have a particular reason for prefacing this suggestion of a higher anthropology by an apology to any genuine biologists who might seem to be included, but are certainly not included, in a protest against cheap popular science. For the first thing to be said about St. Thomas as an anthropologist, is that he is really remarkably like the best sort of modern biological anthropologist; of the sort who would call themselves Agnostics. This fact is so sharp and decisive a turning point in history, that the history really needs to be recalled and recorded.

St. Thomas Aquinas closely resembles the great Professor Huxley, the Agnostic who invented the word Agnosticism. He is like him in his way of starting the argument, and he is unlike everybody else, before and after, until the Huxleyan age. He adopts almost literally the Huxleyan definition of the Agnostic method; "To follow reason as far as it will go"; the only question is--where does it go? He lays down the almost startlingly modern or materialist statement; "Every thing that is in the intellect has been in the senses". This is where he began, as much as any modern man of science, nay, as much as any modern materialist who can now hardly be called a man of science; at the very opposite end of enquiry from that of the mere mystic. The Platonists, or at least the Neo-Platonists, all tended to the view that the mind was lit entirely from within; St. Thomas insisted that it was lit by five windows, that we call the windows of the senses. But he wanted the light from without to shine on what was within. He wanted to study the nature of Man, and not merely of such moss and mushrooms as he might see through the window, and which he valued as the first enlightening experience of man. And starting from this point, he proceeds to climb the House of Man, step by step and story by story, until he has come out on the highest tower and beheld the largest vision.

In other words, he is an anthropologist, with a complete theory of Man, right or wrong. Now the modern Anthropologists, who called themselves Agnostics, completely failed to be Anthropologists at all. Under their limitations, they could not get a complete theory of Man, let alone a complete theory of nature. They began by ruling out something which they called the Unknowable. The incomprehensibility was almost comprehensible, if we could really understand the Unknowable in the sense of the Ultimate. But it rapidly became apparent that all sorts of things were Unknowable, which were exactly the things that a man has got to know. It is necessary to know whether he is responsible or irresponsible, perfect or imperfect, perfectible or unperfectible, mortal or immortal, doomed or free, not in order to understand God, but in order to understand Man. Nothing that leaves these things under a cloud of religious doubt can possibly pretend to be a Science of Man; it shrinks from anthropology as completely as from theology. Has a man free will; or is his sense of choice an illusion? Has he a conscience, or has his conscience any authority; or is it only the prejudice of the tribal past? Is there real hope of settling these things by human reason; and has that any authority? Is he to regard death as final; and is he to regard miraculous help as possible? Now it is all nonsense to say that these are unknowable in any remote sense, like the distinction between the Cherubim and the Seraphim, or the Procession of the Holy Ghost. The Schoolmen may have shot too far beyond our limits in pursuing the Cherubim and Seraphim. But in asking whether a man can choose or whether a man will die, they were asking ordinary questions in natural history; like whether a cat can scratch or whether a dog can smell. Nothing calling itself a complete Science of Man can shirk them. And the great Agnostics did shirk them. They may have said they had no scientific evidence; in that case they failed to produce even a scientific hypothesis. What they generally did produce was a wildly unscientific contradiction. Most Monist moralists simply said that Man has no choice;

but he must think and act heroically as if he had. Huxley made morality, and even Victorian morality, in the exact sense, supernatural. He said it had arbitrary rights above nature; a sort of theology without theism.

I do not know for certain why St. Thomas was called the Angelic Doctor: whether it was that he had an angelic temper, or the intellectuality of an Angel; or whether there was a later legend that he concentrated on Angels--especially on the points of needles. If so, I do not quite understand how this idea arose; history has many examples of an irritating habit of labelling somebody in connection with something, as if he never did any thing else. Who was it who began the inane habit of referring to Dr. Johnson as "our lexicographer"; as if he never did anything but write a dictionary? Why do most people insist on meeting the large and far-reaching mind of Pascal at its very narrowest point: the point at which it was sharpened into a spike by the spite of the Jansenists against the Jesuits? It is just possible, for all I know, that this labelling of Aquinas as a specialist was an obscure depreciation of him as a universalist. For that is a very common trick for the belittling of literary or scientific men. St. Thomas must have made a certain number of enemies, though he hardly ever treated them as enemies. Unfortunately, good temper is sometimes more irritating than bad temper. And he had, after all, done a great deal of damage, as many medieval men would have thought; and, what is more curious, a great deal of damage to both sides. He had been a revolutionist against Augustine and a traditionalist against Averrhoes. He might appear to some to have tried to wreck that ancient beauty of the city of God, which bore some resemblance to the Republic of Plato. He might appear to others to have inflicted a blow on the advancing and levelling forces of Islam, as dramatic as that of Godfrey storming Jerusalem. It is possible that these enemies, by wax of damning with faint praise, talked about his very respectable little work on Angels: as a man might say that Darwin was really reliable when writing on coral-insects; or that some of Milton's Latin poems were very creditable indeed. But this is only a conjecture, and many other conjectures are possible. And I am disposed to think that St. Thomas really was rather specially interested in the nature of Angels, for the same reason that made him even more interested in the nature of Men. It was a part of that strong personal interest in things subordinate and semidependent, which runs through his whole system: a hierarchy of higher and lower liberties. He was interested in the problem of the Angel, as he was interested in the problem of the Man, because it was a problem; and especially because it was a problem of an intermediate creature. I do not pretend to deal here with this mysterious quality, as he conceives it to exist in that inscrutable intellectual being, who is less than God but more than Man. But it was this quality of a link in the chain, or a rung in the ladder, which mainly concerned the theologian, in developing his own particular theory of degrees. Above all, it is this which chiefly moves him, when he finds so fascinating the central mystery of Man. And for him the point is always that Man is not a balloon going up into the sky nor a mole burrowing merely in the earth; but rather a thing like a tree, whose roots are fed from the earth, while its highest branches seem to rise almost to the stars.

I have pointed out that mere modern free-thought has left everything in a fog, including itself. The assertion that thought is free led first to the denial that will is free; but even about that there was no real determination among the Determinists. In practice, they told men that they must treat their will as free though it was not free. In other words, Man must live a double life; which is exactly the old heresy of Siger of Brabant about the Double Mind. In other words, the nineteenth century left everything in chaos: and the importance of Thomism to the twentieth century is that it may give us back a cosmos. We can give here only the rudest sketch of how Aquinas, like the Agnostics, beginning in the cosmic cellars, yet climbed to the cosmic towers.

Without pretending to span within such limits the essential Thomist idea, I may be allowed to throw out a sort of rough version of the fundamental question, which I think I have known myself, consciously or unconsciously since my childhood. When a child looks out of the nursery window and sees anything, say the green lawn of the garden, what does he actually know; or does he know anything? There are all sorts of nursery games of negative philosophy played round this question. A brilliant Victorian scientist delighted in declaring that the child does not see any grass at all; but only a sort of green mist reflected in a tiny mirror of the human eye. This piece of rationalism has always struck me as almost insanely irrational. If he is not sure of the existence of the grass, which he sees through the glass of a window, how on earth can he be sure of the existence of the retina, which he sees through the glass of a microscope? If sight deceives, why can it not go on deceiving? Men of another school answer that grass is a mere green impression on the mind; and that he can be sure of nothing except the mind. They declare that he can only be conscious of his own consciousness; which happens to be the one thing that we know the child is not conscious of at all. In that sense, it would be far truer to say that there is grass and no child, than to say that there is a conscious child but no grass. St. Thomas Aquinas, suddenly intervening in this nursery quarrel, says emphatically that the child is aware of Ens. Long before he knows that grass is grass, or self is self, he knows that something is something. Perhaps it would be best to say very emphatically (with a blow on the table), "There is an Is". That is as much monkish credulity as St. Thomas asks of us at the start. Very few unbelievers start by asking us to believe so little. And yet, upon this sharp pin-point of reality, he rears by long logical processes that have never really been successfully overthrown, the whole cosmic system of Christendom.

Thus, Aquinas insists very profoundly but very practically, that there instantly enters, with this idea of affirmation the idea of contradiction. It is instantly apparent, even to the child, that there cannot be both affirmation and contradiction. Whatever you call the thing he sees, a moon or a mirage or a sensation or a state of consciousness, when he sees it, he knows it is not true that he does not see it. Or whatever you call what he is supposed to be doing, seeing or dreaming or being conscious of an impression, he knows that if he is doing it, it is a lie to say he is not doing it. Therefore there has already entered something beyond even the first fact of being; there follows it like its shadow the first fundamental creed or commandment, that a thing cannot be and not be. Henceforth, in common or popular language, there is a false and true. I say in popular language, because Aquinas is nowhere more subtle than in pointing out that being is not strictly the same as truth; seeing truth must mean the appreciation of being by some mind capable of appreciating it. But in a general sense there has entered that primeval world of pure actuality, the division and dilemma that brings the ultimate sort of war into the world; the everlasting duel between Yes and No. This is the dilemma that many sceptics have darkened the universe and dissolved the mind solely in order to escape. They are those who maintain that there is something that is both Yes and No. I do not know whether they pronounce it Yo.

The next step following on this acceptance of actuality or certainty, or whatever we call it in popular language, is much more difficult to explain in that language. But it represents exactly the point at which nearly all other systems go wrong, and in taking the third step abandon the first. Aquinas has affirmed that our first sense of fact is a fact; and he cannot go back on it without falsehood. But when we come to look at the fact or facts, as we know them, we observe that they have a rather queer character; which has made many moderns grow strangely and restlessly sceptical about them. For instance, they are largely in a state of change, from being one thing to being another; or their qualities are relative to other things; or they appear to move incessantly; or they appear to vanish entirely. At this point, as I say, many sages lose hold of the first principle of reality, which they would concede at first; and fall back on saying that there is nothing except change; or nothing except comparison; or nothing except flux; or in effect that there is nothing at all. Aquinas turns the whole argument the other way, keeping in line with his first realisation of reality. There is no doubt about the being of being, even if it does sometimes look like becoming; that is because what we see is not the fullness of being; or (to continue a sort of colloquial slang) we never see being being as much as it can. Ice is melted into cold water and cold water is heated into hot water; it cannot be all three at once. But this does not make water unreal or even relative; it only means that its being is limited to being one thing at a time. But the fullness of being is everything that it can be; and without it the lesser or approximate forms of being cannot be explained as anything; unless they are explained away as nothing.

This crude outline can only at the best be historical rather than philosophical. It is impossible to compress into it the metaphysical proofs of such an idea; especially in the medieval metaphysical language. But this distinction in philosophy is tremendous as a turning point in history. Most thinkers, on realising the apparent mutability of being, have really forgotten their own realisation of the being, and believed only in the mutability. They cannot even say that a thing changes into another thing; for them there is no instant in the process at which it is a thing at all. It is only a change. It would be more logical to call it nothing changing into nothing, than to say (on these principles) that there ever was or will be a moment when the thing is itself. St. Thomas maintains that the ordinary thing at any moment is something; but it is not everything that it could be. There is a fullness of being, in which it could be everything that it can be. Thus, while most sages come at last to nothing but naked change, he comes to the ultimate thing that is unchangeable, because it is all the other things at once. While they describe a change which is really a change in nothing, he describes a changelessness which includes the changes of everything. Things change because they are not complete; but their reality can only be explained as part of something that is complete. It is God.

Historically, at least, it was round this sharp and crooked corner that all the sophists have followed each other while the great Schoolman went up the high road of experience and expansion; to the beholding of cities, to the building of cities. They all failed at this early stage because, in the words of the old game, they took away the number they first thought of. The recognition of something, of a thing or things, is the first act of the intellect. But because the examination of a thing shows it is not a fixed or final thing, they inferred that there is nothing fixed or final. Thus, in various ways, they all began to see a thing as something thinner than a thing; a wave; a weakness; an abstract instability. St. Thomas, to use the same rude figure, saw a thing that was thicker than a thing; that was even more solid than the solid but secondary facts he had started by admitting as facts. Since we know them to be real, any elusive or bewildering element in their reality cannot really be unreality; and must be merely their relation to the real reality. A hundred human philosophies, ranging over the earth from Nominalism to Nirvana and Maya, from formless evolution to mindless quietism, all come from this first break in the Thomist chain; the notion that, because what we see does not satisfy us or explain itself, it is not even what we see. That cosmos is a contradiction in terms and strangles itself; but Thomism cuts itself free. The defect we see, in what is, is simply that it is not all that is. God is more actual even than Man; more actual even than Matter; for God with all His powers at every instant is immortally in action.

A cosmic comedy of a very curious sort occurred recently; involving the views of very brilliant men, such as Mr. Bernard Shaw and the Dean of St. Paul's. Briefly, freethinkers of many sorts had often said they had no need of a Creation, because the cosmos had always existed and always would exist. Mr. Bernard Shaw said he had become an atheist because the universe had gone on making itself from the beginning or without a beginning; Dean Inge later displayed consternation at the very idea that the universe could have an end. Most modern Christians, living by tradition where medieval Christians could live by logic or reason, vaguely felt that it was a dreadful idea to deprive them of the Day of Judgment. Most modern agnostics (who are delighted to have their ideas called dreadful) cried out all the more, with one accord, that the self-producing, self-existent, truly scientific universe had never needed to have a beginning and could not come to an end. At this very instant, quite suddenly, like the look-out man on a ship who shouts a warning about a rock, the real man of science, the expert who was examining the facts, announced in a loud voice that the universe was coming to an end. He had not been listening, of course, to the talk of the amateurs; he had been actually examining the texture of matter; and he said it was disintegrating: the world was apparently blowing itself up by a gradual explosion called energy; the whole business would certainly have an end and had presumably had a beginning. This was very shocking indeed; not to the orthodox, but rather specially to the unorthodox; who are rather more easily shocked. Dean Inge, who had been lecturing the orthodox for years on their stern duty of accepting all scientific discoveries, positively wailed aloud over this truly tactless scientific discovery; and practically implored the scientific discoverers to go away and discover something different. It seems almost incredible; but it is a fact that he asked what God would have to amuse Him, if the universe ceased. That is a measure of how much the modern mind needs Thomas Aquinas. But even without Aquinas, I can hardly conceive any educated man, let alone such a learned man, believing in God at all without assuming that God contains in Himself every perfection including eternal joy; and does not require the solar system to entertain him like a circus.

To step out of these presumptions, prejudices and private disappointments, into the world of St. Thomas, is like escaping from a scuffle in a dark room into the broad daylight. St. Thomas says, quite straightforwardly, that he himself believes this world has a beginning and end; because such seems to be the teaching of the Church; the validity of which mystical message to mankind he defends elsewhere with dozens of quite different arguments. Anyhow, the Church said the world would end; and apparently the Church was right; always supposing (as we are always supposed to suppose) that the latest men of science are right. But Aquinas says he sees no particular reason, in reason, why this world should not be a world without end; or even without beginning. And he is quite certain that, if it were entirely without end or beginning, there would still be exactly the same logical need of a Creator. Anybody who does not see that, he gently implies, does not really understand what is meant by a Creator.

For what St. Thomas means is not a medieval picture of an old king; but this second step in the great argument about Ens or Being; the second point which is so desperately difficult to put correctly in popular language. That is why I have introduced it here in the particular form of the argument that there must be a Creator even if there is no Day of Creation. Looking at Being as it is now, as the baby looks at the grass, we see a second thing about it; in quite popular language, it looks secondary and dependent. Existence exists; but it is not sufficiently self-existent; and would never become so merely by going on existing. The same primary sense which tells us it is Being, tells us that it is not perfect Being; not merely imperfect in the popular controversial sense of containing sin or sorrow; but imperfect as Being; less actual than the actuality it implies. For instance, its Being is often only Becoming; beginning to Be or ceasing to Be; it implies a more constant or complete thing of which it gives in itself no example. That is the meaning of that basic medieval phrase, "Everything that is moving is moved by another"; which, in the clear subtlety of St. Thomas, means inexpressibly more than the mere Deistic "somebody wound up the clock" with which it is probably often confounded. Anyone who thinks deeply will see that motion has about it an essential incompleteness, which approximates to something more complete.

The actual argument is rather technical; and concerns the fact that potentiality does not explain itself; moreover, in any case, unfolding must be of something folded. Suffice it to say that the mere modern evolutionists, who would ignore the argument do not do so because they have discovered any flaw in the argument; for they have never discovered the argument itself. They do so because they are too shallow to see the flaw in their own argument for the weakness of their thesis is covered by fashionable phraseology, as the strength of the old thesis is covered by old-fashioned phraseology. But for those who really think, there is always something really unthinkable about the whole evolutionary cosmos, as they conceive it; because it is something coming out of nothing; an ever-increasing flood of water pouring out of an empty jug. Those who can simply accept that, without even seeing the difficulty, are not likely to go so deep as Aquinas and see the solution of his difficulty. In a word, the world does not explain itself, and cannot do so merely by continuing to expand itself. But anyhow it is absurd for the Evolutionist to complain that it is unthinkable for an admittedly unthinkable God to make everything out of nothing and then pretend that it is more thinkable that nothing should turn itself into everything.

We have seen that most philosophers simply fail to philosophise about things because they change; they also fail to philosophise about things because they differ. We have no space to follow St. Thomas through all these negative heresies; but a word must be said about Nominalism or the doubt founded on the things that differ. Everyone knows that the Nominalist declared that things differ too much to be really classified; so that they are only labelled. Aquinas was a firm but moderate Realist, and therefore held that there really are general qualities; as that human beings are human, amid other paradoxes. To be an extreme Realist would have taken him too near to being a Platonist. He recognized that individuality is real, but said that it coexists with a common character making some generalisation possible; in fact, as in most things, he said exactly what all common sense would say, if no intelligent heretics had ever disturbed it. Nevertheless, they still continue to disturb it. I remember when Mr. H. G. Wells had an alarming fit of Nominalist philosophy; and poured forth book after book to argue that everything is unique and untypical, as that a man is so much an individual that he is not even a man. It is a quaint and almost comic fact, that this chaotic negation especially attracts those who are always complaining of social chaos, and who propose to replace it by the most sweeping social regulations. It is the very men who say that nothing can be classified, who say that everything must be codified. Thus Mr. Bernard Shaw said that the only golden rule is that there is no golden rule. He prefers an iron rule; as in Russia.

But this is only a small inconsistency in some moderns as individuals. There is a much deeper inconsistency in them as theorists in relation to the general theory called Creative Evolution. They seem to imagine that they avoid the metaphysical doubt about mere change by assuming (it is not very clear why) that the change will always be for the better. But the mathematical difficulty of finding a corner in a curve is not altered by turning the chart upside down, and saying that a downward curve is now an upward curve. The point is that there is no point in the curve; no place at which we have a logical right to say that the curve has reached its climax, or revealed its origin, or come to its end. It makes no difference that they choose to be cheerful about it, and say, "It is enough that there is always a beyond"; instead of lamenting, like the more realistic poets of the past, over the tragedy of mere Mutability. It is not enough that there is always a beyond; because it might be beyond bearing. Indeed the only defence of this view is that sheer boredom is such an agony, that any movement is a relief. But the truth is that they have never read St. Thomas, or they would find, with no little terror, that they really agree with him. What they really mean is that change is not mere change; but is the unfolding of something; and if it is thus unfolded, though the unfolding takes twelve million years, it must be there already. In other words, they agree with Aquinas that there is everywhere potentiality that has not reached its end in act. But if it is a definite potentiality, and if it can only end in a definite act, why then there is a Great Being, in whom all potentialities already exist as a plan of action. In other words, it is impossible even to say that the change is for the better, unless the best exists somewhere, both before and after the change. Otherwise it is indeed mere change, as the blankest sceptics or the blackest pessimists would see it. Suppose two entirely new paths open before the progress of Creative Evolution. How is the evolutionist to know which Beyond is the better; unless he accepts from the past and present some standard of the best? By their superficial theory everything can change; everything can improve, even the nature of improvement. But in their submerged common sense, they do not really think that an ideal of kindness could change to an ideal of cruelty. It is typical of them that they will sometimes rather timidly use the word Purpose; but blush at the very mention of the word Person.

St. Thomas is the very reverse of anthropomorphic, in spite of his shrewdness as an anthropologist. Some theologians have even claimed that he is too much of an agnostic; and has left the nature of God too much of an intellectual abstraction. But we do not need even St. Thomas, we do not need anything but our own common sense, to tell us that if there has been from the beginning anything that can possibly be called a Purpose, it must reside in something that has the essential elements of a Person. There cannot be an intention hovering in the air all by itself, any more than a memory that nobody remembers or a joke that nobody has made. The only chance for those supporting such suggestions is to take refuge in blank and bottomless irrationality; and even then it is impossible to prove that anybody has any right to be unreasonable, if St. Thomas has no right to be reasonable.

In a sketch that aims only at the baldest simplification, this does seem to me the simplest truth about St. Thomas the philosopher. He is one, so to speak, who is faithful to his first love; and it is love at first sight. I mean that he immediately recognised a real quality in things; and afterwards resisted all the disintegrating doubts arising from the nature of those things. That is why I emphasise, even in the first few pages, the fact that there is a sort of purely Christian humility and fidelity underlying his philosophic realism. St. Thomas could as truly say, of having seen merely a stick or a stone, what St. Paul said of having seen the rending of the secret heavens, "I was not disobedient to the heavenly vision". For though the stick or the stone is an earthly vision, it is through them that St. Thomas finds his way to heaven; and the point is that he is obedient to the vision; he does not go back on it. Nearly all the other sages who have led or misled mankind do, on one excuse or another, go back on it. They dissolve the stick or the stone in chemical solutions of scepticism; either in the medium of mere time and change; or in the difficulties of classification of unique units; or in the difficulty of recognising variety while admitting unity. The first of these three is called debate about flux or formless transition; the second is the debate about Nominalism and Realism, or the existence of general ideas; the third is called the ancient metaphysical riddle of the One and the Many. But they can all be reduced under a rough image to this same statement about St. Thomas. He is still true to the first truth and refusing the first treason. He will not deny what he has seen, though it be a secondary and diverse reality. He will not take away the numbers he first thought of, though there may be quite a number of them.

He has seen grass; and will not say he has not seen grass, because it today is and tomorrow is cast into the oven. That is the substance of all scepticism about change, transition, transformism and the rest. He will not say that there is no grass but only growth. If grass grows and withers, it can only mean that it is part of a greater thing, which is even more real; not that the grass is less real than it looks. St. Thomas has a really logical right to say, in the words of the modern mystic, A. E.: "I begin by the grass to be bound again to the Lord".

He has seen grass and grain; and he will not say that they do not differ, because there is something common to grass and grain. Nor will he say that there is nothing common to grass and grain, because they do really differ. He will not say, with the extreme Nominalists, that because grain can be differentiated into all sorts of fruitage, or grass trodden into mire with any kind of weed, therefore there can be no classification to distinguish weeds from slime or to draw a fine distinction between cattle-food and cattle. He will not say with the extreme Platonists, on the other hand, that he saw the perfect fruit in his own head by shutting his eyes, before he saw any difference between grain and grass. He saw one thing and then another thing and then a common quality; but he does not really pretend that he saw the quality before the thing.

He has seen grass and gravel; that is to say, he has seen things really different; things not classified together like grass and grains. The first flash of fact shows us a world of really strange things not merely strange to us, but strange to each other. The separate things need have nothing in common except Being. Everything is Being; but it is not true that everything is Unity. It is here, as I have said, that St. Thomas does definitely one might say defiantly, part company with the Pantheist and Monist. All things are; but among the things that are is the thing called difference, quite as much as the thing called similarity. And here again we begin to be bound again to the Lord, not only by the universality of grass, but by the incompatibility of grass and gravel. For this world of different and varied beings is especially the world of the Christian Creator; the world of created things, like things made by an artist; as compared with the world that is only one thing, with a sort of shimmering and shifting veil of misleading change; which is the conception of so many of the ancient religions of Asia and the modern sophistries of Germany. In the face of these, St. Thomas still stands stubborn in the same obstinate objective fidelity. He has seen grass and gravel; and he is not disobedient to the heavenly vision.

To sum up; the reality of things, the mutability of things, the diversity of things, and all other such things that can be attributed to things, is followed carefully by the medieval philosopher, without losing touch with the original point of the reality. There is no space in this book to specify the thousand steps of thought by which he shows that he is right. But the point is that, even apart from being right he is real. He is a realist in a rather curious sense of his own, which is a third thing, distinct from the almost contrary medieval and modern meanings of the word. Even the doubts and difficulties about reality have driven him to believe in more reality rather than less. The deceitfulness of things which has had so sad an effect on so many sages, has almost a contrary effect on this sage. If things deceive us, it is by being more real than they seem. As ends in themselves they always deceive us; but as things tending to a greater end, they are even more real than we think them. If they seem to have a relative unreality (so to speak) it is because they are potential and not actual; they are unfulfilled, like packets of seeds or boxes of fireworks. They have it in them to be more real than they are. And there is an upper world of what the Schoolman called Fruition, or Fulfillment, in which all this relative relativity becomes actuality; in which the trees burst into flower or the rockets into flame.

Here I leave the reader, on the very lowest rung of those ladders of logic, by which St. Thomas besieged and mounted the House of Man. It is enough to say that by arguments as honest and laborious, he climbed up to the turrets and talked with angels on the roofs of gold. This is, in a very rude outline, his philosophy; it is impossible in such an outline to describe his theology. Anyone writing so small a book about so big a man, must leave out something. Those who know him best will best understand why, after some considerable consideration, I have left out the only important thing.

--/--

VIII THE SEQUEL TO ST. THOMAS

It is often said that St. Thomas, unlike St. Francis, did not permit in his work the indescribable element of poetry. As, for instance, that there is little reference to any pleasure in the actual flowers and fruit of natural things, though any amount of concern with the buried roots of nature. And yet I confess that, in reading his philosophy, I have a very peculiar and powerful impression analogous to poetry. Curiously enough, it is in some ways more analogous to painting, and reminds me very much of the effect produced by the best of the modern painters, when they throw a strange and almost crude light upon stark and rectangular objects, or seem to be groping for rather than grasping the very pillars of the subconscious mind. It is probably because there is in his work a quality which is Primitive, in the best sense of a badly misused word; but any how, the pleasure is definitely not only of the reason, but also of the imagination.

Perhaps the impression is connected with the fact that painters deal with things without words. An artist draws quite gravely the grand curves of a pig; because he is not thinking of the word pig. There is no thinker who is so unmistakably thinking about things and not being misled by the indirect influence of words, as St. Thomas Aquinas. It is true in that sense that he has not the advantage of words, any more than the disadvantage of words. Here he differs sharply, for instance, from St. Augustine who was, among other things a wit. He was also a sort of prose poet, with a power over words in their atmospheric and emotional aspect; so that his books abound with beautiful passages that rise in the memory like strains of music; the illi in vos saeviant; or the unforgettable cry, "Late I have loved thee, O Ancient Beauty!" It is true that there is little or nothing of this kind in St. Thomas; but if he was without the higher uses of the mere magic of words, he was also free from that abuse of it, by mere sentimentalists or self-centred artists, which can become merely morbid and a very black magic indeed. And truly it is by some such comparison with the purely introspective intellectual, that we may find a hint about the real nature of the thing I describe, or rather fail to describe; I mean the elemental and primitive poetry that shines through all his thoughts; and especially through the thought with which all his thinking begins. It is the intense rightness of his sense of the relation between the mind and the real thing outside the mind.

That strangeness of things, which is the light in all poetry, and indeed in all art, is really connected with their otherness; or what is called their objectivity. What is subjective must be stale; it is exactly what is objective that is in this imaginative manner strange. In this the great contemplative is the complete contrary of that false contemplative, the mystic who looks only into his own soul, the selfish artist who shrinks from the world and lives only in his own mind. According to St. Thomas, the mind acts freely of itself, but its freedom exactly consists in finding a way out to liberty and the light of day; to reality and the land of the living. In the subjectivist, the pressure of the world forces the imagination inwards. In the Thomist, the energy of the mind forces the imagination outwards, but because the images it seeks are real things. All their romance and glamour, so to speak, lies in the fact that they are real things; things not to be found by staring inwards at the mind. The flower is a vision because it is not only a vision. Or, if you will, it is a vision because it is not a dream. This is for the poet the strangeness of stones and trees and solid things; they are strange because they are solid. I am putting it first in the poetical manner, and indeed it needs much more technical subtlety to put it in the philosophical manner. According to Aquinas, the object becomes a part of the mind; nay, according to Aquinas, the mind actually becomes the object. But, as one commentator acutely puts it, it only becomes the object and does not create the object. In other words, the object is an object; it can and does exist outside the mind, or in the absence of the mind. And therefore it enlarges the mind of which it becomes a part. The mind conquers a new province like an emperor; but only because the mind has answered the bell like a servant. The mind has opened the doors and windows, because it is the natural activity of what is inside the house to find out what is outside the house. If the mind is sufficient to itself, it is insufficient for itself. For this feeding upon fact is itself; as an organ it has an object which is objective; this eating of the strange strong meat of reality.

Note how this view avoids both pitfalls; the alternative abysses of impotence. The mind is not merely receptive, in the sense that it absorbs sensations like so much blotting-paper; on that sort of softness has been based all that cowardly materialism, which conceives man as wholly servile to his environment. On the other hand, the mind is not purely creative, in the sense that it paints pictures on the windows and then mistakes them for a landscape outside. But the mind is active, and its activity consists in following, so far as the will chooses to follow, the light outside that does really shine upon real landscapes. That is what gives the indefinably virile and even adventurous quality to this view of life; as compared with that which holds that material inferences pour in upon an utterly helpless mind, or that which holds that psychological influences pour out and create an entirely baseless phantasmagoria. In other words, the essence of the Thomist common sense is that two agencies are at work; reality and the recognition of reality; and their meeting is a sort of marriage. Indeed it is very truly a marriage, because it is fruitful; the only philosophy now in the world that really is fruitful. It produces practical results, precisely because it is the combination of an adventurous mind and a strange fact.

M. Maritain has used an admirable metaphor, in his book Theonas, when he says that the external fact fertilises the internal intelligence, as the bee fertilises the flower. Anyhow, upon that marriage, or whatever it may be called, the whole system of St. Thomas is founded; God made Man so that he was capable of coming in contact with reality; and those whom God hath joined, let no man put asunder.

Now, it is worthy of remark that it is the only working philosophy. Of nearly all other philosophies it is strictly true that their followers work in spite of them, or do not work at all. No sceptics work sceptically; no fatalists work fatalistically; all without exception work on the principle that it is possible to assume what it is not possible to believe. No materialist who thinks his mind was made up for him, by mud and blood and heredity, has any hesitation in making up his mind. No sceptic who believes that truth is subjective has any hesitation about treating it as objective.

Thus St. Thomas's work has a constructive quality absent from almost all cosmic systems after him. For he is already building a house, while the newer speculators are still at the stage of testing the rungs of a ladder, demonstrating the hopeless softness of the unbaked bricks, chemically analysing the spirit in the spirit-level, and generally quarrelling about whether they can even make the tools that will make the house. Aquinas is whole intellectual aeons ahead of them, over and above the common chronological sense of saying a man is in advance of his age; he is ages in advance of our age. For he has thrown out a bridge across the abyss of the first doubt, and found reality beyond and begun to build on it. Most modern philosophies are not philosophy but philosophic doubt; that is, doubt about whether there can be any philosophy. If we accept St. Thomas's fundamental act or argument in the acceptance of reality, the further deductions from it will be equally real; they will be things and not words. Unlike Kant and most of the Hegelians, he has a faith that is not merely a doubt about doubt. It is not merely what is commonly called a faith about faith; it is a faith about fact. From this point he can go forward, and deduce and develop and decide, like a man planning a city and sitting in a judgment-seat. But never since that time has any thinking man of that eminence thought that there is any real evidence for anything, not even the evidence of his senses, that was strong enough to bear the weight of a definite deduction.

From all this we may easily infer that this philosopher does not merely touch on social things, or even take them in his stride to spiritual things; though that is always his direction. He takes hold of them, he has not only a grasp of them, but a grip. As all his controversies prove, he was perhaps a perfect example of the iron hand in the velvet glove. He was a man who always turned his full attention to anything; and he seems to fix even passing things as they pass. To him even what was momentary was momentous. The reader feels that any small point of economic habit or human accident is for the moment almost scorched under the converging rays of a magnifying lens. It is impossible to put in these pages a thousandth part of the decisions on details of life that may be found in his work; it would be like reprinting the law-reports of an incredible century of just judges and sensible magistrates. We can only touch on one or two obvious topics of this kind.

I have noted the need to use modern atmospheric words for certain ancient atmospheric things; as in saying that St. Thomas was what most modern men vaguely mean by an Optimist. In the same way, he was very much what they vaguely mean by a Liberal. I do not mean that any of his thousand political suggestions would suit any such definite political creed; if there are nowadays any definite political creeds. I mean, in the same sense, that he has a sort of atmosphere of believing in breadth and balance and debate. He may not be a Liberal by the extreme demands of the moderns for we seem always to mean by the moderns the men of the last century, rather than this. He was very much of a Liberal compared with the most modern of all moderns; for they are nearly all of them turning into Fascists and Hitlerites. But the point is that he obviously preferred the sort of decisions that are reached by deliberation rather than despotic action; and while, like all his contemporaries and co-religionists, he has no doubt that true authority may be authoritative, he is rather averse to the whole savour of its being arbitrary. He is much less of an Imperialist than Dante, and even his Papalism is not very Imperial. He is very fond of phrases like "a mob of free men" as the essential material of a city; and he is emphatic upon the fact that law, when it ceases to be justice, ceases even to be law.

If this work were controversial, whole chapters could be given to the economics as well as the ethics of the Thomist system. It would be easy to show that, in this matter, he was a prophet as well as a philosopher. He foresaw from the first the peril of that mere reliance on trade and exchange, which was beginning about his time; and which has culminated in a universal commercial collapse in our time. He did not merely assert that Usury is unnatural, though in saying that he only followed Aristotle and obvious common sense, which was never contradicted by anybody until the time of the commercialists, who have involved us in the collapse. The modern world began by Bentham writing the Defence of Usury, and it has ended after a hundred years in even the vulgar newspaper opinion finding Finance indefensible. But St. Thomas struck much deeper than that. He even mentioned the truth, ignored during the long idolatry of trade, that things which men produce only to sell are likely to be worse in quality than the things they produce in order to consume. Something of our difficulty about the fine shades of Latin will be felt when we come to his statement that there is always a certain inhonestas about trade. For inhonestas does not exactly mean dishonesty. It means approximately "something unworthy," or, more nearly perhaps, "something not quite handsome." And he was right; for trade, in the modern sense, does mean selling something for a little more than it is worth, nor would the nineteenth century economists have denied it. They would only have said that he was not practical; and this seemed sound while their view led to practical prosperity. Things are a little different now that it has led to universal bankruptcy.

Here, however, we collide with a colossal paradox of history. The Thomist philosophy and theology, quite fairly compared with other philosophies like the Buddhist or the Monist, with other theologies like the Calvinist or the Christian Scientist, is quite obviously a working and even a fighting system; full of common sense and constructive confidence; and therefore normally full of hope and promise. Nor is this hope vain or this promise unfulfilled. In this not very hopeful modern moment, there are no men so hopeful as those who are today looking to

St. Thomas as a leader in a hundred crying questions of craftsmanship and ownership and economic ethics. There is undoubtedly a hopeful and creative Thomism in our time. But we are none the less puzzled by the fact that this did not immediately follow on St. Thomas's time. It is true that there was a great march of progress in the thirteenth century; and in some things, such as the status of the peasant, matters had greatly improved by the end of the Middle Ages. But nobody can honestly say that Scholasticism had greatly improved by the end of the Middle Ages. Nobody can tell how far the popular spirit of the Friars had helped the later popular medieval movements; or how far this great Friar, with his luminous rules of justice and his lifelong sympathy with the poor, may have indirectly contributed to the improvement that certainly occurred. But those who followed his method, as distinct from his moral spirit, degenerated with a strange rapidity; and it was certainly not in the Scholastics that the improvement occurred. Of some of the Scholastics we can only say that they took every thing that was worst in Scholasticism and made it worse. They continued to count the steps of logic; but every step of logic took them further from common sense. They forgot how St. Thomas had started almost as an agnostic; and seemed resolved to leave nothing in heaven or hell about which anybody could be agnostic. They were a sort of rabid rationalists, who would have left no mysteries in the Faith at all. In the earliest Scholasticism there is something that strikes a modern as fanciful and pedantic; but, properly understood, it has a fine spirit in its fancy. It is the spirit of freedom; and especially the spirit of free will. Nothing seems more quaint, for instance, than the speculations about what would have happened to every vegetable or animal or angel, if Eve had chosen not to eat the fruit of the tree. But this was originally full of the thrill of choice; and the feeling that she might have chosen otherwise. It was this detailed detective method that was followed, without the thrill of the original detective story. The world was cumbered with countless tomes, proving by logic a thousand things that can be known only to God. They developed all that was really sterile in Scholasticism, and left for us all that is really fruitful in Thomism.

There are many historical explanations. There is the Black Death, which broke the back of the Middle Ages; the consequent decline in clerical culture, which did so much to provoke the Reformation. But I suspect that there was another cause also; which can only be stated by saying that the contemporary fanatics, who controverted with Aquinas, left their own school behind them; and in a sense that school triumphed after all. The really narrow Augustinians, the men who saw the Christian life only as the narrow way, the men who could not even comprehend the great Dominican's exultation in the blaze of Being, or the glory of God in all his creatures, the men who continued to insist feverishly on every text, or even on every truth, that appeared pessimistic or paralysing, these gloomy Christians could not be extirpated from Christendom; and they remained and waited for their chance. The narrow Augustinians, the men who would have no science or reason or rational use of secular things, might have been defeated in controversy, but they had an accumulated passion of conviction. There was an Augustinian monastery in the North where it was near to explosion.

Thomas Aquinas had struck his blow; but he had not entirely settled the Manichees. The Manichees are not so easily settled; in the sense of settled forever. He had insured that the main outline of the Christianity that has come down to us should be supernatural but not anti-natural; and should never be darkened with a false spirituality to the oblivion of the Creator and the Christ who was made Man. But as his tradition trailed away into less liberal or less creative habits of thought, and as his medieval society fell away and decayed through other causes, the thing against which he had made war crept back into Christendom. A certain spirit or element in the Christian religion, necessary and sometimes noble but always needing to be balanced by more gentle and generous elements in the Faith, began once more to strengthen, as the framework of Scholasticism stiffened or split. The Fear of the Lord, that is the beginning of wisdom, and therefore belongs to the beginnings, and is felt in the first cold hours before the dawn of civilisation; the power that comes out of the wilderness and rides on the whirlwind and breaks the gods of stone; the power before which the eastern nations are prostrate like a pavement; the power before which the primitive prophets run naked and shouting, at once proclaiming and escaping from their god; the fear that is rightly rooted in the beginnings of every religion true or false: the fear of the Lord, that is the beginning of wisdom; but not the end.

It is often remarked as showing the ironical indifference of rulers to revolutions, and especially the frivolity of those who are called the Pagan Popes of the Renaissance, in their attitude to the Reformation, that when the Pope first heard of the first movements of Protestantism, which had started in Germany, he only said in an offhand manner that it was "some quarrel of monks". Every Pope of course was accustomed to quarrels among the monastic orders; but it has always been noted as a strange and almost uncanny negligence that he could see no more than this in the beginnings of the great sixteenth century schism. And yet, in a somewhat more recondite sense, there is something to be said for what he has been blamed for saying. In one sense, the schismatics had a sort of spiritual ancestry even in mediaeval times.

It will be found earlier in this book; and it was a quarrel of monks. We have seen how the great name of Augustine, a name never mentioned by Aquinas without respect but often mentioned without agreement covered an Augustinian school of thought naturally lingering longest in the Augustinian Order. The difference, like every difference between Catholics, was only a difference of emphasis. The Augustinians stressed the idea of the impotence of man before God, the omniscience of God about the destiny of man, the need for holy fear and the humiliation of intellectual pride, more than the opposite and corresponding truths of free will or human dignity or good works. In this they did in a sense continue the distinctive note of St. Augustine, who is even now regarded as relatively the determinist doctor of the Church. But there is emphasis and emphasis; and a time was coming when emphasising the one side was to mean flatly contradicting the other. Perhaps, after all, it did begin with a quarrel of monks; but the Pope was yet to learn how quarrelsome a monk could be. For there was one particular monk in that Augustinian monastery in the German forests, who may be said to have had a single and special talent for emphasis; for emphasis and nothing except emphasis; for emphasis with the quality of earthquake. He was the son of a slatecutter; a man with a great voice and a certain volume of personality; brooding, sincere, decidedly morbid; and his name was Martin Luther. Neither Augustine nor the Augustinians would have desired to see the day of that vindication of the Augustinian tradition; but in one sense, perhaps, the Augustinian tradition was avenged after all.

It came out of its cell again, in the day of storm and ruin, and cried out with a new and mighty voice for an elemental and emotional religion, and for the destruction of all philosophies. It had a peculiar horror and loathing of the great Greek philosophies, and of the scholasticism that had been founded on those philosophies. It had one theory that was the destruction of all theories; in fact it had its own theology which was itself the death of theology. Man could say nothing to God, nothing from God, nothing about God, except an almost inarticulate cry for mercy and for the supernatural help of Christ, in a world where all natural things were useless. Reason was useless. Will was useless. Man could not move himself an inch any more than a stone. Man could not trust what was in his head any more than a turnip. Nothing remained in earth or heaven, but the name of Christ lifted in that lonely imprecation; awful as the cry of a beast in pain.

We must be just to those huge human figures, who are in fact the hinges of history. However strong, and rightly strong, be our own controversial conviction, it must never mislead us into thinking that something trivial has transformed the world. So it is with that great Augustinian monk, who avenged all the ascetic Augustinians of the Middle Ages; and whose broad and burly figure has been big enough to block out for four centuries the distant human mountain of Aquinas. It is not, as the moderns delight to say, a question of theology. The Protestant theology of Martin Luther was a thing that no modern Protestant would be seen dead in a field with; or if the phrase be too flippant, would be specially anxious to touch with a barge-pole. That Protestantism was pessimism; it was nothing but bare insistence on the hopelessness of all human virtue, as an attempt to escape hell. That Lutheranism is now quite unreal; more modern phases of Lutheranism are rather more unreal; but Luther was not unreal. He was one of those great elemental barbarians, to whom it is indeed given to change the world. To compare those two figures hulking so big in history, in any philosophical sense, would of course be futile and even unfair. On a great map like the mind of Aquinas, the mind of Luther would be almost invisible. But it is not altogether untrue to say, as so many journalists have said without caring whether it was true or untrue, that Luther opened an epoch; and began the modern world.

He was the first man who ever consciously used his consciousness or what was later called his Personality. He had as a fact a rather strong personality. Aquinas had an even stronger personality; he had a massive and magnetic presence; he had an intellect that could act like a huge system of artillery spread over the whole world; he had that instantaneous presence of mind in debate, which alone really deserves the name of wit. But it never occurred to him to use anything except his wits, in defence of a truth distinct from himself. It never occurred to Aquinas to use Aquinas as a weapon. There is not a trace of his ever using his personal advantages, of birth or body or brain or breeding, in debate with anybody. In short, he belonged to an age of intellectual unconsciousness, to an age of intellectual innocence, which was very intellectual. Now Luther did begin the modern mood of depending on things not merely intellectual. It is not a question of praise or blame; it matters little whether we say that he was a strong personality, or that he was a bit of a big bully. When he quoted a Scripture text, inserting a word that is not in Scripture, he was content to shout back at all hecklers: "Tell them that Dr. Martin Luther will have it so!" That is what we now call Personality. A little later it was called Psychology. After that it was called Advertisement or Salesmanship. But we are not arguing about advantages or disadvantages. It is due to this great Augustinian pessimist to say, not only that he did triumph at last over the Angel of the Schools, but that he did in a very real sense make the modern world. He destroyed Reason; and substituted Suggestion.

It is said that the great Reformer publicly burned the Summa Theologica and the works of Aquinas; and with the bonfire of such books this book may well come to an end. They say it is very difficult to burn a book; and it must have been exceedingly difficult to burn such a mountain of books as the Dominican had contributed to the controversies of Christendom. Anyhow, there is something lurid and apocalyptic about the idea of such destruction, when we consider the compact complexity of all that encyclopaedic survey of social and moral and theoretical things. All the close-packed definitions that excluded so many errors and extremes; all the broad and balanced judgments upon the clash of loyalties or the choice of evils; all the liberal speculations upon the limits of government or the proper conditions of justice; all the distinctions between the use and abuse of private property; all the rules and exceptions about the great evil of war; all the allowances for human weakness and all the provisions for human health; all this mass of medieval humanism shrivelled and curled up in smoke before the eyes of its enemy; and that great passionate peasant rejoiced darkly, because the day of the Intellect was over. Sentence by sentence it burned, and syllogism by syllogism; and the golden maxims turned to golden flames in that last and dying glory of all that had once been the great wisdom of the Greeks. The great central Synthesis of history, that was to have linked the ancient with the modern world, went up in smoke and, for half the world, was forgotten like a vapour.

For a time it seemed that the destruction was final. It is still expressed in the amazing fact that (in the North) modern men can still write histories of philosophy, in which philosophy stops with the last little sophists of Greece and Rome; and is never heard of again until the appearance of such a third-rate philosopher as Francis Bacon. And yet this small book, which will probably do nothing else, or have very little other value, will be at least a testimony to the fact that the tide has turned once more. It is four hundred years after; and this book, I hope (and I am happy to say I believe) will probably be lost and forgotten in the flood of better books about St. Thomas Aquinas, which are at this moment pouring from every printing-press in Europe, and even in England and America. Compared with such books it is obviously a very slight and amateurish production; but it is not likely to be burned, and if it were, it would not leave even a noticeable gap in the pouring mass of new and magnificent work, which is now daily dedicated to the philosophia perennis; to the Everlasting Philosophy.

THE END

THE MAN WHO WAS THURSDAY

A NIGHTMARE

A WILD, MAD, HILARIOUS AND PROFOUNDLY MOVING TALE

It is very difficult to classify THE MAN WHO WAS THURSDAY. It is possible to say that it is a gripping adventure story of murderous criminals and brilliant policemen; but it was to be expected that the author of the Father Brown stories should tell a detective story like no-one else. On this level, therefore, THE MAN WHO WAS THURSDAY succeeds superbly; if nothing else, it is a magnificent tour-de-force of suspense-writing.

However, the reader will soon discover that it is much more than that. Carried along on the boisterous rush of the narrative by Chesterton's wonderful high-spirited style, he will soon see that he is being carried into much deeper waters than he had planned on; and the totally unforeseeable denouement will prove for the modern reader, as it has for thousands of others since 1908 when the book was first published, an inevitable and moving experience, as the investigators finally discover who Sunday is.

To Edmund Clerihew Bentley

A cloud was on the mind of men, and wailing went the weather,
Yea, a sick cloud upon the soul when we were boys together.
Science announced nonentity and art admired decay;
The world was old and ended: but you and I were gay;
Round us in antic order their crippled vices came—
Lust that had lost its laughter, fear that had lost its shame.
Like the white lock of Whistler, that lit our aimless gloom,
Men showed their own white feather as proudly as a plume.
Life was a fly that faded, and death a drone that stung;
The world was very old indeed when you and I were young.
They twisted even decent sin to shapes not to be named:
Men were ashamed of honour; but we were not ashamed.
Weak if we were and foolish, not thus we failed, not thus;
When that black Baal blocked the heavens he had no hymns from us
Children we were—our forts of sand were even as weak as we,
High as they went we piled them up to break that bitter sea.
Fools as we were in motley, all jangling and absurd,
When all church bells were silent our cap and bells were heard.

Not all unhelped we held the fort, our tiny flags unfurled;
Some giants laboured in that cloud to lift it from the world.
I find again the book we found, I feel the hour that flings

Far out of fish-shaped Paumanok some cry of cleaner things;
And the Green Carnation withered, as in forest fires that pass,
Roared in the wind of all the world ten million leaves of grass;
Or sane and sweet and sudden as a bird sings in the rain—
Truth out of Tusitala spoke and pleasure out of pain.
Yea, cool and clear and sudden as a bird sings in the grey,
Dunedin to Samoa spoke, and darkness unto day.
But we were young; we lived to see God break their bitter charms.
God and the good Republic come riding back in arms:
We have seen the City of Mansoul, even as it rocked, relieved—
Blessed are they who did not see, but being blind, believed.

This is a tale of those old fears, even of those emptied hells,
And none but you shall understand the true thing that it tells—
Of what colossal gods of shame could cow men and yet crash,
Of what huge devils hid the stars, yet fell at a pistol flash.
The doubts that were so plain to chase, so dreadful to withstand—
Oh, who shall understand but you; yea, who shall understand?
The doubts that drove us through the night as we two talked amain,
And day had broken on the streets e'er it broke upon the brain.
Between us, by the peace of God, such truth can now be told;
Yea, there is strength in striking root and good in growing old.
We have found common things at last and marriage and a creed,
And I may safely write it now, and you may safely read.

G. K. C.

CHAPTER I. THE TWO POETS OF SAFFRON PARK

THE suburb of Saffron Park lay on the sunset side of London, as red and ragged as a cloud of sunset. It was built of a bright brick throughout; its sky-line was fantastic, and even its ground plan was wild. It had been the outburst of a speculative builder, faintly tinged with art, who called its architecture sometimes Elizabethan and sometimes Queen Anne, apparently under the impression that the two sovereigns were identical. It was described with some justice as an artistic colony, though it never in any definable way produced any art. But although its pretensions to be an intellectual centre were a little vague, its pretensions to be a pleasant place were quite indisputable. The stranger who looked for the first time at the quaint red houses could only think how very oddly shaped the people must be who could fit in to them. Nor when he met the people was he disappointed in this respect. The place was not only pleasant, but perfect, if once he could regard it not as a deception but rather as a dream. Even if the people were not "artists," the whole was nevertheless artistic. That young man with the long, auburn hair and the impudent face—that young man was not really a poet; but surely he was a poem. That old gentleman with the wild, white beard and the wild, white hat—that venerable humbug was not really a philosopher; but at least he was the cause of philosophy in others. That scientific gentleman with the bald, egg-like head and the bare, bird-like neck had no real right to the airs of science that he assumed. He had not discovered anything new in biology; but what biological creature could he have discovered more singular than himself? Thus, and thus only, the whole place had properly to be regarded; it had to be considered not so much as a workshop for artists, but as a frail but finished work of art. A man who stepped into its social atmosphere felt as if he had stepped into a written comedy.

More especially this attractive unreality fell upon it about nightfall, when the extravagant roofs were dark against the afterglow and the whole insane village seemed as separate as a drifting cloud. This again was more strongly true of the many nights of local festivity, when the little gardens were often illuminated, and the big Chinese lanterns glowed in the dwarfish trees like some fierce and monstrous fruit. And this was strongest of all on one particular evening, still vaguely remembered in the locality, of which the auburn-haired poet was the hero. It was not by any means the only evening of which he was the hero. On many nights those passing by his little back garden might hear his high, didactic voice laying down the law to men and particularly to women. The attitude of women in such cases was indeed one of the paradoxes of the place. Most of the women were of the kind vaguely called emancipated, and professed some protest against male supremacy. Yet these new women would always pay to a man the extravagant compliment which no ordinary woman ever pays to him, that of listening while he is talking. And Mr. Lucian Gregory, the red-haired poet, was really (in some sense) a man worth listening to, even if one only laughed at the end of it. He put the old cant of the lawlessness of art and the art of lawlessness with a certain impudent freshness which gave at least a momentary pleasure. He was helped in some degree by the arresting oddity of his appearance, which he worked, as the phrase goes, for all it was worth. His dark red hair parted in the middle was literally like a woman's, and curved into the slow curls of a virgin in a pre-Raphaelite picture. From within this almost saintly oval, however, his face projected suddenly broad and brutal, the chin carried forward with a look of cockney contempt. This combination at once tickled and terrified the nerves of a neurotic population. He seemed like a walking blasphemy, a blend of the angel and the ape.

This particular evening, if it is remembered for nothing else, will be remembered in that place for its strange sunset. It looked like the end of the world. All the heaven seemed covered with a quite vivid and palpable plumage; you could only say that the sky was full of feathers, and of feathers that almost brushed the face. Across the great part of the dome they were grey, with the strangest tints of violet and mauve and an unnatural pink or pale green; but towards the west the whole grew past description, transparent and passionate, and the last red-hot plumes of it covered up the sun like something too good to be seen. The whole was so close about the earth, as to express nothing but a violent secrecy. The very empyrean seemed to be a secret. It expressed that splendid smallness which is the soul of local patriotism. The very sky seemed small.

I say that there are some inhabitants who may remember the evening if only by that oppressive sky. There are others who may remember it because it marked the first appearance in the place of the second poet of Saffron Park. For a long time the red-haired revolutionary had reigned without a rival; it was upon the night of the sunset that his solitude suddenly ended. The new poet, who introduced himself by the name of Gabriel Syme was a very mild-looking mortal, with a fair, pointed beard and faint, yellow hair. But an impression grew that he was less meek than he looked. He signalised his entrance by differing with the established poet, Gregory, upon the whole nature of poetry. He said that he (Syme) was poet of law, a poet of order; nay, he said he was a poet of respectability. So all the Saffron Parkers looked at him as if he had that moment fallen out of that impossible sky.

In fact, Mr. Lucian Gregory, the anarchic poet, connected the two events.

"It may well be," he said, in his sudden lyrical manner, "it may well be on such a night of clouds and cruel colours that there is brought forth upon the earth such a portent as a respectable poet. You say you are a poet of law; I say you are a contradiction in terms. I only wonder there were not comets and earthquakes on the night you appeared in this garden."

The man with the meek blue eyes and the pale, pointed beard endured these thunders with a certain submissive solemnity. The third party of the group, Gregory's sister Rosamond, who had her brother's braids of red hair, but a kindlier face underneath them, laughed with such mixture of admiration and disapproval as she gave commonly to the family oracle.

Gregory resumed in high oratorical good humour.

"An artist is identical with an anarchist," he cried. "You might transpose the words anywhere. An anarchist is an artist. The man who throws a bomb is an artist, because he prefers a great moment to everything. He sees how much more valuable is one burst of blazing light, one peal of perfect thunder, than the mere common bodies of a few shapeless policemen. An artist disregards all governments, abolishes all conventions. The poet delights in disorder only. If it were not so, the most poetical thing in the world would be the Underground Railway."

"So it is," said Mr. Syme.

"Nonsense!" said Gregory, who was very rational when anyone else attempted paradox. "Why do all the clerks and navvies in the railway trains look so sad and tired, so very sad and tired? I will tell you. It is because they know that the train is going right. It is because they know that whatever place they have taken a ticket for that place they will reach. It is because after they have passed Sloane Square they know that the next station must be Victoria, and nothing but Victoria. Oh, their wild rapture! oh, their eyes like stars and their souls again in Eden, if the next station were unaccountably Baker Street!"

"It is you who are unpoetical," replied the poet Syme. "If what you say of clerks is true, they can only be as prosaic as your poetry. The rare, strange thing is to hit the mark; the gross, obvious thing is to miss it. We feel it is epical when man with one wild arrow strikes a distant bird. Is it not also epical when man with one wild engine strikes a distant station? Chaos is dull; because in chaos the train might indeed go anywhere, to Baker Street or to Bagdad. But man is a magician, and his whole magic is in this, that he does say Victoria, and lo! it is Victoria. No, take your books of mere poetry and prose; let me read a time table, with tears of pride. Take your Byron, who commemorates the defeats of man; give me Bradshaw, who commemorates his victories. Give me Bradshaw, I say!"

"Must you go?" inquired Gregory sarcastically.

"I tell you," went on Syme with passion, "that every time a train comes in I feel that it has broken past batteries of besiegers, and that man has won a battle against chaos. You say contemptuously that when one has left Sloane Square one must come to Victoria. I say that one might do a thousand things instead, and that whenever I really come there I have the sense of hairbreadth escape. And when I hear the guard shout out the word 'Victoria,' it is not an unmeaning word. It is to me the cry of a herald announcing conquest. It is to me indeed 'Victoria'; it is the victory of Adam."

Gregory wagged his heavy, red head with a slow and sad smile.

"And even then," he said, "we poets always ask the question, 'And what is Victoria now that you have got there?' You think Victoria is like the New Jerusalem. We know that the New Jerusalem will only be like Victoria. Yes, the poet will be discontented even in the streets of heaven. The poet is always in revolt."

"There again," said Syme irritably, "what is there poetical about being in revolt? You might as well say that it is poetical to be sea-sick. Being sick is a revolt. Both being sick and being rebellious may be the wholesome thing on certain desperate occasions; but I'm hanged if I can see why they are poetical. Revolt in the abstract is—revolting. It's mere vomiting."

The girl winced for a flash at the unpleasant word, but Syme was too hot to heed her.

"It is things going right," he cried, "that is poetical! Our digestions, for instance, going sacredly and silently right, that is the foundation of all poetry. Yes, the most poetical thing, more poetical than the flowers, more poetical than the stars—the most poetical thing in the world is not being sick."

"Really," said Gregory superciliously, "the examples you choose—"

"I beg your pardon," said Syme grimly, "I forgot we had abolished all conventions."

For the first time a red patch appeared on Gregory's forehead.

"You don't expect me," he said, "to revolutionise society on this lawn?"

Syme looked straight into his eyes and smiled sweetly.

"No, I don't," he said; "but I suppose that if you were serious about your anarchism, that is exactly what you would do."

Gregory's big bull's eyes blinked suddenly like those of an angry lion, and one could almost fancy that his red mane rose.

"Don't you think, then," he said in a dangerous voice, "that I am serious about my anarchism?"

"I beg your pardon?" said Syme.

"Am I not serious about my anarchism?" cried Gregory, with knotted fists.

"My dear fellow!" said Syme, and strolled away.

With surprise, but with a curious pleasure, he found Rosamond Gregory still in his company.

"Mr. Syme," she said, "do the people who talk like you and my brother often mean what they say? Do you mean what you say now?"

Syme smiled.

"Do you?" he asked.

"What do you mean?" asked the girl, with grave eyes.

"My dear Miss Gregory," said Syme gently, "there are many kinds of sincerity and insincerity. When you say 'thank you' for the salt, do you mean what you say? No. When you say 'the world is round,' do you mean what you say? No. It is true, but you don't mean it. Now, sometimes a man like your brother really finds a thing he does mean. It may be only a half-truth, quarter-truth, tenth-truth; but then he says more than he means—from sheer force of meaning it."

She was looking at him from under level brows; her face was grave and open, and there had fallen upon it the shadow of that unreasoning responsibility which is at the bottom of the most frivolous woman, the maternal watch which is as old as the world.

"Is he really an anarchist, then?" she asked.

"Only in that sense I speak of," replied Syme; "or if you prefer it, in that nonsense."

She drew her broad brows together and said abruptly—

"He wouldn't really use—bombs or that sort of thing?"

Syme broke into a great laugh, that seemed too large for his slight and somewhat dandified figure.

"Good Lord, no!" he said, "that has to be done anonymously."

And at that the corners of her own mouth broke into a smile, and she thought with a simultaneous pleasure of Gregory's absurdity and of his safety.

Syme strolled with her to a seat in the corner of the garden, and continued to pour out his opinions. For he was a sincere man, and in spite of his superficial airs and graces, at root a humble one. And it is always the humble man who talks too much; the proud man watches himself too closely. He defended respectability with violence and exaggeration. He grew passionate in his praise of tidiness and propriety. All the time there was a smell of lilac all round him. Once he heard very faintly in some distant street a barrel-organ begin to play, and it seemed to him that his heroic words were moving to a tiny tune from under or beyond the world.

He stared and talked at the girl's red hair and amused face for what seemed to be a few minutes; and then, feeling that the groups in such a place should mix, rose to his feet. To his astonishment, he discovered the whole garden empty. Everyone had gone long ago, and he went himself with a rather hurried apology. He left with a sense of champagne in his head, which he could not afterwards explain. In the wild events which were to follow this girl had no part at all; he never saw her again until all his tale was over. And yet, in some indescribable way, she kept recurring like a motive in music through all his mad adventures afterwards, and the glory of her strange hair ran like a red thread through those dark and ill-drawn tapestries of the night. For what followed was so improbable, that it might well have been a dream.

When Syme went out into the starlit street, he found it for the moment empty. Then he realised (in some odd way) that the silence was rather a living silence than a dead one. Directly outside the door stood a street lamp, whose gleam gilded the leaves of the tree that bent out over the fence behind him. About a foot from the lamp-post stood a figure almost as rigid and motionless as the lamp-post itself. The tall hat and long frock coat were black; the face, in an abrupt shadow, was almost as dark. Only a fringe of fiery hair against the light, and also something aggressive in the attitude, proclaimed that it was the poet Gregory. He had something of the look of a masked bravo waiting sword in hand for his foe.

He made a sort of doubtful salute, which Syme somewhat more formally returned.

"I was waiting for you," said Gregory. "Might I have a moment's conversation?"

"Certainly. About what?" asked Syme in a sort of weak wonder.

Gregory struck out with his stick at the lamp-post, and then at the tree. "About this and this," he cried; "about order and anarchy. There is your precious order, that lean, iron lamp, ugly and barren; and there is anarchy, rich, living, reproducing itself—there is anarchy, splendid in green and gold."

"All the same," replied Syme patiently, "just at present you only see the tree by the light of the lamp. I wonder when you would ever see the lamp by the light of the tree." Then after a pause he said, "But may I ask if you have been standing out here in the dark only to resume our little argument?"

"No," cried out Gregory, in a voice that rang down the street, "I did not stand here to resume our argument, but to end it for ever."

The silence fell again, and Syme, though he understood nothing, listened instinctively for something serious. Gregory began in a smooth voice and with a rather bewildering smile.

"Mr. Syme," he said, "this evening you succeeded in doing something rather remarkable. You did something to me that no man born of woman has ever succeeded in doing before."

"Indeed!"

"Now I remember," resumed Gregory reflectively, "one other person succeeded in doing it. The captain of a penny steamer (if I remember correctly) at Southend. You have irritated me."

"I am very sorry," replied Syme with gravity.

"I am afraid my fury and your insult are too shocking to be wiped out even with an apology," said Gregory very calmly. "No duel could wipe it out. If I struck you dead I could not wipe it out. There is only one way by which that insult can be erased, and that way I choose. I am going, at the possible sacrifice of my life and honour, to prove to you that you were wrong in what you said."

"In what I said?"

"You said I was not serious about being an anarchist."

"There are degrees of seriousness," replied Syme. "I have never doubted that you were perfectly sincere in this sense, that you thought what you said well worth saying, that you thought a paradox might wake men up to a neglected truth."

Gregory stared at him steadily and painfully.

"And in no other sense," he asked, "you think me serious? You think me a flaneur who lets fall occasional truths. You do not think that in a deeper, a more deadly sense, I am serious."

Syme struck his stick violently on the stones of the road.

"Serious!" he cried. "Good Lord! is this street serious? Are these damned Chinese lanterns serious? Is the whole caboodle serious? One comes here and talks a pack of bosh, and perhaps some sense as well, but I should think very little of a man who didn't keep something in the background of his life that was more serious than all this talking—something more serious, whether it was religion or only drink."

"Very well," said Gregory, his face darkening, "you shall see something more serious than either drink or religion."

Syme stood waiting with his usual air of mildness until Gregory again opened his lips.

"You spoke just now of having a religion. Is it really true that you have one?"

"Oh," said Syme with a beaming smile, "we are all Catholics now."

"Then may I ask you to swear by whatever gods or saints your religion involves that you will not reveal what I am now going to tell you to any son of Adam, and especially not to the police? Will you swear that! If you will take upon yourself this awful abnegation if you will consent to burden your soul with a vow that you should never make and a knowledge you should never dream about, I will promise you in return—"

"You will promise me in return?" inquired Syme, as the other paused.

"I will promise you a very entertaining evening." Syme suddenly took off his hat.

"Your offer," he said, "is far too idiotic to be declined. You say that a poet is always an anarchist. I disagree; but I hope at least that he is always a sportsman. Permit me, here and now, to swear as a Christian, and promise as a good comrade and a fellow-artist, that I will not report anything of this, whatever it is, to the police. And now, in the name of Colney Hatch, what is it?"

"I think," said Gregory, with placid irrelevancy, "that we will call a cab."

He gave two long whistles, and a hansom came rattling down the road. The two got into it in silence. Gregory gave through the trap the address of an obscure public-house on the Chiswick bank of the river. The cab whisked itself away again, and in it these two fantastics quitted their fantastic town.

CHAPTER II. THE SECRET OF GABRIEL SYME

THE cab pulled up before a particularly dreary and greasy beershop, into which Gregory rapidly conducted his companion. They seated themselves in a close and dim sort of bar-parlour, at a stained wooden table with one wooden leg. The room was so small and dark, that very little could be seen of the attendant who was summoned, beyond a vague and dark impression of something bulky and bearded.

"Will you take a little supper?" asked Gregory politely. "The pate de foie gras is not good here, but I can recommend the game."

Syme received the remark with stolidity, imagining it to be a joke. Accepting the vein of humour, he said, with a well-bred indifference—

"Oh, bring me some lobster mayonnaise."

To his indescribable astonishment, the man only said "Certainly, sir!" and went away apparently to get it.

"What will you drink?" resumed Gregory, with the same careless yet apologetic air. "I shall only have a crepe de menthe myself; I have dined. But the champagne can really be trusted. Do let me start you with a half-bottle of Pommery at least?"

"Thank you!" said the motionless Syme. "You are very good."

His further attempts at conversation, somewhat disorganised in themselves, were cut short finally as by a thunderbolt by the actual appearance of the lobster. Syme tasted it, and found it particularly good. Then he suddenly began to eat with great rapidity and appetite.

"Excuse me if I enjoy myself rather obviously!" he said to Gregory, smiling. "I don't often have the luck to have a dream like this. It is new to me for a nightmare to lead to a lobster. It is commonly the other way."

"You are not asleep, I assure you," said Gregory. "You are, on the contrary, close to the most actual and rousing moment of your existence. Ah, here comes your champagne! I admit that there may be a slight disproportion, let us say, between the inner arrangements of this excellent hotel and its simple and unpretentious exterior. But that is all our modesty. We are the most modest men that ever lived on earth."

"And who are we?" asked Syme, emptying his champagne glass.

"It is quite simple," replied Gregory. "We are the serious anarchists, in whom you do not believe."

"Oh!" said Syme shortly. "You do yourselves well in drinks."

"Yes, we are serious about everything," answered Gregory.

Then after a pause he added—

"If in a few moments this table begins to turn round a little, don't put it down to your inroads into the champagne. I don't wish you to do yourself an injustice."

"Well, if I am not drunk, I am mad," replied Syme with perfect calm; "but I trust I can behave like a gentleman in either condition. May I smoke?"

"Certainly!" said Gregory, producing a cigar-case. "Try one of mine."

Syme took the cigar, clipped the end off with a cigar-cutter out of his waistcoat pocket, put it in his mouth, lit it slowly, and let out a long cloud of smoke. It is not a little to his credit that he performed these rites with so much composure, for almost before he had begun them the table at which he sat had begun to revolve, first slowly, and then rapidly, as if at an insane seance.

"You must not mind it," said Gregory; "it's a kind of screw."

"Quite so," said Syme placidly, "a kind of screw. How simple that is!"

The next moment the smoke of his cigar, which had been wavering across the room in snaky twists, went straight up as if from a factory chimney, and the two, with their chairs and table, shot down through the floor as if the earth had swallowed them. They went rattling down a kind of roaring chimney as rapidly as a lift cut loose, and they came with an abrupt bump to the bottom. But when Gregory threw open a pair of doors and let in a red subterranean light, Syme was still smoking with one leg thrown over the other, and had not turned a yellow hair.

Gregory led him down a low, vaulted passage, at the end of which was the red light. It was an enormous crimson lantern, nearly as big as a fireplace, fixed over a small but heavy iron door. In the door there was a sort of hatchway or grating, and on this Gregory struck five times. A heavy voice with a foreign accent asked him who he was. To this he gave the more or less unexpected reply, "Mr. Joseph Chamberlain." The heavy hinges began to move; it was obviously some kind of password.

Inside the doorway the passage gleamed as if it were lined with a network of steel. On a second glance, Syme saw that the glittering pattern was really made up of ranks and ranks of rifles and revolvers, closely packed or interlocked.

"I must ask you to forgive me all these formalities," said Gregory; "we have to be very strict here."

"Oh, don't apologise," said Syme. "I know your passion for law and order," and he stepped into the passage lined with the steel weapons. With his long, fair hair and rather foppish frock-coat, he looked a singularly frail and fanciful figure as he walked down that shining avenue of death.

They passed through several such passages, and came out at last into a queer steel chamber with curved walls, almost spherical in shape, but presenting, with its tiers of benches, something of the appearance of a scientific lecture-theatre. There were no rifles or pistols in this apartment, but round the walls of it were hung more dubious and dreadful shapes, things that looked like the bulbs of iron plants, or the eggs of iron birds. They were bombs, and the very room itself seemed like the inside of a bomb. Syme knocked his cigar ash off against the wall, and went in.

"And now, my dear Mr. Syme," said Gregory, throwing himself in an expansive manner on the bench under the largest bomb, "now we are quite cosy, so let us talk properly. Now no human words can give you any notion of why I brought you here. It was one of those quite arbitrary emotions, like jumping off a cliff or falling in love. Suffice it to say that you were an inexpressibly irritating fellow, and, to do you justice, you are still. I would break twenty oaths of secrecy for the pleasure of taking you down a peg. That way you have of lighting a cigar would make a priest break the seal of confession. Well, you said that you were quite certain I was not a serious anarchist. Does this place strike you as being serious?"

"It does seem to have a moral under all its gaiety," assented Syme; "but may I ask you two questions? You need not fear to give me information, because, as you remember, you very wisely extorted from me a promise not to tell the police, a promise I shall certainly keep. So it is in mere curiosity that I make my queries. First of all, what is it really all about? What is it you object to? You want to abolish Government?"

"To abolish God!" said Gregory, opening the eyes of a fanatic. "We do not only want to upset a few despotisms and police regulations; that sort of anarchism does exist, but it is a mere branch of the Nonconformists. We dig deeper and we blow you higher. We wish to deny all those arbitrary distinctions of vice and virtue, honour and treachery, upon which mere rebels base themselves. The silly sentimentalists of the French Revolution talked of the Rights of Man! We hate Rights as we hate Wrongs. We have abolished Right and Wrong."

"And Right and Left," said Syme with a simple eagerness, "I hope you will abolish them too. They are much more troublesome to me."

"You spoke of a second question," snapped Gregory.

"With pleasure," resumed Syme. "In all your present acts and surroundings there is a scientific attempt at secrecy. I have an aunt who lived over a shop, but this is the first time I have found people living from preference under a public-house. You have a heavy iron door. You cannot pass it without submitting to the humiliation of calling yourself Mr. Chamberlain. You surround yourself with steel instruments which make the place, if I may say so, more impressive than homelike. May I ask why, after taking all this trouble to barricade yourselves in the bowels of the earth, you then parade your whole secret by talking about anarchism to every silly woman in Saffron Park?"

Gregory smiled.

"The answer is simple," he said. "I told you I was a serious anarchist, and you did not believe me. Nor do they believe me. Unless I took them into this infernal room they would not believe me."

Syme smoked thoughtfully, and looked at him with interest. Gregory went on.

"The history of the thing might amuse you," he said. "When first I became one of the New Anarchists I tried all kinds of respectable disguises. I dressed up as a bishop. I read up all about bishops in our anarchist pamphlets, in Superstition the Vampire and Priests of Prey. I certainly understood from them that bishops are strange and terrible old men keeping a cruel secret from mankind. I was misinformed. When on my first appearing in episcopal gaiters in a drawing-room I cried out in a voice of thunder, 'Down! down! presumptuous human reason!' they found out in some way that I was not a bishop at all. I was nabbed at once. Then I made up as a millionaire; but I defended Capital with so much intelligence that a fool could see that I was quite poor. Then I tried being a major. Now I am a humanitarian myself, but I have, I hope, enough intellectual breadth to understand the position of those who, like Nietzsche, admire violence—the proud, mad war of Nature and all that, you know. I threw myself into the major. I drew my sword and waved it constantly. I called out 'Blood!' abstractedly, like a man calling for wine. I often said, 'Let the weak perish; it is the Law.' Well, well, it seems majors don't do this. I was nabbed again. At last I went in despair to the President of the Central Anarchist Council, who is the greatest man in Europe."

"What is his name?" asked Syme.

"You would not know it," answered Gregory. "That is his greatness. Caesar and Napoleon put all their genius into being heard of, and they were heard of. He puts all his genius into not being heard of, and he is not heard of. But you cannot be for five minutes in the room with him without feeling that Caesar and Napoleon would have been children in his hands."

He was silent and even pale for a moment, and then resumed—

"But whenever he gives advice it is always something as startling as an epigram, and yet as practical as the Bank of England. I said to him, 'What disguise will hide me from the world? What can I find more respectable than bishops and majors?' He looked at me with his large but indecipherable face. 'You want a safe disguise, do you? You want a dress which will guarantee you harmless; a dress in which no one would ever look for a bomb?' I nodded. He suddenly lifted his lion's voice. 'Why, then, dress up as an anarchist, you fool!' he roared so that the room shook. 'Nobody will ever expect you to do anything dangerous then.' And he turned his broad back on me without another word. I took his advice, and have never regretted it. I preached blood and murder to those women day and night, and—by God!—they would let me wheel their perambulators."

Syme sat watching him with some respect in his large, blue eyes.

"You took me in," he said. "It is really a smart dodge."

Then after a pause he added—

"What do you call this tremendous President of yours?"

"We generally call him Sunday," replied Gregory with simplicity. "You see, there are seven members of the Central Anarchist Council, and they are named after days of the week. He is called Sunday, by some of his admirers Bloody Sunday. It is curious you should mention the matter, because the very night you have dropped in (if I may so express it) is the night on which our London branch, which assembles in this room, has to elect its own deputy to fill a vacancy in the Council. The gentleman who has for some time past played, with propriety and general applause, the difficult part of Thursday, has died quite suddenly. Consequently, we have called a meeting this very evening to elect a successor."

He got to his feet and strolled across the room with a sort of smiling embarrassment.

"I feel somehow as if you were my mother, Syme," he continued casually. "I feel that I can confide anything to you, as you have promised to tell nobody. In fact, I will confide to you something that I would not say in so many words to the anarchists who will be coming to the room in about ten minutes. We shall, of course, go through a form of election; but I don't mind telling you that it is practically certain what the result will be." He looked down for a moment modestly. "It is almost a settled thing that I am to be Thursday."

"My dear fellow." said Syme heartily, "I congratulate you. A great career!"

Gregory smiled in deprecation, and walked across the room, talking rapidly.

"As a matter of fact, everything is ready for me on this table," he said, "and the ceremony will probably be the shortest possible."

Syme also strolled across to the table, and found lying across it a walking-stick, which turned out on examination to be a sword-stick, a large Colt's revolver, a sandwich case, and a formidable flask of brandy. Over the chair, beside the table, was thrown a heavy-looking cape or cloak.

"I have only to get the form of election finished," continued Gregory with animation, "then I snatch up this cloak and stick, stuff these other things into my pocket, step out of a door in this cavern, which opens on the river, where there is a steam-tug already waiting for me, and then—then—oh, the wild joy of being Thursday!" And he clasped his hands.

Syme, who had sat down once more with his usual insolent languor, got to his feet with an unusual air of hesitation.

"Why is it," he asked vaguely, "that I think you are quite a decent fellow? Why do I positively like you, Gregory?" He paused a moment, and then added with a sort of fresh curiosity, "Is it because you are such an ass?"

There was a thoughtful silence again, and then he cried out—

"Well, damn it all! this is the funniest situation I have ever been in in my life, and I am going to act accordingly. Gregory, I gave you a promise before I came into this place. That promise I would keep under red-hot pincers. Would you give me, for my own safety, a little promise of the same kind?"

"A promise?" asked Gregory, wondering.

"Yes," said Syme very seriously, "a promise. I swore before God that I would not tell your secret to the police. Will you swear by Humanity, or whatever beastly thing you believe in, that you will not tell my secret to the anarchists?"

"Your secret?" asked the staring Gregory. "Have you got a secret?"

"Yes," said Syme, "I have a secret." Then after a pause, "Will you swear?"

Gregory glared at him gravely for a few moments, and then said abruptly—

"You must have bewitched me, but I feel a furious curiosity about you. Yes, I will swear not to tell the anarchists anything you tell me. But look sharp, for they will be here in a couple of minutes."

Syme rose slowly to his feet and thrust his long, white hands into his long, grey trousers' pockets. Almost as he did so there came five knocks on the outer grating, proclaiming the arrival of the first of the conspirators.

"Well," said Syme slowly, "I don't know how to tell you the truth more shortly than by saying that your expedient of dressing up as an aimless poet is not confined to you or your President. We have known the dodge for some time at Scotland Yard."

Gregory tried to spring up straight, but he swayed thrice.

"What do you say?" he asked in an inhuman voice.

"Yes," said Syme simply, "I am a police detective. But I think I hear your friends coming."

From the doorway there came a murmur of "Mr. Joseph Chamberlain." It was repeated twice and thrice, and then thirty times, and the crowd of Joseph Chamberlains (a solemn thought) could be heard trampling down the corridor.

CHAPTER III. THE MAN WHO WAS THURSDAY

BEFORE one of the fresh faces could appear at the doorway, Gregory's stunned surprise had fallen from him. He was beside the table with a bound, and a noise in his throat like a wild beast. He caught up the Colt's revolver and took aim at Syme. Syme did not flinch, but he put up a pale and polite hand.

"Don't be such a silly man," he said, with the effeminate dignity of a curate. "Don't you see it's not necessary? Don't you see that we're both in the same boat? Yes, and jolly sea-sick."

Gregory could not speak, but he could not fire either, and he looked his question.

"Don't you see we've checkmated each other?" cried Syme. "I can't tell the police you are an anarchist. You can't tell the anarchists I'm a policeman. I can only watch you, knowing what you are; you can only watch me, knowing what I am. In short, it's a lonely, intellectual duel, my head against yours. I'm a policeman deprived of the help of the police. You, my poor fellow, are an anarchist deprived of the help of that law and organisation which is so essential to anarchy. The one solitary difference is in your favour. You are not surrounded by inquisitive policemen; I am surrounded by inquisitive anarchists. I cannot betray you, but I might betray myself. Come, come! wait and see me betray myself. I shall do it so nicely."

Gregory put the pistol slowly down, still staring at Syme as if he were a sea-monster.

"I don't believe in immortality," he said at last, "but if, after all this, you were to break your word, God would make a hell only for you, to howl in for ever."

"I shall not break my word," said Syme sternly, "nor will you break yours. Here are your friends."

The mass of the anarchists entered the room heavily, with a slouching and somewhat weary gait; but one little man, with a black beard and glasses—a man somewhat of the type of Mr. Tim Healy—detached himself, and bustled forward with some papers in his hand.

"Comrade Gregory," he said, "I suppose this man is a delegate?"

Gregory, taken by surprise, looked down and muttered the name of Syme; but Syme replied almost pertly—

"I am glad to see that your gate is well enough guarded to make it hard for anyone to be here who was not a delegate."

The brow of the little man with the black beard was, however, still contracted with something like suspicion.

"What branch do you represent?" he asked sharply.

"I should hardly call it a branch," said Syme, laughing; "I should call it at the very least a root."

"What do you mean?"

"The fact is," said Syme serenely, "the truth is I am a Sabbatarian. I have been specially sent here to see that you show a due observance of Sunday."

The little man dropped one of his papers, and a flicker of fear went over all the faces of the group. Evidently the awful President, whose name was Sunday, did sometimes send down such irregular ambassadors to such branch meetings.

"Well, comrade," said the man with the papers after a pause, "I suppose we'd better give you a seat in the meeting?"

"If you ask my advice as a friend," said Syme with severe benevolence, "I think you'd better."

When Gregory heard the dangerous dialogue end, with a sudden safety for his rival, he rose abruptly and paced the floor in painful thought. He was, indeed, in an agony of diplomacy. It was clear that Syme's inspired impudence was likely to bring him out of all merely accidental dilemmas. Little was to be hoped from them. He could not himself betray Syme, partly from honour, but partly also because, if he betrayed him and for some reason failed to destroy him, the Syme who escaped would be a Syme freed from all obligation of secrecy, a Syme who would simply walk to the nearest police station. After all, it was only one night's discussion, and only one detective who would know of it. He would let out as little as possible of their plans that night, and then let Syme go, and chance it.

He strode across to the group of anarchists, which was already distributing itself along the benches.

"I think it is time we began," he said; "the steam-tug is waiting on the river already. I move that Comrade Buttons takes the chair."

This being approved by a show of hands, the little man with the papers slipped into the presidential seat.

"Comrades," he began, as sharp as a pistol-shot, "our meeting tonight is important, though it need not be long. This branch has always had the honour of electing Thursdays for the Central European Council. We have elected many and splendid Thursdays. We all lament the sad decease of the heroic worker who occupied the post until last week. As you know, his services to the cause were considerable. He organised the great dynamite coup of Brighton which, under happier circumstances, ought to have killed everybody on the pier. As you also know, his death was as self-denying as his life, for he died through his faith in a hygienic mixture of chalk and water as a substitute for milk, which beverage he regarded as barbaric, and as involving cruelty to the cow. Cruelty, or anything approaching to cruelty, revolted him always. But it is not to acclaim his virtues that we are met, but for a harder task. It is difficult properly to praise his qualities, but it is more difficult to replace them. Upon you, comrades, it devolves this evening to choose out of the company present the man who shall be Thursday. If any comrade suggests a name I will put it to the vote. If no comrade suggests a name, I can only tell myself that that dear dynamiter, who is gone from us, has carried into the unknowable abysses the last secret of his virtue and his innocence."

There was a stir of almost inaudible applause, such as is sometimes heard in church. Then a large old man, with a long and venerable white beard, perhaps the only real working-man present, rose lumberingly and said—

"I move that Comrade Gregory be elected Thursday," and sat lumberingly down again.

"Does anyone second?" asked the chairman.

A little man with a velvet coat and pointed beard seconded.

"Before I put the matter to the vote," said the chairman, "I will call on Comrade Gregory to make a statement."

Gregory rose amid a great rumble of applause. His face was deadly pale, so that by contrast his queer red hair looked almost scarlet. But he was smiling and altogether at ease. He had made up his mind, and he saw his best policy quite plain in front of him like a white road. His best chance was to make a softened and ambiguous speech, such as would leave on the detective's mind the impression that the anarchist brotherhood was a very mild affair after all. He believed in his own literary power, his capacity for suggesting fine shades and picking perfect words. He thought that with care he could succeed, in spite of all the people around him, in conveying an impression of the institution, subtly and delicately false. Syme had once thought that anarchists, under all their bravado, were only playing the fool. Could he not now, in the hour of peril, make Syme think so again?

"Comrades," began Gregory, in a low but penetrating voice, "it is not necessary for me to tell you what is my policy, for it is your policy also. Our belief has been slandered, it has been disfigured, it has been utterly confused and concealed, but it has never been altered. Those who talk about anarchism and its dangers go everywhere and anywhere to get their information, except to us, except to the fountain head. They learn about anarchists from sixpenny novels; they learn about anarchists from tradesmen's newspapers; they learn about anarchists from Ally Sloper's Half-Holiday and the Sporting Times. They never learn about anarchists from anarchists. We have no chance of denying the mountainous slanders which are heaped upon our heads from one end of Europe to another. The man who has always heard that we are walking plagues has never heard our reply. I know that he will not hear it tonight, though my passion were to rend the roof. For it is deep, deep under the earth that the persecuted are permitted to assemble, as the Christians assembled in the Catacombs. But if, by some incredible accident, there were here tonight a man who all his life had thus immensely misunderstood us, I would put this question to him: 'When those Christians met in those Catacombs, what sort of moral reputation had they in the streets above? What tales were told of their atrocities by one educated Roman to another? Suppose' (I would say to him), 'suppose that we are only repeating that still mysterious paradox of history. Suppose we seem as shocking as the Christians because we are really as harmless as the Christians. Suppose we seem as mad as the Christians because we are really as meek.'"

The applause that had greeted the opening sentences had been gradually growing fainter, and at the last word it stopped suddenly. In the abrupt silence, the man with the velvet jacket said, in a high, squeaky voice—

"I'm not meek!"

"Comrade Witherspoon tells us," resumed Gregory, "that he is not meek. Ah, how little he knows himself! His words are, indeed, extravagant; his appearance is ferocious, and even (to an ordinary taste) unattractive. But only the eye of a friendship as deep and delicate as mine can perceive the deep foundation of solid meekness which lies at the base of him, too deep even for himself to see. I repeat, we are the true early Christians, only that we come too late. We are simple, as they revere simple—look at Comrade Witherspoon. We are modest, as they were modest—look at me. We are merciful—"

"No, no!" called out Mr. Witherspoon with the velvet jacket.

"I say we are merciful," repeated Gregory furiously, "as the early Christians were merciful. Yet this did not prevent their being accused of eating human flesh. We do not eat human flesh—"

"Shame!" cried Witherspoon. "Why not?"

"Comrade Witherspoon," said Gregory, with a feverish gaiety, "is anxious to know why nobody eats him (laughter). In our society, at any rate, which loves him sincerely, which is founded upon love—"

"No, no!" said Witherspoon, "down with love."

"Which is founded upon love," repeated Gregory, grinding his teeth, "there will be no difficulty about the aims which we shall pursue as a body, or which I should pursue were I chosen as the representative of that body. Superbly careless of the slanders that represent us as assassins and enemies of human society, we shall pursue with moral courage and quiet intellectual pressure, the permanent ideals of brotherhood and simplicity."

Gregory resumed his seat and passed his hand across his forehead. The silence was sudden and awkward, but the chairman rose like an automaton, and said in a colourless voice—

"Does anyone oppose the election of Comrade Gregory?"

The assembly seemed vague and sub-consciously disappointed, and Comrade Witherspoon moved restlessly on his seat and muttered in his thick beard. By the sheer rush of routine, however, the motion would have been put and carried. But as the chairman was opening his mouth to put it, Syme sprang to his feet and said in a small and quiet voice—

"Yes, Mr. Chairman, I oppose."

The most effective fact in oratory is an unexpected change in the voice. Mr. Gabriel Syme evidently understood oratory. Having said these first formal words in a moderated tone and with a brief simplicity, he made his next word ring and volley in the vault as if one of the guns had gone off.

"Comrades!" he cried, in a voice that made every man jump out of his boots, "have we come here for this? Do we live underground like rats in order to listen to talk like this? This is talk we might listen to while eating buns at a Sunday School treat. Do we line these walls with weapons and bar that door with death lest anyone should come and hear Comrade Gregory saying to us, 'Be good, and you will be happy,' 'Honesty is the best policy,' and 'Virtue is its own reward'? There was not a word in Comrade Gregory's address to which a curate could not have listened with pleasure (hear, hear). But I am not a curate (loud cheers), and I did not listen to it with pleasure (renewed cheers). The man who is fitted to make a good curate is not fitted to make a resolute, forcible, and efficient Thursday (hear, hear)."

"Comrade Gregory has told us, in only too apologetic a tone, that we are not the enemies of society. But I say that we are the enemies of society, and so much the worse for society. We are the enemies of society, for society is the enemy of humanity, its oldest and its most pitiless enemy (hear, hear). Comrade Gregory has told us (apologetically again) that we are not murderers. There I agree. We are not murderers, we are executioners (cheers)."

Ever since Syme had risen Gregory had sat staring at him, his face idiotic with astonishment. Now in the pause his lips of clay parted, and he said, with an automatic and lifeless distinctness—

"You damnable hypocrite!"

Syme looked straight into those frightful eyes with his own pale blue ones, and said with dignity—

"Comrade Gregory accuses me of hypocrisy. He knows as well as I do that I am keeping all my engagements and doing nothing but my duty. I do not mince words. I do not pretend to. I say that Comrade Gregory is unfit to be Thursday for all his amiable qualities. He is unfit to be Thursday because of his amiable qualities. We do not want the Supreme Council of Anarchy infected with a maudlin mercy (hear, hear). This is no time for ceremonial politeness, neither is it a time for ceremonial modesty. I set myself against Comrade Gregory as I would set myself against all the Governments of Europe, because the anarchist who has given himself to anarchy has forgotten modesty as much as he has forgotten pride (cheers). I am not a man at all. I am a cause (renewed cheers). I set myself against Comrade Gregory as impersonally and as calmly as I should choose one pistol rather than another out of that rack upon the wall; and I say that rather than have Gregory and his milk-and-water methods on the Supreme Council, I would offer myself for election—"

His sentence was drowned in a deafening cataract of applause. The faces, that had grown fiercer and fiercer with approval as his tirade grew more and more uncompromising, were now distorted with grins of anticipation or cloven with delighted cries. At the moment when he announced himself as ready to stand for the post of Thursday, a roar of excitement and assent broke forth, and became uncontrollable, and at the same moment Gregory sprang to his feet, with foam upon his mouth, and shouted against the shouting.

"Stop, you blasted madmen!" he cried, at the top of a voice that tore his throat. "Stop, you—"

But louder than Gregory's shouting and louder than the roar of the room came the voice of Syme, still speaking in a peal of pitiless thunder—

"I do not go to the Council to rebut that slander that calls us murderers; I go to earn it (loud and prolonged cheering). To the priest who says these men are the enemies of religion, to the judge who says these men are the enemies of law, to the fat parliamentarian who says these men are the enemies of order and public decency, to all these I will reply, 'You are false kings, but you are true prophets. I am come to destroy you, and to fulfil your prophecies.'"

The heavy clamour gradually died away, but before it had ceased Witherspoon had jumped to his feet, his hair and beard all on end, and had said—

"I move, as an amendment, that Comrade Syme be appointed to the post."

"Stop all this, I tell you!" cried Gregory, with frantic face and hands. "Stop it, it is all—"

The voice of the chairman clove his speech with a cold accent.

"Does anyone second this amendment?" he said. A tall, tired man, with melancholy eyes and an American chin beard, was observed on the back bench to be slowly rising to his feet. Gregory had been screaming for some time past; now there was a change in his accent, more shocking than any scream. "I end all this!" he said, in a voice as heavy as stone.

"This man cannot be elected. He is a—"

"Yes," said Syme, quite motionless, "what is he?" Gregory's mouth worked twice without sound; then slowly the blood began to crawl back into his dead face. "He is a man quite inexperienced in our work," he said, and sat down abruptly.

Before he had done so, the long, lean man with the American beard was again upon his feet, and was repeating in a high American monotone—

"I beg to second the election of Comrade Syme."

"The amendment will, as usual, be put first," said Mr. Buttons, the chairman, with mechanical rapidity.

"The question is that Comrade Syme—"

Gregory had again sprung to his feet, panting and passionate.

"Comrades," he cried out, "I am not a madman."

"Oh, oh!" said Mr. Witherspoon.

"I am not a madman," reiterated Gregory, with a frightful sincerity which for a moment staggered the room, "but I give you a counsel which you can call mad if you like. No, I will not call it a counsel, for I can give you no reason for it. I will call it a command. Call it a mad command, but act upon it. Strike, but hear me! Kill me, but obey me! Do not elect this man." Truth is so terrible, even in fetters, that for a moment Syme's slender and insane victory swayed like a reed. But you could not have guessed it from Syme's bleak blue eyes. He merely began—

"Comrade Gregory commands—"

Then the spell was snapped, and one anarchist called out to Gregory—

"Who are you? You are not Sunday;" and another anarchist added in a heavier voice, "And you are not Thursday."

"Comrades," cried Gregory, in a voice like that of a martyr who in an ecstacy of pain has passed beyond pain, "it is nothing to me whether you detest me as a tyrant or detest me as a slave. If you will not take my command, accept my degradation. I kneel to you. I throw myself at your feet. I implore you. Do not elect this man."

"Comrade Gregory," said the chairman after a painful pause, "this is really not quite dignified."

For the first time in the proceedings there was for a few seconds a real silence. Then Gregory fell back in his seat, a pale wreck of a man, and the chairman repeated, like a piece of clock-work suddenly started again—

"The question is that Comrade Syme be elected to the post of Thursday on the General Council."

The roar rose like the sea, the hands rose like a forest, and three minutes afterwards Mr. Gabriel Syme, of the Secret Police Service, was elected to the post of Thursday on the General Council of the Anarchists of Europe.

Everyone in the room seemed to feel the tug waiting on the river, the sword-stick and the revolver, waiting on the table. The instant the election was ended and irrevocable, and Syme had received the paper proving his election, they all sprang to their feet, and the fiery groups moved and mixed in the room. Syme found himself, somehow or other, face to face with Gregory, who still regarded him with a stare of stunned hatred. They were silent for many minutes.

"You are a devil!" said Gregory at last.

"And you are a gentleman," said Syme with gravity.

"It was you that entrapped me," began Gregory, shaking from head to foot, "entrapped me into—"

"Talk sense," said Syme shortly. "Into what sort of devils' parliament have you entrapped me, if it comes to that? You made me swear before I made you. Perhaps we are both doing what we think right. But what we think right is so damned different that there can be nothing between us in the way of concession. There is nothing possible between us but honour and death," and he pulled the great cloak about his shoulders and picked up the flask from the table.

"The boat is quite ready," said Mr. Buttons, bustling up. "Be good enough to step this way."

With a gesture that revealed the shop-walker, he led Syme down a short, iron-bound passage, the still agonised Gregory following feverishly at their heels. At the end of the passage was a door, which Buttons opened sharply, showing a sudden blue and silver picture of the moonlit river, that looked like a scene in a theatre. Close to the opening lay a dark, dwarfish steam-launch, like a baby dragon with one red eye.

Almost in the act of stepping on board, Gabriel Syme turned to the gaping Gregory.

"You have kept your word," he said gently, with his face in shadow. "You are a man of honour, and I thank you. You have kept it even down to a small particular. There was one special thing you promised me at the beginning of the affair, and which you have certainly given me by the end of it."

"What do you mean?" cried the chaotic Gregory. "What did I promise you?"

"A very entertaining evening," said Syme, and he made a military salute with the sword-stick as the steamboat slid away.

CHAPTER IV. THE TALE OF A DETECTIVE

GABRIEL SYME was not merely a detective who pretended to be a poet; he was really a poet who had become a detective. Nor was his hatred of anarchy hypocritical. He was one of those who are driven early in life into too conservative an attitude by the bewildering folly of most revolutionists. He had not attained it by any tame tradition. His respectability was spontaneous and sudden, a rebellion against rebellion. He came of a family of cranks, in which all the oldest people had all the newest notions. One of his uncles always walked about without a hat, and another had made an unsuccessful attempt to walk about with a hat and nothing else. His father cultivated art and self-realisation; his mother went in for simplicity and hygiene. Hence the child, during his tenderer years, was wholly unacquainted with any drink between the extremes of absinth and cocoa, of both of which he had a healthy dislike. The more his mother preached a more than Puritan abstinence the more did his father expand into a more than pagan latitude; and by the time the former had come to enforcing vegetarianism, the latter had pretty well reached the point of defending cannibalism.

Being surrounded with every conceivable kind of revolt from infancy, Gabriel had to revolt into something, so he revolted into the only thing left—sanity. But there was just enough in him of the blood of these fanatics to make even his protest for common sense a little too fierce to be sensible. His hatred of modern lawlessness had been crowned also by an accident. It happened that he was walking in a side street at the instant of a dynamite outrage. He had been blind and deaf for a moment, and then seen, the smoke clearing, the broken windows and the bleeding faces. After that he went about as usual—quiet, courteous, rather gentle; but there was a spot on his mind that was not sane. He did not regard anarchists, as most of us do, as a handful of morbid men, combining ignorance with intellectualism. He regarded them as a huge and pitiless peril, like a Chinese invasion.

He poured perpetually into newspapers and their waste-paper baskets a torrent of tales, verses and violent articles, warning men of this deluge of barbaric denial. But he seemed to be getting no nearer his enemy, and, what was worse, no nearer a living. As he paced the Thames embankment, bitterly biting a cheap cigar and brooding on the advance of Anarchy, there was no anarchist with a bomb in his pocket so savage or so solitary as he. Indeed, he always felt that Government stood alone and desperate, with its back to the wall. He was too quixotic to have cared for it otherwise.

He walked on the Embankment once under a dark red sunset. The red river reflected the red sky, and they both reflected his anger. The sky, indeed, was so swarthy, and the light on the river relatively so lurid, that the water almost seemed of fiercer flame than the sunset it mirrored. It looked like a stream of literal fire winding under the vast caverns of a subterranean country.

Syme was shabby in those days. He wore an old-fashioned black chimney-pot hat; he was wrapped in a yet more old-fashioned cloak, black and ragged; and the combination gave him the look of the early villains in Dickens and Bulwer Lytton. Also his yellow beard and hair were more unkempt and leonine than when they appeared long afterwards, cut and pointed, on the lawns of Saffron Park. A long, lean, black cigar, bought in Soho for twopence, stood out from between his tightened teeth, and altogether he looked a very satisfactory specimen of the anarchists upon whom he had vowed a holy war. Perhaps this was why a policeman on the Embankment spoke to him, and said "Good evening."

Syme, at a crisis of his morbid fears for humanity, seemed stung by the mere stolidity of the automatic official, a mere bulk of blue in the twilight.

"A good evening is it?" he said sharply. "You fellows would call the end of the world a good evening. Look at that bloody red sun and that bloody river! I tell you that if that were literally human blood, spilt and shining, you would still be standing here as solid as ever, looking out for some poor harmless tramp whom you could move on. You policemen are cruel to the poor, but I could forgive you even your cruelty if it were not for your calm."

"If we are calm," replied the policeman, "it is the calm of organised resistance."

"Eh?" said Syme, staring.

"The soldier must be calm in the thick of the battle," pursued the policeman. "The composure of an army is the anger of a nation."

"Good God, the Board Schools!" said Syme. "Is this undenominational education?"

"No," said the policeman sadly, "I never had any of those advantages. The Board Schools came after my time. What education I had was very rough and old-fashioned, I am afraid."

"Where did you have it?" asked Syme, wondering.

"Oh, at Harrow," said the policeman

The class sympathies which, false as they are, are the truest things in so many men, broke out of Syme before he could control them.

"But, good Lord, man," he said, "you oughtn't to be a policeman!"

The policeman sighed and shook his head.

"I know," he said solemnly, "I know I am not worthy."

"But why did you join the police?" asked Syme with rude curiosity.

"For much the same reason that you abused the police," replied the other. "I found that there was a special opening in the service for those whose fears for humanity were concerned rather with the aberrations of the scientific intellect than with the normal and excusable, though excessive, outbreaks of the human will. I trust I make myself clear."

"If you mean that you make your opinion clear," said Syme, "I suppose you do. But as for making yourself clear, it is the last thing you do. How comes a man like you to be talking philosophy in a blue helmet on the Thames embankment?"

"You have evidently not heard of the latest development in our police system," replied the other. "I am not surprised at it. We are keeping it rather dark from the educated class, because that class contains most of our enemies. But you seem to be exactly in the right frame of mind. I think you might almost join us."

"Join you in what?" asked Syme.

"I will tell you," said the policeman slowly. "This is the situation: The head of one of our departments, one of the most celebrated detectives in Europe, has long been of opinion that a purely intellectual conspiracy would soon threaten the very existence of civilisation. He is certain that the scientific and artistic worlds are silently bound in a crusade against the Family and the State. He has, therefore, formed a special corps of policemen, policemen who are also philosophers. It is their business to watch the beginnings of this conspiracy, not merely in a criminal but in a controversial sense. I am a democrat myself, and I am fully aware of the value of the ordinary man in matters of ordinary valour or virtue. But it would obviously be undesirable to employ the common policeman in an investigation which is also a heresy hunt."

Syme's eyes were bright with a sympathetic curiosity.

"What do you do, then?" he said.

"The work of the philosophical policeman," replied the man in blue, "is at once bolder and more subtle than that of the ordinary detective. The ordinary detective goes to pot-houses to arrest thieves; we go to artistic tea-parties to detect pessimists. The ordinary detective discovers from a ledger or a diary that a crime has been committed. We discover from a book of sonnets that a crime will be committed. We have to trace the origin of those dreadful thoughts that drive men on at last to intellectual fanaticism and intellectual crime. We were only just in time to prevent the assassination at Hartlepool, and that was entirely due to the fact that our Mr. Wilks (a smart young fellow) thoroughly understood a triolet."

"Do you mean," asked Syme, "that there is really as much connection between crime and the modern intellect as all that?"

"You are not sufficiently democratic," answered the policeman, "but you were right when you said just now that our ordinary treatment of the poor criminal was a pretty brutal business. I tell you I am sometimes sick of my trade when I see how perpetually it means merely a war upon the ignorant and the desperate. But this new movement of ours is a very different affair. We deny the snobbish English assumption that the uneducated are the dangerous criminals. We remember the Roman Emperors. We remember the great poisoning princes of the Renaissance. We say that the dangerous criminal is the educated criminal. We say that the most dangerous criminal now is the entirely lawless modern philosopher. Compared to him, burglars and bigamists are essentially moral men; my heart goes out to them. They accept the essential ideal of man; they merely seek it wrongly. Thieves respect property. They merely wish the property to become their property that they may more perfectly respect it. But philosophers dislike property as property; they wish to destroy the very idea of personal possession. Bigamists respect marriage, or they would not go through the highly ceremonial and even ritualistic formality of bigamy. But philosophers despise marriage as marriage. Murderers respect human life; they merely wish to attain a greater fulness of human life in themselves by the sacrifice of what seems to them to be lesser lives. But philosophers hate life itself, their own as much as other people's."

Syme struck his hands together.

"How true that is," he cried. "I have felt it from my boyhood, but never could state the verbal antithesis. The common criminal is a bad man, but at least he is, as it were, a conditional good man. He says that if only a certain obstacle be removed—say a wealthy uncle—he is then prepared to accept the universe and to praise God. He is a reformer, but not an anarchist. He wishes to cleanse the edifice, but not to destroy it. But the evil philosopher is not trying to alter things, but to annihilate them. Yes, the modern world has retained all those parts of police work which are really oppressive and ignominious, the harrying of the poor, the spying upon the unfortunate. It has given up its more dignified work, the punishment of powerful traitors in the State and powerful heresiarchs in the Church. The moderns say we must not punish heretics. My only doubt is whether we have a right to punish anybody else."

"But this is absurd!" cried the policeman, clasping his hands with an excitement uncommon in persons of his figure and costume, "but it is intolerable! I don't know what you're doing, but you're wasting your life. You must, you shall, join our special army against anarchy. Their armies are on our frontiers. Their bolt is ready to fall. A moment more, and you may lose the glory of working with us, perhaps the glory of dying with the last heroes of the world."

"It is a chance not to be missed, certainly," assented Syme, "but still I do not quite understand. I know as well as anybody that the modern world is full of lawless little men and mad little movements. But, beastly as they are, they generally have the one merit of disagreeing with each other. How can you talk of their leading one army or hurling one bolt. What is this anarchy?"

"Do not confuse it," replied the constable, "with those chance dynamite outbreaks from Russia or from Ireland, which are really the outbreaks of oppressed, if mistaken, men. This is a vast philosophic movement, consisting of an outer and an inner ring. You might even call the outer ring the laity and the inner ring the priesthood. I prefer to call the outer ring the innocent section, the inner ring the supremely guilty section. The outer ring—the main mass of their supporters—are merely anarchists; that is, men who believe that rules and formulas have destroyed human happiness. They believe that all the evil results of human crime are the results of the system that has called it crime. They do not believe that the crime creates the punishment. They believe that the punishment has created the crime. They believe that if a man seduced seven women he would naturally walk away as blameless as the flowers of spring. They believe that if a man picked a pocket he would naturally feel exquisitely good. These I call the innocent section."

"Oh!" said Syme.

"Naturally, therefore, these people talk about 'a happy time coming'; 'the paradise of the future'; 'mankind freed from the bondage of vice and the bondage of virtue,' and so on. And so also the men of the inner circle speak—the sacred priesthood. They also speak to applauding crowds of the happiness of the future, and of mankind freed at last. But in their mouths"—and the policeman lowered his voice—"in their mouths these happy phrases have a horrible meaning. They are under no illusions; they are too intellectual to think that man upon this earth can ever be quite free of original sin and the struggle. And they mean death. When they say that mankind shall be free at last, they mean that mankind shall commit suicide. When they talk of a paradise without right or wrong, they mean the grave.

"They have but two objects, to destroy first humanity and then themselves. That is why they throw bombs instead of firing pistols. The innocent rank and file are disappointed because the bomb has not killed the king; but the high-priesthood are happy because it has killed somebody."

"How can I join you?" asked Syme, with a sort of passion.

"I know for a fact that there is a vacancy at the moment," said the policeman, "as I have the honour to be somewhat in the confidence of the chief of whom I have spoken. You should really come and see him. Or rather, I should not say see him, nobody ever sees him; but you can talk to him if you like."

"Telephone?" inquired Syme, with interest.

"No," said the policeman placidly, "he has a fancy for always sitting in a pitch-dark room. He says it makes his thoughts brighter. Do come along."

Somewhat dazed and considerably excited, Syme allowed himself to be led to a side-door in the long row of buildings of Scotland Yard. Almost before he knew what he was doing, he had been passed through the hands of about four intermediate officials, and was suddenly shown into a room, the abrupt blackness of which startled him like a blaze of light. It was not the ordinary darkness, in which forms can be faintly traced; it was like going suddenly stone-blind.

"Are you the new recruit?" asked a heavy voice.

And in some strange way, though there was not the shadow of a shape in the gloom, Syme knew two things: first, that it came from a man of massive stature; and second, that the man had his back to him.

"Are you the new recruit?" said the invisible chief, who seemed to have heard all about it. "All right. You are engaged."

Syme, quite swept off his feet, made a feeble fight against this irrevocable phrase.

"I really have no experience," he began.

"No one has any experience," said the other, "of the Battle of Armageddon."

"But I am really unfit—"

"You are willing, that is enough," said the unknown.

"Well, really," said Syme, "I don't know any profession of which mere willingness is the final test."

"I do," said the other—"martyrs. I am condemning you to death. Good day."

CHAPTER IV. THE TALE OF A DETECTIVE

Thus it was that when Gabriel Syme came out again into the crimson light of evening, in his shabby black hat and shabby, lawless cloak, he came out a member of the New Detective Corps for the frustration of the great conspiracy. Acting under the advice of his friend the policeman (who was professionally inclined to neatness), he trimmed his hair and beard, bought a good hat, clad himself in an exquisite summer suit of light blue-grey, with a pale yellow flower in the buttonhole, and, in short, became that elegant and rather insupportable person whom Gregory had first encountered in the little garden of Saffron Park. Before he finally left the police premises his friend provided him with a small blue card, on which was written, "The Last Crusade," and a number, the sign of his official authority. He put this carefully in his upper waistcoat pocket, lit a cigarette, and went forth to track and fight the enemy in all the drawing-rooms of London. Where his adventure ultimately led him we have already seen. At about half-past one on a February night he found himself steaming in a small tug up the silent Thames, armed with swordstick and revolver, the duly elected Thursday of the Central Council of Anarchists.

When Syme stepped out on to the steam-tug he had a singular sensation of stepping out into something entirely new; not merely into the landscape of a new land, but even into the landscape of a new planet. This was mainly due to the insane yet solid decision of that evening, though partly also to an entire change in the weather and the sky since he entered the little tavern some two hours before. Every trace of the passionate plumage of the cloudy sunset had been swept away, and a naked moon stood in a naked sky. The moon was so strong and full that (by a paradox often to be noticed) it seemed like a weaker sun. It gave, not the sense of bright moonshine, but rather of a dead daylight.

Over the whole landscape lay a luminous and unnatural discoloration, as of that disastrous twilight which Milton spoke of as shed by the sun in eclipse; so that Syme fell easily into his first thought, that he was actually on some other and emptier planet, which circled round some sadder star. But the more he felt this glittering desolation in the moonlit land, the more his own chivalric folly glowed in the night like a great fire. Even the common things he carried with him—the food and the brandy and the loaded pistol—took on exactly that concrete and material poetry which a child feels when he takes a gun upon a journey or a bun with him to bed. The sword-stick and the brandy-flask, though in themselves only the tools of morbid conspirators, became the expressions of his own more healthy romance. The sword-stick became almost the sword of chivalry, and the brandy the wine of the stirrup-cup. For even the most dehumanised modern fantasies depend on some older and simpler figure; the adventures may be mad, but the adventurer must be sane. The dragon without St. George would not even be grotesque. So this inhuman landscape was only imaginative by the presence of a man really human. To Syme's exaggerative mind the bright, bleak houses and terraces by the Thames looked as empty as the mountains of the moon. But even the moon is only poetical because there is a man in the moon.

The tug was worked by two men, and with much toil went comparatively slowly. The clear moon that had lit up Chiswick had gone down by the time that they passed Battersea, and when they came under the enormous bulk of Westminster day had already begun to break. It broke like the splitting of great bars of lead, showing bars of silver; and these had brightened like white fire when the tug, changing its onward course, turned inward to a large landing stage rather beyond Charing Cross.

The great stones of the Embankment seemed equally dark and gigantic as Syme looked up at them. They were big and black against the huge white dawn. They made him feel that he was landing on the colossal steps of some Egyptian palace; and, indeed, the thing suited his mood, for he was, in his own mind, mounting to attack the solid thrones of horrible and heathen kings. He leapt out of the boat on to one slimy step, and stood, a dark and slender figure, amid the enormous masonry. The two men in the tug put her off again and turned up stream. They had never spoken a word.

CHAPTER V. THE FEAST OF FEAR

AT first the large stone stair seemed to Syme as deserted as a pyramid; but before he reached the top he had realised that there was a man leaning over the parapet of the Embankment and looking out across the river. As a figure he was quite conventional, clad in a silk hat and frock-coat of the more formal type of fashion; he had a red flower in his buttonhole. As Syme drew nearer to him step by step, he did not even move a hair; and Syme could come close enough to notice even in the dim, pale morning light that his face was long, pale and intellectual, and ended in a small triangular tuft of dark beard at the very point of the chin, all else being clean-shaven. This scrap of hair almost seemed a mere oversight; the rest of the face was of the type that is best shaven—clear-cut, ascetic, and in its way noble. Syme drew closer and closer, noting all this, and still the figure did not stir.

At first an instinct had told Syme that this was the man whom he was meant to meet. Then, seeing that the man made no sign, he had concluded that he was not. And now again he had come back to a certainty that the man had something to do with his mad adventure. For the man remained more still than would have been natural if a stranger had come so close. He was as motionless as a wax-work, and got on the nerves somewhat in the same way. Syme looked again and again at the pale, dignified and delicate face, and the face still looked blankly across the river. Then he took out of his pocket the note from Buttons proving his election, and put it before that sad and beautiful face. Then the man smiled, and his smile was a shock, for it was all on one side, going up in the right cheek and down in the left.

There was nothing, rationally speaking, to scare anyone about this. Many people have this nervous trick of a crooked smile, and in many it is even attractive. But in all Syme's circumstances, with the dark dawn and the deadly errand and the loneliness on the great dripping stones, there was something unnerving in it.

There was the silent river and the silent man, a man of even classic face. And there was the last nightmare touch that his smile suddenly went wrong.

The spasm of smile was instantaneous, and the man's face dropped at once into its harmonious melancholy. He spoke without further explanation or inquiry, like a man speaking to an old colleague.

"If we walk up towards Leicester Square," he said, "we shall just be in time for breakfast. Sunday always insists on an early breakfast. Have you had any sleep?"

"No," said Syme.

"Nor have I," answered the man in an ordinary tone. "I shall try to get to bed after breakfast."

He spoke with casual civility, but in an utterly dead voice that contradicted the fanaticism of his face. It seemed almost as if all friendly words were to him lifeless conveniences, and that his only life was hate. After a pause the man spoke again.

"Of course, the Secretary of the branch told you everything that can be told. But the one thing that can never be told is the last notion of the President, for his notions grow like a tropical forest. So in case you don't know, I'd better tell you that he is carrying out his notion of concealing ourselves by not concealing ourselves to the most extraordinary lengths just now. Originally, of course, we met in a cell underground, just as your branch does. Then Sunday made us take a private room at an ordinary restaurant. He said that if you didn't seem to be hiding nobody hunted you out. Well, he is the only man on earth, I know; but sometimes I really think that his huge brain is going a little mad in its old age. For now we flaunt ourselves before the public. We have our breakfast on a balcony—on a balcony, if you please—overlooking Leicester Square."

"And what do the people say?" asked Syme.

"It's quite simple what they say," answered his guide.

"They say we are a lot of jolly gentlemen who pretend they are anarchists."

"It seems to me a very clever idea," said Syme.

"Clever! God blast your impudence! Clever!" cried out the other in a sudden, shrill voice which was as startling and discordant as his crooked smile. "When you've seen Sunday for a split second you'll leave off calling him clever."

With this they emerged out of a narrow street, and saw the early sunlight filling Leicester Square. It will never be known, I suppose, why this square itself should look so alien and in some ways so continental. It will never be known whether it was the foreign look that attracted the foreigners or the foreigners who gave it the foreign look. But on this particular morning the effect seemed singularly bright and clear. Between the open square and the sunlit leaves and the statue and the Saracenic outlines of the Alhambra, it looked the replica of some French or even Spanish public place. And this effect increased in Syme the sensation, which in many shapes he had had through the whole adventure, the eerie sensation of having strayed into a new world. As a fact, he had bought bad cigars round Leicester Square ever since he was a boy. But as he turned that corner, and saw the trees and the Moorish cupolas, he could have sworn that he was turning into an unknown Place de something or other in some foreign town.

At one corner of the square there projected a kind of angle of a prosperous but quiet hotel, the bulk of which belonged to a street behind. In the wall there was one large French window, probably the window of a large coffee-room; and outside this window, almost literally overhanging the square, was a formidably buttressed balcony, big enough to contain a dining-table. In fact, it did contain a dining-table, or more strictly a breakfast-table; and round the breakfast-table, glowing in the sunlight and evident to the street, were a group of noisy and talkative men, all dressed in the insolence of fashion, with white waistcoats and expensive button-holes. Some of their jokes could almost be heard across the square. Then the grave Secretary gave his unnatural smile, and Syme knew that this boisterous breakfast party was the secret conclave of the European Dynamiters.

Then, as Syme continued to stare at them, he saw something that he had not seen before. He had not seen it literally because it was too large to see. At the nearest end of the balcony, blocking up a great part of the perspective, was the back of a great mountain of a man. When Syme had seen him, his first thought was that the weight of him must break down the balcony of stone. His vastness did not lie only in the fact that he was abnormally tall and quite incredibly fat. This man was planned enormously in his original proportions, like a statue carved deliberately as colossal. His head, crowned with white hair, as seen from behind looked bigger than a head ought to be. The ears that stood out from it looked larger than human ears. He was enlarged terribly to scale; and this sense of size was so staggering, that when Syme saw him all the other figures seemed quite suddenly to dwindle and become dwarfish. They were still sitting there as before with their flowers and frock-coats, but now it looked as if the big man was entertaining five children to tea.

As Syme and the guide approached the side door of the hotel, a waiter came out smiling with every tooth in his head.

"The gentlemen are up there, sare," he said. "They do talk and they do laugh at what they talk. They do say they will throw bombs at ze king."

And the waiter hurried away with a napkin over his arm, much pleased with the singular frivolity of the gentlemen upstairs.

The two men mounted the stairs in silence.

Syme had never thought of asking whether the monstrous man who almost filled and broke the balcony was the great President of whom the others stood in awe. He knew it was so, with an unaccountable but instantaneous certainty. Syme, indeed, was one of those men who are open to all the more nameless psychological influences in a degree a little dangerous to mental health. Utterly devoid of fear in physical dangers, he was a great deal too sensitive to the smell of spiritual evil. Twice already that night little unmeaning things had peeped out at him almost pruriently, and given him a sense of drawing nearer and nearer to the headquarters of hell. And this sense became overpowering as he drew nearer to the great President.

The form it took was a childish and yet hateful fancy. As he walked across the inner room towards the balcony, the large face of Sunday grew larger and larger; and Syme was gripped with a fear that when he was quite close the face would be too big to be possible, and that he would scream aloud. He remembered that as a child he would not look at the mask of Memnon in the British Museum, because it was a face, and so large.

By an effort, braver than that of leaping over a cliff, he went to an empty seat at the breakfast-table and sat down. The men greeted him with good-humoured raillery as if they had always known him. He sobered himself a little by looking at their conventional coats and solid, shining coffee-pot; then he looked again at Sunday. His face was very large, but it was still possible to humanity.

In the presence of the President the whole company looked sufficiently commonplace; nothing about them caught the eye at first, except that by the President's caprice they had been dressed up with a festive respectability, which gave the meal the look of a wedding breakfast. One man indeed stood out at even a superficial glance. He at least was the common or garden Dynamiter. He wore, indeed, the high white collar and satin tie that were the uniform of the occasion; but out of this collar there sprang a head quite unmanageable and quite unmistakable, a bewildering bush of brown hair and beard that almost obscured the eyes like those of a Skye terrier. But the eyes did look out of the tangle, and they were the sad eyes of some Russian serf. The effect of this figure was not terrible like that of the President, but it had every diablerie that can come from the utterly grotesque. If out of that stiff tie and collar there had come abruptly the head of a cat or a dog, it could not have been a more idiotic contrast.

The man's name, it seemed, was Gogol; he was a Pole, and in this circle of days he was called Tuesday. His soul and speech were incurably tragic; he could not force himself to play the prosperous and frivolous part demanded of him by President Sunday. And, indeed, when Syme came in the President, with that daring disregard of public suspicion which was his policy, was actually chaffing Gogol upon his inability to assume conventional graces.

"Our friend Tuesday," said the President in a deep voice at once of quietude and volume, "our friend Tuesday doesn't seem to grasp the idea. He dresses up like a gentleman, but he seems to be too great a soul to behave like one. He insists on the ways of the stage conspirator. Now if a gentleman goes about London in a top hat and a frock-coat, no one need know that he is an anarchist. But if a gentleman puts on a top hat and a frock-coat, and then goes about on his hands and knees—well, he may attract attention. That's what Brother Gogol does. He goes about on his hands and knees with such inexhaustible diplomacy, that by this time he finds it quite difficult to walk upright."

"I am not good at goncealment," said Gogol sulkily, with a thick foreign accent; "I am not ashamed of the cause."

"Yes you are, my boy, and so is the cause of you," said the President good-naturedly. "You hide as much as anybody; but you can't do it, you see, you're such an ass! You try to combine two inconsistent methods. When a householder finds a man under his bed, he will probably pause to note the circumstance. But if he finds a man under his bed in a top hat, you will agree with me, my dear Tuesday, that he is not likely even to forget it. Now when you were found under Admiral Biffin's bed—"

"I am not good at deception," said Tuesday gloomily, flushing.

"Right, my boy, right," said the President with a ponderous heartiness, "you aren't good at anything."

While this stream of conversation continued, Syme was looking more steadily at the men around him. As he did so, he gradually felt all his sense of something spiritually queer return.

He had thought at first that they were all of common stature and costume, with the evident exception of the hairy Gogol. But as he looked at the others, he began to see in each of them exactly what he had seen in the man by the river, a demoniac detail somewhere. That lop-sided laugh, which would suddenly disfigure the fine face of his original guide, was typical of all these types. Each man had something about him, perceived perhaps at the tenth or twentieth glance, which was not normal, and which seemed hardly human. The only metaphor he could think of was this, that they all looked as men of fashion and presence would look, with the additional twist given in a false and curved mirror.

Only the individual examples will express this half-concealed eccentricity. Syme's original cicerone bore the title of Monday; he was the Secretary of the Council, and his twisted smile was regarded with more terror than anything, except the President's horrible, happy laughter. But now that Syme had more space and light to observe him, there were other touches. His fine face was so emaciated, that Syme thought it must be wasted with some disease; yet somehow the very distress of his dark eyes denied this. It was no physical ill that troubled him. His eyes were alive with intellectual torture, as if pure thought was pain.

He was typical of each of the tribe; each man was subtly and differently wrong. Next to him sat Tuesday, the tousle-headed Gogol, a man more obviously mad. Next was Wednesday, a certain Marquis de St. Eustache, a sufficiently characteristic figure. The first few glances found nothing unusual about him, except that he was the only man at table who wore the fashionable clothes as if they were really his own. He had a black French beard cut square and a black English frock-coat cut even squarer. But Syme, sensitive to such things, felt somehow that the man carried a rich atmosphere with him, a rich atmosphere that suffocated. It reminded one irrationally of drowsy odours and of dying lamps in the darker poems of Byron and Poe. With this went a sense of his being clad, not in lighter colours, but in softer materials; his black seemed richer and warmer than the black shades about him, as if it were compounded of profound colour. His black coat looked as if it were only black by being too dense a purple. His black beard looked as if it were only black by being too deep a blue. And in the gloom and thickness of the beard his dark red mouth showed sensual and scornful. Whatever he was he was not a Frenchman; he might be a Jew; he might be something deeper yet in the dark heart of the East. In the bright coloured Persian tiles and pictures showing tyrants hunting, you may see just those almond eyes, those blue-black beards, those cruel, crimson lips.

Then came Syme, and next a very old man, Professor de Worms, who still kept the chair of Friday, though every day it was expected that his death would leave it empty. Save for his intellect, he was in the last dissolution of senile decay. His face was as grey as his long grey beard, his forehead was lifted and fixed finally in a furrow of mild despair. In no other case, not even that of Gogol, did the bridegroom brilliancy of the morning dress express a more painful contrast. For the red flower in his button-hole showed up against a face that was literally discoloured like lead; the whole hideous effect was as if some drunken dandies had put their clothes upon a corpse. When he rose or sat down, which was with long labour and peril, something worse was expressed than mere weakness, something indefinably connected with the horror of the whole scene. It did not express decrepitude merely, but corruption. Another hateful fancy crossed Syme's quivering mind. He could not help thinking that whenever the man moved a leg or arm might fall off.

Right at the end sat the man called Saturday, the simplest and the most baffling of all. He was a short, square man with a dark, square face clean-shaven, a medical practitioner going by the name of Bull. He had that combination of savoir-faire with a sort of well-groomed coarseness which is not uncommon in young doctors. He carried his fine clothes with confidence rather than ease, and he mostly wore a set smile. There was nothing whatever odd about him, except that he wore a pair of dark, almost opaque spectacles. It may have been merely a crescendo of nervous fancy that had gone before, but those black discs were dreadful to Syme; they reminded him of half-remembered ugly tales, of some story about pennies being put on the eyes of the dead. Syme's eye always caught the black glasses and the blind grin. Had the dying Professor worn them, or even the pale Secretary, they would have been appropriate. But on the younger and grosser man they seemed only an enigma. They took away the key of the face. You could not tell what his smile or his gravity meant. Partly from this, and partly because he had a vulgar virility wanting in most of the others it seemed to Syme that he might be the wickedest of all those wicked men. Syme even had the thought that his eyes might be covered up because they were too frightful to see.

CHAPTER VI. THE EXPOSURE

SUCH were the six men who had sworn to destroy the world. Again and again Syme strove to pull together his common sense in their presence. Sometimes he saw for an instant that these notions were subjective, that he was only looking at ordinary men, one of whom was old, another nervous, another short-sighted. The sense of an unnatural symbolism always settled back on him again. Each figure seemed to be, somehow, on the borderland of things, just as their theory was on the borderland of thought. He knew that each one of these men stood at the extreme end, so to speak, of some wild road of reasoning. He could only fancy, as in some old-world fable, that if a man went westward to the end of the world he would find something—say a tree—that was more or less than a tree, a tree possessed by a spirit; and that if he went east to the end of the world he would find something else that was not wholly itself—a tower, perhaps, of which the very shape was wicked. So these figures seemed to stand up, violent and unaccountable, against an ultimate horizon, visions from the verge. The ends of the earth were closing in.

Talk had been going on steadily as he took in the scene; and not the least of the contrasts of that bewildering breakfast-table was the contrast between the easy and unobtrusive tone of talk and its terrible purport. They were deep in the discussion of an actual and immediate plot. The waiter downstairs had spoken quite correctly when he said that they were talking about bombs and kings. Only three days afterwards the Czar was to meet the President of the French Republic in Paris, and over their bacon and eggs upon their sunny balcony these beaming gentlemen had decided how both should die. Even the instrument was chosen; the black-bearded Marquis, it appeared, was to carry the bomb.

Ordinarily speaking, the proximity of this positive and objective crime would have sobered Syme, and cured him of all his merely mystical tremors. He would have thought of nothing but the need of saving at least two human bodies from being ripped in pieces with iron and roaring gas. But the truth was that by this time he had begun to feel a third kind of fear, more piercing and practical than either his moral revulsion or his social responsibility. Very simply, he had no fear to spare for the French President or the Czar; he had begun to fear for himself. Most of the talkers took little heed of him, debating now with their faces closer together, and almost uniformly grave, save when for an instant the smile of the Secretary ran aslant across his face as the jagged lightning runs aslant across the sky. But there was one persistent thing which first troubled Syme and at last terrified him. The President was always looking at him, steadily, and with a great and baffling interest. The enormous man was quite quiet, but his blue eyes stood out of his head. And they were always fixed on Syme.

Syme felt moved to spring up and leap over the balcony. When the President's eyes were on him he felt as if he were made of glass. He had hardly the shred of a doubt that in some silent and extraordinary way Sunday had found out that he was a spy. He looked over the edge of the balcony, and saw a policeman, standing abstractedly just beneath, staring at the bright railings and the sunlit trees.

Then there fell upon him the great temptation that was to torment him for many days. In the presence of these powerful and repulsive men, who were the princes of anarchy, he had almost forgotten the frail and fanciful figure of the poet Gregory, the mere aesthete of anarchism. He even thought of him now with an old kindness, as if they had played together when children. But he remembered that he was still tied to Gregory by a great promise. He had promised never to do the very thing that he now felt himself almost in the act of doing. He had promised not to jump over that balcony and speak to that policeman. He took his cold hand off the cold stone balustrade. His soul swayed in a vertigo of moral indecision. He had only to snap the thread of a rash vow made to a villainous society, and all his life could be as open and sunny as the square beneath him. He had, on the other hand, only to keep his antiquated honour, and be delivered inch by inch into the power of this great enemy of mankind, whose very intellect was a torture-chamber. Whenever he looked down into the square he saw the comfortable policeman, a pillar of common sense and common order. Whenever he looked back at the breakfast-table he saw the President still quietly studying him with big, unbearable eyes.

In all the torrent of his thought there were two thoughts that never crossed his mind. First, it never occurred to him to doubt that the President and his Council could crush him if he continued to stand alone. The place might be public, the project might seem impossible. But Sunday was not the man who would carry himself thus easily without having, somehow or somewhere, set open his iron trap. Either by anonymous poison or sudden street accident, by hypnotism or by fire from hell, Sunday could certainly strike him. If he defied the man he was probably dead, either struck stiff there in his chair or long afterwards as by an innocent ailment. If he called in the police promptly, arrested everyone, told all, and set against them the whole energy of England, he would probably escape; certainly not otherwise. They were a balconyful of gentlemen overlooking a bright and busy square; but he felt no more safe with them than if they had been a boatful of armed pirates overlooking an empty sea.

There was a second thought that never came to him. It never occurred to him to be spiritually won over to the enemy. Many moderns, inured to a weak worship of intellect and force, might have wavered in their allegiance under this oppression of a great personality. They might have called Sunday the super-man. If any such creature be conceivable, he looked, indeed, somewhat like it, with his earth-shaking abstraction, as of a stone statue walking. He might have been called something above man, with his large plans, which were too obvious to be detected, with his large face, which was too frank to be understood. But this was a kind of modern meanness to which Syme could not sink even in his extreme morbidity. Like any man, he was coward enough to fear great force; but he was not quite coward enough to admire it.

The men were eating as they talked, and even in this they were typical. Dr. Bull and the Marquis ate casually and conventionally of the best things on the table—cold pheasant or Strasbourg pie. But the Secretary was a vegetarian, and he spoke earnestly of the projected murder over half a raw tomato and three quarters of a glass of tepid water. The old Professor had such slops as suggested a sickening second childhood. And even in this President Sunday preserved his curious predominance of mere mass. For he ate like twenty men; he ate incredibly, with a frightful freshness of appetite, so that it was like watching a sausage factory. Yet continually, when he had swallowed a dozen crumpets or drunk a quart of coffee, he would be found with his great head on one side staring at Syme.

"I have often wondered," said the Marquis, taking a great bite out of a slice of bread and jam, "whether it wouldn't be better for me to do it with a knife. Most of the best things have been brought off with a knife. And it would be a new emotion to get a knife into a French President and wriggle it round."

"You are wrong," said the Secretary, drawing his black brows together. "The knife was merely the expression of the old personal quarrel with a personal tyrant. Dynamite is not only our best tool, but our best symbol. It is as perfect a symbol of us as is incense of the prayers of the Christians. It expands; it only destroys because it broadens; even so, thought only destroys because it broadens. A man's brain is a bomb," he cried out, loosening suddenly his strange passion and striking his own skull with violence. "My brain feels like a bomb, night and day. It must expand! It must expand! A man's brain must expand, if it breaks up the universe."

"I don't want the universe broken up just yet," drawled the Marquis. "I want to do a lot of beastly things before I die. I thought of one yesterday in bed."

"No, if the only end of the thing is nothing," said Dr. Bull with his sphinx-like smile, "it hardly seems worth doing."

The old Professor was staring at the ceiling with dull eyes.

"Every man knows in his heart," he said, "that nothing is worth doing."

There was a singular silence, and then the Secretary said—

"We are wandering, however, from the point. The only question is how Wednesday is to strike the blow. I take it we should all agree with the original notion of a bomb. As to the actual arrangements, I should suggest that tomorrow morning he should go first of all to—"

The speech was broken off short under a vast shadow. President Sunday had risen to his feet, seeming to fill the sky above them.

"Before we discuss that," he said in a small, quiet voice, "let us go into a private room. I have something very particular to say."

Syme stood up before any of the others. The instant of choice had come at last, the pistol was at his head. On the pavement before he could hear the policeman idly stir and stamp, for the morning, though bright, was cold.

A barrel-organ in the street suddenly sprang with a jerk into a jovial tune. Syme stood up taut, as if it had been a bugle before the battle. He found himself filled with a supernatural courage that came from nowhere. That jingling music seemed full of the vivacity, the vulgarity, and the irrational valour of the poor, who in all those unclean streets were all clinging to the decencies and the charities of Christendom. His youthful prank of being a policeman had faded from his mind; he did not think of himself as the representative of the corps of gentlemen turned into fancy constables, or of the old eccentric who lived in the dark room. But he did feel himself as the ambassador of all these common and kindly people in the street, who every day marched into battle to the music of the barrel-organ. And this high pride in being human had lifted him unaccountably to an infinite height above the monstrous men around him. For an instant, at least, he looked down upon all their sprawling eccentricities from the starry pinnacle of the commonplace. He felt towards them all that unconscious and elementary superiority that a brave man feels over powerful beasts or a wise man over powerful errors. He knew that he had neither the intellectual nor the physical strength of President Sunday; but in that moment he minded it no more than the fact that he had not the muscles of a tiger or a horn on his nose like a rhinoceros. All was swallowed up in an ultimate certainty that the President was wrong and that the barrel-organ was right. There clanged in his mind that unanswerable and terrible truism in the song of Roland—

"Pagens ont tort et Chretiens ont droit."

which in the old nasal French has the clang and groan of great iron. This liberation of his spirit from the load of his weakness went with a quite clear decision to embrace death. If the people of the barrel-organ could keep their old-world obligations, so could he. This very pride in keeping his word was that he was keeping it to miscreants. It was his last triumph over these lunatics to go down into their dark room and die for something that they could not even understand. The barrel-organ seemed to give the marching tune with the energy and the mingled noises of a whole orchestra; and he could hear deep and rolling, under all the trumpets of the pride of life, the drums of the pride of death.

The conspirators were already filing through the open window and into the rooms behind. Syme went last, outwardly calm, but with all his brain and body throbbing with romantic rhythm. The President led them down an irregular side stair, such as might be used by servants, and into a dim, cold, empty room, with a table and benches, like an abandoned boardroom. When they were all in, he closed and locked the door.

The first to speak was Gogol, the irreconcilable, who seemed bursting with inarticulate grievance.

"Zso! Zso!" he cried, with an obscure excitement, his heavy Polish accent becoming almost impenetrable. "You zay you nod 'ide. You zay you show himselves. It is all nuzzinks. Ven you vant talk importance you run yourselves in a dark box!"

The President seemed to take the foreigner's incoherent satire with entire good humour.

"You can't get hold of it yet, Gogol," he said in a fatherly way. "When once they have heard us talking nonsense on that balcony they will not care where we go afterwards. If we had come here first, we should have had the whole staff at the keyhole. You don't seem to know anything about mankind."

"I die for zem," cried the Pole in thick excitement, "and I slay zare oppressors. I care not for these games of gonzealment. I would zmite ze tyrant in ze open square."

"I see, I see," said the President, nodding kindly as he seated himself at the top of a long table. "You die for mankind first, and then you get up and smite their oppressors. So that's all right. And now may I ask you to control your beautiful sentiments, and sit down with the other gentlemen at this table. For the first time this morning something intelligent is going to be said."

Syme, with the perturbed promptitude he had shown since the original summons, sat down first. Gogol sat down last, grumbling in his brown beard about gombromise. No one except Syme seemed to have any notion of the blow that was about to fall. As for him, he had merely the feeling of a man mounting the scaffold with the intention, at any rate, of making a good speech.

"Comrades," said the President, suddenly rising, "we have spun out this farce long enough. I have called you down here to tell you something so simple and shocking that even the waiters upstairs (long inured to our levities) might hear some new seriousness in my voice. Comrades, we were discussing plans and naming places. I propose, before saying anything else, that those plans and places should not be voted by this meeting, but should be left wholly in the control of some one reliable member. I suggest Comrade Saturday, Dr. Bull."

They all stared at him; then they all started in their seats, for the next words, though not loud, had a living and sensational emphasis. Sunday struck the table.

"Not one word more about the plans and places must be said at this meeting. Not one tiny detail more about what we mean to do must be mentioned in this company."

Sunday had spent his life in astonishing his followers; but it seemed as if he had never really astonished them until now. They all moved feverishly in their seats, except Syme. He sat stiff in his, with his hand in his pocket, and on the handle of his loaded revolver. When the attack on him came he would sell his life dear. He would find out at least if the President was mortal.

Sunday went on smoothly—

"You will probably understand that there is only one possible motive for forbidding free speech at this festival of freedom. Strangers overhearing us matters nothing. They assume that we are joking. But what would matter, even unto death, is this, that there should be one actually among us who is not of us, who knows our grave purpose, but does not share it, who—"

The Secretary screamed out suddenly like a woman.

"It can't be!" he cried, leaping. "There can't—"

The President flapped his large flat hand on the table like the fin of some huge fish.

"Yes," he said slowly, "there is a spy in this room. There is a traitor at this table. I will waste no more words. His name—"

Syme half rose from his seat, his finger firm on the trigger.

"His name is Gogol," said the President. "He is that hairy humbug over there who pretends to be a Pole."

Gogol sprang to his feet, a pistol in each hand. With the same flash three men sprang at his throat. Even the Professor made an effort to rise. But Syme saw little of the scene, for he was blinded with a beneficent darkness; he had sunk down into his seat shuddering, in a palsy of passionate relief.

CHAPTER VII. THE UNACCOUNTABLE CONDUCT OF PROFESSOR DE WORMS

"SIT down!" said Sunday in a voice that he used once or twice in his life, a voice that made men drop drawn swords.

The three who had risen fell away from Gogol, and that equivocal person himself resumed his seat.

"Well, my man," said the President briskly, addressing him as one addresses a total stranger, "will you oblige me by putting your hand in your upper waistcoat pocket and showing me what you have there?"

The alleged Pole was a little pale under his tangle of dark hair, but he put two fingers into the pocket with apparent coolness and pulled out a blue strip of card. When Syme saw it lying on the table, he woke up again to the world outside him. For although the card lay at the other extreme of the table, and he could read nothing of the inscription on it, it bore a startling resemblance to the blue card in his own pocket, the card which had been given to him when he joined the anti-anarchist constabulary.

"Pathetic Slav," said the President, "tragic child of Poland, are you prepared in the presence of that card to deny that you are in this company—shall we say de trop?"

"Right oh!" said the late Gogol. It made everyone jump to hear a clear, commercial and somewhat cockney voice coming out of that forest of foreign hair. It was irrational, as if a Chinaman had suddenly spoken with a Scotch accent.

"I gather that you fully understand your position," said Sunday.

"You bet," answered the Pole. "I see it's a fair cop. All I say is, I don't believe any Pole could have imitated my accent like I did his."

"I concede the point," said Sunday. "I believe your own accent to be inimitable, though I shall practise it in my bath. Do you mind leaving your beard with your card?"

"Not a bit," answered Gogol; and with one finger he ripped off the whole of his shaggy head-covering, emerging with thin red hair and a pale, pert face. "It was hot," he added.

"I will do you the justice to say," said Sunday, not without a sort of brutal admiration, "that you seem to have kept pretty cool under it. Now listen to me. I like you. The consequence is that it would annoy me for just about two and a half minutes if I heard that you had died in torments. Well, if you ever tell the police or any human soul about us, I shall have that two and a half minutes of discomfort. On your discomfort I will not dwell. Good day. Mind the step."

The red-haired detective who had masqueraded as Gogol rose to his feet without a word, and walked out of the room with an air of perfect nonchalance. Yet the astonished Syme was able to realise that this ease was suddenly assumed; for there was a slight stumble outside the door, which showed that the departing detective had not minded the step.

"Time is flying," said the President in his gayest manner, after glancing at his watch, which like everything about him seemed bigger than it ought to be. "I must go off at once; I have to take the chair at a Humanitarian meeting."

The Secretary turned to him with working eyebrows.

"Would it not be better," he said a little sharply, "to discuss further the details of our project, now that the spy has left us?"

"No, I think not," said the President with a yawn like an unobtrusive earthquake. "Leave it as it is. Let Saturday settle it. I must be off. Breakfast here next Sunday."

But the late loud scenes had whipped up the almost naked nerves of the Secretary. He was one of those men who are conscientious even in crime.

"I must protest, President, that the thing is irregular," he said. "It is a fundamental rule of our society that all plans shall be debated in full council. Of course, I fully appreciate your forethought when in the actual presence of a traitor—"

"Secretary," said the President seriously, "if you'd take your head home and boil it for a turnip it might be useful. I can't say. But it might."

The Secretary reared back in a kind of equine anger.

"I really fail to understand—" he began in high offense.

"That's it, that's it," said the President, nodding a great many times. "That's where you fail right enough. You fail to understand. Why, you dancing donkey," he roared, rising, "you didn't want to be overheard by a spy, didn't you? How do you know you aren't overheard now?"

And with these words he shouldered his way out of the room, shaking with incomprehensible scorn.

Four of the men left behind gaped after him without any apparent glimmering of his meaning. Syme alone had even a glimmering, and such as it was it froze him to the bone. If the last words of the President meant anything, they meant that he had not after all passed unsuspected. They meant that while Sunday could not denounce him like Gogol, he still could not trust him like the others.

The other four got to their feet grumbling more or less, and betook themselves elsewhere to find lunch, for it was already well past midday. The Professor went last, very slowly and painfully. Syme sat long after the rest had gone, revolving his strange position. He had escaped a thunderbolt, but he was still under a cloud. At last he rose and made his way out of the hotel into Leicester Square. The bright, cold day had grown increasingly colder, and when he came out into the street he was surprised by a few flakes of snow. While he still carried the swordstick and the rest of Gregory's portable luggage, he had thrown the cloak down and left it somewhere, perhaps on the steam-tug, perhaps on the balcony. Hoping, therefore, that the snow-shower might be slight, he stepped back out of the street for a moment and stood up under the doorway of a small and greasy hair-dresser's shop, the front window of which was empty, except for a sickly wax lady in evening dress.

Snow, however, began to thicken and fall fast; and Syme, having found one glance at the wax lady quite sufficient to depress his spirits, stared out instead into the white and empty street. He was considerably astonished to see, standing quite still outside the shop and staring into the window, a man. His top hat was loaded with snow like the hat of Father Christmas, the white drift was rising round his boots and ankles; but it seemed as if nothing could tear him away from the contemplation of the colourless wax doll in dirty evening dress. That any human being should stand in such weather looking into such a shop was a matter of sufficient wonder to Syme; but his idle wonder turned suddenly into a personal shock; for he realised that the man standing there was the paralytic old Professor de Worms. It scarcely seemed the place for a person of his years and infirmities.

Syme was ready to believe anything about the perversions of this dehumanized brotherhood; but even he could not believe that the Professor had fallen in love with that particular wax lady. He could only suppose that the man's malady (whatever it was) involved some momentary fits of rigidity or trance. He was not inclined, however, to feel in this case any very compassionate concern. On the contrary, he rather congratulated himself that the Professor's stroke and his elaborate and limping walk would make it easy to escape from him and leave him miles behind. For Syme thirsted first and last to get clear of the whole poisonous atmosphere, if only for an hour. Then he could collect his thoughts, formulate his policy, and decide finally whether he should or should not keep faith with Gregory.

He strolled away through the dancing snow, turned up two or three streets, down through two or three others, and entered a small Soho restaurant for lunch. He partook reflectively of four small and quaint courses, drank half a bottle of red wine, and ended up over black coffee and a black cigar, still thinking. He had taken his seat in the upper room of the restaurant, which was full of the chink of knives and the chatter of foreigners. He remembered that in old days he had imagined that all these harmless and kindly aliens were anarchists. He shuddered, remembering the real thing. But even the shudder had the delightful shame of escape. The wine, the common food, the familiar place, the faces of natural and talkative men, made him almost feel as if the Council of the Seven Days had been a bad dream; and although he knew it was nevertheless an objective reality, it was at least a distant one. Tall houses and populous streets lay between him and his last sight of the shameful seven; he was free in free London, and drinking wine among the free. With a somewhat easier action, he took his hat and stick and strolled down the stair into the shop below.

When he entered that lower room he stood stricken and rooted to the spot. At a small table, close up to the blank window and the white street of snow, sat the old anarchist Professor over a glass of milk, with his lifted livid face and pendent eyelids. For an instant Syme stood as rigid as the stick he leant upon. Then with a gesture as of blind hurry, he brushed past the Professor, dashing open the door and slamming it behind him, and stood outside in the snow.

"Can that old corpse be following me?" he asked himself, biting his yellow moustache. "I stopped too long up in that room, so that even such leaden feet could catch me up. One comfort is, with a little brisk walking I can put a man like that as far away as Timbuctoo. Or am I too fanciful? Was he really following me? Surely Sunday would not be such a fool as to send a lame man?"

He set off at a smart pace, twisting and whirling his stick, in the direction of Covent Garden. As he crossed the great market the snow increased, growing blinding and bewildering as the afternoon began to darken. The snow-flakes tormented him like a swarm of silver bees. Getting into his eyes and beard, they added their unremitting futility to his already irritated nerves; and by the time that he had come at a swinging pace to the beginning of Fleet Street, he lost patience, and finding a Sunday teashop, turned into it to take shelter. He ordered another cup of black coffee as an excuse. Scarcely had he done so, when Professor de Worms hobbled heavily into the shop, sat down with difficulty and ordered a glass of milk.

Syme's walking-stick had fallen from his hand with a great clang, which confessed the concealed steel. But the Professor did not look round. Syme, who was commonly a cool character, was literally gaping as a rustic gapes at a conjuring trick. He had seen no cab following; he had heard no wheels outside the shop; to all mortal appearances the man had come on foot. But the old man could only walk like a snail, and Syme had walked like the wind. He started up and snatched his stick, half crazy with the contradiction in mere arithmetic, and swung out of the swinging doors, leaving his coffee untasted. An omnibus going to the Bank went rattling by with an unusual rapidity. He had a violent run of a hundred yards to reach it; but he managed to spring, swaying upon the splash-board and, pausing for an instant to pant, he climbed on to the top. When he had been seated for about half a minute, he heard behind him a sort of heavy and asthmatic breathing.

Turning sharply, he saw rising gradually higher and higher up the omnibus steps a top hat soiled and dripping with snow, and under the shadow of its brim the short-sighted face and shaky shoulders of Professor de Worms. He let himself into a seat with characteristic care, and wrapped himself up to the chin in the mackintosh rug.

Every movement of the old man's tottering figure and vague hands, every uncertain gesture and panic-stricken pause, seemed to put it beyond question that he was helpless, that he was in the last imbecility of the body. He moved by inches, he let himself down with little gasps of caution. And yet, unless the philosophical entities called time and space have no vestige even of a practical existence, it appeared quite unquestionable that he had run after the omnibus.

Syme sprang erect upon the rocking car, and after staring wildly at the wintry sky, that grew gloomier every moment, he ran down the steps. He had repressed an elemental impulse to leap over the side.

Too bewildered to look back or to reason, he rushed into one of the little courts at the side of Fleet Street as a rabbit rushes into a hole. He had a vague idea, if this incomprehensible old Jack-in-the-box was really pursuing him, that in that labyrinth of little streets he could soon throw him off the scent. He dived in and out of those crooked lanes, which were more like cracks than thoroughfares; and by the time that he had completed about twenty alternate angles and described an unthinkable polygon, he paused to listen for any sound of pursuit. There was none; there could not in any case have been much, for the little streets were thick with the soundless snow. Somewhere behind Red Lion Court, however, he noticed a place where some energetic citizen had cleared away the snow for a space of about twenty yards, leaving the wet, glistening cobble-stones. He thought little of this as he passed it, only plunging into yet another arm of the maze. But when a few hundred yards farther on he stood still again to listen, his heart stood still also, for he heard from that space of rugged stones the clinking crutch and labouring feet of the infernal cripple.

The sky above was loaded with the clouds of snow, leaving London in a darkness and oppression premature for that hour of the evening. On each side of Syme the walls of the alley were blind and featureless; there was no little window or any kind of eve. He felt a new impulse to break out of this hive of houses, and to get once more into the open and lamp-lit street. Yet he rambled and dodged for a long time before he struck the main thoroughfare. When he did so, he struck it much farther up than he had fancied. He came out into what seemed the vast and void of Ludgate Circus, and saw St. Paul's Cathedral sitting in the sky.

At first he was startled to find these great roads so empty, as if a pestilence had swept through the city. Then he told himself that some degree of emptiness was natural; first because the snow-storm was even dangerously deep, and secondly because it was Sunday. And at the very word Sunday he bit his lip; the word was henceforth for hire like some indecent pun. Under the white fog of snow high up in the heaven the whole atmosphere of the city was turned to a very queer kind of green twilight, as of men under the sea. The sealed and sullen sunset behind the dark dome of St. Paul's had in it smoky and sinister colours—colours of sickly green, dead red or decaying bronze, that were just bright enough to emphasise the solid whiteness of the snow. But right up against these dreary colours rose the black bulk of the cathedral; and upon the top of the cathedral was a random splash and great stain of snow, still clinging as to an Alpine peak. It had fallen accidentally, but just so fallen as to half drape the dome from its very topmost point, and to pick out in perfect silver the great orb and the cross. When Syme saw it he suddenly straightened himself, and made with his sword-stick an involuntary salute.

He knew that that evil figure, his shadow, was creeping quickly or slowly behind him, and he did not care.

It seemed a symbol of human faith and valour that while the skies were darkening that high place of the earth was bright. The devils might have captured heaven, but they had not yet captured the cross. He had a new impulse to tear out the secret of this dancing, jumping and pursuing paralytic; and at the entrance of the court as it opened upon the Circus he turned, stick in hand, to face his pursuer.

Professor de Worms came slowly round the corner of the irregular alley behind him, his unnatural form outlined against a lonely gas-lamp, irresistibly recalling that very imaginative figure in the nursery rhymes, "the crooked man who went a crooked mile." He really looked as if he had been twisted out of shape by the tortuous streets he had been threading. He came nearer and nearer, the lamplight shining on his lifted spectacles, his lifted, patient face. Syme waited for him as St. George waited for the dragon, as a man waits for a final explanation or for death. And the old Professor came right up to him and passed him like a total stranger, without even a blink of his mournful eyelids.

There was something in this silent and unexpected innocence that left Syme in a final fury. The man's colourless face and manner seemed to assert that the whole following had been an accident. Syme was galvanised with an energy that was something between bitterness and a burst of boyish derision. He made a wild gesture as if to knock the old man's hat off, called out something like "Catch me if you can," and went racing away across the white, open Circus. Concealment was impossible now; and looking back over his shoulder, he could see the black figure of the old gentleman coming after him with long, swinging strides like a man winning a mile race. But the head upon that bounding body was still pale, grave and professional, like the head of a lecturer upon the body of a harlequin.

This outrageous chase sped across Ludgate Circus, up Ludgate Hill, round St. Paul's Cathedral, along Cheapside, Syme remembering all the nightmares he had ever known. Then Syme broke away towards the river, and ended almost down by the docks. He saw the yellow panes of a low, lighted public-house, flung himself into it and ordered beer. It was a foul tavern, sprinkled with foreign sailors, a place where opium might be smoked or knives drawn.

A moment later Professor de Worms entered the place, sat down carefully, and asked for a glass of milk.

CHAPTER VIII. THE PROFESSOR EXPLAINS

WHEN Gabriel Syme found himself finally established in a chair, and opposite to him, fixed and final also, the lifted eyebrows and leaden eyelids of the Professor, his fears fully returned. This incomprehensible man from the fierce council, after all, had certainly pursued him. If the man had one character as a paralytic and another character as a pursuer, the antithesis might make him more interesting, but scarcely more soothing. It would be a very small comfort that he could not find the Professor out, if by some serious accident the Professor should find him out. He emptied a whole pewter pot of ale before the professor had touched his milk.

One possibility, however, kept him hopeful and yet helpless. It was just possible that this escapade signified something other than even a slight suspicion of him. Perhaps it was some regular form or sign. Perhaps the foolish scamper was some sort of friendly signal that he ought to have understood. Perhaps it was a ritual. Perhaps the new Thursday was always chased along Cheapside, as the new Lord Mayor is always escorted along it. He was just selecting a tentative inquiry, when the old Professor opposite suddenly and simply cut him short. Before Syme could ask the first diplomatic question, the old anarchist had asked suddenly, without any sort of preparation—

"Are you a policeman?"

Whatever else Syme had expected, he had never expected anything so brutal and actual as this. Even his great presence of mind could only manage a reply with an air of rather blundering jocularity.

"A policeman?" he said, laughing vaguely. "Whatever made you think of a policeman in connection with me?"

"The process was simple enough," answered the Professor patiently. "I thought you looked like a policeman. I think so now."

"Did I take a policeman's hat by mistake out of the restaurant?" asked Syme, smiling wildly. "Have I by any chance got a number stuck on to me somewhere? Have my boots got that watchful look? Why must I be a policeman? Do, do let me be a postman."

The old Professor shook his head with a gravity that gave no hope, but Syme ran on with a feverish irony.

"But perhaps I misunderstood the delicacies of your German philosophy. Perhaps policeman is a relative term. In an evolutionary sense, sir, the ape fades so gradually into the policeman, that I myself can never detect the shade. The monkey is only the policeman that may be. Perhaps a maiden lady on Clapham Common is only the policeman that might have been. I don't mind being the policeman that might have been. I don't mind being anything in German thought."

"Are you in the police service?" said the old man, ignoring all Syme's improvised and desperate raillery. "Are you a detective?"

Syme's heart turned to stone, but his face never changed.

"Your suggestion is ridiculous," he began. "Why on earth—"

The old man struck his palsied hand passionately on the rickety table, nearly breaking it.

"Did you hear me ask a plain question, you pattering spy?" he shrieked in a high, crazy voice. "Are you, or are you not, a police detective?"

"No!" answered Syme, like a man standing on the hangman's drop.

"You swear it," said the old man, leaning across to him, his dead face becoming as it were loathsomely alive. "You swear it! You swear it! If you swear falsely, will you be damned? Will you be sure that the devil dances at your funeral? Will you see that the nightmare sits on your grave? Will there really be no mistake? You are an anarchist, you are a dynamiter! Above all, you are not in any sense a detective? You are not in the British police?"

He leant his angular elbow far across the table, and put up his large loose hand like a flap to his ear.

"I am not in the British police," said Syme with insane calm.

Professor de Worms fell back in his chair with a curious air of kindly collapse.

"That's a pity," he said, "because I am."

Syme sprang up straight, sending back the bench behind him with a crash.

"Because you are what?" he said thickly. "You are what?"

"I am a policeman," said the Professor with his first broad smile, and beaming through his spectacles. "But as you think policeman only a relative term, of course I have nothing to do with you. I am in the British police force; but as you tell me you are not in the British police force, I can only say that I met you in a dynamiters' club. I suppose I ought to arrest you." And with these words he laid on the table before Syme an exact facsimile of the blue card which Syme had in his own waistcoat pocket, the symbol of his power from the police.

Syme had for a flash the sensation that the cosmos had turned exactly upside down, that all trees were growing downwards and that all stars were under his feet. Then came slowly the opposite conviction. For the last twenty-four hours the cosmos had really been upside down, but now the capsized universe had come right side up again. This devil from whom he had been fleeing all day was only an elder brother of his own house, who on the other side of the table lay back and laughed at him. He did not for the moment ask any questions of detail; he only knew the happy and silly fact that this shadow, which had pursued him with an intolerable oppression of peril, was only the shadow of a friend trying to catch him up. He knew simultaneously that he was a fool and a free man. For with any recovery from morbidity there must go a certain healthy humiliation. There comes a certain point in such conditions when only three things are possible: first a perpetuation of Satanic pride, secondly tears, and third laughter. Syme's egotism held hard to the first course for a few seconds, and then suddenly adopted the third. Taking his own blue police ticket from his own waist coat pocket, he tossed it on to the table; then he flung his head back until his spike of yellow beard almost pointed at the ceiling, and shouted with a barbaric laughter.

Even in that close den, perpetually filled with the din of knives, plates, cans, clamorous voices, sudden struggles and stampedes, there was something Homeric in Syme's mirth which made many half-drunken men look round.

"What yer laughing at, guv'nor?" asked one wondering labourer from the docks.

"At myself," answered Syme, and went off again into the agony of his ecstatic reaction.

"Pull yourself together," said the Professor, "or you'll get hysterical. Have some more beer. I'll join you."

"You haven't drunk your milk," said Syme.

"My milk!" said the other, in tones of withering and unfathomable contempt, "my milk! Do you think I'd look at the beastly stuff when I'm out of sight of the bloody anarchists? We're all Christians in this room, though perhaps," he added, glancing around at the reeling crowd, "not strict ones. Finish my milk? Great blazes! yes, I'll finish it right enough!" and he knocked the tumbler off the table, making a crash of glass and a splash of silver fluid.

Syme was staring at him with a happy curiosity.

"I understand now," he cried; "of course, you're not an old man at all."

"I can't take my face off here," replied Professor de Worms. "It's rather an elaborate make-up. As to whether I'm an old man, that's not for me to say. I was thirty-eight last birthday."

"Yes, but I mean," said Syme impatiently, "there's nothing the matter with you."

"Yes," answered the other dispassionately. "I am subject to colds."

Syme's laughter at all this had about it a wild weakness of relief. He laughed at the idea of the paralytic Professor being really a young actor dressed up as if for the foot-lights. But he felt that he would have laughed as loudly if a pepperpot had fallen over.

The false Professor drank and wiped his false beard.

"Did you know," he asked, "that that man Gogol was one of us?"

"I? No, I didn't know it," answered Syme in some surprise. "But didn't you?"

"I knew no more than the dead," replied the man who called himself de Worms. "I thought the President was talking about me, and I rattled in my boots."

"And I thought he was talking about me," said Syme, with his rather reckless laughter. "I had my hand on my revolver all the time."

"So had I," said the Professor grimly; "so had Gogol evidently."

Syme struck the table with an exclamation.

"Why, there were three of us there!" he cried. "Three out of seven is a fighting number. If we had only known that we were three!"

The face of Professor de Worms darkened, and he did not look up.

"We were three," he said. "If we had been three hundred we could still have done nothing."

"Not if we were three hundred against four?" asked Syme, jeering rather boisterously.

"No," said the Professor with sobriety, "not if we were three hundred against Sunday."

And the mere name struck Syme cold and serious; his laughter had died in his heart before it could die on his lips. The face of the unforgettable President sprang into his mind as startling as a coloured photograph, and he remarked this difference between Sunday and all his satellites, that their faces, however fierce or sinister, became gradually blurred by memory like other human faces, whereas Sunday's seemed almost to grow more actual during absence, as if a man's painted portrait should slowly come alive.

They were both silent for a measure of moments, and then Syme's speech came with a rush, like the sudden foaming of champagne.

"Professor," he cried, "it is intolerable. Are you afraid of this man?"

The Professor lifted his heavy lids, and gazed at Syme with large, wide-open, blue eyes of an almost ethereal honesty.

"Yes, I am," he said mildly. "So are you."

Syme was dumb for an instant. Then he rose to his feet erect, like an insulted man, and thrust the chair away from him.

"Yes," he said in a voice indescribable, "you are right. I am afraid of him. Therefore I swear by God that I will seek out this man whom I fear until I find him, and strike him on the mouth. If heaven were his throne and the earth his footstool, I swear that I would pull him down."

"How?" asked the staring Professor. "Why?"

"Because I am afraid of him," said Syme; "and no man should leave in the universe anything of which he is afraid."

De Worms blinked at him with a sort of blind wonder. He made an effort to speak, but Syme went on in a low voice, but with an undercurrent of inhuman exaltation—

"Who would condescend to strike down the mere things that he does not fear? Who would debase himself to be merely brave, like any common prizefighter? Who would stoop to be fearless—like a tree? Fight the thing that you fear. You remember the old tale of the English clergyman who gave the last rites to the brigand of Sicily, and how on his death-bed the great robber said, 'I can give you no money, but I can give you advice for a lifetime: your thumb on the blade, and strike upwards.' So I say to you, strike upwards, if you strike at the stars."

The other looked at the ceiling, one of the tricks of his pose.

"Sunday is a fixed star," he said.

"You shall see him a falling star," said Syme, and put on his hat.

The decision of his gesture drew the Professor vaguely to his feet.

"Have you any idea," he asked, with a sort of benevolent bewilderment, "exactly where you are going?"

"Yes," replied Syme shortly, "I am going to prevent this bomb being thrown in Paris."

"Have you any conception how?" inquired the other.

"No," said Syme with equal decision.

"You remember, of course," resumed the soi-disant de Worms, pulling his beard and looking out of the window, "that when we broke up rather hurriedly the whole arrangements for the atrocity were left in the private hands of the Marquis and Dr. Bull. The Marquis is by this time probably crossing the Channel. But where he will go and what he will do it is doubtful whether even the President knows; certainly we don't know. The only man who does know is Dr. Bull."

"Confound it!" cried Syme. "And we don't know where he is."

"Yes," said the other in his curious, absent-minded way, "I know where he is myself."

"Will you tell me?" asked Syme with eager eyes.

"I will take you there," said the Professor, and took down his own hat from a peg.

Syme stood looking at him with a sort of rigid excitement.

"What do you mean?" he asked sharply. "Will you join me? Will you take the risk?"

"Young man," said the Professor pleasantly, "I am amused to observe that you think I am a coward. As to that I will say only one word, and that shall be entirely in the manner of your own philosophical rhetoric. You think that it is possible to pull down the President. I know that it is impossible, and I am going to try it," and opening the tavern door, which let in a blast of bitter air, they went out together into the dark streets by the docks.

Most of the snow was melted or trampled to mud, but here and there a clot of it still showed grey rather than white in the gloom. The small streets were sloppy and full of pools, which reflected the flaming lamps irregularly, and by accident, like fragments of some other and fallen world. Syme felt almost dazed as he stepped through this growing confusion of lights and shadows; but his companion walked on with a certain briskness, towards where, at the end of the street, an inch or two of the lamplit river looked like a bar of flame.

"Where are you going?" Syme inquired.

"Just now," answered the Professor, "I am going just round the corner to see whether Dr. Bull has gone to bed. He is hygienic, and retires early."

"Dr. Bull!" exclaimed Syme. "Does he live round the corner?"

"No," answered his friend. "As a matter of fact he lives some way off, on the other side of the river, but we can tell from here whether he has gone to bed."

Turning the corner as he spoke, and facing the dim river, flecked with flame, he pointed with his stick to the other bank. On the Surrey side at this point there ran out into the Thames, seeming almost to overhang it, a bulk and cluster of those tall tenements, dotted with lighted windows, and rising like factory chimneys to an almost insane height. Their special poise and position made one block of buildings especially look like a Tower of Babel with a hundred eyes. Syme had never seen any of the sky-scraping buildings in America, so he could only think of the buildings in a dream.

Even as he stared, the highest light in this innumerably lighted turret abruptly went out, as if this black Argus had winked at him with one of his innumerable eyes.

Professor de Worms swung round on his heel, and struck his stick against his boot.

"We are too late," he said, "the hygienic Doctor has gone to bed."

"What do you mean?" asked Syme. "Does he live over there, then?"

"Yes," said de Worms, "behind that particular window which you can't see. Come along and get some dinner. We must call on him tomorrow morning."

Without further parley, he led the way through several by-ways until they came out into the flare and clamour of the East India Dock Road. The Professor, who seemed to know his way about the neighbourhood, proceeded to a place where the line of lighted shops fell back into a sort of abrupt twilight and quiet, in which an old white inn, all out of repair, stood back some twenty feet from the road.

"You can find good English inns left by accident everywhere, like fossils," explained the Professor. "I once found a decent place in the West End."

"I suppose," said Syme, smiling, "that this is the corresponding decent place in the East End?"

"It is," said the Professor reverently, and went in.

In that place they dined and slept, both very thoroughly. The beans and bacon, which these unaccountable people cooked well, the astonishing emergence of Burgundy from their cellars, crowned Syme's sense of a new comradeship and comfort. Through all this ordeal his root horror had been isolation, and there are no words to express the abyss between isolation and having one ally. It may be conceded to the mathematicians that four is twice two. But two is not twice one; two is two thousand times one. That is why, in spite of a hundred disadvantages, the world will always return to monogamy.

Syme was able to pour out for the first time the whole of his outrageous tale, from the time when Gregory had taken him to the little tavern by the river. He did it idly and amply, in a luxuriant monologue, as a man speaks with very old friends. On his side, also, the man who had impersonated Professor de Worms was not less communicative. His own story was almost as silly as Syme's.

"That's a good get-up of yours," said Syme, draining a glass of Macon; "a lot better than old Gogol's. Even at the start I thought he was a bit too hairy."

"A difference of artistic theory," replied the Professor pensively. "Gogol was an idealist. He made up as the abstract or platonic ideal of an anarchist. But I am a realist. I am a portrait painter. But, indeed, to say that I am a portrait painter is an inadequate expression. I am a portrait."

"I don't understand you," said Syme.

"I am a portrait," repeated the Professor. "I am a portrait of the celebrated Professor de Worms, who is, I believe, in Naples."

"You mean you are made up like him," said Syme. "But doesn't he know that you are taking his nose in vain?"

"He knows it right enough," replied his friend cheerfully.

"Then why doesn't he denounce you?"

"I have denounced him," answered the Professor.

"Do explain yourself," said Syme.

"With pleasure, if you don't mind hearing my story," replied the eminent foreign philosopher. "I am by profession an actor, and my name is Wilks. When I was on the stage I mixed with all sorts of Bohemian and blackguard company. Sometimes I touched the edge of the turf, sometimes the riff-raff of the arts, and occasionally the political refugee. In some den of exiled dreamers I was introduced to the great German Nihilist philosopher, Professor de Worms. I did not gather much about him beyond his appearance, which was very disgusting, and which I studied carefully. I understood that he had proved that the destructive principle in the universe was God; hence he insisted on the need for a furious and incessant energy, rending all things in pieces. Energy, he said, was the All. He was lame, shortsighted, and partially paralytic. When I met him I was in a frivolous mood, and I disliked him so much that I resolved to imitate him. If I had been a draughtsman I would have drawn a caricature. I was only an actor, I could only act a caricature. I made myself up into what was meant for a wild exaggeration of the old Professor's dirty old self. When I went into the room full of his supporters I expected to be received with a roar of laughter, or (if they were too far gone) with a roar of indignation at the insult. I cannot describe the surprise I felt when my entrance was received with a respectful silence, followed (when I had first opened my lips) with a murmur of admiration. The curse of the perfect artist had fallen upon me. I had been too subtle, I had been too true. They thought I really was the great Nihilist Professor. I was a healthy-minded young man at the time, and I confess that it was a blow. Before I could fully recover, however, two or three of these admirers ran up to me radiating indignation, and told me that a public insult had been put upon me in the next room. I inquired its nature. It seemed that an impertinent fellow had dressed himself up as a preposterous parody of myself. I had drunk more champagne than was good for me, and in a flash of folly I decided to see the situation through. Consequently it was to meet the glare of the company and my own lifted eyebrows and freezing eyes that the real Professor came into the room.

"I need hardly say there was a collision. The pessimists all round me looked anxiously from one Professor to the other Professor to see which was really the more feeble. But I won. An old man in poor health, like my rival, could not be expected to be so impressively feeble as a young actor in the prime of life. You see, he really had paralysis, and working within this definite limitation, he couldn't be so jolly paralytic as I was. Then he tried to blast my claims intellectually. I countered that by a very simple dodge. Whenever he said something that nobody but he could understand, I replied with something which I could not even understand myself. 'I don't fancy,' he said, 'that you could have worked out the principle that evolution is only negation, since there inheres in it the introduction of lacuna, which are an essential of differentiation.' I replied quite scornfully, 'You read all that up in Pinckwerts; the notion that involution functioned eugenically was exposed long ago by Glumpe.' It is unnecessary for me to say that there never were such people as Pinckwerts and Glumpe. But the people all round (rather to my surprise) seemed to remember them quite well, and the Professor, finding that the learned and mysterious method left him rather at the mercy of an enemy slightly deficient in scruples, fell back upon a more popular form of wit. 'I see,' he sneered, 'you prevail like the false pig in Aesop.' 'And you fail,' I answered, smiling, 'like the hedgehog in Montaigne.' Need I say that there is no hedgehog in Montaigne? 'Your claptrap comes off,' he said; 'so would your beard.' I had no intelligent answer to this, which was quite true and rather witty. But I laughed heartily, answered, 'Like the Pantheist's boots,' at random, and turned on my heel with all the honours of victory. The real Professor was thrown out, but not with violence, though one man tried very patiently to pull off his nose. He is now, I believe, received everywhere in Europe as a delightful impostor. His apparent earnestness and anger, you see, make him all the more entertaining."

"Well," said Syme, "I can understand your putting on his dirty old beard for a night's practical joke, but I don't understand your never taking it off again."

"That is the rest of the story," said the impersonator. "When I myself left the company, followed by reverent applause, I went limping down the dark street, hoping that I should soon be far enough away to be able to walk like a human being. To my astonishment, as I was turning the corner, I felt a touch on the shoulder, and turning, found myself under the shadow of an enormous policeman. He told me I was wanted. I struck a sort of paralytic attitude, and cried in a high German accent, 'Yes, I am wanted—by the oppressed of the world. You are arresting me on the charge of being the great anarchist, Professor de Worms.' The policeman impassively consulted a paper in his hand, 'No, sir,' he said civilly, 'at least, not exactly, sir. I am arresting you on the charge of not being the celebrated anarchist, Professor de Worms.' This charge, if it was criminal at all, was certainly the lighter of the two, and I went along with the man, doubtful, but not greatly dismayed. I was shown into a number of rooms, and eventually into the presence of a police officer, who explained that a serious campaign had been opened against the centres of anarchy, and that this, my successful masquerade, might be of considerable value to the public safety. He offered me a good salary and this little blue card. Though our conversation was short, he struck me as a man of very massive common sense and humour; but I cannot tell you much about him personally, because—"

Syme laid down his knife and fork.

"I know," he said, "because you talked to him in a dark room."

Professor de Worms nodded and drained his glass.

CHAPTER IX. THE MAN IN SPECTACLES

"BURGUNDY is a jolly thing," said the Professor sadly, as he set his glass down.

"You don't look as if it were," said Syme; "you drink it as if it were medicine."

"You must excuse my manner," said the Professor dismally, "my position is rather a curious one. Inside I am really bursting with boyish merriment; but I acted the paralytic Professor so well, that now I can't leave off. So that when I am among friends, and have no need at all to disguise myself, I still can't help speaking slow and wrinkling my forehead—just as if it were my forehead. I can be quite happy, you understand, but only in a paralytic sort of way. The most buoyant exclamations leap up in my heart, but they come out of my mouth quite different. You should hear me say, 'Buck up, old cock!' It would bring tears to your eyes."

"It does," said Syme; "but I cannot help thinking that apart from all that you are really a bit worried."

The Professor started a little and looked at him steadily.

"You are a very clever fellow," he said, "it is a pleasure to work with you. Yes, I have rather a heavy cloud in my head. There is a great problem to face," and he sank his bald brow in his two hands.

Then he said in a low voice—

"Can you play the piano?"

"Yes," said Syme in simple wonder, "I'm supposed to have a good touch."

Then, as the other did not speak, he added—

"I trust the great cloud is lifted."

After a long silence, the Professor said out of the cavernous shadow of his hands—

"It would have done just as well if you could work a typewriter."

"Thank you," said Syme, "you flatter me."

"Listen to me," said the other, "and remember whom we have to see tomorrow. You and I are going tomorrow to attempt something which is very much more dangerous than trying to steal the Crown Jewels out of the Tower. We are trying to steal a secret from a very sharp, very strong, and very wicked man. I believe there is no man, except the President, of course, who is so seriously startling and formidable as that little grinning fellow in goggles. He has not perhaps the white-hot enthusiasm unto death, the mad martyrdom for anarchy, which marks the Secretary. But then that very fanaticism in the Secretary has a human pathos, and is almost a redeeming trait. But the little Doctor has a brutal sanity that is more shocking than the Secretary's disease. Don't you notice his detestable virility and vitality. He bounces like an india-rubber ball. Depend on it, Sunday was not asleep (I wonder if he ever sleeps?) when he locked up all the plans of this outrage in the round, black head of Dr. Bull."

"And you think," said Syme, "that this unique monster will be soothed if I play the piano to him?"

"Don't be an ass," said his mentor. "I mentioned the piano because it gives one quick and independent fingers. Syme, if we are to go through this interview and come out sane or alive, we must have some code of signals between us that this brute will not see. I have made a rough alphabetical cypher corresponding to the five fingers—like this, see," and he rippled with his fingers on the wooden table—"B A D, bad, a word we may frequently require."

Syme poured himself out another glass of wine, and began to study the scheme. He was abnormally quick with his brains at puzzles, and with his hands at conjuring, and it did not take him long to learn how he might convey simple messages by what would seem to be idle taps upon a table or knee. But wine and companionship had always the effect of inspiring him to a farcical ingenuity, and the Professor soon found himself struggling with the too vast energy of the new language, as it passed through the heated brain of Syme.

"We must have several word-signs," said Syme seriously—"words that we are likely to want, fine shades of meaning. My favourite word is 'coeval'. What's yours?"

"Do stop playing the goat," said the Professor plaintively. "You don't know how serious this is."

"'Lush' too," said Syme, shaking his head sagaciously, "we must have 'lush'—word applied to grass, don't you know?"

"Do you imagine," asked the Professor furiously, "that we are going to talk to Dr. Bull about grass?"

"There are several ways in which the subject could be approached," said Syme reflectively, "and the word introduced without appearing forced. We might say, 'Dr. Bull, as a revolutionist, you remember that a tyrant once advised us to eat grass; and indeed many of us, looking on the fresh lush grass of summer...'"

"Do you understand," said the other, "that this is a tragedy?"

"Perfectly," replied Syme; "always be comic in a tragedy. What the deuce else can you do? I wish this language of yours had a wider scope. I suppose we could not extend it from the fingers to the toes? That would involve pulling off our boots and socks during the conversation, which however unobtrusively performed—"

"Syme," said his friend with a stern simplicity, "go to bed!"

Syme, however, sat up in bed for a considerable time mastering the new code. He was awakened next morning while the east was still sealed with darkness, and found his grey-bearded ally standing like a ghost beside his bed.

Syme sat up in bed blinking; then slowly collected his thoughts, threw off the bed-clothes, and stood up. It seemed to him in some curious way that all the safety and sociability of the night before fell with the bedclothes off him, and he stood up in an air of cold danger. He still felt an entire trust and loyalty towards his companion; but it was the trust between two men going to the scaffold.

"Well," said Syme with a forced cheerfulness as he pulled on his trousers, "I dreamt of that alphabet of yours. Did it take you long to make it up?"

The Professor made no answer, but gazed in front of him with eyes the colour of a wintry sea; so Syme repeated his question.

"I say, did it take you long to invent all this? I'm considered good at these things, and it was a good hour's grind. Did you learn it all on the spot?"

The Professor was silent; his eyes were wide open, and he wore a fixed but very small smile.

"How long did it take you?"

The Professor did not move.

"Confound you, can't you answer?" called out Syme, in a sudden anger that had something like fear underneath. Whether or no the Professor could answer, he did not.

Syme stood staring back at the stiff face like parchment and the blank, blue eyes. His first thought was that the Professor had gone mad, but his second thought was more frightful. After all, what did he know about this queer creature whom he had heedlessly accepted as a friend? What did he know, except that the man had been at the anarchist breakfast and had told him a ridiculous tale? How improbable it was that there should be another friend there beside Gogol! Was this man's silence a sensational way of declaring war? Was this adamantine stare after all only the awful sneer of some threefold traitor, who had turned for the last time? He stood and strained his ears in this heartless silence. He almost fancied he could hear dynamiters come to capture him shifting softly in the corridor outside.

Then his eye strayed downwards, and he burst out laughing. Though the Professor himself stood there as voiceless as a statue, his five dumb fingers were dancing alive upon the dead table. Syme watched the twinkling movements of the talking hand, and read clearly the message—

"I will only talk like this. We must get used to it."

He rapped out the answer with the impatience of relief—

"All right. Let's get out to breakfast."

They took their hats and sticks in silence; but as Syme took his sword-stick, he held it hard.

They paused for a few minutes only to stuff down coffee and coarse thick sandwiches at a coffee stall, and then made their way across the river, which under the grey and growing light looked as desolate as Acheron. They reached the bottom of the huge block of buildings which they had seen from across the river, and began in silence to mount the naked and numberless stone steps, only pausing now and then to make short remarks on the rail of the banisters. At about every other flight they passed a window; each window showed them a pale and tragic dawn lifting itself laboriously over London. From each the innumerable roofs of slate looked like the leaden surges of a grey, troubled sea after rain. Syme was increasingly conscious that his new adventure had somehow a quality of cold sanity worse than the wild adventures of the past. Last night, for instance, the tall tenements had seemed to him like a tower in a dream. As he now went up the weary and perpetual steps, he was daunted and bewildered by their almost infinite series. But it was not the hot horror of a dream or of anything that might be exaggeration or delusion. Their infinity was more like the empty infinity of arithmetic, something unthinkable, yet necessary to thought. Or it was like the stunning statements of astronomy about the distance of the fixed stars. He was ascending the house of reason, a thing more hideous than unreason itself.

By the time they reached Dr. Bull's landing, a last window showed them a harsh, white dawn edged with banks of a kind of coarse red, more like red clay than red cloud. And when they entered Dr. Bull's bare garret it was full of light.

Syme had been haunted by a half historic memory in connection with these empty rooms and that austere daybreak. The moment he saw the garret and Dr. Bull sitting writing at a table, he remembered what the memory was—the French Revolution. There should have been the black outline of a guillotine against that heavy red and white of the morning. Dr. Bull was in his white shirt and black breeches only; his cropped, dark head might well have just come out of its wig; he might have been Marat or a more slipshod Robespierre.

Yet when he was seen properly, the French fancy fell away. The Jacobins were idealists; there was about this man a murderous materialism. His position gave him a somewhat new appearance. The strong, white light of morning coming from one side creating sharp shadows, made him seem both more pale and more angular than he had looked at the breakfast on the balcony. Thus the two black glasses that encased his eyes might really have been black cavities in his skull, making him look like a death's-head. And, indeed, if ever Death himself sat writing at a wooden table, it might have been he.

He looked up and smiled brightly enough as the men came in, and rose with the resilient rapidity of which the Professor had spoken. He set chairs for both of them, and going to a peg behind the door, proceeded to put on a coat and waistcoat of rough, dark tweed; he buttoned it up neatly, and came back to sit down at his table.

The quiet good humour of his manner left his two opponents helpless. It was with some momentary difficulty that the Professor broke silence and began, "I'm sorry to disturb you so early, comrade," said he, with a careful resumption of the slow de Worms manner. "You have no doubt made all the arrangements for the Paris affair?" Then he added with infinite slowness, "We have information which renders intolerable anything in the nature of a moment's delay."

Dr. Bull smiled again, but continued to gaze on them without speaking. The Professor resumed, a pause before each weary word—

"Please do not think me excessively abrupt; but I advise you to alter those plans, or if it is too late for that, to follow your agent with all the support you can get for him. Comrade Syme and I have had an experience which it would take more time to recount than we can afford, if we are to act on it. I will, however, relate the occurrence in detail, even at the risk of losing time, if you really feel that it is essential to the understanding of the problem we have to discuss."

He was spinning out his sentences, making them intolerably long and lingering, in the hope of maddening the practical little Doctor into an explosion of impatience which might show his hand. But the little Doctor continued only to stare and smile, and the monologue was uphill work. Syme began to feel a new sickness and despair. The Doctor's smile and silence were not at all like the cataleptic stare and horrible silence which he had confronted in the Professor half an hour before. About the Professor's makeup and all his antics there was always something merely grotesque, like a gollywog. Syme remembered those wild woes of yesterday as one remembers being afraid of Bogy in childhood. But here was daylight; here was a healthy, square-shouldered man in tweeds, not odd save for the accident of his ugly spectacles, not glaring or grinning at all, but smiling steadily and not saying a word. The whole had a sense of unbearable reality. Under the increasing sunlight the colours of the Doctor's complexion, the pattern of his tweeds, grew and expanded outrageously, as such things grow too important in a realistic novel. But his smile was quite slight, the pose of his head polite; the only uncanny thing was his silence.

"As I say," resumed the Professor, like a man toiling through heavy sand, "the incident that has occurred to us and has led us to ask for information about the Marquis, is one which you may think it better to have narrated; but as it came in the way of Comrade Syme rather than me—"

His words he seemed to be dragging out like words in an anthem; but Syme, who was watching, saw his long fingers rattle quickly on the edge of the crazy table. He read the message, "You must go on. This devil has sucked me dry!"

Syme plunged into the breach with that bravado of improvisation which always came to him when he was alarmed.

"Yes, the thing really happened to me," he said hastily. "I had the good fortune to fall into conversation with a detective who took me, thanks to my hat, for a respectable person. Wishing to clinch my reputation for respectability, I took him and made him very drunk at the Savoy. Under this influence he became friendly, and told me in so many words that within a day or two they hope to arrest the Marquis in France.

"So unless you or I can get on his track—"

The Doctor was still smiling in the most friendly way, and his protected eyes were still impenetrable. The Professor signalled to Syme that he would resume his explanation, and he began again with the same elaborate calm.

"Syme immediately brought this information to me, and we came here together to see what use you would be inclined to make of it. It seems to me unquestionably urgent that—"

All this time Syme had been staring at the Doctor almost as steadily as the Doctor stared at the Professor, but quite without the smile. The nerves of both comrades-in-arms were near snapping under that strain of motionless amiability, when Syme suddenly leant forward and idly tapped the edge of the table. His message to his ally ran, "I have an intuition."

The Professor, with scarcely a pause in his monologue, signalled back, "Then sit on it."

Syme telegraphed, "It is quite extraordinary."

The other answered, "Extraordinary rot!"

Syme said, "I am a poet."

The other retorted, "You are a dead man."

Syme had gone quite red up to his yellow hair, and his eyes were burning feverishly. As he said he had an intuition, and it had risen to a sort of lightheaded certainty. Resuming his symbolic taps, he signalled to his friend, "You scarcely realise how poetic my intuition is. It has that sudden quality we sometimes feel in the coming of spring."

He then studied the answer on his friend's fingers. The answer was, "Go to hell!"

The Professor then resumed his merely verbal monologue addressed to the Doctor.

"Perhaps I should rather say," said Syme on his fingers, "that it resembles that sudden smell of the sea which may be found in the heart of lush woods."

His companion disdained to reply.

"Or yet again," tapped Syme, "it is positive, as is the passionate red hair of a beautiful woman."

The Professor was continuing his speech, but in the middle of it Syme decided to act. He leant across the table, and said in a voice that could not be neglected—

"Dr. Bull!"

The Doctor's sleek and smiling head did not move, but they could have sworn that under his dark glasses his eyes darted towards Syme.

"Dr. Bull," said Syme, in a voice peculiarly precise and courteous, "would you do me a small favour? Would you be so kind as to take off your spectacles?"

The Professor swung round on his seat, and stared at Syme with a sort of frozen fury of astonishment. Syme, like a man who has thrown his life and fortune on the table, leaned forward with a fiery face. The Doctor did not move.

For a few seconds there was a silence in which one could hear a pin drop, split once by the single hoot of a distant steamer on the Thames. Then Dr. Bull rose slowly, still smiling, and took off his spectacles.

Syme sprang to his feet, stepping backwards a little, like a chemical lecturer from a successful explosion. His eyes were like stars, and for an instant he could only point without speaking.

The Professor had also started to his feet, forgetful of his supposed paralysis. He leant on the back of the chair and stared doubtfully at Dr. Bull, as if the Doctor had been turned into a toad before his eyes. And indeed it was almost as great a transformation scene.

The two detectives saw sitting in the chair before them a very boyish-looking young man, with very frank and happy hazel eyes, an open expression, cockney clothes like those of a city clerk, and an unquestionable breath about him of being very good and rather commonplace. The smile was still there, but it might have been the first smile of a baby.

"I knew I was a poet," cried Syme in a sort of ecstasy. "I knew my intuition was as infallible as the Pope. It was the spectacles that did it! It was all the spectacles. Given those beastly black eyes, and all the rest of him his health and his jolly looks, made him a live devil among dead ones."

"It certainly does make a queer difference," said the Professor shakily. "But as regards the project of Dr. Bull—"

"Project be damned!" roared Syme, beside himself. "Look at him! Look at his face, look at his collar, look at his blessed boots! You don't suppose, do you, that that thing's an anarchist?"

"Syme!" cried the other in an apprehensive agony.

"Why, by God," said Syme, "I'll take the risk of that myself! Dr. Bull, I am a police officer. There's my card," and he flung down the blue card upon the table.

The Professor still feared that all was lost; but he was loyal. He pulled out his own official card and put it beside his friend's. Then the third man burst out laughing, and for the first time that morning they heard his voice.

"I'm awfully glad you chaps have come so early," he said, with a sort of schoolboy flippancy, "for we can all start for France together. Yes, I'm in the force right enough," and he flicked a blue card towards them lightly as a matter of form.

Clapping a brisk bowler on his head and resuming his goblin glasses, the Doctor moved so quickly towards the door, that the others instinctively followed him. Syme seemed a little distrait, and as he passed under the doorway he suddenly struck his stick on the stone passage so that it rang.

"But Lord God Almighty," he cried out, "if this is all right, there were more damned detectives than there were damned dynamiters at the damned Council!"

"We might have fought easily," said Bull; "we were four against three."

The Professor was descending the stairs, but his voice came up from below.

"No," said the voice, "we were not four against three—we were not so lucky. We were four against One."

The others went down the stairs in silence.

The young man called Bull, with an innocent courtesy characteristic of him, insisted on going last until they reached the street; but there his own robust rapidity asserted itself unconsciously, and he walked quickly on ahead towards a railway inquiry office, talking to the others over his shoulder.

"It is jolly to get some pals," he said. "I've been half dead with the jumps, being quite alone. I nearly flung my arms round Gogol and embraced him, which would have been imprudent. I hope you won't despise me for having been in a blue funk."

"All the blue devils in blue hell," said Syme, "contributed to my blue funk! But the worst devil was you and your infernal goggles."

The young man laughed delightedly.

"Wasn't it a rag?" he said. "Such a simple idea—not my own. I haven't got the brains. You see, I wanted to go into the detective service, especially the anti-dynamite business. But for that purpose they wanted someone to dress up as a dynamiter; and they all swore by blazes that I could never look like a dynamiter. They said my very walk was respectable, and that seen from behind I looked like the British Constitution. They said I looked too healthy and too optimistic, and too reliable and benevolent; they called me all sorts of names at Scotland Yard. They said that if I had been a criminal, I might have made my fortune by looking so like an honest man; but as I had the misfortune to be an honest man, there was not even the remotest chance of my assisting them by ever looking like a criminal. But at last I was brought before some old josser who was high up in the force, and who seemed to have no end of a head on his shoulders. And there the others all talked hopelessly. One asked whether a bushy beard would hide my nice smile; another said that if they blacked my face I might look like a negro anarchist; but this old chap chipped in with a most extraordinary remark. 'A pair of smoked spectacles will do it,' he said positively. 'Look at him now; he looks like an angelic office boy. Put him on a pair of smoked spectacles, and children will scream at the sight of him.' And so it was, by George! When once my eyes were covered, all the rest, smile and big shoulders and short hair, made me look a perfect little devil. As I say, it was simple enough when it was done, like miracles; but that wasn't the really miraculous part of it. There was one really staggering thing about the business, and my head still turns at it."

"What was that?" asked Syme.

"I'll tell you," answered the man in spectacles. "This big pot in the police who sized me up so that he knew how the goggles would go with my hair and socks—by God, he never saw me at all!"

Syme's eyes suddenly flashed on him.

"How was that?" he asked. "I thought you talked to him."

"So I did," said Bull brightly; "but we talked in a pitch-dark room like a coal-cellar. There, you would never have guessed that."

"I could not have conceived it," said Syme gravely.

"It is indeed a new idea," said the Professor.

Their new ally was in practical matters a whirlwind. At the inquiry office he asked with businesslike brevity about the trains for Dover. Having got his information, he bundled the company into a cab, and put them and himself inside a railway carriage before they had properly realised the breathless process. They were already on the Calais boat before conversation flowed freely.

"I had already arranged," he explained, "to go to France for my lunch; but I am delighted to have someone to lunch with me. You see, I had to send that beast, the Marquis, over with his bomb, because the President had his eye on me, though God knows how. I'll tell you the story some day. It was perfectly choking. Whenever I tried to slip out of it I saw the President somewhere, smiling out of the bow-window of a club, or taking off his hat to me from the top of an omnibus. I tell you, you can say what you like, that fellow sold himself to the devil; he can be in six places at once."

"So you sent the Marquis off, I understand," asked the Professor. "Was it long ago? Shall we be in time to catch him?"

"Yes," answered the new guide, "I've timed it all. He'll still be at Calais when we arrive."

"But when we do catch him at Calais," said the Professor, "what are we going to do?"

CHAPTER IX. THE MAN IN SPECTACLES

At this question the countenance of Dr. Bull fell for the first time. He reflected a little, and then said—

"Theoretically, I suppose, we ought to call the police."

"Not I," said Syme. "Theoretically I ought to drown myself first. I promised a poor fellow, who was a real modern pessimist, on my word of honour not to tell the police. I'm no hand at casuistry, but I can't break my word to a modern pessimist. It's like breaking one's word to a child."

"I'm in the same boat," said the Professor. "I tried to tell the police and I couldn't, because of some silly oath I took. You see, when I was an actor I was a sort of all-round beast. Perjury or treason is the only crime I haven't committed. If I did that I shouldn't know the difference between right and wrong."

"I've been through all that," said Dr. Bull, "and I've made up my mind. I gave my promise to the Secretary—you know him, man who smiles upside down. My friends, that man is the most utterly unhappy man that was ever human. It may be his digestion, or his conscience, or his nerves, or his philosophy of the universe, but he's damned, he's in hell! Well, I can't turn on a man like that, and hunt him down. It's like whipping a leper. I may be mad, but that's how I feel; and there's jolly well the end of it."

"I don't think you're mad," said Syme. "I knew you would decide like that when first you—"

"Eh?" said Dr. Bull.

"When first you took off your spectacles."

Dr. Bull smiled a little, and strolled across the deck to look at the sunlit sea. Then he strolled back again, kicking his heels carelessly, and a companionable silence fell between the three men.

"Well," said Syme, "it seems that we have all the same kind of morality or immorality, so we had better face the fact that comes of it."

"Yes," assented the Professor, "you're quite right; and we must hurry up, for I can see the Grey Nose standing out from France."

"The fact that comes of it," said Syme seriously, "is this, that we three are alone on this planet. Gogol has gone, God knows where; perhaps the President has smashed him like a fly. On the Council we are three men against three, like the Romans who held the bridge. But we are worse off than that, first because they can appeal to their organization and we cannot appeal to ours, and second because—"

"Because one of those other three men," said the Professor, "is not a man."

Syme nodded and was silent for a second or two, then he said—

"My idea is this. We must do something to keep the Marquis in Calais till to-morrow midday. I have turned over twenty schemes in my head. We cannot denounce him as a dynamiter; that is agreed. We cannot get him detained on some trivial charge, for we should have to appear; he knows us, and he would smell a rat. We cannot pretend to keep him on anarchist business; he might swallow much in that way, but not the notion of stopping in Calais while the Czar went safely through Paris. We might try to kidnap him, and lock him up ourselves; but he is a well-known man here. He has a whole bodyguard of friends; he is very strong and brave, and the event is doubtful. The only thing I can see to do is actually to take advantage of the very things that are in the Marquis's favour. I am going to profit by the fact that he is a highly respected nobleman. I am going to profit by the fact that he has many friends and moves in the best society."

"What the devil are you talking about?" asked the Professor.

"The Symes are first mentioned in the fourteenth century," said Syme; "but there is a tradition that one of them rode behind Bruce at Bannockburn. Since 1350 the tree is quite clear."

"He's gone off his head," said the little Doctor, staring.

"Our bearings," continued Syme calmly, "are 'argent a chevron gules charged with three cross crosslets of the field.' The motto varies."

The Professor seized Syme roughly by the waistcoat.

"We are just inshore," he said. "Are you seasick or joking in the wrong place?"

"My remarks are almost painfully practical," answered Syme, in an unhurried manner. "The house of St. Eustache also is very ancient. The Marquis cannot deny that he is a gentleman. He cannot deny that I am a gentleman. And in order to put the matter of my social position quite beyond a doubt, I propose at the earliest opportunity to knock his hat off. But here we are in the harbour."

They went on shore under the strong sun in a sort of daze. Syme, who had now taken the lead as Bull had taken it in London, led them along a kind of marine parade until he came to some cafes, embowered in a bulk of greenery and overlooking the sea. As he went before them his step was slightly swaggering, and he swung his stick like a sword. He was making apparently for the extreme end of the line of cafes, but he stopped abruptly. With a sharp gesture he motioned them to silence, but he pointed with one gloved finger to a cafe table under a bank of flowering foliage at which sat the Marquis de St. Eustache, his teeth shining in his thick, black beard, and his bold, brown face shadowed by a light yellow straw hat and outlined against the violet sea.

CHAPTER X. THE DUEL

SYME sat down at a cafe table with his companions, his blue eyes sparkling like the bright sea below, and ordered a bottle of Saumur with a pleased impatience. He was for some reason in a condition of curious hilarity. His spirits were already unnaturally high; they rose as the Saumur sank, and in half an hour his talk was a torrent of nonsense. He professed to be making out a plan of the conversation which was going to ensue between himself and the deadly Marquis. He jotted it down wildly with a pencil. It was arranged like a printed catechism, with questions and answers, and was delivered with an extraordinary rapidity of utterance.

"I shall approach. Before taking off his hat, I shall take off my own. I shall say, 'The Marquis de Saint Eustache, I believe.' He will say, 'The celebrated Mr. Syme, I presume.' He will say in the most exquisite French, 'How are you?' I shall reply in the most exquisite Cockney, 'Oh, just the Syme—'"

"Oh, shut it," said the man in spectacles. "Pull yourself together, and chuck away that bit of paper. What are you really going to do?"

"But it was a lovely catechism," said Syme pathetically. "Do let me read it you. It has only forty-three questions and answers, and some of the Marquis's answers are wonderfully witty. I like to be just to my enemy."

"But what's the good of it all?" asked Dr. Bull in exasperation.

"It leads up to my challenge, don't you see," said Syme, beaming. "When the Marquis has given the thirty-ninth reply, which runs—"

"Has it by any chance occurred to you," asked the Professor, with a ponderous simplicity, "that the Marquis may not say all the forty-three things you have put down for him? In that case, I understand, your own epigrams may appear somewhat more forced."

Syme struck the table with a radiant face.

"Why, how true that is," he said, "and I never thought of it. Sir, you have an intellect beyond the common. You will make a name."

"Oh, you're as drunk as an owl!" said the Doctor.

"It only remains," continued Syme quite unperturbed, "to adopt some other method of breaking the ice (if I may so express it) between myself and the man I wish to kill. And since the course of a dialogue cannot be predicted by one of its parties alone (as you have pointed out with such recondite acumen), the only thing to be done, I suppose, is for the one party, as far as possible, to do all the dialogue by himself. And so I will, by George!" And he stood up suddenly, his yellow hair blowing in the slight sea breeze.

A band was playing in a cafe chantant hidden somewhere among the trees, and a woman had just stopped singing. On Syme's heated head the bray of the brass band seemed like the jar and jingle of that barrel-organ in Leicester Square, to the tune of which he had once stood up to die. He looked across to the little table where the Marquis sat. The man had two companions now, solemn Frenchmen in frock-coats and silk hats, one of them with the red rosette of the Legion of Honour, evidently people of a solid social position. Besides these black, cylindrical costumes, the Marquis, in his loose straw hat and light spring clothes, looked Bohemian and even barbaric; but he looked the Marquis. Indeed, one might say that he looked the king, with his animal elegance, his scornful eyes, and his proud head lifted against the purple sea. But he was no Christian king, at any rate; he was, rather, some swarthy despot, half Greek, half Asiatic, who in the days when slavery seemed natural looked down on the Mediterranean, on his galley and his groaning slaves. Just so, Syme thought, would the brown-gold face of such a tyrant have shown against the dark green olives and the burning blue.

"Are you going to address the meeting?" asked the Professor peevishly, seeing that Syme still stood up without moving.

Syme drained his last glass of sparkling wine.

"I am," he said, pointing across to the Marquis and his companions, "that meeting. That meeting displeases me. I am going to pull that meeting's great ugly, mahogany-coloured nose."

He stepped across swiftly, if not quite steadily. The Marquis, seeing him, arched his black Assyrian eyebrows in surprise, but smiled politely.

"You are Mr. Syme, I think," he said.

Syme bowed.

"And you are the Marquis de Saint Eustache," he said gracefully. "Permit me to pull your nose."

He leant over to do so, but the Marquis started backwards, upsetting his chair, and the two men in top hats held Syme back by the shoulders.

"This man has insulted me!" said Syme, with gestures of explanation.

"Insulted you?" cried the gentleman with the red rosette, "when?"

"Oh, just now," said Syme recklessly. "He insulted my mother."

"Insulted your mother!" exclaimed the gentleman incredulously.

"Well, anyhow," said Syme, conceding a point, "my aunt."

"But how can the Marquis have insulted your aunt just now?" said the second gentleman with some legitimate wonder. "He has been sitting here all the time."

"Ah, it was what he said!" said Syme darkly.

"I said nothing at all," said the Marquis, "except something about the band. I only said that I liked Wagner played well."

"It was an allusion to my family," said Syme firmly. "My aunt played Wagner badly. It was a painful subject. We are always being insulted about it."

"This seems most extraordinary," said the gentleman who was decore, looking doubtfully at the Marquis.

"Oh, I assure you," said Syme earnestly, "the whole of your conversation was simply packed with sinister allusions to my aunt's weaknesses."

"This is nonsense!" said the second gentleman. "I for one have said nothing for half an hour except that I liked the singing of that girl with black hair."

"Well, there you are again!" said Syme indignantly. "My aunt's was red."

"It seems to me," said the other, "that you are simply seeking a pretext to insult the Marquis."

"By George!" said Syme, facing round and looking at him, "what a clever chap you are!"

The Marquis started up with eyes flaming like a tiger's.

"Seeking a quarrel with me!" he cried. "Seeking a fight with me! By God! there was never a man who had to seek long. These gentlemen will perhaps act for me. There are still four hours of daylight. Let us fight this evening."

Syme bowed with a quite beautiful graciousness.

"Marquis," he said, "your action is worthy of your fame and blood. Permit me to consult for a moment with the gentlemen in whose hands I shall place myself."

In three long strides he rejoined his companions, and they, who had seen his champagne-inspired attack and listened to his idiotic explanations, were quite startled at the look of him. For now that he came back to them he was quite sober, a little pale, and he spoke in a low voice of passionate practicality.

"I have done it," he said hoarsely. "I have fixed a fight on the beast. But look here, and listen carefully. There is no time for talk. You are my seconds, and everything must come from you. Now you must insist, and insist absolutely, on the duel coming off after seven tomorrow, so as to give me the chance of preventing him from catching the 7.45 for Paris. If he misses that he misses his crime. He can't refuse to meet you on such a small point of time and place. But this is what he will do. He will choose a field somewhere near a wayside station, where he can pick up the train. He is a very good swordsman, and he will trust to killing me in time to catch it. But I can fence well too, and I think I can keep him in play, at any rate, until the train is lost. Then perhaps he may kill me to console his feelings. You understand? Very well then, let me introduce you to some charming friends of mine," and leading them quickly across the parade, he presented them to the Marquis's seconds by two very aristocratic names of which they had not previously heard.

Syme was subject to spasms of singular common sense, not otherwise a part of his character. They were (as he said of his impulse about the spectacles) poetic intuitions, and they sometimes rose to the exaltation of prophecy.

He had correctly calculated in this case the policy of his opponent. When the Marquis was informed by his seconds that Syme could only fight in the morning, he must fully have realised that an obstacle had suddenly arisen between him and his bomb-throwing business in the capital. Naturally he could not explain this objection to his friends, so he chose the course which Syme had predicted. He induced his seconds to settle on a small meadow not far from the railway, and he trusted to the fatality of the first engagement.

When he came down very coolly to the field of honour, no one could have guessed that he had any anxiety about a journey; his hands were in his pockets, his straw hat on the back of his head, his handsome face brazen in the sun. But it might have struck a stranger as odd that there appeared in his train, not only his seconds carrying the sword-case, but two of his servants carrying a portmanteau and a luncheon basket.

Early as was the hour, the sun soaked everything in warmth, and Syme was vaguely surprised to see so many spring flowers burning gold and silver in the tall grass in which the whole company stood almost knee-deep.

With the exception of the Marquis, all the men were in sombre and solemn morning-dress, with hats like black chimney-pots; the little Doctor especially, with the addition of his black spectacles, looked like an undertaker in a farce. Syme could not help feeling a comic contrast between this funereal church parade of apparel and the rich and glistening meadow, growing wild flowers everywhere. But, indeed, this comic contrast between the yellow blossoms and the black hats was but a symbol of the tragic contrast between the yellow blossoms and the black business. On his right was a little wood; far away to his left lay the long curve of the railway line, which he was, so to speak, guarding from the Marquis, whose goal and escape it was. In front of him, behind the black group of his opponents, he could see, like a tinted cloud, a small almond bush in flower against the faint line of the sea.

The member of the Legion of Honour, whose name it seemed was Colonel Ducroix, approached the Professor and Dr. Bull with great politeness, and suggested that the play should terminate with the first considerable hurt.

Dr. Bull, however, having been carefully coached by Syme upon this point of policy, insisted, with great dignity and in very bad French, that it should continue until one of the combatants was disabled. Syme had made up his mind that he could avoid disabling the Marquis and prevent the Marquis from disabling him for at least twenty minutes. In twenty minutes the Paris train would have gone by.

"To a man of the well-known skill and valour of Monsieur de St. Eustache," said the Professor solemnly, "it must be a matter of indifference which method is adopted, and our principal has strong reasons for demanding the longer encounter, reasons the delicacy of which prevent me from being explicit, but for the just and honourable nature of which I can—"

"Peste!" broke from the Marquis behind, whose face had suddenly darkened, "let us stop talking and begin," and he slashed off the head of a tall flower with his stick.

Syme understood his rude impatience and instinctively looked over his shoulder to see whether the train was coming in sight. But there was no smoke on the horizon.

Colonel Ducroix knelt down and unlocked the case, taking out a pair of twin swords, which took the sunlight and turned to two streaks of white fire. He offered one to the Marquis, who snatched it without ceremony, and another to Syme, who took it, bent it, and poised it with as much delay as was consistent with dignity.

Then the Colonel took out another pair of blades, and taking one himself and giving another to Dr. Bull, proceeded to place the men.

Both combatants had thrown off their coats and waistcoats, and stood sword in hand. The seconds stood on each side of the line of fight with drawn swords also, but still sombre in their dark frock-coats and hats. The principals saluted. The Colonel said quietly, "Engage!" and the two blades touched and tingled.

When the jar of the joined iron ran up Syme's arm, all the fantastic fears that have been the subject of this story fell from him like dreams from a man waking up in bed. He remembered them clearly and in order as mere delusions of the nerves—how the fear of the Professor had been the fear of the tyrannic accidents of nightmare, and how the fear of the Doctor had been the fear of the airless vacuum of science. The first was the old fear that any miracle might happen, the second the more hopeless modern fear that no miracle can ever happen. But he saw that these fears were fancies, for he found himself in the presence of the great fact of the fear of death, with its coarse and pitiless common sense. He felt like a man who had dreamed all night of falling over precipices, and had woke up on the morning when he was to be hanged. For as soon as he had seen the sunlight run down the channel of his foe's foreshortened blade, and as soon as he had felt the two tongues of steel touch, vibrating like two living things, he knew that his enemy was a terrible fighter, and that probably his last hour had come.

He felt a strange and vivid value in all the earth around him, in the grass under his feet; he felt the love of life in all living things. He could almost fancy that he heard the grass growing; he could almost fancy that even as he stood fresh flowers were springing up and breaking into blossom in the meadow—flowers blood red and burning gold and blue, fulfilling the whole pageant of the spring. And whenever his eyes strayed for a flash from the calm, staring, hypnotic eyes of the Marquis, they saw the little tuft of almond tree against the sky-line. He had the feeling that if by some miracle he escaped he would be ready to sit for ever before that almond tree, desiring nothing else in the world.

But while earth and sky and everything had the living beauty of a thing lost, the other half of his head was as clear as glass, and he was parrying his enemy's point with a kind of clockwork skill of which he had hardly supposed himself capable. Once his enemy's point ran along his wrist, leaving a slight streak of blood, but it either was not noticed or was tacitly ignored. Every now and then he riposted, and once or twice he could almost fancy that he felt his point go home, but as there was no blood on blade or shirt he supposed he was mistaken. Then came an interruption and a change.

At the risk of losing all, the Marquis, interrupting his quiet stare, flashed one glance over his shoulder at the line of railway on his right. Then he turned on Syme a face transfigured to that of a fiend, and began to fight as if with twenty weapons. The attack came so fast and furious, that the one shining sword seemed a shower of shining arrows. Syme had no chance to look at the railway; but also he had no need. He could guess the reason of the Marquis's sudden madness of battle—the Paris train was in sight.

But the Marquis's morbid energy over-reached itself. Twice Syme, parrying, knocked his opponent's point far out of the fighting circle; and the third time his riposte was so rapid, that there was no doubt about the hit this time. Syme's sword actually bent under the weight of the Marquis's body, which it had pierced.

Syme was as certain that he had stuck his blade into his enemy as a gardener that he has stuck his spade into the ground. Yet the Marquis sprang back from the stroke without a stagger, and Syme stood staring at his own sword-point like an idiot. There was no blood on it at all.

There was an instant of rigid silence, and then Syme in his turn fell furiously on the other, filled with a flaming curiosity. The Marquis was probably, in a general sense, a better fencer than he, as he had surmised at the beginning, but at the moment the Marquis seemed distraught and at a disadvantage. He fought wildly and even weakly, and he constantly looked away at the railway line, almost as if he feared the train more than the pointed steel. Syme, on the other hand, fought fiercely but still carefully, in an intellectual fury, eager to solve the riddle of his own bloodless sword. For this purpose, he aimed less at the Marquis's body, and more at his throat and head. A minute and a half afterwards he felt his point enter the man's neck below the jaw. It came out clean. Half mad, he thrust again, and made what should have been a bloody scar on the Marquis's cheek. But there was no scar.

For one moment the heaven of Syme again grew black with supernatural terrors. Surely the man had a charmed life. But this new spiritual dread was a more awful thing than had been the mere spiritual topsy-turvydom symbolised by the paralytic who pursued him. The Professor was only a goblin; this man was a devil—perhaps he was the Devil! Anyhow, this was certain, that three times had a human sword been driven into him and made no mark. When Syme had that thought he drew himself up, and all that was good in him sang high up in the air as a high wind sings in the trees. He thought of all the human things in his story—of the Chinese lanterns in Saffron Park, of the girl's red hair in the garden, of the honest, beer-swilling sailors down by the dock, of his loyal companions standing by. Perhaps he had been chosen as a champion of all these fresh and kindly things to cross swords with the enemy of all creation. "After all," he said to himself, "I am more than a devil; I am a man. I can do the one thing which Satan himself cannot do—I can die," and as the word went through his head, he heard a faint and far-off hoot, which would soon be the roar of the Paris train.

He fell to fighting again with a supernatural levity, like a Mohammedan panting for Paradise. As the train came nearer and nearer he fancied he could see people putting up the floral arches in Paris; he joined in the growing noise and the glory of the great Republic whose gate he was guarding against Hell. His thoughts rose higher and higher with the rising roar of the train, which ended, as if proudly, in a long and piercing whistle. The train stopped.

Suddenly, to the astonishment of everyone the Marquis sprang back quite out of sword reach and threw down his sword. The leap was wonderful, and not the less wonderful because Syme had plunged his sword a moment before into the man's thigh.

"Stop!" said the Marquis in a voice that compelled a momentary obedience. "I want to say something."

"What is the matter?" asked Colonel Ducroix, staring. "Has there been foul play?"

"There has been foul play somewhere," said Dr. Bull, who was a little pale. "Our principal has wounded the Marquis four times at least, and he is none the worse."

The Marquis put up his hand with a curious air of ghastly patience.

"Please let me speak," he said. "It is rather important. Mr. Syme," he continued, turning to his opponent, "we are fighting today, if I remember right, because you expressed a wish (which I thought irrational) to pull my nose. Would you oblige me by pulling my nose now as quickly as possible? I have to catch a train."

"I protest that this is most irregular," said Dr. Bull indignantly.

"It is certainly somewhat opposed to precedent," said Colonel Ducroix, looking wistfully at his principal. "There is, I think, one case on record (Captain Bellegarde and the Baron Zumpt) in which the weapons were changed in the middle of the encounter at the request of one of the combatants. But one can hardly call one's nose a weapon."

"Will you or will you not pull my nose?" said the Marquis in exasperation. "Come, come, Mr. Syme! You wanted to do it, do it! You can have no conception of how important it is to me. Don't be so selfish! Pull my nose at once, when I ask you!" and he bent slightly forward with a fascinating smile. The Paris train, panting and groaning, had grated into a little station behind the neighbouring hill.

Syme had the feeling he had more than once had in these adventures—the sense that a horrible and sublime wave lifted to heaven was just toppling over. Walking in a world he half understood, he took two paces forward and seized the Roman nose of this remarkable nobleman. He pulled it hard, and it came off in his hand.

He stood for some seconds with a foolish solemnity, with the pasteboard proboscis still between his fingers, looking at it, while the sun and the clouds and the wooded hills looked down upon this imbecile scene.

The Marquis broke the silence in a loud and cheerful voice.

"If anyone has any use for my left eyebrow," he said, "he can have it. Colonel Ducroix, do accept my left eyebrow! It's the kind of thing that might come in useful any day," and he gravely tore off one of his swarthy Assyrian brows, bringing about half his brown forehead with it, and politely offered it to the Colonel, who stood crimson and speechless with rage.

"If I had known," he spluttered, "that I was acting for a poltroon who pads himself to fight—"

"Oh, I know, I know!" said the Marquis, recklessly throwing various parts of himself right and left about the field. "You are making a mistake; but it can't be explained just now. I tell you the train has come into the station!"

"Yes," said Dr. Bull fiercely, "and the train shall go out of the station. It shall go out without you. We know well enough for what devil's work—"

The mysterious Marquis lifted his hands with a desperate gesture. He was a strange scarecrow standing there in the sun with half his old face peeled off, and half another face glaring and grinning from underneath.

"Will you drive me mad?" he cried. "The train—"

"You shall not go by the train," said Syme firmly, and grasped his sword.

The wild figure turned towards Syme, and seemed to be gathering itself for a sublime effort before speaking.

"You great fat, blasted, blear-eyed, blundering, thundering, brainless, Godforsaken, doddering, damned fool!" he said without taking breath. "You great silly, pink-faced, towheaded turnip! You—"

"You shall not go by this train," repeated Syme.

"And why the infernal blazes," roared the other, "should I want to go by the train?"

"We know all," said the Professor sternly. "You are going to Paris to throw a bomb!"

"Going to Jericho to throw a Jabberwock!" cried the other, tearing his hair, which came off easily.

"Have you all got softening of the brain, that you don't realise what I am? Did you really think I wanted to catch that train? Twenty Paris trains might go by for me. Damn Paris trains!"

"Then what did you care about?" began the Professor.

"What did I care about? I didn't care about catching the train; I cared about whether the train caught me, and now, by God! it has caught me."

"I regret to inform you," said Syme with restraint, "that your remarks convey no impression to my mind. Perhaps if you were to remove the remains of your original forehead and some portion of what was once your chin, your meaning would become clearer. Mental lucidity fulfils itself in many ways. What do you mean by saying that the train has caught you? It may be my literary fancy, but somehow I feel that it ought to mean something."

"It means everything," said the other, "and the end of everything. Sunday has us now in the hollow of his hand."

"Us!" repeated the Professor, as if stupefied. "What do you mean by 'us'?"

"The police, of course!" said the Marquis, and tore off his scalp and half his face.

The head which emerged was the blonde, well brushed, smooth-haired head which is common in the English constabulary, but the face was terribly pale.

"I am Inspector Ratcliffe," he said, with a sort of haste that verged on harshness. "My name is pretty well known to the police, and I can see well enough that you belong to them. But if there is any doubt about my position, I have a card," and he began to pull a blue card from his pocket.

The Professor gave a tired gesture.

"Oh, don't show it us," he said wearily; "we've got enough of them to equip a paper-chase."

The little man named Bull, had, like many men who seem to be of a mere vivacious vulgarity, sudden movements of good taste. Here he certainly saved the situation. In the midst of this staggering transformation scene he stepped forward with all the gravity and responsibility of a second, and addressed the two seconds of the Marquis.

"Gentlemen," he said, "we all owe you a serious apology; but I assure you that you have not been made the victims of such a low joke as you imagine, or indeed of anything undignified in a man of honour. You have not wasted your time; you have helped to save the world. We are not buffoons, but very desperate men at war with a vast conspiracy. A secret society of anarchists is hunting us like hares; not such unfortunate madmen as may here or there throw a bomb through starvation or German philosophy, but a rich and powerful and fanatical church, a church of eastern pessimism, which holds it holy to destroy mankind like vermin. How hard they hunt us you can gather from the fact that we are driven to such disguises as those for which I apologise, and to such pranks as this one by which you suffer."

The younger second of the Marquis, a short man with a black moustache, bowed politely, and said—

"Of course, I accept the apology; but you will in your turn forgive me if I decline to follow you further into your difficulties, and permit myself to say good morning! The sight of an acquaintance and distinguished fellow-townsman coming to pieces in the open air is unusual, and, upon the whole, sufficient for one day. Colonel Ducroix, I would in no way influence your actions, but if you feel with me that our present society is a little abnormal, I am now going to walk back to the town."

Colonel Ducroix moved mechanically, but then tugged abruptly at his white moustache and broke out—

"No, by George! I won't. If these gentlemen are really in a mess with a lot of low wreckers like that, I'll see them through it. I have fought for France, and it is hard if I can't fight for civilization."

Dr. Bull took off his hat and waved it, cheering as at a public meeting.

"Don't make too much noise," said Inspector Ratcliffe, "Sunday may hear you."

"Sunday!" cried Bull, and dropped his hat.

"Yes," retorted Ratcliffe, "he may be with them."

"With whom?" asked Syme.

"With the people out of that train," said the other.

"What you say seems utterly wild," began Syme. "Why, as a matter of fact—But, my God," he cried out suddenly, like a man who sees an explosion a long way off, "by God! if this is true the whole bally lot of us on the Anarchist Council were against anarchy! Every born man was a detective except the President and his personal secretary. What can it mean?"

"Mean!" said the new policeman with incredible violence. "It means that we are struck dead! Don't you know Sunday? Don't you know that his jokes are always so big and simple that one has never thought of them? Can you think of anything more like Sunday than this, that he should put all his powerful enemies on the Supreme Council, and then take care that it was not supreme? I tell you he has bought every trust, he has captured every cable, he has control of every railway line—especially of that railway line!" and he pointed a shaking finger towards the small wayside station. "The whole movement was controlled by him; half the world was ready to rise for him. But there were just five people, perhaps, who would have resisted him... and the old devil put them on the Supreme Council, to waste their time in watching each other. Idiots that we are, he planned the whole of our idiocies! Sunday knew that the Professor would chase Syme through London, and that Syme would fight me in France. And he was combining great masses of capital, and seizing great lines of telegraphy, while we five idiots were running after each other like a lot of confounded babies playing blind man's buff."

"Well?" asked Syme with a sort of steadiness.

"Well," replied the other with sudden serenity, "he has found us playing blind man's buff today in a field of great rustic beauty and extreme solitude. He has probably captured the world; it only remains to him to capture this field and all the fools in it. And since you really want to know what was my objection to the arrival of that train, I will tell you. My objection was that Sunday or his Secretary has just this moment got out of it."

Syme uttered an involuntary cry, and they all turned their eyes towards the far-off station. It was quite true that a considerable bulk of people seemed to be moving in their direction. But they were too distant to be distinguished in any way.

"It was a habit of the late Marquis de St. Eustache," said the new policeman, producing a leather case, "always to carry a pair of opera glasses. Either the President or the Secretary is coming after us with that mob. They have caught us in a nice quiet place where we are under no temptations to break our oaths by calling the police. Dr. Bull, I have a suspicion that you will see better through these than through your own highly decorative spectacles."

He handed the field-glasses to the Doctor, who immediately took off his spectacles and put the apparatus to his eyes.

"It cannot be as bad as you say," said the Professor, somewhat shaken. "There are a good number of them certainly, but they may easily be ordinary tourists."

"Do ordinary tourists," asked Bull, with the fieldglasses to his eyes, "wear black masks half-way down the face?"

Syme almost tore the glasses out of his hand, and looked through them. Most men in the advancing mob really looked ordinary enough; but it was quite true that two or three of the leaders in front wore black half-masks almost down to their mouths. This disguise is very complete, especially at such a distance, and Syme found it impossible to conclude anything from the clean-shaven jaws and chins of the men talking in the front. But presently as they talked they all smiled and one of them smiled on one side.

CHAPTER XI. THE CRIMINALS CHASE THE POLICE

SYME put the field-glasses from his eyes with an almost ghastly relief.

"The President is not with them, anyhow," he said, and wiped his forehead.

"But surely they are right away on the horizon," said the bewildered Colonel, blinking and but half recovered from Bull's hasty though polite explanation. "Could you possibly know your President among all those people?"

"Could I know a white elephant among all those people!" answered Syme somewhat irritably. "As you very truly say, they are on the horizon; but if he were walking with them... by God! I believe this ground would shake."

After an instant's pause the new man called Ratcliffe said with gloomy decision—

"Of course the President isn't with them. I wish to Gemini he were. Much more likely the President is riding in triumph through Paris, or sitting on the ruins of St. Paul's Cathedral."

"This is absurd!" said Syme. "Something may have happened in our absence; but he cannot have carried the world with a rush like that. It is quite true," he added, frowning dubiously at the distant fields that lay towards the little station, "it is certainly true that there seems to be a crowd coming this way; but they are not all the army that you make out."

"Oh, they," said the new detective contemptuously; "no they are not a very valuable force. But let me tell you frankly that they are precisely calculated to our value—we are not much, my boy, in Sunday's universe. He has got hold of all the cables and telegraphs himself. But to kill the Supreme Council he regards as a trivial matter, like a post card; it may be left to his private secretary," and he spat on the grass.

Then he turned to the others and said somewhat austerely—

"There is a great deal to be said for death; but if anyone has any preference for the other alternative, I strongly advise him to walk after me."

With these words, he turned his broad back and strode with silent energy towards the wood. The others gave one glance over their shoulders, and saw that the dark cloud of men had detached itself from the station and was moving with a mysterious discipline across the plain. They saw already, even with the naked eye, black blots on the foremost faces, which marked the masks they wore. They turned and followed their leader, who had already struck the wood, and disappeared among the twinkling trees.

The sun on the grass was dry and hot. So in plunging into the wood they had a cool shock of shadow, as of divers who plunge into a dim pool. The inside of the wood was full of shattered sunlight and shaken shadows. They made a sort of shuddering veil, almost recalling the dizziness of a cinematograph. Even the solid figures walking with him Syme could hardly see for the patterns of sun and shade that danced upon them. Now a man's head was lit as with a light of Rembrandt, leaving all else obliterated; now again he had strong and staring white hands with the face of a negro. The ex-Marquis had pulled the old straw hat over his eyes, and the black shade of the brim cut his face so squarely in two that it seemed to be wearing one of the black half-masks of their pursuers. The fancy tinted Syme's overwhelming sense of wonder. Was he wearing a mask? Was anyone wearing a mask? Was anyone anything? This wood of witchery, in which men's faces turned black and white by turns, in which their figures first swelled into sunlight and then faded into formless night, this mere chaos of chiaroscuro (after the clear daylight outside), seemed to Syme a perfect symbol of the world in which he had been moving for three days, this world where men took off their beards and their spectacles and their noses, and turned into other people. That tragic self-confidence which he had felt when he believed that the Marquis was a devil had strangely disappeared now that he knew that the Marquis was a friend. He felt almost inclined to ask after all these bewilderments what was a friend and what an enemy. Was there anything that was apart from what it seemed? The Marquis had taken off his nose and turned out to be a detective. Might he not just as well take off his head and turn out to be a hobgoblin? Was not everything, after all, like this bewildering woodland, this dance of dark and light? Everything only a glimpse, the glimpse always unforeseen, and always forgotten. For Gabriel Syme had found in the heart of that sun-splashed wood what many modern painters had found there. He had found the thing which the modern people call Impressionism, which is another name for that final scepticism which can find no floor to the universe.

As a man in an evil dream strains himself to scream and wake, Syme strove with a sudden effort to fling off this last and worst of his fancies. With two impatient strides he overtook the man in the Marquis's straw hat, the man whom he had come to address as Ratcliffe. In a voice exaggeratively loud and cheerful, he broke the bottomless silence and made conversation.

"May I ask," he said, "where on earth we are all going to?"

So genuine had been the doubts of his soul, that he was quite glad to hear his companion speak in an easy, human voice.

"We must get down through the town of Lancy to the sea," he said. "I think that part of the country is least likely to be with them."

"What can you mean by all this?" cried Syme. "They can't be running the real world in that way. Surely not many working men are anarchists, and surely if they were, mere mobs could not beat modern armies and police."

"Mere mobs!" repeated his new friend with a snort of scorn. "So you talk about mobs and the working classes as if they were the question. You've got that eternal idiotic idea that if anarchy came it would come from the poor. Why should it?

The poor have been rebels, but they have never been anarchists; they have more interest than anyone else in there being some decent government. The poor man really has a stake in the country. The rich man hasn't; he can go away to New Guinea in a yacht. The poor have sometimes objected to being governed badly; the rich have always objected to being governed at all. Aristocrats were always anarchists, as you can see from the barons' wars."

"As a lecture on English history for the little ones," said Syme, "this is all very nice; but I have not yet grasped its application."

"Its application is," said his informant, "that most of old Sunday's right-hand men are South African and American millionaires. That is why he has got hold of all the communications; and that is why the last four champions of the anti-anarchist police force are running through a wood like rabbits."

"Millionaires I can understand," said Syme thoughtfully, "they are nearly all mad. But getting hold of a few wicked old gentlemen with hobbies is one thing; getting hold of great Christian nations is another. I would bet the nose off my face (forgive the allusion) that Sunday would stand perfectly helpless before the task of converting any ordinary healthy person anywhere."

"Well," said the other, "it rather depends what sort of person you mean."

"Well, for instance," said Syme, "he could never convert that person," and he pointed straight in front of him.

They had come to an open space of sunlight, which seemed to express to Syme the final return of his own good sense; and in the middle of this forest clearing was a figure that might well stand for that common sense in an almost awful actuality. Burnt by the sun and stained with perspiration, and grave with the bottomless gravity of small necessary toils, a heavy French peasant was cutting wood with a hatchet. His cart stood a few yards off, already half full of timber; and the horse that cropped the grass was, like his master, valorous but not desperate; like his master, he was even prosperous, but yet was almost sad. The man was a Norman, taller than the average of the French and very angular; and his swarthy figure stood dark against a square of sunlight, almost like some allegoric figure of labour frescoed on a ground of gold.

"Mr. Syme is saying," called out Ratcliffe to the French Colonel, "that this man, at least, will never be an anarchist."

"Mr. Syme is right enough there," answered Colonel Ducroix, laughing, "if only for the reason that he has plenty of property to defend. But I forgot that in your country you are not used to peasants being wealthy."

"He looks poor," said Dr. Bull doubtfully.

"Quite so," said the Colonel; "that is why he is rich."

"I have an idea," called out Dr. Bull suddenly; "how much would he take to give us a lift in his cart? Those dogs are all on foot, and we could soon leave them behind."

"Oh, give him anything!" said Syme eagerly. "I have piles of money on me."

"That will never do," said the Colonel; "he will never have any respect for you unless you drive a bargain."

"Oh, if he haggles!" began Bull impatiently.

"He haggles because he is a free man," said the other. "You do not understand; he would not see the meaning of generosity. He is not being tipped."

And even while they seemed to hear the heavy feet of their strange pursuers behind them, they had to stand and stamp while the French Colonel talked to the French wood-cutter with all the leisurely badinage and bickering of market-day. At the end of the four minutes, however, they saw that the Colonel was right, for the wood-cutter entered into their plans, not with the vague servility of a tout too-well paid, but with the seriousness of a solicitor who had been paid the proper fee. He told them that the best thing they could do was to make their way down to the little inn on the hills above Lancy, where the innkeeper, an old soldier who had become devout in his latter years, would be certain to sympathise with them, and even to take risks in their support. The whole company, therefore, piled themselves on top of the stacks of wood, and went rocking in the rude cart down the other and steeper side of the woodland. Heavy and ramshackle as was the vehicle, it was driven quickly enough, and they soon had the exhilarating impression of distancing altogether those, whoever they were, who were hunting them. For, after all, the riddle as to where the anarchists had got all these followers was still unsolved. One man's presence had sufficed for them; they had fled at the first sight of the deformed smile of the Secretary. Syme every now and then looked back over his shoulder at the army on their track.

As the wood grew first thinner and then smaller with distance, he could see the sunlit slopes beyond it and above it; and across these was still moving the square black mob like one monstrous beetle. In the very strong sunlight and with his own very strong eyes, which were almost telescopic, Syme could see this mass of men quite plainly. He could see them as separate human figures; but he was increasingly surprised by the way in which they moved as one man. They seemed to be dressed in dark clothes and plain hats, like any common crowd out of the streets; but they did not spread and sprawl and trail by various lines to the attack, as would be natural in an ordinary mob. They moved with a sort of dreadful and wicked woodenness, like a staring army of automatons.

Syme pointed this out to Ratcliffe.

"Yes," replied the policeman, "that's discipline. That's Sunday. He is perhaps five hundred miles off, but the fear of him is on all of them, like the finger of God. Yes, they are walking regularly; and you bet your boots that they are talking regularly, yes, and thinking regularly. But the one important thing for us is that they are disappearing regularly."

Syme nodded. It was true that the black patch of the pursuing men was growing smaller and smaller as the peasant belaboured his horse.

The level of the sunlit landscape, though flat as a whole, fell away on the farther side of the wood in billows of heavy slope towards the sea, in a way not unlike the lower slopes of the Sussex downs. The only difference was that in Sussex the road would have been broken and angular like a little brook, but here the white French road fell sheer in front of them like a waterfall. Down this direct descent the cart clattered at a considerable angle, and in a few minutes, the road growing yet steeper, they saw below them the little harbour of Lancy and a great blue arc of the sea. The travelling cloud of their enemies had wholly disappeared from the horizon.

The horse and cart took a sharp turn round a clump of elms, and the horse's nose nearly struck the face of an old gentleman who was sitting on the benches outside the little cafe of "Le Soleil d'Or." The peasant grunted an apology, and got down from his seat. The others also descended one by one, and spoke to the old gentleman with fragmentary phrases of courtesy, for it was quite evident from his expansive manner that he was the owner of the little tavern.

He was a white-haired, apple-faced old boy, with sleepy eyes and a grey moustache; stout, sedentary, and very innocent, of a type that may often be found in France, but is still commoner in Catholic Germany. Everything about him, his pipe, his pot of beer, his flowers, and his beehive, suggested an ancestral peace; only when his visitors looked up as they entered the inn-parlour, they saw the sword upon the wall.

The Colonel, who greeted the innkeeper as an old friend, passed rapidly into the inn-parlour, and sat down ordering some ritual refreshment. The military decision of his action interested Syme, who sat next to him, and he took the opportunity when the old innkeeper had gone out of satisfying his curiosity.

"May I ask you, Colonel," he said in a low voice, "why we have come here?"

Colonel Ducroix smiled behind his bristly white moustache.

"For two reasons, sir," he said; "and I will give first, not the most important, but the most utilitarian. We came here because this is the only place within twenty miles in which we can get horses."

"Horses!" repeated Syme, looking up quickly.

"Yes," replied the other; "if you people are really to distance your enemies it is horses or nothing for you, unless of course you have bicycles and motor-cars in your pocket."

"And where do you advise us to make for?" asked Syme doubtfully.

"Beyond question," replied the Colonel, "you had better make all haste to the police station beyond the town. My friend, whom I seconded under somewhat deceptive circumstances, seems to me to exaggerate very much the possibilities of a general rising; but even he would hardly maintain, I suppose, that you were not safe with the gendarmes."

Syme nodded gravely; then he said abruptly—

"And your other reason for coming here?"

"My other reason for coming here," said Ducroix soberly, "is that it is just as well to see a good man or two when one is possibly near to death."

Syme looked up at the wall, and saw a crudely-painted and pathetic religious picture. Then he said—

"You are right," and then almost immediately afterwards, "Has anyone seen about the horses?"

"Yes," answered Ducroix, "you may be quite certain that I gave orders the moment I came in. Those enemies of yours gave no impression of hurry, but they were really moving wonderfully fast, like a well-trained army. I had no idea that the anarchists had so much discipline. You have not a moment to waste."

Almost as he spoke, the old innkeeper with the blue eyes and white hair came ambling into the room, and announced that six horses were saddled outside.

By Ducroix's advice the five others equipped themselves with some portable form of food and wine, and keeping their duelling swords as the only weapons available, they clattered away down the steep, white road. The two servants, who had carried the Marquis's luggage when he was a marquis, were left behind to drink at the cafe by common consent, and not at all against their own inclination.

By this time the afternoon sun was slanting westward, and by its rays Syme could see the sturdy figure of the old innkeeper growing smaller and smaller, but still standing and looking after them quite silently, the sunshine in his silver hair. Syme had a fixed, superstitious fancy, left in his mind by the chance phrase of the Colonel, that this was indeed, perhaps, the last honest stranger whom he should ever see upon the earth.

He was still looking at this dwindling figure, which stood as a mere grey blot touched with a white flame against the great green wall of the steep down behind him. And as he stared over the top of the down behind the innkeeper, there appeared an army of black-clad and marching men. They seemed to hang above the good man and his house like a black cloud of locusts. The horses had been saddled none too soon.

CHAPTER XII. THE EARTH IN ANARCHY

URGING the horses to a gallop, without respect to the rather rugged descent of the road, the horsemen soon regained their advantage over the men on the march, and at last the bulk of the first buildings of Lancy cut off the sight of their pursuers. Nevertheless, the ride had been a long one, and by the time they reached the real town the west was warming with the colour and quality of sunset. The Colonel suggested that, before making finally for the police station, they should make the effort, in passing, to attach to themselves one more individual who might be useful.

"Four out of the five rich men in this town," he said, "are common swindlers. I suppose the proportion is pretty equal all over the world. The fifth is a friend of mine, and a very fine fellow; and what is even more important from our point of view, he owns a motor-car."

"I am afraid," said the Professor in his mirthful way, looking back along the white road on which the black, crawling patch might appear at any moment, "I am afraid we have hardly time for afternoon calls."

"Doctor Renard's house is only three minutes off," said the Colonel.

"Our danger," said Dr. Bull, "is not two minutes off."

"Yes," said Syme, "if we ride on fast we must leave them behind, for they are on foot."

"He has a motor-car," said the Colonel.

"But we may not get it," said Bull.

"Yes, he is quite on your side."

"But he might be out."

"Hold your tongue," said Syme suddenly. "What is that noise?"

For a second they all sat as still as equestrian statues, and for a second—for two or three or four seconds—heaven and earth seemed equally still. Then all their ears, in an agony of attention, heard along the road that indescribable thrill and throb that means only one thing—horses!

The Colonel's face had an instantaneous change, as if lightning had struck it, and yet left it scatheless.

"They have done us," he said, with brief military irony. "Prepare to receive cavalry!"

"Where can they have got the horses?" asked Syme, as he mechanically urged his steed to a canter.

The Colonel was silent for a little, then he said in a strained voice—

"I was speaking with strict accuracy when I said that the 'Soleil d'Or' was the only place where one can get horses within twenty miles."

"No!" said Syme violently, "I don't believe he'd do it. Not with all that white hair."

"He may have been forced," said the Colonel gently. "They must be at least a hundred strong, for which reason we are all going to see my friend Renard, who has a motor-car."

With these words he swung his horse suddenly round a street corner, and went down the street with such thundering speed, that the others, though already well at the gallop, had difficulty in following the flying tail of his horse.

Dr. Renard inhabited a high and comfortable house at the top of a steep street, so that when the riders alighted at his door they could once more see the solid green ridge of the hill, with the white road across it, standing up above all the roofs of the town. They breathed again to see that the road as yet was clear, and they rang the bell.

Dr. Renard was a beaming, brown-bearded man, a good example of that silent but very busy professional class which France has preserved even more perfectly than England. When the matter was explained to him he pooh-poohed the panic of the ex-Marquis altogether; he said, with the solid French scepticism, that there was no conceivable probability of a general anarchist rising. "Anarchy," he said, shrugging his shoulders, "it is childishness!"

"Et ca," cried out the Colonel suddenly, pointing over the other's shoulder, "and that is childishness, isn't it?"

They all looked round, and saw a curve of black cavalry come sweeping over the top of the hill with all the energy of Attila. Swiftly as they rode, however, the whole rank still kept well together, and they could see the black vizards of the first line as level as a line of uniforms. But although the main black square was the same, though travelling faster, there was now one sensational difference which they could see clearly upon the slope of the hill, as if upon a slanted map. The bulk of the riders were in one block; but one rider flew far ahead of the column, and with frantic movements of hand and heel urged his horse faster and faster, so that one might have fancied that he was not the pursuer but the pursued. But even at that great distance they could see something so fanatical, so unquestionable in his figure, that they knew it was the Secretary himself. "I am sorry to cut short a cultured discussion," said the Colonel, "but can you lend me your motor-car now, in two minutes?"

"I have a suspicion that you are all mad," said Dr. Renard, smiling sociably; "but God forbid that madness should in any way interrupt friendship. Let us go round to the garage."

Dr. Renard was a mild man with monstrous wealth; his rooms were like the Musee de Cluny, and he had three motor-cars. These, however, he seemed to use very sparingly, having the simple tastes of the French middle class, and when his impatient friends came to examine them, it took them some time to assure themselves that one of them even could be made to work. This with some difficulty they brought round into the street before the Doctor's house. When they came out of the dim garage they were startled to find that twilight had already fallen with the abruptness of night in the tropics. Either they had been longer in the place than they imagined, or some unusual canopy of cloud had gathered over the town. They looked down the steep streets, and seemed to see a slight mist coming up from the sea.

"It is now or never," said Dr. Bull. "I hear horses."

"No," corrected the Professor, "a horse."

And as they listened, it was evident that the noise, rapidly coming nearer on the rattling stones, was not the noise of the whole cavalcade but that of the one horseman, who had left it far behind—the insane Secretary.

Syme's family, like most of those who end in the simple life, had once owned a motor, and he knew all about them. He had leapt at once into the chauffeur's seat, and with flushed face was wrenching and tugging at the disused machinery. He bent his strength upon one handle, and then said quite quietly—

"I am afraid it's no go."

As he spoke, there swept round the corner a man rigid on his rushing horse, with the rush and rigidity of an arrow. He had a smile that thrust out his chin as if it were dislocated. He swept alongside of the stationary car, into which its company had crowded, and laid his hand on the front. It was the Secretary, and his mouth went quite straight in the solemnity of triumph.

Syme was leaning hard upon the steering wheel, and there was no sound but the rumble of the other pursuers riding into the town. Then there came quite suddenly a scream of scraping iron, and the car leapt forward. It plucked the Secretary clean out of his saddle, as a knife is whipped out of its sheath, trailed him kicking terribly for twenty yards, and left him flung flat upon the road far in front of his frightened horse. As the car took the corner of the street with a splendid curve, they could just see the other anarchists filling the street and raising their fallen leader.

"I can't understand why it has grown so dark," said the Professor at last in a low voice.

"Going to be a storm, I think," said Dr. Bull. "I say, it's a pity we haven't got a light on this car, if only to see by."

"We have," said the Colonel, and from the floor of the car he fished up a heavy, old-fashioned, carved iron lantern with a light inside it. It was obviously an antique, and it would seem as if its original use had been in some way semi-religious, for there was a rude moulding of a cross upon one of its sides.

"Where on earth did you get that?" asked the Professor.

"I got it where I got the car," answered the Colonel, chuckling, "from my best friend. While our friend here was fighting with the steering wheel, I ran up the front steps of the house and spoke to Renard, who was standing in his own porch, you will remember. 'I suppose,' I said, 'there's no time to get a lamp.' He looked up, blinking amiably at the beautiful arched ceiling of his own front hall. From this was suspended, by chains of exquisite ironwork, this lantern, one of the hundred treasures of his treasure house. By sheer force he tore the lamp out of his own ceiling, shattering the painted panels, and bringing down two blue vases with his violence. Then he handed me the iron lantern, and I put it in the car. Was I not right when I said that Dr. Renard was worth knowing?"

"You were," said Syme seriously, and hung the heavy lantern over the front. There was a certain allegory of their whole position in the contrast between the modern automobile and its strange ecclesiastical lamp. Hitherto they had passed through the quietest part of the town, meeting at most one or two pedestrians, who could give them no hint of the peace or the hostility of the place. Now, however, the windows in the houses began one by one to be lit up, giving a greater sense of habitation and humanity. Dr. Bull turned to the new detective who had led their flight, and permitted himself one of his natural and friendly smiles.

"These lights make one feel more cheerful."

Inspector Ratcliffe drew his brows together.

"There is only one set of lights that make me more cheerful," he said, "and they are those lights of the police station which I can see beyond the town. Please God we may be there in ten minutes."

Then all Bull's boiling good sense and optimism broke suddenly out of him.

"Oh, this is all raving nonsense!" he cried. "If you really think that ordinary people in ordinary houses are anarchists, you must be madder than an anarchist yourself. If we turned and fought these fellows, the whole town would fight for us."

"No," said the other with an immovable simplicity, "the whole town would fight for them. We shall see."

While they were speaking the Professor had leant forward with sudden excitement.

"What is that noise?" he said.

"Oh, the horses behind us, I suppose," said the Colonel. "I thought we had got clear of them."

"The horses behind us! No," said the Professor, "it is not horses, and it is not behind us."

Almost as he spoke, across the end of the street before them two shining and rattling shapes shot past. They were gone almost in a flash, but everyone could see that they were motor-cars, and the Professor stood up with a pale face and swore that they were the other two motor-cars from Dr. Renard's garage.

"I tell you they were his," he repeated, with wild eyes, "and they were full of men in masks!"

"Absurd!" said the Colonel angrily. "Dr. Renard would never give them his cars."

"He may have been forced," said Ratcliffe quietly. "The whole town is on their side."

"You still believe that," asked the Colonel incredulously.

"You will all believe it soon," said the other with a hopeless calm.

There was a puzzled pause for some little time, and then the Colonel began again abruptly—

"No, I can't believe it. The thing is nonsense. The plain people of a peaceable French town—"

He was cut short by a bang and a blaze of light, which seemed close to his eyes. As the car sped on it left a floating patch of white smoke behind it, and Syme had heard a shot shriek past his ear.

"My God!" said the Colonel, "someone has shot at us."

"It need not interrupt conversation," said the gloomy Ratcliffe. "Pray resume your remarks, Colonel. You were talking, I think, about the plain people of a peaceable French town."

The staring Colonel was long past minding satire. He rolled his eyes all round the street.

"It is extraordinary," he said, "most extraordinary."

"A fastidious person," said Syme, "might even call it unpleasant. However, I suppose those lights out in the field beyond this street are the Gendarmerie. We shall soon get there."

"No," said Inspector Ratcliffe, "we shall never get there."

He had been standing up and looking keenly ahead of him. Now he sat down and smoothed his sleek hair with a weary gesture.

"What do you mean?" asked Bull sharply.

"I mean that we shall never get there," said the pessimist placidly. "They have two rows of armed men across the road already; I can see them from here. The town is in arms, as I said it was. I can only wallow in the exquisite comfort of my own exactitude."

And Ratcliffe sat down comfortably in the car and lit a cigarette, but the others rose excitedly and stared down the road. Syme had slowed down the car as their plans became doubtful, and he brought it finally to a standstill just at the corner of a side street that ran down very steeply to the sea.

The town was mostly in shadow, but the sun had not sunk; wherever its level light could break through, it painted everything a burning gold. Up this side street the last sunset light shone as sharp and narrow as the shaft of artificial light at the theatre. It struck the car of the five friends, and lit it like a burning chariot. But the rest of the street, especially the two ends of it, was in the deepest twilight, and for some seconds they could see nothing. Then Syme, whose eyes were the keenest, broke into a little bitter whistle, and said,

"It is quite true. There is a crowd or an army or some such thing across the end of that street."

"Well, if there is," said Bull impatiently, "it must be something else—a sham fight or the mayor's birthday or something. I cannot and will not believe that plain, jolly people in a place like this walk about with dynamite in their pockets. Get on a bit, Syme, and let us look at them."

The car crawled about a hundred yards farther, and then they were all startled by Dr. Bull breaking into a high crow of laughter.

"Why, you silly mugs!" he cried, "what did I tell you. That crowd's as law-abiding as a cow, and if it weren't, it's on our side."

"How do you know?" asked the professor, staring.

"You blind bat," cried Bull, "don't you see who is leading them?"

They peered again, and then the Colonel, with a catch in his voice, cried out—

"Why, it's Renard!"

There was, indeed, a rank of dim figures running across the road, and they could not be clearly seen; but far enough in front to catch the accident of the evening light was stalking up and down the unmistakable Dr. Renard, in a white hat, stroking his long brown beard, and holding a revolver in his left hand.

"What a fool I've been!" exclaimed the Colonel. "Of course, the dear old boy has turned out to help us."

Dr. Bull was bubbling over with laughter, swinging the sword in his hand as carelessly as a cane. He jumped out of the car and ran across the intervening space, calling out—

"Dr. Renard! Dr. Renard!"

An instant after Syme thought his own eyes had gone mad in his head. For the philanthropic Dr. Renard had deliberately raised his revolver and fired twice at Bull, so that the shots rang down the road.

Almost at the same second as the puff of white cloud went up from this atrocious explosion a long puff of white cloud went up also from the cigarette of the cynical Ratcliffe. Like all the rest he turned a little pale, but he smiled. Dr. Bull, at whom the bullets had been fired, just missing his scalp, stood quite still in the middle of the road without a sign of fear, and then turned very slowly and crawled back to the car, and climbed in with two holes through his hat.

"Well," said the cigarette smoker slowly, "what do you think now?"

"I think," said Dr. Bull with precision, "that I am lying in bed at No. 217 Peabody Buildings, and that I shall soon wake up with a jump; or, if that's not it, I think that I am sitting in a small cushioned cell in Hanwell, and that the doctor can't make much of my case. But if you want to know what I don't think, I'll tell you. I don't think what you think. I don't think, and I never shall think, that the mass of ordinary men are a pack of dirty modern thinkers. No, sir, I'm a democrat, and I still don't believe that Sunday could convert one average navvy or counter-jumper. No, I may be mad, but humanity isn't."

Syme turned his bright blue eyes on Bull with an earnestness which he did not commonly make clear.

"You are a very fine fellow," he said. "You can believe in a sanity which is not merely your sanity. And you're right enough about humanity, about peasants and people like that jolly old innkeeper. But you're not right about Renard. I suspected him from the first. He's rationalistic, and, what's worse, he's rich. When duty and religion are really destroyed, it will be by the rich."

"They are really destroyed now," said the man with a cigarette, and rose with his hands in his pockets. "The devils are coming on!"

The men in the motor-car looked anxiously in the direction of his dreamy gaze, and they saw that the whole regiment at the end of the road was advancing upon them, Dr. Renard marching furiously in front, his beard flying in the breeze.

The Colonel sprang out of the car with an intolerant exclamation.

"Gentlemen," he cried, "the thing is incredible. It must be a practical joke. If you knew Renard as I do—it's like calling Queen Victoria a dynamiter. If you had got the man's character into your head—"

"Dr. Bull," said Syme sardonically, "has at least got it into his hat."

"I tell you it can't be!" cried the Colonel, stamping.

"Renard shall explain it. He shall explain it to me," and he strode forward.

"Don't be in such a hurry," drawled the smoker. "He will very soon explain it to all of us."

But the impatient Colonel was already out of earshot, advancing towards the advancing enemy. The excited Dr. Renard lifted his pistol again, but perceiving his opponent, hesitated, and the Colonel came face to face with him with frantic gestures of remonstrance.

"It is no good," said Syme. "He will never get anything out of that old heathen. I vote we drive bang through the thick of them, bang as the bullets went through Bull's hat. We may all be killed, but we must kill a tidy number of them."

"I won't 'ave it," said Dr. Bull, growing more vulgar in the sincerity of his virtue. "The poor chaps may be making a mistake. Give the Colonel a chance."

"Shall we go back, then?" asked the Professor.

"No," said Ratcliffe in a cold voice, "the street behind us is held too. In fact, I seem to see there another friend of yours, Syme."

Syme spun round smartly, and stared backwards at the track which they had travelled. He saw an irregular body of horsemen gathering and galloping towards them in the gloom. He saw above the foremost saddle the silver gleam of a sword, and then as it grew nearer the silver gleam of an old man's hair. The next moment, with shattering violence, he had swung the motor round and sent it dashing down the steep side street to the sea, like a man that desired only to die.

"What the devil is up?" cried the Professor, seizing his arm.

"The morning star has fallen!" said Syme, as his own car went down the darkness like a falling star.

The others did not understand his words, but when they looked back at the street above they saw the hostile cavalry coming round the corner and down the slopes after them; and foremost of all rode the good innkeeper, flushed with the fiery innocence of the evening light.

"The world is insane!" said the Professor, and buried his face in his hands.

"No," said Dr. Bull in adamantine humility, "it is I."

"What are we going to do?" asked the Professor.

"At this moment," said Syme, with a scientific detachment, "I think we are going to smash into a lamppost."

The next instant the automobile had come with a catastrophic jar against an iron object. The instant after that four men had crawled out from under a chaos of metal, and a tall lean lamp-post that had stood up straight on the edge of the marine parade stood out, bent and twisted, like the branch of a broken tree.

"Well, we smashed something," said the Professor, with a faint smile. "That's some comfort."

"You're becoming an anarchist," said Syme, dusting his clothes with his instinct of daintiness.

"Everyone is," said Ratcliffe.

As they spoke, the white-haired horseman and his followers came thundering from above, and almost at the same moment a dark string of men ran shouting along the sea-front. Syme snatched a sword, and took it in his teeth; he stuck two others under his arm-pits, took a fourth in his left hand and the lantern in his right, and leapt off the high parade on to the beach below.

The others leapt after him, with a common acceptance of such decisive action, leaving the debris and the gathering mob above them.

"We have one more chance," said Syme, taking the steel out of his mouth. "Whatever all this pandemonium means, I suppose the police station will help us. We can't get there, for they hold the way. But there's a pier or breakwater runs out into the sea just here, which we could defend longer than anything else, like Horatius and his bridge. We must defend it till the Gendarmerie turn out. Keep after me."

They followed him as he went crunching down the beach, and in a second or two their boots broke not on the sea gravel, but on broad, flat stones. They marched down a long, low jetty, running out in one arm into the dim, boiling sea, and when they came to the end of it they felt that they had come to the end of their story. They turned and faced the town.

That town was transfigured with uproar. All along the high parade from which they had just descended was a dark and roaring stream of humanity, with tossing arms and fiery faces, groping and glaring towards them. The long dark line was dotted with torches and lanterns; but even where no flame lit up a furious face, they could see in the farthest figure, in the most shadowy gesture, an organised hate. It was clear that they were the accursed of all men, and they knew not why.

Two or three men, looking little and black like monkeys, leapt over the edge as they had done and dropped on to the beach. These came ploughing down the deep sand, shouting horribly, and strove to wade into the sea at random. The example was followed, and the whole black mass of men began to run and drip over the edge like black treacle.

Foremost among the men on the beach Syme saw the peasant who had driven their cart. He splashed into the surf on a huge cart-horse, and shook his axe at them.

"The peasant!" cried Syme. "They have not risen since the Middle Ages."

"Even if the police do come now," said the Professor mournfully, "they can do nothing with this mob."

"Nonsense!" said Bull desperately; "there must be some people left in the town who are human."

"No," said the hopeless Inspector, "the human being will soon be extinct. We are the last of mankind."

"It may be," said the Professor absently. Then he added in his dreamy voice, "What is all that at the end of the 'Dunciad'?

CHAPTER XII. THE EARTH IN ANARCHY

'Nor public flame; nor private, dares to shine; Nor human light is left, nor glimpse divine! Lo! thy dread Empire, Chaos, is restored; Light dies before thine uncreating word: Thy hand, great Anarch, lets the curtain fall; And universal darkness buries all.'"

"Stop!" cried Bull suddenly, "the gendarmes are out."

The low lights of the police station were indeed blotted and broken with hurrying figures, and they heard through the darkness the clash and jingle of a disciplined cavalry.

"They are charging the mob!" cried Bull in ecstacy or alarm.

"No," said Syme, "they are formed along the parade."

"They have unslung their carbines," cried Bull dancing with excitement.

"Yes," said Ratcliffe, "and they are going to fire on us."

As he spoke there came a long crackle of musketry, and bullets seemed to hop like hailstones on the stones in front of them.

"The gendarmes have joined them!" cried the Professor, and struck his forehead.

"I am in the padded cell," said Bull solidly.

There was a long silence, and then Ratcliffe said, looking out over the swollen sea, all a sort of grey purple—

"What does it matter who is mad or who is sane? We shall all be dead soon."

Syme turned to him and said—

"You are quite hopeless, then?"

Mr. Ratcliffe kept a stony silence; then at last he said quietly—

"No; oddly enough I am not quite hopeless. There is one insane little hope that I cannot get out of my mind. The power of this whole planet is against us, yet I cannot help wondering whether this one silly little hope is hopeless yet."

"In what or whom is your hope?" asked Syme with curiosity.

"In a man I never saw," said the other, looking at the leaden sea.

"I know what you mean," said Syme in a low voice, "the man in the dark room. But Sunday must have killed him by now."

"Perhaps," said the other steadily; "but if so, he was the only man whom Sunday found it hard to kill."

"I heard what you said," said the Professor, with his back turned. "I also am holding hard on to the thing I never saw."

All of a sudden Syme, who was standing as if blind with introspective thought, swung round and cried out, like a man waking from sleep—

"Where is the Colonel? I thought he was with us!"

"The Colonel! Yes," cried Bull, "where on earth is the Colonel?"

"He went to speak to Renard," said the Professor.

"We cannot leave him among all those beasts," cried Syme. "Let us die like gentlemen if—"

"Do not pity the Colonel," said Ratcliffe, with a pale sneer. "He is extremely comfortable. He is—"

"No! no! no!" cried Syme in a kind of frenzy, "not the Colonel too! I will never believe it!"

"Will you believe your eyes?" asked the other, and pointed to the beach.

Many of their pursuers had waded into the water shaking their fists, but the sea was rough, and they could not reach the pier. Two or three figures, however, stood on the beginning of the stone footway, and seemed to be cautiously advancing down it. The glare of a chance lantern lit up the faces of the two foremost. One face wore a black half-mask, and under it the mouth was twisting about in such a madness of nerves that the black tuft of beard wriggled round and round like a restless, living thing. The other was the red face and white moustache of Colonel Ducroix. They were in earnest consultation.

"Yes, he is gone too," said the Professor, and sat down on a stone. "Everything's gone. I'm gone! I can't trust my own bodily machinery. I feel as if my own hand might fly up and strike me."

"When my hand flies up," said Syme, "it will strike somebody else," and he strode along the pier towards the Colonel, the sword in one hand and the lantern in the other.

As if to destroy the last hope or doubt, the Colonel, who saw him coming, pointed his revolver at him and fired. The shot missed Syme, but struck his sword, breaking it short at the hilt. Syme rushed on, and swung the iron lantern above his head.

"Judas before Herod!" he said, and struck the Colonel down upon the stones. Then he turned to the Secretary, whose frightful mouth was almost foaming now, and held the lamp high with so rigid and arresting a gesture, that the man was, as it were, frozen for a moment, and forced to hear.

"Do you see this lantern?" cried Syme in a terrible voice. "Do you see the cross carved on it, and the flame inside? You did not make it. You did not light it. Better men than you, men who could believe and obey, twisted the entrails of iron and preserved the legend of fire. There is not a street you walk on, there is not a thread you wear, that was not made as this lantern was, by denying your philosophy of dirt and rats. You can make nothing. You can only destroy. You will destroy mankind; you will destroy the world. Let that suffice you. Yet this one old Christian lantern you shall not destroy. It shall go where your empire of apes will never have the wit to find it."

He struck the Secretary once with the lantern so that he staggered; and then, whirling it twice round his head, sent it flying far out to sea, where it flared like a roaring rocket and fell.

"Swords!" shouted Syme, turning his flaming face to the three behind him. "Let us charge these dogs, for our time has come to die."

His three companions came after him sword in hand. Syme's sword was broken, but he rent a bludgeon from the fist of a fisherman, flinging him down. In a moment they would have flung themselves upon the face of the mob and perished, when an interruption came. The Secretary, ever since Syme's speech, had stood with his hand to his stricken head as if dazed; now he suddenly pulled off his black mask.

The pale face thus peeled in the lamplight revealed not so much rage as astonishment. He put up his hand with an anxious authority.

"There is some mistake," he said. "Mr. Syme, I hardly think you understand your position. I arrest you in the name of the law."

"Of the law?" said Syme, and dropped his stick.

"Certainly!" said the Secretary. "I am a detective from Scotland Yard," and he took a small blue card from his pocket.

"And what do you suppose we are?" asked the Professor, and threw up his arms.

"You," said the Secretary stiffly, "are, as I know for a fact, members of the Supreme Anarchist Council. Disguised as one of you, I—"

Dr. Bull tossed his sword into the sea.

"There never was any Supreme Anarchist Council," he said. "We were all a lot of silly policemen looking at each other. And all these nice people who have been peppering us with shot thought we were the dynamiters. I knew I couldn't be wrong about the mob," he said, beaming over the enormous multitude, which stretched away to the distance on both sides. "Vulgar people are never mad. I'm vulgar myself, and I know. I am now going on shore to stand a drink to everybody here."

CHAPTER XIII. THE PURSUIT OF THE PRESIDENT

NEXT morning five bewildered but hilarious people took the boat for Dover. The poor old Colonel might have had some cause to complain, having been first forced to fight for two factions that didn't exist, and then knocked down with an iron lantern. But he was a magnanimous old gentleman, and being much relieved that neither party had anything to do with dynamite, he saw them off on the pier with great geniality.

The five reconciled detectives had a hundred details to explain to each other. The Secretary had to tell Syme how they had come to wear masks originally in order to approach the supposed enemy as fellow-conspirators.

Syme had to explain how they had fled with such swiftness through a civilised country. But above all these matters of detail which could be explained, rose the central mountain of the matter that they could not explain. What did it all mean? If they were all harmless officers, what was Sunday? If he had not seized the world, what on earth had he been up to? Inspector Ratcliffe was still gloomy about this.

"I can't make head or tail of old Sunday's little game any more than you can," he said. "But whatever else Sunday is, he isn't a blameless citizen. Damn it! do you remember his face?"

"I grant you," answered Syme, "that I have never been able to forget it."

"Well," said the Secretary, "I suppose we can find out soon, for tomorrow we have our next general meeting. You will excuse me," he said, with a rather ghastly smile, "for being well acquainted with my secretarial duties."

"I suppose you are right," said the Professor reflectively. "I suppose we might find it out from him; but I confess that I should feel a bit afraid of asking Sunday who he really is."

"Why," asked the Secretary, "for fear of bombs?"

"No," said the Professor, "for fear he might tell me."

"Let us have some drinks," said Dr. Bull, after a silence.

Throughout their whole journey by boat and train they were highly convivial, but they instinctively kept together. Dr. Bull, who had always been the optimist of the party, endeavoured to persuade the other four that the whole company could take the same hansom cab from Victoria; but this was over-ruled, and they went in a four-wheeler, with Dr. Bull on the box, singing. They finished their journey at an hotel in Piccadilly Circus, so as to be close to the early breakfast next morning in Leicester Square. Yet even then the adventures of the day were not entirely over. Dr. Bull, discontented with the general proposal to go to bed, had strolled out of the hotel at about eleven to see and taste some of the beauties of London. Twenty minutes afterwards, however, he came back and made quite a clamour in the hall. Syme, who tried at first to soothe him, was forced at last to listen to his communication with quite new attention.

"I tell you I've seen him!" said Dr. Bull, with thick emphasis.

"Whom?" asked Syme quickly. "Not the President?"

"Not so bad as that," said Dr. Bull, with unnecessary laughter, "not so bad as that. I've got him here."

"Got whom here?" asked Syme impatiently.

"Hairy man," said the other lucidly, "man that used to be hairy man—Gogol. Here he is," and he pulled forward by a reluctant elbow the identical young man who five days before had marched out of the Council with thin red hair and a pale face, the first of all the sham anarchists who had been exposed.

"Why do you worry with me?" he cried. "You have expelled me as a spy."

"We are all spies!" whispered Syme.

"We're all spies!" shouted Dr. Bull. "Come and have a drink."

Next morning the battalion of the reunited six marched stolidly towards the hotel in Leicester Square.

"This is more cheerful," said Dr. Bull; "we are six men going to ask one man what he means."

"I think it is a bit queerer than that," said Syme. "I think it is six men going to ask one man what they mean."

They turned in silence into the Square, and though the hotel was in the opposite corner, they saw at once the little balcony and a figure that looked too big for it. He was sitting alone with bent head, poring over a newspaper. But all his councillors, who had come to vote him down, crossed that Square as if they were watched out of heaven by a hundred eyes.

They had disputed much upon their policy, about whether they should leave the unmasked Gogol without and begin diplomatically, or whether they should bring him in and blow up the gunpowder at once. The influence of Syme and Bull prevailed for the latter course, though the Secretary to the last asked them why they attacked Sunday so rashly.

"My reason is quite simple," said Syme. "I attack him rashly because I am afraid of him."

They followed Syme up the dark stair in silence, and they all came out simultaneously into the broad sunlight of the morning and the broad sunlight of Sunday's smile.

"Delightful!" he said. "So pleased to see you all. What an exquisite day it is. Is the Czar dead?"

The Secretary, who happened to be foremost, drew himself together for a dignified outburst.

"No, sir," he said sternly "there has been no massacre. I bring you news of no such disgusting spectacles."

"Disgusting spectacles?" repeated the President, with a bright, inquiring smile. "You mean Dr. Bull's spectacles?"

The Secretary choked for a moment, and the President went on with a sort of smooth appeal—

"Of course, we all have our opinions and even our eyes, but really to call them disgusting before the man himself—"

Dr. Bull tore off his spectacles and broke them on the table.

"My spectacles are blackguardly," he said, "but I'm not. Look at my face."

"I dare say it's the sort of face that grows on one," said the President, "in fact, it grows on you; and who am I to quarrel with the wild fruits upon the Tree of Life? I dare say it will grow on me some day."

"We have no time for tomfoolery," said the Secretary, breaking in savagely. "We have come to know what all this means. Who are you? What are you? Why did you get us all here? Do you know who and what we are? Are you a half-witted man playing the conspirator, or are you a clever man playing the fool? Answer me, I tell you."

"Candidates," murmured Sunday, "are only required to answer eight out of the seventeen questions on the paper. As far as I can make out, you want me to tell you what I am, and what you are, and what this table is, and what this Council is, and what this world is for all I know. Well, I will go so far as to rend the veil of one mystery. If you want to know what you are, you are a set of highly well-intentioned young jackasses."

"And you," said Syme, leaning forward, "what are you?"

"I? What am I?" roared the President, and he rose slowly to an incredible height, like some enormous wave about to arch above them and break. "You want to know what I am, do you? Bull, you are a man of science. Grub in the roots of those trees and find out the truth about them. Syme, you are a poet. Stare at those morning clouds. But I tell you this, that you will have found out the truth of the last tree and the top-most cloud before the truth about me. You will understand the sea, and I shall be still a riddle; you shall know what the stars are, and not know what I am. Since the beginning of the world all men have hunted me like a wolf—kings and sages, and poets and lawgivers, all the churches, and all the philosophies. But I have never been caught yet, and the skies will fall in the time I turn to bay. I have given them a good run for their money, and I will now."

Before one of them could move, the monstrous man had swung himself like some huge ourang-outang over the balustrade of the balcony. Yet before he dropped he pulled himself up again as on a horizontal bar, and thrusting his great chin over the edge of the balcony, said solemnly—

"There's one thing I'll tell you though about who I am. I am the man in the dark room, who made you all policemen."

With that he fell from the balcony, bouncing on the stones below like a great ball of india-rubber, and went bounding off towards the corner of the Alhambra, where he hailed a hansom-cab and sprang inside it. The six detectives had been standing thunderstruck and livid in the light of his last assertion; but when he disappeared into the cab, Syme's practical senses returned to him, and leaping over the balcony so recklessly as almost to break his legs, he called another cab.

He and Bull sprang into the cab together, the Professor and the Inspector into another, while the Secretary and the late Gogol scrambled into a third just in time to pursue the flying Syme, who was pursuing the flying President. Sunday led them a wild chase towards the north-west, his cabman, evidently under the influence of more than common inducements, urging the horse at breakneck speed. But Syme was in no mood for delicacies, and he stood up in his own cab shouting, "Stop thief!" until crowds ran along beside his cab, and policemen began to stop and ask questions. All this had its influence upon the President's cabman, who began to look dubious, and to slow down to a trot. He opened the trap to talk reasonably to his fare, and in so doing let the long whip droop over the front of the cab. Sunday leant forward, seized it, and jerked it violently out of the man's hand. Then standing up in front of the cab himself, he lashed the horse and roared aloud, so that they went down the streets like a flying storm. Through street after street and square after square went whirling this preposterous vehicle, in which the fare was urging the horse and the driver trying desperately to stop it. The other three cabs came after it (if the phrase be permissible of a cab) like panting hounds. Shops and streets shot by like rattling arrows.

At the highest ecstacy of speed, Sunday turned round on the splashboard where he stood, and sticking his great grinning head out of the cab, with white hair whistling in the wind, he made a horrible face at his pursuers, like some colossal urchin. Then raising his right hand swiftly, he flung a ball of paper in Syme's face and vanished. Syme caught the thing while instinctively warding it off, and discovered that it consisted of two crumpled papers. One was addressed to himself, and the other to Dr. Bull, with a very long, and it is to be feared partly ironical, string of letters after his name. Dr. Bull's address was, at any rate, considerably longer than his communication, for the communication consisted entirely of the words:—

"What about Martin Tupper now?"

"What does the old maniac mean?" asked Bull, staring at the words. "What does yours say, Syme?"

Syme's message was, at any rate, longer, and ran as follows:—

"No one would regret anything in the nature of an interference by the Archdeacon more than I. I trust it will not come to that. But, for the last time, where are your goloshes? The thing is too bad, especially after what uncle said."

The President's cabman seemed to be regaining some control over his horse, and the pursuers gained a little as they swept round into the Edgware Road. And here there occurred what seemed to the allies a providential stoppage. Traffic of every kind was swerving to right or left or stopping, for down the long road was coming the unmistakable roar announcing the fire-engine, which in a few seconds went by like a brazen thunderbolt. But quick as it went by, Sunday had bounded out of his cab, sprung at the fire-engine, caught it, slung himself on to it, and was seen as he disappeared in the noisy distance talking to the astonished fireman with explanatory gestures.

"After him!" howled Syme. "He can't go astray now. There's no mistaking a fire-engine."

The three cabmen, who had been stunned for a moment, whipped up their horses and slightly decreased the distance between themselves and their disappearing prey. The President acknowledged this proximity by coming to the back of the car, bowing repeatedly, kissing his hand, and finally flinging a neatly-folded note into the bosom of Inspector Ratcliffe. When that gentleman opened it, not without impatience, he found it contained the words:—

> *"Fly at once. The truth about your trouser-stretchers is known. —A FRIEND."*

The fire-engine had struck still farther to the north, into a region that they did not recognise; and as it ran by a line of high railings shadowed with trees, the six friends were startled, but somewhat relieved, to see the President leap from the fire-engine, though whether through another whim or the increasing protest of his entertainers they could not see. Before the three cabs, however, could reach up to the spot, he had gone up the high railings like a huge grey cat, tossed himself over, and vanished in a darkness of leaves.

Syme with a furious gesture stopped his cab, jumped out, and sprang also to the escalade. When he had one leg over the fence and his friends were following, he turned a face on them which shone quite pale in the shadow.

"What place can this be?" he asked. "Can it be the old devil's house? I've heard he has a house in North London."

"All the better," said the Secretary grimly, planting a foot in a foothold, "we shall find him at home."

"No, but it isn't that," said Syme, knitting his brows. "I hear the most horrible noises, like devils laughing and sneezing and blowing their devilish noses!"

"His dogs barking, of course," said the Secretary.

"Why not say his black-beetles barking!" said Syme furiously, "snails barking! geraniums barking! Did you ever hear a dog bark like that?"

He held up his hand, and there came out of the thicket a long growling roar that seemed to get under the skin and freeze the flesh—a low thrilling roar that made a throbbing in the air all about them.

"The dogs of Sunday would be no ordinary dogs," said Gogol, and shuddered.

Syme had jumped down on the other side, but he still stood listening impatiently.

"Well, listen to that," he said, "is that a dog—anybody's dog?"

There broke upon their ear a hoarse screaming as of things protesting and clamouring in sudden pain; and then, far off like an echo, what sounded like a long nasal trumpet.

"Well, his house ought to be hell!" said the Secretary; "and if it is hell, I'm going in!" and he sprang over the tall railings almost with one swing.

The others followed. They broke through a tangle of plants and shrubs, and came out on an open path. Nothing was in sight, but Dr. Bull suddenly struck his hands together.

"Why, you asses," he cried, "it's the Zoo!"

As they were looking round wildly for any trace of their wild quarry, a keeper in uniform came running along the path with a man in plain clothes.

"Has it come this way?" gasped the keeper.

"Has what?" asked Syme.

"The elephant!" cried the keeper. "An elephant has gone mad and run away!"

"He has run away with an old gentleman," said the other stranger breathlessly, "a poor old gentleman with white hair!"

"What sort of old gentleman?" asked Syme, with great curiosity.

"A very large and fat old gentleman in light grey clothes," said the keeper eagerly.

"Well," said Syme, "if he's that particular kind of old gentleman, if you're quite sure that he's a large and fat old gentleman in grey clothes, you may take my word for it that the elephant has not run away with him. He has run away with the elephant. The elephant is not made by God that could run away with him if he did not consent to the elopement. And, by thunder, there he is!"

There was no doubt about it this time. Clean across the space of grass, about two hundred yards away, with a crowd screaming and scampering vainly at his heels, went a huge grey elephant at an awful stride, with his trunk thrown out as rigid as a ship's bowsprit, and trumpeting like the trumpet of doom. On the back of the bellowing and plunging animal sat President Sunday with all the placidity of a sultan, but goading the animal to a furious speed with some sharp object in his hand.

"Stop him!" screamed the populace. "He'll be out of the gate!"

"Stop a landslide!" said the keeper. "He is out of the gate!"

And even as he spoke, a final crash and roar of terror announced that the great grey elephant had broken out of the gates of the Zoological Gardens, and was careening down Albany Street like a new and swift sort of omnibus.

"Great Lord!" cried Bull, "I never knew an elephant could go so fast. Well, it must be hansom-cabs again if we are to keep him in sight."

As they raced along to the gate out of which the elephant had vanished, Syme felt a glaring panorama of the strange animals in the cages which they passed. Afterwards he thought it queer that he should have seen them so clearly. He remembered especially seeing pelicans, with their preposterous, pendant throats. He wondered why the pelican was the symbol of charity, except it was that it wanted a good deal of charity to admire a pelican. He remembered a hornbill, which was simply a huge yellow beak with a small bird tied on behind it. The whole gave him a sensation, the vividness of which he could not explain, that Nature was always making quite mysterious jokes. Sunday had told them that they would understand him when they had understood the stars. He wondered whether even the archangels understood the hornbill.

The six unhappy detectives flung themselves into cabs and followed the elephant sharing the terror which he spread through the long stretch of the streets. This time Sunday did not turn round, but offered them the solid stretch of his unconscious back, which maddened them, if possible, more than his previous mockeries. Just before they came to Baker Street, however, he was seen to throw something far up into the air, as a boy does a ball meaning to catch it again. But at their rate of racing it fell far behind, just by the cab containing Gogol; and in faint hope of a clue or for some impulse unexplainable, he stopped his cab so as to pick it up. It was addressed to himself, and was quite a bulky parcel. On examination, however, its bulk was found to consist of thirty-three pieces of paper of no value wrapped one round the other. When the last covering was torn away it reduced itself to a small slip of paper, on which was written:—

"The word, I fancy, should be 'pink'."

The man once known as Gogol said nothing, but the movements of his hands and feet were like those of a man urging a horse to renewed efforts.

Through street after street, through district after district, went the prodigy of the flying elephant, calling crowds to every window, and driving the traffic left and right. And still through all this insane publicity the three cabs toiled after it, until they came to be regarded as part of a procession, and perhaps the advertisement of a circus. They went at such a rate that distances were shortened beyond belief, and Syme saw the Albert Hall in Kensington when he thought that he was still in Paddington. The animal's pace was even more fast and free through the empty, aristocratic streets of South Kensington, and he finally headed towards that part of the sky-line where the enormous Wheel of Earl's Court stood up in the sky. The wheel grew larger and larger, till it filled heaven like the wheel of stars.

The beast outstripped the cabs. They lost him round several corners, and when they came to one of the gates of the Earl's Court Exhibition they found themselves finally blocked. In front of them was an enormous crowd; in the midst of it was an enormous elephant, heaving and shuddering as such shapeless creatures do. But the President had disappeared.

"Where has he gone to?" asked Syme, slipping to the ground.

"Gentleman rushed into the Exhibition, sir!" said an official in a dazed manner. Then he added in an injured voice: "Funny gentleman, sir. Asked me to hold his horse, and gave me this."

He held out with distaste a piece of folded paper, addressed: "To the Secretary of the Central Anarchist Council."

The Secretary, raging, rent it open, and found written inside it:—

> *"When the herring runs a mile, Let the Secretary smile; When the herring tries to fly, Let the Secretary die. Rustic Proverb."*

"Why the eternal crikey," began the Secretary, "did you let the man in? Do people commonly come to your Exhibition riding on mad elephants? Do—"

"Look!" shouted Syme suddenly. "Look over there!"

"Look at what?" asked the Secretary savagely.

"Look at the captive balloon!" said Syme, and pointed in a frenzy.

"Why the blazes should I look at a captive balloon?" demanded the Secretary. "What is there queer about a captive balloon?"

"Nothing," said Syme, "except that it isn't captive!"

They all turned their eyes to where the balloon swung and swelled above the Exhibition on a string, like a child's balloon. A second afterwards the string came in two just under the car, and the balloon, broken loose, floated away with the freedom of a soap bubble.

"Ten thousand devils!" shrieked the Secretary. "He's got into it!" and he shook his fists at the sky.

The balloon, borne by some chance wind, came right above them, and they could see the great white head of the President peering over the side and looking benevolently down on them.

"God bless my soul!" said the Professor with the elderly manner that he could never disconnect from his bleached beard and parchment face. "God bless my soul! I seemed to fancy that something fell on the top of my hat!"

He put up a trembling hand and took from that shelf a piece of twisted paper, which he opened absently only to find it inscribed with a true lover's knot and, the words:—

"Your beauty has not left me indifferent.—From LITTLE SNOWDROP."

There was a short silence, and then Syme said, biting his beard—

"I'm not beaten yet. The blasted thing must come down somewhere. Let's follow it!"

CHAPTER XIV. THE SIX PHILOSOPHERS

ACROSS green fields, and breaking through blooming hedges, toiled six draggled detectives, about five miles out of London. The optimist of the party had at first proposed that they should follow the balloon across South England in hansom-cabs. But he was ultimately convinced of the persistent refusal of the balloon to follow the roads, and the still more persistent refusal of the cabmen to follow the balloon. Consequently the tireless though exasperated travellers broke through black thickets and ploughed through ploughed fields till each was turned into a figure too outrageous to be mistaken for a tramp. Those green hills of Surrey saw the final collapse and tragedy of the admirable light grey suit in which Syme had set out from Saffron Park. His silk hat was broken over his nose by a swinging bough, his coat-tails were torn to the shoulder by arresting thorns, the clay of England was splashed up to his collar; but he still carried his yellow beard forward with a silent and furious determination, and his eyes were still fixed on that floating ball of gas, which in the full flush of sunset seemed coloured like a sunset cloud.

"After all," he said, "it is very beautiful!"

"It is singularly and strangely beautiful!" said the Professor. "I wish the beastly gas-bag would burst!"

"No," said Dr. Bull, "I hope it won't. It might hurt the old boy."

"Hurt him!" said the vindictive Professor, "hurt him! Not as much as I'd hurt him if I could get up with him. Little Snowdrop!"

"I don't want him hurt, somehow," said Dr. Bull.

"What!" cried the Secretary bitterly. "Do you believe all that tale about his being our man in the dark room? Sunday would say he was anybody."

"I don't know whether I believe it or not," said Dr. Bull. "But it isn't that that I mean. I can't wish old Sunday's balloon to burst because—"

"Well," said Syme impatiently, "because?"

"Well, because he's so jolly like a balloon himself," said Dr. Bull desperately. "I don't understand a word of all that idea of his being the same man who gave us all our blue cards. It seems to make everything nonsense. But I don't care who knows it, I always had a sympathy for old Sunday himself, wicked as he was. Just as if he was a great bouncing baby. How can I explain what my queer sympathy was? It didn't prevent my fighting him like hell! Shall I make it clear if I say that I liked him because he was so fat?"

"You will not," said the Secretary.

"I've got it now," cried Bull, "it was because he was so fat and so light. Just like a balloon. We always think of fat people as heavy, but he could have danced against a sylph. I see now what I mean. Moderate strength is shown in violence, supreme strength is shown in levity. It was like the old speculations—what would happen if an elephant could leap up in the sky like a grasshopper?"

"Our elephant," said Syme, looking upwards, "has leapt into the sky like a grasshopper."

"And somehow," concluded Bull, "that's why I can't help liking old Sunday. No, it's not an admiration of force, or any silly thing like that. There is a kind of gaiety in the thing, as if he were bursting with some good news. Haven't you sometimes felt it on a spring day? You know Nature plays tricks, but somehow that day proves they are good-natured tricks. I never read the Bible myself, but that part they laugh at is literal truth, 'Why leap ye, ye high hills?' The hills do leap—at least, they try to.... Why do I like Sunday?... how can I tell you?... because he's such a Bounder."

There was a long silence, and then the Secretary said in a curious, strained voice—

"You do not know Sunday at all. Perhaps it is because you are better than I, and do not know hell. I was a fierce fellow, and a trifle morbid from the first. The man who sits in darkness, and who chose us all, chose me because I had all the crazy look of a conspirator—because my smile went crooked, and my eyes were gloomy, even when I smiled. But there must have been something in me that answered to the nerves in all these anarchic men. For when I first saw Sunday he expressed to me, not your airy vitality, but something both gross and sad in the Nature of Things. I found him smoking in a twilight room, a room with brown blind down, infinitely more depressing than the genial darkness in which our master lives. He sat there on a bench, a huge heap of a man, dark and out of shape. He listened to all my words without speaking or even stirring. I poured out my most passionate appeals, and asked my most eloquent questions. Then, after a long silence, the Thing began to shake, and I thought it was shaken by some secret malady. It shook like a loathsome and living jelly. It reminded me of everything I had ever read about the base bodies that are the origin of life—the deep sea lumps and protoplasm. It seemed like the final form of matter, the most shapeless and the most shameful. I could only tell myself, from its shudderings, that it was something at least that such a monster could be miserable. And then it broke upon me that the bestial mountain was shaking with a lonely laughter, and the laughter was at me. Do you ask me to forgive him that? It is no small thing to be laughed at by something at once lower and stronger than oneself."

"Surely you fellows are exaggerating wildly," cut in the clear voice of Inspector Ratcliffe. "President Sunday is a terrible fellow for one's intellect, but he is not such a Barnum's freak physically as you make out. He received me in an ordinary office, in a grey check coat, in broad daylight. He talked to me in an ordinary way. But I'll tell you what is a trifle creepy about Sunday. His room is neat, his clothes are neat, everything seems in order; but he's absent-minded. Sometimes his great bright eyes go quite blind. For hours he forgets that you are there. Now absent-mindedness is just a bit too awful in a bad man. We think of a wicked man as vigilant. We can't think of a wicked man who is honestly and sincerely dreamy, because we daren't think of a wicked man alone with himself. An absentminded man means a good-natured man. It means a man who, if he happens to see you, will apologise. But how will you bear an absentminded man who, if he happens to see you, will kill you? That is what tries the nerves, abstraction combined with cruelty. Men have felt it sometimes when they went through wild forests, and felt that the animals there were at once innocent and pitiless. They might ignore or slay. How would you like to pass ten mortal hours in a parlour with an absent-minded tiger?"

"And what do you think of Sunday, Gogol?" asked Syme.

"I don't think of Sunday on principle," said Gogol simply, "any more than I stare at the sun at noonday."

"Well, that is a point of view," said Syme thoughtfully. "What do you say, Professor?"

The Professor was walking with bent head and trailing stick, and he did not answer at all.

"Wake up, Professor!" said Syme genially. "Tell us what you think of Sunday."

The Professor spoke at last very slowly.

"I think something," he said, "that I cannot say clearly. Or, rather, I think something that I cannot even think clearly. But it is something like this. My early life, as you know, was a bit too large and loose.

"Well, when I saw Sunday's face I thought it was too large—everybody does, but I also thought it was too loose. The face was so big, that one couldn't focus it or make it a face at all. The eye was so far away from the nose, that it wasn't an eye. The mouth was so much by itself, that one had to think of it by itself. The whole thing is too hard to explain."

He paused for a little, still trailing his stick, and then went on—

"But put it this way. Walking up a road at night, I have seen a lamp and a lighted window and a cloud make together a most complete and unmistakable face. If anyone in heaven has that face I shall know him again. Yet when I walked a little farther I found that there was no face, that the window was ten yards away, the lamp ten hundred yards, the cloud beyond the world. Well, Sunday's face escaped me; it ran away to right and left, as such chance pictures run away. And so his face has made me, somehow, doubt whether there are any faces. I don't know whether your face, Bull, is a face or a combination in perspective. Perhaps one black disc of your beastly glasses is quite close and another fifty miles away. Oh, the doubts of a materialist are not worth a dump. Sunday has taught me the last and the worst doubts, the doubts of a spiritualist. I am a Buddhist, I suppose; and Buddhism is not a creed, it is a doubt. My poor dear Bull, I do not believe that you really have a face. I have not faith enough to believe in matter."

Syme's eyes were still fixed upon the errant orb, which, reddened in the evening light, looked like some rosier and more innocent world.

"Have you noticed an odd thing," he said, "about all your descriptions? Each man of you finds Sunday quite different, yet each man of you can only find one thing to compare him to—the universe itself. Bull finds him like the earth in spring, Gogol like the sun at noonday. The Secretary is reminded of the shapeless protoplasm, and the Inspector of the carelessness of virgin forests. The Professor says he is like a changing landscape. This is queer, but it is queerer still that I also have had my odd notion about the President, and I also find that I think of Sunday as I think of the whole world."

"Get on a little faster, Syme," said Bull; "never mind the balloon."

"When I first saw Sunday," said Syme slowly, "I only saw his back; and when I saw his back, I knew he was the worst man in the world. His neck and shoulders were brutal, like those of some apish god. His head had a stoop that was hardly human, like the stoop of an ox. In fact, I had at once the revolting fancy that this was not a man at all, but a beast dressed up in men's clothes."

"Get on," said Dr. Bull.

"And then the queer thing happened. I had seen his back from the street, as he sat in the balcony. Then I entered the hotel, and coming round the other side of him, saw his face in the sunlight. His face frightened me, as it did everyone; but not because it was brutal, not because it was evil. On the contrary, it frightened me because it was so beautiful, because it was so good."

"Syme," exclaimed the Secretary, "are you ill?"

"It was like the face of some ancient archangel, judging justly after heroic wars. There was laughter in the eyes, and in the mouth honour and sorrow. There was the same white hair, the same great, grey-clad shoulders that I had seen from behind. But when I saw him from behind I was certain he was an animal, and when I saw him in front I knew he was a god."

"Pan," said the Professor dreamily, "was a god and an animal."

"Then, and again and always," went on Syme like a man talking to himself, "that has been for me the mystery of Sunday, and it is also the mystery of the world. When I see the horrible back, I am sure the noble face is but a mask. When I see the face but for an instant, I know the back is only a jest. Bad is so bad, that we cannot but think good an accident; good is so good, that we feel certain that evil could be explained. But the whole came to a kind of crest yesterday when I raced Sunday for the cab, and was just behind him all the way."

"Had you time for thinking then?" asked Ratcliffe.

"Time," replied Syme, "for one outrageous thought. I was suddenly possessed with the idea that the blind, blank back of his head really was his face—an awful, eyeless face staring at me! And I fancied that the figure running in front of me was really a figure running backwards, and dancing as he ran."

"Horrible!" said Dr. Bull, and shuddered.

"Horrible is not the word," said Syme. "It was exactly the worst instant of my life. And yet ten minutes afterwards, when he put his head out of the cab and made a grimace like a gargoyle, I knew that he was only like a father playing hide-and-seek with his children."

"It is a long game," said the Secretary, and frowned at his broken boots.

"Listen to me," cried Syme with extraordinary emphasis. "Shall I tell you the secret of the whole world? It is that we have only known the back of the world. We see everything from behind, and it looks brutal. That is not a tree, but the back of a tree. That is not a cloud, but the back of a cloud. Cannot you see that everything is stooping and hiding a face? If we could only get round in front—"

"Look!" cried out Bull clamorously, "the balloon is coming down!"

There was no need to cry out to Syme, who had never taken his eyes off it. He saw the great luminous globe suddenly stagger in the sky, right itself, and then sink slowly behind the trees like a setting sun.

The man called Gogol, who had hardly spoken through all their weary travels, suddenly threw up his hands like a lost spirit.

"He is dead!" he cried. "And now I know he was my friend—my friend in the dark!"

"Dead!" snorted the Secretary. "You will not find him dead easily. If he has been tipped out of the car, we shall find him rolling as a colt rolls in a field, kicking his legs for fun."

"Clashing his hoofs," said the Professor. "The colts do, and so did Pan."

"Pan again!" said Dr. Bull irritably. "You seem to think Pan is everything."

"So he is," said the Professor, "in Greek. He means everything."

"Don't forget," said the Secretary, looking down, "that he also means Panic."

Syme had stood without hearing any of the exclamations.

"It fell over there," he said shortly. "Let us follow it!"

Then he added with an indescribable gesture—

"Oh, if he has cheated us all by getting killed! It would be like one of his larks."

He strode off towards the distant trees with a new energy, his rags and ribbons fluttering in the wind. The others followed him in a more footsore and dubious manner. And almost at the same moment all six men realised that they were not alone in the little field.

Across the square of turf a tall man was advancing towards them, leaning on a strange long staff like a sceptre. He was clad in a fine but old-fashioned suit with knee-breeches; its colour was that shade between blue, violet and grey which can be seen in certain shadows of the woodland. His hair was whitish grey, and at the first glance, taken along with his knee-breeches, looked as if it was powdered. His advance was very quiet; but for the silver frost upon his head, he might have been one to the shadows of the wood.

"Gentlemen," he said, "my master has a carriage waiting for you in the road just by."

"Who is your master?" asked Syme, standing quite still.

"I was told you knew his name," said the man respectfully.

There was a silence, and then the Secretary said—

"Where is this carriage?"

"It has been waiting only a few moments," said the stranger. "My master has only just come home."

CHAPTER XIV. THE SIX PHILOSOPHERS

Syme looked left and right upon the patch of green field in which he found himself. The hedges were ordinary hedges, the trees seemed ordinary trees; yet he felt like a man entrapped in fairyland.

He looked the mysterious ambassador up and down, but he could discover nothing except that the man's coat was the exact colour of the purple shadows, and that the man's face was the exact colour of the red and brown and golden sky.

"Show us the place," Syme said briefly, and without a word the man in the violet coat turned his back and walked towards a gap in the hedge, which let in suddenly the light of a white road.

As the six wanderers broke out upon this thoroughfare, they saw the white road blocked by what looked like a long row of carriages, such a row of carriages as might close the approach to some house in Park Lane. Along the side of these carriages stood a rank of splendid servants, all dressed in the grey-blue uniform, and all having a certain quality of stateliness and freedom which would not commonly belong to the servants of a gentleman, but rather to the officials and ambassadors of a great king. There were no less than six carriages waiting, one for each of the tattered and miserable band. All the attendants (as if in court-dress) wore swords, and as each man crawled into his carriage they drew them, and saluted with a sudden blaze of steel.

"What can it all mean?" asked Bull of Syme as they separated. "Is this another joke of Sunday's?"

"I don't know," said Syme as he sank wearily back in the cushions of his carriage; "but if it is, it's one of the jokes you talk about. It's a good-natured one."

The six adventurers had passed through many adventures, but not one had carried them so utterly off their feet as this last adventure of comfort. They had all become inured to things going roughly; but things suddenly going smoothly swamped them. They could not even feebly imagine what the carriages were; it was enough for them to know that they were carriages, and carriages with cushions. They could not conceive who the old man was who had led them; but it was quite enough that he had certainly led them to the carriages.

Syme drove through a drifting darkness of trees in utter abandonment. It was typical of him that while he had carried his bearded chin forward fiercely so long as anything could be done, when the whole business was taken out of his hands he fell back on the cushions in a frank collapse.

Very gradually and very vaguely he realised into what rich roads the carriage was carrying him. He saw that they passed the stone gates of what might have been a park, that they began gradually to climb a hill which, while wooded on both sides, was somewhat more orderly than a forest. Then there began to grow upon him, as upon a man slowly waking from a healthy sleep, a pleasure in everything. He felt that the hedges were what hedges should be, living walls; that a hedge is like a human army, disciplined, but all the more alive. He saw high elms behind the hedges, and vaguely thought how happy boys would be climbing there. Then his carriage took a turn of the path, and he saw suddenly and quietly, like a long, low, sunset cloud, a long, low house, mellow in the mild light of sunset. All the six friends compared notes afterwards and quarrelled; but they all agreed that in some unaccountable way the place reminded them of their boyhood. It was either this elm-top or that crooked path, it was either this scrap of orchard or that shape of a window; but each man of them declared that he could remember this place before he could remember his mother.

When the carriages eventually rolled up to a large, low, cavernous gateway, another man in the same uniform, but wearing a silver star on the grey breast of his coat, came out to meet them. This impressive person said to the bewildered Syme—

"Refreshments are provided for you in your room."

Syme, under the influence of the same mesmeric sleep of amazement, went up the large oaken stairs after the respectful attendant. He entered a splendid suite of apartments that seemed to be designed specially for him. He walked up to a long mirror with the ordinary instinct of his class, to pull his tie straight or to smooth his hair; and there he saw the frightful figure that he was—blood running down his face from where the bough had struck him, his hair standing out like yellow rags of rank grass, his clothes torn into long, wavering tatters. At once the whole enigma sprang up, simply as the question of how he had got there, and how he was to get out again. Exactly at the same moment a man in blue, who had been appointed as his valet, said very solemnly—

"I have put out your clothes, sir."

"Clothes!" said Syme sardonically. "I have no clothes except these," and he lifted two long strips of his frock-coat in fascinating festoons, and made a movement as if to twirl like a ballet girl.

"My master asks me to say," said the attendant, "that there is a fancy dress ball tonight, and that he desires you to put on the costume that I have laid out. Meanwhile, sir, there is a bottle of Burgundy and some cold pheasant, which he hopes you will not refuse, as it is some hours before supper."

"Cold pheasant is a good thing," said Syme reflectively, "and Burgundy is a spanking good thing. But really I do not want either of them so much as I want to know what the devil all this means, and what sort of costume you have got laid out for me. Where is it?"

The servant lifted off a kind of ottoman a long peacock-blue drapery, rather of the nature of a domino, on the front of which was emblazoned a large golden sun, and which was splashed here and there with flaming stars and crescents.

"You're to be dressed as Thursday, sir," said the valet somewhat affably.

"Dressed as Thursday!" said Syme in meditation. "It doesn't sound a warm costume."

"Oh, yes, sir," said the other eagerly, "the Thursday costume is quite warm, sir. It fastens up to the chin."

"Well, I don't understand anything," said Syme, sighing. "I have been used so long to uncomfortable adventures that comfortable adventures knock me out. Still, I may be allowed to ask why I should be particularly like Thursday in a green frock spotted all over with the sun and moon. Those orbs, I think, shine on other days. I once saw the moon on Tuesday, I remember."

"Beg pardon, sir," said the valet, "Bible also provided for you," and with a respectful and rigid finger he pointed out a passage in the first chapter of Genesis. Syme read it wondering. It was that in which the fourth day of the week is associated with the creation of the sun and moon. Here, however, they reckoned from a Christian Sunday.

"This is getting wilder and wilder," said Syme, as he sat down in a chair. "Who are these people who provide cold pheasant and Burgundy, and green clothes and Bibles? Do they provide everything?"

"Yes, sir, everything," said the attendant gravely. "Shall I help you on with your costume?"

"Oh, hitch the bally thing on!" said Syme impatiently.

But though he affected to despise the mummery, he felt a curious freedom and naturalness in his movements as the blue and gold garment fell about him; and when he found that he had to wear a sword, it stirred a boyish dream. As he passed out of the room he flung the folds across his shoulder with a gesture, his sword stood out at an angle, and he had all the swagger of a troubadour. For these disguises did not disguise, but reveal.

CHAPTER XV. THE ACCUSER

AS Syme strode along the corridor he saw the Secretary standing at the top of a great flight of stairs. The man had never looked so noble. He was draped in a long robe of starless black, down the centre of which fell a band or broad stripe of pure white, like a single shaft of light. The whole looked like some very severe ecclesiastical vestment. There was no need for Syme to search his memory or the Bible in order to remember that the first day of creation marked the mere creation of light out of darkness. The vestment itself would alone have suggested the symbol; and Syme felt also how perfectly this pattern of pure white and black expressed the soul of the pale and austere Secretary, with his inhuman veracity and his cold frenzy, which made him so easily make war on the anarchists, and yet so easily pass for one of them. Syme was scarcely surprised to notice that, amid all the ease and hospitality of their new surroundings, this man's eyes were still stern. No smell of ale or orchards could make the Secretary cease to ask a reasonable question.

If Syme had been able to see himself, he would have realised that he, too, seemed to be for the first time himself and no one else. For if the Secretary stood for that philosopher who loves the original and formless light, Syme was a type of the poet who seeks always to make the light in special shapes, to split it up into sun and star. The philosopher may sometimes love the infinite; the poet always loves the finite. For him the great moment is not the creation of light, but the creation of the sun and moon.

As they descended the broad stairs together they overtook Ratcliffe, who was clad in spring green like a huntsman, and the pattern upon whose garment was a green tangle of trees. For he stood for that third day on which the earth and green things were made, and his square, sensible face, with its not unfriendly cynicism, seemed appropriate enough to it.

They were led out of another broad and low gateway into a very large old English garden, full of torches and bonfires, by the broken light of which a vast carnival of people were dancing in motley dress. Syme seemed to see every shape in Nature imitated in some crazy costume. There was a man dressed as a windmill with enormous sails, a man dressed as an elephant, a man dressed as a balloon; the two last, together, seemed to keep the thread of their farcical adventures. Syme even saw, with a queer thrill, one dancer dressed like an enormous hornbill, with a beak twice as big as himself—the queer bird which had fixed itself on his fancy like a living question while he was rushing down the long road at the Zoological Gardens. There were a thousand other such objects, however. There was a dancing lamp-post, a dancing apple tree, a dancing ship. One would have thought that the untamable tune of some mad musician had set all the common objects of field and street dancing an eternal jig. And long afterwards, when Syme was middle-aged and at rest, he could never see one of those particular objects—a lamppost, or an apple tree, or a windmill—without thinking that it was a strayed reveller from that revel of masquerade.

On one side of this lawn, alive with dancers, was a sort of green bank, like the terrace in such old-fashioned gardens.

Along this, in a kind of crescent, stood seven great chairs, the thrones of the seven days. Gogol and Dr. Bull were already in their seats; the Professor was just mounting to his. Gogol, or Tuesday, had his simplicity well symbolised by a dress designed upon the division of the waters, a dress that separated upon his forehead and fell to his feet, grey and silver, like a sheet of rain. The Professor, whose day was that on which the birds and fishes—the ruder forms of life—were created, had a dress of dim purple, over which sprawled goggle-eyed fishes and outrageous tropical birds, the union in him of unfathomable fancy and of doubt. Dr. Bull, the last day of Creation, wore a coat covered with heraldic animals in red and gold, and on his crest a man rampant. He lay back in his chair with a broad smile, the picture of an optimist in his element.

One by one the wanderers ascended the bank and sat in their strange seats. As each of them sat down a roar of enthusiasm rose from the carnival, such as that with which crowds receive kings. Cups were clashed and torches shaken, and feathered hats flung in the air. The men for whom these thrones were reserved were men crowned with some extraordinary laurels. But the central chair was empty.

Syme was on the left hand of it and the Secretary on the right. The Secretary looked across the empty throne at Syme, and said, compressing his lips—

"We do not know yet that he is not dead in a field."

Almost as Syme heard the words, he saw on the sea of human faces in front of him a frightful and beautiful alteration, as if heaven had opened behind his head. But Sunday had only passed silently along the front like a shadow, and had sat in the central seat. He was draped plainly, in a pure and terrible white, and his hair was like a silver flame on his forehead.

For a long time—it seemed for hours—that huge masquerade of mankind swayed and stamped in front of them to marching and exultant music. Every couple dancing seemed a separate romance; it might be a fairy dancing with a pillar-box, or a peasant girl dancing with the moon; but in each case it was, somehow, as absurd as Alice in Wonderland, yet as grave and kind as a love story. At last, however, the thick crowd began to thin itself. Couples strolled away into the garden-walks, or began to drift towards that end of the building where stood smoking, in huge pots like fish-kettles, some hot and scented mixtures of old ale or wine. Above all these, upon a sort of black framework on the roof of the house, roared in its iron basket a gigantic bonfire, which lit up the land for miles. It flung the homely effect of firelight over the face of vast forests of grey or brown, and it seemed to fill with warmth even the emptiness of upper night. Yet this also, after a time, was allowed to grow fainter; the dim groups gathered more and more round the great cauldrons, or passed, laughing and clattering, into the inner passages of that ancient house. Soon there were only some ten loiterers in the garden; soon only four. Finally the last stray merry-maker ran into the house whooping to his companions. The fire faded, and the slow, strong stars came out. And the seven strange men were left alone, like seven stone statues on their chairs of stone. Not one of them had spoken a word.

They seemed in no haste to do so, but heard in silence the hum of insects and the distant song of one bird. Then Sunday spoke, but so dreamily that he might have been continuing a conversation rather than beginning one.

"We will eat and drink later," he said. "Let us remain together a little, we who have loved each other so sadly, and have fought so long. I seem to remember only centuries of heroic war, in which you were always heroes—epic on epic, iliad on iliad, and you always brothers in arms. Whether it was but recently (for time is nothing), or at the beginning of the world, I sent you out to war. I sat in the darkness, where there is not any created thing, and to you I was only a voice commanding valour and an unnatural virtue. You heard the voice in the dark, and you never heard it again. The sun in heaven denied it, the earth and sky denied it, all human wisdom denied it. And when I met you in the daylight I denied it myself."

Syme stirred sharply in his seat, but otherwise there was silence, and the incomprehensible went on.

"But you were men. You did not forget your secret honour, though the whole cosmos turned an engine of torture to tear it out of you. I knew how near you were to hell. I know how you, Thursday, crossed swords with King Satan, and how you, Wednesday, named me in the hour without hope."

There was complete silence in the starlit garden, and then the black-browed Secretary, implacable, turned in his chair towards Sunday, and said in a harsh voice—

"Who and what are you?"

"I am the Sabbath," said the other without moving. "I am the peace of God."

The Secretary started up, and stood crushing his costly robe in his hand.

"I know what you mean," he cried, "and it is exactly that that I cannot forgive you. I know you are contentment, optimism, what do they call the thing, an ultimate reconciliation. Well, I am not reconciled. If you were the man in the dark room, why were you also Sunday, an offense to the sunlight? If you were from the first our father and our friend, why were you also our greatest enemy? We wept, we fled in terror; the iron entered into our souls—and you are the peace of God! Oh, I can forgive God His anger, though it destroyed nations; but I cannot forgive Him His peace."

Sunday answered not a word, but very slowly he turned his face of stone upon Syme as if asking a question.

"No," said Syme, "I do not feel fierce like that. I am grateful to you, not only for wine and hospitality here, but for many a fine scamper and free fight. But I should like to know. My soul and heart are as happy and quiet here as this old garden, but my reason is still crying out. I should like to know."

Sunday looked at Ratcliffe, whose clear voice said—

"It seems so silly that you should have been on both sides and fought yourself."

Bull said—

"I understand nothing, but I am happy. In fact, I am going to sleep."

"I am not happy," said the Professor with his head in his hands, "because I do not understand. You let me stray a little too near to hell."

And then Gogol said, with the absolute simplicity of a child—

"I wish I knew why I was hurt so much."

Still Sunday said nothing, but only sat with his mighty chin upon his hand, and gazed at the distance. Then at last he said—

"I have heard your complaints in order. And here, I think, comes another to complain, and we will hear him also."

The falling fire in the great cresset threw a last long gleam, like a bar of burning gold, across the dim grass. Against this fiery band was outlined in utter black the advancing legs of a black-clad figure. He seemed to have a fine close suit with knee-breeches such as that which was worn by the servants of the house, only that it was not blue, but of this absolute sable. He had, like the servants, a kind of sword by his side. It was only when he had come quite close to the crescent of the seven and flung up his face to look at them, that Syme saw, with thunder-struck clearness, that the face was the broad, almost ape-like face of his old friend Gregory, with its rank red hair and its insulting smile.

"Gregory!" gasped Syme, half-rising from his seat. "Why, this is the real anarchist!"

"Yes," said Gregory, with a great and dangerous restraint, "I am the real anarchist."

"'Now there was a day,'" murmured Bull, who seemed really to have fallen asleep, "'when the sons of God came to present themselves before the Lord, and Satan came also among them.'"

"You are right," said Gregory, and gazed all round. "I am a destroyer. I would destroy the world if I could."

A sense of a pathos far under the earth stirred up in Syme, and he spoke brokenly and without sequence.

"Oh, most unhappy man," he cried, "try to be happy! You have red hair like your sister."

"My red hair, like red flames, shall burn up the world," said Gregory. "I thought I hated everything more than common men can hate anything; but I find that I do not hate everything so much as I hate you!"

"I never hated you," said Syme very sadly.

Then out of this unintelligible creature the last thunders broke.

"You!" he cried. "You never hated because you never lived. I know what you are all of you, from first to last—you are the people in power! You are the police—the great fat, smiling men in blue and buttons! You are the Law, and you have never been broken. But is there a free soul alive that does not long to break you, only because you have never been broken? We in revolt talk all kind of nonsense doubtless about this crime or that crime of the Government. It is all folly! The only crime of the Government is that it governs. The unpardonable sin of the supreme power is that it is supreme. I do not curse you for being cruel. I do not curse you (though I might) for being kind. I curse you for being safe! You sit in your chairs of stone, and have never come down from them. You are the seven angels of heaven, and you have had no troubles. Oh, I could forgive you everything, you that rule all mankind, if I could feel for once that you had suffered for one hour a real agony such as I—"

Syme sprang to his feet, shaking from head to foot.

"I see everything," he cried, "everything that there is. Why does each thing on the earth war against each other thing? Why does each small thing in the world have to fight against the world itself? Why does a fly have to fight the whole universe? Why does a dandelion have to fight the whole universe? For the same reason that I had to be alone in the dreadful Council of the Days. So that each thing that obeys law may have the glory and isolation of the anarchist. So that each man fighting for order may be as brave and good a man as the dynamiter. So that the real lie of Satan may be flung back in the face of this blasphemer, so that by tears and torture we may earn the right to say to this man, 'You lie!' No agonies can be too great to buy the right to say to this accuser, 'We also have suffered.'

"It is not true that we have never been broken. We have been broken upon the wheel. It is not true that we have never descended from these thrones. We have descended into hell. We were complaining of unforgettable miseries even at the very moment when this man entered insolently to accuse us of happiness. I repel the slander; we have not been happy. I can answer for every one of the great guards of Law whom he has accused. At least—"

He had turned his eyes so as to see suddenly the great face of Sunday, which wore a strange smile.

"Have you," he cried in a dreadful voice, "have you ever suffered?"

As he gazed, the great face grew to an awful size, grew larger than the colossal mask of Memnon, which had made him scream as a child. It grew larger and larger, filling the whole sky; then everything went black. Only in the blackness before it entirely destroyed his brain he seemed to hear a distant voice saying a commonplace text that he had heard somewhere, "Can ye drink of the cup that I drink of?"

* * *

When men in books awake from a vision, they commonly find themselves in some place in which they might have fallen asleep; they yawn in a chair, or lift themselves with bruised limbs from a field. Syme's experience was something much more psychologically strange if there was indeed anything unreal, in the earthly sense, about the things he had gone through. For while he could always remember afterwards that he had swooned before the face of Sunday, he could not remember having ever come to at all. He could only remember that gradually and naturally he knew that he was and had been walking along a country lane with an easy and conversational companion. That companion had been a part of his recent drama; it was the red-haired poet Gregory. They were walking like old friends, and were in the middle of a conversation about some triviality. But Syme could only feel an unnatural buoyancy in his body and a crystal simplicity in his mind that seemed to be superior to everything that he said or did. He felt he was in possession of some impossible good news, which made every other thing a triviality, but an adorable triviality.

Dawn was breaking over everything in colours at once clear and timid; as if Nature made a first attempt at yellow and a first attempt at rose. A breeze blew so clean and sweet, that one could not think that it blew from the sky; it blew rather through some hole in the sky. Syme felt a simple surprise when he saw rising all round him on both sides of the road the red, irregular buildings of Saffron Park. He had no idea that he had walked so near London. He walked by instinct along one white road, on which early birds hopped and sang, and found himself outside a fenced garden. There he saw the sister of Gregory, the girl with the gold-red hair, cutting lilac before breakfast, with the great unconscious gravity of a girl.

"THE KINGDOM OF GOD IS WITHIN YOU"
CHRISTIANITY NOT AS A MYSTIC RELIGION
BUT AS A NEW THEORY OF LIFE
LEO TOLSTOY
Benediction Classics, 2011
298 pages
ISBN: 978-1-84902-474-7

Available from www.amazon.com,
www.amazon.co.uk

A new edition of Tolstoy's non-fiction magnum opus. Gandhi regarded this book, banned in Tolstoy's native Russia, as one of the three greatest influences on him. The ideas Tolstoy that expounds so clearly were revolutionary in his day and still are relevant and challenging today.

On the Christian Life
John Calvin
Benediction Classics, 2011
58 pages
ISBN: 978-1-84902-426-6

Available from www.amazon.com, www.amazon.co.uk

John Calvin (1509 - 1564) was an influential French theologian and pastor during the Protestant Reformation. This book is an abridged version of Calvin's "Institutes". The language has been translated into crisper English, making it very readable. Calvin's positive theological statements and arguments are included, while the bitter polemics that Calvin often used have been removed. Hence, it is possible to see the flow of Calvin's arguments without being distracted by the denunciations of those who disagreed with him. The abridgement has been skilfully executed, enabling the reader to see the coherent argument at the centre of Calvin's theology. This edition comes complete with the original title page, outline of the book, an index of scriptures and an index of French words and phrases.

SELECTED ESSAYS
Søren Kierkegaard
Benediction Classics, 2011
192 pages
ISBN: 978-1-84902-457-0

Available from www.amazon.com, www.amazon.co.uk

Soren Kierkegaard (1813 - 1855) was a prominent Danish Christian philosopher. This book contains five of his essays and some selections from "The Present Moment". This collection is varied in theme and a good representation of Kierkegaard's literature. Readers will find his philosophy thought-provoking and meticulously well thought through. The essays included are: The Crowd Is Untruth Diapsalmata In Vino Veritas (The Banquet) Fear And Trembling Preparation For A Christian Life Selections From The Present Moment.

The Imitation Of Christ - with indexes of Biblical References, People Names and Subject Matter
Thomas à Kempis
Benediction Classics, 2011
190 pages
ISBN: 978-1-78139-038-2

Available from www.amazon.com, www.amazon.co.uk

The Imitation of Christ by Thomas à Kempis is the most widely read Christian devotional book next to the Bible. It was written in Latin five hundred years ago and now brings comfort to millions of readers in over fifty languages. The Imitation is based on meditations on the life and teachings of Jesus, and emphasises the interior life and the centrality of the Eucharist rather than an active imitation of Christ. This version has an index of Biblical references, an index of names and an index of subjects.

Also from Benediction Books ...

Wandering Between Two Worlds: Essays on Faith and Art
Anita Mathias
Benediction Books, 2007
152 pages
ISBN: 0955373700

Available from www.amazon.com, www.amazon.co.uk

In these wide-ranging lyrical essays, Anita Mathias writes, in lush, lovely prose, of her naughty Catholic childhood in Jamshedpur, India; her large, eccentric family in Mangalore, a sea-coast town converted by the Portuguese in the sixteenth century; her rebellion and atheism as a teenager in her Himalayan boarding school, run by German missionary nuns, St. Mary's Convent, Nainital; and her abrupt religious conversion after which she entered Mother Teresa's convent in Calcutta as a novice. Later rich, elegant essays explore the dualities of her life as a writer, mother, and Christian in the United States-- Domesticity and Art, Writing and Prayer, and the experience of being "an alien and stranger" as an immigrant in America, sensing the need for roots.

About the Author

Anita Mathias is the author of *Wandering Between Two Worlds: Essays on Faith and Art*. She has a B.A. and M.A. in English from Somerville College, Oxford University, and an M.A. in Creative Writing from the Ohio State University, USA. Anita won a National Endowment of the Arts fellowship in Creative Non-fiction in 1997. She lives in Oxford, England with her husband, Roy, and her daughters, Zoe and Irene.

Anita's website:
http://www.anitamathias.com, and
Anita's blog Dreaming Beneath the Spires:
http://dreamingbeneaththespires.blogspot.com

The Church That Had Too Much
Anita Mathias
Benediction Books, 2010
52 pages
ISBN: 9781849026567

Available from www.amazon.com, www.amazon.co.uk

The Church That Had Too Much was very well-intentioned. She wanted to love God, she wanted to love people, but she was both hampered by her muchness and the abundance of her possessions, and beset by ambition, power struggles and snobbery. Read about the surprising way The Church That Had Too Much began to resolve her problems in this deceptively simple and enchanting fable.

About the Author

Anita Mathias is the author of *Wandering Between Two Worlds: Essays on Faith and Art*. She has a B.A. and M.A. in English from Somerville College, Oxford University, and an M.A. in Creative Writing from the Ohio State University, USA. Anita won a National Endowment of the Arts fellowship in Creative Non-fiction in 1997. She lives in Oxford, England with her husband, Roy, and her daughters, Zoe and Irene.

Anita's website:
    http://www.anitamathias.com, and
Anita's blog Dreaming Beneath the Spires:
    http://dreamingbeneaththespires.blogspot.com

Milton Keynes UK
Ingram Content Group UK Ltd.
UKHW021500010724
444990UK00045B/1281

9 781789 432909